Lecture Notes in Computer Science

Lecture Notes in Artificial Intelligence   15359

Founding Editor

Jörg Siekmann

Series Editors

Randy Goebel, *University of Alberta, Edmonton, Canada*
Wolfgang Wahlster, *DFKI, Berlin, Germany*
Zhi-Hua Zhou, *Nanjing University, Nanjing, China*

The series Lecture Notes in Artificial Intelligence (LNAI) was established in 1988 as a topical subseries of LNCS devoted to artificial intelligence.

The series publishes state-of-the-art research results at a high level. As with the LNCS mother series, the mission of the series is to serve the international R & D community by providing an invaluable service, mainly focused on the publication of conference and workshop proceedings and postproceedings.

Derek F. Wong · Zhongyu Wei · Muyun Yang
Editors

Natural Language Processing and Chinese Computing

13th National CCF Conference, NLPCC 2024
Hangzhou, China, November 1–3, 2024
Proceedings, Part I

 Springer

Editors
Derek F. Wong 🆔
University of Macau
Macao, China

Zhongyu Wei 🆔
Fudan University
Shanghai, China

Muyun Yang
Harbin Institute of Technology
Harbin, China

ISSN 0302-9743   ISSN 1611-3349 (electronic)
Lecture Notes in Artificial Intelligence
ISBN 978-981-97-9430-0   ISBN 978-981-97-9431-7 (eBook)
https://doi.org/10.1007/978-981-97-9431-7

LNCS Sublibrary: SL7 – Artificial Intelligence

Preface

Welcome to NLPCC 2024, the thirteenth CCF International Conference on Natural Language Processing and Chinese Computing. Following the success of previous conferences held in Beijing (2012), Chongqing (2013), Shenzhen (2014), Nanchang (2015), Kunming (2016), Dalian (2017), Hohhot (2018), Dunhuang (2019), Zhengzhou (2020), Qingdao (2021), Guilin (2022), and Foshan (2023), this year's NLPCC convened in Hangzhou. It was organized by the China Computer Federation and hosted by Westlake University. As a premier international conference on natural language processing and Chinese computing, organized by the CCF-NLP (Technical Committee of Natural Language Processing, China Computer Federation, formerly known as Technical Committee of Chinese Information, China Computer Federation), NLPCC serves as a vital forum for researchers and practitioners from academia, industry, and government to share their ideas, research results, and experiences, and to promote their research and technical innovations.

The fields of natural language processing (NLP) and Chinese computing (CC) have seen remarkable growth in recent years. In keeping with NLPCC's tradition, we welcomed submissions in ten areas for the main conference: Fundamentals of NLP; Information Extraction and Knowledge Graph; Information Retrieval, Dialogue Systems, and Question Answering; Large Language Models and Agents; Machine Learning for NLP; Machine Translation and Multilinguality; Multimodality and Explainability; NLP Applications and Text Mining; Sentiment Analysis, Argumentation Mining, and Social Media; Summarization and Generation. This year, we received 451 submissions by the submission deadline.

After a thorough review process, including meta reviewing, out of 451 valid submissions (some were withdrawn by authors or desk-rejected due to policy violations), 161 papers were accepted as regular papers to be presented at the main conference. Among them, 40 papers (9% of submissions) were presented orally. Additionally, these papers were featured in the poster sessions, offering further opportunities for discussion and engagement. Another 121 papers (27%) were exclusively presented as posters. Five papers were nominated by our area chairs for the best and outstanding paper awards. An independent best paper award committee was formed to select the top papers from the shortlist. Eventually, we selected one best paper, one best student paper, and three outstanding papers. Differing from past years, the conference only accepted English papers. In addition to the main proceedings, 33 papers were accepted for the Evaluation workshops.

We were honored to have four internationally renowned keynote speakers, Kam-Fai Wong (Chinese University of Hong Kong), Ehud Reiter (University of Aberdeen), Minlie Huang (Tsinghua University), and Fei Liu (Emory University), who shared their recent research progress and achievements in natural language processing.

We would like to express our gratitude to all those who contributed to NLPCC 2024. First, we extend our thanks to our 31 area chairs for their diligent work in recruiting reviewers, monitoring the review and discussion processes, and carefully rating and recommending submissions. We are also thankful to all 491 reviewers for their time and effort in reviewing the submissions, especially acknowledging the 35 reviewers selected as the best reviewers, as nominated by the area chairs for their exceptional contributions. Our appreciation goes to the general chairs, Anna Korhonen and Xiaojun Wan, and to the organization committee chairs, Yue Zhang and Haofen Wang. Special thanks to Muyun Yang, the publication chair, for his invaluable assistance.

Finally, we thank all the authors who submitted their work to NLPCC 2024 and our sponsors for their contributions to the conference. Without your support, we could not have assembled such a strong conference program.

We were pleased to welcome you to NLPCC 2024 in Hangzhou and hope you enjoyed the conference!

September 2024

Derek F. Wong
Zhongyu Wei

Organization

General Chairs

Anna Korhonen   University of Cambridge, UK
Xiaojun Wan   Peking University, China

Program Committee Chairs

Derek F. Wong   University of Macau, China
Zhongyu Wei   Fudan University, China

Workshop Chairs

Ruifeng Xu   Harbin Institute of Technology (Shenzhen), China
Xu Chen   Renmin University of China, China
Tao Gui   Fudan University, China

Evaluation Chairs

Yunbo Cao   PLA Academy of Military Science, China
Meishan Zhang   Harbin Institute of Technology (Shenzhen), China

Tutorial Chairs

Yi Cai   South China University of Technology, China
Jing Li   Hong Kong Polytechnic University, China

Publication Chair

Muyun Yang   Harbin Institute of Technology, China

Sponsorship Chairs

Zhongqing Wang	Soochow University, China
Piji Li	Nanjing University of Aeronautics and Astronautics, China

Publicity Chairs

Min Yang	Shenzhen Institute of Advanced Technology, Chinese Academy of Sciences, China
Libo Qin	Central South University, China
Xiangyu Zhao	City University of Hong Kong, China

Organization Chairs

Yue Zhang	Westlake University, China
Haofen Wang	Tongji University, China

Area Chairs

IR/Dialogue Systems/Question Answering

Zhaochun Ren	Leiden University, The Netherlands
Libo Qin	Central South University, China
Jing Ma	Hong Kong Baptist University, China
Shen Gao	University of Electronic Science and Technology of China, China

Fundamentals of NLP

Longyue Wang	Alibaba Group, China
Hao Fei	National University of Singapore, Singapore

Information Extraction and Knowledge Graph

Yangqiu Song	Hong Kong University of Science and Technology, China

Yubo Chen   Institute of Automation, Chinese Academy of
                                 Sciences, China
Qin Chen   East China Normal University, China
Yixin Cao   Singapore Management University, Singapore

Large Language Models and Agents

Yuxuan Lai   Open University of China, China
Junxian He   Hong Kong University of Science and
                                 Technology, China
Siyuan Wang   University of Southern California, USA
Wei Chen   Huazhong University of Science and Technology,
                                 China

Machine Learning for NLP

Chenliang Li   Wuhan University, China
Linfeng Song   Tencent AI Lab, China

Machine Translation and Multilinguality

Yang Feng   Institute of Computing Technology, Chinese
                                 Academy of Sciences, China
Chenhui Chu   Kyoto University, Japan

Multimodality and Explainability

Tong Xu   University of Science and Technology of China,
                                 China
Jiatao Gu   Apple, USA

NLP Applications/Text Mining

Jing Li   Hong Kong Polytechnic University, China
Xiaocheng Feng   Harbin Institute of Technology, China
Chenghua Lin   University of Manchester, UK
Xuebo Liu   Harbin Institute of Technology, Shenzhen, China
Yue Feng   University of Birmingham, UK

Summarization and Generation

Piji Li	Nanjing University of Aeronautics and Astronautics, China
Yi Ren Fung	University of Illinois Urbana-Champaign, USA

Sentiment Analysis/Argumentation Mining/Social Media

Fei Li	Wuhan University, China
Lin Gui	King's College London, UK
Bin Liang	Chinese University of Hong Kong, China
Jianfei Yu	Nanjing University of Science and Technology, China

Poster Chairs

Xuebo Liu	Harbin Institute of Technology, Shenzhen, China
Longyue Wang	Alibaba Group, China

OpenReview Co-chairs

Yuhang Lai	Fudan University, China
Shudong Liu	University of Macau, China

Program Committee

Ang Li	Harbin Institute of Technology, China
Ante Wang	Xiamen University, China
Bang Liu	University of Montreal, Canada
Bei Li	Meituan, China
Benfeng Xu	University of Science and Technology of China, China
Benyou Wang	Chinese University of Hong Kong, Shenzhen, China
Bin Li	Nanjing Normal University, China
Bin Liang	Chinese University of Hong Kong, Hong Kong, China
Bingbing Wang	Harbin Institute of Technology, Shenzhen, China
Bingqing Wang	Bosch Research Center North America, USA

Binyuan Hui	Alibaba Group, China
Bo Chen	Minzu University of China, China
Bo Wang	Beijing Institute of Technology, China
Bo Xu	Dalian University of Technology, China
Bobo Li	Wuhan University, China
Boyang Wang	Beijing University of Aeronautics and Astronautics, China
Caixia Yuan	Beijing University of Post and Telecommunication, China
Changmeng Zheng	Hong Kong Polytechnic University, Hong Kong, China
Changyi Xiao	University of Science and Technology of China, China
Changzhi Sun	ByteDance, China
Chao Huang	University of California, Davis, USA
Chao Jiang	Georgia Institute of Technology, USA
Chen Jia	SI-TECH Information Technology Co., Ltd, China
Chen Qiu	Wuhan University of Science and Technology, China
Chen Shi	Alibaba Group, China
Chen Xu	Harbin Engineering University, China
Chen Zhang	Beijing Institute of Technology, China
Chen Zhang	Peking University, China
Chen Zheng	Open University of China, China
Cheng Jiayang	Hong Kong University of Science and Technology, Hong Kong, China
Chengjie Sun	Harbin Institute of Technology, China
Chenhao Wang	Institute of Automation, Chinese Academy of Sciences, China
Chong Feng	University of Science and Technology of China, China
Chong Li	Institute of Automation, Chinese Academy of Sciences, China
Chuan-Ju Wang	Academia Sinica, Taiwan
Chuanyi Li	Nanjing University, China
Chunkit Chan	Hong Kong University of Science and Technology, Hong Kong, China
Chunli Xiang	Hubei University of Technology, China
Chunxia Zhang	Beijing Institute of Technology, China
Claudia Marzi	Italian CNR, Italy
Cunxiang Wang	Westlake University, China

Da Ren	Hong Kong Polytechnic University, Hong Kong, China
Danqing Zhang	Amazon, USA
Deqing Yang	Fudan University, China
Di Wang	King Abdullah University of Science and Technology, Saudi Arabia
Dingcheng Li	Baidu, China
Dongfang Li	Harbin Institute of Technology, China
Dongji Feng	Gustavus Adolphus College, USA
Dongning Rao	Guangdong University of Technology, China
Dongwei Jiang	Johns Hopkins University, USA
Dongyuan Li	Tokyo Institute of Technology, Japan
Emmanuele Chersoni	Hong Kong Polytechnic University, Hong Kong, China
Erxin Yu	Hong Kong Polytechnic University, Hong Kong, China
Fanfan Wang	Nanjing University of Science and Technology, China
Fangfang Su	Hangzhou Dianzi University, China
Fei Cheng	Kyoto University, Japan
Feilong Chen	Institute of Automation, Chinese Academy of Sciences, China
Fengran Mo	Université de Montréal, Canada
Gao Zuchen	Hong Kong Polytechnic University, Hong Kong, China
Ge Zhang	University of Waterloo, Canada
Gongbo Tang	Beijing Language and Culture University, China
Guanglin Niu	Beihang University, China
Guanhua Chen	Southern University of Science and Technology, China
Guanhua Chen	University of Macau, China
Guanyi Chen	Central China Normal University, China
Guoxin Wang	Microsoft, USA
Hai Wang	Amazon, USA
Haidong Xu	Harbin Institute of Technology, Shenzhen, China
Haiyue Song	National Institute of Information and Communications Technology, Japan
Han Liu	Dalian University of Technology, China
Hang Chen	Xi'an Jiaotong University, China
Hanzhuo Tan	Hong Kong Polytechnic University, Hong Kong, China
Hanzi Xu	Temple University, USA
Hao Wang	Nanyang Technological University, Singapore

Hao Wang	Shanghai University, China
Hao Xiong	Chinese Academy of Sciences, China
Hao Yan	Huazhong University of Science and Technology, China
Haojing Huang	Tsinghua University, China
Haonan Li	Mohamed bin Zayed University of Artificial Intelligence, UAE
Haoran Li	Hong Kong University of Science and Technology, Hong Kong, China
Haoran Luo	Beijing University of Posts and Telecommunications, China
Haoyu Wang	Amazon, USA
Heng Yu	Chinese Academy of Sciences, China
Henghui Zhu	Amazon, USA
Hengtong Lu	Beijing University of Posts and Telecommunications, China
Hen-Hsen Huang	Institute of Information Science, Academia Sinica, Taiwan
Herun Wan	Xi'an Jiaotong University, China
Hexuan Deng	Harbin Institute of Technology, Shenzhen, China
Hongfei Wang	Tokyo Metropolitan University, Japan
Hongfei Xu	Zhengzhou University, China
Hongjie Cai	Nanjing University of Science and Technology, China
Hongkun Hao	Shanghai Jiao Tong University, China
Hongliang Dai	Nanjing University of Aeronautics and Astronautics, China
Hongqiu Wu	Shanghai Jiao Tong University, China
Hongyu Zhang	University of Newcastle, Australia
Hou Pong Chan	Alibaba Group, Singapore
Hui Li	Xiamen University, China
Jiachun Li	Institute of Automation, Chinese Academy of Sciences, China
Jiahao Xu	Nanyang Technological University, Singapore
Jiahao Ying	Singapore Management University, Singapore
Jiaju Lin	Pennsylvania State University, USA
Jiajun Li	Huawei Technologies Ltd., China
Jiale Han	Hong Kong University of Science and Technology, Hong Kong, China
Jiali Cheng	University of Massachusetts at Lowell, USA
Jialu Li	University of North Carolina at Chapel Hill, USA
Jian Liu	Beijing Jiaotong University, China
Jiangen He	University of Tennessee, Knoxville, USA

Jiangping Huang	Nanyang Technological University, Singapore
Jianhui Pang	University of Macau, China
Jiani Huang	University of Pennsylvania, USA
Jiaxin Bai	Hong Kong University of Science and Technology, Hong Kong, China
Jiaxin Mao	Renmin University of China, Tsinghua University, China
Jiaxin Qin	Renmin University of China, China
Jiayi Chen	University of Virginia, USA
Jiazhan Feng	Peking University, China
Jiazhao Li	University of Michigan - Ann Arbor, USA
Jie Zhu	Alibaba Group, China
Jin Wang	Yunnan University, China
Jing Luo	Xi'an Jiaotong University, China
Jingcong Liang	Fudan University, China
Jinghan Zhang	Hong Kong University of Science and Technology, Hong Kong, China
Jinghang Gu	Hong Kong Polytechnic University, Hong Kong, China
Jinghui Lu	ByteDance, China
Jingjie Zeng	Dalian University of Technology, China
Jingjing Wang	Soochow University, China
Jingqing Zhang	Pangaea Data Limited, UK
Jingwen Wang	Elizabethtown College, USA
Jinliang Lu	Institute of Automation, Chinese Academy of Sciences, China
Jinzhi Liao	National University of Defense Technology, China
Jitai Hao	Shandong University, China
Jun Rao	Harbin Institute of Technology, China
Jun Zhou	Wuhan University, China
Junchao Wu	University of Macau, China
Junchen Zhao	University of California, Irvine, USA
Jundong Xu	National University of Singapore, Singapore
Junfeng Tian	East China Normal University, China
Junguo Zhu	Kunming University of Technology, China
Junhao Liu	University of California, Irvine, USA
Junhui Li	Soochow University, China
Junjie Chen	University of Tokyo, Japan
Junjie Wu	Hong Kong University of Science and Technology, Hong Kong, China
Junjie Ye	Fudan University, China

Junnan Zhu	Institute of Automation, Chinese Academy of Sciences, China
Junshuang Wu	Beijing Jinghang Research Institute of Computing and Communication, China
Junteng Liu	Shanghai Jiao Tong University, China
Junwen Duan	Central South University, China
Jyotika Singh	Placemakr, USA
Kai Chen	National University of Defense Technology, China
Kai Xiong	Harbin Institute of Technology, China
Kai Yang	Zhongguancun Lab, China
Kai Zhang	Ohio State University, USA
Kai Zhang	University of Science and Technology of China, China
Kailai Yang	University of Manchester, UK
Kaixin Lan	University of Macau, China
Kang Xu	Nanjing University of Posts and Telecommunications, China
Ke Deng	Tsinghua University, China
Ke Li	University of Exeter, UK
Kexiang Wang	Alibaba Group, USA
Keyang Ding	Harbin Institute of Technology, China
Khanh Duy Nguyen	University of Illinois at Urbana-Champaign, USA
Lei Chen	Fudan University, China
Lei Hou	Tsinghua University, China
Lei Zhang	Guizhou University, China
Lei Zhang	Meta, USA
Leilei Gan	Zhejiang University, China
Li Du	Harbin Institute of Technology, China
Li Zheng	Wuhan University, China
Liang Ding	Zhejiang University, China
Liang Pang	Institute of Computing Technology, Chinese Academy of Sciences, China
Liangxin Liu	Harbin Institute of Technology, China
Lianwei Wu	Northwestern Polytechnical University, China
Libo Sun	Fudan University, China
Li-Ming Zhan	Hong Kong Polytechnic University, Hong Kong, China
Ling Luo	Dalian University of Technology, China
Lingling Mu	Zhengzhou University, China
Lingyong Yan	Baidu, China
Lingzhi Wang	Chinese University of Hong Kong, Hong Kong, China

Linhai Zhang	Southeast University, China
Linqi Song	City University of Hong Kong, Hong Kong, China
Linyang Li	Fudan University, China
Liwei Wang	Chinese University of Hong Kong, Hong Kong, China
Liwen Zhang	Alibaba Group, China
Long Bai	Institute of Computing Technology, Chinese Academy of Sciences, China
Longfei Yang	Tokyo Institute of Technology, Japan
Lucy H. Lin	Spotify, Sweden
Luo Xuan	Harbin Institute of Technology, China
Luwei Xiao	Nanyang Technological University, Singapore
Luyang Lin	Chinese University of Hong Kong, Hong Kong, China
Mengjie Zhao	Sony, Japan
Mengxiang Wang	Beijing Union University, China
Min Yu	Institute of Information Engineering, Chinese Academy of Sciences, China
Ming Li	University of Maryland, College Park, USA
Ming Liao	Hong Kong Polytechnic University, Hong Kong, China
Mingda Li	Amazon, USA
Minghao Wu	Monash University, Australia
Minghuan Tan	Shenzhen Institute of Advanced Technology, Chinese Academy of Sciences, China
Mingming Yang	Tencent AI Lab, China
Mingxu Tao	Peking University, China
Mingyang Song	Tencent, China
Minjie Qiang	Suzhou University, China
Muyun Yang	Harbin Institute of Technology, China
Nan Jiang	Purdue University, USA
Nayu Liu	University of the Chinese Academy of Sciences, China
Ning Lu	Hong Kong University of Science and Technology, Hong Kong, China
Pei Zhang	Carnegie Mellon University, USA
Peiyu Liu	Zhejiang University, China
Peng Wang	Central South University, China
Pengyu Xu	Beijing Jiaotong University, China
Pengyuan Liu	Beijing Language and Culture University, China
Pengzhi Gao	Baidu, China
Ping Jian	Beijing Institute of Technology, China

Qi Hu	Hong Kong University of Science and Technology, Hong Kong, China
Qi Jia	National University of Singapore, Singapore
Qian Li	Beijing University of Posts and Telecommunications, China
Qian Li	Shandong University, China
Qiang Sheng	Institute of Computing Technology, Chinese Academy of Sciences, China
Qiang Yang	University of Florida, USA
Qianglong Chen	Zhejiang University, China
Qianhui Wu	Microsoft, USA
Qiguang Chen	Harbin Institute of Technology, China
Qiji Zhou	Westlake University, China
Qin Liu	University of California, Davis, USA
Qinghua Zhao	Beijing University of Aeronautics and Astronautics, China
Qingming Tang	Amazon, USA
Qingyun Wang	University of Illinois Urbana-Champaign, USA
Qintong Li	University of Hong Kong, Hong Kong, China
Qiuhao Lu	UTHealth Houston, USA
Qiushi Sun	University of Hong Kong, Hong Kong, China
Quan Guo	Sichuan University, China
Qun Liu	Chongqing University of Posts and Telecommunications, China
Quzhe Huang	Peking University, China
Renhao Li	University of Macau, China
Renliang Sun	International Digital Economy Academy, China
Rui Chen	Zhengzhou University of Light Industry, China
Ruifan Li	Beijing University of Post and Telecommunication, China
Ruiqi Yang	Brown University, USA
Ruixiang Zhang	Mila, UdeM, Canada
Runzhe Zhan	University of Macau, China
Ruoqing Zhao	Nanjing University of Aeronautics and Astronautics, China
Ruoyao Wang	University of Arizona, USA
Shangjian Yin	South China Agricultural University, China
Shaolei Zhang	Institute of Computing Technology, Chinese Academy of Sciences, China
Shaolin Zhu	Tianjin University, China
Shengbin Yue	Fudan University, China
Shengjie Li	University of Texas at Dallas, USA
Shi Feng	Northeastern University, China

Shi Wang	Institute of Computing Science, Chinese Academy of Sciences, China
Shibo Hong	University of Hong Kong, Hong Kong, China
Shijie Wang	Hong Kong Polytechnic University, Hong Kong, China
Shu Zhao	Anhui University, China
Shuai Zhao	Beijing University of Posts and Telecommunications, China
Shucheng Zhu	Tsinghua University, China
Shufang Xie	Renmin University of China, China
Shuichiro Shimizu	Kyoto University, Japan
Shujian Huang	Nanjing University, China
Shujun Liu	Fudan University, China
Shumin Deng	National University of Singapore, Singapore
Si Sun	Tsinghua University, China
Sijia Wang	Virginia Polytechnic Institute and State University, USA
Siqi Wang	Hong Kong Polytechnic University, Hong Kong, China
Siru Ouyang	University of Illinois Urbana-Champaign, USA
Sixing Wu	Yunnan University, China
Siyu Yuan	Fudan University, China
Siyuan Wang	University of Southern California, USA
Song Wang	Microsoft Azure AI, USA
Songsheng Wang	University of Macau, China
Taiqiang Wu	University of Hong Kong, Hong Kong, China
Tao Fang	University of Macau, China
Tao He	Harbin Institute of Technology, China
Tao Ji	Fudan University, China
Tao Qian	Hubei University of Science and Technology, China
Tengfei Yu	Harbin Institute of Technology, China
Tianbao Xie	University of Hong Kong, Hong Kong, China
Tianhao Shen	Tianjin University, China
Tianlin Zhang	University of Manchester, UK
Tianshi Zheng	Hong Kong University of Science and Technology, Hong Kong, China
Tianyong Hao	South China Normal University, China
Ting-En Lin	Alibaba Group, China
Tong Xiao	Northeastern University, China
Victor Junqiu Wei	Hong Kong University of Science and Technology, Hong Kong, China
Wang Chen	Google, USA

Wang Xu	Harbin Institute of Technology, China
Wei Emma Zhang	University of Adelaide, Australia
Wei Liu	Hong Kong University of Science and Technology, Hong Kong, China
Wei Liu	Huazhong University of Science and Technology, China
Wei Shao	City University of Hong Kong, Hong Kong, China
Wei Tang	University of Science and Technology of China, China
Wei Xiang	Huazhong University of Science and Technology, China
Wei Zhang	Saks Fifth Avenue, USA
Wei Zhu	University of Hong Kong, Hong Kong, China
Weibo Gao	University of Science and Technology of China, China
Weixiang Zhao	Harbin Institute of Technology, China
Wei-Yao Wang	University of California, Los Angeles, USA
Weizhe Lin	University of Cambridge, UK
Wen Zhang	Xiaomi AI Lab, China
Wen Zhang	Zhejiang University, China
Wenduan Xu	Quantinuum, UK
Wenliang Dai	NVIDIA, USA
Wenqi Zhang	Zhejiang University, China
Winston Wu	University of Hawaii at Hilo, USA
Xi Wang	University of Sheffield, UK
Xiabing Zhou	Soochow University, China
Xiachong Feng	University of Hong Kong, Hong Kong, China
Xian Wu	Tencent, China
Xiang Zhang	Institute of Automation, Chinese Academy of Sciences, China
Xiangci Li	Google, USA
Xiangdong Su	Inner Mongolia University, China
Xiangrui Cai	Nankai University, China
Xianjun Yang	University of California, Santa Barbara, USA
Xian-Ling Mao	Beijing Institute of Technology, China
Xianming Li	Hong Kong Polytechnic University, Hong Kong, China
Xiao Li	Nanjing University, China
Xiao Liu	Microsoft Research Asia, China
Xiao Liu	Peking University, China
Xiao Wang	Fudan University, China
Xiaoang Xu	Harbin University of Science and Technology, China

Xiaobo Liang	Soochow University, China
Xiaocui Yang	Northeastern University, China
Xiaohan Yu	Huawei Technologies Ltd., China
Xiaojun Zhang	Xi'an Jiaotong-Liverpool University, China
Xiaolong Wang	Tsinghua University, China
Xiaomian Kang	Institute of Automation, Chinese Academy of Sciences, China
Xiaowen Sun	Peking University, China
Xiaoyi Bao	Hong Kong Polytechnic University, Hong Kong, China
Xiaoyu Yang	LG AI Lab, Korea
Xihong Yang	National University of Defense Technology, China
Xin Liu	Peng Cheng Laboratory, China
Xin Wu	South China University of Technology, China
Xingyu Shen	Peking University, China
Xinhao Wang	University of Macau, China
Xinnong Zhang	Fudan University, China
Xinshi Lin	Chinese University of Hong Kong, Hong Kong, China
Xinsong Zhang	Bytedance AI Lab, China
Xinting Huang	Tencent AI Lab, China
Xinting Liao	Zhejiang University, China
Xintong Wang	University of Hamburg, Germany
Xinyi Mou	Fudan University, China
Xinyu Ma	University of Macau, China
Xiucheng Ly	Harbin Institute of Technology, China
Xu Wang	Hebei University of Technology, China
Xuefeng Bai	Harbin Institute of Technology, China
Xuehang Guo	University of Pittsburgh, USA
Xueqing Wu	University of California, Los Angeles, USA
Xunzhu Tang	University of Luxemburg, Luxembourg
Xutai Ma	Meta, USA
Xuxi Chen	University of Texas at Austin, USA
Yafu Li	Westlake University, China
Yan Xu	Hong Kong University of Science and Technology, Hong Kong, China
Yang Deng	Singapore Management University, Singapore
Yang Sun	Harbin Institute of Technology, China
Yang Xiang	Peng Cheng Laboratory, China
Yang Xu	Southern University of Science and Technology, China

Yang Zhao   Institute of Automation, Chinese Academy of
                             Sciences, China
Yang Zhong   University of Pittsburgh, USA
Yanguang Wang   Xiamen University, China
Yanhao Wang   East China Normal University, China
Yanxia Qin   National University of Singapore, Singapore
Yanyue Zhang   Southeast University, China
Yanzeng Li   Peking University, China
Yanzheng Xiang   King's College London, UK
Yao Wan   Huazhong University of Science and Technology,
                             China
Yao Zhang   Nankai University, China
Yaojie Lu   Institute of Software, Chinese Academy of
                             Sciences, China
Yaoyiran Li   University of Cambridge, UK
Yaqian Zhou   Fudan University, China
Yaqiang Wang   Chengdu University of Information Technology,
                             China
Yauwai Yim   Hong Kong University of Science and
                             Technology, Hong Kong, China
Yazhou Zhang   Zhengzhou University of Light Industry, China
Ye Liu   National University of Singapore, Singapore
Ye Wang   Fudan University, China
Ye Yuan   Peking University, China
Yekun Chai   Baidu, China
Yi Feng   Nanjing University, China
Yi Xu   Shanghai Jiao Tong University, China
Yibo Sun   Baidu, China
Yichen Jiang   University of North Carolina at Chapel Hill, USA
Yicheng Zou   Fudan University, China
Yidong Chen   Xiamen University, China
Yifei Yuan   Copenhagen University, Denmark
Yige Xu   Nanyang Technological University, Singapore
Yi-Hsin Hung   Tsinghua University, China
Yile Wang   Shenzhen University, China
Yilun Zhao   Yale University, USA
Yimeng Wu   Huawei Technologies Ltd., China
Ying Chen   China Agricultural University, China
Ying Zhang   RIKEN, Japan
Yinghui Li   Tsinghua University, China
Yingjie Li   Westlake University, China
Yinglong Ma   North China Electric Power University, China

Yinhe Zheng	Alibaba Group, China
Yinxia Lou	Jianghan University, China
Yiquan Wu	Zhejiang University, China
Yitong Li	Huawei Technologies Ltd., China
Yiwei Wang	University of California, Merced, USA
Yixia Li	Southern University of Science and Technology, China
Yong Dai	Tencent AI Lab, China
Yongbin Liu	University of South China, China
Yongheng Zhang	Central South University, China
Yougang Lyu	Shandong University, China
Youyuan Lin	Kyoto University, Tokyo Institute of Technology, Japan
Yu Cao	University of Sydney, Australia
Yu Wang	Xi'an Jiaotong University, China
Yu Zhao	Tianjin University, China
Yuan Zhang	Microsoft, USA
Yuan Zhuang	University of Utah, USA
Yuanbin Wu	East China Normal University, China
Yuanhang Yang	Harbin Institute of Technology, Shenzhen, China
Yuanliang Meng	Tsinghua University, China
Yuanxing Liu	Harbin Institute of Technology, China
Yuanyuan Lei	Texas A&M University - College Station, USA
Yuanzhe Zhang	Institute of Automation, Chinese Academy of Sciences, China
Yubo Ma	Nanyang Technological University, Singapore
Yue Feng	University College London, UK
Yue Wang	Soochow University, China
Yue Zhang	Michigan State University, USA
Yufei Wang	Huawei Technologies Ltd., China
Yuhang Wang	Beijing Jiaotong University, China
Yuji Zhang	Hong Kong Polytechnic University, Hong Kong, China
Yun Chen	Shanghai University of Finance and Economics, China
Yunfan Shao	Fudan University, China
Yunfei Long	University of Essex, UK
Yuntao Wen	University of Electronic Science and Technology of China, China
Yunyi Zhang	University of Illinois Urbana-Champaign, USA
Yunzhi Yao	Zhejiang University, China
Yuqing Xie	NetFlix, USA

Yusong Wang   Tokyo Institute of Technology, Japan
Yuting Wu   Beijing Jiaotong University, China
Yuting Zhao   Kyushu University, Japan
Yutong Wang   Harbin Institute of Technology, China
Yutong Yao   University of Macau, China
Yuxiang Jia   Zhengzhou University, China
Yuxiang Nie   Hong Kong University of Science and
                              Technology, Hong Kong, China
Yuxuan Gu   Harbin Institute of Technology, China
Yuyue Zhao   University of Science and Technology of China,
                              China
Yuzhen Huang   Hong Kong University of Science and
                              Technology, Hong Kong, China
Zecheng Tang   Soochow University, China
Zejun Li   Fudan University, China
Zhang Zhuocheng   Institute of Computing Technology, Chinese
                              Academy of Sciences, China
Zhangyin Feng   Harbin Institute of Technology, China
Zhaocong Li   University of Macau, China
Zhaoyang Wang   University of North Carolina at Chapel Hill, USA
Zhe Hu   Baidu, China
Zhe Yang   Institute of Computing Technology, Chinese
                              Academy of Sciences, China
Zhen Wan   Kyoto University, Japan
Zhen Wang   University of California, San Diego, USA
Zhen Xu   Tencent, China
Zhengfu He   Fudan University, China
Zhenghao Liu   Northeastern University, China
Zhengliang Shi   Shandong University, China
Zhengrui Ma   Institute of Computing Technology, Chinese
                              Academy of Sciences, China
Zhenhailong Wang   University of Illinois Urbana-Champaign, USA
Zhenjie Zhao   Nankai University, China
Zhenxi Lin   Tencent, China
Zhexuan Wang   Harbin Institute of Technology, China
Zheye Deng   Hong Kong University of Science and
                              Technology, Hong Kong, China
Zhichun Wang   Beijing Normal University, China
Zhidan Wang   Tsinghua University, China
Zhihan Zhang   Singapore Management University, Singapore
Zhihao Fan   Alibaba Group, China
Zhihua Jiang   Jinan University, China
Zhijun Wang   Nanjing University, China

Zhitao He	Institute of Automation, Chinese Academy of Sciences, China
Zhiwen Tang	Yunnan University, China
Zhixu Li	Fudan University, China
Zhiyang Teng	ByteDance, China
Zhiyi Hou	Harbin Institute of Technology, China
Zhiyuan Fan	Tianjin University, China
Zhiyuan Liu	National University of Singapore, Singapore
Zhiyuan Wen	Harbin Institute of Technology, China
Zhiyue Liu	Guangxi University, China
ZhiZheng Wang	National Institutes of Health, USA
Zhong Zhang	Tsinghua University, China
Zhuang Chen	Tsinghua University, China
Zhuang Li	Monash University, Australia
Zhuang Liu	Dongbei University of Finance and Economics, China
Zhuohan Long	Tongji University, China
Zhuoxuan Jiang	Shanghai Business School, China
Zifeng Wang	University of Illinois Urbana-Champaign, USA
Zihan Wang	University of Amsterdam, Netherlands
Zihao Fu	University of Oxford, UK
Zihao Li	Wuhan University, China
Zihao Wang	Hong Kong University of Science and Technology, Hong Kong, China
Zihao Zhou	Xi'an Jiaotong-Liverpool University, China
Zixian Huang	Nanjing University, China
Zixuan Liu	University of Washington, USA
Ziyang Chen	National University of Defense Technology, China
Ziyang Li	University of Pennsylvania, USA
Ziyang Luo	National University of Singapore, Singapore
Ziyang Wang	University of North Carolina at Chapel Hill, USA
Zi-Yi Dou	University of California, Los Angeles, USA
Zongcheng Ji	Ping An Technology, China
Zonglin Yang	Nanyang Technological University, Singapore
Zuchao Li	Wuhan University, China
Zuoli Tang	Wuhan University, China

Best Reviewers

Bin Li	Nanjing Normal University, China
Boyang Wang	Beijing University of Aeronautics and Astronautics, China
Changyi Xiao	University of Science and Technology of China, China
Guoxin Wang	Microsoft, USA
Haiyue Song	National Institute of Information and Communications Technology, Japan
Haonan Li	Mohamed bin Zayed University of Artificial Intelligence, UAE
Hongfei Xu	Zhengzhou University, China
Hou Pong Chan	Alibaba Group, Singapore
Hui Li	Xiamen University, China
Jiachun Li	Institute of Automation, Chinese Academy of Sciences, China
Jiaju Lin	Pennsylvania State University, USA
Jiani Huang	University of Pennsylvania, USA
Jinghan Zhang	Hong Kong University of Science and Technology, Hong Kong, China
Jundong Xu	National University of Singapore, Singapore
Junhui Li	Soochow University, China
Ke Li	University of Exeter, UK
Libo Sun	Fudan University, China
Lucy H. Lin	Spotify, Sweden
Min Yu	Institute of Information Engineering, Chinese Academy of Sciences, China
Mingxu Tao	Peking University, China
Peiyu Liu	Zhejiang University, China
Peng Wang	Central South University, China
Shaolin Zhu	Tianjin University, China
Shi Feng	Northeastern University, China
Shucheng Zhu	Tsinghua University, China
Si Sun	Tsinghua University, China
Tao Fang	University of Macau, China
Wei Emma Zhang	University of Adelaide, Australia
Winston Wu	University of Hawaii at Hilo, USA
Xinting Huang	Tencent AI Lab, China
Yi-Hsin Hung	Tsinghua University, China
Yutong Yao	University of Macau, China

Zhenjie Zhao   Nankai University, China
Zuchao Li   Wuhan University, China

Organizers

Organized by

China Computer Federation, China

Hosted by

Westlake University

In Cooperation with

Lecture Notes in Computer Science

Springer

Sponsoring Institutions

Main Sponsor

Cloud Town

Diamond Sponsors

OPPO

Alibaba Cloud

JDT

Platinum Sponsors

HUAWEI

ZTE

XIAOMI

Lenovo Research

Golden Sponsors

GTCOM

PARATERA

Douyin Group

ModelBest

DataOcean AI

Zhipu AI

NiuTrans

Scietrain

Baidu

Contents – Part I

IR/Dialogue Systems/Question Answering

Fundamentals of NLP

Information Extraction and Knowledge Graph

IR/Dialogue Systems/Question Answering

Overcoming Rigid and Monotonous: Enhancing Knowledge-Grounded Conversation Generation via Multi-granularity Knowledge

Xingsheng Zhang[1,2], YiFan Deng[1,2], Yue Hu[1,2(✉)], Yunpeng Li[1,2], and Ping Guo[1,2]

[1] Institute of Information Engineering, Chinese Academy of Sciences, Beijing, China
{zhangxingsheng,dengyifan,liyunpeng,guoping,huyue}@iie.ac.cn
[2] School of Cyber Security, University of Chinese Academy of Sciences, Beijing, China

Abstract. Knowledge-grounded conversation (KGC) shows great potential in building an engaging and reliable chatbot, in which knowledge-aware generation is a key ingredient in it. Traditional methods, which usually generate responses based on sentence-level knowledge, are unable to locate the suitable knowledge pieces exactly, leading to insufficient utilization of knowledge and monotonous and rigid responses. In this paper, we propose a Multi-granularity Knowledge-aware Adaptive Generation (MKAG) model, which can adaptively select knowledge units from coarse to fine-grained based on various semantic segments in the response, as well as generating knowledgeable and informative responses. Specifically, an expandable knowledge supporter is devised to split knowledge units of various granularities according to semantics for positioning knowledge precisely. Besides, we design a segmentation-based decoding method, which is capable of generating multiple semantic segments sequentially, and each semantic segment can adaptively select the corresponding granularity of knowledge units for the generation. Experimental results show that MKAG significantly outperforms state-of-the-art methods in terms of both automatic and human evaluations, indicating that it can alleviate the issue of monotonous and rigid replies effectively.

Keywords: Knowledge-grounded conversation · Multi-granularity Knowledge · Segmentation-based decoding

1 Introduction

Open-domain conversation systems often produce bland responses due to reliance solely on context. Knowledge-Grounded Conversation (KGC) [2,23] addresses this by integrating external knowledge to enhance informativeness. However, the challenge lies in effectively incorporating diverse knowledge pieces to avoid

D. F. Wong et al. (Eds.): NLPCC 2024, LNAI 15359, pp. 3–15, 2025.
https://doi.org/10.1007/978-981-97-9431-7_1

monotonous responses. Knowledge-aware generation (KG) integrates knowledge into conversations, which is crucial for KGC. Existing KG methods often rely on latent variables [23] or copying generation [18], resulting in rigid and monotonous texts. These methods typically use coarse-grained, sentence-level knowledge, making it difficult to control knowledge usage, leading to either underutilization or overuse, and limiting responses' diversity and informativeness.

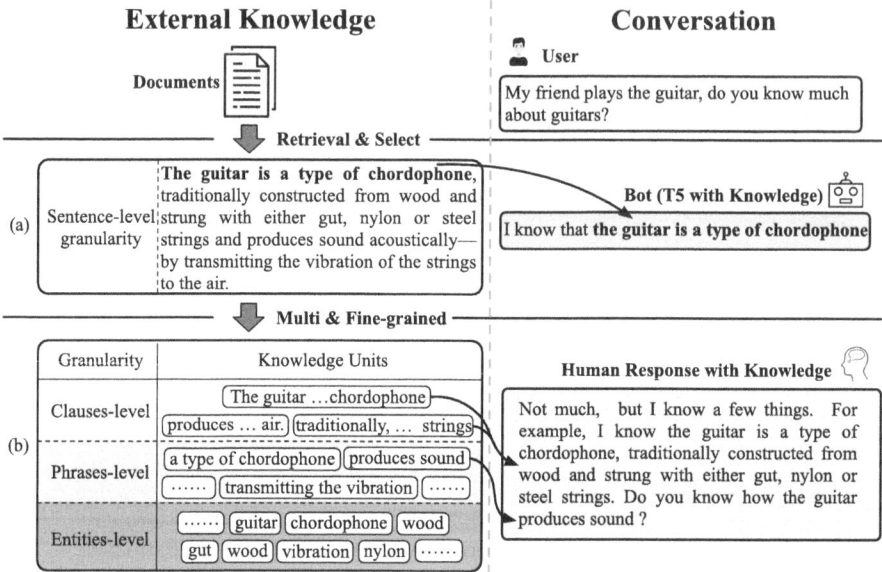

Fig. 1. (a) rigid response with **bold** (knowledge used). (b)-left: multiple knowledge units of varying granularity. (b)-right: Engaging response with different semantic segments.

Incorporating fine-grained knowledge can help models tackle the above issue. As shown in Fig. 1, the Bot generates dull responses by mechanically copying short knowledge pieces, while engaging responses often contain multiple semantic segments, each conveying different content and intents. We propose decomposing responses into non-overlapping semantic segments, each focusing on knowledge units of varying granularities to generate more informative responses. Fine-grained knowledge units enhance the naturalness and memorability of responses.

In this paper, we introduce a **M**ulti-granularity **K**nowledge-aware **A**daptive **G**eneration (MKAG) model to infuse the multi-granularity knowledge units into the response generation. Specifically, an expandable knowledge supporter module is devised to decompose the coarse-level knowledge into various fine-grained units through several knowledge extractors. A segmentation-based decoding method is designed to guide the model to generate the response segment by segment. To model the mapping from semantic segments to various granularity knowledge units, a knowledge linker is introduced to format the training target, enabling the model could select reasonable knowledge units adaptively for each semantic segment generation while training. Thus, the model is capable of utilizing external knowledge effectively to generate knowledgeable responses.

Extensive experiments on FaithDial demonstrate that MKAG outperforms existing models in response diversity and informativeness. Both automatic and human evaluations validate the benefits of incorporating multi-granularity knowledge units and the segment-based decoding method.

The key contributions of this work are: (1) proposing MKAG, a model grounded by multi-granularity knowledge units for knowledge-aware generation; (2) designing an expandable knowledge supporter and a segmentation-based decoding method to incorporate various granularity knowledge units; and (3) empirically validating MKAG's efficacy through extensive experiments on a KGC dataset.

2   Related Work

Recently, various neural models have been proposed for KGC [2,11]. Existing methods often decompose the task into two sub-problems [5]: (1) knowledge selection: retrieving relevant knowledge from external sources, e.g. knowledge graph [23], unstructured knowledge corpus [1], parametric models [8]. (2) knowledge-aware generation: injecting external knowledge to generate responses. Our work focuses on the KG task. Existing approaches include latent variable models [23], copying generation [18], and infusing knowledge via prompts [8]. Rely solely on sentence-level, causing issues of knowledge underutilization or overuse. Our work introduces multiple granularity knowledge units to address these limitations.

Our work also relates to segment generation, which has been applied in many NLP tasks. In text generation, Wiseman et al. [17] develop a neural template-like generation model with a hidden semi-markov model (HSMM) decoder, and each cell in the template represents a segment in the response. In open-domain conversation, Yang et al. [19] proposed the templates estimated from the unpaired data to guide the process of response generation; Zou et al. [24] employed a customized Insertion Transformer that performs concept-guided non-autoregressive generation to complete a response; Zhao et al. [22] proposed a segmentation-based model with sequential latent variables for segment positioning and categorization. These methods often involve complex model architectures and increased computation. In contrast, our novel decoding method enables adaptive response generation efficiently, without additional computation.

3   Task Formulation

Given a conversation corpus $\mathcal{D}$ with N cases, and every case is in the format of (C, K, R), where $C = (u_1, u_2, \ldots, u_{l_c})$ is the context of the conversation consists of a sequence of l_c previous utterances, $R = (r_1, r_2, \ldots, r_{l_r})$ is the response. And

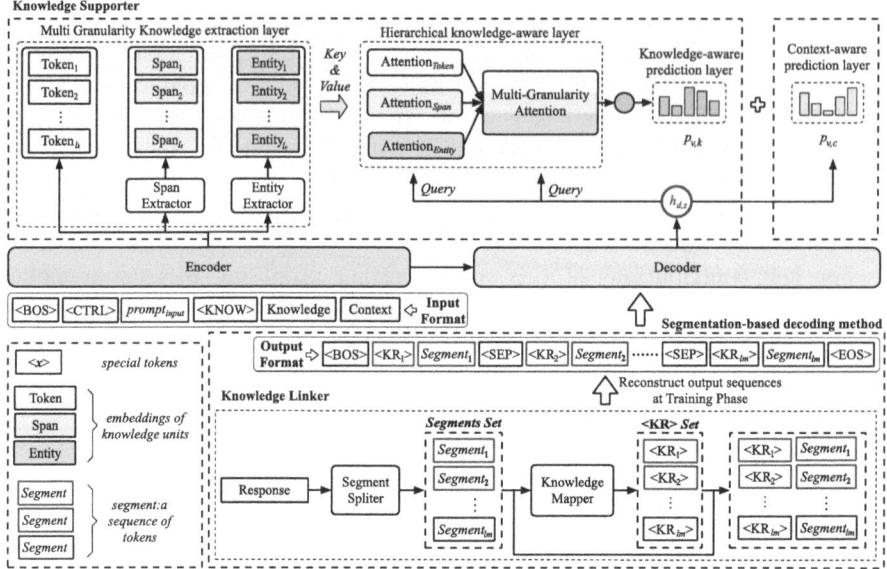

Fig. 2. An overview of MKAG.

$K = (k_1, \ldots, k_{l_k})$ serves as the external knowledge sentence with l_k tokens. Our goal is to learn a generation model $p_\theta(R \mid C, K)$ (θ denotes the parameters of the model) from $\mathcal{D}$ that could generate a knowledgeable and informative response R based on conversation context C and external knowledge K.

4   Methodology

The proposed MKAG framework, illustrated in Fig. 2, comprises three modules: (1) **Encoder**: encodes the conversation context and external knowledge into contextual representations h_C and h_K; (2) **Knowledge Supporter**: obtains multiple units from coarse to fine-grained via various extractors and outputs a knowledge-aware vocabulary distribution $p_{v,k}$ by a hierarchical knowledge-aware layer. (3) **Decoder**: generate the output sequence step wisely. It predicts the context-aware distribution $p_{v,c}$ at each step and queries over knowledge units. The segmentation-based decoding method forces the decoder to sequentially embed appropriate knowledge units into each segment. During training, the Knowledge Linker refashions training targets to align with the segmented structure.

4.1   Encoder

We exploit the pre-trained language model T5 [15] as the backbone. The input consists of three parts: (a) Context part: insert speaker ID (either <user>

or <bot>) into C to tag the roles; (b) Knowledge part: prepend the special token <KNOW> to the knowledge sequence K for separating. (c) Prompt part: inspired by natural language input prompts used in DialCTRL [16] to represent control codes. The input sequence of the encoder can be formatted as: $Input_{format} = (<\text{BOS}>, <\text{CTRL}>, prompt_{input}, <\text{KNOW}>, K, C)$, <BOS> is the special token as T5, and <CTRL> for separating. To this end, the encoder can be formulated as follows:

$$h_x = \text{Encoder}\,(Input_{format}) \tag{1}$$

where $h_x \in \mathbb{R}^{l_x \times d}$, l_x is the length of the total input sequence and d is the hidden size. The knowledge contextual representation $h_K = \{h_{k,1}, h_{k,2}, \ldots, h_{k,l_k}\} \in \mathbb{R}^{l_k \times d}$ can be split from h_x according to the index of K in $Input_{format}$. Similarly, h_C represents the conversation context.

4.2   Knowledge Supporter

To improve knowledge locate during generation, we designed a Knowledge Supporter module with three layers: (1) Multi-granularity Knowledge Extraction Layer: Extracts fine-grained knowledge units from sentences; (2) Hierarchical Knowledge-Aware Layer: Softly integrates the appropriate knowledge unit at each decoding step; (3) Knowledge-Aware Prediction Layer: Predicts the next token distribution based on the fused latent representation of knowledge. This module can theoretically extract knowledge units at any granularity level. In this paper, we use sentence-level, span-level, and entity-level granularities to balance detail and efficiency, with future work to explore optimal granularity combinations.

Multi-granularity Knowledge Extraction Layer. Given the sentence-level knowledge K as a coarse-grained unit, this layer employs various extractors to obtain fine-grained knowledge units. As for span-level granularity, StanfordNLP toolkit [10] parses K into spans, with each span's embedding obtained via maxpooling over its token embeddings (a span usually covers multiple tokens). The span representations set $h_S = \{h_{s,1}, \ldots, h_{s,l_s}\} \in \mathbb{R}^{d \times l_s}$, where l_s is the number of spans. For entity-level, the spacy toolkit [4] extracts entities from K, which is also derived through max-pooling. The entity representation set $h_E = \{h_{e,1}, h_{e,2}, \ldots, h_{e,l_e}\} \in \mathbb{R}^{d \times l_e}$, and l_e is the number of entities.

Hierarchical Knowledge-Aware Layer. To locate the knowledge evidence from multiple granularity knowledge units for generation, this layer integrates the knowledge from single-granularity to multi-granularity in a hierarchical manner. The single-granularity sub-layer captures the relationships within each granularity using scaled dot-product attention. Given the decoder hidden state $h_{d,z}$ of decoding step z as query and the knowledge unit representations set of a granularity(either h_K or h_S or h_E) as key and value, the process as follows:

$$\tilde{h}_t = \text{Softmax}\left(\frac{h_{d,z}\,(h_t)^{\mathsf{T}}}{\sqrt{d}}\right) h_t, \quad t \in \{K, S, E\} \tag{2}$$

where $\tilde{h}_t \in \mathbb{R}^{d\times 1}$. Next, the multi-granularity sub-layer addresses the interconnections among different granularities as:

$$\tilde{h}_{d,z} = \text{Softmax}\left(\frac{h_{d,z}[\tilde{h}_K \cdot \tilde{h}_S \cdot \tilde{h}_E]^{\mathsf{T}}}{\sqrt{d}}\right) [\tilde{h}_K \cdot \tilde{h}_S \cdot \tilde{h}_E] \tag{3}$$

$h_{d,z}$ as query and the concatenated knowledge representations $[\tilde{h}_K \cdot \tilde{h}_S \cdot \tilde{h}_E] \in \mathbb{R}^{d\times 3}$ as key and value, $\cdot$ refers to the concatenation between vectors.

Knowlegde-Aware Prediction Layer: Knowledge-aware prediction head predicts the vocab distribution $p_{v,k}$ based on the representation $\tilde{h}_{d,z}$:

$$p_{v,k} = \text{Softmax}\left(\mathbf{W^K}\tilde{h}_{d,z} + \mathbf{b^K}\right) \tag{4}$$

where $\mathbf{W^K} \in \mathbb{R}^{d\times|v|}$ and $\mathbf{b^K}$ are the parameters. And $|v|$ is vocab size.

4.3 Decoder

Prediction. Following the T5 model, the decoder predicts the output distribution token-by-token using the hidden representation h_x. At decoding step z, the hidden state $h_{d,z}$ updated as:

$$h_{d,z} = \text{Decoder}\left([h_x; h_{d,1}, \dots, h_{d,z-1}], y_{z-1}\right) \tag{5}$$

The hidden state $h_{d,z}$ locates the knowledge units in the knowledge supporter module. Meanwhile, the context-aware vocab distribution is predicted:

$$p_{v,c} = \text{Softmax}(\mathbf{W^C}h_{d,z} + \mathbf{b^C}) \tag{6}$$

where $\mathbf{W^C} \in \mathbb{R}^{d\times|v|}$ and $\mathbf{b^C}$ are parameters. Considering the coherence and the informativeness of responses, we adopt a scale hyperparameter λ to balance knowledge-aware and context-aware distribution:

$$p_{y,z} = \lambda p_{v,k} + (1 - \lambda)\,p_{v,c} \tag{7}$$

Segmentation-Based Decoding Method. The general greedy decoding method ignores the intrinsic feature that a response contains multiple segments, making it difficult to locate suitable knowledge pieces from various granularities. Therefore, we propose a segmentation-based decoding method, modifying the output format to enable sequential generation of semantic segments and adaptive retrieval of appropriate knowledge units. This method generates the output sequence token-by-token. Next, we first introduce the output format in this method and then describe the knowledge linker module which constructs the output sequences during training.

Output Format. Unlike the traditional methods that directly regard the original response R as the output sequence y, we attempt to inject separate tokens <SEP> to discriminate different segments. To link semantic segments with corresponding knowledge units, we propose a knowledge mapper function to measure the degree of knowledge usage for each segment.

Intuitively, the degrees of knowledge usage are directly related to the granularity of the knowledge unit. Specifically, we devise three degrees of knowledge usage, "no_know": segment is independent of external knowledge; "low_know": segment partially relies on external knowledge; "high_know": segment mostly relies on external knowledge. Accordingly, three kinds of knowledge-based guiding tokens <KR> $\in$ {<no_know>, <low_know>, <high_know>} to guide the model adaptively retrieve the appropriate knowledge units for each segment. Given a response R contains several semantic segments $\{m_1, m_1, \ldots, m_{l_m}\}$ in order, and each segment m_i associated with a guiding token KR_i obtained through knowledge mapper, The formatted output sequence $\tilde{y}$ includes separate tokens between segments and prepends the guiding tokens to each segment:

$$\tilde{y} = (\text{<BOS>}, \text{<KR}_1\text{>}, m_1, \text{<SEP>}, \ldots, \text{<KR}_{l_m}\text{>}, m_{l_m}, \text{<EOS>}) \qquad (8)$$

During training, we reconstruct the responses into $\tilde{y}$ through knowledge linker and regard $\tilde{y}$ as training targets to optimize the model. After training, the model can automatically generate sequences in this format during inference. We filter out the special tokens(e.g. <SEP>, <KR>) by post-processing to get a pure response.

Knowledge Linker. splits responses into segments and assigns knowledge-based guiding tokens to each segment. And Segment Splitter use StanfordNLP toolkit [10] to split the response into several segments:

$$\{m_1, m_2, \ldots, m_{l_m}\} = \text{SemanticSplitter}(R) \qquad (9)$$

where l_m is the number of segments. For i-th segment m_i, knowledge linker calculates F1-score between m_i and external knowledge K as knowledge mapper function to assign knowledge-based guiding token <KR$_i$> for segment m_i:

$$
\begin{aligned}
KR_i &= \text{KnowledgeMapper}(m_i), i \in \{1, 2, \ldots, l_m\} \\
&= \begin{cases}
\text{<no\_know>} & \text{if} \quad \text{F1Score}(m_i, K) == 0 \\
\text{<low\_know>} & \text{if} \quad \text{F1Score}(m_i, K) <= \alpha \\
\text{<high\_know>} & \text{if} \quad \text{F1Score}(m_i, K) > \alpha
\end{cases}
\end{aligned} \qquad (10)
$$

where the function $\text{F1Score}(m_i, K)$ counting the number of matched tokens between m_i and K. α is a threshold to distinguish degrees of knowledge usage,

4.4   Training Loss Function

Given a training sequence $\tilde{y}$, we train the whole model end-to-end with the negative log-likelihood loss (NLL) function defined as:

$$\mathcal{L}_{\mathrm{NLL}}(\theta) = -\sum_{i=1}^{|\tilde{y}|} \log p\left(\tilde{y}_i \mid \tilde{y}_{<i}, C, K\right) \tag{11}$$

where θ denotes all the trainable model parameters and y_i is the i-th token; $r_{<i}$ are the tokens up to the $(i$-1)-th decoding step. $|\tilde{y}|$ is the length of $\tilde{y}$.

5   Experimental Setup

5.1   Datasets

Experiments were conducted on the FaithDial dataset [3], which enhances responses from the Wow dataset [2] to be more informative and engaging. Unlike Wow and Holl_E [11], which contain many dull responses, FaithDial offers more knowledgeable and challenging conversations.

5.2   Baselines

For the Knowledge-aware Generation task, we compare MKAG with several state-of-the-art models: (1) **GPT2** [14]: A Transformer-based [2] pre-trained language model that generates text autoregressively; (2) **DialoGPT** [21]: A dialogue generation model trained on a dialogue corpus, using the same Transformer architecture as GPT-2; (3) **DoHA** [13]: Enhances BART with a two-view attention mechanism for document-grounded generation, focusing on context-driven representation. (4) **T5** [15]: A unified framework that converts text-based language problems into a text-to-text format, using a Transformer encoder-decoder architecture; (5) **DialCTRL** [16]: Uses control tokens (<objective-voice>, <lexical-overlap>, <entailment>) to manage response styles, implemented with T5 and showing state-of-the-art results on the FaithDial dataset.

5.3   Evaluation Metrics

We use both automatic metrics and human ratings to evaluate MKAG's performance.

Automatic Metrics. We assess generated responses from three perspectives: **Appropriateness**: Using BLEU [12][1], ROUGE-L [7] to evaluate relevance to ground-truth responses; **Distinctness**: Using Distinct-1/2 [6] to measure the diversity of responses by the ratio of distinct unigrams and bigrams; **Knowledgeability**: Using BERTScore [20] and Know-F1 to evaluate the informativeness of responses. BERTScore measures semantic similarity with BERT embeddings, while Know-F1 measures token-level lexical overlap.

---

[1] https://github.com/mjpost/sacrebleu.

Huamn Meterics. We randomly sample 200 examples from the FaithDial test set and have three volunteers rate them based on: **Relevance**: How well the utterance fits the conversation context; **Engagingness**: How attractive and fluent the utterance is; **Knowledgeability**: Whether the response is informative. Evaluators score on a scale of 1–5, and agreement is measured using Fleiss' kappa.

Table 1. Automatic results on FaithDial. Numbers in **bold** mean that the improvement to the best performing baseline is statistically significant (t-test with p-value < 0.05)

Models	Knowledgeability		Appropriateness		Diversity	
	BERTScore	F1	BLEU	ROUGE	DIST-1	DIST-2
GPT2	0.36	50.41	9.50	33.43	–	–
DIALOGPT	0.36	52.25	9.63	33.13	–	–
DoHA	0.39	58.32	9.89	31.78	–	–
T5	0.41	59.22	10.31	33.89	0.10	0.32
DialCTRL	0.46	62.21	10.41	**33.97**	0.11	0.34
MKAG	**0.48**	**65.08**	**12.10**	33.50	**0.11**	**0.35**

5.4 Implementation Details

Following [3,16], we use the HuggingFace library versions of T5-base[2] as our underlying model. We train our models for 10 epochs on batch size of 8 via accumulating gradients for 4 steps, and use AdamW [9] with a learning rate of 6.25e-5 that warms up for 4% of training steps. The maximum input and output sequence are set to 256 and 128 respectively. For encoding, the maximum dialogue history length is set to 5 utterances. For decoding, we use nucleus sampling with p = 0.6. The maximum dialogue history length of 3 utterances. The hyperparameters λ in Eq.(7) is set to 0.5 and α in Eq. (10) is set to 0.21. We trained our model on a single NVIDIA Tesla V100 GPU with 32 GB memory.

6 Experiment Results

6.1 Automatic Evaluation

As shown in Table 1, our method outperforms state-of-the-art baselines in most metrics, demonstrating the empirical effectiveness of MKAG. In terms of knowledgeability, MKAG significantly surpasses all baselines, producing more informative and knowledgeable responses. While DialCTRL achieves competitive results, it still lags behind MKAG. Integrating multiple granularity knowledge units is

---

[2] https://huggingface.co/t5-base.

crucial for this improvement. For appropriateness, MKAG excels in the BLEU metric, indicating that its responses are both fluent and contextually coherent. However, MKAG slightly underperforms T5 and DialCTRL in the ROUGE metric, likely due to the segmentation-based decoding method, which may disrupt response consistency. Future work will explore better patterns to establish segment correlations. Regarding diversity, we reproduced the strongest baselines (T5 and DialCTRL) to calculate diversity metrics, as they were not provided in [3]. MKAG outperforms these baselines overall, benefiting from the injection of suitable knowledge units into semantic segments during generation.

Table 2. Human evaluation on FaithDial. Numbers in **bold** that the improvement to the best performing baseline is statistically significant (t-test with p-value < 0.05).

Models	Relevance	Engagingness	Knowledgeability
T5	3.08	4.21	3.43
DialCTRL	3.13	4.24	3.56
MKAG	**3.29**	**4.37**	**3.84**

6.2   Human Evaluation

Given the time and cost of human evaluation, we only included the competitive baselines T5 and DialCTRL. As shown in Table 2, our model outperforms these baselines across all metrics. The relevance and knowledgeability results align with automatic evaluations, confirming the benefits of multi-granularity knowledge units and the effectiveness of MKAG. Additionally, MKAG achieved the highest engagement scores, indicating that its responses are more attractive. Despite minor losses in the ROUGE metric, the significant improvement in engagement suggests that the segmentation-based decoding method enhances the informativeness of the generated text.

Table 3. Ablation study on knowledge unit granularity. **Bolded** indicate best performance. All variants uses the segmentation-based decoding method.

Models	BERTScore	F1	BLEU	ROUGE
MKAG	**0.48**	**65.08**	12.10	33.50
w/o. *sentence*	0.47	64.61	11.88	32.90
w/o. *span*	0.46	63.84	11.95	32.91
w/o. *entity*	0.47	64.42	**12.13**	**33.51**

Table 4. Ablation study for knowledge-based guiding tokens. **Bolded** indicate best performance. All variants are equipped with the Knowledge supporter.

Models	BERTScore	F1	BLEU	ROUGE
MKAG	**0.48**	**65.08**	**12.10**	33.50
w/o. *high_know*	0.47	64.87	11.91	**36.10**
w/o. *low_know*	0.48	63.82	11.86	33.08
w/o. *no_know*	0.47	63.82	11.88	33.30

Table 5. Knowledge units infused in response are highlighted(Sentence , Span , Entity). **Gold** indicates reference response. Know. means knowledgeable response.

Knowledge	Sentence	The domestic dog ("Canis lupus familiaris" or "Canis familiaris") is a member of the genus "Canis" (canines), which forms part of the wolf-like canids, and is the most widely abundant terrestrial carnivore
	Spans	a member of the genus "Canis" (canines); the most widely abundant terrestrial carnivore
	Enitities	Canis lupus familiaris; Canis familiaris
Context		<user>I have two dogs! Do you have any dogs, or a favorite breed?

Gold: As I am a bot I don't really have favorites. Did you know that they are the terrestrial carnivore that is the most abundant widely?

T5: I don't have any favorites, but I know that dogs are part of the genus Canis. (Monotonous)

DialCTRL: I don't have any favorites, but I know that dogs are part of the genus Canis. (Monotonous)

MKAG: I don't have a favorite breed, but I do know that the domestic dog is the most widely abundant terrestrial carnivore . (Know.)

6.3   Ablation Study

Next we are especially interested in some research questions:

1. **RQ1** How does each granularity of knowledge units in knowledge supporter contribute to the performance of our model?
2. **RQ2** How does each kind of guiding token in the segmentation-based decoding method contribute to the performance of our model?

To address RQ1, we conduct an ablation study comparing the full model with several variants: (1) w/o. *sentence*: Remove sentence-level knowledge units; (2) w/o. *span*: Remove span-level knowledge units; (3) w/o. *entity*: Remove entity-level knowledge units. As shown in Table 3, we observed: (1) all variants exhibit a degeneration at BERTScore and F1 metrics, highlighting the necessity of multiple knowledge units for informativeness. (2) Removing sentence-level and span-level units degraded BLEU and ROUGE scores, indicating that different response segments prefer different knowledge granularities, enhancing fluency. (3) Removing entity-level units slightly improved BLEU and ROUGE scores, as entity knowledge units can disrupt fluency due to their semantic independence.

To address RQ2, we evaluated the impact of removing different knowledge-based guiding tokens (<KR>) from the segmentation-based decoding method. As shown in Table 4: Removing guiding tokens significantly decreased BERTScore, F1, and BLEU metrics, demonstrating their role in effectively injecting knowledge units for informative and fluent responses. Removing *high_know* tokens improved ROUGE scores, suggesting that fewer disruptions in sentence consistency enhance response coherence.

6.4   Case Study

To illustrate our method's advantages, Table 5 presents a case sampled from the FaithDial test set with gold responses. In Case, T5 and DialCTRL understand the context, they fail to select appropriate knowledge pieces, resulting in monotonous responses. In contrast, MKAG uses multi-granularity knowledge units to incorporate suitable knowledge into segment generation, creating more engaging responses.

7   Conclusion

In this work, we propose MKAG, which incorporates the multiple granularity knowledge units into knowledge-aware generation for informative and knowledge-able responses. Knowledge supporter provides coarse-to-fine-grained knowledge units, and segmentation-based decoding method guides the injection of suitable knowledge units response segment. For future work, we would like to incorporate multiple granularity knowledge units into the pre-training process.

References

1. Chen, X., et al.: Bridging the gap between prior and posterior knowledge selection for knowledge-grounded dialogue generation. In: Proceedings of EMNLP (2020)
2. Dinan, E., Roller, S., Shuster, K., Fan, A., Auli, M., Weston, J.: Wizard of Wikipedia: knowledge-powered conversational agents. In: Proceedings of ICLR (2019)
3. Dziri, N., et al.: FaithDial: a faithful benchmark for information-seeking dialogue. Trans. Assoc. Comput. Linguist. **10**, 1473–1490 (2022)
4. Honnibal, M., Montani, I.: spaCy 2: natural language understanding with Bloom embeddings, convolutional neural networks and incremental parsing (2017)
5. Kim, B., Ahn, J., Kim, G.: Sequential latent knowledge selection for knowledge-grounded dialogue. In: Proceedings of ICLR (2020)
6. Li, J., Galley, M., Brockett, C., Gao, J., Dolan, B.: A diversity-promoting objective function for neural conversation models. In: Proceedings of NAACL (2016)

7. Lin, C.Y.: ROUGE: a package for automatic evaluation of summaries. In: Text Summarization Branches Out (2004)
8. Liu, Z., et al.: Multi-stage prompting for knowledgeable dialogue generation. In: Proceedings of ACL Findings (2022)
9. Loshchilov, I., Hutter, F.: Decoupled weight decay regularization. In: Proceedings of ICLR (2019)
10. Manning, C., Surdeanu, M., Bauer, J., Finkel, J., Bethard, S., McClosky, D.: The Stanford CoreNLP natural language processing toolkit. In: Proceedings of ACL (2014)
11. Moghe, N., Arora, S., Banerjee, S., Khapra, M.M.: Towards exploiting background knowledge for building conversation systems. In: Proceedings of EMNLP (2018)
12. Papineni, K., Roukos, S., Ward, T., Zhu, W.J.: BLEU: a method for automatic evaluation of machine translation. In: Proceedings of ACL (2002)
13. Prabhumoye, S., Hashimoto, K., Zhou, Y., Black, A.W., Salakhutdinov, R.: Focused attention improves document-grounded generation. In: Proceedings of NAACL (2021)
14. Radford, A., Wu, J., Child, R., Luan, D., Amodei, D., Sutskever, I.: Language models are unsupervised multitask learners (2019)
15. Raffel, C., et al.: Exploring the limits of transfer learning with a unified text-to-text transformer. J. Mach. Learn. Res. **21**, 1–67 (2022)
16. Rashkin, H., Reitter, D., Tomar, G.S., Das, D.: Increasing faithfulness in knowledge-grounded dialogue with controllable features. In: Proceedings of ACL (2021)
17. Wiseman, S., Shieber, S., Rush, A.: Learning neural templates for text generation. In: Proceedings of EMNLP (2018)
18. Wu, S., Li, Y., Wang, M., Zhang, D., Zhou, Y., Wu, Z.: More is better: enhancing open-domain dialogue generation via multi-source heterogeneous knowledge. In: Proceedings of EMNLP (2021)
19. Yang, Z., Wu, W., Yang, J., Xu, C., Li, Z.: Low-resource response generation with template prior. In: Proceedings of EMNLP (2019)
20. Zhang*, T., Kishore*, V., Wu*, F., Weinberger, K.Q., Artzi, Y.: BERTScore: evaluating text generation with BERT. In: Proceedings of ICLR (2020)
21. Zhang, Y., et al.: DIALOGPT: large-scale generative pre-training for conversational response generation. In: Proceedings of ACL (2020)
22. Zhao, X., Fu, T., Tao, C., Wu, W., Zhao, D., Yan, R.: Learning to express in knowledge-grounded conversation. In: Proceedings of NAACL (2022)
23. Zhou, H., Young, T., Huang, M., Zhao, H., Xu, J., Zhu, X.: Commonsense knowledge aware conversation generation with graph attention. In: Proceedings of IJCAI (2018)
24. Zou, Y., Liu, Z., Hu, X., Zhang, Q.: Thinking clearly, talking fast: concept-guided non-autoregressive generation for open-domain dialogue systems. In: Proceedings of EMNLP (2021)

Learning to Generate Style-Specific Adapters for Stylized Dialogue Generation

Jinpeng Li[1], Yuhang Chen[1], Pengfei Wu[1], Yingce Xia[2], Shufang Xie[4], Dongyan Zhao[1,3(✉)], and Rui Yan[4]

[1] Wangxuan Institute of Computer Technology, Peking University, Beijing, China
{lijinpeng,pengfeiwu1999,zhaody}@stu.pku.edu.cn
[2] Microsoft Research, Beijing, China
yingce.xia@microsoft.com
[3] National Key Laboratory of General Artificial Intelligence, Beijing, China
[4] Gaoling School of Artifical Intelligence, Renmin University of China, Beijing, China
{shufangxie,ruiyan}@ruc.edu.cn

Abstract. Stylized dialogue generation is capable of producing highly creative and engaging responses, making it an indispensable feature of intelligent dialogue systems. However, a major challenge to this task is the paucity of supervised data, resulting in suboptimal performance. Although some unsupervised methods have emerged, they tend to handle only a limited range of dialogue styles simultaneously. Retraining becomes necessary when new dialogue styles are introduced, leading to increased training overhead and model redundancy. Furthermore, the large language model shows exciting performance, it still falls short on some specific tasks. To address the data limitations and training overhead, we propose a Multi-Stylized Adapter Dialogue Generation (MultiSADG) model, which generates multiple stylized adapters by using representations from different stylized corpora. Specifically, we generate style-specific adapters for modeling both contexts and stylized responses. These style-specific adapters are generated by a hypernetwork trained on multiple stylized corpora. In addition, for unseen stylized texts, Multi-SADG uses the stylized corpus to generate style-specific adapters through the hypernetwork to deal with the zero-shot scenario. MultiSADG is evaluated on five stylized dialogue data, and the experimental results show its satisfactory performance in both automatic and manual evaluation.

Keywords: Stylized dialogue generation · Adapter · Hypernetwork

1 Introduction

In recent years, dialogue systems have attracted considerable research attention and achieved remarkable success [21,24,27,32]. With the development of deep learning, there has been an increasing demand for intelligent dialogue systems. Researchers envision systems that can automatically generate responses in specific styles, known as stylized dialogue generation, which has shown significant attention in dialogue systems.

© The Author(s), under exclusive license to Springer Nature Singapore Pte Ltd. 2025
D. F. Wong et al. (Eds.): NLPCC 2024, LNAI 15359, pp. 16–28, 2025.
https://doi.org/10.1007/978-981-97-9431-7_2

Unfortunately, stylized dialogue generation faces a challenge due to the lack of parallel training data between contexts and responses in desired styles, which limits the performance of data-driven models. Strengthening the connection between different hidden space vectors is a natural solution. [5] propose to bridge conversation modeling and non-parallel style transfer text by sharing a structured latent space. Another research direction involves establishing pseudo pairs between contexts and responses of style using unsupervised or semi-supervised learning. [25] introduce a diversifying dialogue model based on iterative back translation [22]. [33] propose a style routing approach with a joint training process, utilizing an inverse model to generate pseudo pairs and train the model. While previous work has made progress, they have generally been able to generate only one or two dialogue styles. Expanding to multiple styles of responses often requires retraining a new model, which incurs significant costs, especially when working with pre-trained models. In addition, although large language models show exciting performance, they still fall short on some specific tasks, such as stylized dialogues The ability to generate specific responses for various constantly emerging styles without retraining the entire model is an invaluable capability known as lifelong learning [14], which enables models to continually acquire knowledge and adapt to new tasks and data. The continuous emergence of new styles places greater demands on existing generation methods.

To tackle these challenges, we propose a new model, Multi-Stylized Adapter Dialogue Generation (MultiSADG), which enhances the capability of generating dialogues with multiple styles. Our approach integrates style-specific adapters into a pre-trained dialogue model so as to enable multi-style response generation without compromising overall performance. In MultiSADG, the parameters of the adapters are generated by a hypernetwork module [6], which takes several style sentences as input, learns their style features and generates style-related parameters. The adapters are lightweight, which can efficiently handle multiple domains [2]. The style sentences are retrieved from a style corpus, which has similar content to the context. This approach empowers our model to generate responses through the trained hypernetwork in unseen styles during the zero-shot scenario, without the need for retraining. This capability relies solely on the available corpus. Additionally, our method also leverages back translation [23], which generates pseudo-parallel data to further enhance performance. We conduct extensive experiments on five stylized dialogue styles, including Formal, Informal, arXiv, Holmes, and Shakespearean responses. The experimental results demonstrate significant improvements in automatic and manual evaluations compared to the baselines. In addition, our approach achieves comparable performance on the basis of a much smaller number of parameters than the large language model. In summary, the contributions can be summarized as follows:

- We propose a Multi-stylized adapter dialogue generation model to handle multiple styles of response generation simultaneously.
- We address the zero-shot scenario by generating style-specific adapter parameters using the stylized corpus, eliminating the need for retraining when generating responses in unseen styles.

- We incorporate joint training of the hypernetwork and back translation modules, and experiments conducted on five stylized datasets show that our model outperforms baselines in both automatic and manual evaluations.

2   Related Work

Adapter is a lightweight component that can be inserted into a large model. These adapters typically consist of two-level projection layers and can be inserted into the attention or residual parts of a Transformer block. By doing so, adapters significantly reduce the number of trainable parameters while preserving the overall capabilities of model [8]. Besides, it can separate the parameters in a multi-lingual model [2]. Therefore, Transformer equipped with multiple adapters can be employed in multi-task scenarios without a substantial increase in model parameters or computational overhead [13]. **Hypernetwork** involves training one model to generate parameters for another network [6]. A specific type of hypernetwork, known as the contextual parameter generator, generates parameters based on input features, such as language embeddings [18] or task description [30]. By utilizing these parameters in downstream tasks, the model facilitates information sharing across languages without requiring model retraining when a new language appears. Users only need to provide language-specific features, and the hypernetwork can generate corresponding parameters [1,19,26]. **Stylized Dialogue Generation** is a more demanding style transfer that aims to generate content-related and style-specific responses. Due to the challenge of collecting parallel sentences for the original and target styles, research on unsupervised methods for stylized dialogue generation has been growing in recent years. Research on stylized response generation includes approaches such as space fusion [5], back-translation [33] and token-sentences level guided method [29].

3   Methodology

3.1   Problem Formulation

The proposed MultiSADG model consists of two main components: the encoder-decoder framework and the hypernetwork module, as shown in Fig. 1. Specifically, the encoder-decoder framework includes a stylized dialogue model (forward model) that generates stylized responses based on the input context. Additionally, a reverse model (backward model), similar to [33], is employed to generate a pseudo context $\hat{x}$ from a target stylized text y. To handle various stylized responses, a hypernetwork is incorporated to generate adapter parameters, which are then inserted into the transformer blocks. The objective is to generate multiple types of stylized dialogues using limited dialogue datasets. We have dialogue dataset $D_p = \{(x_1, y_1), ..., (x_N, y_N)\}$ with style S_0 is used for training. Here, x and y represent the context and response, respectively. There are k types of unpaired texts $D_{s_k} = \{t_{sk,1}, ..., t_{sk,M}\}$, where $t_{sk,i}$ is the i-th sentence in the S_k style. When provided with a specific style type S_k and context x, the model generates a coherent stylized response y' by selecting the $y' = \mathrm{argmax}_{y'} p(y'|x, S_k)$.

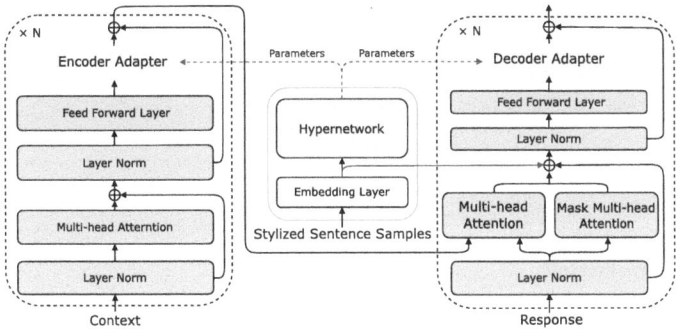

Fig. 1. The framework of MultiSADG model. The solid blue line represents the style features related to the current context, while the dashed blue line represents the generated style parameters, which are used as parameters for the adapter. (Color figure online)

3.2 Style Feature Modeling

To model style features from different styles in a flexible manner, we employ a style extractor based on the approach proposed in [20] to extract style embedding features. First, we sample contexts and retrieve a set of sentences from the target stylized corpus that have the highest semantic similarity to the context using SimCSE [4]. To ensure sufficient style information collection, we search for multiple semantically similar stylized sentences and concatenate them for each context. We also delete tokens that appear in all styles to improve the feature information in each sentence. Next, to model style features from these sentences, we construct the style extractor based on the embedding layer of GPT-2. We multiply the tokens of the sentence by this embedding matrix and calculate their mean value to form the style embedding for the samples as follows:

$$s_k = \text{Mean}(W_e \cdot [t_{k1}, ..., t_{kn}]), \tag{1}$$

where s_k represents the feature embedding in style S_k, W_e is embedding matrix, and t_{ki} represents the i-th token of sampled stylized sentence. Unlike previous approaches that use one-hot feature embeddings, we enhance the style feature by extracting real stylized sentences. We then average the style embeddings with decoder attention to guide the style relevance of generated responses.

3.3 Multi-stylized Adapter

Recent research has suggested that fine-tuning all parameters of a language model may lead to sub-optimal solutions, particularly for low-resource datasets [17]. To address this issue and control the modeling of different styles, we employ the adapter module, which efficiently adapts to new styles by inserting it into the encoder and decoder blocks of the forward model. Adapters are bottleneck architectures that consist of a down-projection, GELU non-linearity [7], and up-projection. Let h_i denote the output of the hidden state in layer i with dimension b of forward Transformers block. The adapter applies an affine transformation and a ReLU activation function as follows:

$$z_i = (W_{up}(\text{GELU}(W_{dw}h_i + B_{dw})) + B_{up}) + h_i, \tag{2}$$

where $W_{dw} \in \mathbb{R}^{d \times b}$, $W_{up} \in \mathbb{R}^{b \times d}$ $(d < b)$, and B_{dw} and B_{up} are bias.

3.4   Hypernetwork

To generate the parameters for the Adapter, we construct a hypernetwork module based on GPT-2. First, we specify the target transfer style for each batch, meaning that all sample sentences in a batch have the same style. Next, we use the embedding matrix mentioned in Sect. 3.2 to convert the input sample sentences into embedding sequences s_k, which are then fed into the GPT-2 model as input. To integrate as much information as possible from multiple stylized sentences in a batch, we perform average pooling on the tensor obtained from the above step to form a unified parameter vector $H_{s_k} = f_{\text{hyp}}(s_k)$, where f_{hyp} is the hypernetwork function. Afterward, we use a two-layer parameter generation head to generate parameters P_θ of the adapter, $\theta \in \{W_{dw}, W_{up}, B_{dw}, B_{up}\}$:

$$P_\theta = W_{L2}(\text{ReLU}(W_{L1}H_{s_k} + B_{L1})) + B_{L2}, \tag{3}$$

In the generation head, W_{L1} transform H_{s_k} into a lower-dimensional space with the bias B_{L1}. This projection reduces the number of parameters in the hypernetwork. Subsequently, W_{L2} and B_{L2} project the hidden state to create the parameters of the adapter. For W_{dw} and W_{up}, the output of the hypernetwork is a $d \times b$ vector that is reshaped before being injected into the adapter. For B_{dw} and B_{up}, the output of the hypernetwork is a d-dimensional and b-dimensional vector, respectively.

3.5   Training Strategy

The training process in our model consists of two stages. In the first stage, we optimize the model without the hypernetwork and adapter. In the second stage, we incorporate the hypernetwork and freeze most of the parameters of the Transformer. Following previous work [26], we do not freeze the parameters of the language model head. This training method allows us to avoid the computational costs associated with the hypernetwork while still benefiting from the performance of the Transformer. The encoders and decoders of the dialogue model and reverse model are denoted as e, $\hat{e}$, d, and $\hat{d}$, respectively. Both stages share the same training objective, which is to optimize the losses on dialogue pairs in dialogue dataset D_p:

$$\mathcal{L}_{p2r} = -\log(y|e(x), S_0), \tag{4}$$

$$\mathcal{L}_{r2p} = -\log(x|\hat{e}(y), S_0). \tag{5}$$

The reverse model is similarly defined for stylized text to context, which uses pseudo context and stylized text as a dialogue pair to train dialogue model:

$$\mathcal{L}_{style} = -\log(t|e(\hat{d}(\hat{e}(t))), S_k), \tag{6}$$

where t is a text in target style S_k. The total loss for optimizing the MultiSADG is calculated as the weighted sum of the losses mentioned above:

$$\mathcal{L} = \lambda_1 \mathcal{L}_{p2r} + \lambda_2 \mathcal{L}_{p2r} + \lambda_3 \mathcal{L}_{style}, \tag{7}$$

where λ_1, λ_2, and λ_3 are the weighted hyper-parameters. Our training process follows a two-stage schedule. In the first stage, we train the main network using a pre-trained model to ensure that our model possesses the capability for stylized dialogue generation. Once a certain threshold is reached, the hypernetwork is introduced into the main network, and model is trained to learn style-specific adapters while keeping the main network frozen in second stage.

4   Experiments

Datasets. To train a multiple stylized dialogue system and evaluate its zero-shot ability, we use a dialogue dataset and five stylized text corpus. TCFC [28]: TCFC is a dataset that has an informal style dialogue corpus and a formal text corpus. We used $217k$ informal dialogue pairs and $500k$ formal texts. We also regard the response of informal dialogue as a separate kind of style text. arXiv and Holmes: We use the pipeline in [5] to construct an arXiv-style text corpus. We sample about $290k$ sentences from arXiv articles. For Holmes-style texts, we use the $38k$ data provided by StyleDGPT. In order to keep consistent with StyleDGPT, we also randomly selected 2,000 pieces of samples as test sets and each context has at least 4 responses. Shakespeare is the aligned modern version of Shakespearean plays on the supervised style transfer task. We sample $112.7k$ unpaired corpus and 1,000 manually craft dialogue pairs from [10]. Shakespeare is used as the zero-shot dataset in experiment, we only calculate its style feature and not use any of its sentences to perform the training process.

Baselines. We compare our model with the baselines: 1) MTask: a multi-task model proposed by [12], which is trained by both dialogue and stylized datasets. 2) StyleFusion: a multi-task model proposed by [5] which builds latent space to draw sentences with the same style closer. 3) SRJT: SRJT is a back-translation based model proposed by [33]. It includes an inverse model and a joint training strategy. 4) StyleDGPT: It combines token-level and sentence-level style control, and uses a language model and style classifier to guide model in generating stylized responses [29]. 5) ChatGPT: We use version gpt-3.5-turbo of the advanced large-scale language model ChatGPT [15], and the results demonstrate that our method and ChatGPT are comparable.

Experimental Setting. We utilize the pre-trained DialoGPT [31] model[1] as the initialization for both dialogue module and back-translation module. For the hypernetwork, we use GPT-2 to initialize its parameters with word embedding size of 768 and hidden state dimension of 128. The output dimension for the parameter head of the hypernetwork is set to 768×128 for the adapter down-projection weights, 128×768 for the adapter up-projection weights. Each parameter head in each block for the encoder and decoder has separate parameters. The training of the MultiSADG model is conducted on NVIDIA GTX3090 machines. In the first stage (without hypernetwork), the model is trained with a batch size of 28 and a gradient accumulation of 2. In the second stage (with hypernetwork), the model is trained with a batch size of 10 and a gradient accumulation of 8. To extract style features, we sample 15 related stylized sentences for each context. We use the Adam optimizer and perform grid search to tune the hyper-parameters. The learning rate for the generation model is set to $2.25e-4$.

Table 1. Evaluation results on automatic metrics (BLEU-1 and BLEU-2). Note that the results of ChatGPT and MultiSADG use one model to generate four stylized responses, and other baselines come from four different models.

Model	BLEU-1					BLEU-2				
	Informal	Formal	arXiv	Holmes	Average	Informal	Formal	arXiv	Holmes	Average
MTask	<u>7.41</u>	6.36	16.85	**29.88**	15.13	0.24	0.50	4.67	8.31	3.43
SFusion	4.61	5.51	**19.07**	<u>29.70</u>	14.72	0.22	0.28	4.74	7.10	3.09
StyleDGPT	4.30	10.05	17.22	24.62	14.05	0.22	1.02	<u>6.55</u>	7.20	3.75
SRJT	6.69	<u>15.10</u>	<u>18.23</u>	27.07	<u>16.77</u>	0.67	<u>1.71</u>	**7.14**	**9.03**	**4.64**
ChatGPT	5.18	13.76	13.23	22.53	13.68	<u>0.82</u>	1.44	5.73	7.86	3.96
MultiSADG	**8.97**	**15.77**	17.70	25.80	**17.06**	**1.00**	**1.74**	6.30	<u>8.82</u>	<u>4.47</u>

Table 2. Evaluation results on automatic metrics (Dist-2 and BERT).

Model	Dist-2					BERT				
	Informal	Formal	arXiv	Holmes	Average	Informal	Formal	arXiv	Holmes	Average
MTask	4.12	29.30	16.77	16.81	16.75	**99.89**	37.30	4.90	55.47	49.39
SFusion	**62.80**	**61.00**	17.10	9.18	37.52	70.30	21.90	42.31	55.47	47.50
StyleDGPT	52.93	<u>55.43</u>	**77.23**	49.55	**58.79**	<u>92.98</u>	78.59	43.80	29.37	61.19
SRJT	49.40	43.40	53.27	**66.24**	53.08	69.40	**97.30**	<u>97.86</u>	<u>97.53</u>	**90.52**
ChatGPT	41.77	47.02	<u>73.05</u>	<u>65.70</u>	<u>56.89</u>	23.85	<u>95.93</u>	15.00	7.32	35.53
MultiSADG	<u>57.30</u>	43.10	61.99	64.37	56.69	59.20	95.48	**98.15**	**98.29**	<u>87.78</u>

---

[1] https://github.com/huggingface/transformers.

5   Results and Analysis

5.1   Automatic and Manual Evaluation

Automatic Evaluation. To assess the quality of our stylized responses, we employ both content, diversity and style evaluations in automatic evaluation. For content and diversity, we use BLEU [16] and Dist-2 [11]. Regarding style, we use pre-trained BERT [3] to determine whether the content we generate conforms to the expected style. To ensure consistency with the baseline, we train style classifier on both informal style and the target style. The accuracy on validation set for formal and informal is 98.5%, for arXiv is 99.9%, for holmes is 99.4%, and for Shakespearean is 99.3%. We present the aggregated results in Table 1 and Table 2, which demonstrate the performance of our proposed Multi-SADG model in generating high-quality stylized responses. Note that, compared to baselines that can only generate one or two types of stylized responses, our model exhibits the ability to produce multiple styles simultaneously while maintaining high performance in each style. In terms of BLEU-1, MultiSADG achieves the highest average scores in five styles. Furthermore, our model demonstrates competitive diversity in generating stylized responses. Although the Dist-2 score is slightly lower than that of StyleDGPT, StyleDGPT generates many non-target style words leads to a high Dist-2 but low content relevance and style features. In terms of style consistency, MultiSADG achieves comparable results. While its style score is lower than that of SRJT, it still outperforms other baselines. Especially MTask and SFusion, which show minimal style transfer in the arXiv and Holmes domains. This suggests that the supervision signal obtained through back-translation is superior to implicit methods such as language models. Additionally, MultiSADG effectively utilizes adapters for different styles, resulting in good performance across all styles. Besides, the overall performance of MultiSADG (Based-on GPT-2) is superior to ChatGPT, which further illustrates the success of our method. In summary, MultiSADG achieves the highest automatic performance in terms of content consistency. It demonstrates competitive performance in generating diverse responses and achieving style consistency.

Table 3. Manual evaluation on formal responses and Shakespearean responses.

Model	Fluency	Relevance	Style
The target style is formal response (low-resource)			
StyleDGPT	0.55	0.34	0.42
SRJT	0.84	0.69	0.59
MultiSADG	**0.89**	**0.77**	**0.63**
The target style is Shakespearean response (zero-shot)			
StyleDGPT	0.24	0.27	0.19
SRJT	0.37	0.32	0.26
MultiSADG	**0.65**	**0.40**	**0.38**

Manual Evaluation. In addition to automatic evaluation, we conduct manual evaluation in three aspects: (1) *Fluency* indicates how smooth the sentence is; (2) *Relevance* shows the content of the response is consistent with the context; (3) *Style consistency* evaluates how the response style matches the target domain. For a fair comparison, all generated responses are re-capitalized, de-tokenized and shuffled in order. We sample 100 instances from test set and employ three graduated annotators to rate each context-response pair. The scores range from 0 to 1, with 1 indicating the best. The generated responses from the models are provided to annotators for evaluation. The final scores are averaged across different judges. Table 3 presents the results of manual evaluation, showing that MultiSADG significantly outperforms baselines. Specifically, for formal response, where the models are trained in a low-resource scenario, our method achieves the highest manual evaluation scores. In the zero-shot scenario for Shakespearean style, MultiSADG again achieves the best scores, indicating the effectiveness of our approach. This can be attributed to the hypernetwork, which has the ability to generate parameters for unseen style texts. The kappa statistics indicate substantial agreement between annotators[2], with the values of 0.68, 0.62, and 0.69 for Fluency, Relevance, and Style Consistency, respectively.

Table 4. Automatic evaluation for Shakespearean responses.

Model	BLEU-1	BLEU-2	Dist-2	BERT
Low-resource Scenario				
StyleDGPT	4.89	0.25	**61.42**	70.54
SRJT	11.72	1.15	50.91	**98.44**
Zero-shot Scenario				
StyleDGPT	3.34	0.86	13.98	0
SRJT	7.08	0.25	46.18	1.27
MultiSADG	**14.20**	**1.26**	46.63	25.58

5.2 Discussions

Analysis of Zero-Shot Scenario. To evaluate the ability to generate dialogue in the zero-shot scenario, we conducted experiments using the Shakespearean style as input to the hypernetwork to generate a stylized dialogue adapter. Since other models lack the ability to generate responses in a zero-shot scenario, we used SRJT and StyleDGPT trained on the TCFC dialogue dataset as baselines. In addition, we also compare low-resource scenario where SRJT and StyleDGPT are trained on Shakespeare texts. The results can be seen in Table 4, indicate that our responses are more consistent with the reference compared to the baselines. MultiSADG achieved the highest BLEU-1 and BLEU-2 scores in zero-shot

---

[2] Following [9], we use characterize kappa values in 0.61–0.80 as substantial agreement.

scenario, surpassing both baselines. In terms of style scores, our model obtained a lower score compared to SRJT and StyleDGPT in low-resource scenario. This is attributed to the lack of supervised signal from back-translation or a stylized language model. However, the BERT classifier recognized that some of the responses generated by MultiSADG exhibited the style of Shakespeare in zero-shot scenario, indicating the effectiveness of our proposed style feature and the ability of the hypernetwork to learn the connection between different styles.

Table 5. Ablation study of automatic evaluation with average scores.

Model	BLEU-1	BLEU-2	Dist-2
Low-resource Scenario			
MultiSADG	**17.06**	4.47	56.68
w/o Hypernetwork	16.68	4.34	57.87
w/o Pre-trained	16.88	4.41	54.78
w/o Parameter Generator	15.73	3.73	37.76
w/o Freezing Parameters	16.97	**4.51**	58.82
Pseudo-Context Only	16.61	4.46	**59.46**
Zero-shot Scenario			
MultiSADG	**14.20**	**1.26**	46.63
w/o Hypernetwork	10.99	0.36	42.94
w/o Pre-trained	13.54	0.95	44.33
w/o Freezing Parameters	12.24	1.14	49.56
Pseudo-Context Only	12.86	1.18	**51.33**

Ablation Study. To validate the effectiveness of our model, we conduct an ablation study on both the low-resource scenario (four styles) and the zero-shot scenario (Shakespeare) as presented in Table 5. The "w/o Hypernetwork" refers to the removal of the hypernetwork module to evaluate the performance improvement it provides. We fine-tune the parameters on the original Transformer. The "w/o pre-training model" explores the role of the GPT-2 components in the hypernetwork by replacing it with two linear network parameter generation heads. In the "w/o parameter generator" scenario, we solely employ separate adapters to generate responses in various styles. In the "w/o freezing parameters" scenario, we adopt a training method without freezing parameters. In the "pseudo-context only" scenario, We solely utilize pseudo-contexts for training. The experimental results revealed the following insights: 1) After removing hypernetwork or pre-trained module, the overall performance decrease to varying degrees, with Shakespeare style being particularly affected. 2) In low-resource scenarios, removing the hypernetwork achieves relatively higher diversity but also sacrificed some content relevance. 3) In zero-shot scenario, the removal of the hypernetwork led to a decrease of 2.63 points in BLEU-1, demonstrating that our proposed method can generate better stylized responses without the need for retraining. 4) In the setting without the parameter generator, the model can achieve performance similar to MultiSADG, because different adapters can focus more on generating one style. However, if the parameter generator is removed, the model is incapable of performing zero-shot task, because when a new style appears, it cannot automatically generate new adapter parameters. 5) Although the outcomes of not freezing parameters are similar to those when parameters are frozen, freezing parameters can significantly save memory usage. 6) When only using pseudo data, the absence of guidance from real data leads to a decrease in model performance. These findings support the validity of our model and emphasize the importance of the hypernetwork module and the pre-training model components in achieving improved performance.

6 Conclusions

In this paper, we introduce the multi-stylized adapter dialogue generation model, which utilizes the hypernetwork and adapter techniques to generate multi-stylized responses. These enable the generation of style-specific adapters and enhance the ability to produce diverse and style-consistent responses. Unlike previous approaches, MultiSADG can handle multiple styles and adapt to unseen styles without the need for retraining. Experimental results on five stylized dialogue datasets demonstrate the effectiveness of our proposed method in both low-resource and zero-shot scenarios. In future work, we plan to explore the integration of more controllable attributes into dialogue generation for interactive dialogue systems. This could involve incorporating additional style-related features or exploring other methods to enhance the controllability and diversity of generated responses. In addition, we plan to incorporate this technology into large-scale language models to explore even more powerful generative capabilities. Overall, the proposed method opens up new possibilities for generating multi-stylized responses in dialogue systems, providing a more flexible and adaptive approach to stylized dialogue generation.

References

1. Ansell, A., et al.: MAD-G: multilingual adapter generation for efficient cross-lingual transfer. In: Proceedings of the Conference on Empirical Methods in Natural Language Processing (2021)
2. Bapna, A., Arivazhagan, N., Firat, O.: Simple, scalable adaptation for neural machine translation. In: Proceedings of the Conference on Empirical Methods in Natural Language Processing (2019)
3. Devlin, J., Chang, M.W., Lee, K., Toutanova, K.: BERT: pre-training of deep bidirectional transformers for language understanding. arXiv abs/1810.04805 (2019)
4. Gao, T., Yao, X., Chen, D.: SimCSE: simple contrastive learning of sentence embeddings. In: Proceedings of the Conference on Empirical Methods in Natural Language Processing (2021)

5. Gao, X., et al.: Structuring latent spaces for stylized response generation. In: Proceedings of the Conference on Empirical Methods in Natural Language Processing (2019)
6. Ha, D., Dai, A.M., Le, Q.V.: Hypernetworks. arXiv: abs/1609.09106 (2016)
7. Hendrycks, D., Gimpel, K.: Gaussian error linear units (GELUs). arXiv Learning (2016)
8. Houlsby, N., et al.: Parameter-efficient transfer learning for NLP. In: International Conference on Machine Learning (2019)
9. Landis, J.R., Koch, G.G.: The measurement of observer agreement for categorical data. Biometrics **33**, 159–174 (1977)
10. Li, J., Xia, Y., Yan, R., Sun, H., Zhao, D., Liu, T.Y.: Stylized dialogue generation with multi-pass dual learning. In: Advances in Neural Information Processing Systems (2021)
11. Li, J., Galley, M., Brockett, C., Gao, J., Dolan, W.B.: A diversity-promoting objective function for neural conversation models. In: Proceedings of NAACL-HLT (2015)
12. Luan, Y., Brockett, C., Dolan, W.B., Gao, J., Galley, M.: Multi-task learning for speaker-role adaptation in neural conversation models. In: Proceedings of the Eighth International Joint Conference on Natural Language Processing (2017)
13. Madotto, A., Lin, Z., Bang, Y., Fung, P.: The adapter-bot: all-in-one controllable conversational model. In: Proceedings of the AAAI Conference on Artificial Intelligence (2020)
14. Mazumder, P., Singh, P., Rai, P.: Few-shot lifelong learning. In: Proceedings of the AAAI Conference on Artificial Intelligence (2021)
15. Ouyang, L., et al.: Training language models to follow instructions with human feedback. In: Advances in Neural Information Processing Systems (2022)
16. Papineni, K., Roukos, S., Ward, T., Zhu, W.J.: BLEU: a method for automatic evaluation of machine translation. In: Proceedings of the 40th Annual Meeting of the Association for Computational Linguistics (2002)
17. Peters, M.E., Ruder, S., Smith, N.A.: To tune or not to tune? Adapting pretrained representations to diverse tasks. arXiv: abs/1903.05987 (2019)
18. Platanios, E.A., Sachan, M., Neubig, G., Mitchell, T.M.: Contextual parameter generation for universal neural machine translation. In: Proceedings of the 2018 Conference on Empirical Methods in Natural Language Processing (2018)
19. Ponti, E., Vulic, I., Cotterell, R., Reichart, R., Korhonen, A.: Towards zero-shot language modeling. In: Proceedings of the 2019 Conference on Empirical Methods in Natural Language Processing and the 9th International Joint Conference on Natural Language Processing (2019)
20. Riley, P., Constant, N., Guo, M., Kumar, G., Uthus, D.C., Parekh, Z.: TextSETTR: few-shot text style extraction and tunable targeted restyling. In: Proceedings of the 59th Annual Meeting of the Association for Computational Linguistics and the 11th International Joint Conference on Natural Language Processing (2020)
21. Ritter, A., Cherry, C., Dolan, W.: Data-driven response generation in social media. In: Proceedings of the Conference on Empirical Methods in Natural Language Processing (2011)
22. Sennrich, R., Haddow, B., Birch, A.: Improving neural machine translation models with monolingual data. In: Proceedings of the 54th Annual Meeting of the Association for Computational Linguistics (2016)
23. Sennrich, R., Haddow, B., Birch, A.: Improving neural machine translation models with monolingual data. In: Proceedings of the 54th Annual Meeting of the Association for Computational Linguistics (2015)

24. Shang, L., Lu, Z., Li, H.: Neural responding machine for short-text conversation. In: Proceedings of the 53rd Annual Meeting of the Association for Computational Linguistics and the 7th International Joint Conference on Natural Language Processing (2015)
25. Su, H., et al.: Diversifying dialogue generation with non-conversational text. In: Proceedings of the 58th Annual Meeting of the Association for Computational Linguistics (2020)
26. Ustun, A., Bisazza, A., Bouma, G., van Noord, G.: UDapter: language adaptation for truly universal dependency parsing. In: Proceedings of the 2020 Conference on Empirical Methods in Natural Language Processing (2020)
27. Wang, Y., Liu, C., Huang, M., Nie, L.: Learning to ask questions in open-domain conversational systems with typed decoders. In: Proceedings of the 56th Annual Meeting of the Association for Computational Linguistics (2018)
28. Wu, Y., Wang, Y., Liu, S.: A dataset for low-resource stylized sequence-to-sequence generation. In: Proceedings of the AAAI Conference on Artificial Intelligence (2020)
29. Yang, Z., et al.: StyleDGPT: stylized response generation with pre-trained language models. In: Findings of Empirical Methods in Natural Language Processing (2020)
30. Ye, Q., Ren, X.: Learning to generate task-specific adapters from task description. In: Proceedings of the 59th Annual Meeting of the Association for Computational Linguistics and the 11th International Joint Conference on Natural Language Processing (2021)
31. Zhang, Y., et al.: DialoGPT: large-scale generative pre-training for conversational response generation. In: Proceedings of the 58th Annual Meeting of the Association for Computational Linguistics (2020)
32. Zhao, X., Wu, W., Tao, C., Xu, C., Zhao, D., Yan, R.: Low-resource knowledge-grounded dialogue generation abs/2002.10348 (2020)
33. Zheng, Y., Chen, Z., Zhang, R., Huang, S., Mao, X.X., Huang, M.: Stylized dialogue response generation using stylized unpaired texts. In: Proceedings of the AAAI Conference on Artificial Intelligence (2020)

Hierarchical Knowledge Aggregation
for Personalized Response Generation
in Dialogue Systems

Yuezhou Dong[1,2], Ke Qin[1,2(✉)], and Shuang Liang[1]

[1] The National Key Laboratory of Intelligent Collaborative Computing, University of Electronic Science and Technology of China, Chengdu 611731, Sichuan, China
`yuezhou.dong@std.uestc.edu.cn, {qinke,shuangliang}@uestc.edu.cn`
[2] School of Computer Science and Engineering, University of Electronic Science and Technology of China, Chengdu 611731, Sichuan, China

Abstract. Personalized Dialogue Response Generation, which aims to emulate human-like and customized responses, has attracted considerable research interest. Recent advances in this field have integrated external knowledge to enhance models' language comprehension. However, the generic nature of this external knowledge is inadequate for the generation of personalized responses for a diverse range of users. Moreover, the redundancy of external knowledge diverts models' attention to other topics. To address these challenges, we propose a novel GNN-based approach, Hierarchical Knowledge Aggregation (HKA), which hierarchically aggregates both external knowledge and knowledge from the dialogue context. Additionally, we introduce a dialogue relation recognition task to enhance the accurate modeling of structural information. The results of our experiments, conducted on the ConvAI2 and PersonalDialog datasets, demonstrate that HKA outperforms existing baselines in generating personalized responses.

Keywords: Personalized Dialogue Systems · Knowledge Graph · Graph Neural Network

1 Introduction

The evolution of language modeling and natural language generation (NLG) techniques has significantly advanced the development of personalized dialogue systems. These systems have become proficient at understanding user messages and generating natural language responses [1–6]. The core task of these systems is personalized dialogue generation to emulate human dialogue and generate diverse content for various users. However, many dialogue systems produce customized responses that lack engagement and relevance, failing to provide the depth and informative content.

To enhance dialogue systems' capacity for generating contextually relevant and informative responses, researchers have integrated external knowledge, including both unstructured [7–12] and structured data [5, 15–18]. This external knowledge fosters a deeper semantic understanding of the dialogue context, enriching responses with related

D. F. Wong et al. (Eds.): NLPCC 2024, LNAI 15359, pp. 29–42, 2025.
https://doi.org/10.1007/978-981-97-9431-7_3

concepts through both explicit and implicit knowledge integration techniques. Despite these advancements, there remains a deficiency in generating personalized responses due to **(1) the generic nature of external knowledge**, which is insufficient for customization and leads to inconsistent persona for user and agent, and **(2) the redundancy of external knowledge**, which distracts the model and leads to irrelevant responses. As illustrated in Fig. 1, external knowledge contains three categories: knowledge that is relevant (entities circled by red dashed boxes), weakly relevant (entities circled by blue dashed boxes), and irrelevant (other entities) to the persona. Responses generated with reference to relevant knowledge tend to satisfy users, whereas responses with reference to weakly relevant and irrelevant knowledge tend to dissatisfy users. Therefore, there are challenges to achieve personalized responses: (1) how to obtain user-specific knowledge rather than common knowledge, (2) how to selectively use knowledge for responses that are relevant, informative, and personalized.

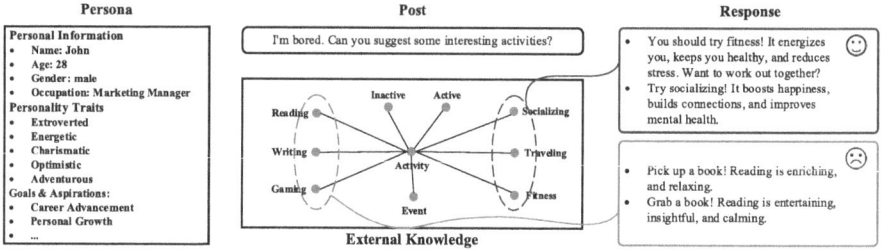

Fig. 1. An example of generic nature and redundancy of external knowledge

In real conversations, although dialogue starts similar, subsequent interactions with different people lead to considerable divergence in content, suggesting that the necessity of incorporating user-specific knowledge to generate personalized responses. However, previous works focus on incorporating external knowledge, ignoring the generic nature of external knowledge which often leads to informative but un-personalized responses. Fu et al. [11] append selected knowledge after the dialogue context and input it into BERT for encoding. INFO [10] composes dialogue history, persona and knowledge as a query for retrieving responses. In contrast to INFO, we suggest integrating knowledge from external knowledge graphs and the dialogue context to form user-specific knowledge, rather than being based on a generic knowledge for personalization. Moreover, Lao et al. [19] propose a denoising strategy to remove noise in knowledge graphs through entity selection. INFO [10] proposes a dialogue context-aware knowledge/persona selection mechanism to effectively ground dialogue models with external knowledge and persona simultaneously. Fu et al. [11] introduce personal information into knowledge selection building on the work of INFO. The objective of the aforementioned works is to eliminate redundancy and enhance the relevance of knowledge through the implementation of a knowledge selecting process, which ultimately contributes to the accuracy of subsequent information modelling. Therefore, we introduce the Hierarchical Knowledge Aggregation (HKA) algorithm, which merges knowledge from external knowledge graphs with the dialogue context. This integration leverages a hierarchical aggregation algorithm to model structural information and combines it with semantic information derived from the dialogue context to guide the response generation process. Besides, we introduce an auxiliary dialogue relation recognition task. This task identifies relationships between keywords within the dialogue context and aligns them with relationships in a commonsense knowledge graph, creating a homogeneous graph. We do not utilize the large language model (LLM) in this work. Because our objective is to substantiate the significance of user-specific knowledge that is graph-structured, while LLM does not demonstrate the requisite capacity to adapt effectively to graph-structured data inputs. The utilization of graph-structured data as textual input in existing works results in the partial loss of the original structured information inherent to the data. Furthermore, the LLM displays a certain degree of knowledge bias. In response to unspecified knowledge and information, LLM is inclined to produce output that aligns with its inherent distribution, a phenomenon known as "hallucination". Given that the maladaptation of the LLM, we are concerned about whether the graph-structured user-specific knowledge can prompt the LLM for personalized response generation. We summarize our contributions as follows:

1. We propose a hierarchical knowledge aggregation algorithm that combines knowledge from the dialogue context and external knowledge graphs, and hierarchically aggregates structural information to guide personalized response generation.
2. We incorporate dialogue relation recognition task during the training phase to improve accuracy of structural information modeling and response personalization.
3. Our algorithm is validated through experiments conducted on the ConvAI2 [21] and PersonalDialog [22] datasets, using ConceptNet [23] as the external knowledge. Results demonstrate significant improvements in generating personalized responses.

2   Related Work

2.1   Knowledge-Aware Dialogue System

External knowledge utilized in dialogue systems can broadly be categorized into two types: structured and unstructured. Numerous studies have focused on unstructured data. PersonaTKG [12] integrates personas, dialogue utterances, and external text knowledge in a unified graph, and employs a GCN mechanism to identify addressee in multi-party dialogue. SAFARI [8] utilizes LLMs as planners to selectively retrieve information from multiple knowledge sources. Several studies utilize structured data to enhance personalization and context richness. He et al. [16] employ a key-value memory network to store external knowledge for efficient knowledge utilization. Ain et al. [17] and Wang et al. [18] generate personal knowledge graphs to model user information for recommendation and emotional response generation.

2.2   Personalized Dialogue Generation

A growing number of researchers are focusing on the personalization of dialogue systems. Tang et al. [1] employ GPT-2 as both an encoder and a decoder to combine persona, facilitating the generation of personalized dialogue. Liu et al. [2] adopt a two-step strategy to first retrieve the best persona, and then encode the retrieved information based on the dialogue context. Song et al. [3] stack two decoders for response generation and regularization separately, which benefits model learning from smaller training data. Huang et al. [4] propose a customized attention to adaptively adjust the weight between persona and context depending on different dialogue situations. Ashby et al. [5] consider in-game context as a kind of persona, and merge it with generated content to produce dialogue content in role-playing games, utilizing large language models.

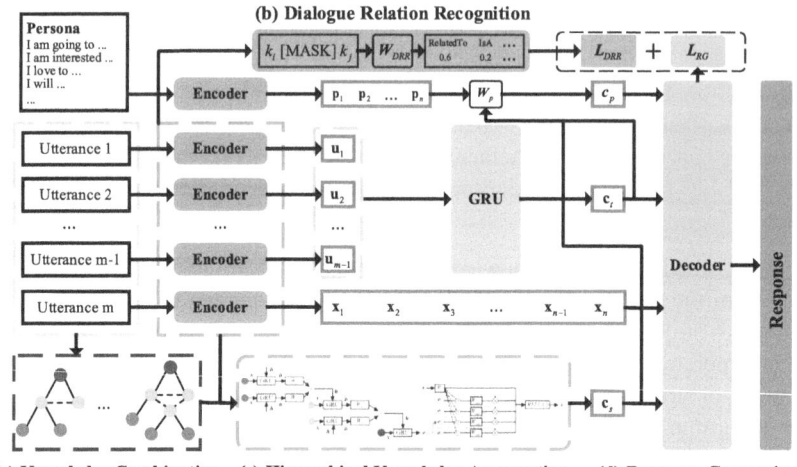

Fig. 2. The architecture diagram of HKA.

3 Method

3.1 Problem Formulation

For response generation in personalized dialogue systems, models process the dialogue context $U = \{u_1, \ldots, u_m\}$, persona $P = \{p_1, \ldots, p_n\}$ and knowledge graph G, where u_i is the i-th utterance and $u_i = \{x_1^i, \ldots, x_n^i\}$. The objective is to generate response $Y = \{y_1, \ldots, y_n\}$. We present the architecture diagram of HKA in Fig. 2.

3.2 Knowledge Combination

To form user-specific knowledge, HKA integrates knowledge by connecting multiple sub-graphs from a commonsense knowledge graph based on the linkages identified within the dialogue content. Initially, word frequencies are calculated. Words, that are verbs and nouns, with frequencies surpassing a threshold are identified as keywords, recognizing that not all words convey meaningful semantics [24]. Several keyword graphs are then constructed, with nodes representing keywords and edges representing relations derived after the dialogue relation recognition task.

To improve the generalization of model, combination graphs are formed by traversing commonsense knowledge graph with each keyword, extracting relevant factual triples. Filtering rules are employed to limit the number of triples due to the extensive dialogue content. These rules include inclusion of triples only if their confidence levels meet or exceed a threshold, and exclusion of seldom-encountered concepts. A pseudo node is devised to link keywords within the same utterance, creating a more cohesive structure and facilitating better integration of knowledge into the dialogue context.

3.3 Dialogue Encoder

To facilitate the understanding of the dialogue context U, we utilize the Gated Recurrent Neural Networks (GRUs) are utilized to encode dialogue history information c_t.

$$c_t = GRU(\boldsymbol{u}_1, \boldsymbol{u}_2, \ldots, \boldsymbol{u}_{m-1}) \tag{1}$$

$$\boldsymbol{u}_i = Enc(u_i), i \in (1, m-1) \tag{2}$$

$$\left\{x_1^m, \ldots, x_n^m\right\} = Enc(u_m) \tag{3}$$

$$\boldsymbol{p}_i = Enc(p_i) \tag{4}$$

where $\boldsymbol{u}$ and $\boldsymbol{p}$ are the first token embedding of encoder output; Enc represents the encoder part of the BART [25]; $\boldsymbol{x}_n^m$ is the embedding of the token x_n^m in the post. To improve accuracy of dialogue relation recognition and effectiveness of knowledge selection, we design a special template T for encoder input, where $\left[MASK_1^{ijk}\right]$ and $\left[MASK_2^{ijk}\right]$ are two [MASK] tokens, and x_i^k and x_j^k are two keywords.

$$T = x_i^k \left[MASK_1^{ijk}\right] x_j^k \left[MASK_2^{ijk}\right] u_k \tag{5}$$

3.4 Dialogue Relation Recognition

To obtain more accurate structural information and improve response personalization, we introduce an auxiliary task that forces the model to recognize the dialogue relation between keywords extracted in Sect. 3.2. Assume that x_i^k and x_j^k are two keywords, we predict the relation label between these two keywords using BART by concatenating keywords with the utterance they are located in as an input text, T. The hidden states from [MASK] tokens are fed into a fully-connected layer to recognize dialogue relations. We utilize the cross-entropy loss function to optimize the parameters:

$$P\left(r_{ij} | u_k, x_i^k, x_j^k\right) = softmax\left(W_{RDD} e_{MASK_1^{ijk}}\right) \tag{6}$$

$$L_{DRR} = -\frac{1}{n} \sum_{i=1}^{n} \sum_{j \in Nr_i} \hat{r}_{ij} log P\left(r_{ij} | u_k, x_i^k, x_j^k\right) \tag{7}$$

where Nr_i represents the neighboring nodes set of x_i^k, $\hat{r}_{ij}$ is the truth label of relation.

3.5 Hierarchical Knowledge Aggregation

To avoid the knowledge redundancy and achieve personalized knowledge selection, HKA implements GRUs and GNNs to model structural information in combination graph under guidance of semantic information from $\left[MASK_1^{ijk}\right]$ and $\left[MASK_2^{ijk}\right]$. Then, attention mechanism evaluates the significance of structural information from each utterance. Figure 3 illustrates the process of hierarchical knowledge aggregation, with blue/yellow/purple circle denoting concept/keyword/pseudo node. The $\oplus$/$\otimes$/ⓒrepresent operations of element-wise addition/multiplication and concatenation.

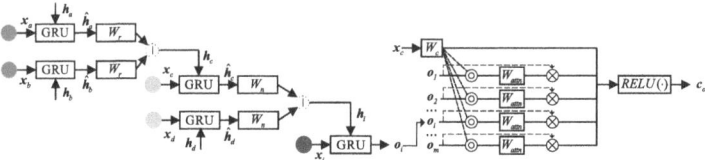

Fig. 3. Hierarchical Knowledge Aggregation.

Specifically, each keyword node connects to a sub-graph extracted from Concept-Net. The intuition is to aggregate the information from neighboring nodes to update representations of central nodes. A GNN-based algorithm is utilized on the sub-graph to aggregate structural information, while a GRU module updates node representation:

$$\hat{h}_i^{(l)} = GRU\left(x_i, h_i^{(l-1)}\right) \tag{8}$$

$$h_i^{(l-1)} = \sum_{j \in Nr_i} s_{ij} W_r \hat{h}_j^{(l-1)} \tag{9}$$

$$s_{ij} = cos\left(e_{MASK_1^{ijk}}, e_{MASK_2^{ijk}}\right) \tag{10}$$

where x is embedding of token x; $\hat{h}_i^{(l)}$ is hidden state of node i at l-th layer; W_r is a trainable weight matrix specific for relation type r; cos indicates the cosine similarity.

After message propagation, the hidden state of pseudo nodes k can be derived by integrating its latest embedding x_k and latest hidden state h_k into GRU, marked as o_k. Since embedding of pseudo node cannot be derived from the vocabulary due to the lack of textual representation, we define it as: $x_k^{(l)} = \sum_{p \in N_k} h_p^{(l-1)}$, where N_k represents the set of all keywords in the k-th utterance. Then, we acquire a set of hidden states $O = \{o_1, o_2, \ldots, o_m\}$, which potentially contribute differently to the composite structural information representing the dialogue context. To optimally integrate these hidden states into a unified representation, an attention mechanism is utilized as follows:

$$c_s = ReLU\left(W_c x_c + \sum_{o_i \in O} \mu_i o_i\right) \tag{11}$$

$$\mu_i = \frac{exp\{PReLU[W_{attn}(W_c x_c; o_i)]\}}{\sum_{o_j \in O} exp\{PReLU[W_{attn}(W_c x_c; o_j)]\}} \tag{12}$$

$$x_c = \sum_{i \in N_a} x_i \tag{13}$$

where W_c represents a linear transformation that projects the feature of context vector x_c into a hidden representation space, derived by summing the embeddings of all keywords across the entire dialogue session. W_{attn} signifies linear transformation utilized within the attention mechanism. The concatenation operation is denoted by [;]. The coefficient μ_i reflects the significance of the hidden representation o_i, with higher values of μ_i, indicating greater importance of o_i. $PReLU$ represents the parametric rectifier function; N_a denotes the set of all keyword nodes. Then, we model persona information according to structural and semantic information of the dialogue context.

$$c_p = ReLU \left(\sum_{p_i \in P} \sigma_i p_i \right) \tag{14}$$

$$\sigma_i = \frac{exp\{W_p(p_i;c_t;c_s)\}}{\sum_{p_j \in P} exp\{W_p(p_j;c_t;c_s)\}} \tag{15}$$

3.6 Response Generation

The structural information is integrated into decoder to enhance the personalization. This integration facilitates the combination of semantic and structural information, resulting in augmented embeddings for tokens. To address the issue of extensive dialogue context, only the post is input into the decoder. Context semantic information is introduced to circumvent the issue of responses becoming irrelevant due to information loss:

$$\hat{x}_i^m = W_{cat}\left(x_i^m; c_p; c_s; c_t\right) \tag{16}$$

where x_i^m represents the embedding of the token in the post. W_{cat} is defined as a trainable fully-connected layer. The decoding process involves generating the token y_t of the response, utilizing the contextual tokens and the sequentially preceding tokens $y_{<t}$:

$$y_t = Softmax\left(W_H \cdot Dec\left(\hat{x}_1^m, \ldots, \hat{x}_n^m, y_{<t}\right)\right) \tag{17}$$

We use the cross-entropy loss function to optimize the model for the generation task:

$$L_{RG} = -\frac{1}{n} \sum_{t=1}^n \sum_{w \in V} l(y_t) \log p(y_t) \tag{18}$$

where $l(y_t)$ refers to the truth label of token y_t.

3.7 Loss Functions

The training loss of the model consists of two parts: the dialogue relation recognition loss L_{RDD} and the response generation loss L_{RG}. Following multi-task learning principle, the overall loss L is defined as follows with an adjustable hyperparameter α:

$$L = L_{RG} + \alpha * L_{RDD} \tag{19}$$

4   Experiment Results and Analysis

4.1   General Settings

Dataset. All experiments are conducted on the ConvAI2 and PersonalDialog datasets. The ConvAI2 focuses on conversations about personal interests, comprising 17,878 training pairs, 1,000 validation pairs, and 1,015 testing pairs. The PersonalDialog augments dialogue context with speaker traits, totally 20.83M sessions. The ConceptNet contains 120,850 triples, 21,471 concepts, and 47 types of relations.

Baselines. IMPACT mines implicit user information from dialogue history and employs it in conjunction with explicit user information. GSMN proposes split memory network to store user information and history message separately. KnowPAML framework represents a novel integration of knowledge-enhanced approaches and meta-learning. It introduces a knowledge aggregation mechanism combining external knowledge with user-specific information to produce personalized and contextually rich dialogue responses. BeCand and INFO employ knowledge, dialogue history, and persona sentences. The former utilizes top-k relevant knowledge for responses generation, while the latter combines them as a query for response retrieval. CLV [1] refines the use of sparse and dense persona, incorporating dialogue history to jointly guide response generation. BART combines both bidirectional encoding and autoregressive decoding, and is a powerful generative model that is often used in text generation tasks.

Evaluation Metrics. For automatic evaluation, responses are assessed in three dimensions: relevance, diversity, and novelty. Relevance measures similarity between generated and golden responses. Diversity measures variation among generated responses. Novelty measures the ability to introduce new words. Bleu-1 [26], Rouge-L [27], and Meteor [28] measure the relevance and novelty of generated responses. Dist-2 [29] and Ent-4 [30] metrics quantify the diversity of generated responses. For human evaluation, responses are assessed in persona consistency, appropriateness and informativeness. Persona consistency evaluates whether the response aligned with the user persona. Appropriateness assesses how well the response aligns with the topic of given dialogue context, and informativeness evaluates the diversity and specificity of the response.

Implement Details. We employ Pytorch for our model which consists of 6 layers for encoder, 6 layers for decoder with a hidden state size of 768. Our model is trained with a batch size of 10, a learning rate set at $3e-5$, and the Adam optimizer is employed. For hyper-parameters, the thresholds of word/concept frequency and triple confidence are set to 13, 10, 1.0, respectively, and coefficient of multi-task learning α is set to 0.1.

4.2   Automatic Evaluation

The results highlighted in bold denote the most superior outcomes across all experiments. Results marked with (*) identify the best outcomes without ablation variations. As detailed in Table 1, our model exhibits superior performance in relevance compared to all baselines. While BART shows commendable performance, it slightly lags behind INFO, underscoring the pivotal roles of persona information and knowledge guidance in augmenting generated responses. The HKA model surpassing INFO indicates that user-specific knowledge with hierarchical knowledge aggregation significantly contributes to performance. Table 2 elucidates that both HKA and BART exhibit commendable performance across diversity and novelty metrics. The HKA model enhances diversity, which is attributed to the incorporation of user-specific knowledge. This broadens the selection of candidate tokens that are factually relevant yet textually varied in relation to the dialogue context. Additionally, the knowledge selection mechanism filters unrelated knowledge, achieving personalized knowledge aggregation. The comparison between HKA and baselines demonstrates the efficacy of user-specific knowledge in addressing the lack of personalization in response content due to the generic nature of external knowledge. In terms of novelty, BART's relatively constrained performance is linked to its intrinsic structure which tend to reiterating tokens presented in the input. The comparative analysis between HKA and BART demonstrates that HKA's innovative application of combined knowledge and aggregation algorithms disrupts the output distribution favorably, fostering the generation of novel tokens within responses.

Table 1. Automatic Evaluation on Relevance ($\uparrow$).

Model	ConvAI2			PersonalDialog		
	Bleu	Rouge	Meteor	Bleu	Rouge	Meteor
IMPACT [7]	0.1336	0.1498	0.0773	0.0315	0.1613	0.1157
GSMN [13]	0.1069	0.1502	0.0797	0.0311	0.1690	0.1988
KnowPAML [15]	0.1397	0.1552	0.0838	0.0387	0.1757	0.1192
BeCand [9]	0.1368	0.1588	0.0861	0.0376	0.1609	0.1135
CLV[1]	0.1326	0.1533	0.0824	0.0368	0.1647	0.1152
INFO [10]	0.1423	0.1715	0.0898	0.0412	0.1709	0.1302
BART [25]	0.1318	0.1371	0.0764	0.0397	0.1673	0.1298
HKA (ours)	**0.1447**[*]	**0.1729**[*]	**0.0925**[*]	**0.0428**[*]	**0.1739**[*]	**0.1340**[*]
-w/o K	0.1413	0.1475	0.0716	0.0378	0.1657	0.1096
-w/o UK	0.1405	0.1329	0.0760	0.0403	0.1716	0.0883
-w/o CK	0.1416	0.1469	0.0747	0.0418	0.1703	0.0894
-w/o DRR	0.1407	0.1428	0.0737	0.0410	0.1827	0.1155
-w/o HKA	0.1332	0.1261	0.0684	0.0357	0.1607	0.0864
-w/o HKA + UK	0.1353	0.1496	0.0744	0.0395	0.1690	0.1011

4.3 Human Evaluation

Human evaluation contains 100 cases randomly chosen for pairwise comparison. Three human judges were instructed to rate each response on a scale from 1 to 5. Table 3 presents two metrics: average scores and best@1 ratio. The former reflects the mean value of

Table 2. Automatic Evaluation on Diversity ($\uparrow$) and Novelty ($\downarrow$).

Model	Diversity				Novelty			
	ConvAI2		PersonalDialog		ConvAI2		PersonalDialog	
	Dist	Ent	Dist	Ent	Bleu	Rouge	Bleu	Rouge
IMPACT	15.94	4.955	18.03	8.680	1.25	5.66	3.09	12.00
GSMN	13.00	4.135	13.62	6.733	1.10	5.68	3.29	11.72
KnowPAML	18.06	5.309	19.97	9.384	1.15	5.01	2.38	11.69
BeCand	17.82	5.366	19.14	9.184	1.20	5.12	2.67	11.24
CLV	17.57	5.318	19.22	9.193	1.27	5.35	2.86	11.65
INFO	18.84	6.085	20.73	9.825	1.05	4.49	2.41	10.75
BART	17.34	5.687	21.60	10.066	2.39	8.91	6.01	22.18
HKA (ours)	**19.15***	**6.238***	**21.74***	**10.544***	0.98*	3.94*	2.29*	10.06*
-w/o K	16.03	5.659	13.40	8.989	1.38	5.12	2.38	12.98
-w/o UK	15.95	5.670	16.79	9.078	0.92	**3.40**	**1.98**	**9.25**
-w/o CK	15.43	5.633	14.25	9.026	1.13	3.93	2.15	10.37
-w/o DRR	16.54	5.791	18.73	9.497	**0.80**	3.59	2.01	9.49
-w/o HKA	16.64	5.836	16.27	9.176	1.20	3.91	2.23	10.89
-w/o HKA + UK	15.35	5.646	13.91	8.974	1.04	3.87	2.17	9.85

the ratings, while the latter highlights the frequency with which response received the highest score compared to its counterparts. HKA demonstrates superior performance across metrics, affirming its capability to produce personalized responses characterized by persona consistency, readability, and informativeness.

4.4   Ablation Study

Effectiveness of User-Specific Knowledge. We devise three variants: "-w/o K" removing all knowledge, "-w/o UK" removing the user-specific knowledge and utilizing only external knowledge, and "-w/o CK" removing external knowledge and utilizing only keyword graph. The results in Tables 1 and 2 demonstrate that the full model consistently outperforms in the majority of evaluated dimensions, thereby substantiating the efficacy of the knowledge combination. However, the variant "-w/o UK" shows better performance in novelty compared to the full model. One possible reason is that user-specific knowledge limits knowledge coverage, constraining the model's output.

Effectiveness of Dialogue Relation Recognition. We conduct an ablation experiment with the variant "-w/o DRR". This variant removes dialogue relation recognition, leading to a heterogeneous graph due to non-relational edges in the keyword graph. The results in Tables 1 and 2 reveal that the full model outperforms the variant "-w/o DRR" in

Table 3. Human Evaluation on Persona Consistency (Per.) (↑), Appropriateness (App.) (↑) and Informativeness (Inf.) (↑).

Model	Average Score			Best@1 Ratio		
	Per	App	Inf	Per	App	Inf
IMPACT	2.0857	2.2685	2.0034	8.5%	9.1%	9.2%
GSMN	1.8754	1.2614	1.9985	4.3%	6.6%	10.4%
KnowPAML	2.6125	2.3848	2.0093	10.1%	11.1%	11.0%
BeCand	2.5449	2.4359	1.1039	9.9%	12.6%	5.9%
CLV	2.4197	2.3961	2.2166	9.5%	12.2%	12.1%
INFO	2.8275	2.7534	2.5631	16.2%	17.3%	14.3%
BART	2.6706	2.4534	2.3391	13.3%	12.1%	13.5%
HKA (ours)	**3.3428**	**3.2050**	**2.7692**	**28.1%**	**18.9%**	**23.5%**

relevance and diversity. This shows that more accurate structural information helps maintain dialogue context consistency and personalization.

Effectiveness of Hierarchical Knowledge Aggregation. We design two ablation variants: "-w/o HKA" employs conventional knowledge aggregation instead of HKA, where the hidden state o_i is the sum of embeddings of nodes in i-th utterance, and "-w/o HKA+UK" removes user-specific knowledge on the basis of "-w/o HKA". As detailed in Table 1 and 2, the comparison among full model, "-w/o HKA" and "-w/o HKA+UK" indicates that HKA is capable of leveraging user-specific knowledge more effectively than traditional knowledge aggregation. The variant "-w/o HKA+UK" exhibits better performance to the variant "-w/o HKA" in relevance, suggesting that introduced knowledge cause information interference without effective knowledge aggregation algorithms, making the responses less relevant. However, its lag in diversity indicates that without the guidance of specific information, the inclusion of external knowledge does not significantly increase the diversity of responses.

4.5   Case Study

Table 4 offers an evaluation of generation performance across two dialogue cases, involving three models: INFO, BART, and HKA. In the first case, the response from INFO is contextually relevant but not appropriate, and there is a contradiction between the personal information and the response from BART. HKA provides a concise and appropriate response, leveraging persona to answer the question directly without extending the topic unnecessarily. In the second scenario, HKA demonstrates knowledge reasoning ability by directing the conversation to 'skiing' based on the persona.

Table 4. Two Cases from Test Dataset with Responses Generated from Different Models.

Sample #1	**Persona B:** I love Italian food and garlic bread my favorite color is yellow I'm a gold medalist Olympian I workout four hours a day	
Context	A: B: A: B: A:	What sport do you like? A runner sports is a good thing Running is awesome but gymnastics is better I too did gymnastics, but my passion is with running How much time do you spend every day for running?
INFO	B:	Thanks. I run every day. Do you run every day?
BART	B:	I don't like sports, but I won an Olympic gold medal
HKA (ours)	B:	I exercise four hours every day
Sample #2	**Persona B:** I won a gold medal in the 1992 Olympics I love cats and have two cats I have a hat collection of over 1000 hats I have a weakness for vanilla ice cream My favorite season is winter	
Context	A: B: A:	Do you have any hobbies? I really love sky diving, rollercoasters and cooking shows I like vanilla ice cream. What is best for you? Sounds yummy. Watching an adventure action movie and eating some popcorn. Do you like movie?
INFO	B:	I'm a big fan of films. I love films about cats
BART	B:	Not at all, but I like to run
HKA (ours)	B:	I don't like watching films. I like sports, especially skiing

5 Conclusion

In this paper, we introduce Hierarchical Knowledge Aggregation (HKA) to improve personalized dialogue systems. Our methodology uniquely addresses the generic nature of external knowledge by integrating a keyword graph derived from dialogue content with a commonsense knowledge graph, and mitigates the effects of knowledge redundancy by hierarchical knowledge aggregation. The efficacy of the HKA approach has been validated through both automated metrics and human evaluations. The results demonstrate that HKA enhances the relevance, diversity, and personalization of generated responses, outperforming baseline models. Our future works will focus on refining the knowledge aggregation algorithm within the constructed combination graph and applying the concept of combination knowledge into large language models to further improve the capabilities and performance of personalized dialogue systems. Furthermore, we will investigate the capacity of large language models to autonomously extract subgraphs and user information from dialogue content.

References

1. Tang, Y., et al.: Enhancing personalized dialogue generation with contrastive latent variables: combining sparse and dense persona. In: ACL, pp. 5456–5468, Toronto (2023)
2. Liu, S., et al.: RECAP: retrieval-enhanced context-aware prefix encoder for personalized dialogue response generation. In: ACL, pp. 8404–8419, Toronto (2023)
3. Song, H., et al.: A stack-propagation framework for low-resource personalized dialogue generation. ACM Trans. Inf. Syst. 41(3), 68:1–68:36 (2023)
4. Huang, Q., et al.: Personalized dialogue generation with persona-adaptive attention. In: AAAI, pp. 12916–12923, Washington (2023)
5. Ashby, T., et al.: Personalized quest and dialogue generation in role-playing games: a knowledge graph- and language model-based approach. In: CHI, pp. 290:1–290:20, Hamburg (2023)
6. Yu, J., et al.: Dial-QP: a multi-tasking and keyword-guided approach for enhancing conversational query production. In: NLPCC, pp. 840–852, Foshan (2023)
7. Xu, F., et al.: Exploring implicit persona knowledge for personalized dialogue generation. J. Supercomput. 79(13), 14545–14570 (2023)
8. Wang, H., et al.: Large language models as source planner for personalized knowledge-grounded dialogues. In: EMNLP, pp. 9556–9569, Singapore (2023)
9. Lim, J., et al.: Beyond candidates: adaptive dialogue agent utilizing persona and knowledge. In: EMNLP, pp. 7950–7963, Singapore (2023)
10. Lim, J., et al.: You truly understand what i need: intellectual and friendly dialogue agents grounding knowledge and persona. CoRR, abs/2301.02401 (2023)
11. Fu, T., et al.: There are a thousand hamlets in a thousand people's eyes: enhancing knowledge-grounded dialogue with personal memory. In: ACL, pp. 3901–3913, Dublin (2022)
12. Ju, D., et al.: Learning to improve persona consistency in multi-party dialogue generation via text knowledge enhancement. In: COLING, pp. 298–309, Gyeongju (2022)
13. Wu, Y., et al.: Personalized response generation via generative split memory network. In: NAACL-HLT, pp. 1956–1970, Online (2021)
14. Wang, Y., et al.: Improving persona understanding for persona-based dialogue generation with diverse knowledge selection. In: IEEE, pp. 1915–1921, Montreal (2023)
15. Shukla, A., et al.: KnowPAML: a knowledge enhanced framework for adaptable personalized dialogue generation using meta-learning. In: ICON, pp. 194–203, New Delhi (2022)
16. He, M., et al.: Conversation and recommendation: knowledge-enhanced personalized dialog system. Knowl. Inf. Syst. 65(1), 261–279 (2023)
17. Ain, Q., et al.: Learner modeling and recommendation of learning resources using personal knowledge graphs. In: ACM, pp. 273–283, Kyoto (2024)
18. Wang, W., et al.: Emily: developing an emotion-affective open-domain chatbot with knowledge graph-based persona. CoRR, abs/2109.08875 (2021)
19. Lao, L., et al.: A noise-removal of knowledge graph framework for profile-based spoken language understanding. In: NLPCC, pp. 814–826, Foshan (2023)
20. Wang, H., et al.: Discourse relation-aware multi-turn dialogue response generation. In: NLPCC, pp. 853–865, Foshan (2023)
21. Dinan, E., et al.: The second conversational intelligence challenge (ConvAI2). CoRR, abs/1902.00098 (2019)

22. Zheng, Y., et al.: Personalized dialogue generation with diversified traits. CoRR, abs/1901.09672 (2019)
23. Speer, R., et al.: ConceptNet 5.5: an open multilingual graph of general knowledge. In: AAAI, pp. 4444–4451, San Francisco (2017)
24. Si, P., et al.: Guiding topic flows in the generative chatbot by enhancing the ConceptNet with the conversation corpora. CoRR, abs/2109.05406 (2021)
25. Lewis, M., et al.: BART: denoising sequence-to-sequence pre-training for natural language generation, translation, and comprehension. In: ACL, pp. 7871–7880, Online (2020)
26. Papineni, K., et al.: BLEU: a method for automatic evaluation of machine translation. In: ACL, pp. 311–318, Philadelphia (2002)
27. Lin, C.: ROUGE: a package for automatic evaluation of summaries. In: Text Summarization Branches Out, pp. 74–81, Barcelona (2004)
28. Lavie, A., Agarwal, A.: METEOR: an automatic metric for MT evaluation with high levels of correlation with human judgments. In: WMT, pp. 228–231, Prague (2007)
29. Li, J., et al.: A diversity-promoting objective function for neural conversation models. In: NAACL, pp. 110–119, San Diego, California (2016)
30. Zhang, Y., et al.: Generating informative and diverse conversational responses via adversarial information maximization. In: NIPS, pp. 1815–1825. MIT, Montreal (2018)

Multi-hop Reading Comprehension Model Based on Abstract Meaning Representation and Multi-task Joint Learning

Peiyu Zhao, Zhujian Zhang, and Bo Liu[✉]

College of Information Science and Technology, Jinan University,
Guangzhou 510632, China
{jnuzpy,zzj2021}@stu2021.jnu.edu.cn,
tlbxldd@jnu.edu.cn

Abstract. In recent years, the issue of document-based extractive reading comprehension has been widely studied. Multi-hop reading comprehension requires obtaining supporting facts from multiple paragraphs in the document and reasoning to get the answer. But some problems have not been well solved: during the process of extracting the answer, it is often disturbed by the non-real answer (i.e. similar answer) in the document; the lack of a related expression mechanism for multiple scattered evidences in the paragraph affects the extraction of the answer. To address these issues, this paper proposes a multi-hop reading comprehension method based on Abstract Meaning Representation (AMR) and contrastive learning, which combines graph neural network (GNN) and answer verification for multi-task joint learning to reduce the interference of confusing information and enhance the robustness of the model. Experiments were conducted on datasets including HotpotQA and MuSiQue. The results show that the method proposed in this paper performs better than some competitive baselines in terms of exact match (EM) and F1 score evaluation.

Keywords: AMR · Contrastive Learning · Multi-hop Reading Comprehension · Graph Neural Network · Expected Calibration Error

1 Introduction

In single-hop reading comprehension tasks [1,2], the answer can often be deduced from a single paragraph [3]. With the advancement of computational power and the emergence of pre-training models, the level of single-hop reading comprehension is close to human performance. In recent years, many machine reading comprehension studies have shifted their focus to multi-hop reasoning across multiple documents or paragraphs, such as HotpotQA [4], and MuSiQue [5]. Unlike single-hop reading comprehension, multi-hop reading comprehension requires the integration of multiple sentences or paragraphs for reasoning, such as comparison,

D. F. Wong et al. (Eds.): NLPCC 2024, LNAI 15559, pp. 43–55, 2025.
https://doi.org/10.1007/978-981-97-9431-7_4

| Paragraph1:David Weissman |
| "David Weissman is a screenwriter and director.His film credits include "The Family Man" (2000), "Evolution" (2001), and "When in Rome" (2010)". |
| Paragraph2:The Family Man |
| "The Family Man is a 2000 American romantic comedy-drama film directed by Brett Ratner, written by David Diamond and David Weissman, and starring Nicolas Cage and Tea Leoni. Cage's production company, Satum Films, helped produce the film.The film centers on a man who sees what could have been had he made a different decision 13 years prior." |

| Question: "What screenwriter with credits for "Evolution" co-wrote a film starring Nicolas Cage and Tea Leoni?" |
| Answer: "David Weissman" |
| Support fact:["David Weissman",0],["David Weissman",1],["The Family Man",0] |

Fig. 1. An example of multi-hop question answering from HotpotQA.

bridge, etc., and these tasks generally require the provision of interpretable evidence. The current paradigm for Multi-Hop Reading Comprehension (Multi-Hop RC) tasks is the "Retriever+Reader" [6]. This paradigm first uses the retriever to search for relevant context information composed of sentences or paragraphs from multiple candidate paragraphs, and then the reader performs reading comprehension based on the retrieved context to infer the answer. In addition to annotating the answers, some datasets (such as HotpotQA [4]) also provide supporting facts (namely [paragraph title,sentence number]) to explain the results of the predicted answers, as shown in Fig. 1.

Current research in multi-hop reading comprehension [6,10,11] is dedicated to applying Graph Neural Network (GNN) to the Reader model to enhance its reasoning ability. The current evaluation results of these GNN-based models on the HotpotQA dataset show that they perform very well in terms of supporting fact evaluation, but still have low Exact Match (EM) and F1 scores in answer extraction. One speculated reason is the way of predicting supporting facts and answers. Specifically, the Reader generally uses binary classification to judge whether a sentence is a supporting fact, while the Reader typically predicts the start and end positions to extract the answer. Although the answer usually only consists of a few tokens, there are many short spans that are very similar to the real answer, which leads to the Reader having incorrect information about the start and end positions.

Figure 1 presents an example of a multi-hop reading comprehension task, in which the answer cannot be provided using information from either the first or second paragraph alone. Although traditional multi-hop models can leverage the information provided by the question, bridging from the first to the second paragraph for subsequent answer inference, they may struggle to accurately distinguish between "David Weissman" and "David Diamond" due to their semantic similarity. This could lead the model to potentially predict incorrect answer.

We have observed that Multi-Hop RC models, during the answer extraction process, are often interfered by non-actual answers (i.e. similar answers) in the document. Moreover, the lack of a mechanism to express the correlation among multiple dispersed pieces of evidence within a paragraph can further affect the extraction of the answer.

To address the issues present in Multi-Hop RC models, we proposes a Graph Network model based on AMR and contractive learning (called AGN), which consists of core modules including graph construction, contrastive learning, answer verification, and multi-task joint learning. Firstly, the graph construction module filters sentences in the document paragraph based on the question, and extracts concepts and relationships from the filtered sentences using the Abstract Meaning Representation (AMR) graph construction method, thereby constructing a multi-granularity hierarchical graph (MGH-Graph). Secondly, a contrastive learning module is introduced and combined with the GNN to realize multi-task joint learning. The model improves the ability to extract answers and predict supporting facts by sharing multi-task information, and enhancing the model's resistance to interference data.

The main contributions of this paper are as follows:

1. To address the issue of dispersed evidence in Multi-Hop RC, we propose a multi-granularity hierarchical graph (MGH-Graph) construction method based on AMR.
2. To enhance the robustness of the model, we employ contrastive learning to improve the model's contextual representation space, thereby further enhancing the model's learning ability at the sentence level.
3. To strengthen the model's ability to discern answers, we utilize an answer verification module with answer candidates and expected calibration error (ECE) conditional constraints, which assists the model in selecting correct and reliable answers from multiple similar answer candidates.

2   Related Work

Multi-Hop RC Current research on Multi-Hop RC has achieved some results, mainly involving technologies such as information retrieval, deep learning, and contrastive learning.

Multi-hop RC models based on GNN adopt different graph constructions. For instance, HGN [10], and SAE Graph [11] construct heterogeneous graphs using information of different granularities such as entities, sentences, and paragraphs, enabling rich information interactions between different types of nodes during the inference process. MHQA-GRN [12] constructs an entity graph using methods such as named entity recognition and relational parsing, and uses different GNN to propagate information. Lee et al. [13] improved retrieval performance by incorporating phrase retrieval into a coarse-grained retrieval model. Compared to other methods, most GNN-based methods exhibit better reading comprehension performance. Therefore, we adopt Graph Neural Networks as the basic structure for the AGN.

In recent years, contrastive learning techniques have also been applied to multiple fields such as question-answer pair ranking [14] and sentence representation learning [15]. In the field of question answering and reading comprehension, DPR [17] uses a rule-based method to construct positive and negative samples, then employs contrastive learning to retrieve paragraphs related to the question. Structural dropout and representation dropout enhancement strategies. To

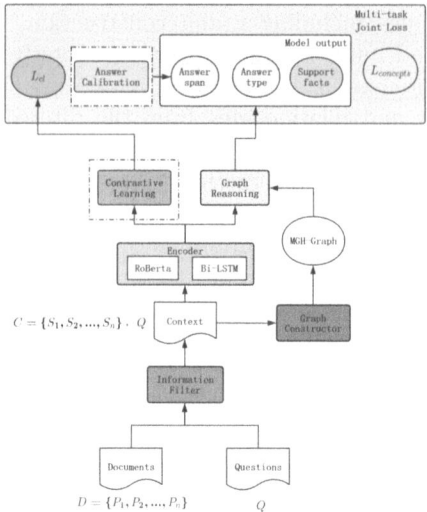

Fig. 2. Overview of AGN.

improve model robustness and enhance learning capability through fine-grained representation considering the contextual situation, they employed a contrastive learning module for joint training.

3   The Proposed Model

The AGN framework proposed in this study is shown in Fig. 2. Where D is the input documents, which are composed of multiple paragraphs, Q is the question associated with the documents. The framework consists of the following main parts: Graph Constructor, Context Encoder, Graph Reasoning, Contrastive Learning, Answer Calibration, Multi-task Joint Training. Contrastive Learning and Answer Calibration are two auxiliary task modules that are only used in the training process.

3.1   Graph Constructor

The construction of the MGH-Graph is carried out in two steps: (i) screening relevant reasoning information; (ii) adding edges in the filtered information that represent the relationships between sentences and concepts.

Information Filtering. In the process of reasoning out answers, the most important information is the question and the sentences related to the question, as the required supporting facts are often found within these related sentences. Based on this idea, this paper adopts the concept of multi-round iterative retrieval. Starting from the question, the top-k sentences most relevant to the

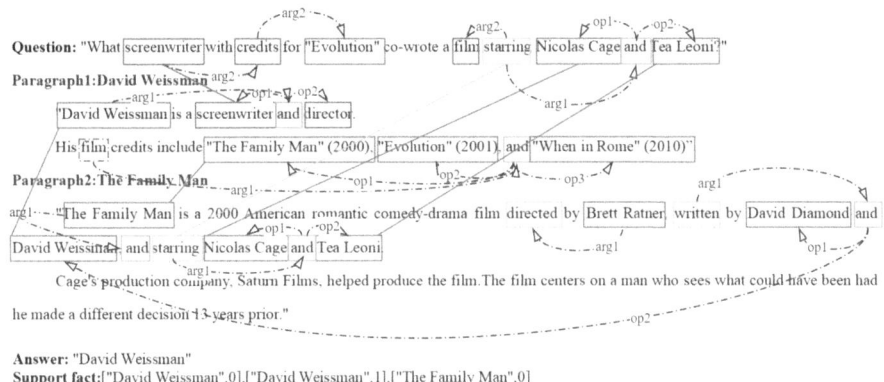

Fig. 3. An example of MGH-Graph construction based on AMR. Concepts are boxed with rectangles. "arg1" represents the prototype patient, "arg2" represents indirect objects, tools, etc., and "op" represents parallel/choice relationships, special date formats, quantities, etc. Some concepts and connection are omitted for simplicity.

question are selected as information candidates in each round, and are concatenated with the question to start the next round of iteration. The ultimate goal is to ensure that the supporting facts are included in the selected candidate sentence set.

Nodes and Edges. Use the AMR (Abstract Meaning Representation) tool to extract concept entities from candidate sentences. Compared to other semantic parsing methods such as named entity recognition, AMR uses graph structures to better describe phenomena such as argument sharing where a noun is dominated by multiple predicates, and AMR also allows for the addition of implicit or omitted components in the sentence to restore more complete sentence semantics. An example of AMR concept extraction is shown in Fig. 3. Take the candidate sentences and concept entities as nodes, and add edges between sentences that belong to the same paragraph. Edges between the concepts are then added based on the following rules:

(i) For all concepts in a sentence, edges are added between the concept nodes.
(ii) Edges are added for the same concepts in different sentences.
(iii) To enhance the conceptual connections between different sentences calculate the similarity between different sentence concepts. If the similarity is greater than a certain threshold, an edge is drawn between the two concepts.
(iv) If two concepts from different sentences are semantically connected in the AMR semantic graph, an edge is drawn between these two concepts.

In the MGH-Graph, the types of nodes capture semantics from different information sources.

3.2   Context Encoding

After constructing the MGH-Graph, the next step is to obtain the initial representations of the graph nodes. All selected candidate sentences are first combined into the context C, which is then connected with the question Q and input into the pre-trained RoBerta, followed by a bidirectional attention layer. The encoded representation of the question is denoted as $Q = \{q_0, q_1, \ldots, q_{m-1}\} \in R^{m \times d}$, and the encoded representation of the context as $C = \{c_0, c_1, \ldots, c_{n-1}\} \in R^{n \times d}$, where m is the length of the question and n is the length of the context, each $q_i, c_j \in R^d$

A shared BiLSTM is applied on top of the context representation C, and different node representations are extracted from the output of the BiLSTM, denoted as $M \in R^{n \times 2d}$. For concept/sentence nodes. For the question node, a max pooling layer is used to obtain its representation, as follows:

$$s_i = MLP_1\left(\left[M\left[S^i_{\text{start}}\right][d:]; M\left[S^i_{\text{start}}\right][:d]\right]\right) \tag{1}$$

$$e_i = MLP_2\left(\left[M\left[E^i_{\text{start}}\right][d:]; M\left[E^i_{\text{start}}\right][:d]\right]\right) \tag{2}$$

$$q = \text{max\_pooling}(Q) \tag{3}$$

where S^i_{start}, E^i_{start} denotes the start position of the sentence/concept entity node, and similarly S^i_{end}, E^i_{end} denotes the corresponding end position. In summary, after context encoding, $s_i, e_i \in R^d$ serves as the representation of the i-th sentence/concept entity node. The question node is represented by $q \in R^d$.

3.3   Graph Reasoning

After the context encoding, the AGN carries out inference on MGH-Graph, where the contextualized representations of all graph nodes are transformed into high-level representations through the graph neural network. Specifically, let $S = \{s_i\}_{i=1}^{n_s}$ and $E = \{e_i\}_{i=1}^{n_e}$, where n_s, n_e denote the number of sentences and concepts in the graph, respectively. The representation is $H = \{q, S, E\} \in R^{g \times d}$, where d is the feature dimension of each node, $g = n_s + n_e + 1$.

For graph information propagation, the Graph Attention Network (GAT) [18] to perform message passing on the MGH-Graph. Specifically, GAT takes all nodes as input and updates h'_i features through neighboring node N_i in the graph, specifically as follows:

$$h'_i = LeakyRelu\left(\sum_{j \in N_i} \alpha_{ij} h_j W\right) \tag{4}$$

where h_j is the j-th vector starting from H, $W \in R^{d \times d}$ is the weight matrix to be learned, and α_{ij} is the attention coefficient, calculated as follows:

$$\alpha_{ij} = \frac{\exp\left(f\left([h_i; h_j]\, w_{e_{ij}}\right)\right)}{\sum_{k \in N_i} \exp\left(f\left([h_i; h_k]\, w_{e_{ik}}\right)\right)} \tag{5}$$

where $w_{e_{ij}} \in R^{2d}$ is the weight vector corresponding to the edge type e_{ij} between the i-th and j-th nodes. $f(.)$ is the LeakyReLU activation function. In summary, after graph reasoning, we obtain $H' = \{h'_0, h'_1, \ldots, h'_g\} \in R^{g \times d}$, from which we can obtain the updated representations of various types of nodes.

Then, graph propagation will further provide contextual information for predicting answers and supporting facts. The context representation M and graph representation H' are combined through the gated attention mechanism:

$$C = Relu\left(MW_m\right) \cdot Relu\left(H'W'_m\right)^T \tag{6}$$

$$\bar{H} = Softmax(C) \cdot H' \tag{7}$$

$$G = \sigma\left([M; \bar{H}]W_s\right) \cdot Tanh\left([M; \bar{H}]W_t\right) \tag{8}$$

where $W_m \in R^{2d \times 2d}$, $W'_m \in R^{2d \times 2d}$, $W_s \in R^{4d \times 4d}$, $W_t \in R^{4d \times 4d}$ are the weight matrix to be learned, $G \in R^{n \times 4d}$ is gated representation, will be used for span extraction in answering.

3.4 Contrastive Learning

In order to enhance the learning capability of the model and improve its robustness, a contrastive learning module is introduced for joint training. Referring to the method proposed by Gao et al. [15], positive and negative samples are generated through random Dropout of the filtered sentence set C.

The sentences in C are transformed into vector representations $cl\_output \in R^{n \times d}$ through the encoder and mean pooling, where n represents the number of sentences in C, and d is the dimension of the hidden layer. The loss function is represented by L_{cl}:

$$L_{cl} = -\log\left(\frac{e^{S\left(z_i, z'_i\right)/r}}{\sum_{j=0}^{n} e^{S(z_i, z_j)/r}}\right) \tag{9}$$

where $S(.)$ represents the cosine similarity function, r is a hyper-parameter, z_i represents the original golden sample. z'_i represents positive samples, z_j represents negative samples.

3.5 Multi-task Joint Training

After graph inference, the updated node representations are used for different subtasks. Support fact prediction is based on sentence nodes, while answer prediction is based on concept entity nodes and context representation G.

For support fact prediction, two-layer MLP is are used as a binary classifiers:

$$O_{\text{sent}} = MLP(S') \tag{10}$$

where $O_{\text{sent}} \in R^{n_s}$ represents whether a sentence is selected as a supporting fact.

The concept entity prediction is regarded as a multi-classification problem which predicts the entities included in the answer. The candidate entity set

E' include all entities in the question and entities that match the titles in the paragraphs. If the true answer exists in the predicted entity set, the entity loss is recorded as 0. Specifically, it is as follows:

$$O_{\text{concept}} = MLP(E') \qquad (11)$$

The loss is used as a regularization term and denoted as $L_{concept}$.

Similarly, the type of answer needs to be identified, which includes span, yes/no, and no-answer types. Based on the first dimension representation of G, MLP is used for answer type classification:

$$O_{\text{type}} = MLP(G[0]) \qquad (12)$$

In the decoding process, we first determine the answer type. If it is "yes" or "no", we directly return it as the answer. If it is a "no-answer" type, we do not answer.

Regarding answer span prediction, the logarithms of the start and end points of the span are calculated based on the dual-layer MLP of G:

$$O_{start} = MLP(G) \qquad (13)$$

$$O_{end} = MLP(G) \qquad (14)$$

In order to ensure the most reliable prediction of the answer, an answer calibration module is introduced in the answer prediction, which includes answer verification and confidence calibration constraints. Regarding answer candidates, according to $\left(p_s^{\text{start}}, p_e^{\text{end}}\right)$ take the top-k candidate span representations, the candidate span representations are input into two offline projection layers to calculate the overall confidence score c of the final predicted answer ans. For training samples, the real answer label δ is constructed as:

$$\delta = \begin{cases} 1, & \text{if } ans \text{ is the correct answer} \\ 0, & \text{otherwise} \end{cases} \qquad (15)$$

If the ans output by the answer prediction module is correct, then $\delta = 1$. Therefore, binary cross-validation is performed as an uncertainty estimation, and the possibility of correct answer prediction is learned through self-supervised learning. The loss function of answer verification is as follows as cross entropy:

$$L_{\text{ans\_ver}} = -\delta \log c - (1 - \delta) \log(1 - c) \qquad (16)$$

If only cross-entropy loss optimization is considered in answer verification, it will lead to overconfidence and mis-calibration of prediction probability. In order to consider the overall generalization ability of the model and the guarantee of answer reliability, confidence calibration constraints [16] are introduced to make its prediction confidence more consistent with its accuracy, so as to produce more calibrated and reliable prediction probabilities. For its prediction interval, the difference between accuracy and confidence is weighted average estimation, and the loss is calculated as follows:

$$L_{ece} = \sum_{m=1}^{M} \frac{|B_m|}{n} |acc(B_m) - conf(B_m)| \tag{17}$$

The overall loss calculation of the answer calibration module is as follows:

$$L_{ans\_calibration} = L_{ans\_ver} + L_{ece} \tag{18}$$

The overall loss of the model is as follows:

$$L_{out} = L_{start} + L_{end} + L_{sent} \tag{19}$$

$$L_{joint} = L_{out} + \gamma_1 L_{concept} + \gamma_2 L_{type} + \gamma_3 L_{cl} + \gamma_4 L_{ans\_calibration} \tag{20}$$

The overall training goal is to enhance the robustness and reliability of the model.

Table 1. HotpotQA Experiment results

Row	Model	Ans EM	Ans F1	Sup Em	Sup F1	Joint EM	Joint F1
1	Baseline [4]	44.44	58.28	21.95	66.66	11.56	40.86
2	DFGN [6]	55.66	69.34	53.10	82.24	33.68	59.86
3	LongFormer-large [8]	68.00	81.00	63.09	85.80	45.91	71.40
4	SAE(RoBERTa) [11]	67.70	80.75	63.30	87.38	46.81	72.75
5	QUARK [7]	67.75	81.21	60.72	86.97	44.35	72.76
6	HGN [10]	69.22	82.19	62.76	88.47	47.11	74.21
7	Beam Retrieval [9]	72.25	85.30	67.25	90.43	–	–
8	AGN(ours)	**72.42**	**85.38**	**67.52**	**90.61**	**49.33**	**77.35**

Table 2. MuSiQue-ans Experiment results

Row	Model	Ans F1	Sup F1
1	Select+Answer Model [5]	52.30	75.20
2	Step Execution by End2End Model [5]	49.00	80.60
3	Step Execution by Select+Answer [5]	46.40	78.10
4	End2End Model [5]	40.70	69.40
5	Beam Retrieval [9]	**69.20**	91.40
6	AGN(ours)	67.80	**91.90**

4   Experiments

In this section, the experimental results of AGN are compared with relevant methods, and the results are analyzed.

4.1   Dataset and Evaluation Measures

This paper evaluates the performance of the AGN using the HotpotQA [4] and MuSiQue [5] multi-hop reading comprehension benchmark datasets. Each dataset includes two subtasks: (i) answer prediction, and (ii) supporting fact prediction. For each subtask, the model's performance is evaluated using exact match (EM) and F1 score. The final performance is measured using a joint score of EM and F1. EM requires the predicted answer to be exactly the same as the real answer.

The conduct experiment is on RTX 4090 GPU. In the information filtering stage, the uncased Roberta Tokenizer [19] is used to tokenize all sentences and questions. The encoding vector of the sentence pairs is generated using the pre-trained Roberta-large model. In the graph construction phase, the pre-trained AMR model of CoreNLP is used to extract the conceptual entities in the sentence. The maximum number of conceptual entities in the graph is set to 40, and the maximum number of sentences is limited to 20. During training, the training set is fine-tuned for 8 epochs, with a batch size of 8. For optimization, the Adam Optimizer is chosen, with an initial learning rate of 1e−5.

4.2   Experimental Results

Tables 1 and 2 show the results of the method proposed in this paper compared to other baseline models. The best results obtained from our model are displayed in bold font. From these tables, it can be seen that the proposed AGN method achieves good results on most evaluation metrics. It performs better on the answer metrics than most competitive baselines, as the answer verification module helps the model to choose more reliable and confident answers. Similarly, it performs better on the supporting fact metrics than most competitive baselines, as the contrastive learning module extracts sentences containing contextual information from the context as positive and negative samples, expanding the distance between the answer sentence and other sentences in the context. Therefore, in terms of the Sup F1 and Sup Em evaluation metrics, the performance of AGN surpasses other models under the same conditions. However, in Table 2, our method is slightly inferior to Beam Retrieval on Ans_F1. We speculate that due to the larger training data used upstream by Beam Retrieval, it performs slightly better on datasets with higher inference difficulty.

4.3   Ablation Experiments

In order to verify the role of the contrastive learning module in AGN, an ablation experiment is conducted by removing the contrastive learning module from the model (denoted as w/o cl_module). The results are given in Table 3, which show that the contrastive learning module helps to some extent improves the prediction effect of the model.

Table 3. ablation experiments of contrastive learning on HotpotQA

Dataset	Model	Ans-F1(%)	Sup-F1(%)
MuSiQue	w/o cl_module	65.10	88.30
	AGN	67.80	91.90
HotpotQA	w/o cl_module	84.64	89.24
	AGN	85.38	90.61

In order to verify whether the answer calibration module really helps the model prediction, we conduct the experiment by removing the answer calibration module from the model (denoted as w/o ver_ece). As shown in Table 4, with the help of the answer verification module, AGN can produce well-calibrated prediction probabilities, thus avoiding the generation of unreliable answers.

Table 4. ablation experiments of the answer calibration on HotpotQA

Dataset	Model	Ans-F1(%)	Sup-F1(%)
MuSiQue	w/o ver_ece	64.90	91.20
	AGN	67.80	91.90
HotpotQA	w/o ver_ece	84.24	89.93
	AGN	85.38	90.61

5   Conclusion

This paper mainly studies complex multi-hop reading comprehension tasks, and proposes a multi-hop reading comprehension model based on MGH-Graph, contrastive learning, and answer verification. By introducing a MGH-Graph and applying GAT, the method of answering multi-hop questions is improved; by using contrastive learning, the anti-interference ability of the model are improved; the answer verification module is added to select the most reasonable and reliable answer. In the future, we will further explore reading comprehension models for other types of answers, such as aggregated answers.

References

1. Rajpurkar, P., Zhang, J., Lopyrev, K.: SQuAD: 100,000+ questions for machine comprehension of text. In: Proceedings of the 2016 Conference on Empirical Methods in Natural Language Processing, pp. 2383–2392 (2016)
2. Trischler, A., Wang, T., Yuan, X.: NewsQA: a machine comprehension dataset. In: Proceedings of the 2nd Workshop on Representation Learning for NLP, pp. 191–200 (2017)
3. Devlin, J., Chang, M., Lee, K.: BERT: pre-training of deep bidirectional transformers for language understanding. In: Proceedings of NAACL-HLT, pp. 4171–4186 (2019)
4. Yang, Z., Qi, P., Zhang, S.: HotpotQA: a dataset for diverse, explainable multi-hop question answering. In: Proceedings of the 2018 Conference on Empirical Methods in Natural Language Processing, pp. 2369–2380 (2018)
5. Trivedi, H., Balasubramanian, N., Khot, T.: MuSiQue: multihop questions via single-hop question composition. Trans. Assoc. Comput. Linguist. **10**, 539–554 (2022)
6. Qiu, L., Xiao, Y., Qu, Y.: Dynamically fused graph network for multi-hop reasoning. In: Proceedings of the 57th Annual Meeting of the Association for Computational Linguistics, pp. 6140–6150 (2019)
7. Groeneveld, D., Khot, T., Sabharwal, A.: A simple yet strong pipeline for HotpotQA. In: Proceedings of the 2020 Conference on Empirical Methods in Natural Language Processing (EMNLP), pp. 8839–8845 (2020)
8. Beltagy, I., Peters, M.E., Cohan, A.: LongFormer: the long-document transformer. arXiv preprint arXiv:2004.05150 (2020)
9. Zhang, J., Zhang, H., Zhang, D., et al.: Beam retrieval: general end-to-end retrieval for multi-hop question answering. arXiv preprint arXiv:2308.08973 (2023)
10. Fang, Y., Sun, S., Gan, Z.: Hierarchical graph network for multi-hop question answering. In: Proceedings of the 2020 Conference on Empirical Methods in Natural Language Processing (EMNLP), pp. 8823–8838 (2020)
11. Tu, M., Huang, K., Wang, G.: Select, answer and explain: interpretable multi-hop reading comprehension over multiple documents. Proc. AAAI Conf. Artif. Intell. **34**(05), 9073–9080 (2020)
12. Song, L., Wang, Z., Yu, M.: Exploring graph-structured passage representation for multi-hop reading comprehension with graph neural networks. arXiv preprint arXiv:1809.02040 (2018)
13. Lee, J., Wettig, A., Chen, D.: Phrase retrieval learns passage retrieval, too. In: Proceedings of the 2021 Conference on Empirical Methods in Natural Language Processing, pp. 3661–3672 (2021)
14. Deng, Y., Zhang, W., Lam, W.: Learning to rank question answer pairs with bilateral contrastive data augmentation. In: Proceedings of the Seventh Workshop on Noisy User-Generated Text (W-NUT 2021), pp. 175–181 (2021)
15. Gao, T., Yao, X., Chen, D.: SimCSE: simple contrastive learning of sentence embeddings. In: 2021 Conference on Empirical Methods in Natural Language Processing, EMNLP 2021. Association for Computational Linguistics (ACL), pp. 6894–6910 (2021)
16. Guo, C., Pleiss, G., Sun, Y.: On calibration of modern neural networks. In: International Conference on Machine Learning, pp. 1321–1330. PMLR (2017)
17. Karpukhin, V., Oğuz, B., Min, S.: Dense passage retrieval for open-domain question answering. In: Proceedings of the 2020 Conference on Empirical Methods in Natural Language Processing (EMNLP), pp. 6769–6781 (2020)

18. Veličković, P., Cucurull, G., Casanova, A.: Graph attention networks. Stat **1050**, 4 (2018)
19. Liu, Y., Ott, M., Goyal, N.: RoBERTa: a robustly optimized BERT pretraining approach. arXiv preprint arXiv:1907.11692 (2019)

Leveraging Large Language Models for QA Dialogue Dataset Construction and Analysis in Public Services

Chaomin Wu[1], Di Wu[2], Yushan Pan[3], and Hao Wang[1]($\boxtimes$)

[1] Xidian University, Xi'an 710126, China
23151214136@stu.xidian.edu.cn
[2] Norwegian University of Science and Technology, 6009 Ålesund, Norway
[3] Xi'an Jiaotong-Liverpool University, Suzhou 215123, China

Abstract. This paper identifies the limitations of current AI datasets within the public service sector, specifically concerning the human-robot interaction (HRI) context. Existing datasets often lack the necessary interactive features for effective and efficient interactions, hindering the development of customized and emotionally responsive systems. As public service demands become more diverse and complex in HRI, traditional datasets fail to support high-quality interactions, necessitating significant improvements. To address this issue, we introduce a QA dialogue dataset specifically tailored for public service applications, comprising 1208 pairs generated by large language model. This dataset integrates textual and emotional data, providing detailed annotations for interaction quality and emotional accuracy. Our method includes four stages: data generation, annotation, emotion analysis, and performance evaluation. During the data generation stage, GPT-4 is employed to create a diverse set of dialogues. In the annotation stage, these dialogues are meticulously labeled for quality and emotional content. The emotion analysis stage utilizes various recognition algorithms to process the data. Finally, the performance evaluation stage involves experiments to validate the dataset's effectiveness. Comparative experiments demonstrate the dataset's efficacy in enhancing the adaptability and performance of public service robots, underscoring its potential for training AI models to effectively handle real-world dialogues.

Keywords: Human-Robot Interaction · Public Service · Emotion Analysis · QA Dialogue Datasets

1 Introduction

Over the past decade, significant progress in artificial intelligence (AI) has been driven by general datasets like ImageNet [1] for image recognition and Penn Treebank for natural language processing. These resources have advanced deep learning and computer vision, improving static image analysis and grammatical

D. F. Wong et al. (Eds.): NLPCC 2024, LNAI 15359, pp. 56–68, 2025.
https://doi.org/10.1007/978-981-97-9431-7_5

structure modeling. However, their narrow focus limits applicability to dynamic and interactive scenarios, crucial for robotic navigation and public systems [2,3]. This dichotomy in AI research shows that technological advancements in data-driven models haven't fully translated into broader applicability, especially in the public sector.

Despite the utility of general datasets, they significantly limit addressing the specific needs of complex service sectors like public service. The need for a specialized dataset arises because existing datasets do not capture the intricacies and emotional complexity of human-robot interactions in public service settings [4–6]. Public service environments involve complex, emotionally charged communication, revealing a critical gap in AI research-the lack of datasets tailored to the unique challenges of public service robotics [7,8]. This shortcoming hinders the ability of robots to enhance efficiency and responsiveness in public service delivery.

To tackle these challenges, this study introduces a novel dataset created using large language model (LLM), designed for public service scenarios to simulate authentic dialogues between robots and citizens. Previous research highlighted GPT-3.5's robust capabilities in synthetic QA dialogue generation and textual analysis [9]. Building on these strengths, GPT-4 shows enhanced sensitivity to linguistic and emotional contexts, generating detailed, context-aware conversations [10]. These attributes are crucial for developing a dataset with fine-grained annotations that capture nuanced interactions. The dataset includes comprehensive annotations for specific public operations, evaluating relevance, timeliness, efficiency, emotional accuracy, and overall interaction quality. It also assesses user emotional tendencies and the emotional tendencies in the robots' responses, crucial for improving interaction quality in emotionally charged scenarios.

By integrating detailed annotations of emotional and contextual dialogue dimensions, we enhance the development of emotionally intelligent and contextually adaptive AI systems. The study validates the dataset's efficacy through comparative experiments with classic fine-tuning algorithms, showing that even small datasets can meet public service needs. These findings underscore the dataset's potential to enhance the comprehension and adaptability of public service robots, enabling effective management of complex interactions. By incorporating realistic scenarios, this context-rich dataset facilitates nuanced analysis and training of AI models, improving their ability to handle real-world dialogues. This specialized dataset boosts general AI models' performance through fine-tuning, providing valuable resources for developing emotionally intelligent and contextually adaptive AI systems in public service. The primary contributions of this paper include:

– This study presents the first QA dialogue dataset for public service applications, featuring rich contextual information. It enhances empirical research and development of AI-driven public service interactions, enabling nuanced analysis and training of AI models to handle real-world dialogues effectively.
– Integrating detailed annotations that capture emotional and contextual dialogue dimensions enhances the development of emotionally intelligent and

contextually adaptive AI systems. These annotations, covering relevance, efficiency, timeliness, emotional accuracy, interactivity, user emotional tendency, and answer emotional tendency, enrich the dataset for training sophisticated AI models capable of nuanced human-computer interactions.

– The study shows the dataset's effectiveness in comparative experiments with traditional fine-tuning algorithms, revealing its ability to create domain-specific datasets for public service needs from small datasets. These findings highlight its potential to enhance general AI model performance through fine-tuning, offering valuable resources for specialized AI systems in the public service sector.

2 Related Work

2.1 Existing General Datasets

Traditional datasets like ImageNet [11], COCO [12], and MNIST [13] have been foundational in advancing computer vision and machine learning. ImageNet, developed by Stanford University, includes over 14 million images across thousands of categories, serving as a crucial resource for training and testing image recognition systems. COCO offers extensive image annotations for tasks like object detection, segmentation, and captioning, while MNIST features a large collection of handwritten digits widely used for evaluating pattern recognition [14] and machine learning algorithms [15]. Despite their significance, these datasets are predominantly generalized and often fail to adequately address domain-specific tasks or contexts, particularly those requiring specialized knowledge or unique environmental considerations. Similarly, QA datasets like SQuAD [16], MS MARCO [17], and CoQA [18], which are tailored for natural language understanding and information retrieval, assess models' abilities to comprehend questions and generate accurate responses. While they have propelled advancements in conversational systems, search engines, and machine reading comprehension, they also highlight challenges in handling specialized domain-specific scenarios. Unlike existing datasets, our proposed dataset captures the nuances and complexities inherent in human-robot interactions within public service environments, providing a more relevant and robust foundation for developing and evaluating AI models in this domain.

2.2 Generating QA Datasets with Large Language Model

Since the introduction of OpenAI's generative pre-trained transformer (GPT) series, these models have revolutionized natural language processing by excelling in generating coherent and semantically rich texts. GPT-3, trained with 175 billion parameters, exhibits human-like performance across diverse linguistic tasks, influencing applications in automated QA systems and programming [19]. Building on these advancements, GPT-4 enhances text generation and annotation capabilities, particularly in simulating public affairs dialogues. This research leverages Large Language Models (LLMs) to develop a dataset tailored for public affairs dialogues. The dataset demonstrates LLM's proficiency in generating practical and relevant text and introduces comprehensive emotion annotations to analyze interactions between robots and citizens. Prompt design ensures the dataset reflects authentic public interactions [20]. By integrating advanced text generation with emotion annotation, this dataset equips robots to navigate complex emotional and contextual nuances in public service dialogues effectively. This innovative dataset addresses the limitations of traditional datasets in specialized domains and enhances emotional intelligence in public service robots. The meticulous prompt design captures the intricacies of public-citizen interactions, maximizing its relevance and practical utility in real-world applications.

2.3 Emotion Analysis in Human-Robot Interaction

Emotion analysis in human-robot interaction (HRI) [21] has evolved significantly over time. Initially, research focused on identifying basic emotional states using direct cues like facial expressions and vocal intonation. Early systems utilized visual processing techniques, such as the Facial Action Coding System (FACS) by Ekman and Friesen [22], to decode emotions through facial expressions.

As technology advanced, researchers expanded their scope to include auditory emotion detection. Schuller *et al.*. [23] demonstrated the effectiveness of analyzing vocal intonation in detecting emotions. Moreover, understanding the influence of contextual background on emotional interpretation became crucial, as highlighted by Devillers *et al.*. [24]. Recent advancements, such as multimodal approaches integrating visual, auditory, and textual data, have significantly improved emotion detection accuracy in HRI, as shown by Poria *et al.*. [25]. These developments reflect a shift from recognizing emotions based on single cues to a more comprehensive multimodal understanding. By incorporating facial expressions, vocal intonation, and contextual cues, robots can engage with humans more empathetically and effectively in various interaction scenarios.

3   Method

3.1 Dataset Construction

This section details the method for developing the dataset, including dialogue generation via LLM, the annotation framework for categorizing interactions, and quality assurance protocols to ensure consistency and reliability.

Dataset Generation via LLM. The dataset was generated using LLM to produce dialogues simulating exchanges between individuals and robots in public affairs halls. The prompts for LLM were strategically crafted to cover various public service types, ensuring a comprehensive representation of real-world inquiries. Specifically, the public service scenarios included in the dataset encompass a wide range of common government services, such as Household Registration, ID Card Services, Passport Services, Visa Services, Residence Permit Services, Social Security, Traffic Violation, Public Service Complaints and Feedback, Payment Services, and other miscellaneous government-related inquiries. Each of these scenarios was chosen to reflect the diversity of interactions that occur in public service contexts, providing a comprehensive foundation for evaluating AI-driven public service robots. Each directive required generating QA-style interactive dialogues, maintaining user anonymity, and constructing all dialogues in English. Instructions for LLM emphasized excluding personal identifiers, focusing solely on informational exchanges relevant to public services. The specific prompt was: "Change the type of public affairs business and generate a QA-style interactive dialogue between a group of natural persons and the robot in the public affairs hall. The public affairs business should fall within the hall's scope. The user's name should not appear, and the dialogue should be in English." This methodology enabled the creation of dialogues across ten distinct public service categories, ensuring the dataset's relevance to real-world applications. By encompassing such diverse scenarios, the dataset not only reflects typical conversational frameworks in service environments but also provides a robust foundation for training and evaluating AI systems. This enhances the dataset's

Table 1. Quantitative Performance and Emotional Interaction Metrics

Quantitative Performance Metrics		Emotional Interaction Metrics	
Category	Description	Category	Description
Relevance		**Emotional Accuracy**	
1	Completely irrelevant	1	Completely inappropriate emotional tone
2	Minimally relevant	2	Emotional tone feels unnatural
3	Partially relevant with some misalignment	3	Generally matches user's emotional state but could be improved
4	Highly relevant, providing almost all necessary information	4	Matches user's emotional state well, with minor discrepancies
5	Completely relevant, directly and comprehensively addressing the user's question	5	Perfectly matches user's emotional state and needs
Efficiency		**Interactivity**	
1	Slow or requires multiple interactions	1	Poor interaction, with frequent interruptions
2	Requires several steps	2	Interaction is somewhat poor, needing more clarification
3	Resolves the question but not with optimal efficiency	3	Moderate interaction, generally fluid with occasional clarifications
4	Quick and direct with minimal unnecessary interactions	4	Good, fluid interaction with rare clarifications
5	Extremely efficient, resolving the question concisely	5	Excellent, fluid interaction without clarifications needed
Timeliness		**User Emotional Tendency**	Enjoyment, Negative Emotion, Novelty, and Satisfaction
1	Severely delayed	**Answer Emotional Tendency**	Utility and Courtesy
2	Slightly delayed		
3	On time		
4	Provided quickly		
5	Very rapid, exceeding expected speed		

utility in simulating realistic service interactions, thereby supporting comprehensive assessments of robot response efficacy across varied public service scenarios. In addition, to ensure the dataset's relevance and reliability, we employed a multi-step data generation process. Initially, prompts were designed to cover a broad spectrum of public service scenarios, followed by iterative refinement to enhance the accuracy and diversity of the dialogues. This involved multiple rounds of dialogue generation, where the output from the LLM was reviewed and refined based on predefined criteria, ensuring that each generated dialogue met the standards for inclusion in the dataset. This iterative process was crucial in capturing the nuances of real-world interactions and ensuring that the dataset is both comprehensive and reflective of actual public service encounters.

Dataset Annotation Protocol. The dataset annotations were conducted by feeding the generated dialogues back into LLM, which uses an annotation protocol to evaluate each QA dialogue based on predefined labels. This ensures consistent standards across all interactions, as outlined in Table 1. The labels include:

Quantitative Performance Metrics

- **Relevance:** Scored from 1 (completely irrelevant) to 5 (completely relevant), assessing how well responses address the user's inquiry. High scores indicate on-topic and useful responses, reducing follow-up questions.
- **Efficiency:** Rated from 1 (inefficient, requiring multiple interactions) to 5 (extremely efficient, resolving the query concisely). Efficiency improves user experience by minimizing the time and effort needed for accurate information.
- **Timeliness:** Evaluated from 1 (severely delayed) to 5 (exceedingly prompt), measuring response speed. Timeliness is crucial for maintaining conversation flow and preventing user frustration.

Emotional Interaction Metrics

- **Emotional Accuracy:** Scored from 1 (completely inappropriate) to 5 (perfectly matches the user's emotional state), gauging the alignment of the response's emotional tone with the user's needs. Emotional accuracy affects user satisfaction and perception of the service.
- **Interactivity:** Scored from 1 (ineffective) to 5 (highly engaging), assessing the fluidity and responsiveness of the dialogue. High scores indicate smooth and engaging interactions.
- **User Emotional Tendency:** Identifies the emotional state of the user as negative, neutral, or positive. This helps in tailoring responses to user emotions.
- **Answer Emotional Tendency:** Evaluates the emotional attributes of the response, emphasizing utility and courtesy. This metric ensures responses are useful and polite, enhancing user perception of the service's professionalism.

First, quantitative performance metrics: relevance, efficiency, and timeliness: evaluate the chatbot's functional effectiveness in public service contexts. Relevance measures how well responses address user inquiries. Efficiency assesses the chatbot's ability to resolve queries concisely, reducing user effort. Timeliness evaluates response speed to maintain smooth interaction flow. Embedding these metrics ensures models deliver accurate answers promptly, meeting user expectations and enhancing satisfaction. Second, emotional interaction metrics-emotional accuracy, interactivity, user emotional tendency, and answer emotional tendency-provide qualitative insights. Emotional accuracy ensures responses align with user emotions, fostering empathetic interactions. Interactivity measures dialogue fluidity, reflecting seamless engagement. User emotional tendency and answer emotional tendency analyze emotional impacts post-interaction, guiding courteous responses. Understanding these metrics enhances chatbot design for appropriate emotional responses, improving engagement and satisfaction. Integrating both sets of metrics ensures a holistic evaluation of chatbot performance, balancing factual accuracy with emotional intelligence. This approach supports effective user interactions in public service, where meeting both informational needs and emotional expectations is crucial.

Quality Control. To ensure the integrity and utility of our dataset of QA pairs from public service robot interactions, we implemented a meticulous quality control (QC) process. This protocol involves multiple stages to uphold the highest standards of data accuracy, annotation reliability, and model validation.

– **Accuracy and Relevance of Dialogue Pairs:** Experts review interactions for grammar and relevance, ensuring suitability for public service scenarios. Automated checks ensure responses align with queries and adhere to public procedures.
– **Annotation Quality Assurance:** Annotators receive training on relevance, timeliness, efficiency, emotional accuracy, and interactivity. LLM provides guidelines, supplemented by secondary human review.
– **Sampling and Validation of Annotations:** A random sample (e.g., 5% of the dataset) undergoes secondary review to ensure high quality. Multiple user-generated labels validate these annotations.
– **Model Validation:** Classification models are tested on a validation set excluded from training. The dataset is validated through comparisons with baseline models like BERT, DistilBERT, ALBERT, RoBERTa, XLNet, and GPT-2, using the macro-averaged F1 score to measure performance.
– **Continuous Monitoring and Feedback Loop:** The QC process includes regular reassessments to maintain consistency. Feedback refines guidelines and training, improving dataset quality.

By combining LLM's review and labeling capabilities with human oversight and rigorous quality control, we established a robust QC process for this dataset. Comparative experiments further verify the dataset's labeling quality and emotional distribution.

3.2 Dataset Evaluation

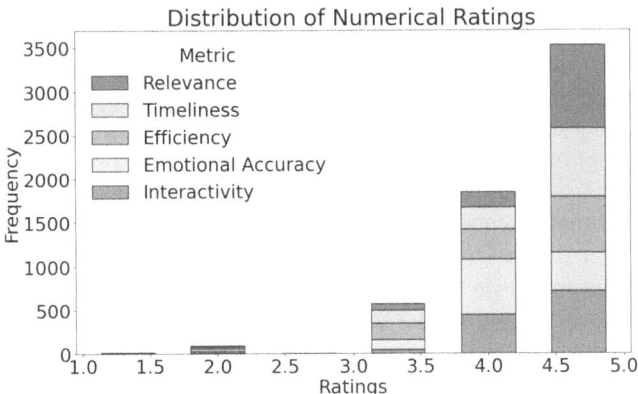

Fig. 1. Distribution of Numerical Ratings

Assessment of User Engagement and Robot Response Effectiveness.
The histograms depicting numerical ratings show predominantly positive evaluations across relevance, timeliness, efficiency, emotional accuracy, and interactivity (Fig. 1). The concentration of ratings towards higher scores (4 and 5 points) suggests overall satisfaction with robotic performance. Lower scores are rare, indicating effective service delivery.

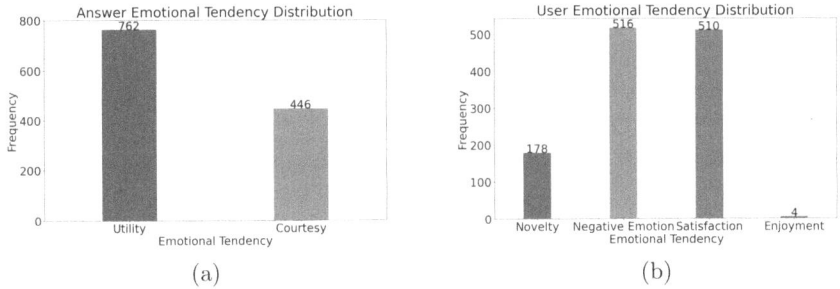

Fig. 2. Distribution of Emotional Tendency

Figure 2 (a) illustrates a diverse emotional landscape among users, highlighting prevalent expressions of "negative emotion" and "satisfaction." This suggests users predominantly interact with the service during moments of dissatisfaction or approval, rather than seeking novelty or enjoyment. Figure 2 (b) shows prevalent emotional dispositions, emphasizing the robot's primary strategies of "utility" and "courtesy." "utility" reflects its focus on providing useful information, while "courtesy" underscores efforts to maintain respectful communication. This strategy enhances user engagement and satisfaction by aligning responses with the emotional context of inquiries.

Enhancing Satisfaction Through Adaptive Responses in Public Services. Upon analyzing the dataset, a clear pattern emerges where user satisfaction ratings increase from 3 to 4, despite prevalent "negative emotion". This observation was based on the progression of interactions, where initial user dissatisfaction stemmed from issues such as delays or generic responses, resulting in lower satisfaction ratings. As the interactions continued, the robot adapted its responses by offering quicker solutions and streamlining processes in reaction to user feedback, directly addressing immediate concerns and leading to improved response effectiveness, which corresponded with higher satisfaction ratings. Additionally, the tone of the robot's responses evolved from being purely utilitarian to more empathetic, better aligning with the emotional states of users. This shift, particularly in addressing frustration or dissatisfaction, played a significant role in enhancing user satisfaction. The conclusion that adaptive responses improve satisfaction was drawn from these observed patterns: as the robot adjusted both its operational approach and tone in response to user needs, user satisfaction consistently improved. This underscores the importance of adaptive, emotionally intelligent AI responses in public service interactions, where meeting both practical and emotional needs can significantly enhance user satisfaction.

4   Experiments

4.1   Data Preprocessing

During initial data preprocessing, we thoroughly cleaned and validated QA pairs from public service robot interactions. Domain experts reviewed a subset of dialogues for grammatical accuracy and contextual relevance. Automated consistency checks used advanced NLP techniques, including TF-IDF vectorization and cosine similarity, to ensure logical coherence and internal consistency.

4.2   Baselines Settings

This study evaluates six state-of-the-art pre-trained language models: BERT, RoBERTa, DistilBERT, ALBERT, XLNet, and GPT-2 on sentiment and emotion analysis using a newly developed dataset. These models are renowned for their performance across various NLP tasks. To prevent overfitting, L2 regularization [26] was applied during the training process, and k-fold cross-validation was implemented to evaluate model performance across different subsets of the data, ensuring that the model does not overfit to a specific subset. For sentiment analysis, the models were assessed on their ability to classify QA dialogue pairs into neutral and negative categories, with the macro-averaged F1 score as the primary metric. In emotion analysis, the models were tested on their ability to classify QA dialogues into three categories: negative emotion, novelty, and satisfaction. These categories are crucial in public service contexts for identifying distress, evaluating innovative solutions, and measuring user satisfaction. The evaluation also used the macro-averaged F1 score to assess performance across these categories.

4.3   Experiment Implementation

The experimental setup involved fine-tuning and evaluating pre-trained language models on sentiment and emotion analysis tasks using a dataset from public service robot interactions. The dataset was split into training (80%), validation (10%), and test (10%) sets. Tokenizers specific to each model (BERT, RoBERTa, DistilBERT, ALBERT, XLNet, and GPT-2) were used to tokenize the input texts, with padding and truncation to ensure uniform input lengths. The tokenized data was converted into a PyTorch dataset object. Each model was fine-tuned using the Hugging Face Transformers library with the AdamW optimizer, a learning rate of 2×10^{-5}, batch size of 32, and training for 5 epochs, incorporating early stopping based on validation loss. Training was conducted on an NVIDIA GeForce RTX 4070 Laptop GPU. The primary evaluation metric was the macro-averaged F1 score, with additional metrics including precision and recall.

4.4   Results and Discussion

Table 2 presents the evaluation outcomes of six models on the newly curated dataset, showing results both before and after fine-tuning. The outcomes illustrate the models' capabilities in sentiment and emotion analysis within public service dialogues. In sentiment analysis, post-fine-tuning results show marked improvement across all models. XLNet achieved the highest macro-averaged F1

Table 2. F1 scores for Sentiment and Emotion analysis using various models

Models	Sentiment			Emotion			
	Neutral	Negative	Average(MF1)	Negative Emotion	Novelty	Satisfaction	Average(MF1)
BERT	0.87	0.84	0.86	0.83	0.63	0.75	0.55
	0.93	**0.90**	**0.92**	**0.97**	**0.87**	**0.92**	**0.94**
RoBERTa	0.86	0.84	0.85	0.86	0.59	0.75	0.55
	0.91	**0.87**	**0.89**	**0.97**	**0.88**	**0.93**	**0.86**
DistilBERT	0.88	0.86	0.87	0.81	0.64	0.72	0.54
	0.89	**0.93**	**0.91**	**0.97**	**0.89**	**0.92**	**0.95**
ALBERT	0.85	0.82	0.83	0.81	0.63	0.74	0.54
	0.87	**0.89**	**0.88**	**0.95**	**0.88**	**0.92**	**0.69**
XLNet	0.89	0.87	0.88	0.82	0.57	0.72	0.53
	0.96	**0.92**	**0.94**	**0.96**	**0.91**	**0.94**	**0.70**
GPT-2	0.86	0.84	0.85	0.78	**0.64**	0.71	0.53
	0.91	**0.83**	**0.87**	**0.83**	0.61	**0.75**	**0.76**

score of 0.94, underscoring its enhanced ability to distinguish between Neutral and Negative sentiments. Similarly, DistilBERT's performance increased to a macro-averaged F1 score of 0.91, indicating that streamlined models can maintain robust performance while benefiting substantially from fine-tuning. These findings highlight the critical role of fine-tuning in improving models' proficiency in identifying prevalent sentiments in public QA dialogues, essential for effectively addressing public concerns.

In emotion analysis, BERT and RoBERTa excelled in identifying negative emotion post-fine-tuning, each achieving a score of 0.97. Prompt detection of negative emotions is vital in public service as it informs policy adjustments and enhances citizen engagement. Their relatively lower scores in novelty and satisfaction before fine-tuning (BERT scoring 0.63 and 0.75, and RoBERTa 0.59 and 0.75) significantly improved after fine-tuning (BERT scoring 0.87 and 0.92, and RoBERTa 0.88 and 0.93). These advancements suggest that fine-tuning helps models better detect nuanced emotional states in public dialogues. The results indicate that overall emotion detection is more challenging than sentiment analysis in public interactions due to the complexity and subtlety of emotional expressions. The macro-averaged F1 scores for emotion analysis were generally lower before fine-tuning, reflecting the difficulties faced by public service robots in identifying innovative thinking, creativity, and citizen satisfaction. For instance, XLNet's score in novelty detection improved from 0.57 to 0.91 post-fine-tuning, reflecting its enhanced capability to interpret and respond to less frequent but significant emotional states.

5   Conclusion

This study identifies limitations in current general datasets for public service and introduces a new Large Language Model-generated dataset simulating interactions between public service robots and citizens. It includes rich contextual information and detailed annotations like relevance, efficiency, timeliness, emotional accuracy, interactivity, user emotional tendency, and answer emotional tendency. These enrichments support training sophisticated AI models for nuanced human-computer interaction, demonstrating efficacy through comparative experiments with fine-tuning algorithms. The dataset's potential lies in enhancing AI performance tailored to public service needs, aiming to improve interaction quality and satisfaction in public service environments.

6   Future Work

While our QA dialogue dataset is a significant step forward, we acknowledge its limitations and areas for improvement. We plan to expand the dataset by incorporating a wider variety of public service scenarios and user interactions, ensuring more comprehensive coverage. To address potential biases from relying on GPT-4, we will diversify the dataset by including data generated from multiple language models. Additionally, we will use bias detection techniques and involve domain experts in reviewing the data. Expanding the range of emotional categories and interaction scenarios, as well as integrating multi-modal data like voice tone and facial expressions, will further enhance the dataset. These efforts will help develop more robust and adaptable AI models for complex public service applications.

References

1. Russakovsky, O., et al.: ImageNet large scale visual recognition challenge. Int. J. Comput. Vision **115**(3), 211–252 (2015)
2. Chen, Y., Zhao, F., Lou, Y.: Interactive model predictive control for robot navigation in dense crowds. IEEE Trans. Syst. Man Cybern. Syst. **52**(4), 2289–2301 (2021)
3. Trautman, P., Ma, J., Murray, R.M., Krause, A.: Robot navigation in dense human crowds: statistical models and experimental studies of human-robot cooperation. Int. J. Robot. Res. **34**(3), 335–356 (2015)
4. Engin, Z., Treleaven, P.: Algorithmic government: automating public services and supporting civil servants in using data science technologies. Comput. J. **62**(3), 448–460 (2019)
5. Tiddi, I., Bastianelli, E., Daga, E., d'Aquin, M., Motta, E.: Robot-city interaction: mapping the research landscape-a survey of the interactions between robots and modern cities. Int. J. Soc. Robot. **12**, 299–324 (2020)
6. Chibani, A., Amirat, Y., Mohammed, S., Matson, E., Hagita, N., Barreto, M.: Ubiquitous robotics: recent challenges and future trends. Robot. Auton. Syst. **61**(11), 1162–1172 (2013)
7. Li, Y., Jiang, Y., Tian, D., Hu, L., Lu, H., Yuan, Z.: AI-enabled emotion communication. IEEE Network **33**(6), 15–21 (2019)
8. Guzman, A.L., Lewis, S.C.: Artificial intelligence and communication: a human-machine communication research agenda. New Media Soc. **22**(1), 70–86 (2020)
9. Raposo, G., Coheur, L., Martins, B.: Prompting, retrieval, training: an exploration of different approaches for task-oriented dialogue generation. In: Proceedings of the 24th Annual Meeting of the Special Interest Group on Discourse and Dialogue, pp. 400–412 (2023)
10. Goldman, D.S.: A Stateful Multi-Context Aware Design Using OpenAI's GPT (Towards Digital Sentience) (2023)
11. Deng, J., Dong, W., Socher, R., Li, L.-J., Li, K., Fei-Fei, L.: ImageNet: a large-scale hierarchical image database. In: 2009 IEEE Conference on Computer Vision and Pattern Recognition, pp. 248–255. IEEE (2009)
12. Lin, T.-Y., et al.: Microsoft COCO: common objects in context. In: Fleet, D., Pajdla, T., Schiele, B., Tuytelaars, T. (eds.) Computer Vision-ECCV 2014: 13th European Conference, Zurich, Switzerland, 6–12 September 2014, Proceedings, Part V, LNCS, vol. 8693, pp. 740–755. Springer, Heidelberg (2014). https://doi.org/10.1007/978-3-319-10602-1_48
13. Xiao, H., Rasul, K., Vollgraf, R.: Fashion-MNIST: a novel image dataset for benchmarking machine learning algorithms. arXiv preprint arXiv:1708.07747 (2017)
14. Jain, A.K., Duin, R.P.W., Mao, J.: Statistical pattern recognition: a review. IEEE Trans. Pattern Anal. Mach. Intell. **22**(1), 4–37 (2020)
15. Sarker, I.H.: Machine learning: algorithms, real-world applications and research directions. SN Comput. Sci. **2**(3), 160 (2021)

16. Rajpurkar, P., Zhang, J., Lopyrev, K., Liang, P.: SQuAD: 100,000+ questions for machine comprehension of text. arXiv preprint arXiv:1606.05250 (2016)
17. Nguyen, T., et al.: MS MARCO: a human-generated machine reading comprehension dataset (2016)
18. Reddy, S., Chen, D., Manning, C.D.: CoQA: a conversational question answering challenge. Trans. Assoc. Comput. Linguist. **7**, 249–266 (2019)
19. Winkler, D., Biffl, S.: Improving quality assurance in automation systems development projects. In: Quality Assurance and Management, pp. 20–40 (2012)
20. Willems, J., Schmidthuber, L., Vogel, D., Ebinger, F., Vanderelst, D.: Ethics of robotized public services: the role of robot design and its actions. Gov. Inf. Q. **39**(2), 101683 (2022)
21. Szabóová, M., Sarnovský, M., Krešňáková, V.M., Machová, K.: Emotion analysis in human-robot interaction. Electronics **9**(11), 1761 (2020)
22. Friesen, E., Ekman, P.: Facial action coding system: a technique for the measurement of facial movement. Palo Alto **3**(2), 5 (1978)
23. Schuller, B., Rigoll, G., Lang, M.: Speech emotion recognition combining acoustic features and linguistic information in a hybrid support vector machine-belief network architecture. In: 2004 IEEE International Conference on Acoustics, Speech, and Signal Processing, vol. 1, pp. I-577. IEEE (2004)
24. Devillers, L., Vidrascu, L.: Real-life emotions detection with lexical and paralinguistic cues on human-human call center dialogs. In: Ninth International Conference on Spoken Language Processing (2006)
25. Majumder, N., Hazarika, D., Gelbukh, A., Cambria, E., Poria, S.: Multimodal sentiment analysis using hierarchical fusion with context modeling. Knowl.-Based Syst. **161**, 124–133 (2018)
26. Zeng, S., Gou, J., Deng, L.: An antinoise sparse representation method for robust face recognition via joint l1 and l2 regularization. Expert Syst. Appl. **82**, 1–9 (2017)

MCFC: A Momentum-Driven Clicked Feature Compressed Pre-trained Language Model for Information Retrieval

Dongyang Li[1,2], Ruixue Ding[2], Pengjun Xie[2], and Xiaofeng He[1(✉)]

[1] East China Normal University, Shanghai, China
hexf@cs.ecnu.edu.cn
[2] Alibaba Group, Hangzhou, China
{ada.drx,chengchen.xpj}@alibaba-inc.com

Abstract. Information Retrieval (IR) pre-trained language models are trained from large-scale retrieval-based corpora to promote the task-specific knowledge capacity. Previous works focus on general retrieval pre-trained datasets, which cover inter-document data and intra-document data, paying less attention to the important asset of clicked data which is commonly adopted in recommendation domain. However, the utilization of easily accessible clicked data is a non-trivial operation due to its characteristics of large volume and insufficient refinement, which affect model learning efficiency and imply the risk of distorting learning directions. In this paper, we propose a **M**omentum-Driven **C**licked **F**eature **C**ompressed Pre-trained Language Models for Information Retrieval (MCFC). Specifically, to tackle the effective learning pace on large amounts of data, we generalize multiple similar feature instances and compress the dispersed knowledge together at the query granularity, named Multi-Instance Information Integration. Meanwhile, more relevant detection between queries and documents is eager in coarse clicked data background, we leverage a momentum-driven adjusting mechanism to refine the text representations, named Continuous Debiasing Calibration. Extensive experiments on downstream datasets validate the superiority of our work to other recent strong baselines.

Keywords: Pre-trained Language Model · Information Retrieval · Clicked Feature

1 Introduction

Pre-trained language models (PLMs) for specific IR task are learned from document collections and are tailored by customized objectives. Compared with general PLMs (i.e., BERT [9], RoBERTa [19], GPT [32] etc.), IR PLMs perform professionally on retrieval tasks, such as ad-hoc retrieval [4,25], dense retrieval [4,25], dense retrieval [10,22], and ranking [41,45]. Recently, large language models (LLMs) [30,37] also introduce retrieval to alleviate the hallucination problem

D. F. Wong et al. (Eds.): NLPCC 2024, LNAI 15359, pp. 69–82, 2025.
https://doi.org/10.1007/978-981-97-9431-7_6

Type	#ORCAS	#MS MARCO	#ORCAS/ #MS MARCO
Queries	10,405,342	367,013	28.4 times
QRELs	18,823,602	384,597	48.9 times
Top 100 Candidates	982,951,086	36,701,116	26.8 times

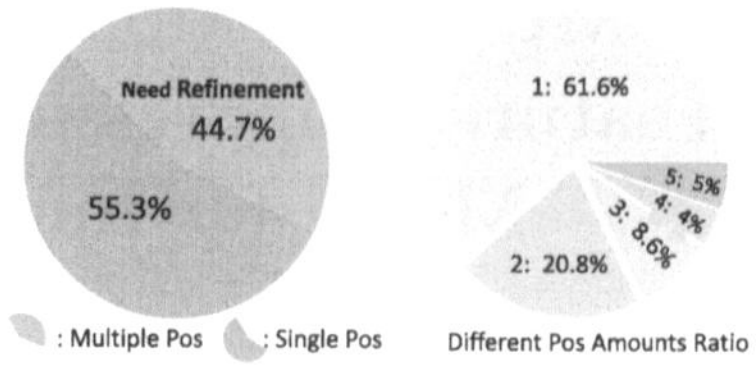

Need Refinement 44.7%

55.3%

: Multiple Pos   : Single Pos

1: 61.6%

2: 20.8%   3: 8.6%   4: 4%   5: 5%

Different Pos Amounts Ratio

Fig. 1. The detailed analysis of ORCAS dataset characteristics.

and to augment the model with relevant knowledge. And conversely, retrieval models [8,35] consider the data generated by LLMs to promote the performance in few-shot and zero-shot scenarios. LLMs and retrieval models are co-dependent and co-boosting with each other.

Existing works utilize diverse document collections to train the task-specific model, they concentrate on inter-document data [25,44] to explore the connection by hyperlinks and anchors, and intra-document data [16,22] to leverage HTML information and well-formed Wiki-articles. These works neglect the recommendation commonly used clicked data to introduce extra knowledge. ORCAS[1] [5] is a typical clicked data collection in web search scenario, which records queries that have been repeated across many anonymized users. It focuses on query-document connections, which are important assets and have not been sufficiently exploited. [2,27] demonstrate the performance improvement with the assistance of ORCAS. As the left part of Fig. 1 shows, in terms of the dataset size, ORCAS is significantly times larger than MS MARCO[2] [28]. Since the large volume ORCAS dataset is coarsely collected from click logs and no supervised human annotation during the data collection stage, there exists an uncertain quality problem, such as multiple positive documents related to one query and the scattered distribution of profitable document information. Additionally, Compressive Sensing Theory [31] in the signal processing domain mentions also acts as the support theory here, which declares that a low dimension representation contains enough information to recover the original signal when the signal could be compressed, and its transform domain is sparse. Thus, we need generalized operations to compress redundant information and purify the samples.

The middle part of Fig. 1 demonstrates the proportion of multiple positive and single positive documents in the ORCAS QRELs file. In human-annotated supervised cases, each query is mapped to only one positive document. However, the multiple positive documents ratio in ORCAS reaches 44.7%, covering nearly half of the total set, which needs to be refined with finer-grained treatment. The right part of Fig. 1 indicates the detail rate of different positive documents amounts corresponding to one query, there are only 61.6% queries that have one positive document, and the rest of the queries all need further detection to filter out worth limited samples. The false positive and false negative samples affect

---

[1] https://microsoft.github.io/msmarco/ORCAS.

[2] https://microsoft.github.io/msmarco/Datasets.html.

the model performance and disturb the relevance judgment of the query and document. Therefore, the calibration of these uncertain data should be considered to enhance reliability.

To overcome the challenges mentioned above, we propose a pre-trained language model for information retrieval based on a **M**omentum-Driven **C**licked **F**eature **C**ompressed (MCFC) mechanism, which facilities knowledge compressing and refining to obtain more accurate representations:

(1) Multi-Instance Information Integration: To address the large volume characteristic of clicked data, we introduce the distantly supervised multi-instance learning [43] strategy to collect and compress the similar feature to a bag. Thus, the sparse scattered information is unified, we apply the unified bag representations to represent the same query's multiple relevant samples. The redundant and less informative data is folded to save the compute consumption.

(2) Continuous Debiasing Calibration: To further refine the noisy data in large volume ORCAS, we utilize a parameters continuously-evolving momentum model to lead the original model update forward. The momentum model produces soft pseudo targets for queries, we treat these soft pseudo targets as additional supervision for the original model, avoiding the model distorting overly on updating direction due to noise. The negative sample range is also enlarged at the contrastive learning stage.

2   Related Work

2.1   Pre-trained Language Models for IR

Customizing pre-trained language models to specific task promotes professionalism for certain applicable situations. Recent IR PLMs are proposed in two types, (1) Mono-modal based. The mono-modal based IR PLMs are trained with text only inter and intra-document data. [16,22,25,44] attempt to exploit the connections between documents to enhance the connections. Intra-document data works and integrate the structured data (i.e., HTML, tables, etc.) to obtain the hierarchical relevance. [3,23] also design task objectives for IR pre-training stage, such as Inverse Cloze Task(ICT), Body First Selection (BFS), Wiki Link Prediction (WLP) and Words Prediction (ROP). (2) Multi-modal based, MILES [14] utilizes an extra encoder to produce labels for masked video patch prediction and is trained with a video-text alignment objective. GilBERT [17] proposes a generative visual-linguistic retrieval model by modality pairs completion and image-text data representation generation. However, less attention has been paid to utilizing click data to pre-train the model, which records important relevant information.

2.2   Clicked Data Utilization

(1) Utilization In Recommendation Domain. Research works in the recommendation domain are mainstream applications of clicked data, which concentrate

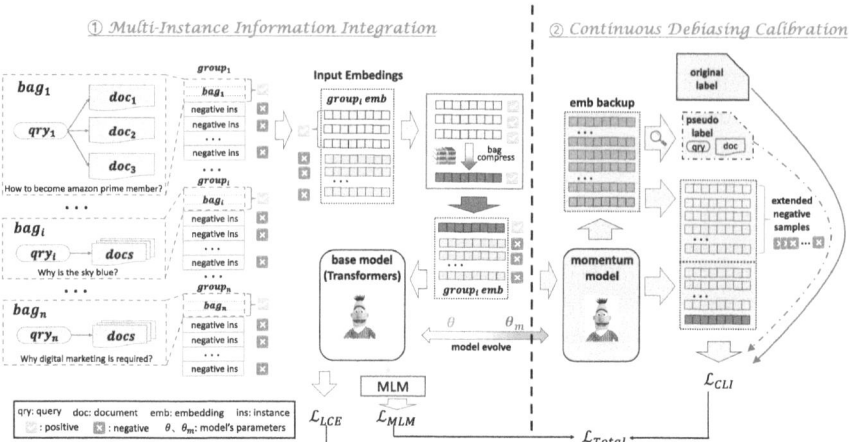

Fig. 2. The model architecture of MCFC. Each group combines three positive instances (in green color) from the bag and several randomly sampled negative instances (in gray color). (Color figure online)

on catching the user behavior knowledge for accurate recommendation in industrial Engineering usage. [1] facilitates the position information to encourage the model to capture user behaviors by probability distribution calculation. [18] produce a confidence estimator by a few labeled data and apply a pairwise learn to rank strategy on gradient boosting decision tree. These works above are probability-based researches and not main Transformer-based methods. (2) Utilization In Computer Vision domain. Click data features are dug to enhance the image recognition task. [42] considers an image dataset containing click information to assist the model understand the image semantics and perform well on three image recognition datasets. [38] combines the image recognition and click prediction tasks in a unified framework to settle limit model performance and multi-domain knowledge transfer problems. However, applying click data to deep neural pre-trained language models is seldom taken into consideration.

3   Methodology

3.1   Model Overview and Notations

The model architecture is shown in Fig. 2. To sufficiently facilitate the knowledge in the large volume clicked data, our work proposes a model with two functional components: (1) Multi-Instance Information Integration treats the large size data as a distantly supervised scene to effectively accelerate the corpora procedure. (2) Continuous Debiasing Calibration leverages the idea of the momentum model to create pseudo targets as the additional supervised tags and extend the negative sample range at the learning stage.

In MCFC's training dataset, the i-th query contains $|q_i|$ tokens, $qry_i = \{t_{q_i}^1, t_{q_i}^2, \cdots, t_{q_i}^{|q_i|}\}$. The i-th bag bag_i is consist of the specific i-th query qry_i and its related document collection, the j-th document of bag bag_i is composed of $|d_{ij}|$ tokens $doc_{ij} = \{t_{d_{ij}}^1, t_{d_{ij}}^2, \cdots, t_{d_{ij}}^{|d_{ij}|}\}$. The base encode model is represented as $\mathcal{M}$ with θ to denote the model parameters, and the momentum model is $\widetilde{\mathcal{M}}$ with a parameters collection $\widetilde{\theta}$. The model's hidden state dimension is denoted as d.

3.2   Multi-instance Information Integration

We introduce the large volume clicked data ORCAS to inject abundant query and document relevant information to the model. The ORCAS's size is tens of times larger than the commonly utilized dataset MS MARCO. Meanwhile, ORCAS records query and document clicked history in the web search engine. However, the uncertain quality problem exists in the dataset, such as the clickbait issue, ambiguous queries, mistake click operation, and so on. The ORCAS's features of convenient access and large volume inspire us to model this scene as a distantly supervised problem.

When a specific query is searched in the web search engine, ORCAS records the corresponding clicked document information of different users. And the clicked documents can be collected together and regarded as the specific query's related documents. We cluster all of the clicked documents under a specific query search scenario and the specific query itself together to form a distantly supervised bag bag_i. We suppose there exists at least one document that indeed contains high relevant semantics to the specific query, and this situation satisfies the assumption of distantly supervised multi-instance learning [43].

In order to measure the relevance between query and document, we employ a base model to obtain the sequence representations and calculate the relevance score of the queries and documents by a linear function. During the data pre-processing stage, the training dataset offers us the clicked document URL, document title, and the document content body, we combine these components in the following order:

$$doc_{ij} = \{URL_{ij} \ || \ title_{ij} \ || \ body_{ij}\} \tag{1}$$

where "$||$" means the string concatenation. We set the URL as the first part of document components because users tend to choose the mainstream websites to acquire the information, the URL part carries certain indicative messages. Next, the i-th query is concatenated with the j-th clicked document to form an instance sequence $ins_{ij} = \{qry_i \ || \ doc_{ij}\}$. We encode the instance sequence with a Transformer-based model (e.g., BERT) and select the pooled [CLS] token embedding as the instance representations:

$$H_{ins_{ij}}^{CLS} = \mathcal{M}(t_{q_i}^1, \cdots, t_{q_i}^{|q_i|}, t_{d_{ij}}^1, \cdots, t_{d_{ij}}^{|d_{ij}|}) \tag{2}$$

where $H_{ins_{ij}}^{CLS} \in \mathbb{R}^d$.

The bag bag_i is formulated by the instances with a query and its highly relevant documents in the QRELs file, which is treated as the ground truth of the dataset, $bag_i = \{g\_ins_{i1}, g\_ins_{i2}, \cdots, g\_ins_{i|b_i|}\}$, where $|b_i|$ is the total instance count of bag_i. To integrate the multi-instance knowledge and fold the trivial parts into an ensemble, we leverage the mean-pooling strategy at bag level to obtain the bag representation, the hidden state of a bag is formulated as:

$$H_{bag_i}^{CLS} = MeanPool(H_{g\_ins_{i1}}^{CLS}, H_{g\_ins_{i2}}^{CLS}, \cdots, H_{g\_ins_{i|b_i|}}^{CLS}) \tag{3}$$

where $H_{bag_i}^{CLS} \in \mathbb{R}^d$. The aggregated bag representation packages the scattered information together instead of calculating each sample respectively to save the computation consumption. Then, we arrange the bag at the front with several randomly sampled instances followed to form a group.

The relevance score $S(qry_i, doc_{ij})$ of a general instance's[3] query and document is calculated by a linear function with the instance representation $H_{ins_{ij}}^{CLS}$.

$$S(qry_i, doc_{ij}) = W_{ins} H_{ins_{ij}}^{CLS} + b_{ins} \tag{4}$$

where $W_{ins} \in \mathbb{R}^{1 \times d}$ is the trainable transformation matrix, b_{ins} is the bias.

The goal of our task is to detect the query's highly relevant document and push the irrelevant document distant. Following the traditional retrieval task-handling manner, we apply contrastive learning to the training process. The pooled bag representation is treated as the positive instance, and we randomly select other documents from the query's top-100 relevant retrieval results to construct negative instances. For adapting the design of the group with front positive and subsequent randomly sampled negative instances, we utilize Localized Contrastive Estimation (LCE) loss [11] as the loss function instead of other standard contrastive learning loss [29,34,36]. The above relevance score is treated as the distance in the contrastive learning loss function.

$$\mathcal{L}_{LCE} = \frac{1}{|N_{qry}|} \sum_{i=1}^{|N_{qry}|} -log \frac{exp(S(H_{bag_i}^{CLS}))}{\sum_{m=1}^{|G|} exp(S(H_{neg\_ins_{ij}}^{CLS}))} \tag{5}$$

where $|N_{qry}|$ is the batch query count, $|G|$ is the group size with one positive sample and several non-relevant samples, $H_{neg\_ins_{ij}}^{CLS}$ is the negative instances representation.

3.3   Continuous Debiasing Calibration

Since the ORCAS is the document clicked history records data, there exists noise and mistake click operation. In detail, the false positive samples are probably due to the intentionally misleading document with a misguided attractive title and unintended error click operation. The false negative samples are generated

---

[3] The general instance is a naive sample of a group, it could be the pooled bag or a random sampled instance.

by the unconscious omission and low rank of highly related documents. We need to detect whether the document is relevant or not with accurate model representations. Thus, we consider the continuously-evolving momentum model to produce pseudo-targets for the sample to alleviate the bias in the clicked data. Meanwhile, the extended negative sample ranges promote contrastive learning effectiveness.

The momentum model is a continuously-moving model whose parameters $\widetilde{\theta}$ are updated via the indication of base model's parameters θ:

$$\widetilde{\theta}_{m+1} = \alpha\widetilde{\theta}_m + (1 - \alpha)\theta_m \tag{6}$$

where m is the iteration step index, α is the continuously-evolving parameter of the base model and momentum model. We input the query and documents independently to the momentum model to produce the momentum-driven representations respectively:

$$\widetilde{H}_{qry_i}^{CLS} = \widetilde{\mathcal{M}}(t_{q_i}^1, t_{q_i}^2, \cdots, t_{q_i}^{|q_i|}) \qquad \widetilde{H}_{doc_{ij}}^{CLS} = \widetilde{\mathcal{M}}(t_{d_{ij}}^1, t_{d_{ij}}^2, \cdots, t_{d_{ij}}^{|d_{ij}|}) \tag{7}$$

We attain the similarity between query and document by a dot-product function:

$$S(qry_i, doc_{ij}) = H_{qry_i}^{CLS} \cdot H_{doc_{ij}}^{CLS} \qquad \widetilde{S}(qry_i, doc_{ij}) = \widetilde{H}_{qry_i}^{CLS} \cdot \widetilde{H}_{doc_{ij}}^{CLS} \tag{8}$$

where $H_{qry_i}^{CLS}$ and $H_{doc_{ij}}^{CLS}$ are the query and document representations of base model. The softmax-normalized similarity of a query and a specific document text is measured by the representation similarity between the two elements, which is formulated as:

$$p_{ij}^{q \cdot d} = \frac{exp(S(qry_i, doc_{ij})/\tau)}{\sum_{x=1}^{|N_{neg}|} exp(S(qry_i, doc_{ij})/\tau)} \qquad \widetilde{p}_{ij}^{q \cdot d} = \frac{exp(\widetilde{S}(qry_i, doc_{ij})/\tau)}{\sum_{x=1}^{|N_{neg}|} exp(\widetilde{S}(qry_i, doc_{ij})/\tau)} \tag{9}$$

where τ is the temperature controlling parameter, $p_{ij}^{q \cdot d}$ is the base model produced representations softmax-normalized similarity, $\widetilde{p}_{ij}^{q \cdot d}$ is the momentum model produced representations softmax-normalized similarity. $\widetilde{p}_{ij}^{q \cdot d}$ is utilized to be the pseudo-targets for the base model predicting result to calibrate and debias the model representation. We combine of base model cross-entropy loss $\mathcal{L}_{c.e.}$ and Kullback-Leibler divergence expectation to construct the calibration loss.

$$\mathcal{L}_{CLI} = \mu\mathbb{E}_{(qry,doc)\sim T}[\mathcal{L}_{c.e.}(y_{ij}, p_{ij}^{q \cdot d})] + (1 - \mu)\mathbb{E}_{(qry,doc)\sim T}[KL(p_{ij}^{q \cdot d} \mid \widetilde{p}_{ij}^{q \cdot d})] \tag{10}$$

where T means the total training dataset samples, μ is the ratio control parameter, y_{ij} is the ground truth sample of the query in the QRELs file. Additionally, to improve the efficiency of contrastive learning, we enlarge the negative sample range by randomly selecting samples from a maintained embedding backup queue that stores history representations.

3.4 Training Objective

To further develop the model representation output ability, we leverage the mask language modeling (MLM) task to train the model. The input sequence tokens are randomly masked by the special token, and we encourage the context text to predict the masked token labels. The MLM loss can be represented as:

$$\mathcal{L}_{MLM} = - \sum_{t_{mask} \sim C_{mask}^{i}} log P(t_{mask} | ins_{mask}^{i}) \qquad (11)$$

where C_{mask}^{i} is the masked token collection, and ins_{mask}^{i} means the masked instance sequence. Therefore, we joint all three loss functions to constitute the total loss.

$$\mathcal{L}_{Total} = \lambda_1 \mathcal{L}_{LCE} + \lambda_2 \mathcal{L}_{CLI} + \lambda_3 \mathcal{L}_{MLM} \qquad (12)$$

where where λ_k is the control hyper-parameter and $\sum_{k=1}^{3} \lambda_k = 1$, denoting the weight of each component.

4 Experiments

4.1 Datasets

The pre-training corpus of our work is the clicked dataset ORCAS [5], which is collected from the web search engine logs. We utilize the MS MARCO Document ranking dataset [28] and the TREC 2019 Deep Learning Track dataset [6] to fine-tune the MCFC. We utilize the metric Mean Reciprocal Rank at 100 and 10 (MRR@100 and MRR@10) on the MS MARCO dataset. For TREC DL 2019 dataset, the Normalized Discounted Cumulative Gain at rank 100 and 10 (NDCG@100 and NDCG@10) metrics are leveraged for evaluations.

4.2 Experiments Settings

Pre-training Settings. During the pre-training stage, we utilize the BERT base model as the backbone, which includes 12 Transformer layers and 12 self-attention heads. The context-aware representation dimension of each token is 768. The maximum sequence length is 512. We choose the AdamW [20] as the optimizer with 5e-6 as the learning rate and 1e-5 as the weight decay. The pre-training group size for contrastive learning is set to 10 for 3 positive samples and 7 negative samples, when the count of positive samples is less than 3, we randomly sample the query's existing samples to reach 3. The batch size is 4 and the model is trained for 2 epochs. The pre-training stage's learning rate is 2e-5. The MLM is executed on the setting of 15% randomly selected masked tokens, in all these masked tokens, 80% are replaced by [MASK] token, 10% are randomly replaced by other tokens, and 10% remain unchanged. The continuously-evolving parameter of the base model and momentum model α is 0.995. We set the softmax-normalized similarity tempreture τ to 0.5, the ratio control parameter μ in $\mathcal{L}_{CLI}$ is 0.4. The λ of total loss $\mathcal{L}_{Total}$ is set to 0.35, 0.4, 0.25. We run our pre-training stage on 8 NVIDA A100 80G GPUs for 5 days.

Fine-tuning Settings. We fine-tune the pre-trained model on two commonly used datasets, MS MARCO Dev document set and TREC DL 2019. We only test the model performance on the reranking task with two different candidate document datasets, ANCE Top100, and Official Top100. The ANCE Top100 is the retrieval result from the ANCE model [40] and the Official Top100 is acquired from the official site. The fine-tuning group size is 8 for 1 positive sample and 7 negative samples. We fine-tune the model at the batch size of 1 and the epoch is set to 3. The learning rate of this fine-tuning stage is 1e-5 and the weight decay is 0.01. We employ AdamW to optimize the model and set the warm-up ratio to 0.1. The model's input sequence maximum length is 512. We fine-tune the model on 8 NVIDA V100 32G GPUs.

4.3   Baselines

We compare our method with two traditional models: QL [13], BM25 [33], three neural models: DRMM [15], KNRM [39], Conv-KNRM [7], and seven pre-trained models: $BERT_{base}$ [9], $PROP_{marco}$ [24], COSTA [22], SEED [21], ARES [4], HARP [25], Webformer [16].

4.4   General Experimental Results

We validate our model on two common retrieval datasets, MS MARCO DEV and TREC DL 2019. The performance under four metrics is listed in Table 1. From the results, we can observe that: (1) MCFC outperforms common models and recently released retrieval models, owing to the assistance of the refined quality clicked knowledge contained in ORCAS. (2) The performance on TREC

Table 1. General experimental results of MCFC and baselines on two downstream datasets. Best scores are in bold and second best scores are underlined. The t-tests demonstrate the improvements of MCFC are statistically significant with $p < 0.05$ level.

Model Type	Model	MS MARCO DEV				TREC DL 2019			
		ANCE		OFFICIAL		ANCE		OFFICIAL	
		MRR@100	MRR@10	MRR@100	MRR@10	NDCG@100	NDCG@10	NDCG@100	NDCG@10
Traditional Models	QL	23.25	22.45	21.74	20.08	46.44	53.70	46.94	43.54
	BM25	24.77	23.13	22.51	21.56	46.92	54.11	48.19	46.81
NeuralModels	DRMM	11.06	10.02	10.43	9.95	38.12	30.85	40.99	30.00
	KNRM	26.94	25.29	25.81	24.64	46.71	54.91	47.27	43.19
	Conv-KNRM	30.37	29.30	27.26	25.11	48.76	59.90	52.21	58.99
Pre-trainedModels	$BERT_{base}$	36.80	35.13	37.08	36.86	49.07	60.54	52.89	63.58
	$PROP_{marco}$	<u>41.59</u>	39.67	38.19	37.32	48.94	61.66	52.42	62.08
	COSTA	40.73	39.88	<u>38.64</u>	37.57	48.72	61.93	53.11	62.60
	SEED	40.81	39.52	37.70	37.13	49.14	62.75	52.85	60.50
	ARES	40.68	40.14	37.92	36.49	<u>49.71</u>	<u>62.58</u>	<u>53.53</u>	65.05
	HARP	41.02	<u>40.77</u>	38.37	37.25	49.49	62.02	53.37	**65.62**
	Webformer	40.54	39.95	38.45	<u>37.74</u>	49.67	62.00	53.35	64.79
Ours	MCFC	**41.75**	**41.26**	**39.84**	**39.31**	**51.00**	**65.35**	**53.64**	<u>65.52</u>

DL 2019 (ANCE) at NDCG@10 metric of MCFC surpasses two special pre-trained models, HARP ($62.02 \rightarrow 65.35$) and Webformer ($62.00 \rightarrow 65.35$), which are all pre-trained with web related data, such as hyperlinks and web pages. This phenomenon demonstrates that the clicked history data carries effective information to support the model to rank high related documents at the front. (3) Our model has higher scores than COSTA which utilizes group-wise contrastive learning on every evaluation metric. This advantages of MCFC indicate the momentum-driven mechanism and contrastive design work well on pulling the more semantic similar text close. In general, it can be seen from Table 1 that the specific design of our two modules facilitates the clicked feature to behave well on the retrieval tasks.

Table 2. Ablation study our model on TREC dataset. "-" means removing the module behind.

Dataset	TREC DL 2019			
Model	ANCE		OFFICIAL	
	NDCG@100	NDCG@10	NDCG@100	NDCG@10
MCFC (Ours)	**51.00**	**65.35**	**53.64**	**65.52**
- Multi-Ins. Inf. Int.	49.51	64.02	52.37	63.43
- Con. Deb. Cal.	48.63	62.94	51.45	62.11
- MLM	45.19	61.16	50.78	62.35
- LCE	42.33	59.57	49.61	60.67

5   Detailed Analysis of MCFC

5.1   Ablation Study

In order to prove the effectiveness of our model's components, we conduct ablation experiments on the TREC DL 2019 dataset. As shown in Table 2, (1) When we remove the Mutil-instance Information Integration module, the clicked data stays in the original form and the queries' multiple related documents are trained respectively without integration. The performance of MCFC drops 1.49 at NDCG@100 metric in terms of ANCE, due to the integration operation's value on effectively solving the uncertain quality data problem. (2) We remove the Continuous Debiasing Calibration module by cutting off the momentum-based manipulation continuously, the model is trained only by the loss function of LCE and MLM. The results further decrease by 1.05 on average on four different experimental settings, revealing that the Continuous Debiasing Calibration module is helpful to exclude the influence of noisy information. (3) The removal of LCE loss means we only retain MLM loss at the training stage, similarly, the removal of MLM loss means only keeping LCE loss. These two removal leads to performance decline and the descent of LCE loss is larger than the MLM, which reflects that the contrastive LCE loss is more significant than MLM in this retrieval scenario.

5.2   The Influence of Multi-instance Information Integration

In order to further probe the significance of Multi-Instance Information Integration, we randomly sample three queries that have 10 positive documents[4] and plot each query's positive documents representations in Fig. 3 after the t-SNE [26] dimensional reduction. The Mean Integration means we utilize the Mean-Pooling mechanism to integrate instances, the No Integration means we maintain the instances as the original state and train the instances independently. From Fig. 3, we can observe that the representations after mean integration are more centralized than no integration. This phenomenon demonstrates the Multi-Instance Information Integration's superiority in promoting the representation space distribution more reasonable and accurate.

5.3   The Influence of Continuous Debiasing Calibration

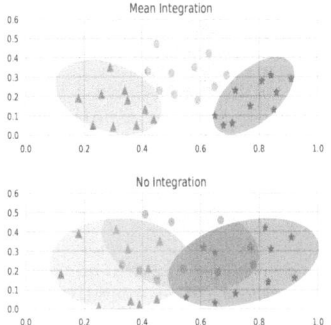

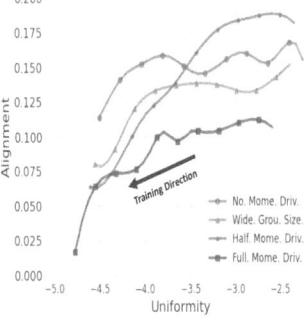

Fig. 3. Representations comparison between Mean Integration and No Integration after the t-SNE dimensional reduction. The ellipses represent the representation ranges of each category sample.

Fig. 4. Alignment and uniformity comparison of different calibration skills. The arrow indicates the training direction.

To analyze the effectiveness of our Continuous Debiasing Calibration module, we leverage the alignment and uniformity metrics to validate the features of the training stage. We calculate the samples' alignment and uniformity [12] during the training process. Both alignment and uniformity's smaller values represent better contrastive learning performance, which means the moving tendency towards the bottom left corner indicates the effective learning process. In Fig. 4, we record the representation samples of four different calibration skills and

---

[4] In this retrieval scenario, multiple positive documents of one query are treated as highly relevant samples to each other.

plot the smooth trend with the help of the interpolation method. No Momentum Driven means we dropout the learning skill of the momentum model and extended negative sample range, Widen Group Size denotes we enlarge the group size number, but this is a limited operation because of the fixed GPU memory. Half and Full Momentum Driven represent the half and full negative range settings of the samples. As shown in Fig. 4, the full momentum-driven manner achieves the best scores and has relatively lower values of alignment and uniformity during the whole training process. These performances indicate the effectiveness of the Continuous Debiasing Calibration module.

6   Conclusion

In this paper, we propose a pre-trained language model for information retrieval, named MCFC, based on the momentum-driven clicked feature compression. The Multi-Instance Information Integration provides an effective mechanism for accelerating the pre-training pace and shrinking the influence of the uncertain quality data. The Continuous Debiasing Calibration refines the large volume ORCAS by extending the negative sample range of contrastive learning with the assistance of an additional momentum model. Experiments on two common retrieval datasets validate the significance of MCFC and the ablation study further explains the efficiency of two component modules.

References

1. Agarwal, A., Wang, X., Li, C., Bendersky, M., Najork, M.: Addressing trust bias for unbiased learning-to-rank. In: WWW, pp. 4–14 (2019)
2. Alexander, D., Kusa, W., de Vries, A.P.: ORCAS-I: queries annotated with intent using weak supervision. In: SIGIR, pp. 3057–3066 (2022)
3. Chang, W., Yu, F.X., Chang, Y., Yang, Y., Kumar, S.: Pre-training tasks for embedding-based large-scale retrieval. In: ICLR (2020)
4. Chen, J., et al.: Axiomatically regularized pre-training for ad hoc search. In: SIGIR, pp. 1524–1534 (2022)
5. Craswell, N., Campos, D., Mitra, B., Yilmaz, E., Billerbeck, B.: ORCAS: 18 million clicked query-document pairs for analyzing search. CoRR abs/2006.05324 (2020)
6. Craswell, N., Mitra, B., Yilmaz, E., Campos, D., Voorhees, E.M.: Overview of the TREC 2019 deep learning track. CoRR abs/2003.07820 (2020)
7. Dai, Z., Xiong, C., Callan, J., Liu, Z.: Convolutional neural networks for soft-matching n-grams in ad-hoc search. In: WSDM, pp. 126–134 (2018)
8. Dai, Z., et al.: Promptagator: Few-shot dense retrieval from 8 examples. CoRR abs/2209.11755 (2022)
9. Devlin, J., Chang, M., Lee, K., Toutanova, K.: BERT: pre-training of deep bidirectional transformers for language understanding. In: NAACL-HLT, pp. 4171–4186 (2019)
10. Gao, L., Callan, J.: Unsupervised corpus aware language model pre-training for dense passage retrieval. In: ACL, pp. 2843–2853 (2022)

11. Gao, L., Dai, Z., Callan, J.: Rethink training of BERT rerankers in multi-stage retrieval pipeline. In: Hiemstra, D., Moens, M.-F., Mothe, J., Perego, R., Potthast, M., Sebastiani, F. (eds.) ECIR 2021. LNCS, vol. 12657, pp. 280–286. Springer, Cham (2021). https://doi.org/10.1007/978-3-030-72240-1_26

12. Gao, T., Yao, X., Chen, D.: SimCSE: simple contrastive learning of sentence embeddings. In: EMNLP, pp. 6894–6910 (2021)

13. Gaussier, É.: Statistical language models for information retrieval. Comput. Linguist. **36**(2), 279–281 (2010)

14. Ge, Y., et al.: MILES: visual BERT pre-training with injected language semantics for video-text retrieval. In: Avidan, S., Brostow, G., Cissé, M., Farinella, G.M., Hassner, T. (eds.) Computer Vision – ECCV 2022. ECCV 2022. LNCS, vol. 13695, pp. 691–708. Springer, Cham (2022). https://doi.org/10.1007/978-3-031-19833-5_40

15. Guo, J., Fan, Y., Ai, Q., Croft, W.B.: A deep relevance matching model for ad-hoc retrieval. In: CIKM, pp. 55–64. ACM (2016)

16. Guo, Y., et al.: WebFormer: pre-training with web pages for information retrieval. In: SIGIR, pp. 1502–1512 (2022)

17. Hong, W., Ji, K., Liu, J., Wang, J., Chen, J., Chu, W.: GilBERT: generative vision-language pre-training for image-text retrieval. In: SIGIR, pp. 1379–1388 (2021)

18. Lee, J., Song, Y., Haam, D., Lee, S., Choi, W., Lee, J.: Bridging the gap between click and relevance for learning-to-rank with minimal supervision. In: CIKM, pp. 2109–2112 (2020)

19. Liu, Y., et al.: RoBERTa: A robustly optimized BERT pretraining approach. CoRR abs/1907.11692 (2019)

20. Loshchilov, I., Hutter, F.: Fixing weight decay regularization in adam. CoRR abs/1711.05101 (2017)

21. Lu, S., et al.: Less is more: Pretrain a strong siamese encoder for dense text retrieval using a weak decoder. In: EMNLP (2021)

22. Ma, X., Guo, J., Zhang, R., Fan, Y., Cheng, X.: Pre-train a discriminative text encoder for dense retrieval via contrastive span prediction. In: SIGIR, pp. 848–858 (2022)

23. Ma, X., Guo, J., Zhang, R., Fan, Y., Ji, X., Cheng, X.: PROP: pre-training with representative words prediction for ad-hoc retrieval. In: WSDM, pp. 283–291 (2021)

24. Ma, X., Guo, J., Zhang, R., Fan, Y., Li, Y., Cheng, X.: B-PROP: bootstrapped pre-training with representative words prediction for ad-hoc retrieval. In: SIGIR, pp. 1318–1327 (2021)

25. Ma, Z., et al.: Pre-training for ad-hoc retrieval: hyperlink is also you need. In: CIKM, pp. 1212–1221 (2021)

26. van der Maaten, L., Hinton, G.: Visualizing data using t-SNE. pp. 2579–2605 (2008)

27. Mitra, B., Hofstätter, S., Zamani, H., Craswell, N.: Improving transformer-kernel ranking model using conformer and query term independence. In: SIGIR, pp. 1697–1702 (2021)

28. Nguyen, T., et al.: MS MARCO: a human generated machine reading comprehension dataset. In: NIPS. CEUR Workshop Proceedings, vol. 1773 (2016)

29. van den Oord, A., Li, Y., Vinyals, O.: Representation learning with contrastive predictive coding. CoRR abs/1807.03748 (2018)

30. Patil, S.G., Zhang, T., Wang, X., Gonzalez, J.E.: Gorilla: Large language model connected with massive APIs. arXiv preprint arXiv:2305.15334 (2023)

31. Qaisar, S.B., Bilal, R.M., Iqbal, W., Naureen, M., Lee, S.: Compressive sensing: from theory to applications, a survey. J. Commun. Networks **15**(5), 443–456 (2013)

32. Radford, A., Narasimhan, K., Salimans, T., Sutskever, I., et al.: Improving language understanding by generative pre-training (2018)

33. Robertson, S.E., Zaragoza, H.: The probabilistic relevance framework: BM25 and beyond. Found. Trends Inf. Retr. **3**(4), 333–389 (2009)
34. Robinson, J.D., Chuang, C., Sra, S., Jegelka, S.: Contrastive learning with hard negative samples. In: ICLR. OpenReview.net (2021)
35. Saad-Falcon, J., et al.: UDAPDR: unsupervised domain adaptation via LLM prompting and distillation of rerankers. CoRR abs/2303.00807 (2023)
36. Schroff, F., Kalenichenko, D., Philbin, J.: FaceNet: a unified embedding for face recognition and clustering. In: CVPR, pp. 815–823 (2015)
37. Srinivasan, K., Raman, K., Samanta, A., Liao, L., Bertelli, L., Bendersky, M.: QUILL: query intent with large language models using retrieval augmentation and multi-stage distillation. In: EMNLP, pp. 492–501 (2022)
38. Tan, M., Yu, J., Zhang, H., Rui, Y., Tao, D.: Image recognition by predicted user click feature with multidomain multitask transfer deep network. IEEE Trans. Image Process. **28**(12), 6047–6062 (2019)
39. Xiong, C., Dai, Z., Callan, J., Liu, Z., Power, R.: End-to-end neural ad-hoc ranking with kernel pooling. In: SIGIR, pp. 55–64 (2017)
40. Xiong, L., et al.: Approximate nearest neighbor negative contrastive learning for dense text retrieval. In: ICLR (2021)
41. Yan, M., Li, C., Bi, B., Wang, W., Huang, S.: A unified pretraining framework for passage ranking and expansion. In: AAAI, pp. 4555–4563 (2021)
42. Yu, J., Tan, M., Zhang, H., Rui, Y., Tao, D.: Hierarchical deep click feature prediction for fine-grained image recognition. IEEE Trans. Pattern Anal. Mach. Intell. **44**(2), 563–578 (2022)
43. Zeng, D., Liu, K., Chen, Y., Zhao, J.: Distant supervision for relation extraction via piecewise convolutional neural networks. In: EMNLP, pp. 1753–1762 (2015)
44. Zhou, J., et al.: Hyperlink-induced pre-training for passage retrieval in open-domain question answering. In: ACL, pp. 7135–7146 (2022)
45. Zhu, X., Hao, T., Cheng, S., Wang, F.L., Liu, H.: A self-supervised joint training framework for document reranking. In: Findings of NAACL, pp. 1056–1065 (2022)

Integrating Syntax Tree and Graph Neural Network for Conversational Question Answering over Heterogeneous Sources

Meiwen Li, Tianyu Cai, Lingyan Wu, Li Chen, and Shenggen Ju[✉]

College of Computer Science, Sichuan University, Chengdu, China
jsg@scu.edu.cn

Abstract. Conversational question answering (ConvQA) over heterogeneous sources leverages information from heterogeneous sources to enhance answer coverage, thereby improving the performance of ConvQA systems. Current mainstream methods rely on neural Seq2Seq models focusing on the complete conversation history. These models extract question entities and relation phrases implicit in the conversation history through sequence generation. However, numerous errors occur in extracting question entities because the conversation history contains irrelevant noise, and the sequence generation approach may lead to inaccuracies. To address this problem, we propose a model that incorporates a syntax tree and a graph neural network for ConvQA over heterogeneous sources. The model constructs a syntax tree by syntactically analyzing the user's question and conversation history. It then learns node representations and predicts node scores of the word nodes in the tree. This is based on the node's entity information and its relevance to the current question within the neighborhood. A graph neural network that includes entity-level attention is used to complete the extraction of the question entities. Experiments on the ConvMix and ConvQuestions datasets verify the overall performance improvement and validate the effectiveness of the proposed model.

Keywords: Conversational Question Answering · Graph Neural Network · Constituency Parsing

1 Introduction

Conversational question answering (ConvQA) over heterogeneous sources facilitates a conversation between a user and a system by integrating information from various structures. In this process, the user and the system engage in multiple dialog turns on one or more topics [4,5,17]. The user's questions may contain unspecified context that requires an understanding of the conversation history. The primary challenge is incorporating the conversation history to understand the user's question fully.

D. F. Wong et al. (Eds.): NLPCC 2024, LNAI 15359, pp. 83–96, 2025.
https://doi.org/10.1007/978-981-97-9431-7_7

Mainstream approaches for ConvQA over heterogeneous sources use neural Seq2Seq models to process the entire conversation history and current question to understand the user's question [4, 6]. These models generate a structured representation to extract entities and relation phrases related to the current question from the conversation history while simultaneously generating the expected answer type. However, these approaches still suffer from incorrectly extracting question entities for two main reasons:

1) The Seq2Seq model frequently makes errors in extracting relevant entities from the conversation history because it processes the entire history, making it challenging to differentiate which entity is relevant to the current question. As shown in Fig. 1, the Seq2Seq model may incorrectly identify *Harry Potter* or *movies* as the question entity, thus affecting the answer.
2) The Seq2Seq model extracts question entities through sequence generation, which can result in generating texts that are contextually irrelevant or logically incoherent during the decoding phase, leading to false identification of question entities.

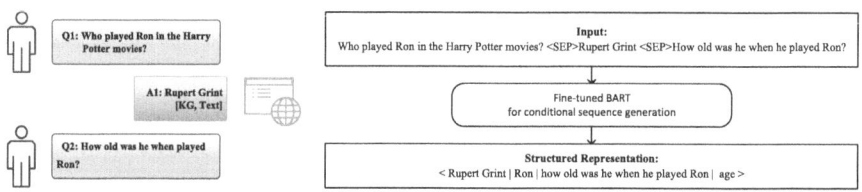

Fig. 1. The generating process of structured representation in conversational question answering over heterogeneous sources.

To address the issue of inaccuracies in extracting question entities, we propose a model that integrates a syntax tree and a graph neural network (GNN) for ConvQA over heterogeneous sources. The model comprises three modules:

1) **Question Understanding Module.** Construct a syntax tree based on the user's question and conversation history, then use a GNN to extract entities related to the current question from the tree. A Seq2Seq model is used to generate the relation and answer type. A structured representation can be obtained by combining the question entities, relation, and answer type.
2) **Evidence Retrieval Module.** Retrieve relevant evidences from heterogeneous sources, including a knowledge graph, a text corpus, a collection of tables, and infoboxes.
3) **Answer Generation Module.** Construct a graph based on these evidences, then iteratively compute the best answer and supporting evidence using GNNs.

Our main contributions are as follows:

- Proposing a ConvQA model over heterogeneous sources by fusing syntax trees and graph neural networks to enhance the extraction of question entities.
- Developing an attention mechanism ensures that only entity-relevant information is spread over the local neighborhoods during message passing.
- Experiments on two datasets show that the proposed model helps improve overall performance.

2   Concepts and Notation

Conversation. A conversation C is a sequence of question-answer pairs $\langle (q^1, a^1), (q^2, a^2), \cdots, (q^{t-1}, a^{t-1}), (q^t, a^t) \rangle$, each called a turn t. The initial question q^1 contains complete information, while follow-up questions q^t $(t > 1)$ may be incomplete, such as *Who created Iron Man?* (information is complete) or *How many minutes is the movie?* (information is implied and the *movie* refers to *Iron Man*).

Evidence. An evidence ϵ is a short textual fragment that can come from a knowledge graph (KG), a text corpus, a table, and an infobox.

Structured Representation. A structured representation SR is an intent-explicit version of a question. The SR used in [4,5] consists of four parts: (1) context entity; (2) question entity; (3) relation; and (4) expected answer type. In order to reduce the complexity of the structured representation and to improve the extraction effect of the structured representation, we use three slots to represent the current question: (1) question entity (related to the current question); (2) relation; and (3) answer type. This intent-explicit representation can be represented in linear form as a single string, using delimiters to separate slots ('|' in our case).

Conversation Graph. A conversation graph CG represents the graph of conversation history, consisting of the syntax tree corresponding to each turn in a conversation. Nodes in a CG correspond to nodes in the syntax tree.

3   Our Approach

The architecture of our model (Fig. 2) follows a pipeline form. The following subsections discuss the model's three modules: question understanding, evidence retrieval, and answer generation.

3.1   Question Understanding Module

The question understanding module (QU) takes the conversation history and current question q^t as inputs, outputting a structured representation SR with complete information and clear intent. It comprises five parts: graph construction, node encodings, message passing, node scoring, and relation and answer type generation.

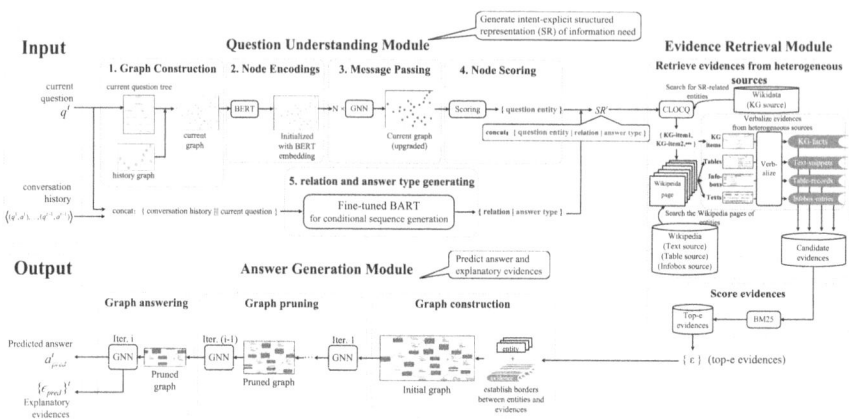

Fig. 2. An overview of the three main modules of the approach.

Graph Construction. Unlike the Seq2Seq model, which relies on attention mechanisms to understand semantics, syntactic analysis goes deeper into the sentence structure, identifying constituents and their relationships to form a tree-structured representation.

The Stanford NLP tool [22] is used to analyze the q^t, obtain the syntactic tree, and fuse it with the CG of the previous turn to form the current CG. After the system answers, the same process is repeated, and the CG is updated. Although follow-up questions are incomplete, syntactic analysis still helps to understand the sentence structure.

Node Encodings. The GNN incrementally updates node encodings in local neighborhoods to predict graph node scores via a message-passing algorithm. First, node texts, entity labels, and the question are sliced into token sequences and fed into a pre-trained language model to obtain node encodings $n^0 \in \mathbb{R}^d$, entity label encodings $bio^0 \in \mathbb{R}^d$, and question encoding $Q \in \mathbb{R}^d$. These encodings use the same language model whose parameters are updated during GNN training to adapt to entity labels and the syntactic structure of the CG.

Message Passing. The core of GNN is the message passing [21] procedure, which propagates information among neighboring nodes through the graph structure. We focus on entity-relevant information rather than general information. Therefore, a new attention mechanism is proposed to re-weight the messages based on the entity label information of the word nodes. This attention is computed by $\alpha_{e,n}^l (\in \mathbb{R})$.

$$
\begin{aligned}
\alpha_{e,n}^l &= \underset{\mathcal{N}(e)}{softmax}(lin_{\alpha_c}^l(n^{l-1}) \cdot bio_n) \\
&= \frac{lin_{\alpha_c}^l(n^{l-1}) \cdot bio_n}{\sum_{n_i \in \mathcal{N}(e)} lin_{\alpha_c}^l(n_i^{l-1}) \cdot bio_{n_i}}
\end{aligned}
\tag{1}
$$

where n denotes the neighboring nodes of e, first project the node encoding using a linear transformation ($lin_{\alpha_c}^l : \mathbb{R}^d \to \mathbb{R}^d$) and then multiply it with the corresponding entity label encoding of the neighboring nodes ($n \in \mathcal{N}(e)$) to obtain a score, and then apply the softmax function to all the neighboring nodes. Thus, a node can obtain a different attention score for each neighbor node based on the scores of other neighbor nodes.

Then, the messages are aggregated using the attention scores and projected through another linear layer:

$$
m_e^l = lin_{m_c}^l \left(\sum_{n \in \mathcal{N}(e)} \alpha_{e,n}^l \cdot n^{l-1} \right)
\tag{2}
$$

where $lin_{m_c}^l$ is a linear layer ($lin_{m_c}^l : \mathbb{R}^d \to \mathbb{R}^d$).

The updated node encoding is then obtained by adding the evidence encoding from the previous layer e^{l-1} and the messages from the neighbors m_e^l, which are activated by a ReLU function:

$$
e^l = ReLU(m_e^l + e^{l-1})
\tag{3}
$$

The intuition here is to ensure that entity-related information from neighboring nodes is passed and merged into the current node encoding at each update, thereby improving question entity extraction.

Node Scoring. With l message passing steps, we obtain the final node encodings. We model the question entity extraction task as a node classification task [9,21] and compute the scores of leaf nodes in the question entity slot. The question's relevance is also considered when calculating the question entity score for each node. The calculation of the question entity score s_e mirrors the process of calculating the attention score:

$$
s_e = \underset{E}{softmax}(lin_e(e^L) \cdot Q)
\tag{4}
$$

where e^L is the final representation of the node, Q is the representation of the current problem, and lin_e is the linear layer ($lin_e : \mathbb{R}^d \to \mathbb{R}^d$).

A threshold is set to obtain question entity nodes and splice word texts as question entities. This combines semantic information, reduces the error rate, and avoids phantom problems.

Relation and Answer Type Generating. Since the question entities are extracted from the original content of the conversation, and the relation and answer type are based on the newly generated text of the conversation, the generative method is utilized for generating the relation and answer type [5, 14].

Generation is accomplished by fine-tuning a pre-trained sequence generation model, where the input consists of conversation history and q^t, and the output is spliced text of relation and answer type. Eventually, the question entities, relation, and answer type are connected with separators to form a SR.

Learning. In this paper, we use binary cross entropy as a loss function $\mathcal{L}1$ for question entity score prediction and train the GNN architecture to reason about the input graph at once:

$$\mathcal{L}1 = -\frac{1}{E} \sum_{i=1}^{E} [y_i \cdot \log p(y_i) + (1 - y_i) \cdot \log p(1 - y_i)] \tag{5}$$

where y_i is the actual class and $p(y_i)$ is the probability of predicting the class y_i.

The cross-entropy between the decoder output and the correct output is used as the loss function $\mathcal{L}2$ for relation and answer type generation:

$$\mathcal{L}2 = -\sum_{i} y_i \cdot \log p(y_i) \tag{6}$$

where y_i is the actual output probability and $p(y_i)$ is the predicted output probability.

3.2 Evidence Retrieval Module

The evidence retrieval module retrieves candidate evidences from heterogeneous sources based on the SR and performs sorting and filtering. For KG evidences, we use the CLOCQ [3] method to retrieve relevant KG facts and serialize them as candidate evidences. Meanwhile, we retrieve Wikipedia pages for each KG entity, segment the text into sentences as candidate evidences, and use serialized tables and infoboxes as information sources [9]. Since the number of candidate evidences could be enormous, we utilize the BM25 [19] scoring model to rank them and retain the most relevant ones. Finally, the evidence retrieval module outputs a collection of the top-k evidences.

3.3 Answer Generation Module

The answer generation module combines the retrieved evidences to reason out the correct answer. We employ the iterative GNN method proposed in EXPLAIGNN

[5] to generate the final answer. First, a graph comprising entity and evidence nodes is constructed based on retrieved evidences. Then, the node encodings are initialized using a pre-trained language model. The iterative GNN updates the node encoding through a message-passing algorithm, and the graph structure propagates information between neighboring nodes. Finally, each node is scored by a classification task to determine whether it represents an answer.

4   Experiments

4.1   Settings

Datasets. The experiments are conducted on two publicly available datasets: ConvMix [4] and ConvQuestions [2]. ConvMix is designed for ConvQA over heterogeneous sources, covering five domains: books, movies, soccer, music, and TV shows, while ConvQuestions contains questions from the same domains, covering comparison, aggregation, combination, and temporal reasoning complex question types. The test set of the ConvMix includes not only conventional dialogues (5T, with five rounds for each conversation) but also more challenging unconventional dialogues (10T, with ten rounds for each conversation). The questions in ConvMix-10T are much more incomplete; for example, when a user asks *CR7* with the question *born?*, it requires contextual understanding to determine whether the user is inquiring *Where was CR7 born?* or *When was CR7 born?*.

Metrics. To evaluate the model's ability to understand the problem, we choose Recall as the primary metric to measure the accuracy of problem entity prediction. To assess the model's answering performance, the P@1 metric is used to measure the effectiveness of factual QA methods, and the ranking ability of different methods is further investigated using MRR and Hit@5. To assess the retrieval quality, we introduce the answer presence rate (Ans. Pres.) to measure whether the list of evidences contains the correct answer.

Baselines. On the ConvMix dataset [4], we compare the proposed models with mainstream approaches [4,5,18,20]. **Question Resolution** method [20] transforms context disambiguation into a term classification task by adding a term classification header; **Question Rewriting** method based on T5 [18] is fine-tuned to adapt to the ConvMix dataset; The **CONVINSE** model [4] applies BART [14] to generate structured representations of the processing of user questions and dialog history; The **EXPLAIGNN** model is based on CONVINSE with improved responses but still errors in question understanding and evidence retrieval (53.9% of error cases) [5].

Configurations. We use a GPU (NVIDIA Tesla V100S PCIe 32GB) to train and evaluate the model. Wikidata was used as the knowledge graph, and the same version as in the earlier work (2022-01-31) was used, ensuring that the results are comparable to those provided earlier.

We use a bert-base model as the encoder. GNN is trained in 5 rounds. We choose an epoch-wise evaluation strategy and keep the parameters that yield the best performance on the validation set. AdamW is used as the optimizer with a learning rate of 10^{-5}, a batch size of 1, and a weight decay of 0.01. The bart-base model is trained in 5 rounds with a batch size of 10. The ER and AG modules were initialized using code and data from EXPLAIGNN [5].

4.2 Main Results

This section presents the results of the overall model performance analysis. All provided metrics are obtained by averaging over all problems in the dataset. Bold in each column of the table indicates the experimental results of our model.

Our Approach Improves the Question Entity Predicting Performance. The experimental results in Table 1 show that the proposed model outperforms the baseline methods in question entity prediction. The baselines rely on Seq2Seq processing conversation and fail to capture word-to-word and word-to-question relations. We extract the question entity through syntax tree and GNN, improve the node representation, and optimize the recall rate by combining the current question information, which proves that this method is effective in extracting the question entity information.

Our Approach Improves the Answering Performance. The experimental results in Table 2 show that the proposed model outperforms the baseline methods in terms of response performance, benefiting from the optimization of the question understanding module, which improves the prediction of question entities and reduces the impact of errors on subsequent modules (2.0% relative improvement in P@1, 5.3% relative improvement in MRR, 7.1% relative improvement in Hit@5).

The Performance is Stable over Different Domains and Sources. We conducted experiments on questions from different domains (book, movie, music, TV and soccer) and information sources (KG, text, table and infobox). The experimental results in Table 3 and Fig. 3 show that the model performance is stable over different domains and sources. The proposed model performs better in KG and infobox source, while the table information processing is the worst. Also, it performs best in the TV Series domain.

Generalizability. The model trained on the ConvMix dataset [4] is tested on the ConvQuestions dataset [2] without additional training or fine-tuning to

Table 1. Comparison of question entity recall on the ConvMix test set.

QU Method	Recall
Q.Res.(2020) [20]	0.374
Q.Rew.(2021) [18]	0.636
Convinse [4] (original)(2022)	0.550
Convinse [4] (top-k FiD)(2022)	0.550
Explaignn(2023) [5]	0.555
Ours	**0.654**

Table 2. Comparison of answering performance on the ConvMix test set.

Method	P@1	MRR	Hit@5
Q.Res.(2020) [20]	0.282	0.289	0.297
Q.Rew.(2021) [18]	0.271	0.278	0.285
Convinse [4] (original)(2022)	0.342	0.365	0.386
Convinse [4] (top-k FiD)(2022)	0.343	0.378	0.431
Explaignn(2023) [5]	0.406	0.471	0.561
Ours	**0.414**	**0.496**	**0.601**

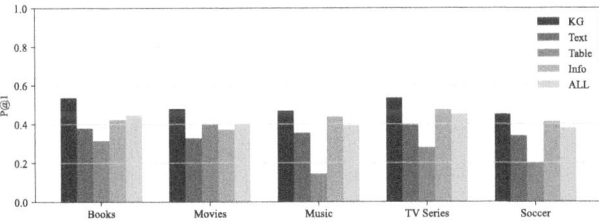

Fig. 3. Domain-wise results (ours P@1).

evaluate its generalizability. The experimental results in Table 4 show that this model performs best on the MRR and Hit@5 metrics, while the KRR [12] method is optimal on the P@1 metric.

4.3   Analysis

Feasibility Analysis. The model proposed effectively handles the incomplete questions on heterogeneous sources, and the answer presence rate is improved to 60.8% after QU and ER (as shown in Table 5, bold indicates the experimental results of our model, the experimental setup is the same as CONVINSE). The Prepend method [4] is also considered: (1) add only the initial turn $\langle q^0, a^0 \rangle$ (**Prepend init**); (2) add only the previous turn $\langle q^{t-1}, a^{t-1} \rangle$ (**Prepend prev**); (3) add both initial and previous turns (**Prepend init+prev**); and (4) add all turns (**Prepend all**).

Comparison with LLMs. Through specific case studies over different domains (as shown in Fig. 4), we illustrate scenarios where large language models (LLMs) make mistakes while our model performs better. While LLMs [23] demonstrate impressive generative capabilities when handling complex queries, they could

Table 3. Source-wise results.

Source	P@1	MRR	Hit@5
KG	0.495	0.577	0.688
Text	0.359	0.442	0.544
Table	0.272	0.348	0.439
Info	0.425	0.505	0.612
KG+Text	0.435	0.518	0.624
KG+Tables	0.441	0.522	0.629
KG+Info	0.465	0.546	0.655
Text+Tables	0.334	0.415	0.514
Text+Info	0.392	0.473	0.577
Table+Info	0.381	0.459	0.562
All	**0.414**	**0.496**	**0.601**

Table 4. Generalizability of the model, without further training or fine-tuning, on the ConvQuestions benchmark.

Method	P@1	MRR	Hit@5
Convex(2019) [2]	0.184	0.200	0.219
Focal Entity Model(2021) [13]	0.248	0.248	0.248
OAT(2021) [15]	0.166	0.175	–
Conquer(2021) [11]	0.240	0.279	0.329
Praline(2022) [10]	0.294	0.373	0.464
KRR(2022) [12]	0.397	0.397	0.397
Explaignn(2023) [5]	0.330	0.399	0.480
Ours	**0.333**	**0.405**	**0.500**

Table 5. Comparison of answer presence within top-100 retrieved evidences after QU + ER on the ConvMix test set.

QU+ER Method	KG	Text	Table	Info	KGText	KGTable	KGInfo	TextTable	TextInfo	TableInfo	All
Prepend init	0.380	0.298	0.120	0.331	0.415	0.386	0.406	0.297	0.329	0.331	0.419
Prepend prev	0.342	0.284	0.095	0.295	0.382	0.347	0.372	0.284	0.317	0.306	0.392
Prepend init+prev	0.440	0.366	0.137	0.420	0.486	0.443	0.479	0.359	0.407	0.409	0.495
Prepend all	0.431	0.367	0.148	0.430	0.476	0.437	0.468	0.361	0.411	0.419	0.482
Q.Res. [20]	0.414	0.311	0.115	0.329	0.445	0.419	0.437	0.312	0.356	0.341	0.453
Q.Rew. [18]	0.434	0.315	0.114	0.347	0.460	0.435	0.461	0.319	0.362	0.336	0.465
Convinse [4]	0.475	0.352	0.117	0.369	0.528	0.486	0.507	0.353	0.408	0.381	0.542
Explaignn [5]	0.476	0.350	0.119	0.370	0.526	0.486	0.505	0.351	0.406	0.382	0.543
Ours	**0.446**	**0.341**	**0.076**	**0.270**	**0.569**	**0.464**	**0.516**	**0.360**	**0.424**	**0.301**	**0.608**

also encounter the phenomenon of hallucination in some cases (as shown in cases 1-5). Moreover, we observe that even with Retrieval-Augmented Generation (RAG) [7], LLMs can still make mistakes when presented with inaccurate (as shown in case 2, case 3, and case 5) or noisy information (as shown in case 1 and case 4). In the future, further exploring how to combine our model's advantages in question entity extraction with LLM+RAG to enhance the performance of ConvQA systems is a worthwhile research direction.

Ablation Studies. Table 6 shows the results of the ablation studies. We conducted experiments on the question understanding module after eliminating the entity-level attention mechanism, the syntax tree structure, and the two mechanisms simultaneously. The paper finds that each of these mechanisms helps the model to improve question entity prediction. The most decisive factor is the syntax tree structure, which ensures that word-to-word information can be propagated among the correct neighbors. Without this component, the performance drops dramatically (Recall from 0.654 to 0.254).

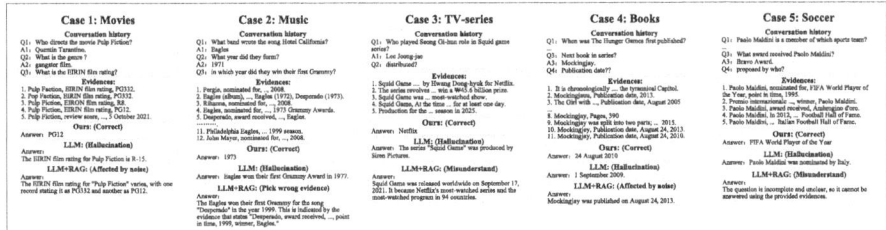

Fig. 4. Comparison with LLMs.

Experiment of Hyper-Parameters. Table 7 shows that 3-layer GNN works best on question entity prediction. Although 1-layer GNN performs well, it cannot learn the node representations well, resulting in noise. In less than or equal to three layers, the information spreads moderately, which helps to learn; in more than three layers, the information spreads excessively, weakening the prediction ability.

Error Analysis. We identify four key sources of error: (1) correct question entities not appearing in (34.6% of error cases), as well as the QU module incorrectly predicting irrelevant words as question entities as well, generating noise that affects the subsequent modules; (2) answers not being in the initial list of evidences (21.8% of error cases); (3) answers being lost when pruning the graph (as shown in Fig. 5) (8.2%)), as well as lost when answering based on the pruned graph (10.3%); and (4) answer appeared in the final graph but were not identified as the correct answer (30.7%).

5   Related Work

Conversational QA. In recent years, ConvQA approaches have involved structured data, semi-structured data, or unstructured text sources. Some approaches

Table 6. Ablation study on question understanding: assessing the contributions of entity-level attention, syntax tree and their combination.

Method	Recall
Ours	0.654
w/o attention	0.637
w/o syntax-tree	0.254
w/o both	0.247

Table 7. Effectiveness in predicting question entity with different GNN layers (dev set).

Method	Recall
Ours(i=2)	0.438
Ours(i=3; proposed)	0.472
Ours(i=4)	0.455
Ours(i=5)	0.429
Ours(i=6)	0.444

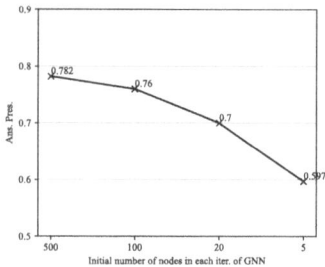

Fig. 5. Changes in answer presence in the answer generation process.

to structured data retrieve answers by mapping questions to logical forms of knowledge graphs [12,15], while other approaches construct a context graph to search for answers [2,11,13]. Approaches to Semi-structured data obtain answers through logical forms or graph encoding [16]. Approaches to unstructured text treat ConvQA as a machine reading comprehension task [1,8] and rely on techniques such as question rewriting [18,20].

ConvQA over Heterogeneous Sources. The fusion of heterogeneous sources is intended to extend the answer coverage. Literature [4] uses the Seq2Seq model to generate structured representation, then retrieves evidences from heterogeneous sources and generates final answers. Literature [6] processes mathematical operators to implement numerical reasoning tasks. Literature [5] constructs a graph and uses GNN to reason and predict answer nodes. However, these approaches rely excessively on the Seq2Seq model in understanding the current question and conversation history, which may lead to entity extraction errors and phantom phenomena.

6   Conclusion

This paper proposes a model incorporating syntax tree and GNN for ConvQA over heterogeneous sources to address the problem of wrong extraction of question entities in question understanding. By converting the conversation and current question into a syntax tree and learning node encodings using GNN, the model significantly improves question entity extraction on the ConvMix [4] and ConvQuestions [2] datasets. Future research will focus on optimizing the evidence retrieval module and answer generation module.

Acknowledgments. This work is supported to grant from the Key Program of National Natural Science Foundation of China (No. 62137001), the Sichuan Provincial Key Research and Development Program (2023YFG0265).

Disclosure of Interests. The authors have no competing interests to declare that are relevant to the content of this article.

References

1. Choi, E., et al.: QuAC: question answering in context. arXiv preprint arXiv:1808.07036 (2018)
2. Christmann, P., Saha Roy, R., Abujabal, A., Singh, J., Weikum, G.: Look before you hop: conversational question answering over knowledge graphs using judicious context expansion. In: Proceedings of the 28th ACM International Conference on Information and Knowledge Management, pp. 729–738 (2019)
3. Christmann, P., Saha Roy, R., Weikum, G.: Beyond NED: fast and effective search space reduction for complex question answering over knowledge bases. In: Proceedings of the Fifteenth ACM International Conference on Web Search and Data Mining, pp. 172–180 (2022)
4. Christmann, P., Saha Roy, R., Weikum, G.: Conversational question answering on heterogeneous sources. In: Proceedings of the 45th International ACM SIGIR Conference on Research and Development in Information Retrieval, pp. 144–154 (2022)
5. Christmann, P., Saha Roy, R., Weikum, G.: Explainable conversational question answering over heterogeneous sources via iterative graph neural networks. In: Proceedings of the 46th International ACM SIGIR Conference on Research and Development in Information Retrieval, pp. 643–653 (2023)
6. Deng, Y., Lei, W., Zhang, W., Lam, W., Chua, T.S.: Pacific: towards proactive conversational question answering over tabular and textual data in finance. arXiv preprint arXiv:2210.08817 (2022)
7. Gao, Y., et al.: Retrieval-augmented generation for large language models: a survey. arXiv:2312.10997 (2024)
8. Huang, H.Y., Choi, E., Yih, W.T.: FlowQA: grasping flow in history for conversational machine comprehension. arXiv preprint arXiv:1810.06683 (2018)
9. Jia, Z., Pramanik, S., Saha Roy, R., Weikum, G.: Complex temporal question answering on knowledge graphs. In: Proceedings of the 30th ACM International Conference on Information & Knowledge Management, pp. 792–802 (2021)
10. Kacupaj, E., Singh, K., Maleshkova, M., Lehmann, J.: Contrastive representation learning for conversational question answering over knowledge graphs. In: Proceedings of the 31st ACM International Conference on Information & Knowledge Management, pp. 925–934 (2022)
11. Kaiser, M., Saha Roy, R., Weikum, G.: Reinforcement learning from reformulations in conversational question answering over knowledge graphs. In: Proceedings of the 44th International ACM SIGIR Conference on Research and Development in Information Retrieval, pp. 459–469 (2021)
12. Ke, X., et al.: Knowledge-augmented self-training of a question rewriter for conversational knowledge base question answering. In: Findings of the Association for Computational Linguistics: EMNLP 2022, pp. 1844–1856 (2022)
13. Lan, Y., Jiang, J.: Modeling transitions of focal entities for conversational knowledge base question answering. In: Proceedings of the 59th Annual Meeting of the Association for Computational Linguistics and the 11th International Joint Conference on Natural Language Processing (Volume 1: Long Papers), pp. 3288–3297 (2021)
14. Lewis, M., et al.: BART: denoising sequence-to-sequence pre-training for natural language generation, translation, and comprehension. arXiv preprint arXiv:1910.13461 (2019)

15. Marion, P., Nowak, P.K., Piccinno, F.: Structured context and high-coverage grammar for conversational question answering over knowledge graphs. arXiv preprint arXiv:2109.00269 (2021)
16. Mueller, T., Piccinno, F., Nicosia, M., Shaw, P., Altun, Y.: Answering conversational questions on structured data without logical forms. arXiv preprint arXiv:1908.11787 (2019)
17. Qu, C., Yang, L., Chen, C., Qiu, M., Croft, W.B., Iyyer, M.: Open-retrieval conversational question answering. In: Proceedings of the 43rd International ACM SIGIR conference on research and development in Information Retrieval, pp. 539–548 (2020)
18. Raposo, G., Ribeiro, R., Martins, B., Coheur, L.: Question rewriting? assessing its importance for conversational question answering. In: Hagen, M., et al. (eds.) ECIR 2022. LNCS, vol. 13186, pp. 199–206. Springer, Cham (2022). https://doi.org/10.1007/978-3-030-99739-7_23
19. Robertson, S., Zaragoza, H.: The probabilistic relevance framework: BM25 and beyond. Found. Trends Inf. Retrieval **3**(4), 333–389 (2009)
20. Voskarides, N., Li, D., Ren, P., Kanoulas, E., de Rijke, M.: Query resolution for conversational search with limited supervision. In: Proceedings of the 43rd International ACM SIGIR conference on research and development in Information Retrieval, pp. 921–930 (2020)
21. Yasunaga, M., Ren, H., Bosselut, A., Liang, P., Leskovec, J.: QA-GNN: reasoning with language models and knowledge graphs for question answering. arXiv preprint arXiv:2104.06378 (2021)
22. Zeman, D., et al.: CoNLL 2018 shared task: multilingual parsing from raw text to universal dependencies. In: Proceedings of the CoNLL 2018 Shared Task: Multilingual parsing from raw text to universal dependencies, pp. 1–21 (2018)
23. Zhao, W.X., et al.: A survey of large language models. arxiv:2303.18223 (2023)

PqE: Zero-Shot Document Expansion for Dense Retrieval with Large Language Models

Jiyuan Liu, Dongsheng Zou[✉], Naiquan Chai, Yuming Yang, Hao Wang, and Xinyi Song

School of Computer Science, Chongqing University, Chongqing, China
{jiyuanliu,haowang}@stu.cqu.edu.cn,
{dszou,naiquanchai,ymyang,xinyisong}@cqu.edu.cn

Abstract. The dense retrieval model offers remarkable capabilities, yet it exhibits inconsistencies in the embedding space of queries and documents due to its dual-encoder structure. Addressing this limitation, we introduce Pseudo-query Embedding (PqE), a document expansion approach that eliminates the need for supervised data. By zero-shot prompting large language models (LLMs), we generate a specific number of pseudo-queries for each document, which are used to mitigate inconsistencies in the embeddings between queries and documents. This innovative strategy employs a multi-stage retrieval process to expand documents, enhancing the performance of the dense retrieval model without unduly impacting retrieval time. Experimental results demonstrate the efficacy of PqE. On the TREC DL dataset, PqE enhances the nDCG@10 metric of the unsupervised dense retrieval model Contriever by 7% points, and the Recall@1k metric by 4% points, surpassing the performance of the BM25 algorithm. Even for contriever[FT], fine-tuned on the massive dataset MS-MARCO, and BGE, trained on hundreds of millions of query-document pairs, PqE boosts their Recall@1k metrics on the TREC DL dataset by 1 to 2% points. Notably, on out-of-domain datasets from BEIR, PqE elevates the performance of most models across all metrics.

Keywords: Dense retrieval models · Large language models · Document expansion

1 Introduction

Dense retrieval model [1, 2] utilizes high-dimensional vectors to represent sentence semantics, thereby facilitating semantic-level retrieval and effectively retrieving relevant documents for queries of varying lengths. The remarkable success of the dense retrieval model is evident across diverse scenarios, including web search and question answering. To achieve efficient retrieval, dense retrieval models commonly embrace a dual-encoder architecture. This structure employs

D. F. Wong et al. (Eds.): NLPCC 2024, LNAI 15359, pp. 97–109, 2025.
https://doi.org/10.1007/978-981-97-9431-7_8

two encoders to map queries and documents to n-dimensional vectors, respectively. The similarity between the query and the document through methods such as vector inner-product [3,4].

However, in the dual-encoder structure, the interaction between the query encoder and the document encoder lacks depth, posing challenges in effectively capturing profound information between the query and the document. Despite the retrieval model being trained on extensive supervised datasets [5,6], inconsistencies persist in the embedding space of the query and the document, resulting in inaccurate similarity computation. This issue becomes particularly pronounced in out-of-domain zero-shot tasks, where mapping the query and document to the same embedding space becomes more challenging. To address these concerns, query expansion [7,8] and document expansion [9,10] stand out as key techniques to alleviate the embedding space inconsistencies between queries and documents. Traditional expansion methods, including RM3 [8,11] and doc2query [9], are primarily designed for sparse retrieval models, while most dense retrieval models do not adopt these techniques. Large language models [12–14] have demonstrated strong language understanding and generation capabilities in recent years. Approaches like HyDE [15] and query2doc [16] leverage the power of large language models for query expansion, thereby enhancing the retrieval outcomes of dense retrieval models. However, this improvement comes at the cost of a notable increase in retrieval time.

In this paper, we propose a generalized zero-shot document expansion methodology for diverse dense retrieval models, enhancing retrieval effectiveness in both in-domain and out-of-domain tasks with little increase in retrieval time. Our proposed method, called Pseudo-query Embedding (PqE), employs LLMs as document expansion models. First, PqE generates a collection of pseudo-queries by zero-shot prompting LLMs for each document, which contains several pseudo-queries, setting the prompt to be "Please generate five questions based on the above passage". Figure 1 shows an illustration of PqE zero-shot prompting. We expect at least one of the generated pseudo-queries can capture the "relevance" with the real query. Subsequently, a multi-stage retrieval is employed to choose the pseudo-query that is most similar to the query and surpasses a predefined similarity threshold for document expansion. Specifically, the multi-stage retrieval comprises three stages: Stage 1 involves retrieving the top-N documents, Stage 2 focuses on expanding the top-N documents, and Stage 3 entails retrieving the top-K documents from the expanded top-N documents. It is worth noting that our approach does not require additional training for any of the models during the entire procedure.

For the in-domain evaluation, we utilize the TREC DL19 [17] and TREC DL20 [18] datasets, which are based on the MS-MARCO [5] dataset. For the out-of-domain evaluation, we select datasets from five different tasks in BEIR [19]. Pseudo-queries are generated using the large language model zephyr [20] (zephyr-7b-beta). The experimental results demonstrate that PqE significantly improves the retrieval performance of the unsupervised dense retrieval model Contriever [3], outperforming the BM25 algorithm on most datasets. Notably,

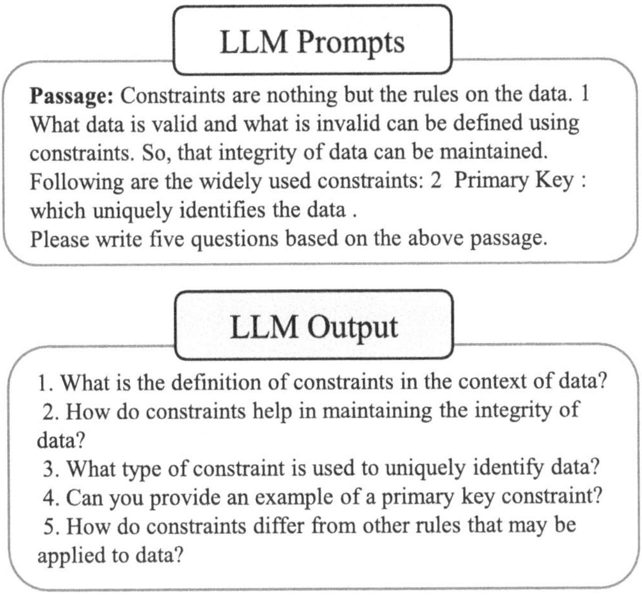

LLM Prompts

Passage: Constraints are nothing but the rules on the data. 1 What data is valid and what is invalid can be defined using constraints. So, that integrity of data can be maintained. Following are the widely used constraints: 2 Primary Key : which uniquely identifies the data .

Please write five questions based on the above passage.

LLM Output

1. What is the definition of constraints in the context of data?
2. How do constraints help in maintaining the integrity of data?
3. What type of constraint is used to uniquely identify data?
4. Can you provide an example of a primary key constraint?
5. How do constraints differ from other rules that may be applied to data?

Fig. 1. Illustration of PqE zero-shot prompting.

PqE yields improvements even for models like Contriever^{FT} [3], trained on the MS-MARCO dataset, and BGE [6], trained on hundreds of millions of query-document pairs.

The primary contribution of our work is to propose a document expansion approach for enhancing the performance of various dense retrieval models. More specifically, we propose:

(1) Generating several pseudo-queries for each document using a large language model without additional training.
(2) Expanding documents with pseudo-queries through multi-stage retrieval, which improves retrieval performance with minimal impact on retrieval time.
(3) The approach can be applied to any dense retrieval model, improving its retrieval performance on both in-domain and out-of-domain data.

2   Related Works

2.1   Dense Retrieval

Dense retrieval models have made significant progress since the advent of BERT [21]. However, sparse retrieval models like BM25 remain competitive for out-of-domain data. To enhance the performance of dense retrieval models, researchers investigated methods such as unsupervised contrast learning [3,4] and negative sampling [22]. These approaches facilitated more accurate capture of semantic information by enabling models to learn similarities and differences. At the same time, researchers tried to train on larger datasets [6], aiming to improve the generalization ability of the model and make it better for domain migration.

2.2   Large Language Models(LLMs)

LLMs pre-trained on large-scale corpora containing hundreds of millions of tokens, such as GPT3 [12], LLaMA [13], Mistral [14], etc., successfully gained the ability to understand instructions and follow them through methods such as instruction fine-tuning. The instruction fine-tuned LLMs are able to follow given instructions in zero-shot scenarios [23,24], which enables us to migrate LLMs to zero-shot tasks.

2.3   Query Expansion and Document Expansion

In the field of information retrieval, query expansion and document expansion are two common techniques to mitigate the distributional differences between queries and documents. Traditional query expansion techniques typically rewrite queries using relevance feedback [7,8] or lexical resources [25] to reduce the disparity between queries and documents in terms of vocabulary and length. On the other hand, document expansion enriches the document representation by adding additional information to the document. Document expansion methods, such as doc2query [9], generated pseudo-queries by training a seq2seq model. These pseudo-queries were then spliced after the original document. SPLADE [26] also employed an end-to-end learning approach for determining vocabulary weights. However, most advanced dense retrieval models do not adopt these techniques.

As LLMs show strong understanding and generation capabilities, researchers have started to utilize LLMs for query expansion. HyDE [15] used GPT3 [12] to generate n pseudo-documents based on a query, and employed vector averaging to expand the query. Similarly, query2doc [16] used GPT3 to generate one pseudo-document based on the query and added the generated pseudo-document directly after the original query.

3   Method

Our approach, Pseudo-query Embedding (PqE), comprises two modules: pseudo-queries generation and multi-stage retrieval. The multi-stage retrieval process is subdivided into three stages. The comprehensive schematic representation of our approach is illustrated in Fig. 2.

3.1   Preliminaries

The dense retrieval model typically adopts the structure of dual-encoder, which consists of two encoders, enc_q and enc_d. Here, enc_q is used to map query q to an n-dimensional vector v_q, and enc_d is used to map document d to an n-dimensional

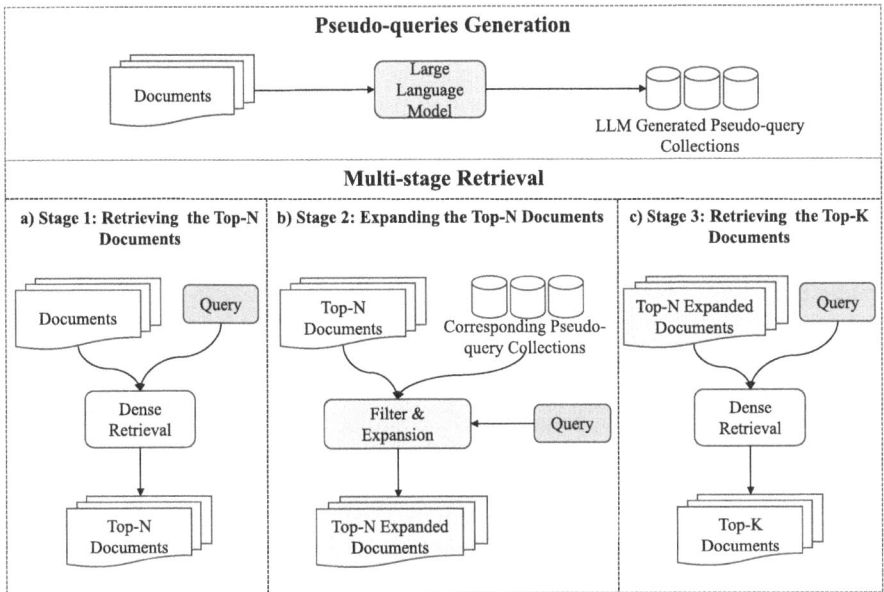

Fig. 2. Overall structure of PqE

vector v_d. Typically, the document collection $D = \{d_1, d_2..., d_L\}$ is pre-encoded using enc_d, resulting in a collection of document vectors $v_D = \{v_{d1}, v_{d2}, ..., v_{dL}\}$. Let d_i represent the i-th document in D, and v_{di} represent the embedding vector of d_i. When a query q is received, enc_q is used to map q into v_q, the similarity score between v_q and each v_{di} in v_D is computed using vector inner-product, and retrieval top-K documents based on their similarity to q in descending order, denoted as $D_{top-K} = \{d_{K1}, d_{K2}, ..., d_{KK}\}$.

$$v_d = enc_d(d) \tag{1}$$

$$Sim(q, d) = \langle enc_q(q), v_d \rangle = \langle v_q, v_d \rangle \tag{2}$$

$\langle ; , ; \rangle$represents vector inner-product.

3.2   Pseudo-queries Generation

For each document d_i in D, prompting the LLM to generate n pseudo-queries based on d_i by instruction in zero-shot, denoted as $Q'_i = \{q'_{i1}, q'_{i2}, ..., q'_{in}\}$, q'_{ij} denotes the j-th pseudo-query in the pseudo-query collection Q'_i. The pseudo-query collection corresponding to the document collection D is denoted as $Q'_D = \{Q'_1, Q'_2, ..., Q'_L\}$.

$$Q'_i = LLM(d_i, instruction) \tag{3}$$

3.3   Multi-stage Retrieval

Most of the pseudo-queries in the pseudo-query collection are not related to the actual query q, and filtering the generated pseudo-queries can avoid adding too much noise during document expansion. For each pseudo-query collection Q'_i in Q'_D, the similarity between q and each pseudo-query q'_{ij} in Q'_i is computed using the formula (2), and the pseudo-query q^*_i that is the most similar to q is selected to expand document d_i. In order not to significantly increase the retrieval time, a kind of multi-stage retrieval is used to avoid the pseudo-query filtering for all pseudo-query collections in Q'_D.

Stage 1: Retrieving the Top-N Documents. For a given query q, the similarity between q and each document d_i in D is calculated using the formula (2), and retrieval top-N documents based on their similarity to q in descending order, denoted as $D_{top-N} = \{d_{N1}, d_{N2}, ..., d_{NN}\}$, and its corresponding pseudo-query collections is denoted as $Q'_{top-N} = \{Q'_{N1}, Q'_{N2}, ..., Q'_{NN}\}$. d_{Ni} is denoted as the i-th document in D_{top-N}, Q'_{Ni} is denoted as the collection of pseudo-queries corresponding to d_{Ni}, and q'_{Ni_j} is denoted as the j-th pseudo-query in Q'_{Ni}.

Stage 2: Expanding the Top-N Documents. Calculate the similarity between query q and each pseudo-query q'_{Ni_j} in Q'_{top-N} using the formula (2), and select the most similar pseudo-query q^*_{Ni} to q from each pseudo-query collection Q'_{Ni}. A similarity threshold s is also set, if $\langle enc_q(q), enc_q(q^*_{Ni}) \rangle$ is greater than s, the document d_{Ni} is expanded using q^*_{Ni}, if it is less than s, the document d_{Ni} is not expanded. Vector averaging is used for document expansion to obtain the expanded document vector $v_{d^*_{Ni}}$ corresponding to document d_{Ni}. Denote,

$$v_{d^*_{Ni}} = \begin{cases} (v_{d_{Ni}} + v_{q^*_{Ni}})/2 & \text{if } \langle q, q^*_{Ni} \rangle > s \\ v_{d_{Ni}} & \text{else} \end{cases} \tag{4}$$

$v_{d_{Ni}}$ represents the vector of d_{Ni}, $v_{q^*_{Ni}}$ represents the vector of q^*_{Ni}.

Stage 3: Retrieving the Top-K Documents. The inner-product of v_q and each $v_{d^*_{Ni}}$ is computed as the similarity score between the query q and the document d_{Ni}, and retrieval top-K documents based on the scores to q in descending order.

4   Experiments

4.1   Datasets

For in-domain evaluation, we consider TREC DL19 [17] and DL20 [18], they are based on the MS-MARCO [5] dataset, evaluation metrics include MAP, nDCG@10 and Recall@1K. For zero-shot out-of-domain evaluation, we select datasets from five different tasks in BEIR [19], evaluation metrics include nDCG@10 and Recall@100.

TREC DL
Passage:[PASSAGE]
Please write five questions based on the above passage.

SciFact
Passage:[PASSAGE]
Please write five scientific claims to support/refute the above passage.

ArguAna
Passage:[PASSAGE]
Please write a counter argument for the above passage.

SCIDOCS
Passage:[PASSAGE]
Please write five titles for the above passage.

FiQA-2018
Passage:[PASSAGE]
Please write five financial questions based on the above passage.

NFCorpus
Passage:[PASSAGE]
Please write five short topics about health in plain English based on the above passage.

Fig. 3. Prompt for each dataset.

4.2 Implementation

We employ the large language model zephyr [20] (zephyr-7b-beta) to generate five pseudo-queries at once for each document in a greedy decoding approach.

Table 1. Results on DL19/20. Best performing w/o Fine-tuning and w/ Fine-tuning are marked **bold**. Contriever[FT] and BGE are in-domain supervised models that the training data includes the training set of MS-MARCO.

	DL19			DL20		
	MAP	nDCG@10	Recall@1k	map	nDCG@10	Recall@1k
w/o Fine-tuning						
BM25	30.1	50.6	75.0	28.6	48.0	78.6
Contriever	26.6	45.5	77.5	25.5	44.8	77.3
+PqE	$\mathbf{32.8}^{+6.2}$	$\mathbf{52.5}^{+7.0}$	$\mathbf{81.5}^{+4.0}$	$\mathbf{32.3}^{+6.8}$	$\mathbf{52.3}^{+7.5}$	$\mathbf{81.4}^{+4.1}$
w/ Fine-tuning						
Contriever[FT]	45.2	67.5	84.3	46.8	66.6	86.2
+PqE	$44.4^{-0.8}$	$68.1^{+0.6}$	$86.0^{+1.7}$	$46.1^{-0.7}$	$65.9^{-0.7}$	$\mathbf{87.4}^{+1.2}$
BGE	46.0	**72.4**	85.0	46.9	**70.5**	85.2
+PqE	$\mathbf{46.5}^{+0.5}$	$71.0^{-1.4}$	$\mathbf{87.1}^{+2.1}$	$\mathbf{47.1}^{+0.2}$	$69.8^{-0.7}$	$87.0^{+1.8}$

Table 2. Five tasks from BEIR. Best performing w/o Fine-tuning and w/ Fine-tuning are marked **bold**.

	SciFact	ArguAna	SCIDOCS	FiQA-2018	NFCorpus
nDCG@10					
w/o Fine-tuning					
BM25	**67.9**	39.7	14.9	23.6	32.2
Contriever	64.9	37.9	14.9	24.5	31.7
+PqE	$67.5^{+2.6}$	$\mathbf{45.2}^{+7.3}$	$\mathbf{16.3}^{+1.4}$	$\mathbf{29.1}^{+4.6}$	$\mathbf{34.4}^{+2.7}$
w/ Fine-tuning					
Contriever^{FT}	67.7	44.7	16.5	33.0	32.8
+PqE	$70.9^{+3.2}$	$51.3^{+6.6}$	$17.0^{+0.5}$	$33.8^{+0.8}$	$35.3^{+2.5}$
BGE	74.0	63.6	21.7	40.6	37.4
+PqE	$\mathbf{76.5}^{+2.5}$	$\mathbf{65.9}^{+2.3}$	$\mathbf{22.7}^{+1.0}$	$\mathbf{40.8}^{+0.2}$	$\mathbf{38.4}^{+1.0}$
Recall@100					
w/o Fine-tuning					
BM25	92.5	93.2	34.8	54.0	24.6
Contriever	92.6	90.1	36.0	56.2	29.4
+PqE	$\mathbf{94.1}^{+1.5}$	$\mathbf{96.4}^{+6.3}$	$\mathbf{38.4}^{+2.4}$	$\mathbf{62.6}^{+6.4}$	$\mathbf{31.6}^{+2.2}$
w/ Fine-tuning					
Contriever^{FT}	94.7	97.7	37.8	65.6	30.1
+PqE	$95.2^{+0.5}$	$98.2^{+0.5}$	$38.8^{+1.0}$	$66.5^{+0.9}$	$31.1^{+1.0}$
BGE	96.7	99.2	49.6	**74.2**	33.7
+PqE	$\mathbf{97.3}^{+0.6}$	$\mathbf{99.4}^{+0.2}$	$\mathbf{51.5}^{+1.9}$	$74.0^{-0.2}$	$\mathbf{35.5}^{+1.8}$

The prompt for each dataset is shown in Fig. 3. For DL19 and DL20 datasets, using zephyr to generate pseudo-queries for all documents requires a significant amount of time due to the large number of documents. Therefore, we use zephyr to generate pseudo-queries for 60000 randomly selected documents and train a T5 [27] (flan-t5-base) model using these document-pseudo-query pairs. Subsequently, this T5 model is used to generate pseudo-queries for all documents. During multi-stage retrieval, we set N to 30,000 in stage 1 and K to 1,000 in stage 3. For datasets in BEIR, zephyr is employed to generate pseudo-queries for all documents. Considering that the query length in the arguana dataset is long, it is difficult to generate five long pseudo-queries in a single generation, so random sampling is used to generate five pseudo-queries. In stage 1 of the multi-stage retrieval, N is set to 1,000, and in stage 3, K is set to 100. Retrieval models include the unsupervised dense retrieval model Contriever [3], and its fine-tuned version on the MS-MARCO dataset, Contriever^{FT} [3] (contriever-msmarco). Additionally, we incorporate one of the state-of-the-art retrieval models, BGE [6] (bge-base-en-v1.5), which is trained on extensive supervised datasets comprising hundreds of millions of instances. For Contriever, considering the absence of supervised fine-tuning, the similarity threshold s in document expansion is designated as 0. The similarity threshold s for Contriever^{FT} is configured as 1.1. For BGE, its similarity threshold s is set to 0.7 on FiQA and TREC DL datasets, and 0.5 on other datasets. A FlatIP index is constructed using Faiss [28], and Pyserini [29] is employed for the computation of evaluation metrics.

4.3   Main Results

In Table 1, we show the results on the TREC DL dataset. For unsupervised retrieval models, "Contriever+PqE" outperforms the BM25 algorithm and brings more than 7% points of improvement over Contriever. For supervised dense retrieval models, all types of models combined with PqE outperform the corresponding original models in the metric Recall@1k. However, there is a slight decrease in MAP and nDCG@10, which may be due to the noise from the pseudo-queries generated by T5 that reduces the sorting ability of the retrieval models.

In Table 2, we show the retrieval results of zero-shot on out-of-domain datasets. Except for Recall@100 of BGE on the FiQA dataset, which drops slightly, all models combined with PqE outperform their corresponding baselines on all evaluation metrics for all datasets.

5   Analysis

5.1   Effect of the Number of Retrieved Documents in Stage 1 of a Multi-stage Retrieval

Table 3 shows the effect of different number of retrieved documents N on retrieval effectiveness and retrieval time in Stage 1 of multi-stage retrieval by Contriever^{FT} on TREC DL19 and SCIDOCS datasets, respectively. N=0 represents the original contriever^{FT}. The experimental results show that choosing the appropriate

Table 3. Impact of the number of retrieved documents(N) on the retrieval effectiveness and retrieval time of contriever^{FT} on TREC DL19 dataset.

TREC DL19					SCIDOCS			
N	MAP	nDCG@10	Recall@1k	time	N	nDCG@10	Recall@100	time
0	45.2	67.5	84.3	2.44 s	0	16.5	37.8	16ms
2000	44.2	68.1	85.3	2.56 s	200	17.0	38.3	19ms
5000	44.3	68.1	85.6	2.56 s	500	17.0	38.7	25ms
10000	44.3	68.1	85.8	2.57 s	1000	17.0	38.8	31ms
20000	44.3	68.1	85.8	2.67 s	2000	17.0	38.8	45ms
30000	44.4	68.1	86.0	2.77 s	5000	17.0	38.8	85ms
40000	44.4	68.1	86.0	2.78 s	10000	17.0	38.8	148ms
50000	44.4	68.1	86.0	3.04 s	20000	17.0	38.8	253ms

Table 4. Impact of the number of generating pseudo-queries(n) on the retrieval effectiveness of contriever^{FT} on TREC DL19 and SCIDOCS datasets.

	TREC DL19			SCIDOCS	
n	MAP	nDCG@10	Recall@1k	nDCG@10	Recall@100
0	45.2	67.5	84.3	16.5	37.8
1	41.0	66.6	84.7	16.1	36.8
2	42.5	66.9	85.2	16.6	37.7
3	43.8	67.4	85.8	16.7	37.9
4	43.8	68.1	86.0	17.0	38.5
5	44.4	68.1	86.0	17.0	38.8

Table 5. Impact of the similarity threshold(s) on the retrieval effectiveness of contriever^{FT} and BGE on TREC DL19 and SCIDOCS datasets.

	contriever^{FT}		BGE	
s	DL19	SCIDOCS	DL19	SCIDOCS
0	84.5	38.4	86.0	50.8
0.5	84.6	38.4	86.2	51.6
0.6	84.6	38.7	86.6	51.8
0.7	84.8	38.8	87.1	51.7
0.8	84.9	38.9	85.7	51.5
0.9	85.1	38.9	–	–
1.0	85.6	38.8	–	–
1.1	85.8	38.8	–	–
1.2	85.6	38.6	–	–
1.3	85.4	38.1	–	–

N can improve the retrieval effect with almost no increase in retrieval time. When the number of retrieved documents reaches a certain level, continuing to increase the number of documents retrieved in stage one has only a small gain and increases the retrieval time.

5.2   Effect of the Number of Pseudo-Queries Generated

Table 4 shows the effect of generating different number of pseudo-queries on retrieval results for contriever^{FT} on TREC DL19 and SCIDOCS datasets. $n=0$ represents the original contriever^{FT}. When the number of generated pseudo-queries is smaller, it leads to a negative gain. As the number of pseudo-queries increases, the gain gradually changes from negative to positive and brings more improvement as the number of pseudo-queries increases.

Table 6. Impact of language model on the retrieval effectiveness of contriever^{FT} on SCIDOCS dataset.

model	SCIDOCS	
	nDCG@10	Recall@100
Contriever^{FT}	16.5	37.8
PqE		
w/ Contriever^{FT}		
w/ TinyLlama(1.1B)	16.6	38.6
w/ zephyr(7B)	17.0	38.8

5.3   Effect of Similarity Threshold

Table 5 shows the effect of different similarity thresholds on the Recall metrics of contriever^{FT} and BGE on the TREC DL19 and SCIDOCS datasets. The experimental results show that an appropriate threshold can effectively filter out the noise in the pseudo-queries, while a smaller threshold will lead to adding too much noise and a larger threshold will lead to too many documents not being expanded.

5.4   Effect of Language Model

Table 6 shows the effect of using different language models to generate pseudo-queries on the retrieval results of contriever^{FT} on the SCIDOCS dataset. In particular, we consider TinyLlama-1.1B-Chat-v1.0 [30] and zephyr-7b-beta. From the experimental results, we observe a positive correlation between the effectiveness of PqE and the language model's capabilities, but even the 1.1B model can still bring some improvement.

5.5   Limitations

To accelerate pseudo-query selection, we store all pseudo-query vectors in memory. In our approach, we generate n pseudo-queries for each document, which requires n times more memory compared to the original retrieval method. If the dataset size is too large to fit all pseudo-query vectors into memory, an alternative is to use a vector database to store the pseudo-query vectors. However, this still necessitates n times the storage space compared to the original approach. In practical usage, the choice of the number of generated pseudo-queries should be based on resource constraints.

6   Conclusion

In this study, we introduce a straightforward yet versatile method for expanding documents in dense retrieval models. Initially, we employ LLMs to generate a set of pseudo-queries for each document, utilizing zero-shot prompting. Subsequently, Through a multi-stage retrieval process, we select the pseudo-query that exhibits the greatest similarity to the current query and exceeds a predefined threshold for document expansion. This approach mitigates the inconsistency in the embedding space between queries and documents. The underlying rationale behind this method is to leverage the knowledge encapsulated within LLMs to enrich document representation. Notably, despite its simplicity, experimental results demonstrate the consistent efficacy of this approach across diverse datasets and dense retrieval models.

References

1. Lee, K., Chang, M.W., Toutanova, K.: Latent retrieval for weakly supervised open domain question answering. In: Proceedings of the 57th Annual Meeting of the Association for Computational Linguistics, pp. 6086–6096 (2019)
2. Karpukhin, V., et al.: Dense passage retrieval for open-domain question answering. In: Proceedings of the 2020 Conference on Empirical Methods in Natural Language Processing (EMNLP), pp. 6769–6781 (2020)
3. Izacard, G., et al.: Unsupervised dense information retrieval with contrastive learning. arXiv preprint arXiv:2112.09118 (2021)
4. Gao, L., Callan, J.: Unsupervised corpus aware language model pre-training for dense passage retrieval. In: Proceedings of the 60th Annual Meeting of the Association for Computational Linguistics, vol. 1 (2022)
5. Bajaj, P., et al.: MS MARCO: a human generated machine reading comprehension dataset. arXiv preprint arXiv:1611.09268 (2016)
6. Xiao, S., Liu, Z., Zhang, P., Muennighof, N.: C-Pack: packaged resources to advance general Chinese embedding. arXiv preprint arXiv:2309.07597 (2023)
7. Rocchio Jr, J.J.: Relevance feedback in information retrieval. The SMART Retrieval System: Experiments in Automatic Document Processing (1971)
8. Lavrenko, V., Croft, W.B.: Relevance-based language models. In: ACM SIGIR Forum, vol. 51, pp. 260–267. ACM New York, NY, USA (2017)
9. Nogueira, R., Lin, J., Epistemic, A.: From doc2query to docTTTTTquery. Online Prep. **6**, 2 (2019)
10. Nogueira, R., Yang, W., Lin, J., Cho, K.: Document expansion by query prediction. arXiv preprint arXiv:1904.08375 (2019)
11. Lv, Y., Zhai, C.: A comparative study of methods for estimating query language models with pseudo feedback. In: Proceedings of the 18th ACM Conference on Information and Knowledge Management, pp. 1895–1898 (2009)
12. Brown, T., et al.: Language models are few-shot learners. In: Advances in Neural Information Processing Systems, vol. 33, pp. 1877–1901 (2020)
13. Touvron, H., et al.: LLaMA 2: open foundation and fine-tuned chat models. arXiv preprint arXiv:2307.09288 (2023)
14. Jiang, A.Q., et al.: Mistral 7B. arXiv preprint arXiv:2310.06825 (2023)
15. Gao, L., Ma, X., Lin, J., Callan, J.: Precise zero-shot dense retrieval without relevance labels. In: Proceedings of the 61st Annual Meeting of the Association for Computational Linguistics (Volume 1: Long Papers), pp. 1762–1777 (2023)
16. Wang, L., Yang, N., Wei, F.: Query2doc: query expansion with large language models. In: The 2023 Conference on Empirical Methods in Natural Language Processing (2023)

17. Craswell, N., Mitra, B., Yilmaz, E., Campos, D., Voorhees, E.M.: Overview of the TREC 2019 deep learning track. arXiv preprint arXiv:2003.07820 (2020)
18. Craswell, N., Mitra, B., Yilmaz, E., Campos, D.: Overview of the TREC 2020 deep learning track. arXiv:2102.07662 (2021)
19. Thakur, N., Reimers, N., Rücklé, A., Srivastava, A., Gurevych, I.: BEIR: a heterogeneous benchmark for zero-shot evaluation of information retrieval models. In: Thirty-fifth Conference on Neural Information Processing Systems Datasets and Benchmarks Track (Round 2) (2021)
20. Tunstall, L., et al.: Zephyr: direct distillation of LM alignment. arXiv preprint arXiv:2310.16944 (2023)
21. Devlin, J.: BERT: pre-training of deep bidirectional transformers for language understanding. In: Proceedings of NAACL-HLT, vol. 2019, p. 4171 (2018)
22. Xiong, L., et al.: Approximate nearest neighbor negative contrastive learning for dense text retrieval. In: International Conference on Learning Representations (2020)
23. Sanh, V., et al.: Multitask prompted training enables zero-shot task generalization. In: International Conference on Learning Representations (2021)
24. Ouyang, L., et al.: Training language models to follow instructions with human feedback. In: Advances in Neural Information Processing Systems, vol. 35, pp. 27730–27744 (2022)
25. Miller, G.A.: WordNet: a lexical database for English. Commun. ACM **38**(11), 39–41 (1995)
26. Formal, T., Piwowarski, B., Clinchant, S.: SPLADE: sparse lexical and expansion model for first stage ranking. In: Proceedings of the 44th International ACM SIGIR Conference on Research and Development in Information Retrieval, pp. 2288–2292 (2021)
27. Chung, H.W., et al.: Scaling instruction-finetuned language models. J. Mach. Learn. Res. **25**(70), 1–53 (2024)
28. Johnson, J., Douze, M., Jégou, H.: Billion-scale similarity search with GPUs. IEEE Trans. Big Data **7**(3), 535–547 (2019)
29. Lin, J., Ma, X., Lin, S.C., Yang, J.H., Pradeep, R., Nogueira, R.: Pyserini: a python toolkit for reproducible information retrieval research with sparse and dense representations. In: Proceedings of the 44th International ACM SIGIR Conference on Research and Development in Information Retrieval, pp. 2356–2362 (2021)
30. Zhang, P., Zeng, G., Wang, T., Lu, W.: TinyLlama: an open-source small language model. arXiv preprint arXiv:2401.02385 (2024)

CKF: Conditional Knowledge Fusion Method for CommonSense Question Answering

Minghui Xie, Chuzhan Hao, Peng Zhang$^{(\boxtimes)}$, and XinDian Ma

College of Intelligence and Computing, Tianjin University, Tianjin, China
{minghuixie,chuzhanhao,pzhang,xindianma}@tju.edu.cn

Abstract. Augmenting pretrained language model (PLM) with knowledge graph (KG) has demonstrated superior performance for commonsense question answering (CSQA). In the knowledge fusion process, existing KG-augmented methods ignore (i) *exploiting the knowledge of PLM* and (ii) *the supervisory role of PLM*. As a result, the noise of KG cannot be filtered effectively in the knowledge fusion process. In this paper, we propose a **C**onditional **K**nowledge **F**usion method (CKF) (https://github.com/Xie-Minghui/CKF/). to enhance the commonsense reasoning ability of PLM. First, we apply the prompt learning method to *exploit the knowledge of PLM* which can provide a better semantic supervision signal for the knowledge fusion process. Second, we design a conditional fusion module to *filter out the noise of KG*. To further improve performance, we design a re-attention mechanism to supplement PLM with commonsense knowledge. Experimental results demonstrate the superior effectiveness of CKF through considerable performance gains across three popular benchmark datasets.

Keywords: Conditional knowledge fusion · Commonsense reasoning · Question answering

1 Introduction

Commonsense question answering requires selecting the answer to the question from candidate choices. It requires system to learn commonsense knowledge and reasoning skills, which are the critical gap between artificial intelligence and human intelligence [1]. Although large PLM implicitly contain abundant knowledge [2], they cannot cover all commonsense due to the limitation of pre-training corpus. Therefore, many works enhance PLM with external knowledge graph. Existing methods usually follow a retrieval-then-modeling paradigm. First, they extract subgraphs related to the given question based on string matching or semantic similarity. Second, they design elaborate GNN to learn commonsense knowledge from the retrieved subgraphs. They finally fuse the knowledge of PLM and GNN to make prediction.

© The Author(s), under exclusive license to Springer Nature Singapore Pte Ltd. 2025
D. F. Wong et al. (Eds.): NLPCC 2024, LNAI 15359, pp. 110–122, 2025.
https://doi.org/10.1007/978-981-97-9431-7_9

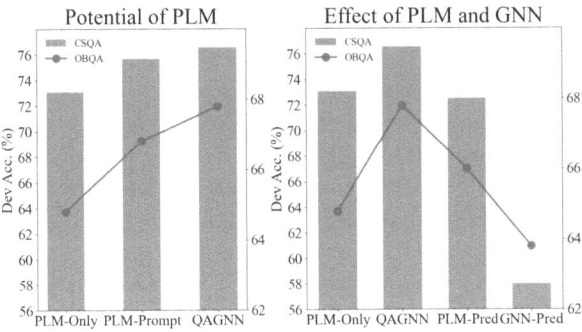

Fig. 1. Performance comparison on CSQA and OBQA dataset. The left index belongs to CSQA and the right index belongs to OBQA. *PLM-Only* indicates only PLM is used for training and prediction. *PLM-Pred* and *GNN-Pred* indicate that only PLM or GNN of the QAGNN [3] is used for prediction respectively. *PLM-Prompt* indicates that pure PLM is enhanced by prompt learning method (prompt ① on Table 5). The result of *PLM-Prompt* in left chart is pretty close to QAGNN, which means the potential of PLM has not been fully exploited. The results in right chart prove that PLM is more important than GNN for commonsense reasoning.

However, these methods have two main issues. **First, they ignore exploiting the knowledge of PLM.** They primarily focus on designing elaborate GNN, such as various node and edge attention in message passing [3,4] and relational path modeling methods [5,6]. But as shown in the left chart of Fig. 1, the result of *PLM-Prompt* is very close to the classical KG-augmented method QAGNN [3], indicating that PLM can achieve the effect similar to QAGNN through prompt learning without the help of KG. **Second, they put too much emphasis on the role of KG and ignore the supervisory role of PLM in the knowledge fusion process.** But the results of the right chart in Fig. 1 suggest that PLM contributes the most to the commonsense reasoning. GNN cannot perform effective reasoning independently, but can enhance PLM as the auxiliary role [7]. Existing methods [3,8,9] often treat PLM and GNN as equivalent roles during knowledge fusion process and design fusion mechanisms similar to cross-attention mechanism. However, the retrieved KGs contain much noise. The previous fusion mode causes the noise of KG to interfere too much with PLM, which will mislead the final prediction.

In response, we propose a conditional knowledge fusion method to enhance the commonsense reasoning ability of PLM. First, we adopt prompt learning method to exploit the potential of PLM. Specially, we reconstruct the textual input using designed prompt to obtain more distinguishable sentence embeddings of question-choice (q-c) pairs. They not only directly guide the knowledge fusion process, but also are important evidence for the final prediction. Second, we design a conditional fusion module to guide the knowledge selection of GNN. This module can filter noise at a more fine-grained feature level and avoid noise interfering PLM directly. To further improve performance, we design a re-attention mechanism to supplement PLM with commonsense knowledge. Because when PLM lacks commonsense knowledge about q-c pair, it will assign less attention to keywords. Therefore, we use the commonsense knowledge learned by GNN to redistribute the attention of PLM.

Our key contributions are as follows: (1) We propose a conditional knowledge fusion method to enhance the commonsense reasoning ability of PLM. CKF uses prompt learning method to obtain more distinguishable sentence embeddings, and introduces the conditional fusion module to filter out noise at a more fine-grained feature level without interfering PLM directly. Finally, it supplements the commonsense knowledge to PLM with the re-attention mechanism. (2) Experimental results show CKF is superior to most existing KG-augmented methods. New state-of-the art result on MedQA-USMLE demonstrates CKF can be effectively migrated to other domains.

2   Related Work

CSQA with LM+KG. Existing methods for CSQA often supplement commonsense knowledge to PLM using knowledge graph. One part of them focuses on designing elaborate GNN. The main difference between this part is how they design elaborate node and edge attention mechanisms in message passing [3,9], or how to model the relational path [5]. The other part focuses on how to fuse PLM and KG [4,8,10,11]. For example, GREASELM [8] uses modality interaction layer to fuse information of two modalities. HamQA [4] propose a hierarchy-aware multi-hop QA framework on KG to align the mutual hierarchical information between question contexts and KGs. These fusion methods allow KG to be deeply involved in the encoding process of PLM, which causes the noise of KG to interfere too much with PLM.

Prompt Learning in CSQA. Prompt learning methods aim to re-frame the original input into prompts based on the training input form of PLM. They can exploit the potential of PLM [12], which gains increasing research interests recently. Some works [13,14] apply them in CSQA task from the perspective of natural language generation. Prompt templates are designed to prompt PLM to generate related commonsense knowledge about question.

Feature-Wise Linear Module. FiLM [15] applies a feature-wise affine transformation in the intermediate features of neural network based on conditional information. This method is effective in the Visual Quenstion Answering (VQA) task and has been widely used in subsequent works [16,17]. In VQA task, question is usually fed into the FiLM generator as condition to generate feature-wise transformation parameters for image processing module. Perez [15] points out that FiLM adaptively and radically alters the behavior of image processing as a function of the input question, allowing the model to carry out reasoning tasks. Similar in CSQA task, the learning process of GNN should also be guided by the semantics of the q-c pair. Inspired by this, we propose a conditional fusion module based on FiLM. FiLM in VQA is used to fuse the two modalities while we use FiLM to fuse PLM and GNN.

3   Methodology

The architecture of CKF is shown in Fig. 2. We retrieve a KG $\mathcal{G}_i$ for each q-c pair. Following QAGNN [3], we add each q-c pair as a virtual node e_0 to the $\mathcal{G}_i$ and make connection with question and choice nodes in KG individually.

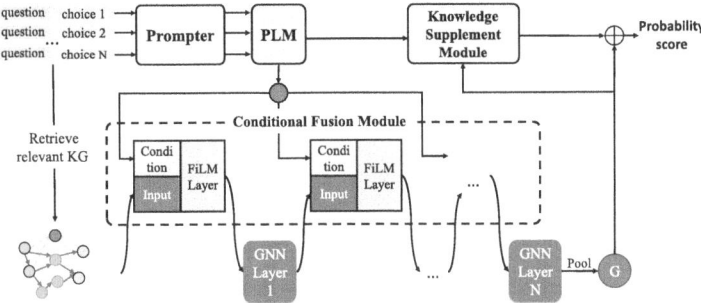

Fig. 2. The schematic diagram of CKF. The PLM enhanced with the prompt learning method will obtain more distinguishable sentence embeddings of q-c pairs, which are used as conditions for conditional fusion module. The node and edge features of GNN are used as the input. After the fusion of FiLM layer, these features will be more relevant to the q-c pair and irrelevant noises will be filtered out. The knowledge learned by GNN will be supplemented for PLM through the knowledge supplement module.

3.1   Prompt Enhanced Sentence Embedding

In CSQA task, distinguishable sentence embeddings of q-c pairs are crucial for the subsequent selection of relevant knowledge. However, recent studies [18,19] show that the anisotropy or token embeddings biases in PLM will result in a high similarity between sentence pairs. Besides, there are only small textual differences between different q-c pairs, which are differences in the text of choices. This will cause the sentence embeddings of q-c pairs are too similar to distinguish in the subsequent learning process. Promptbert [19] demonstrates that prompt learning methods can increase distinctions between different sentence embeddings. Therefore, we propose to apply prompt learning method to enhance the ability of PLM to distinguish similar q-c pairs. We search for several kinds of prompt templates in Sect. 5.2, including hard prompts and soft prompts. Then we use PLM to obtain the sentence embedding $\mathcal{C}^{LM1}$ of reconstructed input x. The detailed process is as follow:

$$x = f_{prompt}(q, c_i), \mathcal{C}^{LM1} = PLM(x), \tag{1}$$

where $f_{prompt}()$ converts the input into a specific prompting form.

3.2   Conditional Fusion Module

The retrieved knowledge graph usually contains many noisy entities and relations with little relevance to the q-c pairs. These noise is usually filtered through the semantics of q-c pairs in the knowledge fusion process. As shown in Fig. 3, existing methods use traditional knowledge fusion method, which is similar to cross attention mechanism. The traditional knowledge fusion method will make the noise of KG interfere too much with the prediction of PLM. The above problem can be abstracted as a condition modeling problem $g(f_2|q\text{-}c, f_1)$, which means how to obtain the node and edge features on KG under the condition of q-c pair. f_1 are the original node and edge features and f_2 are the corresponding transformed features. The representations of q-c pair and KG are usually located in different representation spaces. This is similar to the difference in representation spaces between two modalities, like vision and language.

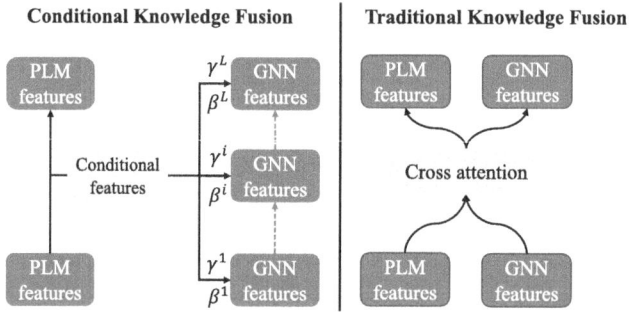

Fig. 3. The difference between conditional knowledge fusion and traditional knowledge fusion. β^* and γ^* are parameters that are generated based on conditional features and used to transform GNN features.

Motivated by the success FiLM in VQA, we propose a conditional fusion module to filter out noise at a more fine-grained feature level and avoid noise interfering PLM directly. Specially, we use the enhanced sentence embedings of q-c pair as the condition to determine the element-wise affine transformation of node and edge features in GNN. This allows CKF to dynamically up-weight and down-weight features to filter out irrelevant noise. The process is as follow:

$$\beta_n, \gamma_n = g^n(\mathcal{C}^{LM1}), \tilde{h}_n = \gamma_n h_n + \beta_n,, \tag{2}$$

$$\beta_e, \gamma_e = g^e(\mathcal{C}^{LM1}), \tilde{r}_e = \gamma_e r_e + \beta_e, \tag{3}$$

where β_n, γ_n and β_e, γ_e are the element-wise transformation parameters of node feature h_n and edge feature r_e. g^n and g^e are the FiLM generators of node and edge features respectively. Implementing g^* as a single linear layer works well.

3.3 GNN Module

Message Passing. To get more distinguishing edge features, we use all kinds of edge information, including source/target node types and edge type. We obtain the edge feature r_{st}^ℓ at layer ℓ from node s to node t as follows:

$$r_{st}^\ell = f_r(e_{st}, u_s, u_t), \tag{4}$$

where $u_s, u_t \in \{0,1\}^T$ are one-hot embeddings indicating the node types of s and t, $e_{st} \in \{0,1\}^{|\mathcal{R}|}$ is a one-hot embedding indicating the relation type of edge $s \to t$. $f_r \colon \mathbb{R}^{|\mathcal{R}|+2|T|} \to \mathbb{R}^D$ is a 2-layer MLP. As shown in Eq. 2 and Eq. 3, we utilize the conditional fusion module to transform the edge feature r_{st}^ℓ and the node feature h_s^ℓ at the ℓ-th layer. Then, we use the transformed edge feature $\tilde{r}_{st}^\ell$ and node feature $\tilde{h}_s^\ell$ to compute the message m_{st}^ℓ from s to t:

$$\boldsymbol{m}_{st}^\ell = f_m(\tilde{h}_s^\ell, \tilde{r}_{st}^\ell). \tag{5}$$

where $f_m \colon \mathbb{R}^{2.5D} \to \mathbb{R}^D$ is a linear transformation.

Message Aggregation. For each layer, the update rule of the node feature $h_t^\ell \in \mathbb{R}^D$ is as follows:

$$\boldsymbol{h}_t^{\ell+1} = f_n \left(\sum_{s \in \mathcal{N}_t \cup \{t\}} \alpha_{st} \boldsymbol{m}_{st}^\ell \right) + h_t^\ell, \tag{6}$$

where $\mathcal{N}_t$ represents the neighborhood of an arbitrary node t, and f_n is a 2-layer MLP. α_{st} is the attention weight from node s to node t. The query and key vectors of attention mechanism can be obtained as follows:

$$q_s = f_q(m_{st}^\ell), k_t = f_k(h_t^\ell), \gamma_{st} = \frac{q_s^\top k_t}{\sqrt{D}}, \alpha_{st} = \frac{exp(\gamma_{st})}{\sum_{s' \in \mathcal{N}(t)} exp(\gamma_{s't})}, \tag{7}$$

where q_s and k_t respectively denote the query vector for node s and the key vector for node t in the attention mechanism, f_q and f_k denote linear layers, γ_{st} denotes the attention vector used to compute the final attention weights, and D denotes the hidden layer dimension of the key vector k_t. γ_{st} denotes the attention weights for all neighboring nodes $s' \in \mathcal{N}_t$ of the source node s with respect to the target node t, exp denotes the exponential operation.

3.4 Knowledge Supplement Module

After learning commonsense knowledge through GNN module, existing methods usually concatenate commonsense knowledge with PLM output. This supplemental approach cannot provide PLM prior commonsense knowledge about q-c pair to enhance the attention weights of keywords, which are necessary to understand the meaning of q-c pair. Therefore, we design a re-attention mechanism, which uses the commonsense knowledge learned by GNN to redistribute the attention weights of PLM. This will obtain new q-c pair representation $\mathcal{C}^{LM2}$, which has commonsense knowledge as prior knowledge. The process is as follows:

$$G = \sum_{t \in \mathcal{G}} \alpha_{et} h_t^\ell, \mathcal{C}^{LM2} = softmax(\frac{G^\mathsf{T} H}{\sqrt{D'}})H, \tag{8}$$

where G is the result of attention pooling applied to the node features h_t^ℓ of GNN, which represents the commonsense knowledge learned by GNN. α_{et} represents the attention scores of the virtual node e_0 towards all other nodes t. These attention scores are calculated through Eq. 7 in the message aggregation process of GNN. H denotes the last hidden states of PLM and D' represents the hidden layer dimension of H. The re-attention mechanism treats G as the query vector and H as the key and value vectors of the self-attention mechanism.

3.5   Inference and Learning

Finally, we use $\mathcal{C}^{LM1}$, $\mathcal{C}^{LM2}$ and G to calculate the score P_{c_i} for each choice c_i being the correct answer. The detailed process is as follows:

$$P_{c_i} = \frac{(\mathcal{F}^1(\mathcal{C}^{LM1}, G) + \mathcal{F}^2(\mathcal{C}^{LM2}, G))}{2}. \tag{9}$$

The reason why we added $\mathcal{C}^{LM1}$ is to further emphasize the role of PLM, kind of like residual connection. $\mathcal{F}^1$ and $\mathcal{F}^2$ are linear layers. The whole method is totally differentiable and trained end-to-end using the cross entropy loss.

4   Experiments

4.1   Experimental Settings

Datasets. CommonsenseQA [1] is a 5-way multiple-choice QA dataset of 12,102 questions that require background commonsense beyond surface language understanding. The test set is not publicly available. We conduct experiments using the in-house (IH) data split of Kagnet [5]. **OpenBookQA** [20] (OBQA) is a 4-way multiple choice QA dataset of 5,957 questions that require elementary science knowledge. **MedQA-USMLE** [21] is a 4-way multiple choice QA dataset of 12,723 questions that require biomedical and clinical knowledge.

Implementation Details. For CommonsenseQA and OpenBookQA, we use ConceptNet [22] as knowledge source. For MedQA-USMLE, we use the KG constructed by QAGNN [3]. Given each q-c pair, we retrieve the top 200 nodes and adjacent edge according the node relevance score following QAGNN [3]. We set the dimension (D = 200) and number of GNN layers (L = 5) with dropout rate 0.2. The batch sizes on CommonsenseQA, OpenBookQA and MedQA-USMLE are set as {64, 128, 256} respectively. We train the model with the RAdam optimizer [23] using two GPUs (Tesla V100). We use separate learning rates for the

PLM and GNN, which are set as {1e-5, 2e-5, 3e-5} and {5e-4, 1e-3, 2e-3} respectively. We use RoBERTa-Large for CommonsenseQA, RoBERTa-Large [24] and AristoRoBERTa [25] for OpenBookQA and SapBERT for MedQA-USMLE.

Compared Methods. The purpose of our work is to leverage structured external knowledge for improving the reasoning ability of PLM on knowledge question answering tasks. Therefore, we only compare with the models that enhance PLM with similar KGs, not the models using other KG retrieval methods. Here are our baselines. **MHGRN** [6] proposes multi-hop message passing mechanism to model paths. **HGN** [26] proposes edge-weighted attention to guide the message passing. The other part focuses on how to fuse PLM and KG. **QAGNN** [3] introduces a QA context node in the subgraph for joint reasoning over the QA context and KG. **JointLK** [10] designs a dense bidirectional LM-KG attention to integrate LM and KG deeply. **GREASELM** [8] uses modality interaction layer to fuse PLM and GNN. **SAFE** [7] encodes relation paths using a simple two-layer MLP ranther than GNN. **HamQA** [4] propose a hierarchy-aware multi-hop QA framework to align the mutual hierarchical information between question and KG.

4.2   Main Results

Table 1 and Table 2 show the results on CommonsenseQA and OpenBookQA respectively. We repeat each experiment 4 times and report the mean and standard deviation of accuracy following QAGNN. CKF achieves higher accuracy on both development and test sets compared to other methods on CommonSenseQA. On the OpenBookQA, CKF combined with RoBERTa-Large significantly outperforms other methods, while its performance combined with AristoRoBERTa is weaker than SAFE. This is mainly because AristoRoBERTa is pre-trained on a collection of science datasets relevant to the questions, thus the gain from fine-tuning to enhance the PLM may not be as effective as with the RoBERTa-Large. The performance of CKF combined with AristoRoBERTa is consistently better than that combined with RoBERTa-Large, mainly because AristoRoBERTa is an enhanced RoBERTa-Large model pre-trained on more scientific data. In summary, these results suggest that exploring the potential of PLM during the knowledge fusion process and employing conditional fusion method can effectively help model select and integrate different knowledge.

The results on MedQA-USMLE are shown in Table 3. CKF performs significantly better than other methods. This may be attributed to the fact that the questions in the MedQA-USMLE dataset involve medical expertise and require more accurate external knowledge. The conditional knowledge fusion method can better select relevant knowledge, leading to greater performance improvement.

5   Analysis

5.1   Low-Resource Studies

Prompt learning methods can not only exploit the potential of PLM, but also generally improve the performance at the low resource setting. Figure 4 show

Table 1. Performance comparison on CommonsenseQA.

Methods	IHdev-Acc. (%)	IHtest-Acc. (%)
RoBERTa-Large	73.07 (±0.45)	68.69 (±0.56)
+MHGRN	74.45 (±0.10)	71.11 (±0.81)
+HGN	-	73.64 (±0.30)
+QAGNN	76.54 (±0.21)	73.41 (±0.92)
+JointLK	77.88 (±0.25)	74.43 (±0.83)
+GREASELM	78.50 (±0.50)	74.20 (±0.40)
+SAFE	-	74.03
+HamQA	76.90	73.90
+CKF (**Ours**)	**79.34** (±0.44)	**75.31** (±0.57)

Table 2. Performance comparison on OpenBookQA.

Methods	RoBERTa-Large	AristoRoBERTa
Fine-tuned LMs	64.80 (±2.37)	78.40 (±1.64)
+MHGRN	66.85 (±1.19)	80.60
+QAGNN	67.80 (±2.75)	82.77 (±1.56)
+JointLK	70.34 (±0.75)	84.92 (±1.07)
+GREASELM	-	84.80
+SAFE	69.20	**87.13**
+HamQA	-	84.60
+CKF (**Ours**)	**72.10** (±0.74)	86.96 (±0.82)

the results of CKF and baselines when trained with different portions of the training data on CommonsenseQA and OpenBookQA. CKF performances better under most settings. The main reason is that prompt learning can enhance the ability of PLM to distinguish similar q-c pairs, thus reducing the need for training resources. In scenarios with limited training data, improvements to the knowledge-agnostic baseline (LM Fine-tuning) are typically more pronounced, indicating that integrating external knowledge is beneficial in low-resource environments.

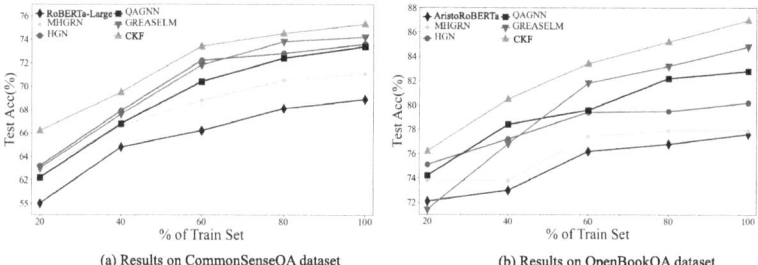

(a) Results on CommonSenseQA dataset   (b) Results on OpenBookQA dataset

Fig. 4. Experimental results when training with different portions of training data on CSQA and OBQA dataset with AristoRoBERTa.

5.2   Prompt Search

In this section, we explore the performance of different implementations of $f_{prompt}()$ in Sect. 3.1. ① refers to the successful template of PromptBERT [19], where [MASK] represent the meaning of q-c pair. Following the classical OptiPrompt [27], we design template ② and initialize it as the hard template ①. [V1...5] are virtual tokens which are not corresponding to real words. The [MASK] token in template ③ represents the meaning of *right* or *wrong*. The design of template ④ refers to the common setting in Natural Language Inference (NLI), because the CSQA and NLI tasks are very similar. The supplementary fact texts in CSQA can be viewed as the premise in NLI and q-c pair in CSQA as the hypothesis in NLI. Template ⑤ represents the same simple concatenation as other methods.

Table 3. Performance comparison on MedQA-USMLE.

Methods	Test Acc.(%)
SapBERT	37.2
+QAGNN	38.0
+GREASELM	38.5
+HamQA	38.5
+CKF(**Ours**)	**39.7**

Table 4. Ablation study of CKF on CSQA and OBQA.

Methods	CSQA	OBQA
Roberta + GNN	73.41	82.77
(a) w/ Prompt	74.28	85.20
(b) w/ FiLM	74.62	85.90
(c) w/ re-attention	74.04	84.88
(d) w/all (**final**)	**75.31**	**86.96**

Table 5. Experimental results of different prompt templates on CSQA IHtest set and OBQA with AristoRoBERTa.

Prompt	CSQA	OBQA
①The question is [question]. The candidate answer is [choice]. This means [MASK]. *(hard prompt)*	**75.31**	**86.96**
②The question is [question].[V1][V2][V3][V4][choice]. [V4][V5][MASK]. *(soft prompt)*	75.10	86.2
③The question is [question]. [choice] is the [MASK] answer for the question. *(hard prompt)*	73.35	83.8
④premise:[fact]. hypothesis:[question][choice]. *(hard prompt)*	–	85.5
⑤[question][choice]. *(no prompt)*	73.98	84.0

As shown in Table 5, template ① performs best, which is chosen as our final prompt. By comparing the results of template ① and ③, we find that although the final goal is to judge right or wrong, using the semantics of q-c pair can better guide GNN to learn commonsense knowledge, which is more helpful to the final goal. One possible reason why template ② (*soft prompt*) perform worse than template ① (*hard prompt*) is that it overfits to the training context. It performs worse in the new context of the test set.

5.3 Ablation Studies

We further conduct specific experiments to investigate the effectiveness of different components in CKF. We add each module onto the backbone structure consisting of Roberta-Large and GNN individually and report the accuracy on CommonsenseQA and OpenBookQA following JointLK [10].

As shown in Table 4, taking the CommonSenseQA dataset as an example, adding the prompt learning method provides a 0.87% performance improvement for CKF. This proves that prompt learning method can further utilize the potential of PLM. The gain of 0.63% can be obtained by adding the FiLM layer alone, indicating that the conditional fusion module is very effective. The performance gain from adding the re-attention mechanism indicates that it is useful to redistribute the attention weight of sentences using prior commonsense knowledge.

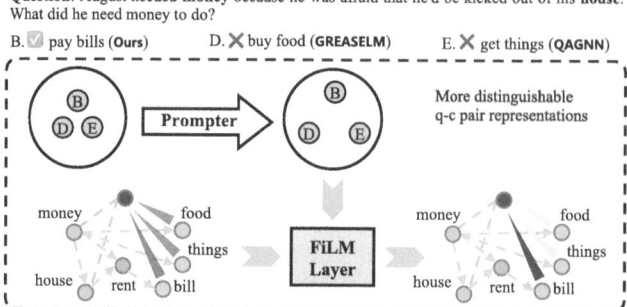

Fig. 5. Part of the reasoning process of CKF in a question from CSQA dataset. The darker the purple arrow, the greater the attention weight. After PLM is enhanced by prompter, the euclidean distance between the sentence embeddings of confusing choices is increased, which makes them easier to distinguish and provides better supervision signals for later modules. The FiLM layer will increases the attention weight of GNN to the right answer, while weakening the wrong answers. (Color figure online)

5.4   Case Study

As shown in Fig. 5, we calculate the euclidean distance of sentence embeddings between q-c pairs before and after PLM is enhanced by prompt learning method. We find prompt learning method can increase the distance between confusing choices. The same phenomenon is observed in Promptbert [19], which proposes the first prompt-based sentence embeddings method for more distinguishable sentence representation. This can make them easier to distinguish and provide better supervision signals for later modules. We calculate the attention weights of the virtual node to different choices before and after adding the FiLM layer. The attention weight on the right choice is strengthened and other confusing choices are weakened, suggesting FiLM can effectively filter noise of KG. Benefiting from these improvements, CKF predicts the right answer from confusing choices.

6   Conclusions

In this paper, we design a conditional knowledge fusion method to enhance the commonsense reasoning ability of PLM. CKF first uses prompt learning method to increase the distinction between different q-c pairs. Then it uses the conditional fusion module to guide the knowledge selection of GNN and filter out noise at a more fine-grained feature level. Finally, it supplements the commonsense knowledge to PLM through the re-attention mechanism. Experimental results show that CKF is superior to most existing KG-augmented methods. In future work, we plan to investigate further on how to use prompt learning method to better integrate structured knowledge.

Acknowledgments. This work is supported in part by the Natural Science Foundation of China (grant No. 62276188).

References

1. Talmor, A., Herzig, J., Lourie, N., Berant, J.: Commonsenseqa: a question answering challenge targeting commonsense knowledge. In: Proceedings of the North American Chapter of the Association for Computational Linguistics (NAACL), pp. 4149–4158 (2019)
2. Jiang, Z., Xu, F.F., Araki, J., Neubig, G.: How can we know what language models know? Trans. Assoc. Comput. Linguistics (ACL) **8**, 423–438 (2020)
3. Yasunaga, M., Ren, H., Bosselut, A., Liang, P., Leskovec, J.: Qagnn: reasoning with language models and knowledge graphs for question answering. In: Proceedings of the North American Chapter of the Association for Computational Linguistics (NAACL), pp. 535–546 (2021)
4. Dong, J., Zhang, Q., Huang, X., Duan, K., Tan, Q., Jiang, Z.: Hierarchy-aware multi-hop question answering over knowledge graphs. In: Proceedings of the ACM Web Conference 2023, pp 2519–2527 (2023)
5. Lin, B.Y., Chen, X., Chen, J., Ren, X.: KagNet: knowledge-aware graph networks for commonsense reasoning. In: Proceedings of the Conference on Empirical Methods in Natural Language Processing (EMNLP) and the International Joint Conference on Natural Language Processing (IJCNLP), pp. 2829–2839 (2019)
6. Feng, Y., Chen, X., Lin, B.Y., Wang, P., Yan, J., Ren, X.: Scalable multi-hop relational reasoning for knowledge-aware question answering. In: Proceedings of the Conference on Empirical Methods in Natural Language Processing (EMNLP), pp. 1295–1309 (2020)
7. Jiang, J., Zhou, K., Zhao, W.X., Wen, J.-R.: Great truths are always simple: a rather simple knowledge encoder for enhancing the commonsense reasoning capacity of pre-trained models. In: Findings of the Association for Computational Linguistics (ACL), pp. 1730–1741 (2022)
8. Zhang, X., Bosselut, A., Yasunaga, M., Ren, H., Liang, P., Manning, C.D.: Greaselm: graph reasoning enhanced language models for question answering. In: Proceedings of the International Conference on Learning Representations (ICLR), Vancouver, Canada (2022)
9. Zhang, Q., Chen, S., Fang, M., Chen, X.: Joint reasoning with knowledge subgraphs for multiple choice question answering. Inf. Process. Manage. **60**(3), 103297 (2023)
10. Sun, Y., Shi, Q., Qi, L., Zhang, Y.: Jointlk: joint reasoning with language models and knowledge graphs for commonsense question answering. In: Proceedings of the North American Chapter of the Association for Computational Linguistics (NAACL), pp. 5049–5060 (2022)
11. Zhang, L., Li, R.: KE-GCL: knowledge enhanced graph contrastive learning for commonsense question answering. In: Goldberg, Y., Kozareva, Z., Zhang, Y., (eds.) Findings of the Conference on Empirical Methods in Natural Language Processing (EMNLP), pp. 76–87, Abu Dhabi, United Arab Emirates (2022)
12. Liu, P., Yuan, W., Fu, J., Jiang, Z., Hayashi, H., Neubig: Pre-train, prompt, and predict: a systematic survey of prompting methods in natural language processing. ACM Comput. Surv. **55**(9), 1–35 (2023)
13. Liu, J., et al.: Generated knowledge prompting for commonsense reasoning. In: Proceedings of the the Association for Computational Linguistics (ACL), pp. 3154–3169 (2022)
14. Huang, Z., Wu, A., Zhou, J., Gu, Y., Zhao: clues before answers: generation-enhanced multiple-choice qa. In: Proceedings of the North American Chapter of the Association for Computational Linguistics (NAACL), pp. 3272–3287 (2022)

15. Perez, E., Strub, F., De Vries, H., Dumoulin, V., Courville, A.: Film: visual reasoning with a general conditioning layer. In: Proceedings of the Association for the Association for the Advancement of Artificial Intelligence (AAAI) 32, pp. 3942–3951 (2018)

16. Strub, F., et al.: Visual reasoning with multi-hop feature modulation. In: Proceedings of the European Conference on Computer Vision (ECCV), pp. 784–800 (2018)

17. Qiu, Y., Satoh, Y., Suzuki, R., Iwata, K., Kataoka: multi-view visual question answering with active viewpoint selection. Sensors **20**(8), 2281 (2020)

18. Li, B., Zhou, H., He, J., Wang, M., Yang, Y., Li, L.: On the sentence embeddings from pre-trained language models. In: Proceedings of the Empirical Methods in Natural Language Processing (EMNLP), pp. 9119–9130 (2020)

19. Jiang, T., et al.: Promptbert: improving bert sentence embeddings with prompts. In: Proceedings of the Empirical Methods in Natural Language Processing (EMNLP), pp. 8826–8837 (2022)

20. Mihaylov, T., Clark, P., Khot, T., Sabharwal, A.: Can a suit of armor conduct electricity? a new dataset for open book question answering. In: Proceedings of the Conference on Empirical Methods in Natural Language Processing (EMNLP), pp. 2381–2391, Brussels, Belgium (2018)

21. Jin, D., Pan, E., Oufattole, N., Weng, W.-H., Fang, H., Szolovits, P.: What disease does this patient have? a large-scale open domain question answering dataset from medical exams. Appl. Sci. **11**(14), 6421 (2021)

22. Speer, R., Chin, J.: Conceptnet: an open multilingual graph of general knowledge. In: Proceedings of the Association for the Advancement of Artificial Intelligence (AAAI) Conference, pp. 4444–4451 (2017)

23. Liu, L., et al.: On the variance of the adaptive learning rate and beyond (iclr). In: Proceedings International Conference on Learning Representations (2020)

24. Liu, Y., et al.: Roberta: a robustly optimized bert pretraining approach. ArXiv preprint, abs/1907.11692 (2019)

25. Clark, P., et al.: From 'f' to 'a' on the ny regents science exams: an overview of the aristo project. AI Magazine **41**(4), 39–53 (2020)

26. Yan, J., et al.: Learning contextualized knowledge structures for commonsense reasoning. In: Findings of the Association for Computational Linguistics and International Joint Conference on Natural Language Processing (ACL-IJCNLP), pp. 4038–4051 (2021)

27. Zhong, Z., Friedman, D., Chen, D.: Factual probing is [MASK]: learning vs. learning to recall. In: Proceedings of the North American Chapter of the Association for Computational Linguistics (NAACL), pp. 5017–5033 (2021)

MPPQA: Structure-Aware Extractive Multi-span Question Answering for Procedural Documents

Bihan Zhou[1,2], Haopeng Ren[1,2], Yi Cai[1,2(✉)], Zetao Lian[1,2], Pinli Zhu[1,2], and Yushi Zeng[1,2]

[1] School of Software Engineering, South China University of Technology, Guangzhou, China
ycai@scut.edu.cn
[2] Key Laboratory of Big Data and Intelligent Robot, (South China University of Technology) Ministry of Education, Guangzhou, China

Abstract. Procedural documents, which provide procedural knowledge with step-by-step instructions to help achieve specific goals, have shown growing popularity in both industry workflows and daily routines. Particularly, answering prerequisite associated questions facilitates thorough preparation for procedures and supports the execution of the subsequent operations. However, most prevailing researches in procedural knowledge primarily concentrate on the task of entity state tracking or "What if" reasoning, typically formulated as single-span extraction or multiple-choice question answering. Due to the limitation of single-span extraction format or disregard for leveraging the structural procedural knowledge within procedural document, existing question answering methods still struggle to accurately answer multi-span prerequisite associated questions. In this paper, we explore the problem of prerequisite associated question answering task to extract multi-span style answers from the procedural documents, and propose a key procedure concentrated question answering model SAPE integrated with structure-aware module. Additionally, a new dataset MPPQA is built and extensive experiments are conducted to evaluate the effectiveness of our proposed model.

Keywords: Structural procedural knowledge · Prerequisite associated question · Multi-span question answering

1 Introduction

Procedural knowledge, often presented as a series of procedures or actions aimed at achieving a particular goal (e.g., welding lead, installing an operating system) within procedural document (e.g., recipes, teaching manuals, and user guides), is prevalent in both industry processes and daily routines. Under the guidance

---

B. Zhou and H. Ren—Contribute equally to this paper.

© The Author(s), under exclusive license to Springer Nature Singapore Pte Ltd. 2025
D. F. Wong et al. (Eds.): NLPCC 2024, LNAI 15359, pp. 123–135, 2025.
https://doi.org/10.1007/978-981-97-9431-7_10

of autonomous agents by answering the procedural questions, which rank as the second largest query set to web engines after factoid question [2], the individuals are able to accomplish certain tasks more conveniently.

Given a procedural document, answering prerequisites for accomplishing a specific procedure or step facilitates the correctness judgement of current operation and the proceeding of the subsequent operation. In the procedural execution workflow depicted in Fig. 1a, it is crucial for the baker to fulfill the necessary prerequisites including factors and components (e.g., ingredients) to make a bread, thus enabling the next baking operation. According to the question patterns of "<WH><Prerequisite><X>" shown in Fig. 1b, where "<X>" denotes the specific goal and "<Prerequisite>" denotes the required preparation in the process, it is classified as prerequisite associated questions [2].

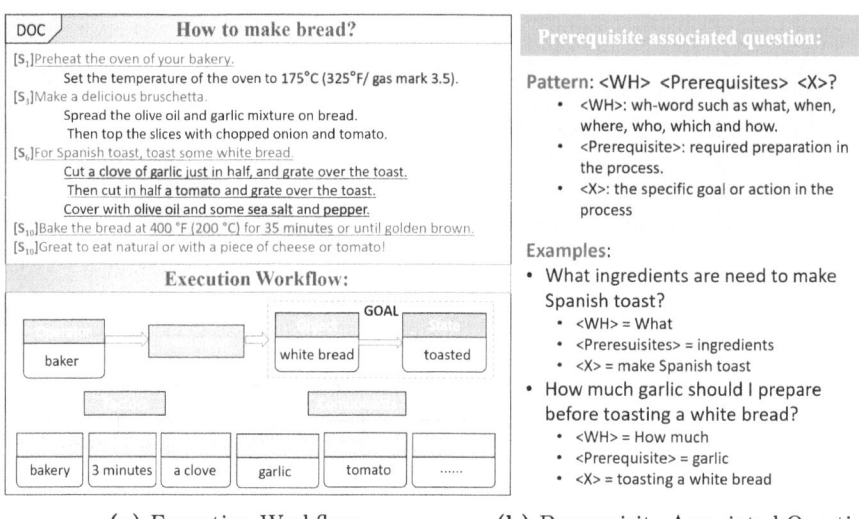

(a) Execution Workflow.   **(b)** Prerequisite Associated Question.

Fig. 1. The Workflow of the Procedure and Pattern of Prerequisite Associated Question.

Moreover, as shown in Fig. 1a, prerequisites of a procedure are mostly distributed discontinuously throughout the execution steps of long procedural documents in realistic scenarios, which require step-by-step reasoning over multiple relevant procedures. Existing work [29] infers precondition by constructing dependency structure, but is incapable of specifically and quickly answering necessary prerequisites for a given goal. In that case, traditional single-span style answer extraction models [17,23] can only extract a continuous span of text as answer and thus struggle to provide precise and comprehensive answers to prerequisite associated question. Considering the limitation of single-span extraction model, some [10,15] propose multi-span question answering methods.

Since procedures within procedural documents are constantly organized into various structures, featuring multiple ordering relations among operations, existing multi-span question answering methods fail to accurately identify the relevant procedures and lead to the lack or redundancy of answer span.

In this paper, to accurately obtain prerequisite from the procedural document, we introduce prerequisite associated multi-span style extractive question answering task. In this task, multi-span style answers to prerequisite associated questions are extracted given the procedural document, thus guiding the execution of instruction. From the case in Fig. 2, it can be observed that integrating structural knowledge from the constructed procedural graph contributes to extracting answers from discontinuous relevant procedure fragments. Given a procedural document introducing the process of making bread and a prerequisite associated question asking about the ingredients required for making Spanish toast, a procedural graph containing structural knowledge can be constructed based on the classification of sentence node types and relation types. Subsequently, a procedure fragment (from sentence S_6 to S_9) with branch structure detailing the process of making Spanish toast is inferred from the procedural graph according to the structure and semantic relevancy with question, and the answer spans are extracted from the concentrated procedural fragment.

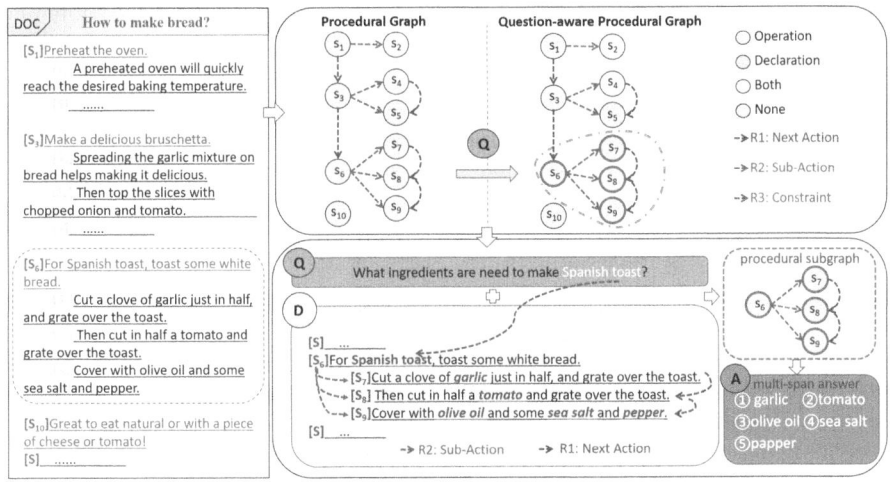

Fig. 2. An Example of Answering Prerequisite Associated Question on Procedural Document with Structure Information.

Additionally, we propose a **Structure-A**ware model to integrate **P**rocedural knowledg**E** for answering multi-span prerequisite associated questions in procedural documents (**SAPE**). The overview of our method is shown in Fig. 3. Specifically, a procedure embedding and attention module is designed to integrate structural knowledge from constructed procedural graph and distinguish the relevant procedural fragments. Moreover, a knowledge fusion and reasoning module is designed to infer multi-span answers by incorporating structural and semantic information. To explore the problem of extracting **M**ulti-span answers from **P**rocedural document to **P**rerequisite associated questions, we construct a new **Q**uestion **A**nswering dataset **MPPQA** which covers multiple domains of procedure and take long procedural documents into consideration, and we conduct extensive experiments to evaluate the effectiveness of our design model.

2   Related Work

2.1   Question Answering on Procedural Document

Procedural knowledge finds extensive applications in enhancing productivity across industrial sector [4] and guiding various daily activities (e.g., cooking recipes) [8,30]. There has been a notable interest in extracting and comprehending procedural knowledge from procedural documents. In this regard, the task of tracking entity state changes [3,19,27] involves monitoring the attributes and states of entities throughout the procedure. Beyond entity-level reasoning over procedural knowledge, "What if" reasoning task [26,32] aims to assess the effects of given conditions on a process and trace the resulting influence chains. While the above procedure-related question answering tasks are lacking in consideration for inferring the prerequisites of procedure, a precondition identification and generation task [13] and a Knowing-how & Knowing-that user manuals reading comprehension task [16] are proposed. To be noticed, prerequisite to a specific procedure constantly derives from multiple relevant steps, which limits the performance of single-span extractive question answering methods [17,23] since it can only extract answer from a single continuous span of text. Recognizing the prevalence of the multi-span answer style, several multi-span extractive question answering methods [6,9,10,14,15,18] are designed. Nevertheless, they predominantly focus on descriptive knowledge and can not effectively leverage structural procedural knowledge to address prerequisite associated questions. Moreover, there exist multiple generative models [5,7,28,31] including large language model with outperforming semantic understanding ability. However, limitations such as factual accuracy, limited context length, and computing resource restrict their applications in realistic scenarios. Consequently, we introduce prerequisite associated multi-span style extractive question answering task on procedural document, to facilitate thorough preparation for procedures and support the execution of the subsequent operation.

2.2   Structure Modeling on Procedural Knowledge

For utilizing the structural aspects (e.g., dependency relations and node types) of procedural documents, efforts to obtain structural procedural knowledge have led to the development of both entity-level and sentence-level methods. Entity-level methods [11,20,22,30,33] involve extracting predefined entities and their relations from unstructured procedural documents. In contrast, sentence-level based methods [21,24] are designed to construct flow graphs at the sentence level within procedural documents, aiming to mitigate the limitations of massive fine-grained annotation effort required by entity-level approaches. Specifically, the recognition of multiple sentence types (e.g., operation, declaration, and both) and dependency relations (e.g., next action, sub-action, and constraint) [24] contributes positive feedback to prerequisite associated procedural question answering task. Furthermore, an action-condition inference task that predicts the pre- and postcondition relations of actions from procedural text [29] is proposed. Integrating the structural procedural knowledge, we propose a key procedure concentrated multi-span question answering model SAPE and construct a new multi-span style extractive question answering dataset MPPQA based on WikiHow knowledge base[1] to evaluate the effectiveness of the model.

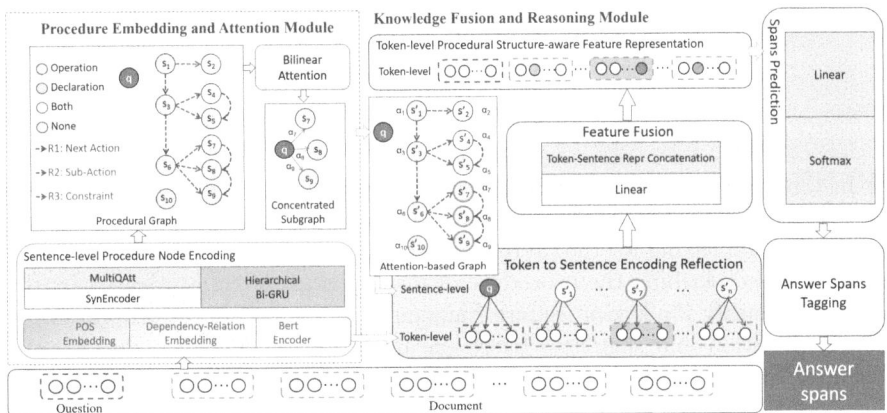

Fig. 3. The Overview of Our Proposed Model SAPE.

3   Model

3.1   Problem Definition and Notations

Given a procedural document $D = \{d_i\}_{i=1}^{n}$ with n tokens and a prerequisite associated procedural question $Q = \{q_i\}_{i=1}^{l}$ with l tokens, we construct a procedural graph G_D with m sentence nodes $S = \{s_i\}_{i=1}^{m} \in D$ and extract multi-span answer $A = \{a_i\}_{i=1}^{k}$. As illustrated in Fig. 3, our model SAPE is comprised of two modules: (1) procedure embedding and attention module, and (2) knowledge fusion and reasoning module. The former module encodes the sentence-level procedural graph feature and applies bilinear attention mechanism to capture the key procedure fragments. The latter module adopts the BIO tagging scheme [25] to extract multi-span answer by fusing token-level semantic knowledge with sentence-level structure knowledge.

---

[1] https://www.wikihow.com/Main-Page.

3.2   Procedure Embedding and Attention Module

Following procedural graph construction technique [24] whose efficacy in representing procedural knowledge has been well-established, we derive the sentence representation v_i^{graph} of the procedure document by concatenating the syntactic feature representation v_i^{syn} and semantic feature representation v_i^{gru} of the procedural graph, as follows:

$$v_i^{graph} = [v_i^{syn}; v_i^{gru}] \tag{1}$$

where $[\cdot; \cdot]$ denotes the concatenation operation for both vectors. Given the embedding vector of each sentence in document D, the syntactic feature representation $V^{syn} = \{v_i^{syn}\}_{i=1}^m$ is obtained by applying syntactic RGCN encoder and Multi-query syntactic aware attention [24], and the semantic feature representation $V^{gru} = \{v_i^{gru}\}_{i=1}^m$ is obtained by a hierarchical Bi-GRU encoder [24]:

$$V^{syn} = \text{MultiQAtt}(\text{SynEncoder}(D)) \tag{2}$$

$$V^{gru} = \text{Bi-GRU}(\text{Encoder}(D)) \tag{3}$$

For instance illustrated in Fig. 2, key sentences S_6 to S_9 with branch structure describing detailed procedure for making Spanish toast provide additional clues for the question asking for the prerequisite ingredients, compared to the preceding sentences describing the procedure of making bruschetta. Motivated by the above, we identify the key procedure fragments by calculating the relevant score between question and sentences based on attention mechanism. Subsequently, we integrate the procedure relevance information to obtain the sentence-level procedure feature representation $V_D^{sent} = \{v_i^{sent}\}_{i=1}^m$:

$$V_D^{sent} = \text{FFN}(\sum_i^m \alpha_i v_i^{graph}),$$
$$\alpha_i \propto exp(F^D(v^Q, v_i^{graph})) \tag{4}$$

where attention function F^D adheres to bilinear form [12]. The parameter α_i denotes the relevant score between the question and the corresponding sentence, which positively correlates with the calculated attention score, and v^Q is the sentence-level representation of the question.

3.3   Knowledge Fusion and Reasoning Module

Considering the multi-span distribution phenomenon, we approach this task as a sequence-to-sequence tagging problem with the BIO scheme. Specifically, we concatenate the tokenized question Q and document D as input, and add the special token "[CLS]" before the question, as well as the token "[SEP]" to separate the sentences. Subsequently, we obtain token-level procedural document feature $V_D^{token} = \{v_i^{token}\}_{i=1}^s \in \mathbb{R}^{s \times h}$ with a hidden size h and input length s

by employing a shared BERT of sentence-level procedure embedding module as encoder:

$$V_{CLS}, V_Q, V_{SEP}, V_D^{token} = \text{BERT}([CLS]; Q; [SEP]; D) \tag{5}$$

To obtain the fused representation $v_i \in \mathbb{R}^p$ with a dimension of p by integrating structural knowledge with semantic knowledge, we concatenate the attention-based sentence-level procedural feature representation v_j^{sent} with token-level document feature representation v_i^{token} for each token i belonging to sentence j:

$$v_i = [v_i^{token}; v_j^{sent}] \tag{6}$$

Instead of locating the starting and ending answer tokens of traditional single-span models, we obtain the multi-span answer by fetching the BIO tags of each token. Therefore, we feed the fused token-level procedure feature into a linear classifier and calculate the probability p_i of the answer tag by softmax layer:

$$p_i = \text{softmax}(\text{FFN}(v_i)) \tag{7}$$

Then we obtain the predicted answer spans $A_D \in \mathbb{R}^{n \times t}$, where $t = 3$ in BIO tagging scheme.

Given the training dataset M, the training objective is defined as below:

$$\mathcal{L}(M, \theta) = \sum_{D,Q \in M} (\mathcal{L}_{spans}(D, Q; \theta) + \lambda \mathcal{L}_{sent}(D, Q; \theta)) \tag{8}$$

where $\mathcal{L}_{spans}(D, Q; \theta)$ represents the cross-entropy loss function for answer span tagging after softmax operation, and $\mathcal{L}_{sent}(D, Q; \theta)$ represents the binary cross-entropy focal loss with a loss weight λ, which deals with the imbalanced distribution of key sentences tags.

4 Experiment

4.1 Dataset Collection and Annotation

To evaluate the performance of our model, we build a new dataset MPPQA which consists of 1236 triples comprising a procedural document, a prerequisite associated question, and a set of multi-span answer. The original corpus is collected from 379 procedural documents of online wikiHow knowledge base [1] which features *how-to* procedural articles describing procedures to accomplish a certain goal, covering the fields of *Food, Craft, Vehicle* and *Gardening*. Extra dataset statistics are illustrated in Table 1, where MPPQA features longer document lengths and is specialized in procedural documents and prerequisite associated questions. During the annotation process, we employ three well-educated annotators to manually annotate prerequisite associated questions and answers for the procedural documents, and adhere to the following key principles: (1)

Documents lacking procedural knowledge or incapable of answering the question should be discarded. (2) Annotate the answer span with continuous phrases as concise as possible to answer the question. (3) Retain long document which is challenging for users to quickly browse for answers. Additionally, each annotation underwent manual cross verification by each annotator and is eventually examined by most experienced annotator given the confidence score to ensure high-quality annotations.

Besides, we manually collect the distribution statistics of answer spans and the first <WH> token of questions in dataset MPPQA, as depicted in Fig. 4. It can be observed that multi-span answers constitute a relatively high portion of the dataset, and questions beginning with "What" comprise the majority of the prerequisite associated question.

Table 1. Dataset Statistics.

Dataset	#QA Pairs	Avg. Token Num. of Doc.	Max. Token Num. of Doc.	Avg. Len. of Question	Avg. Span Num. of Answer	Doc. Type	Prerequisite Associated
QUOREF[6]	2208	391.18	1333	16.93	2.5	Descriptive	-
MASH-QA[15]	6536	250.36	1182	9.03	4.2	Descriptive	-
MPPQA	1236	1478.78	4685	12.75	2.4	Procedural	√

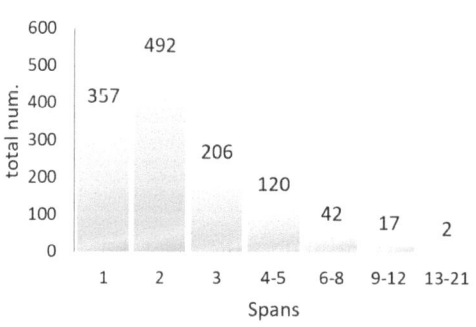

(a) Distribution of Answer Spans.

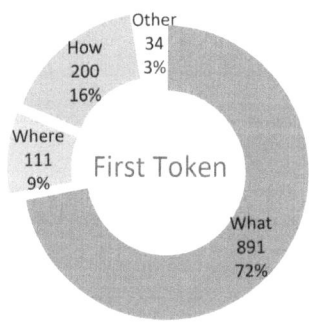

(b) Distribution of First <WH> Token of Questions.

Fig. 4. Distribution Statistics of MPPQA.

Table 2. The Experiment Results with Exact Match and Partial Match Metrics on MPPQA.

Methods	Exact Match			Partial Match		
	P(%)	R(%)	F1(%)	P(%)	R(%)	F1(%)
$TASE_{IO}$+SSE_{BERT_base} [25]	13.07	11.61	12.29	32.36	30.49	31.40
$TASE_{IO}$+SSE_{BERT_large} [25]	30.12	33.56	31.75	51.46	54.09	52.74
$TASE_{BIO}$+SSE_{BERT_base} [25]	16.55	12.44	14.20	36.37	32.52	34.34
$TASE_{BIO}$+SSE_{BERT_large} [25]	28.17	17.86	21.86	43.98	34.84	38.88
$MTMSN_{BERT\_base}$ [9]	21.58	15.82	18.25	41.58	39.53	40.53
$MTMSN_{BERT\_large}$ [9]	22.31	18.71	20.35	42.24	43.94	43.07
MultiSpanQA(joint)$_{BERT\_base}$ [15]	31.34	30.27	30.79	53.89	42.59	47.58
MultiSpanQA(joint)$_{BERT\_large}$ [15]	41.64	40.65	41.14	62.44	54.08	57.96
MultiSpanQA(full)$_{BERT\_base}$ [15]	31.19	28.06	29.54	53.10	40.86	46.18
MultiSpanQA(full)$_{BERT\_large}$ [15]	42.62	39.80	41.16	62.92	53.32	57.72
SpanQualifier$_{BERT\_base}$ [10]	18.12	25.51	21.19	50.09	45.09	47.46
SpanQualifier$_{BERT\_large}$ [10]	9.43	41.50	15.37	30.93	62.87	41.46
FlAN-T5-Small$_{zero-shot}$ [5]	17.00	7.13	10.05	38.74	36.04	37.34
FlAN-T5-Small$_{finetune}$ [5]	24.83	12.56	16.69	44.85	43.96	44.40
FLAN-T5-Base$_{zero-shot}$ [5]	21.05	8.83	12.44	46.76	49.38	48.03
FLAN-T5-Base$_{one-shot}$ [5]	18.22	7.64	10.77	43.99	43.84	43.92
Llama-2-7b-chat-hf$_{zero-shot}$ [28]	2.01	4.41	2.76	11.65	64.42	19.73
DeepSeek-llm-7b-chat$_{zero-shot}$ [7]	7.42	16.64	10.27	21.35	70.14	32.73
$SAPE_{BERT\_base}$ w/o Structure(Ours)	35.41	32.82	34.07	58.34	47.08	52.11
$SAPE_{BERT\_large}$ w/o Structure(Ours)	39.77	41.33	40.53	63.04	55.54	59.06
$SAPE_{BERT\_base}$(Ours)	36.83	38.78	37.78	57.98	51.51	54.55
$SAPE_{BERT\_large}$(Ours)	41.40	45.41	**43.31**	65.80	60.82	**63.21**

4.2 Baseline

Extractive Model. **TASE+SSE** [25] combines tag-based span extraction with traditional single-span extraction method and dynamically decide which span extraction method to utilize by multi-head model. We select $BERT_{base}$ and $BERT_{large}$ as base models and adopt both BIO and IO tagging scheme method to test the model performance. **MTMSN** [9] integrates a gating mechanism with the standard decoding strategy and adopts the non-maximum suppression algorithm to extract non-overlapped spans. **MultiSpanQA** [15] combines a sequence tagger with a span number predictor, span structure predictor, and span adjustment module. As the state-of-the-art multi-span model on the leaderboard, **SpanQualifier** [10] implements a span-centric scheme with stacked modules and spans interaction layers to extract multi-span answers.

Generative Model. We conduct finetuning operation, zero-shot and one-shot testing on instruction-finetuned language model **FLAN-T5** [5] with encoder-decoder architecture, and conduct zero-shot testing on large language model **Llama-2-7b-chat-hf** [28] and **DeepSeek-llm-7b-chat** [7] with decoder-only architecture. Due to resource constraints, Llama-2 and DeepSeek are not fine-tuned.

4.3   Evaluation Metrics

Exact Match (EM). Prediction of a sample is considered correct for exact match if it fully matches one of the ground-truth answer spans.

Partial Match (PM). The overlap between the prediction and ground-truth answer regarded as a string is measured by micro-averaged F1 score.

4.4   Experiment Settings

The experiment is conducted on our annotated dataset MPPQA which is split into training and testing sets with a ratio of 8:2. We utilize the pretrained procedural graph construction model [24] to capture structure information. We set loss weight λ to 0.02, optimize the model with Adam optimizer, with an initial learning rate of 8e-6 and a dropout rate of 0.2, and perform finetuning on A40(48GB) with a batch size of 2 for 10 epochs.

4.5   Result Analysis

Main Result. We conduct comparative experiments with both extractive and generative baselines outlined in Sect. 4.2, and use EM and PM metrics with micro-averaged F1 score. From the experiment results shown in Table 2, we can observe: (1) SAPE significantly outperforms previous multi-span extractive question answering model in MPPQA on both EM and PM metrics. (2) The design of structure-aware module shows effectiveness in capturing the key structural procedure information. Viewed as a sequence labeling problem, it is assumed that current multi-span extractive models are lacking in leveraging the structural procedural knowledge to identify relevant procedure fragments, resulting in a performance gap in answering prerequisite associated questions. Regarding generative models, it is noticed that FLAN-T5-Small exhibits improved performance after finetuning, and one-shot performance of FLAN-T5-Base is worse than zero-shot. It is suggested that one-shot with longer input introduces extra difficulty for the model to capture relevant information thus harming the performance. Besides, it is observed that both decoder-only architecture large language models, Llama-2-7b-chat-hf and DeepSeek-llm-7b-chat, demonstrate worse performances on the EM metric and large deviation between precision and recall scores on the PM metric. It is owing to their tendency to generate extraneous irrelevant results since there are inherent challenges in fully comprehending the instructions. Observed from the statistics in Table 1, massive scale of the document input also brings challenge to LLM with limited context length. In comparison, the effectiveness of our designed structure aware module is verified in extracting multi-span answer by integrating procedural knowledge.

Ablation Study. To comprehensively evaluate the effectiveness of our designed module, we conduct an ablation experiment, as shown in Table 2. It can be observed that after removing the structure information of procedure embedding and attention module, the performance of $SAPE_{BERT\_base}$ drops by 3.71% in exact match f1 score and 2.44% in partial match f1 score, respectively. From the ablation experiment result, the necessity of structure-aware module is proved, since it can effectively concentrate on the key procedure fragments by capturing the structural procedure information to answer prerequisite associated question.

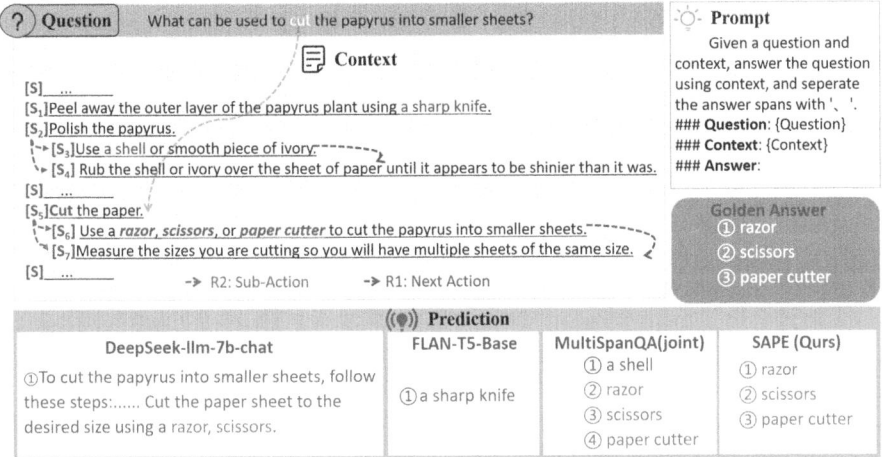

Fig. 5. Case Study for the Example of MPPQA.

Case Study. As depicted in Fig. 5, we conduct a case study to intuitively evaluate the effectiveness of our proposed model compared with other representative models. In the example, a procedural document detailing the tutorial of making Papyrus is provided, accompanied by a question regarding the prerequisite tools required for cutting the papyrus in the procedure. Upon analysis, it is observed that MultiSpanQA is distracted by unrelated procedure, resulting in redundant incorrect prediction, FLAN-T5-Base generates incorrect answer relevant to the other procedure given the prompt, and DeepSeek-llm-7b-chat generates extra knowledge and fails to provide an adequate answer span due to misunderstanding the instructions. In comparison, our model correctly identifies relevant procedure fragments with branch structure to acquire prerequisites for cutting the paper. Therefore, the above highlights the effectiveness of our structure-aware model in procedural extractive question answering task.

5 Conclusion

In this paper, we introduce the task of extracting multi-span style answers to prerequisite associated questions, and construct a new dataset MPPQA on procedural corpus to explore the problem. We resolve it by designing a structure-aware extractive question answering model SAPE that integrates structural procedural knowledge with contextualized information. Extensive experiments are conducted on MPPQA to evaluate the effectiveness of our designed model.

Acknowledgments. This research is supported by the National Natural Science Foundation of China (62076100, 62476097), the Fundamental Research Funds for the Central Universities, South China University of Technology (x2rjD2240100), the Science and Technology Planning Project of Guangdong Province (2020B0101100002), Guangdong Provincial Fund for Basic and Applied Basic Research–Regional Joint Fund Project (Key Project) (2023B1515120078), Guangdong Provincial Natural Science Foundation for Outstanding Youth Team Project (2024B1515040010), the China Computer Federation (CCF)-Zhipu AI Large Model Fund.

References

1. Anthonio, T., Bhat, I., Roth, M.: wikihowtoimprove: a resource and analyses on edits in instructional texts. In: LREC, pp. 5721–5729 (2020)
2. Banerjee, S., Bandyopadhyay, S.: Question classification and answering from procedural text in english. In: Proceedings of the Workshop on Question Answering for Complex Domains, pp. 11–26 (2012)
3. Bosselut, A., et al.: Simulating action dynamics with neural process networks. In: ICLR (2018)
4. Cao, J., He, Y.L., Zhu, Q.: An ontology-based procedure knowledge framework for the process industry. CJCE **99**(2), 530–542 (2021)
5. Chung, H.W., et al.: Scaling instruction-finetuned language models (2022)
6. Dasigi, P., et al.: Quoref: a reading comprehension dataset with questions requiring coreferential reasoning. In: EMNLP-IJCNLP, pp. 5924–5931 (2019)
7. DeepSeek-AI, et al.: Deepseek llm: scaling open-source language models with longtermism (2024)
8. Haopeng, R., et al.: Grounded multimodal procedural entity recognition for procedural documents: a new dataset and baseline. In: LREC-COLING 2024, pp. 7971–7981. ELRA and ICCL, Torino, Italia, May 2024
9. Hu, M., et al.: A multi-type multi-span network for reading comprehension that requires discrete reasoning. In: EMNLP-IJCNLP 2019, pp. 1596–1606 (2019)
10. Huang, Z., et al.: Spans, not tokens: a span-centric model for multi-span reading comprehension. In: CIKM 2023 (2023)
11. Jiang, Y., et al.: Recipe instruction semantics corpus (risec): resolving semantic structure and zero anaphora in recipes. In: AACL, pp. 821–826 (2020)
12. Kim, J.H., Jun, J., Zhang, B.T.: Bilinear attention networks. In: NeurIPS 2018, pp. 1571–1581 (2018)
13. Kwon, H., et al.: Modeling preconditions in text with a crowd-sourced dataset. In: EMNLP Findings 2020, pp. 3818–3828 (2020)
14. Lee, S., Kim, H., Kang, J.: Liquid: a framework for list question answering dataset generation. In: AAAI, vol. 37, pp. 13014–13024 (2023)

15. Li, H., et al.: Multispanqa: A dataset for multi-span question answering. In: NAACL 2022, pp. 1250–1260 (2022)
16. Liang, H., et al.: Knowing-how & knowing-that: a new task for machine comprehension of user manuals. In: ACL Findings, pp. 10550–10564 (01 2023)
17. Luo, M., et al.: Choose your qa model wisely: a systematic study of generative and extractive readers for question answering. In: Spa-NLP 2022, pp. 7–22 (2022)
18. Luo, Z., Zhang, Y., Luo, S.: A token-based transition-aware joint framework for multi-span question answering. IPM **61**(3), 103678 (2024)
19. Mishra, B.D., et al.: Tracking state changes in procedural text: a challenge dataset and models for process paragraph comprehension. In: Proceedings of NAACL-HLT, pp. 1595–1604 (2018)
20. Mysore, S., et al.: The materials science procedural text corpus: Annotating materials synthesis procedures with shallow semantic structures. In: LAW 2019, pp. 56–64 (2019)
21. Pal, K.K., et al.: Constructing flow graphs from procedural cybersecurity texts. In: ACL-IJCNLP Findings 2021, pp. 3945–3957 (2021)
22. Qian, C., et al.: An approach for process model extraction by multi-grained text classification. In: CAiSE, pp. 268–282 (2020)
23. Rajpurkar, P., et al.: Squad: 100,000+ questions for machine comprehension of text. In: EMNLP 2016, pp. 2383–2392, November 2016
24. Ren, H., et al.: Constructing procedural graphs with multiple dependency relations: a new dataset and baseline. In: ACL Findings 2023, pp. 8474–8486 (2023)
25. Segal, E., et al.: A simple and effective model for answering multi-span questions. In: EMNLP 2020, pp. 3074–3080 (2020)
26. Tandon, N., et al.: Wiqa: a dataset for "what if..." reasoning over procedural text. In: EMNLP-IJCNLP 2019, pp. 6076–6085 (2019)
27. Tandon, N., et al.: A dataset for tracking entities in open domain procedural text. In: EMNLP 2020, pp. 6408–6417 (2020)
28. Touvron, H., et al.: Llama 2: open foundation and fine-tuned chat models (2023)
29. Wu, T.L., et al.: Learning action conditions from instructional manuals for instruction understanding. In: ACL, pp. 3023–3043, July 2023
30. Yamakata, Y., Mori, S., Carroll, J.A.: English recipe flow graph corpus. In: LREC 2020, pp. 5187–5194 (2020)
31. Yuan, L., et al.: Hierarchical template transformer for fine-grained sentiment controllable generation. Inf. Process. Manag. **59**(5), 103048 (2022)
32. Zheng, C., Kordjamshidi, P.: Relevant commonsense subgraphs for "what if..." procedural reasoning. In: ACL Findings 2022, pp. 1927–1933 (2022)
33. Zhou, Y., Feng, Y.: Improve discourse dependency parsing with contextualized representations. In: NAACL Findings 2022, pp. 2250–2261 (2022)

GraphLLM: A General Framework for Multi-hop Question Answering over Knowledge Graphs Using Large Language Models

Zijian Qiao[1,2], Nan Li[2], Chenxi Huang[1], Gangliang Wang[2,3], Shenglin Liang[3], Hui Lin[2], and Qinglang Guo[2(✉)]

[1] School of Informatics, Xiamen University, Xiamen, China
{zjqiao,supermonkeyxi}@xmu.edu.cn
[2] CETC Academy of Electronics and Information Technology Group Co., Ltd., Beijing, China
gql1993@mail.ustc.edu.cn
[3] Xidian University, Xi'an, China
wgl@stu.xidian.edu.cn

Abstract. The task of multi-hop question answering over knowledge graphs (KGQA) is designed to identify answer entities for a given question through reasoning across multiple edges over KGs. This task presents persistent challenges: as the number of hops increases, both the reasoning complexity and the pool of candidate answers expand, resulting in suboptimal outcomes. Due to the powerful semantic understanding and logical reasoning capabilities of large language models, we propose a general framework for multi-hop KQGA using large language models (LLMs), named **GraphLLM**. Specifically, GraphLLM involves employing the semantic understanding and reasoning abilities of LLMs to decompose multi-hop questions through a **Divide-And-Conquer** approach and construct sub-graphs, transforming complex problems into several simple sub-questions. We obtain the ultimate answer by iteratively using Graph Neural Networks (GNNs) to solve sub-questions. By conducting experiments on benchmarks WebQSP and MetaQA, results indicate that GraphLLM exhibits outstanding performance compared to leading methods. We successfully demonstrate a collaborative example of LLMs and GNNs, offering a novel approach to addressing intricate multi-hop KGQA.

Keywords: Large Language Model · Knowledge Graph · Multi-hop Question Answering · Graph Neural Network

1 Introduction

Knowledge Graphs (KGs) are structured semantic knowledge bases that store information through "Entity-Relation-Entity" triplets, forming a graph-structured data model or topology with nodes and edges. Multi-hop Question

---

Z. Qiao and N. Li—Contribute equally to this work.

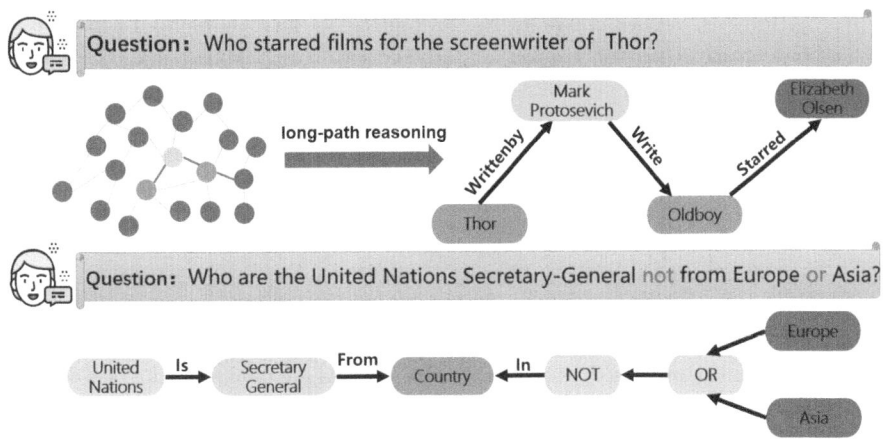

Fig. 1. Two challenges of muti-hop KGQA tasks. The first one is an example of long-distance reasoning, and the second one is an example of complex logical reasoning.

Answering over KGs (KGQA) task involves providing a natural language question and KGs, and ultimately finding the answer entity through perform reasoning over multiple edges [25]. Multi-hop KGQA systems hold crucial significance in various practical applications, including intelligent assistants, recommendation systems, and semantic search.

However, current studies [2,6,27] suggest that multi-hop KGQA tasks still present significant challenges. We illustrate an example in Fig. 1. The first challenge is long-path reasoning: with an escalation in the number of reasoning hops, the search space on the KGs expands substantially, resulting in a decrease in answer precision. The second challenge is complex logical reasoning: questions involving logical relationship reasoning, such as negation or conditional relationships.

To alleviate the issue of long-path reasoning, recent efforts [16,30] have employed semantic embedding methods to find latent relationships. However, training semantic embedding models requires a substantial amount of data, bring high costs and difficult to transfer to other domains. To address complex logical relationships, researchers [6,13,16] have introduced inference methods based on logical rule querying. By generating logical query statements, entities corresponding to the query are retrieved from the KG. Nevertheless, above methods still struggle to handle intricate knowledge inquiries. In recent years, large language models (LLMs), such as GPT [1], LLaMA [24], GLM [8], have achieved impressive advancements in the field of natural language processing (NLP) due to LLM's powerful semantic understanding and text generation capabilities. Recent studies [6,14] have also shown that LLMs trained on massive corpora have demonstrated strong logical reasoning abilities and can handle complex reasoning tasks.

We propose a general framework for multi-hop KGQA using LLMs based on a **divide-and-conquer** approach, named GraphLLM. Harnessing the robust semantic comprehension capabilities of LLMs, we use LLMs to decompose complex problems into simpler sub-problems. Unlike approaches such as StructGPT [12] and KG-GPT [15], which generate structured query statements, we employ Graph Neural Networks (GNNs) for iterative reasoning to achieve explainable answer.

In a nutshell, GraphLLM, the combination of problem decomposition using LLMs and GNNs, is able to reduce the complexity of problems. To evaluate the effectiveness of our work, we conducted experiments on multi-hop question answering datasets based on KGs, including WebQSP [28] and MetaQA [32]. The experimental results demonstrate that GraphLLM achieves favorable performance in most multi-hop question answering task, particularly in reasoning with long paths and complex questions. The contributions of our work can be summarized as follows:

- GraphLLM is the first framework to combine LLMs with GNNs for this task and particularly effective in performing long-path and complex logical reasoning.
- We leverage the semantic understanding and logical reasoning capabilities of LLMs to transform complex problems in a divide-and-conquer way, reducing the complexity of the problems and thereby improving accuracy.
- The experimental results demonstrate that our framework exhibits outstanding performance and strong applicability. Our work generates insights for the future integration of LLMs and KGs, paving the way for explainable question answering tasks.

2   Related Work

2.1   Multi-hop Question Answering over Knowledge Graph

Multi-hop KGQA aims to find answer entities that are multiple hops away from the topic entities in a large-scale KG. Existing work typically can currently be categorized into two categories: information retrieval methods and semantic parsing methods. Semantic parsing methods translate natural language questions into logical query statements, which are then used to query KGs to determine the answers. STAGG [29], QGG [16] and AQGnet [4] attempt to obtain correct answer entities by parsing questions and generating appropriate query graphs. However, their effectiveness is limited by the accumulation of errors in complex pipelines. Information retrieval method utilizes effective information retrieval from the knowledge graph by matching the question with entities and relationships to find relevant facts or triples. KV-Mem [20], KSR [11], and BAMnet [5] enhance the representation of questions by capturing correlations between sparse graphs using memory networks, thereby improving the ability to infer answers. GRAFT-NET [22] and PullNet [21] achieve better representation of the knowledge graph by constructing question sub-graphs and employing GNNs which lack generalization.

2.2   LLMs for KGQA

With the success of pre-trained models (PLMs) such as RoBERTa [18] and T5 [1], researchers have begun applying PLMs to multi-hop KGQA tasks. Several studies attempt to fuse the representation of the KGs into the PLMs. QA-GNN [27] integrates pre-training to combine natural language questions and knowledge graph representations, employing GNN to update the scores of KG nodes or paths to determine answers. With the launch of ChatGPT, open-source LMs with larger parameter scales built on the research foundation of PLMs have demonstrated stronger capabilities [3,23]. Especially in tasks involving arithmetic or reasoning, Chain of Though (CoT) [26] has been shown to significantly improve the correctness of generated answers. StructGPT [12] proposes an Iterative Reading-then-Reasoning framework for LLMs to utilize interfaces to solve tasks, but still unable to overcome the challenges posed by long-path reasoning. In contrast, ChatKBQA [19] introduces a generate-then-retrieve approach, fine-tuning LLMs to generate graph query statements which relies on the accuracy of generated statements.

3   Method

3.1   Problem Definition And Overview

A knowledge graph composed of fact triples is a graphical structure used to represent knowledge, expressed as $\mathcal{G} = \{(e, r, e') \mid e, e' \in V, r \in E\}$, where V and E respectively denote the entity set and relation set. (e, r, e') represents a fact triplet, where e denotes the head entity, r is the relationship, and e' denotes the tail entity. Given natural language question q and a series of answer choices $a \in C$, the objective of KGQA is to find the correct answer a from a structured knowledge graph $\mathcal{G}$. Following previous work [27], we define the entities involved in the question q as topic entities $e_{topic} \subset E$, which have already been linked with entities on KG. We propose a general framework that combines LLMs and GNNs to alleviate the challenges of long-path reasoning and complex logical reasoning, called **GraphLLM**. It refers a divide-and-conquer method, using LLMs to decompose a complex question to several simple sub-questions and construct sub-graphs for GNNs. The overview architecture is illustrated in Fig. 2.

3.2   Question Decomposing

Existing researches [8,10,24] indicate that LLMs show remarkable generalization capabilities through training on extensive corpora. However, the performance of LLMs often leaves much to be desired due to the lack of training data for multi-hop KGQA tasks. To address this, we specifically propose to use the semantic understanding and logical reasoning capabilities of LLMs to address complex multi-hop questions without high training cost. It can be divided into two modules: Named Entity Recognition (NER) and Decomposition.

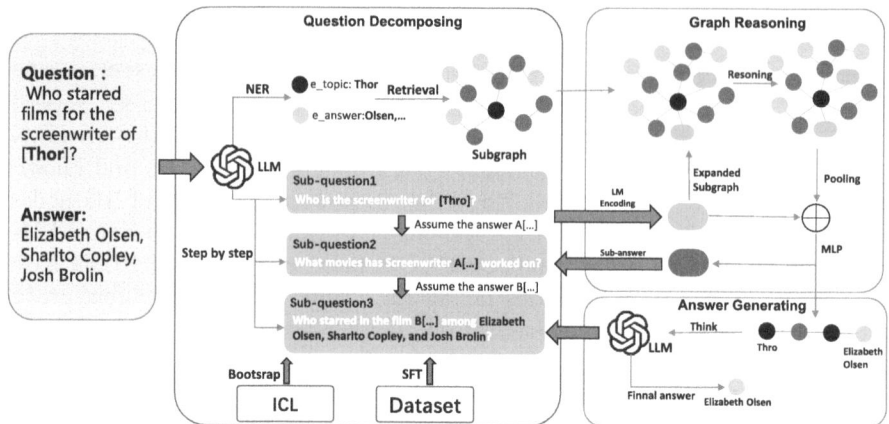

Fig. 2. An overview of GraphLLM. The framework includes three sub-modules: Question Decomposing, Graph Reasoning and Answer Generating.

Named Entity Recognition: Given a natural language question q, we identify and extract important entities (e.g., people, places, and times) as topic entities e_{topic} from q using LLMs. The input candidate answers $a \in C$ can be directly donated as answer entities e_{answer}. Specifically, we guide the generation of the target response by inputting a prompt P and q into a well-trained LLM, the objective is to maximize the conditional probability in an auto-regressive formulation:

$$p_\theta \left(e_{topic} | q, P \right) = \prod_{i=1}^{m} p_\theta \left(e^i | q, P, e < i \right) \tag{1}$$

where θ is a trainable parameter of LLM. In order to minimize the size of the candidate entity sets, we construct an inference sub-graph based on topic entities e_{topic}, answer entities e_{answer}, and the factual knowledge graph. We connect e_{topic} with e_{answer} based on the retrieval results of factual KG structure by Dijkstra's algorithm [9] and extend each entity by k-hops, avoiding sacrificing the recall of answers.

Decomposition: Given a question q, we guide LLMs to decompose q into a series of simple sub-questions $[q_1, q_2, ..., q_n]$ step by step through COT based on a Divide-and-Conquer method. While generating the first sub-question, we teach the LLM to assume an unknown answer sequence $X [x_1, x_2, ..., x_n]$ corresponding to the sub-question, thereby assisting in generating the next sub-question more effectively, until the process concludes. Sub-questions and corresponding unknown answer sequences $[q_n; X_n]$ can be described as follows:

$$[q_n; X_n] = LLM(q_{n-1}, P', X_{n-1}) \tag{2}$$

where P' is a prompt used for decomposition. Specifically, for questions involving logical reasoning, we incorporate additional prompts and auxiliary information to assist LLMs in accurately discerning logical relationships. The information includes common logical vocabulary and symbols (e.g., or, not, and¬), mitigating inconspicuous yet critical logical errors.

We additionally employ Supervised Fine-Tuning (SFT) [19] and In-Context Learning [1] (ICL) to enhance the capability of LLMs for more accurate subgraph construction and decomposition. We use GPT-4 API to generate data and manually rewrite to construct an instruction fine-tuning dataset which contains 2,135 examples of questions to enhance capability of LLMs in NER and decomposition. Recent studies [12,19] have shown that incorporating few shots in downstream tasks can effectively enhance LLMs. We study the impact of input demonstrations into prompts to improving the performance of LLMs and find the best shots.

3.3 Graph Reasoning

We obtain context sub-questions and a retrieval sub-graph with two different knowledge structures after decomposing the question. The Graph Reasoning module interacts with LLMs to solve sub-questions one by one. To conduct effective graph reasoning, we refer to existing method [27] to introduce a new representation node for each sub-question and connect it with the entity nodes to build a joint sub-graph if the entity nodes can be found in either the sub-question or answers portion of the context. We initialize the sub-question representation q_n^{LM} by using BGE-M3 and compute node embeddings, where triples of KG are transformed into sentences using predefined relation templates.

We utilize GNNs to perform inference on the sub-graph representation and employ a graph attention framework to better capture graph structure and representation information. Specifically, in the L-th layer of the GNN, we update the representation of node embeddings $\left[e_0^l, e_1^l, ..., e_n^l\right]$ by referencing and improving the method of GreaseLM [31]. We achieve message passing by updating the representation of central nodes by aggregating neighboring nodes.

$$e_n^{l+1} = f_n \left(\sum_{s \in N_n \cup \{n\}} \alpha_{sn} m_{sn} \right) + e_n^l \tag{3}$$

where N_n represents the neighborhood of node t, f_n is a 2-layer MLP, m_{sn} denotes the message from each neighbor node $e_s \rightarrow e_n$, and α_{sn} is an attention weight that scales each message m_{sn}. We obtain representation of u_s's node type and embed the relationshipr_{sn} between $e_s \rightarrow e_n$, thus compute the message.

$$m_{sn} = f_m \left(e_s^{(l)}, u_s, r_{sn} \right) \tag{4}$$

where f_m is a linear transformation. We employ scaled dot-product attention as scoring function, and obtain a probability distribution over values corresponding to keys through pooling operations. The representations of the query and key vectors Q_s and K_n are defined as follows:

$$Q_s = f_Q(e_s^l, u_s) \qquad\qquad K_n = f_K(e_n^l, u_n, r_{sn}) \qquad (5)$$

where f_Q and f_K are linear transformations. The attention weight α_{sn} is defined as follows:

$$\alpha_{sn} = softmax(\frac{Q_s^\top K_n}{\sqrt{d}}) \qquad (6)$$

We regard the entities present within the sub-graph as candidate answer entities in relation to the corresponding sub-question, with probabilities as follows: $p(e \mid q_n) \propto \exp(MLP(q_n^{LM}, e_n^L, g))$ where g denotes the pooling of all the entity representations in the sub-graph, and q_n^{LM}, e_n^L are defined the same as above. We choose cross-entropy loss to optimize the model and choose the entity with the highest probability as answer returned to question decomposing module, until all sub-questions are solved.

3.4 Answer Generating

Due to LLM's robust generalization and inference capabilities, we propose a method for assessing results given relevant knowledge. Specifically, we use the graph and inference outcomes to obtain triples as reference knowledge and construct inference paths. Subsequently, After inputting the question, candidate answers, and triples into LLMs, we evaluate the validity of the reasoning process through a meticulously designed prompt. If it is deemed irrational, the answer generating and graph reasoning will be repeated. Table 1 provides an illustration of answer generating prompt. To mitigate the potential impact of LLM's Pre-trained knowledge on the results which may conflict with the factual knowledge graph, we emphasis on the imperative reliance on the provided knowledge triplets for factual inference.

4   Experiments

4.1 Datasets

We evaluate GraphLLM on two question answering datasets: WebQuestionSP [28] and MetaQA [32]. These datasets have been divided into training, validation, and testing set by previous works.

WebQuestionSP is a QA dataset generated based on web queries, consisting of 4,737 questions and the questions cover various types involving logical reasoning, common sense queries, with most having 1-hop and 2-hop relationships.

MetaQA consists of over 400k questions and question hop counts include 1-hop, 2-hop, and 3-hop. Furthermore, we select and rewrite 1,346 questions

Table 1. The illustration of answer generating prompt.

Answer Generating Prompt
You are a question-answering assistant. Below, I will provide you with a question and candidate answers. Please evaluate the validity of the given reasoning path.   QUESTION: *< Who starred films for the screenwriter of Thor? >*   ANSWERS: *< Elizabeth Olsen, Sharlto Copley, Josh Brolin >*   REASONING PATH: *< (Thor, Writtenby, Mark Protosevich), (Mark Protosevich, Write, Old Boy), (Old Boy, Star, Elizabeth Olsen)>*   Remember, rely on the provided reasoning path above as reference knowledge; Do not use your own knowledge!

Table 2. Evaluation results (*Hits@1*) of GraphLLM on WebQuestionSP and MetaQA datasets.

Methods	WebQSP	MetaQA		
		1-hop	2-hop	3-hop
KV-Mem	46.7	96.2	82.7	48.9
VRN	–	97.5	89.9	62.5
GraftNet	66.4	97.0	94.8	77.7
UniKGQA	75.1	97.5	99.0	99.1
PullNet	68.1	97.0	**99.9**	91.4
QA-GNN	73.0	–	–	–
EmbedKGQA	66.6	97.5	98.8	94.8
DCRN	67.8	97.5	**99.9**	**99.3**
ChatGPT	61.2	61.9	31.0	43.2
ChatKBQA	83.5	–	–	–
GraphLLM(Ours)	**84.7**	**97.7**	98. 0	97.2

pertaining to logical reasoning relationships from the MetaQA dataset to evaluate GraphLLM's sensitivity when face complex logical questions. And we select "not", "and", and "or" as the keywords for logical reasoning and the questions contain one to two of these keywords, covering the majority of logical reasoning scenarios.

4.2   Main Results

Table 2 presents a comprehensive evaluation results (*Hits@1*) of GraphLLM framework when applied to the WebQuestionSP and MetaQA datasets. The empirical findings delineate that, in comparison to existing baseline for multi-hop KGQA, our framework procures superior performance on both the WebQSP and the 1-hop subset of the MetaQA dataset. Notably, the disparities in the outcomes among the baseline approaches are observed to be nominal for single-hop queries, a phenomenon that lines with our initial expectation.

Table 3. Evaluation results (*Hits*@1) of GraphLLM on MetaQA datasets which randomly drop 50% of the triplets or consist of logic reasoning.

Methods	Drop 50%			Logic Reasoning		
	1-hop	2-hop	3-hop	AND	OR	NOT
KV-Mem	63.6	41.8	37.6	33.8	31.1	43.4
GraftNet	64.0	52.6	59.2	45.7	30.8	40.6
PullNet	65.1	52.1	59.7	62.4	47.4	50.7
EmbedKGQA	83.9	91.8	70.3	58.4	55.3	53.2
ChatGPT	61.8	32.4	43.1	58.4	55.3	53.2
GraphLLM(Ours)	**94.5**	**92.3**	**90.4**	**70.2**	**62.1**	**68.5**

Although our approach does not manifest an exceptional performance in the 2-hop and 3-hop segments of the MetaQA dataset, the observed decrement in performance is marginal, with only a 0.5% diminution in accuracy accompanying an escalation in the number of hops. In contrast, KV-Mem, VRN and GraftNet which relying on sub-graph retrieval are significantly affected when facing long-path reasoning questions due to the rapid expansion of their search space with increasing hop distances. This can be attributed to the efficacy of the divide-and-conquer strategy that we have integrated into our framework, which bolsters the robustness of the GraphLLM and mitigates the adverse impact of increased complexity in multi-hop KGQA scenarios.

Our framework exhibits a slight disadvantage on the MetaQA dataset compared to models such as PullNet and EmbedKGQA. However, we offer strong traceability and correctability for GraphLLM compared to other models. We can systematically deconstruct complex problems by using the reasoning capability of LLM and iteratively derive a comprehensive reasoning path step by step.

In order to evaluate the efficacy of these models in scenarios that necessitate long-path reasoning, we have adopted an approach similar from prior work [2], which involves the random deletion of 50% of the triplets present in the knowledge graph. As shown in Table 3, the results reveal that GraphLLM surpasses other baseline when operating over an incomplete knowledge graph. The capability of ChatGPT remain unaffected due to its rich training knowledge without knowledge graph. It becomes evident that both ChatGPT and our method exhibit a diminished susceptibility to the impact of missing relations within the knowledge graph. This resilience renders our model more suitable for practical applications, contrasting with the performance of other models which are more significantly affected by such omissions. This comparative analysis suggests that LLMs compensate for missing knowledge graph in multi-hop KGQA tasks through its existing pre-training knowledge.

In order to verify the ability of GraphLLM in complex logical reasoning, we specifically select 1,346 questions from the MetaQA dataset and rewrite them, targeting those that contain common logical relation terms (e.g., 'and', 'or', 'not'). Table 3 demonstrates that our method surpasses other singular method-ologies when assessed on datasets that demand logical reasoning capabilities.

Table 4. Ablation study of major components in GraphLLM.

Methods	WebQSP	MetaQA	
		3-hop	logical reasoning
GraphLLM (Ours)	**84.7**	**97.2**	**66.9**
-Question Decomposing	64.2	51.7	38.5
-Graph Reasoning	45.3	35.4	34.6
-Answer Generating	70.2	86.1	62.4
only LLM (Llama2-13B)	41.3	31.2	32.3
only Graph Reasoning	62.4	49.3	34.7

4.3 Ablation Study

The ablation study is conduct to assess the impact of three essential components in GraphLLM on three representative tasks: WebQSP, MetaQA (3-hop), and MetaQA (logical reasoning). As shown in Table 4, the most significant improvement is observed: when the question decomposing module is missing, the performance of GraphLLM quickly deteriorates, especially on multi-hop and complex logical reasoning tasks. This demonstrates that our proposed divide-and-conquer approach can effectively handle long-path and logical reasoning problems in multi-hop KGQA tasks. We find that the answer generating module has less impact on the model compared to other modules. This is because it primarily serves as a validation component, filtering out only incorrect answers. However, it is necessary to use LLMs for answer generating, which can effectively leverage existing resources and improve accuracy.

Besides, we construct a supervised fine-tuning dataset and train LLMs to enhance the ability of GraphLLM in question decomposing. As shown in Table 5, the results on WebQSP and MetaQA (logical reasoning) datasets ultimately demonstrate that SFT effectively enhances performance, which aids our method in executing decomposing instructions and accomplishing the question decomposing task effectively. While current researches [7,19] suggest that different SFT methods may exert different influences on the result, it is not the primary focus of our paper and is not discussed here.

We attempt to incorporate varying numbers of references to guide LLM and draw inspiration from some in-context learning researches [1,17] and choose for one-shot learning, which can surpass few-shot in most time. Table 5 indicates that the inclusion of ICL has led to significant improvements in performance, particularly in the logical reasoning task which require higher reasoning capability of LLMs without additional training.

Table 5. Ablation study of Question Decomposing on WebSQP and MetaQA (logical reasoning) .

Methods	WebSQP	MetaQA
GraphLLM(Ours)	**84.7**	66.9
- SFT	75.2	54.3
- ICL	75.4	60.7

5   Conclusion

This paper addresses the critical challenges of long-path reasoning and complex logical reasoning in multi-hop Question Answering over Knowledge Graph. Our work proposes a combination of LLMs and GNN algorithms based on the divide-and-conquer approach and has a **plug-and-play** characteristics, allowing for the swift replacement of LLMs to adapt to various requirements. We successfully demonstrate a collaborative example of LLMs and GNNs, offering a novel approach to for multi-hop KGQA task.

While the proposed GraphLLM alleviates performance degradation caused by long-path and logical reasoning in multi-hop KGQA, the integration of LLMs also introduces significant resource consumption. One possible strategy is to reduce the resource consumption of LLM during runtime by accelerating and optimizing.

Acknowledgments. This study was funded by the National Key Research and Development Program of China (2021YFC3300500).

References

1. Bubeck, S., et al.: Sparks of artificial general intelligence: early experiments with GPT-4, March 2023
2. Cai, J., Zhang, Z., Wu, F., Wang, J.: Deep cognitive reasoning network for multi-hop question answering over knowledge graphs. In: Findings of the Association for Computational Linguistics: ACL-IJCNLP 2021, January 2021
3. Chai, Z., et al.: GraphLLM: boosting graph reasoning ability of large language model (2023). https://arxiv.org/abs/2310.05845
4. Chen, Y., Li, H., Hua, Y., Qi, G.: Formal query building with query structure prediction for complex question answering over knowledge base. In: Proceedings of the Twenty-Ninth International Joint Conference on Artificial Intelligence, July 2020
5. Chen, Y., Wu, L., Zaki, M.J.: Bidirectional attentive memory networks for question answering over knowledge bases. In: Proceedings of the 2019 Conference of the North, January 2019
6. Choudhary, N., Reddy, C.: Complex logical reasoning over knowledge graphs using large language models, May 2023
7. Dettmers, T., Pagnoni, A., Holtzman, A., Zettlemoyer, L.: Qlora: efficient finetuning of quantized llms (2024)
8. Du, Z., et al.: GLM: general language model pretraining with autoregressive blank infilling (2021)
9. Feijen, W., Schäfer, G.: Dijkstras algorithm with predictions to solve the single-source many-targets shortest-path problem, December 2021
10. Ghosal, D., Chia, Y.K., Majumder, N., Poria, S.: Flacuna: unleashing the problem solving power of vicuna using flan fine-tuning (2023)

11. Huang, J., Zhao, W.X., Dou, H., Wen, J.R., Chang, E.Y.: Improving sequential recommendation with knowledge-enhanced memory networks. In: The 41st International ACM SIGIR Conference on Research & Development in Information Retrieval, June 2018

12. Jiang, J., Zhou, K., Dong, Z., Ye, K., Zhao, W., Wen, J.R.: StructGPT: a general framework for large language model to reason over structured data (2023)

13. Jiang, J., Zhou, K., Zhao, W., Li, Y., Wen, J.R.: ReasoningLM: enabling structural subgraph reasoning in pre-trained language models for question answering over knowledge graph (2023)

14. Khot, T., et al.: Decomposed prompting: a modular approach for solving complex tasks, October 2022

15. Kim, J., Kwon, Y., Jo, Y., Choi, E.: Kg-GPT: a general framework for reasoning on knowledge graphs using large language models, October 2023

16. Lan, Y., Jiang, J.: Query graph generation for answering multi-hop complex questions from knowledge bases. In: Proceedings of the 58th Annual Meeting of the Association for Computational Linguistics, January 2020

17. Liu, X., et al.: WebGLM: towards an efficient web-enhanced question answering system with human preferences (2023)

18. Liu, Y., et al.: Roberta: a robustly optimized bert pretraining approach, July 2019

19. Luo, H., et al.: ChatKBQA: a generate-then-retrieve frame-work for knowledge base question answering with fine-tuned large language models (2023)

20. Miller, A., Fisch, A., Dodge, J., Karimi, A.H., Bordes, A., Weston, J.: Key-value memory networks for directly reading documents. In: Proceedings of the 2016 Conference on Empirical Methods in Natural Language Processing, January 2016

21. Sun, H., Bedrax-Weiss, T., Cohen, W.: Pullnet: open domain question answering with iterative retrieval on knowledge bases and text. In: Proceedings of the 2019 Conference on Empirical Methods in Natural Language Processing and the 9th International Joint Conference on Natural Language Processing, January 2019

22. Sun, H., Dhingra, B., Zaheer, M., Mazaitis, K., Salakhutdinov, R., Cohen, W.: Open domain question answering using early fusion of knowledge bases and text. In: Proceedings of the 2018 Conference on Empirical Methods in Natural Language Processing, January 2018

23. Tang, J., et al.: GraphGPT: graph instruction tuning for large language models (2024). https://arxiv.org/abs/2310.13023

24. Touvron, H., et al.: Llama: open and efficient foundation language models (2023)

25. Wang, Q., Mao, Z., Wang, B., Guo, L.: Knowledge graph embedding: a survey of approaches and applications. IEEE Trans. Knowl. Data Eng. **29**(12), 2724–2743 (2017)

26. Wei, J., et al.: Chain of thought prompting elicits reasoning in large language models (2022)

27. Yasunaga, M., Ren, H., Bosselut, A., Liang, P., Leskovec, J.: QA-GNN: reasoning with language models and knowledge graphs for question answering. In: Proceedings of the 2021 Conference of the North American Chapter of the Association for Computational Linguistics: Human Language Technologies, January 2021

28. Yih, W.t., Chang, M.W., He, X., Gao, J.: Semantic parsing via staged query graph generation: question answering with knowledge base. In: Proceedings of the 53rd Annual Meeting of the Association for Computational Linguistics and the 7th International Joint Conference on Natural Language Processing, January 2015

29. Yih, W.t., Richardson, M., Meek, C., Chang, M.W., Suh, J.: The value of semantic parse labeling for knowledge base question answering. In: Proceedings of the 54th Annual Meeting of the Association for Computational Linguistics, January 2016

30. Zhang, L., et al.: FC-KBQA: a fine-to-coarse composition framework for knowledge base question answering, June 2023
31. Zhang, X., et al.: GreaseLM: graph reasoning enhanced language models for question answering, January 2022
32. Zhang, Y., Dai, H., Kozareva, Z., Smola, A., Song, L.: Variational reasoning for question answering with knowledge graph, April 2018

Local or Global Optimization for Dialogue Discourse Parsing

Chengrui Wang[1,2], Shaoming Ji[1,2], and Fang Kong[1,2(✉)]

[1] Laboratory for Natural Language Processing, Soochow University, Suzhou, China
{20234227065,20214227062}@stu.suda.edu.cn
[2] School of Computer Science and Technology, Soochow University, Suzhou, China
kongfang@suda.edu.cn

Abstract. Dialogue Discourse Parsing aims to identify the discourse links and relations between utterances, which has attracted more interest in recent years. Previous studies either adopt local optimization to independently select one parent for each utterance or use global optimization to directly get the tree representing the dialogue structure. However, the influence of these two optimization methods remains less explored. In this paper, we aim to systematically inspect their performance. Specifically, for local optimization, we use local loss during the training stage and a greedy strategy during the inference stage. For global optimization, We implement optimization of unlabeled and labeled trees by structured losses including Max-Margin and TreeCRF, and exploit Chu-Liu-Edmonds algorithm during the inference stage. Experiments shows that the performance of these two optimization methods is closely related to the characteristics of the dataset, and global optimization can reduce the burden of identifying long-range dependency relations.

Keywords: Dialogue discourse parsing · Local optimization · Global optimization

1 Introduction

Dialogue discourse parsing can reveal the discourse structure of a dialogue and provide better understanding of disorder dialogue content so that it is helpful for many other natural language processing (NLP) tasks, such as dialogue comprehension [7], dropped pronoun recovery [17] and so on.

As shown in Fig. 1, we can parse the dialogue structure from two perspectives: local optimization and global optimization. The former formalizes this task as optimizing each dependency edge independently, and then select its parent node for each utterance while the later directly optimize a tree[1] globally, and then find the highest-scoring tree representing the dialogue structure. Among the deep learning methods, most previous studies start from the perspective of

---

[1] In general, the structure of a dialogue is a Directed Acyclic Graph(DAG), but for simplicity, we follow previous studies to predict it as a tree structure during both training and inference.

© The Author(s), under exclusive license to Springer Nature Singapore Pte Ltd. 2025
D. F. Wong et al. (Eds.): NLPCC 2024, LNAI 15359, pp. 149–161, 2025.
https://doi.org/10.1007/978-981-97-9431-7_12

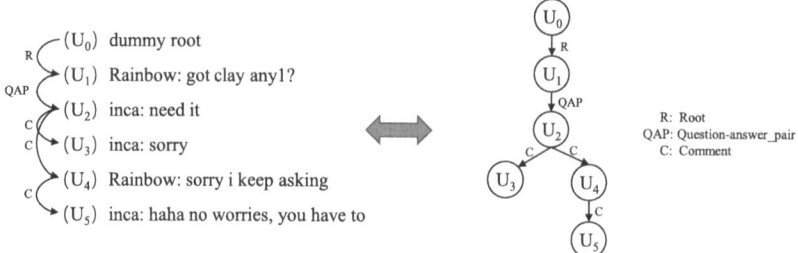

Fig. 1. Perspectives from local optimization and global optimization

local optimization. Only Chi and Rudnicky [4] perform structured dialogue discourse parsing, which is the first attempt to optimize a labeled non-projective tree by TreeCRF loss during training and obtain a labeled highest-scoring tree by modified Chu-Liu-Edmonds during inference. They only compare their principled model with other local optimization-based baselines but ignore the deeper comparison and analysis of these two types of optimization methods.

According to above discussion, no research systematically considers the impact of local optimization and global optimization. Therefore, in this paper, we put our sight on exploring these two perspectives. In detail, during the training phase, for local optimization, we use local loss to optimize each dependency edge. For global optimization, to the best of our knowledge, there are two typical types of structured training strategies, Max-Margin and TreeCRF, to impose structured constraints. During the inference phase, for local optimization, we use a greedy strategy to find the parent for each utterance in a dialogue, while for global optimization, we use the Chu-Liu-Edmonds algorithm to decode the highest-scoring tree.

2   Related Work

Research on dialogue discourse parsing can be divided into two stages: methods based on traditional manual features and methods based on deep learning. Methods based on traditional manual features adopt a two-stage strategy: first estimating the local probability between any two utterances, and then parsing the dialogue structure with decoding algorithms such as maximum spanning tree [1] or integer linear programming [12]. Methods based on deep learning adopt deep neural networks to realize feature learning and label mapping and can be categorized into two types according to different optimization perspectives.

Local Optimization-Based Methods: For better and richer representations, different features are extracted and fused, such as historical paths [13], implicit structural information [16], contextual information [11], speaker interactions [18], the interaction of two paradigms [6], beneficial assistance from other tasks [5,7, 17] and so on.

Global Optimization-Based Models: To the best of our knowledge, in dialogue discourse parsing task, Chi and Rudnicky [4] is the first attempt to conduct global optimization during training. Regarding the dialogue structure as a labeled multi-root non-projective tree, they optimize each gold tree by TreeCRF loss based on pairwise encoding model during training and decode a maximum spanning tree by modified Chu-Liu-Edmonds during inference.

3 Methodology

3.1 Model

Inspired by Chi and Rudnicky [4], we will adopt pairwise context encoding. Figure 2 shows the locally optimized model architecture and it mainly includes three steps: pairwise encoding, context-aware encoding and edge scoring.

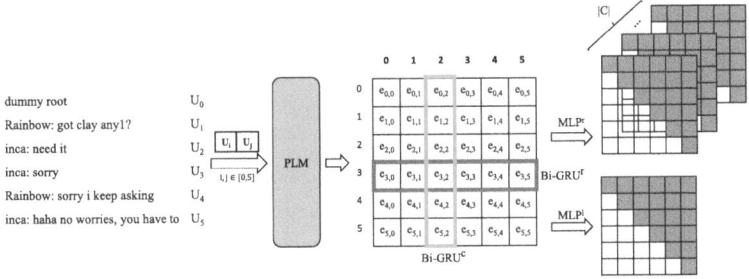

Fig. 2. The architecture of local optimization.

Pairwise Encoding. Given a dialogue D consisting n utterances (aka EDUs) $\{u_i\}_{i=1}^{n}$, we follow previous works to add a dummy root u_0[2] at the beginning of the dialogue. Any utterance pair is encoded by RoBERTa. A special token $<s>$ is prepended before the concatenation of two arbitrary utterances u_i and u_j. We simply reserve the representation of $<s>$ as the utterance pair representation $e_{i,j}$, i.e., edge representation between u_i and u_j. This calculation can be formalized as follows:

$$e_{ij} = RoBERTa(u_i, u_j) \tag{1}$$

---

[2] We use the utterance "this is the start of dialogue" in this work since root utterance can be chosen arbitrarily.

Context-Aware Encoding. Contextual information between utterance pairs, i.e. edges, is ignored in Eq. (1). To encode contextual information, we apply Bi-GRU separately on the row and column where the utterance pair is located because as shown in Fig. 1, the representation of an utterance pair is contextually related to the row and column in which it is located. Concretely, the context-aware representations of $e_{i,j}$ in its row and column are $e_{i,j}^r$ and $e_{i,j}^c$:

$$\{e_{i,j}^r\}_{j=0}^n = BiGRU^r(\{e_{i,j}^r\}_{j=0}^n) \tag{2}$$

$$\{e_{i,j}^c\}_{i=0}^n = BiGRU^c(\{e_{i,j}^c\}_{i=0}^n) \tag{3}$$

The final context-aware utterance pair representation of u_i and u_j is:

$$e_{i,j}^{'} = e_{i,j}^r + e_{i,j}^c \tag{4}$$

Edge Scoring. Regardless of the optimization approach used, edge scoring is necessary. Here, we use a multi-layer perceptron(MLP) for edge scoring. Equation(5) scores the edge between the utterance pair u_i and u_j. Equation(6) scores all edge types if the edge between u_i and u_j exists. It is worth noting that if dependency links and relations are predicted jointly, only Eq. 6 is required.

$$s_{i,j}^l = MLP^l(e_{i,j}^{'}) \tag{5}$$

$$s_{i,j}^r = MLP^r(e_{i,j}^{'}) \tag{6}$$

where $s_{i,j}^l \in R$ and $s_{i,j}^r \in R^{|c|}$ denote the edge score and type scores separately, $|c|$ is the number of discourse relations.

3.2   Training

In this section, we will introduce the details of local and global optimization during the training stage. For local optimization, we use local loss to independently optimize each local dependency edge. For global optimization, we comprehensively consider two types of structured losses including Max-Margin loss and TreeCRF loss to optimize an unlabeled tree and a labeled tree.

Local Training. In the setting of local optimization, the training goal is to independently select a parent for each utterance. Considering the fact that the parent of each utterance must be chosen from the utterances proceding itself in this task, we need to apply an upper triangular mask to the score matrices S^l and S^r coming from edge scoring module.

To realize the goal of local optimization, we follow most previous works to minimize the cross-entropy of gold pair for link prediction and gold relation for relation classification. This is what we call local loss $\mathcal{L}(\Theta)$:

$$\mathcal{L}(\Theta) = \mathcal{L}^l(\Theta) + \mathcal{L}^r(\Theta) \tag{7}$$

$$\mathcal{L}^l(\Theta) = -\sum_{x \in \mathcal{X}} \sum_{i=1}^{n} log P(p_i = p_i^* | S_{i,<i}^l; \Theta) \qquad (8)$$

$$\mathcal{L}^r(\Theta) = -\sum_{x \in \mathcal{X}} \sum_{i=1}^{n} log P(r_{ji} = r_{ji}^* | s_{i,j}^r, u_j = p_i^*; \Theta) \qquad (9)$$

$$P(p_i = p_i^* | S_{i,<i}^l; \Theta) = softmax(S_{i,<i}^l) \qquad (10)$$

$$P(r_{ji} = r_{ji}^* | s_{i,j}^r, u_j = p_i^*; \Theta) = softmax(s_{i,j}^r) \qquad (11)$$

where Θ denotes the set of model parameters, x is a dialogue, $\mathcal{X}$ is the training data, n indicates the utterance number of x, p_i^* and r_{ji}^* denote the gold parent and corresponding gold relation of u_i and $S_{i,<i}^l = [s_{i,0}^l, s_{i,1}^l, ..., s_{i,i-1}^l]$.

Max-Margin Training. In the setting of global optimization, the output is regarded as a non-projective tree and all dependency arcs have the same direction. In order to facilitate the realization of global optimization, we define the direction from front to back, so the score matrices of edges and types needs a lower triangular mask to impose $i < j$ constraints.

The goal of max-margin training is to make the score of the golden standard dependency tree higher than other incorrect dependency trees. To improve the generalization ability of the model, there is also a certain gap between their scores, which depends on the number of incorrect dependency edges.

Unlabeled Tree Learning. In the setting of global optimization of unlabeled trees, Eq. (10) is retained for relation classification and for link prediction, Eq. (9) is replaced by:

$$\mathcal{L}^l(\Theta) = \sum_{x \in \mathcal{X}} (\max_{\hat{y}^l \in Y^l(x)} (Score(x, \hat{y}^l; \Theta) + \Delta(\hat{y}^l, y^l; \Theta)) - Score(x, y^l; \Theta)) \quad (12)$$

where y^l is gold unlabeled tree, $\hat{y}^l$ is the predicted unlabeled tree with the highest scores, $Y^l(x)$ denotes all possible unlabeled trees of this instance, $Score(x, y^l; \Theta)$ is the sum of all gold arc scores and denotes the score of the gold unlabeled tree y^l, $Score(x, \hat{y}^l; \Theta)$ is the sum of all arc scores in the predicted unlabeled tree $\hat{y}^l$ and denotes the score of the predicted unlabeled tree, and $\Delta(\hat{y}^l, y^l; \Theta)$ is the error number between $\hat{y}^l$ and y^l.

Labeled Tree Learning. In the setting of labeled trees optimization[3], Eq. (10) for relation classification is also need to replaced by:

$$\mathcal{L}^r(\Theta) = \sum_{x \in \mathcal{X}} (\max_{\hat{y}^r \in Y^r(x)} (Score(x, \hat{y}^r; \Theta) + \Delta(\hat{y}^r, y^r; \Theta)) - Score(x, y^r; \Theta)) \quad (13)$$

---

[3] It is too hard for the model to directly learn a labeled tree by max-margin training. Therefore, we follow previous works to learn a labeled tree on its gold unlabeled tree, resulting in much better performance.

where y^r is the gold labeled tree, $\hat{y}^r$ is the predicted labeled tree with the highest scores, $Y^r(x)$ denotes all possible labeled trees of this instance, $Score(x, y^r; \Theta)$ is the sum of all gold type scores and denotes the score of the gold labeled tree y^r, $Score(x, \hat{y}^r; \Theta)$ is the sum of all type scores in the predicted labeled tree $\hat{y}^r$ and denotes the score of the predicted labeled tree, and $\Delta(\hat{y}^r, y^r; \Theta)$ is the error number between $\hat{y}^r$ and y^r.

TreeCRF Training. Similar to max-margin learning, we also need to impose a lower triangular mask on the edge score matrix and the three dimensional vector of relation type scores by Eq. (13). The goal of TreeCRF training is to maximize the probability of the golden-standard tree. It is worth noting that in this setting, the score of a tree is the product of weights of all dependency arcs in the tree.

Unlabeled Tree Training. Optimizing an unlabeled tree, for relation classification, we continue using Eq. (10) and for link prediction, we need to replace Eq. (9) with:

$$\mathcal{L}^l(\Theta) = - \sum_{x \in \mathcal{X}} logP(y^l|x; \Theta) \tag{14}$$

where $P(y^l|x; \Theta)$ is the probability of the gold standard unlabeled tree.

$$P(y^l|x; \Theta) = \frac{Score(x, y^l; \Theta)}{Z(x; \Theta)} \tag{15}$$

In order to calculate this probability value, it is necessary to calculate the molecular $Score(x, y^l; \Theta)$ and the denominator $Z(x; \Theta)$. Koo et al. [8] and Smith et al. [14] have given the method of calculating the denominator, namely the partition function, through the matrix-tree theory [15]. Here we briefly review the calculation process. Firstly, we need to apply non-negative weights to the arcs of a unidirectional directed graph, yielding the following weighted adjacency matrix $A(\Theta) \in R^{(n+1) \times (n+1)}$:

$$A_{i,j}(\Theta) = \begin{cases} 0 & \text{if } i \geq j \\ \exp\left(s_{i,j}^l\right) & \text{otherwise} \end{cases} \tag{16}$$

According to the definition [8], the score of any directed spanning tree is the product of the weights $A_{i,j}^l(\Theta)$ for the arcs in that tree:

$$Score(x, y^l; \Theta) = \prod_{(i,j) \in y^l} A_{i,j}(\Theta) \tag{17}$$

According to Koo et al. [8], the denominator value is equal to the minor of $L(\Theta)$ at (0, 0), which is L(0, 0):

$$Z(x; \Theta) = L^{(0,0)}(\Theta) \tag{18}$$

$$L(\Theta) = D(\Theta) - A(\Theta) \tag{19}$$

$$D_{i,j}(\Theta) = \begin{cases} \sum\limits_{i'=0}^{n} A_{i',j}(\Theta) & \text{if } i = j \\ 0 & \text{otherwise} \end{cases} \tag{20}$$

where $D(\Theta)$ is the weighted degree matrix, $L(\Theta)$ is the Laplacian matrix and $L^{(0,0)}(\Theta)$ is the determinant of the submatrix constructed by removing the first row and the first column of $L(\Theta)$, which denotes the sum of the scores of all possible unlabeled trees rooted at the added dummy root utterance.

Labeled Tree Training. The techniques mentioned above can be easily extended to the labeled tree. Formally, the labeled version can be easily calculated by only changing the way of obtaining weighted adjacency matrix $A(\Theta)$:

$$A_{i,j}(\Theta) = \sum_{k=0}^{16} exp(s_{i,j,k}^r) \tag{21}$$

where $s_{i,j,k}^r$ is the type score from the edge scoring module and there are 16 discourse relation types in two datasets and the added type 0 denotes to the edges where utterances are connected to dummy root. Other steps are similar to the unlabeled version. It is noted that a labeled tree can be directly learned in this setting and in other words, link prediction and relation classification can be conducted jointly. Hence, unlike previous separate training, the final loss only includes the labeled tree loss:

$$\mathcal{L}(\Theta) = \mathcal{L}^r(\Theta) \tag{22}$$

$$\mathcal{L}^r(\Theta) = -\sum_{x \in \mathcal{X}} log P(y^r | x; \Theta) \tag{23}$$

where y^r denotes the gold labeled tree, $P(y^r | x; \Theta)$ can be calculated same with the unlabeled version except the calculation of the adjacency matrix $A(\Theta)$.

3.3   Inference

In this section, we will introduce different inference methods according to different training objectives. In brief, we greedily select a parent for each utterance when optimizing local pair independently but we use Chu-Liu-Edmonds to decode an unlabeled maximum spanning tree or modified Chu-Liu-Edmonds for labeled maximum spanning tree in the setting of global optimization.

Greedy Inference. For each utterance u_i, we will choose the parent with the highest score:

$$p_i = \underset{j \in [0, i-1]}{argmax}(s_{i,j}^l) \tag{24}$$

where $s_{i,j}^l$ is from edge scoring, the parent of u_i is prior to u_i and p_i denotes the predicted parent of u_i.

After identifying the dependency link, we will greedily choose the relation type with the highest score. Assuming the predicted parent is u_j, i.e., $p_i = u_j$, this step can be formalized as:

$$r_{ji} = \underset{k \in [0,16]}{argmax}(s^r_{i,j,k}) \tag{25}$$

where $s^r_{i,j,k}$ is from edge scoring, 17 types are contained in two datasets and r_{ji} denotes the predicted relation type between u_j and u_i.

Unlabeled Tree Inference. Because of the presence of crossing dependencies in the dialogue, the structure is better represented by non-projective trees, and Chu-Liu-Edmonds is a typical algorithm for non-projective tree parsing. Here we list the execution process.

Algorithm 1: Chu-Liu-Edmonds

   Input   : G: Directed Weighted Graph $G = (V, E)$
                  Score: Edge Weight Function *Score*
   Output: G_M: The Maximum Spanning Tree of G
1 initialization: $M \leftarrow []$;
2 **for** v *in* V **do**
3 | $v^* = argmax_{v'} Score(v', v)$;
4 | $M = M \cup (v^*, v)$;
5 **end**
6 $G_M = (V, M)$;
7 **if** G_M *has no cycles* **then**
8 | **return** G_M;
9 **else**
10 | find a cycle C in G_M;
11 | $G_C = $ contract$(G, C, Score)$;
12 | $y = $ Chu-Liu-Edmonds$(G_C, Score)$;
13 | $G_M = $ expand(y, C);
14 | **return** G_M;
15 **end**

It is worth noting that dependency arcs in dialogues have the same direction, so for each utterance node, after finding its highest-scoring incoming edge, it is impossible to form a cycle so that the algorithm ends at step 8 without executing the branch in the *else* statement.

In summary, this algorithm can be simplified as greedily selecting the head with the highest score for each utterance.

Labeled Tree Inference. The labeled tree inference is only used in directly predicting a labeled tree, i.e., in the setting of TreeCRF training of labeled trees.

To get a highest-scoring labeled tree, we have to first choose the type with the highest type score in $S^r \in (n+1) \times (n+1) \times |c|$ to get $\widetilde{S^r} \in (n+1) \times (n+1)$:

$$\widetilde{s^r_{i,j}} = \max_k(s^r_{i,j,k}) \tag{26}$$

where $\widetilde{s^r_{i,j}}$ and $s^r_{i,j,k}$ denote any item in $\widetilde{S^r}$ and S^r separately.

Then $\widetilde{S^r}$ can be feed into Chu-Liu-Edmonds to find the highest-scoring tree. This approach is easy to prove by contradiction: suppose that the optimal labeled tree contains an arc whose score is not the highest, then the arc can be substituted with the highest-scoring one to get a better tree (contradiction) [4].

4   Experiments

4.1   Experimental Settings

Molweni [9] and STAC [2] are used in our experiments. There are 9000, 500 and 500 dialogues collected from an online forum for training, validation and testing in Molweni. There are 1062 and 111 dialogues collected from an online game for training and testing in STAC. We preprocess these two datasets following Chi and Rudnicky [4] and RoBERTa-Base uncased pretrained checkpoint is used for a fair comparison. The learning rate of RoBERTa-Base is set to 2e–5 and the learning rate of other modules is set to 3e–4. The epoch number is set differently on Molweni and STAC, 10 and 20 respectively. To prevent overfitting, the L2 is set to 0.01. For stable training, warmup strategy is adopted and its radio is set to 0.1. We optimize model parameters by AdamW.

4.2   Baselines

We compare our work with following single-task and multi-task models.

Single-task: **MST** [1]: It first calculates local probability between two utterances and then decodes a tree by maximum spanning tree algorithm. **ILP** [12]: It can get a more general DAG structure by integer linear programming. **DeepSequential** [13]: It predicts dependency relations and construct a dialogue structure alternatively and jointly. **Hierarchical** [11]: It proposes a hierarchical utterance encoding model. **SSA** [16]: To avoid error propagation in DeepSequential [13], it extracts implicit structural features by edge-centric fully connected graphs. **DAMT** [6]: It combines the advantages of graph-based and transition-based paradigms to enhance utterance representations. **SA_DPMD** [18]: It extracts features from the same speaker and different speakers to get speaker-aware utterance representations. **BERTLine** [3]:It uses a BERT-based double-headed multi-task learning model. **DialogueDP** [10]:It combines bottom-up and top-down parsing strategies through a two-way self-supervision mechanism. **SDDP** [4]: It conducts global optimization during both training and inference.

Multi-task: **DiscProReco** [17],**DPRC** [7],**TST** [5] : These models are jointly learned with dropped pronoun recovery, dialogue reading comprehension and addressee recognition separately.

Table 1. Performance comparison. US and LS denotes unlabeled tree optimization and labeled tree optimization.

Model		Molweni		STAC	
		Link	Link&Rel	Link	Link&Rel
Single-Task	ChatGPT	59.9	25.3	63.8	23.9
	MST	69.0	48.7	69.6	52.1
	ILP	67.3	48.3	69.0	53.1
	DeepSequential	76.1	53.3	73.2	54.4
	Hierarchical	80.1	56.1	73.1	57.1
	SSA	81.6	58.4	73.4	57.3
	DAMT	82.5	58.9	73.6	57.4
	SA_DPMD	83.7	59.4	73.0	57.4
	BERTLine	–	–	73.1	56.3
	DialogueDP	83.2	59.8	73.0	58.5
	SDDP	83.5	59.9	74.4	59.6
Multi-Task	DiscProReco	–	–	74.1	57.0
	DPRC	80.0	57.0	–	–
	TST	**85.3**	**60.9**	73.7	57.6
Ours	Local	83.3	59.2	73.3	57.1
	Max-Margin(US)	84.0	59.7	75.1	59.8
	Max-Margin(LS)	83.3	59.1	**76.2**	**59.8**
	TreeCRF(US)	84.0	60.0	75.3	59.3
	TreeCRF(LS)	82.9	59.5	74.7	59.1

4.3 Main Results

Table 1 shows the main results of our model with different training objectives as well as previous dialogue discourse parsers.

Firstly, compared with single-task and multi-task baselines, the model with different optimization methods on Molweni and STAC has achieved comparable results, and even Max-Margin (LS) has achieved the best results.

Secondly, taking a look at local optimization and global optimization, i.e. comparing Local and Max-Margin/TreeCRF(US/LS), on Molweni, whether it is TreeCRF or Max-Margin, global optimization of unlabeled trees or labeled trees, the results are comparable to local optimzation. However, on STAC, the results of all global optimization methods are much higher than those of local optimization. This may be related to the data characteristics of the two datasets. This will be discussed in 4.4.

4.4 Analysis

Intuitively, global optimization is better at parsing structures of long dialogues than local optimization, because it can parse the dialogue structure from a global perspective, thereby reducing the difficulty of predicting long-distance dependencies. Therefore, this paper analyzes the length of macro-dialogue and the distance of micro-dependency respectively.

Table 2. Comparison of Link&Rel across different length intervals in the test set of Molweni and STAC.

Models	Molweni		STAC			
	<=10	<=20	<=10	<=20	<=30	<=40
Local	59.3	59.0	72.6	55.3	44.1	35.8
Max-margin(US)	**60.1**	58.9	74.5	**58.3**	46.0	**42.1**
Max-margin(LS)	59.4	58.3	74.0	57.7	**48.9**	39.6
TreeCRF(US)	60.0	**60.0**	**74.6**	57.3	47.3	37.4
TreeCRF(LS)	59.5	59.3	73.4	56.9	47.6	40.8

Table 3. Comparison of Link&Rel on short-distance dependencies ($=1$) and long-distance dependencies (>1) in the test set of Molweni and STAC.

Models	Molweni		STAC	
	1	>1	1	>1
Local	66.9	42.4	65.7	43.2
Max-margin(US)	66.8	44.6	67.6	46.7
Max-margin(LS)	66.2	44.0	67.1	**48.0**
TreeCRF(US)	**67.0**	**44.9**	**67.9**	45.8
TreeCRF(LS)	66.7	43.2	67.2	46.5

From Table 2, we can find that all models show a decreasing tendency, especially on STAC, which indicates that it is more challenging to parse the structure when the dialogue becomes longer. Global optimization does not show any prominent advantage over local optimization on Molweni whose dialogues are all brief and concentrated between 7 and 14 utterances. However, on all length intervals, all global optimization methods perform much better than local optimization on STAC whose dialogues vary greatly in length. In terms of dialogue length, the results of local and global optimization are greatly influenced by the characteristics of the dataset itself.

From Table 3, we can find that it is relatively difficult to predict long-distance dependency relations. Another important finding is that all global optimization methods perform much better on long-distance dependency relation classification on both Molweni and STAC, which indicates that global optimization can lower the burden of the parser to predict long-distance dependencies.

5   Conclusion

In this paper, we realize local optimization and global optimization during both training and inference, and compare the influences of local optimization and global optimization. Experiments show that the results of local and global optimization are greatly influenced by the characteristic of the dataset and global optimization performs much better on predicting long-distance dependency relations. In the future, we will continue to explore domain adaptation in order to better parse real-world conversations.

Acknowledgments. This work was supported by the Project 62276178 under the National Natural Science Foundation of China, the Key Project 23KJA520012 under the Natural Science Foundation of Jiangsu Higher Education Institutions and the Priority Academic Program Development of Jiangsu Higher Education Institutions.

Disclosure of Interests. The authors have no competing interests to declare that are relevant to the content of this article.

References

1. Afantenos, S., Kow, E., Asher, N., Perret, J.: Discourse parsing for multi-party chat dialogues. In: Proceedings of the 2015 Conference on Empirical Methods in Natural Language Processing (2015)
2. Asher, N., Hunter, J., Morey, M., Benamara, F., Afantenos, S.: Discourse structure and dialogue acts in multiparty dialogue: the STAC corpus. In: 10th International Conference on Language Resources and Evaluation (LREC 2016), pp. 2721–2727 (2016)
3. Bennis, Z., Hunter, J., Asher, N.: A simple but effective model for attachment in discourse parsing with multi-task learning for relation labeling. In: 17th Conference of the European Chapter of the Association for Computational Linguistics (EACL 2023), pp. 3412–3417. ACL (2023)
4. Chi, T.C., Rudnicky, A.: Structured dialogue discourse parsing. In: Proceedings of the 23rd Annual Meeting of the Special Interest Group on Discourse and Dialogue, pp. 325–335 (2022)
5. Fan, Y., Jiang, F., Li, P., Kong, F., Zhu, Q.: Improving dialogue discourse parsing via reply-to structures of addressee recognition. In: Proceedings of the 2023 Conference on Empirical Methods in Natural Language Processing, pp. 8484–8495 (2023)
6. Fan, Y., Li, P., Kong, F., Zhu, Q.: A distance-aware multi-task framework for conversational discourse parsing. In: Proceedings of the 29th International Conference on Computational Linguistics, pp. 912–921 (2022)
7. He, Y., Zhang, Z., Zhao, H.: Multi-tasking dialogue comprehension with discourse parsing (2021)
8. Koo, T., Globerson, A., Carreras Pérez, X., Collins, M.: Structured prediction models via the matrix-tree theorem. In: Joint Conference on Empirical Methods in Natural Language Processing and Computational Natural Language Learning (EMNLP-CoNLL), pp. 141–150 (2007)
9. Li, J., et al.: Molweni: a challenge multiparty dialogues-based machine reading comprehension dataset with discourse structure. arXiv preprint arXiv:2004.05080 (2020)
10. Li, W., Zhu, L., Shao, W., Yang, Z., Cambria, E.: Task-aware self-supervised framework for dialogue discourse parsing. In: Findings of the Association for Computational Linguistics: EMNLP 2023, pp. 14162–14173 (2023)
11. Liu, Z., Chen, N.F.: Improving multi-party dialogue discourse parsing via domain integration. arXiv e-prints (2021)
12. Perret, J., Afantenos, S., Asher, N., Morey, M.: Integer linear programming for discourse parsing. In: Proceedings of the 2016 Conference of the North American Chapter of the Association for Computational Linguistics: Human Language Technologies (2016)

13. Shi, Z., Huang, M.: A deep sequential model for discourse parsing on multi-party dialogues. In: Proceedings of the AAAI Conference on Artificial Intelligence, vol. 33, pp. 7007–7014 (2019)
14. Smith, D.A., Smith, N.A.: Probabilistic models of nonprojective dependency trees. In: EMNLP-CoNLL 2007, Proceedings of the 2007 Joint Conference on Empirical Methods in Natural Language Processing and Computational Natural Language Learning, June 28-30, 2007, Prague, Czech Republic (2007)
15. Tutte, W.: Graph theory, encyclopedia of mathematics and it applications (1984)
16. Wang, A., et al.: A structure self-aware model for discourse parsing on multi-party dialogues. In: International Joint Conference on Artificial Intelligence (2021)
17. Yang, J., Xu, K., Xu, J., Li, S., Wen, J.R.: A joint model for dropped pronoun recovery and conversational discourse parsing in chinese conversational speech. In: Proceedings of the 59th Annual Meeting of the Association for Computational Linguistics and the 11th International Joint Conference on Natural Language Processing (Volume 1: Long Papers) (2021)
18. Yu, N., Fu, G., Zhang, M.: Speaker-aware discourse parsing on multi-party dialogues. In: Proceedings of the 29th International Conference on Computational Linguistics, pp. 5372–5382 (2022)

Structure and Behavior Dual-Graph Reasoning with Integrated Key-Clue Parsing for Multi-party Dialogue Reading Comprehension

Rui Cao, Xiabing Zhou$^{(\boxtimes)}$, and Guodong Zhou

School of Computer Science and Technology, Soochow University, Suzhou, China
rcaocaorui@stu.suda.edu.cn, {zhouxiabing,gdzhou}@suda.edu.cn

Abstract. Multi-party Dialogue Reading Comprehension is a reading comprehension task that involves comprehending dialogue with multiple interlocutors and answering questions. Research on MDRC faces enormous challenges because of the multiple parties involved and the frequent changes in the chat topic. Previous work has explored in mining and modeling dialogue context features on the basis of pre-trained models and graph-based models. However, two issues exist: insufficient connection between the behavioral events of dialogue participants and excessive information irrelevant to the question during reasoning. In this paper, we propose a dual-graph reasoning with integrated key-clue parsing approach. We utilize the dual-graph reasoning strategy to capture the global structure and internal dynamics of the dialogue. Moreover, we design the key-clue parsing module to prioritize essential dialogue content, which significantly reduces the burden on the model and enhances the accuracy of our model. The experiments on the benchmark dataset show that our approach yields stable and substantial improvements, and outperforms the state-of-the-art methods.

Keywords: Multi-party Dialogue Reading Comprehension ·
Structure-aware Graph · Behavior-aware Graph · Key-Clue Parsing

1 Introduction

Multi-party Dialogue Reading Comprehension (MDRC) aims at comprehending and answering questions according to the whole dialogue with multiple participants. Distinct from traditional Machine Reading Comprehension (MRC), MDRC has the following characteristics: (i) Its intricate discourse structure arises from the frequent switch in interlocutors and shifting chat topics. As depicted in Fig. 1, U_4 alters the topic and responds to U_2, resulting in a dialogue process with multiple information flows. For Question 1, the model must attend to the structural relationship between U_0 and U_1 to arrive at an answer. (ii) The unique expression intent and style of each interlocutor introduce complex co-referential

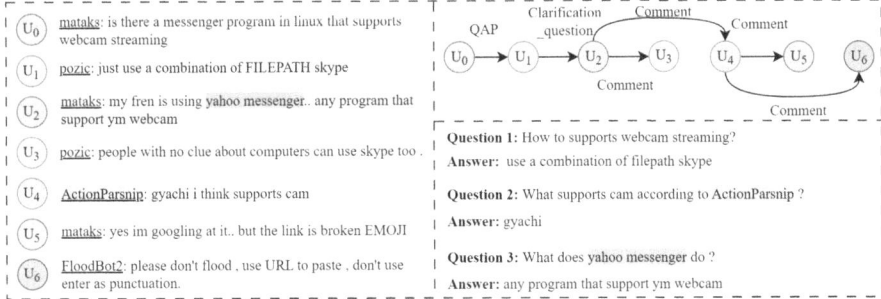

Fig. 1. An example of multi-party dialogue

information into the dialogue. Managing these referential relations and analyzing speaker behavior enhances contextual comprehension. For instance, both "ActionParsnip" in Question 2 and "i" in U_4 refer to the same speaker "ActionParsnip" (marked in green). The answer "gyachi" is tied to the specific actions of "ActionParsnip". (iii) Answers tend to occur in utterances that resemble the question. For instance, U_2 contains the answer "any program that supports ym webcam" for Question 3, which is highly similar to the question itself (marked in red).

Currently, some progress has been made in the work regarding MDRC. The pre-trained models, such as BERT, have shown effective performance [6,25,29]. These models, when incorporated with speaker information, structure information, or co-attentive mechanisms, demonstrate efficient contextual modeling. Further, graph-based models have emerged as a suitable approach for dialogue tasks, due to their ability to naturally represent and manipulate complex relationships within a dialogue [4,11,19]. Li et al. [13] and Ma et al. [9] have successfully utilized Graph Convolutional Networks (GCN) and Graph Attention Networks (GAT) to capture structural information in dialogue contexts.

However, two phenomena still have not been well considered: (i) The lack of connectivity among the behavior events of dialogue participants across the entire dialogue, which is crucial for capturing nuanced details and comprehending extensive dialogue content. (ii) The reasoning process often involves excessive irrelevant information, adding unnecessary complexity to the model's modeling process.

Accordingly, we propose a Dual-Graph Reasoning with Integrated Key-Clue Parsing (DGKC) model. It encodes two graphs: a structure-aware graph that captures global structural interaction and a role behavior-aware graph that retrieves rich content interaction. The structure-aware graph leverages conversational discourse structures to associate utterances spanning the entire dialogue. Meanwhile, the role behavior-aware graph models the behavioral events of dialogue participants, facilitating an understanding of the content details within the utterances. It further utilizes coreference resolution to integrate global dialogue content interaction. Moreover, to prioritize essential dialogue content, we conduct key-clue parsing by considering the question context, enabling the model to consciously attend to crucial dialogue segments. We have validated our proposed method on a public dataset, and the results demonstrated that our approach achieved superior performance, effectively capturing the inter-dependencies and correlations among the behavioral events of dialogue participants. Additionally, considering the relevance of the question can also help extract key content.

In summary, our contributions include: (i) We propose dual-graph reasoning strategy to mining the global structure and features of the dialogue, which helps capture the dialogue dynamics more comprehensively and accurately, and enables the model to produce a more informed and effective understanding. (ii) We design key-clue parsing to prioritize essential dialogue content, enabling the model to consciously attend to crucial dialogue segments. This significantly reduces the burden on the model and enhances the accuracy of answer prediction. (iii) Experimental results on a dataset with the MDRC task show that the model proposed in this paper substantially outperforms a powerful baseline model.

2   Related Work

We briefly overview the related work for MDRC in this section.

Multi-party Dialogue Modeling. Recent studies have shown that MDRC is more complex than traditional MRC [2, 5, 28]. In MDRC, each utterance includes the speaker's role, disrupting the flow found in non-dialogue texts. Past research has focused on modeling speakers and discourse structures to solve referential issues in dialogues. RAMPNet [7] address the unique aspects of multiparty dialogues by integrating role and speaker information into the dialogue. Li and Zhao [14] use self-supervised tasks to identify key dialogue elements. BiDeN [15] is designed to capture the temporal features of dialogue. Li et al. [12] develop CADA, which profiles utterances and models interactions, allowing for their combination.

Graph-Based Models. Graph-based models are popular in dialogue modeling for their ability to handle complex interactions [24, 27, 33] For the MDRC, Liu et al. [16] create a "relation graph" to structure dialogue, using edges to show relationships between utterances. Hu et al. [8] introduced a Graph-Structured neural Network (GSN) to track information flow for the same speakers. Li et al. [11] apply GCN to conduct graph reasoning by using discourse dependency links. Recently, Li et al. [9] develop QuISG to connect questions, speakers, and utterances. Ma et al. [19] created two heterogeneous graph networks to capture speaker properties and discourse relations. Li et al. [13] propose a question-aware reasoning approach, moving from a global graph to local details. Gao et al. [4] use a hierarchical graph convolutional neural network to model explicit dialogue information.

Different from the previous work, our model better captures the latent semantics and intent information in the dialogue context, and performs dual-graph joint reasoning for the global structure and internal details.

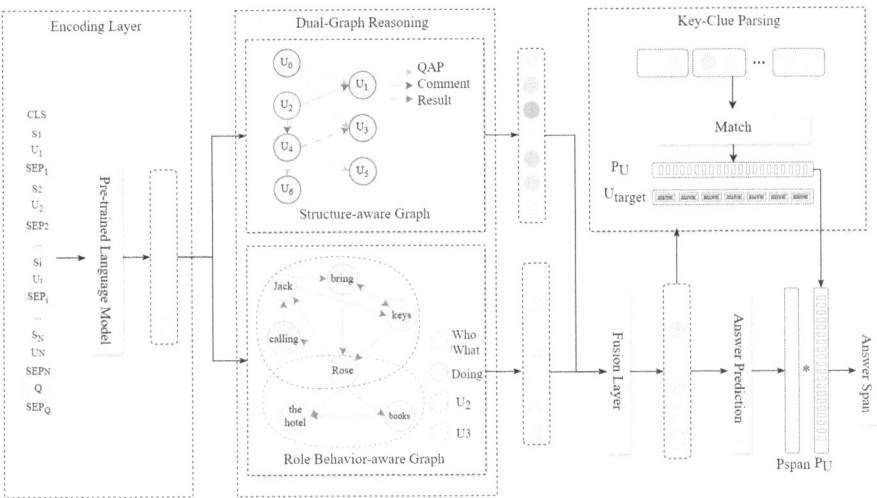

Fig. 2. An overview of DGKC. It contains (i) the PLM for encoding, (ii) the Dual-Graph Reasoning module, (iii) the Key-Clue Parsing, Fusion Layer, and Answer Prediction module. The behavioral structures generated by U_2 and U_3 in the Role Behavior-aware graph are marked with different colored dashes. They share the common node "Rose," indicating the co-referential links among utterances.

3   Method

The general architecture of our model is shown in Fig. 2, and we will introduce it in the following sections.

3.1   Encoding Layer

First of all, we obtain the preliminary representation by concatenating the dialogue $D = \{U_0, U_1, ..., U_N\}$ with N utterances and a corresponding question Q. Specifically, we form the input sequence X using special tokens $[CLS]$ and $[SEP]$ as follow:

$$X = \{[CLS], Q, [SEP], U_0, [SEP], U_1, \ldots, U_N, [SEP]\} \tag{1}$$

Then, the input sequence is fed into a Pre-trained Language Model (PLM) to gain its contextualized representation $H_c \in R^{n \times d}$, where n represents the length of the input sequence and d represents the dimension of hidden state.

3.2   Dual-Graph Reasoning

To provide a more precise answer, it is imperative to have a thorough understanding of both the discourse structure and the content of dialogue. The discourse structure aids in comprehending the coherence and flow of the dialogue, as well as the interactive relationships between the utterances. Meanwhile, analyzing the roles and actions within the dialogue establishes a global connection between the participants, their behaviors, and the events mentioned, thereby capturing the context internal details and enhancing the comprehension of the overall content. Therefore, we propose the dual-graph reasoning to capture the structure and behavior information through the structure-aware graph and role behavior-aware graph.

Structure-Aware Graph. The utterances in a dialogue exhibit coherence, and analyzing the discourse structure aids in understanding global utterance interactions. Molweni dataset [10] provides discourse structure annotations with 16 relation types, such as QAP (Question-answer pair), Comment, etc. Based on these, we build a structure-aware graph $G_s = (V_s, E_s)$, where each utterance U_i is represented as a vertex $v_i^s \in V_s$ and edge e_{ij}^s represent annotated relation r_{ij} between v_i^s and v_j^s. Figure 2 exemplifies this with a five-vertex graph, showing three discourse relations, where vertices are utterances, edges represent natural connections, and edge types correspond to annotated relations.

After constructing structure-aware graph, we utilize the two-layer graph convolution operation to aggregate the utterances and corresponding discourse relations [26]. The formula is as follows:

$$
\begin{aligned}
h_i^{(1)} &= \sigma \left(\sum_{r \in R} \sum_{j \in N_i^r} \frac{1}{c_{i,r}} W_r^{(1)} v_j^s + W_0^{(1)} v_i^s \right) \\
h_i^{(2)} &= \sigma \left(\sum_{j \in N_i^r} W^{(2)} h_j^{(1)} + W_0^{(2)} h_j^{(1)} \right)
\end{aligned}
\tag{2}
$$

where, N_i^r is the set of neighbours of vertex v_i^s connected by relation r, and R is the set of relations. $c_{i,r}$ is the element number of N_i^r used for normalization. We use trainable parameter matrices $W_r^{(1)}, W_0^{(1)}, W^{(2)}, W_0^{(2)}$ and an activation function σ to perform message passing between related vertices. This results in a discourse structure-aware feature vector $H_s \in R^{N \times d}$ for N utterance unites.

Role Behavior-Aware Graph. Role behavior-aware graph is proposed to understand the content information in dialogue, including dialogue participants and the behaviors they have done. To better extract specific details of what is happening in the dialogue, we follow these steps:

1) Replace the first/second person pronouns with the speakers' name;
2) Utilize FastCoref [22] to replace all third-person pronouns in the co-reference clusters of the dialogue;
3) Extract "Who-Doing-What" triples using the OpenIE system [1].

For example, combining contextual information of the dialogue, an sentence "I will book it with you tomorrow" is transformed into "Jack will book the hotel with Rose tomorrow", and triples that match the "WHO-DOING-WHAT" structure, like "(Jack, book, the hotel)" and "(Jack, book, with Rose)" are extracted. Those "Who-Doing-What" triples are word-level structural information that provides an explicit visualization of the dialogue participants and their behaviors.

Based on the extracted triples, we build a role behavior-aware graph $G_b = (V_b, E_b)$, where V_b represents triple nodes. The representation of each vertex $v_i^b \in V_b$, denoted by h_i, can be obtained from the encoding H_c. Edge e_{ij}^b is set to 1 if two nodes v_i^b and v_j^b belong to the same triad. We then apply GAT [31] to propagate and aggregate messages between nodes in the graph, which is calculated as follows:

$$h_i^{(l+1)} = \Sigma_{j \in N_i} \alpha_{ij}^{(l)} W^{(l)} h_j^{(l)}$$
$$\alpha_{ij}^{(l)} = \frac{\exp\left(f\left(\left[h_i^{(l)}; h_j^{(l)}\right], W_0^{(l)}\right)\right)}{\Sigma_{h_k \in N_i} \exp\left(f\left(\left[h_i^{(l)}; h_k^{(l)}\right], W_0^{(l)}\right)\right)} \qquad (3)$$

where N_i represents the neighbors of vertex v_i^b. α_{ij} measures the attention between h_i and h_j. GAT computes this attention at each layer l by concatenating h_i and h_j, passing them through a LeakyReLU [20] activation function, and multiplying by trainable parameters $W^{(l)}$ and $W_0^{(l)}$. After L layers of GAT, we get h_i^L, which represents the hidden state of all tokens in node i. Collecting these for all nodes gives us the role behavior-aware feature vector $H_b = \left\{h_i^L \in R^d\right\}_{i=1}^m$ where m is the total number of nodes.

Fusion Layer. From the dual-graph construction, we obtain utterance-level representation H_s and token-level representation H_b. To better fuse the multi-feature, we first extend H_s and H_b to token-level representation so that they are aligned with H_c. Then, we use the attention mechanism for two-way integration, combine the role behavior information with discourse structure information, and obtain the represented by H_s' and H_b', respectively. This method effectively integrates two pieces of information to improve the understanding and expression of the conversation content. Finally, we concatenate H_c, H_s' and H_b' to obtain the o obtain the feature representation H that contains the global structure and internal details of the dialogue context by $H = [H_c, H_s', H_b']$.

3.3 Key-Clue Parsing

Using the contextualized representation H from Sect. 3.2, we collect the $[SEP]$ token representations and use them as the utterance representations in the dialogue context, initializing N utterance nodes $H_U = \left\{H_{Ui} \in R^d\right\}_{i=1}^N$ and a question node $h_Q \in R^d$. Then, h_Q is paired with each H_{Ui} to implement the key-clue parsing task. Specifically, inspired by the heuristic matching mechanism [21], we define a matching function $Match(X, Y, \sigma)$ to calculate the matching scores s,

$$G = [X; Y; X - Y; X \odot Y] \in R^{N \times 4d}$$
$$s = \sigma\left(aG^T\right) \in R^N \qquad (4)$$

Here, $\odot$ denotes element-by-element multiplication, $a \in R^{4d}$ is a vector with trainable weights, and σ is an activation function to obtain a probability distribution according to the downstream loss function, which can be chosen from *softmax* and *sigmoid*. We set the key-clue parsing target based on the start and end positions of the answer span, and define $U^{target} = i$ as the target, where i is the index of the utterance containing the answer span. We calculate the probability distribution of key clues by $P_U^{pred} = Match(H_U, H_Q, soft \max)$, where $H_Q \in R^{N \times d}$ is extended by h_Q. The loss function is:

$$L_u = -\log \left(P_U^{pred} \left[U^{target} \right] \right) \tag{5}$$

We extend $P_U^{pred} \in R^N$ to the length of the token-level representation yields, denoted as $P_U^{extend} \in R^n$, which will be fed into the Answer Prediction and Training Module to filter noisy utterances in the fused representation.

3.4 Answer Prediction and Training

The MDRC task finally needs to locate the position of the answer, thus we get the answer span by:

$$P_{start} = soft \max \left(W_{start}^T H \right) \odot P_U^{extend}$$
$$P_{end} = soft \max \left(W_{end}^T H \right) \odot P_U^{extend} \tag{6}$$

where W_{start}^T and W_{end}^T are trainable weight vectors, $P_U^{\exp end}$ is defined in Sect. 2.4, and $\odot$ represents element-by-element multiplication. In addition, considering that there are some questions that cannot be answered, we have added a judgment on the existence of the answer. At last, the loss function for answer span L_{span} and answer existence L_a are derived from the cross-entropy. The overall training objective of our model is $L = L_{span} + L_a + L_u$.

4 Experiments

4.1 Experimental Setting

Dataset. We train and evaluate our model on a MDRC dataset, Molweni, which is constructed by Li et al. [10] and widely used in MDRC. It includes 9,754 conversations, 30,066 questions and 78,245 discourse relations, which is a large-scale and the most popular dataset in the field of MDRC. We follow the common practice [4,10,13] to split it into the training, validation and test sets, and use EM-score and F1-score as the evaluation.

Baseline and Compared Models. We use BERT-Base-Uncased ($BERT_{base}$) and BERT-Large-Uncased ($BERT_{large}$) [3] as baseline. To verify the effectiveness of our model, we compare the following existing models, including **SKIDB** [14], **BiDeN** [15], **CADA** [12], and graph-based models **DAD-graph** [11], **ESA** [19], **Dis-QueGCN** [4], **GLGR** [13].

Implementation Details. All models are implemented based on Transformers [32]. Exact Matching (EM) and F1 scores are the metrics to measure performance. Fine-tuning was performed using the AdamW optimizer [18]. For experiments on the Molweni dataset, we set the batch size to 2 for $BERT_{base}$ and 4 for

Table 1. Experimental results on Molweni

Model	$BERT_{base}$		$BERT_{large}$	
	EM	F1	EM	F1
Baseline	45.3	58.0	52.3	65.7
DADGraph [11]	46.5	61.5	–	–
SKIDB [14]	49.2	64.0	–	–
BiDeN [15]	48.1	63.2	–	–
CADA [12]	**49.9**	63.9	52.9	67.6
ESA [19]	49.7	**64.4**	52.9	66.9
Dis-QueGCN [4]	47.7	63.6	–	–
GLGR [13]	48.2	**64.4**	53.7	67.5
DGKC (Ours)	**49.9**	63.9	**53.8**	**67.8**

We only show the results presented in the published papers.
The bold values indicate the best result.

$BERT_{large}$. The learning rates of $BERT_{base}$ and $BERT_{large}$ are set to 1.8e-5 and 1.6e-5, respectively.

4.2 Main Results

The results of the comparison experiments between our model and the related models are shown in Table 1. When we use $BERT_{base}$ as the backbone, our model achieves 49.9% and 63.9% in EM-score and F1-score, which outperforms the baseline model. Although the F1 score is close to the ESA model, the EM value of our model remains competitive, demonstrating its ability to precisely capture and extract core information from dialogue for high-matching answers. Moreover, DGKC exhibits significant improvements over $BERT_{large}$, notably outperforming most of the state-of-the-art MDRC models.

4.3 Analysis

Ablation Study We performed an ablation analysis to assess the impact of each module. By removing the Structure-ware Graph, Role behavior-aware Graph, and Key-Clue Parsing modules from DGKC, we observe distinct effects on performance. Similarly, adding these modules to the baselines highlights their individual contributions. As shown in Table 2, all three modules enhance the final performance of DGKC, with the Key-Clue Parsing module contributing the most. This is because dialogue contexts in Molweni are short with less turns, where key clues are crucial for answering questions. Both the Structure-ware Graph and Role behavior-aware Graph improve the baselines by approximately 1.5% in EM and 1.8% in F1, demonstrating their comparable and essential contributions.

Analysis on Different Speaker and Utterance Number. Figure 3 illustrates the performance of our model on Molweni varies with the number of speakers and utterances. For smaller numbers, the baseline and our model perform

Table 2. Results of ablation study

Model	EM	F1
$DGKC$ ($BERT_{base}$)	**49.9**	**63.9**
-Structure-aware Graph	47.9	61.2
-Role behavior-aware Graph	48.4	62.1
-Key-Clue Parsing	47.8	61.2
$BERT_{base}$	45.3	58.0
+Structure-aware Graph	47.2	61.4
+Role behavior-aware Graph	47.3	61.5
+Key-Clue Parsing	48.6	63.2

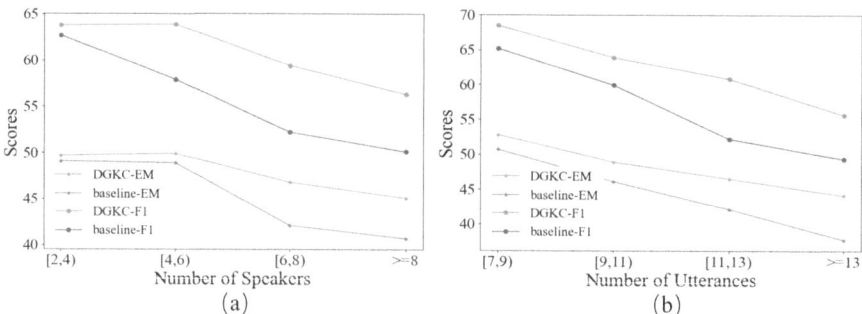

Fig. 3. Results on different (a) speaker numbers or (b) utterance numbers

similarly. However, with a large number of speakers and utterances, performance declines for both models due to increased noise. Notably, the performance gap widens as the number of speakers and utterances grows, indicating the robustness of our model in handling more complex dialogue environments.

Analysis on Different Interrogative Words. To further analyze the performance of DGKC, we evaluate its improvement on questions with different interrogative words, including *Who, How, Why, Where*, and *What*, categorizing "Whose" under "Who". Table 3 summarizes the score of $BERT_{base}$ and our model for each question type, revealing the following insights: (i) DGKC improves performance across all question types, which is consistent with our main experiment. (ii) *Who* questions have the most improved scores (9.1 EM and 11.1 F1). We consider the Role Behavior Graph Reasoning module to be a major contributor to the *Who* questions, because it performs co-referential parsing and gives the model insight into the speaker's behavior. In addition, the benefits of modeling discourse structure are mainly seen in *How* questions, because it enhances the model's ability to reason among utterances. And we believe that the Key Clues Parsing module helps solve most of the questions well, because it enhances the connection between the question and context of the dialogue. (iii) Both models struggle with *How* and *Why* questions, requiring attention to multiple utterances and a deep understanding of relevant context.

Table 3. Results on questions with different interrogative words

Type	Pro.	EM	F1
What	74.6%	49.9(↑ 1.5)	64.9(↑ 3.6)
How	8.3%	45.8(↑ 8.7)	54.9(↑ 4.4)
Why	4.4%	40.1(↑ 1.8)	55.2(↑ 3.8)
Where	4.3%	51.9(↑ 0.7)	62.9(↑ 2.2)
Who	3.8%	49.6(↑ 9.1)	61.3(↑ 11.1)

4.4 Case Study

In this section, following early work, we analyze a test case from the Molweni dataset and compare the result with the baseline. Figure 4 shows one of the results. While the baseline failed to match the ground truth, our model accurately predicted the answer span. According to the discourse dependencies and co-referential information (such as words highlighted in blue in the context) existing between U5 and U6, as well as the behavioral structures of *Gabz* and *mbd* that are represented in the role-behavior-aware graph, our model strengthens token connections utilizing the dual-graph-reasoning module. Additionally, our model incorporate the key clues probability distribution predicted by the key-clue parsing module (highlighted in the heatmap, U5 and U6 are the most critical clues), and derives the answer span prediction.

4.5 LLMs for MDRC

The development of large models has impacted many tasks in the field of natural language processing [17,23,30], but their capabilities on MDRC remains to be explored. To preliminarily evaluate their performance on MDRC tasks, we experiment with three representative LLMs (ChatGPT[1] LLaMA-2-13b-chat3[2] LLaMA-2-7b4[3]) in zero-shot mode on Molweni. Given that the mentioned models are generative and may yield non-answer content, we consider a model's output correct if it includes the answer. Our experiments show that ChatGPT, LLaMA-2-13b-chat3, and LLaMA-2-7b4 achieved accuracies of 52%, 40.9%, and 40.6%, respectively, lagging behind our model's 67.9%. This may be attributed to: (i) the technical nature of the Molweni dataset, which even humans struggle with, affecting the zero-shot performance of LLMs. (ii) our tailored modeling strategy for MDRC, which enables a deeper understanding of specialized dialogues. LLMs require more task-specific prompts to enhance their performance.

---

[1] https://openai.com/blog/chatgpt/.
[2] https://huggingface.co/meta-llama/Llama-2-13bchat.
[3] https://huggingface.co/meta-llama/Llama-2-7b.

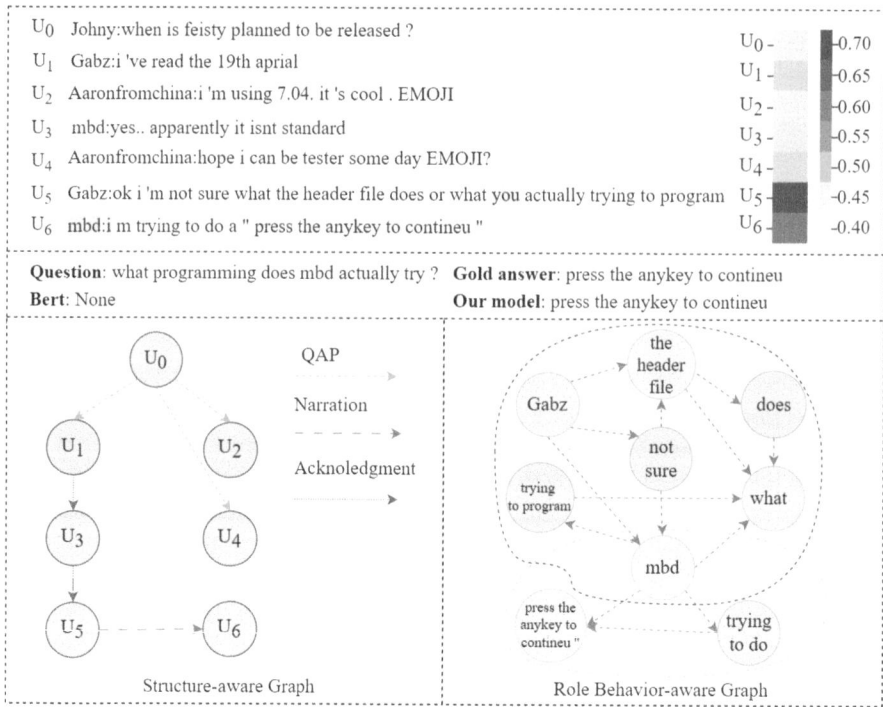

Fig. 4. A case study for DGKC. It shows the structure-aware graph of the dialogue and portion of the role behavior-aware graph. The heatmap shows the probability distribution of the key clues.

5   Conclusion

We propose a dual-graph reasoning with integrated key-clue parsing approach towards MDRC, which captures the global discourse structure and behavioral event interaction. Experimental results show that our method demonstrates stable and substantial improvements when adopting different PLMs as backbones, and achieves state-of-the-art results. We analyze the contribution of each module through ablation studies. Moreover, we investigate the effect of data features on the model performance, including the number of speakers and utterances, the type of interrogative words. The case study and corresponding visualization validate the effectiveness of our model.

References

1. Angeli, G., Johnson Premkumar, M.J., Manning, C.D.: Leveraging linguistic structure for open domain information extraction. In: ACL 2015, July 26-31, 2015, Beijing, China, pp. 344–354. The Association for Computer Linguistics (2015)
2. Asher, N., Hunter, J., Morey, M., Benamara, F., Afantenos, S.: Discourse structure and dialogue acts in multiparty dialogue: the STAC corpus. In: LREC 2016, Portorož, Slovenia, pp. 2721–2727. ELRA (2016)
3. Devlin, J., Chang, M.W., Lee, K., Toutanova, K.: Bert: pre-training of deep bidirectional transformers for language understanding. In: NAACL-HLT 2019, Minneapolis, MN, USA, pp. 4171–4186. Association for Computational Linguistics (2019)
4. Gao, X., Zhou, X., Zhang, M.: A multi-information perception based method for question answering in multi-party conversation. Acta Scientiarum Naturalium Universitatis Pekinensis, pp. 21–29 (2023)
5. Gu, J.C., Tao, C., Ling, Z.H.: Who says what to whom: a survey of multi-party conversations. In: IJCAI 2022, Vienna, Austria, pp. 5486–5493. ijcai.org (2022)
6. He, Z., Tavabi, L., Lerman, K., Soleymani, M.: Speaker turn modeling for dialogue act classification. In: EMNLP 2021, Virtual Event/Punta Cana, Dominican Republic, pp. 2150–2157. Association for Computational Linguistics (2021)
7. Hsu, J.H., Shen, P.W., Su, H.T., Chang, C.H., Yeh, J.F., Hsu, W.H.: Role aware multi-party dialogue question answering. In: ICASSP 2021, Toronto, ON, Canada, pp. 7813–7817. IEEE (2021)
8. Hu, W., Chan, Z., Liu, B., Zhao, D., Ma, J., Yan, R.: GSN: a graph-structured network for multi-party dialogues, pp. 5010–5016 (2019)
9. Li, J., et al.: Question-interlocutor scope realized graph modeling over key utterances for dialogue reading comprehension, pp. 4956–4968 (2023)
10. Li, J., et al.: Molweni: a challenge multiparty dialogues-based machine reading comprehension dataset with discourse structure. In: COLING 2020, Barcelona, Spain, pp. 2642–2652. International Committee on Computational Linguistics (2020)
11. Li, J., et al.: DADgraph: a discourse-aware dialogue graph neural network for multiparty dialogue machine reading comprehension. In: IJCNN 2021, Shenzhen, China, pp. 1–8. IEEE (2021)
12. Li, Y., Zou, B., Fan, Y., Dong, M., Hong, Y.: Coreference-aware double-channel attention network for multi-party dialogue reading comprehension. In: IJCNN 2023, Gold Coast, Australia, pp. 1–8. IEEE (2023)
13. Li, Y., Zou, B., Fan, Y., Li, X., Aw, A., Hong, Y.: GLGR: question-aware global-to-local graph reasoning for multi-party dialogue reading comprehension. In: EMNLP 2023, Singapore, pp. 1817–1826. Association for Computational Linguistics (2023)
14. Li, Y., Zhao, H.: Self-and pseudo-self-supervised prediction of speaker and key-utterance for multi-party dialogue reading comprehension. In: EMNLP 2021, Virtual Event/Punta Cana, Dominican Republic, pp. 2053–2063. Association for Computational Linguistics (2021)
15. Li, Y., Zhao, H., Zhang, Z.: Back to the future: bidirectional information decoupling network for multi-turn dialogue modeling, pp. 2761–2774. Association for Computational Linguistics (2022)
16. Liu, J., Sui, D., Liu, K., Zhao, J.: Graph-based knowledge integration for question answering over dialogue. In: COLING 2020, Barcelona, Spain, pp. 2425–2435. International Committee on Computational Linguistics (2020)
17. Liu, Y., Iter, D., Xu, Y., Wang, S., Xu, R., Zhu, C.: G-Eval: NLG evaluation using GPT-4 with better human alignment. arXiv preprint arXiv:2303.16634 (2023)

18. Loshchilov, I., Hutter, F.: Decoupled weight decay regularization. In: ICLR 2019, New Orleans, LA, USA. OpenReview.net (2019)

19. Ma, X., Zhang, Z., Zhao, H.: Enhanced speaker-aware multi-party multi-turn dialogue comprehension. IEEE/ACM Trans. Audio Speech Lang. Process. **31**, 2410–2423 (2023)

20. Maas, A.L.: Rectifier nonlinearities improve neural network acoustic models (2013)

21. Mou, L., et al.: Natural language inference by tree-based convolution and heuristic matching. In: ACL 2016, Berlin, Germany. The Association for Computer Linguistics (2016)

22. Otmazgin, S., Cattan, A., Goldberg, Y.: F-coref: fast, accurate and easy to use coreference resolution. In: AACL/IJCNLP 2022 - System Demostrations, Taipei, Taiwan, pp. 48–56. Association for Computational Linguistics (2022)

23. Qin, C., Zhang, A., Zhang, Z., Chen, J., Yasunaga, M., Yang, D.: Is ChatGPT a general-purpose natural language processing task solver? pp. 1339–1384 (2023)

24. Qin, L., Li, Z., Che, W., Ni, M., Liu, T.: Co-gat: a co-interactive graph attention network for joint dialog act recognition and sentiment classification. In: AAAI 2021, pp. 13709–13717. AAAI Press (2021)

25. Qin, X., et al.: BERT-ERC: fine-tuning BERT is enough for emotion recognition in conversation. In: AAAI 2023, Washington, DC, USA, pp. 13492–13500. AAAI Press (2023)

26. Schlichtkrull, M., Kipf, T.N., Bloem, P., van den Berg, R., Titov, I., Welling, M.: Modeling relational data with graph convolutional networks. In: Gangemi, A., et al. (eds.) ESWC 2018. LNCS, vol. 10843, pp. 593–607. Springer, Cham (2018). https://doi.org/10.1007/978-3-319-93417-4_38

27. Shen, W., Wu, S., Yang, Y., Quan, X.: Directed acyclic graph network for conversational emotion recognition. In: ACL/IJCNLP 2021, pp. 1551–1560. Association for Computational Linguistics (2021)

28. Shi, Z., Huang, M.: A deep sequential model for discourse parsing on multi-party dialogues. In: AAAI, pp. 7007–7014. AAAI Press (2019)

29. Sultana, M., Zaíane, O.R.: Exploring dialog act recognition in open domain conversational agents. In: Wrembel, R., Gamper, J., Kotsis, G., Tjoa, A.M., Khalil, I. (eds.) Big Data Analytics and Knowledge Discovery, DaWaK 2023, LNCS, vol. 14148, pp. 233–247. Springer, Cham (2023). https://doi.org/10.1007/978-3-031-39831-5_22

30. Sun, W., Yan, L., Ma, X., Ren, P., Yin, D., Ren, Z.: Is chatgpt good at search? investigating large language models as re-ranking agent, pp. 14918–14937 (2023)

31. Velickovic, P., Cucurull, G., Casanova, A., Romero, A., Lio, P., Bengio, Y., et al.: Graph attention networks. Stat **1050**(20), 10–48550 (2017)

32. Wolf, T., et al.: Transformers: state-of-the-art natural language processing. In: EMNLP 2020 - Demos, pp. 38–45. Association for Computational Linguistics (2020)

33. Yasunaga, M., Ren, H., Bosselut, A., Liang, P., Leskovec, J.: QA-GNN: reasoning with language models and knowledge graphs for question answering. In: NAACL-HLT 2021, 6–11 June 2021, pp. 535–546. Association for Computational Linguistics (2021)

Enhancing Emotional Support Conversation with Cognitive Chain-of-Thought Reasoning

Yaru Cao[1], Zhuang Chen[2], Guanqun Bi[2], Yulin Feng[3], Min Chen[3], Fucheng Wan[3], Minlie Huang[2], and Hongzhi Yu[3(✉)]

[1] Department of Chinese Language and Literature, Northwest Minzu University, Lanzhou 730030, China
y222240011@stu.xbmu.edu.cn

[2] Department of Computer Science and Technology, Tsinghua University, Beijing 100084, China

[3] Key Laboratory of Linguistic and Cultural Computing Ministry of Education, Northwest Minzu University, Lanzhou 730030, China
yhz@xbmu.edu.cn

Abstract. Emotional support conversation can reduce mental stress and provide social benefits. However, the help seeker's mental state often lies beneath the surface utterance in conversation, making it difficult to understand the seeker's deep status and provide effective emotional support through mere dialogue modeling. To address this challenge, we propose CogChain, a cognitive chain-of-thought (CoT) reasoning framework that mimics a human supporter's cognitive process for emotional support conversation. Specifically, CogChain employs a chained structure to *analyze* the seeker's *issues*, *infer* internal *thoughts*, *determine* behavioral *intentions*, and *select* appropriate *strategies* to *achieve* support *goals*. We further design an in-context learning pipeline using large language models to efficiently generate CogChain for any given dialogue content. To validate the effectiveness of CogChain, we incorporate it in the frequently used ESConv dataset and accordingly train enhanced machine supporters with CoT reasoning ability. Extensive automatic and human evaluations show that, CogChain not only improves the machine supporter's performance for in-domain seen scenarios but also enhances its generalizability to out-of-domain unseen scenarios, demonstrating the importance of cognitive reasoning for emotional support conversation (Our resources are available at https://github.com/YaruCao-AI/CogChain).

Keywords: Emotional Support Conversation · Chain-of-Thought Reasoning · Large Language Models

1 Introduction

In today's fast-paced society, an increasing number of individuals face emotional stress, leading to a growing demand for emotional therapy. Emotional

---

Y. Cao, Z. Chen, G. Bi—Equal contribution.

© The Author(s), under exclusive license to Springer Nature Singapore Pte Ltd. 2025
D. F. Wong et al. (Eds.): NLPCC 2024, LNAI 15359, pp. 175–187, 2025.
https://doi.org/10.1007/978-981-97-9431-7_14

support conversation (ESC) plays a crucial role in helping people alleviate distress, understand their emotions, and cope with life's challenges through social interactions [3,10,14]. ESC has profound implications in various fields like psychological counseling and emotional companionship, playing a crucial role in building and maintaining harmonious social relationships [12].

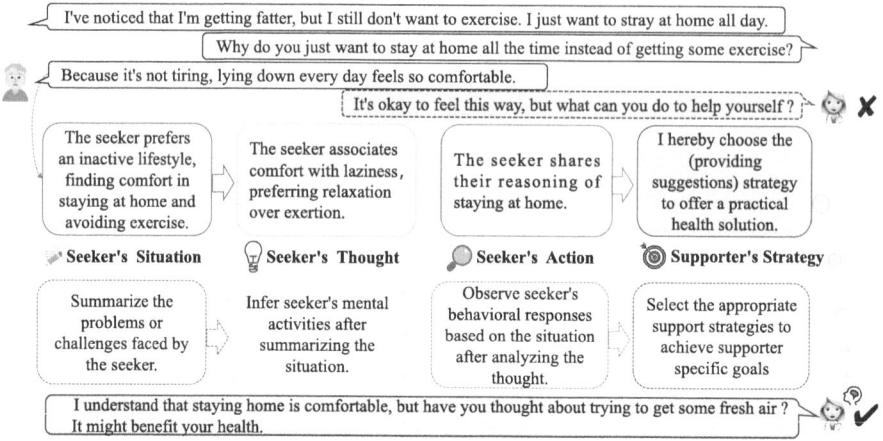

Fig. 1. An illustration of the CogChain framework in a conversation.

However, in emotional support conversation, the help seeker's mental states are often implicit and underlying beneath surface utterances, making it complex to understand their deep status and provide appropriate support. As shown in Fig. 1, when a seeker struggling with weight loss says, "*Because it (staying at home) is not tiring, lying down every day feels so comfortable*", they are not merely describing their comfort. Instead, this reflects their anxiety about gaining weight and failing to find suitable exercise routines (otherwise, they would not be seeking help). Therefore, a supporter cannot just respond with empathy but must offer concrete advice to help the seeker find appropriate exercise methods. Existing studies mainly attempt to enhance the process of emotional support in two ways. One involves injecting knowledge or commonsense to understand the seeker's utterances [9,16]. However, understanding meaning beyond the literal level requires reasoning, and merely incorporating concepts is insufficient to grasp deeper thoughts or intentions. The other approach directly guides supporter responses through predefined strategies [7,14,19,26], but it neither explains why a particular strategy is chosen nor clarifies the goal of using that strategy, making it difficult for the dialogue model to learn the decision-making motivation and process behind the strategy.

To address these challenges, we get inspiration from the dual-process theory of human thinking, which suggests that humans utilize both fast and slow thinking processes [8]. In this context, instead of relying on "fast thinking" - which involves instant and intuitive (often suboptimal) responses - we model emotional support as a "slow thinking" step-by-step reasoning process. Before a supporter responds, they should understand the seeker's deep status and choose an appropriate strategy. Further refined by the concepts from cognitive behavioral therapy [2], we propose **CogChain**, a **Cog**nitive **Chain**-of-thought (CoT) reasoning framework that mimics a human supporter's comprehensive cognitive process. CogChain employs a chained structure containing four components: *seeker's situation, seeker's thought, seeker's action*, and *supporter's strategy*. Specifically, CogChain first analyzes the seeker's situation, then infers internal thoughts, determines behavioral intentions, and finally selects appropriate strategies to achieve specific support goals. As shown in Fig. 1, through deliberate reasoning, the supporter can accurately understand the seeker's status, choose a suitable strategy, and respond with "*I understand that staying home is comfortable, but have you thought about trying to get some fresh air? It might benefit your health*". Beyond the structure design, we further design an in-context learning pipeline using large language models like GPT-3.5 to efficiently generate CogChain for any dialogue.

To validate the effectiveness of CogChain, we incorporate it into the widely used ESConv dataset [14] for emotional support conversation. For each dialogue turn in ESConv, we employ the previously mentioned pipeline to automatically supplement the cognitive CoT reasoning process, resulting in an enhanced dataset named ESChain. Subsequently, we train the large language model LLaMA-2 [18] on ESChain to obtain an enhanced machine supporter equipped with cognitive reasoning abilities. Keeping the training data unchanged, we conduct experiments on two test sets. In the in-domain ESConv test set, experimental results indicate that the supporter with CogChain significantly outperforms the supporter without CogChain in both automatic and human evaluations. Additionally, we examine the supporter on the out-of-domain ExTES dataset [26], which features more diverse dialogue topics compared to ESConv. The results demonstrate that CogChain markedly improves the machine supporter's generalizability to handle unseen scenarios in ExTES.

2   Related Work

2.1   Emotional Support Conversation

Emotional support (ES) [3] aims to alleviate individuals' emotional stress and help seekers address their challenges. Unlike emotional chatting [27] that generates responses consistent with preset emotions, and empathetic responses [17] that acknowledge the seeker's implied feelings, ES conversations involve higher-level abilities. Liu et al. [14] introduce the task of emotional support conversations (ESC), which use strategies to offer support to help-seekers. Various models have been proposed to enhance ESC: Tu et al. [19] develop a mixed-strategy model using commonsense knowledge. Peng et al. [16] use a hierarchical graph network to model global commonsense causes and local contextual intentions. Zhao et al. [25] explore state transitions in dialogues. Cheng et al. [6] add the user's persona information. Deng et al. [9] propose a system enhanced with a mental health knowledge graph. Zhou et al. [28] use reinforcement learning to elicit positive emotions in multi-turn dialogues. Chen et al. [5] develop a causal-aware model to identify emotional causes and effects. Xu et al. [22] use cognitive relations to guide response generation. Most existing models use fragmented, non-continuous information for guidance. In contrast, our approach employs a complete cognitive chain of thought, extending from the seeker's mental states to the supporter's strategic goals, thereby providing more targeted and effective responses.

2.2 Chain-of-Thought Prompting

Wei et al. [21] initially introduce Chain-of-Thought (CoT) Prompting to mimic the human reasoning process. Subsequently, researchers leverage CoT to enable large language models (LLMs) to handle complex reasoning tasks, such as Auto-CoT [24] and PsyCoT [23]. To apply CoT prompting in dialogue systems, Chae et al. [4] proposed DialogueCoT to decompose commonsense reasoning into steps, and provide CoT rationales for response generation to facilitate dialogue CoT reasoning. Wang et al. [20] introduced CueCoT, which prompts the system to first infer the seeker's mental states and then generate a response based on the dialogue context and those inferred states. Our work aims to enhance emotional support capabilities by exploring cognitive chain-of-thought reasoning that simulates the human emotional support process.

3 Methodology

We propose CogChain, a cognitive CoT reasoning framework that mimics a human supporter's comprehensive cognitive process. The effectiveness of our framework is validated by integrating it into each supporter's utterance in ESConv dataset. As depicted in Fig. 2, the process involves four main steps: (1) designing the CogChain framework, (2) constructing a CogChain example as the demonstration of LLMs, (3) augmenting the ESConv dataset with CogChain generated by LLMs and forming the new enhanced dataset ESChain, and (4) controlling data quality and fine-tuning LLaMA-2 to obtain the machine supporter.

3.1 Task Definition

Let $D = \{x_1, y_1, \ldots, x_N, y_N\}$ denote a conversation, where x represents the seeker's utterances, y represents the supporter's utterances, and N is the number of dialogue turns. Our approach involves generating a cognitive chain-of-thought (CogChain) for each utterance from the supporter. We denote a specific CogChain as c. Subsequently, the supporter's response y is generated based on the flattened dialogue history and its corresponding CogChain c.

$$\mathbb{P}(\tilde{y}|x) = \prod_{i=1}^{|c|} \mathbb{P}(c_i|x, c_{<i}) \prod_{j=1}^{|y|} \mathbb{P}(y_j|x, c, y_{<j}) \tag{1}$$

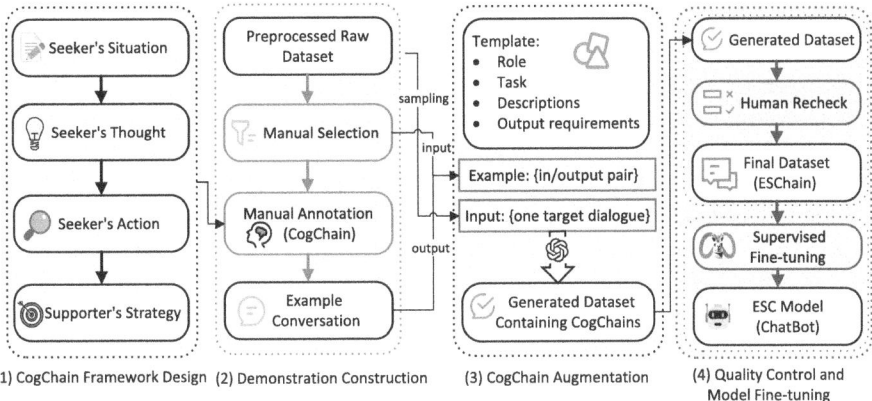

Fig. 2. The pipeline of our methodology, which includes CogChain Framework Design(§3.2), Demonstration Construction(§3.3), CogChain Augmentation(§3.3), as well as Quality Control (§3.4) and Model Fine-tuning(§4).

where $\tilde{y} = c \oplus y$ is the output of our model. The CogChain serves as a foundational framework guiding the generation process, as it encapsulates essential contextual and strategic information necessary for crafting relevant and supportive responses.

3.2 CogChain Framework Design

Limited utterances often fail to convey the seeker's complex emotional states. Inspired by CBT's principle that human thoughts, feelings, and actions are interconnected [2], we mimic the human emotional support process by dynamically summarizing the seeker's current situation, mental state, and behavioral intentions. This allows us analyze the underlying mental states beneath the seeker's surface utterances. People have preset goals when choosing strategies [8], thus, we emulate human supporters by selecting strategies and setting goals based on our analysis of the seeker, thereby reflecting the supporter's intentions. We hereby design a novel cognitive chain-of-thought reasoning framework containing the below four types of elements:

– **Seeker's Situation**: This element refers to the supporter's inference of the specific circumstances the seeker is facing in the dialogue. By understanding the seeker's real-life situation, the supporter can more accurately grasp the context and challenges of the conversation.
– **Seeker's Thought**: This element involves the supporter's inference of the seeker's mental states. This includes understanding the seeker's emotional state and expectations. By inferring the seeker's thoughts, the supporter can gain a deeper understanding of the seeker's needs and intentions.
– **Seeker's Action**: This element involves the supporter's observation and analysis of the seeker's behavior in the dialogue. By observing the seeker's

words and actions, the supporter can gather clues about the seeker's behavioral intentions and attitudes.

- **Supporter's Strategy**: This element involves the supporter's chosen emotional support strategies and corresponding goals. Based on the inferences about the seeker's situation, thoughts, and behaviors, the supporter selects appropriate strategies and clarifies the purpose of using those strategies to maximally help the seeker cope with emotional distress.

3.3   ESChain Construction

Demonstration Construction. In ESConv, there are instances where seekers and supporters consecutively speak multiple utterances, and these utterances are recorded separately. To ensure that the conversation strictly follows a turn-taking pattern, as required to supplement CogChain, we first preprocess the raw ESConv data. Specifically, we concatenate consecutive utterances by the same speakers in ESConv into a complete utterance, including the strategy used in each supporter utterance. For example, a dialogue "$Seeker\text{-}u_1$, $Seeker\text{-}u_2$, $Supporter\text{-}(s_3,\ u_3)$, $Supporter\text{-}(s_4,\ u_4)$" is transformed into "$Seeker\text{-}(u_1, u_2)$, $Supporter\text{-}(s_3, s_4,\ u_3, u_4)$", where s represents strategy, u represents utterance. To emulate a real help-seeking environment, we restructure each dialogue to start with the seeker and end with the supporter. Then we carefully select conversations from the original ESConv dataset, adhering to criteria such as high Seeker feedback scores, significant reduction in emotional intensity, and completeness of strategy types. Subsequently, we recruit psychology students to annotate the cognitive chain-of-thought reasoning for each supporter's utterance in the conversations based on the CogChain framework. After careful inspection and correction of the supplemented CogChain, the quality of both the conversations and the CogChains was ensured. This process is illustrated in Fig. 2 (2).

CogChain Augmentation. By utilizing the in-context learning potential of LLMs, we prompt GPT-3.5-turbo to construct the ESChain dataset with cognitive chain-of-thought reasoning for the processed ESConv dataset. Specifically, we design a template (refer to Fig. 2 (3)) to define role tasks, describe the cognitive chain-of-thought framework and strategy definitions, and specify output requirements. We combine the manually selected raw data with meticulously designed examples to form an input-output pair, using the input-output pair with cognitive reasoning as demonstrations. We supplement the input dialogues sampled from the preprocessed ESConv dataset with the generated cognitive chain-of-thought reasoning for supporters, while keeping the utterance portion consistent with the input.

3.4   Quality Control

To ensure the quality of the ESChain dataset generated by GPT-3.5-turbo, we perform multiple manual iterations involving review, correction, and regeneration. We focus on the following aspects: (1) Dialogue completeness and accuracy:

ensuring that the output dialogue matches the input and includes all turns. (2) Presence and completeness of CogChain: verifying that each supporter's utterance includes a complete CogChain with no missing elements. (3) Quality of CogChain: confirming that the situation, thought, and action elements are contextually relevant, detailed, and accurate, and ensuring that strategy names match the input and that strategy intentions align with the responses. Through multiple rounds of manual and automated checks, we ensure the quality of the CogChains in the ESChain dataset.

Table 1. Rationality evalution of CogChain in the ESChain.

	Situation	Thought	Action	Strategy	Overall
Score	2.9	2.83	2.9	3	2.87

To evaluate the quality of CogChain in the ESChain dataset, we manually evaluated their rationality across four key elements: *seeker's situation, seeker's thought, seeker's action*, and *supporter's strategy*. We randomly selected 100 CogChains and rated each element on a 0 to 3 Likert scale for rationality. As shown in Table 1 The average scores range from 2.83 to 3.0, with the strategy element achieving a perfect score. These results indicate the high rationality of the CogChains generated in the ESChain dataset.

3.5   Statistics of Dataset

This section presents the statistical overview of the ESChain dataset after quality control. As shown in Table 2, ESChain contains 1,300 dialogues with an average of 22.5 turns each. The dataset includes 14,617 seeker and supporter utterances, with each supporter utterance supplemented by a CogChain, totaling 14,617 CogChains.

Table 2. Statistics of ESChain.

Dialogue		CogChain	
Num. of Dialogues	1300	Num.of CogChain/Sit./Thou./Act./Stra.	14617
Avg Len. of Dialogue	22.5	Avg. Len. of CogChain	52.1
Num. of Seeker Utterance	14617	Avg. Len. of Seeker's Situation	10.9
Num. of Supporter Utterance	14617	Avg. Len. of Seeker's Thought	10
Avg. Len. of Seeker Utterance	19.9	Avg. Len. of Seeker's Action	7.7
Avg. Len. of Supporter Utterance	22.3	Avg. Len. of Supporter's Strategy	15.5

ESChain consists of two main parts: dialogue utterances and CogChains. Each CogChain includes four elements: *Seeker's Situation, Seeker's Thought, Seeker's Action*, and *Supporter's Strategy*, ensuring completeness. The average length of CogChains is relatively long, reflecting detailed reasoning. The Strategy element includes both the strategy term and its goal, enhancing the interpretability and credibility of emotional support responses.

4   Experiments

To evaluate the effectiveness of the proposed cognitive chain-of-thought reasoning, we conduct a comprehensive set of experiments focusing on two critical research problems: (**Q1**) Does CogChain enhance the model's emotional support capabilities? (**Q2**) Does CogChain improve the model's generalizability?

4.1   Datasets

The training dataset for the experiments consists of ESConv and ESChain, which are divided into three categories: ESConv without strategy, ESConv with strategy, and ESChain. The data is split according to the ESConv train/test ratio (9:1), corresponding to 1170/130 dialogues, respectively. We use two types of test sets: in-domain (Q1) and out-of-domain (Q2). The in-domain test set, derived from the ESConv test set [11], includes 130 randomly selected dialogues. The out-of-domain test set, taken from the ExTES test set [22], includes 200 randomly selected dialogues. This out-of-domain test set features topic types that the model has not encountered during training [26], includes 200 randomly selected dialogues. This out-of-domain test set features topic types that the model has not encountered during training.

4.2   Comparison Methods and Implementation Details

We use LLaMA2-7B as the backbone model and fine-tune it on three different datasets, resulting in three model variants. Additionally, we train a smaller model, BlendBot-small. The evaluation focuses solely on the quality of generated responses, excluding strategy or CogChain components.

The training experiments are conducted using an NVIDIA Tesla V100-SXM2-32G GPU and adopt the PyTorch framework. The training process involves 2–4 epochs with a batch size set to 2 and gradient accumulation steps set to 4. The learning rate is set to 5e-5, and we use fp16 with a maximum input length of 4096.

4.3   Automatic Evaluation

Following previous works [14], the automatic evaluation metrics used in this study include BLEU-2/3/4 (B-n) [15], Distinct-1/2/3 (D-n) [11], METEOR (Met.) [1], and ROUGE-L (R-L) [13].

As shown in Table 3, we have the following observations: (1) Models trained on ESChain outperform other models on most metrics in both in-domain

Table 3. Automatic evaluation results on in-domain and out-of-domain test sets.

Test Set	Model	Train Set	D-2	D-3	B-1	B-2	B-3	B-4	Met.	R-L
ESConv (In-domain)	Blender-Bot	**ESChain(Our)**	23.41	46.01	**22.29**	**9.08**	**4.54**	**2.65**	**17.46**	**18.89**
		ESConv-nostra	**26.06**	**50.1**	20.08	8.25	4.12	2.29	16.34	17.99
	LLaMA	**ESChain(Our)**	33.19	**61.12**	**19.71**	**8.27**	**4.21**	**2.43**	**16.36**	**18.9**
		ESConv-stra	**33.55**	60.69	16.71	7.02	3.55	2.05	15.31	18.66
		ESConv-nostra	31.19	57.4	17.93	7.53	3.84	2.24	15.65	18.55
ExTES (Out-of-domain)	LLaMA	**ESChain(Our)**	**26.13**	**50.03**	**22.22**	**10.78**	**6.17**	**3.86**	**19.66**	22.13
		ESConv-stra	25.32	48.39	20.69	10.25	6.03	3.86	19.15	**22.31**
		ESConv-nostra	24.28	46.03	19.49	9.69	5.75	3.68	18.57	21.67

and out-of-domain test sets. This suggests that incorporating cognitive reasoning before generating responses improves model performance, possibly because the reasoning process aids model learning. (2) The model's performance also improves in out-of-domain experiments, indicating that datasets with cognitive chain-of-thought reasoning processes have better generalizability. (3) The model trained on ESChain outperforms the model trained on ESConv-stra across most metrics, suggesting that analyzing the Seeker's Situation, Thought, and Action before selecting a strategy leads to better performance than directly selecting a strategy. (4) The small model shows significant improvements in B-n, METEOR, and R-L metrics. However, the D-n metric is lower, likely because responses closer to real responses naturally exhibit less diversity.

4.4   Human Evaluation

To thoroughly evaluate the effectiveness of the proposed cognitive chain-of-thought reasoning, we adopt widely used settings to manually assess the emotional support responses generated by different models. We perform both static evaluation and dynamic human interactive evaluation, following the evaluation protocol: Fluency (Flu.), Identification (Ide.), Comforting (Com.), Suggestion (Sug.), and Overall (All.) [14]. The final statistics are reported as Win, Loss, and Tie.

Static Evaluation Setting. For static evaluation, we randomly select 100 samples from the ESConv test set and recruit three graduate students to evaluate the responses generated by the models and the real human responses, averaging the scores of the two. Considering the variability between individuals, we perform human A/B testing to directly compare our paradigm with other models. Fleiss's kappa is used to analyze the consistency of evaluations, with kappa values ranging from 0.44 to 0.89 for each metric. The results of human static evaluation are shown in Table 4.

Interactive Evaluation Setting. For human interactive evaluation, we recruit 30 students from different majors, collecting a total of 90 interactive conversations and ratings (each participant contributes three conversations). Each participant is asked to discuss the same emotional issue with three different bots, which accept the same first informative utterances. Each conversation lasts at least 8 turns (8 utterances from participants and 8 from bots). Notably, we adopt an open-domain setting, allowing participants to talk about any topic they desire, unrestricted by predefined categories. This differs from the setup in [14], where participants are limited to discussing specific in-domain topics. Participants are asked to rate the performance of the three bots based on the evaluation protocol. The results of human interactive evaluation are shown in Table 4.

Table 4. Results of human static and interactive evaluation (%). Ties are not shown. $\dagger/\ddagger$ denote p-value $< 0.1/0.05$ respectively in significance test.

ESChain vs.	ESConv-noStra				ESConv-Stra				Human	
	Static Eval.		Inter. Eval.		Static Eval.		Inter. Eval.		Static Eval.	
	Win	Loss	Win	Loss	Win	Loss	Win	Loss	Win	Loss
Flu.	$40^{\ddagger}$	5	$50^{\ddagger}$	3	$27^{\ddagger}$	6	$30^{\ddagger}$	3	$19^{\dagger}$	10
Ide.	$47^{\ddagger}$	10	$70^{\ddagger}$	3	$45^{\ddagger}$	14	$57^{\ddagger}$	7	$26^{\ddagger}$	1
Com.	$50^{\ddagger}$	16	$60^{\ddagger}$	7	$46^{\ddagger}$	20	$63^{\ddagger}$	10	$36^{\dagger}$	24
Sug.	$48^{\ddagger}$	10	$63^{\ddagger}$	3	$48^{\ddagger}$	13	$50^{\ddagger}$	23	25	25
All.	$66^{\ddagger}$	12	$73^{\ddagger}$	3	$60^{\ddagger}$	17	$50^{\ddagger}$	10	41	30

Human Evaluation Results. The comparative results in Table 4 demonstrate the following findings: (1) Fine-tuning LLM on our ESChain dataset performs best in all metrics during both static and interactive evaluations, indicating that CogChain-guided models have superior emotional support capabilities. (2) The version using CogChain outperforms both the strategy-based version and the version without strategies in all metrics and overall performance, showing that a complete cognitive reasoning process is more effective than mere strategy words in guiding emotional support responses. (3) Notably, our model is generally more preferred by seekers compared to the original human-provided gold responses.

4.5   Ablation Study

To investigate the impact of different elements of the CogChain on generating responses, we perform an ablation study, and the results are reported in Table 5. Specifically, we remove certain nodes of the chain and perform LoRA fine-tuning on the LLaMA model for each configuration. The evaluation is performed on the ESConv test set.

Table 5 shows that responses using the complete CogChain (rows 1) achieve the best performance, indicating the importance of all elements in enhancing emotional support. Removing any elements (rows 2 to 4) leads to a decline in performance, but results are still better than the baseline (row 5), where no ESConv elements are used. This confirms that each element of the cognitive chain improves the model's emotional support capability.

Table 5. Ablation study on different elements of CogChian.

	Setting				Result							
Row	Sit.	Tho.	Act.	Str.	D-2	D-3	B-1	B-2	B-3	B-4	Met.	R-L
1	✓	✓	✓	✓	**33.19**	**61.12**	**19.71**	**8.27**	**4.21**	**2.43**	**16.36**	**18.9**
2	–	✓	✓	✓	32.98	60.7	17.92	7.39	3.82	2.25	15.88	18.86
3	✓	–	✓	✓	32.69	60.81	18.36	7.5	3.74	2.2	15.83	18.68
4	✓	✓	–	✓	32.4	60.03	18.32	7.57	3.89	2.28	15.66	18.47
5	–	–	–	–	31.19	57.4	17.93	7.53	3.84	2.24	15.65	18.55

4.6   Case Study

The case in Table 6 demonstrates that our model better recognizes the seeker's situation in long conversations and identifies their needs, thereby providing more effective suggestions. The other three models do not accurately understand the seeker's true needs, and even fail to recognize what the seeker has already mentioned, such as *I have not been able to connect with the teacher ... .* In contrast, our CogChain focuses on critical information, such as the seeker's need for more learning resources, resulting in a more reasonable and helpful response.

Table 6. Case study.

Dialogue Context	Seeker: ...I have not been able to connect with the teacher enough to know...You mentioned online sites...
	Supporter: Khan Academy is absolutely fantastic! ... I can recommend other resources if you'd like.
	Seeker: Thank you, just a couple more if you have them.
	Human Response: If this is an upper level math course, you can go to university sites! They always have lessons.
LLaMA2 +ESConv +ESConv-Stra	Yes, I have the last two.
	I would suggest reaching out to your professor for help if you can!
	I would recommend using a planner.
+ESChain(our)	**Seeker's Situation:** The seeker is seeking more learning resources to prepare for a test
	Seeker's Thought: The seeker hopes to receive reliable advice and resources to improve their math skills.
	Seeker's Action: The Seeker wants some additional resources.
	Supporter's Strategy: I hereby choose the (Information) strategy to recommend another potential helpful resource.
	Response: There are a lot of great sites! One that I use is IXL.com. It is a bit pricey, but you can get a free trial!

5   Conclusion

In this paper, we propose CogChain, a cognitive chain-of-thought reasoning framework for mimicking the human supporter's thinking process in emotional suppport conversation. Instead of instant and intuitive responding, the machine supporter first understands the situation, thought, and behavior of the seeker, and then selects an appropriate strategy to achieve specific support goals. We further design an LLM-based pipeline for generating CogChain and incorporate it with the ESConv dataset, and accordingly train enhanced machine supporters equipped with CoT reasoning ability. Extensive experiments and comprehensive evaluations demonstrate that step-by-step cognitive reasoning can enhance the emotional support capability of machine supporters, and further improve their generalizability to unseen support scenarios.

Acknowledgement. This research was Supported by the National Natural Science Foundation of China (No. 62366045, 62366046), the Fundamental Research Innovation Group Project (No. 24JRRA154), and the Fundamental Research Funds for the Central Universities (No. 31920240127).

References

1. Banerjee, S., Lavie, A.: METEOR: an automatic metric for MT evaluation with improved correlation with human judgments. In: Proceedings of IEEvaluation@ACL, pp. 65–72 (2005)
2. Beck, J.S.: Cognitive Behavior Therapy: Basics and Beyond. Guilford Publications, New York (2020)
3. Burleson, B.R.: Emotional support skills. In: Handbook of Communication and Social Interaction Skills, pp. 551–594. Lawrence Erlbaum Associates Publishers (2003)
4. Chae, H., et al.: Dialogue chain-of-thought distillation for commonsense-aware conversational agents. In: Proceedings of the EMNLP, pp. 5606–5632 (2023)
5. Chen, W., et al.: Cauesc: a causal aware model for emotional support conversation. CoRR **abs/2401.17755** (2024)
6. Cheng, J., Sabour, S., Sun, H., Chen, Z., Huang, M.: PAL: persona-augmented emotional support conversation generation. In: Findings of the ACL, pp. 535–554 (2023)
7. Cheng, Y., et al.: Improving multi-turn emotional support dialogue generation with lookahead strategy planning. In: Proceedings of the EMNLP, pp. 3014–3026 (2022)
8. Daniel, K.: Thinking, Fast and Slow. Farrar, Straus and Giroux, New York (2011)
9. Deng, Y., Zhang, W., Yuan, Y., Lam, W.: Knowledge-enhanced mixed-initiative dialogue system for emotional support conversations. In: Proceedings of the ACL, pp. 4079–4095 (2023)
10. Langford, C.P.H., Bowsher, J.E., Maloney, J.P., Lillis, P.P.: Social support: a conceptual analysis. J. Adv. Nurs. **25**(1), 95–100 (1997)
11. Li, J., Galley, M., Brockett, C., Gao, J., Dolan, B.: A diversity-promoting objective function for neural conversation models. In: Conference of the NAACL-HLT, pp. 110–119 (2016)
12. Li, Y., Li, K., Ning, H., Xia, X., Guo, Y., Wei, C., Cui, J., Wang, B.: Towards an online empathetic chatbot with emotion causes. In: Proceedings of the ACM SIGIR, pp. 2041–2045 (2021)
13. Lin, C.Y.: ROUGE: A package for automatic evaluation of summaries. In: Text Summarization Branches Out, pp. 74–81. Association for Computational Linguistics, Barcelona, Spain, July 2004
14. Liu, S., Zheng, C., Demasi, O., Sabour, S., Li, Y., Yu, Z., Jiang, Y., Huang, M.: Towards emotional support dialog systems. In: Proceedings of the ACL/IJCNLP, pp. 3469–3483 (2021)
15. Papineni, K., Roukos, S., Ward, T., Zhu, W.: Bleu: a method for automatic evaluation of machine translation. In: Proceedings of the ACL, pp. 311–318 (2002)
16. Peng, W., Hu, Y., Xing, L., Xie, Y., Sun, Y., Li, Y.: Control globally, understand locally: a global-to-local hierarchical graph network for emotional support conversation. In: Proceedings of the IJCAI, pp. 4324–4330 (2022)

17. Rashkin, H., Smith, E.M., Li, M., Boureau, Y.: Towards empathetic open-domain conversation models: a new benchmark and dataset. In: Proceedings of the ACL, pp. 5370–5381. Association for Computational Linguistics (2019)
18. Touvron, H., Martin, L., Stone, K., Albert, et al.: Llama 2: open foundation and fine-tuned chat models. arXiv preprint arXiv:2307.09288 (2023)
19. Tu, Q., Li, Y., Cui, J., Wang, B., Wen, J., Yan, R.: MISC: a mixed strategy-aware model integrating COMET for emotional support conversation. In: Proceedings of the ACL, 22–27 May 2022, pp. 308–319 (2022)
20. Wang, H., et al.: Cue-cot: chain-of-thought prompting for responding to in-depth dialogue questions with llms. In: Findings of EMNLP, pp. 12047–12064 (2023)
21. Wei, J., et al.: Chain-of-thought prompting elicits reasoning in large language models. In: NeurIPS (2022)
22. Xu, Z., Chen, D., Kuang, J., Yi, Z., Li, Y., Shen, Y.: Dynamic demonstration retrieval and cognitive understanding for emotional support conversation. arXiv preprint arXiv:2404.02505 (2024)
23. Yang, T., et al.: PsyCoT: psychological questionnaire as powerful chain-of-thought for personality detection. In: Findings of the EMNLP, pp. 3305–3320 (2023)
24. Zhang, Z., Zhang, A., Li, M., Smola, A.: Automatic chain of thought prompting in large language models. In: ICLR (2023)
25. Zhao, W., Zhao, Y., Wang, S., Qin, B.: TransESC: smoothing emotional support conversation via turn-level state transition. In: Findings of the ACL, pp. 6725–6739 (2023)
26. Zheng, Z., Liao, L., Deng, Y., Nie, L.: Building emotional support chatbots in the era of llms. CoRR **abs/2308.11584** (2023)
27. Zhou, H., Huang, M., Zhang, T., Zhu, X., Liu, B.: Emotional chatting machine: emotional conversation generation with internal and external memory. In: Proceedings of the AAAI, pp. 730–739 (2018)
28. Zhou, J., Chen, Z., Wang, B., Huang, M.: Facilitating multi-turn emotional support conversation with positive emotion elicitation: a reinforcement learning approach. In: Proceedings of the ACL (2023)

A Simple and Effective Span Interaction Modeling Method for Enhancing Multiple Span Question Answering

Yingying Zhang, Zhiyi Luo[✉], and Zuohua Ding[✉]

Zhejiang Sci-Tech University, Hangzhou, China
luozhiyi@zstu.edu.cn, zouhuading@hotmail.com

Abstract. Although multi-span question-answering tasks align more closely with the complex demands of the real world, existing models often struggle to effectively model the dependencies and overall semantic structure between multiple answer spans. Therefore, we propose a concise and effective method for modeling span interactions, which primarily includes: 1) a Span Representation Module that utilizes SpanBERT to enhance span information within tokens; and 2) a Span Interaction Module that leverages two contrastive learning tasks to reinforce answer spans' interaction within token representation. On one hand, we use the [CLS] token as an intermediary variable to carry information of span interaction, and on the other hand, we employ prompt-based tasks to further strengthen the multi-span question-answering reasoning capabilities of encoder and the span aggregation ability of the CLS token. Experiments demonstrate that baselines, on MultiSpanQA, incorporating our strategy achieved an improvement in EM F1 ranging from 2.88 to 11.27, achieving state-of-the-art (SOTA) results at equivalent model scales.

Keywords: Reading Comprehension · Multi-Span Question Answering · Span Modeling · Contrastive Learning

1 Introduction

Extractive question-answering can be divided into Single-Span QA and Multiple-Span QA (MSQA), based on the number of answer spans. Benefiting from its versatile task formulation, MSQA offers more flexible application scenarios that align closely with real-world requirements, but are also more challenging, prompting recent research into this issue (Li et al., 2022 [1]; Luo et al., 2024 [2]). However, existing models still underperform in MSQA, and according to our experiments, even ChatGPT, widely recognized for its generalization and comprehension abilities, struggles with this. Because the answer spans in MSQA are interdependent, requiring the combination of multiple spans to form a complete answer. Furthermore, crafting a comprehensive answer in MSQA depends on both the question and the core semantic of the context, making the MSQA task more complex. Among previous studies, only SpanQualifier [3] has tried to model the interactions among potential answer spans in MSQA using Convolutional

© The Author(s), under exclusive license to Springer Nature Singapore Pte Ltd. 2025
D. F. Wong et al. (Eds.): NLPCC 2024, LNAI 15359, pp. 188–200, 2025.
https://doi.org/10.1007/978-981-97-9431-7_15

Neural Networks (CNN). However, SpanQualifier has its limitations that it needs to enumerate all possible spans, leading to substantial computational demand and possible missing critical spans in long contexts, arising from the limited input length of Pre-trained Language Models (PLMs).

Therefore, to address the following three critical issues: 1) effectively representing spans; 2) modeling interactions between spans; and 3) ensuring the broad applicability of our method across various model architectures, we have developed a straightforward yet effective approach to model span interactions in this task. This method involves the following steps: 1) We employ SpanBERT [4] as the foundational encoder to achieve robust span representations. Thanks to its Span-Boundary Objective (SBO) during pre-training, SpanBERT can naturally integrates span information into token representations. 2) Building on this, we use the MultiSpanQA benchmark to construct sets of positive and negative pairs for contrastive learning during continued pre-training. These tasks allow encoders to infuse global answer span information into the [CLS] token, creating a task-adapted encoder. 3) Consequently, during the fine-tuning phase, the [CLS] token acts as an intermediary, with model leveraging the attention layer to model span interactions within token representations via interactions between the [CLS] and other tokens.

Table 1. Example

Question	What are the names of Tagore's three most famous poems?
Context	Tagore was able to boldly innovate in poetry. His works reflect the strong desire of the Indian people to change their fate under the oppression of imperialism and the feudal caste system, depicting their unyielding resistance struggle, filled with vivid patriotism and democratic spirit
	Here are three of his most famous poems. Let's appreciate them together!
	"The Champa Flower": If I were to become a champaka flower…
	"The End": It is time for me to go, mother; I am going…
	"The Banyan Tree": O you shaggy-headed banyan tree standing on…

Firstly, we have designed a contrastive learning task that treats "question-context" and "question-answer" pairs as positive pairs, referred to here as "QC-QA" pairs. In this task, a question is regarded as an intent directive, ensuring that the "question-context" aligns semantically with the answer sequence at its core. Particularly under the attention mechanisms, the "question-context" sequence's semantic focus is concentrated on the context fragment indicated by the question. This design mirrors human cognitive patterns; for instance, in the provided example showed in Table 1, although the context includes details such as a personal introduction to Tagore, his poetic style, and his famous works, the question's intent naturally shifts attention to the names of his three most famous poems, while other information is overlooked. Since the [CLS] token generally encapsulates the overall semantics of the input sequence, strengthening the proximity between the [CLS] representations of "question-context" and "question-answer" enhances the semantic linkage between the [CLS] token and the candidate answer tokens.

Totally, this task aims to enable the [CLS] token to capture complete answer span information, thereby positioning it as an intermediary variable that embodies the global answer span knowledge during fine-tuning.

Additionally, considering that the sentence classification tasks during the pre-training phase of BERT family are simple, these models, despite their robust token representation capabilities, exhibit weaker [CLS] representation abilities. Therefore, beyond the aforementioned tasks, we have introduced another learning objective in the continued pre-training phase. Specifically, we have designed a prompting template that merge questions with their context into a single sentence, utilizing [MASK] tokens within the template to capture the global representation of the answer in the merged sequence. Subsequently, we use the representation of these [MASK] tokens alongside the [CLS] representation of the answer sequence as positive pairs in contrastive learning, which we refer to as "PQC-A" pairs. Overall, this task aims to transform the strong token representation capabilities of the BERT series encoders into global representation capabilities, enhance the model's question-answering reasoning abilities and also enrich the global answer span information within the [CLS] representation.

Based on aforementioned design, we developed SpanInteractor, an encoder with enhanced span interaction knowledge, through a task-adaptive continued pre-training process. Experiments show that baselines incorporating our strategy achieved an improvement in EM F1 scores ranging from 2.88 to 11.27, on MultiSpanQA benchmark, achieving state-of-the-art-results at equivalent model scales. In summary, our contributions are as follows:

- Supporting by SpanBERT, our method centers on modeling span interactions, which naturally aligns with the requirements of multi-span question-answering tasks. It optimizes the use of token answers and, in experimental comparisons, surpasses the performance of the current best models at equivalent model scales.
- Starting from the core semantics of question-based sequences, we proposed a contrastive learning strategy based on "question-context" and "question-answer" pairs. Innovatively, we utilized the [CLS] token as an intermediary that integrates global answer span information. This approach models interactions between spans through the interactions of tokens within the attention layer.
- We developed a contrastive learning strategy based on prompt templates, designed to enhance the representational capability of the [CLS] token, improve question-answering reasoning, and augment the global answer span information contained within the [CLS] token.

2 Related Work

2.1 Neural Networks for MultiSpanQA

Existing research on MSQA can generally be divided into two categories: the first involves improving task performance through model architecture enhancements, and the second involves expanding training data via data augmentation without altering the model structure (Lee et al., 2023 [5]). From the perspective of model enhancement, current architectures can be categorized into four types: First, token-level sequence tagging models (e.g., Segal et al., 2020 [6]; Li et al., 2022 [1]; Luo et al., 2023 [7]), which label each token in a sequence as one of three categories, {B, I, O}, with the first token of an answer span marked as B (Beginning), subsequent tokens within the answer span as I (Inside), and tokens not part of any answer span as O (Outside). Second, span-level classification models (Huang et al., 2023 [3]), which identify predicted answer spans by exhaustively labeling all possible spans. Third, iterative single-span extraction models (Zhang et al., 2023 [8]), which sequentially extract a span of answer using a single-span model, and integrate extracted answer spans into new question using well-designed templates to facilitate the extraction of remaining answers spans. Finally, generation-based Seq2Seq architectures use prompts to constrain the output of generative models, yielding the corresponding extracted answers.

Research on model improvements has focused on token-level sequence tagging architectures. Segal et al. (2020) [6] pioneered the formulation of the MSQA task as a sequence tagging task to overcome the limitations posed by existing span boundary prediction paradigms, referring to this architecture as TASE. Building on this, Li et al. (2020) introduced an average pooling layer that transforms the representations of tokens predicted as beginning (B) or inside (I) into representations of predicted answer spans. They also introduced a joint learning framework, named TASE-SNP, which considers both the number and structure of answers. Moreover, Luo et al. (2023) [7] designed TOAST that capturing transition within adjacent token to delineate answer span boundaries, significantly enhancing the model's performance in answering descriptive questions.

To address the inability of token sequence tagging models to capture dependencies between spans, Huang et al. (2023) [3] developed a model called SpanQualifier. This model utilizes boundaries of spans for modeling and classifying answer spans and then incorporates a CNN to model dependencies between spans. Zhang et al. (2023) [8] took a more exploratory approach, systematically analyzing the multi-span question answering paradigms. Their work categorizes common multi-span QA instances and explores the effectiveness of 4 paradigms: sequence tagging, select answers by predicting the number of answer spans and ranking candidate spans, iterative extraction using single-span model, and answer generation by constraining generative model.

Compared to extractive models, generative commonly face issues with uncontrolled generation. To address this, current works based on generative architectures can be divided into two categories. The first focuses on improving generative models (such as BART and Llama) by fine-tuning them to learn an extractive QA paradigm. Apart from generative paradigm discussed by Zhang et al. (2023) [8], Ai et al. (2024) [9] have incorporated a question-attended span extraction (QASE) module into generative model. The second enhances the reasoning capabilities of Large Language Models (LLMs) on MSQA through designed prompting strategies. For instance, Huang et al. (2023) [10] have expanded conventional few-shot learning prompting templates by incorporating human feedback to regulate LLM outputs.

Overall, the community has made significant strides in MSQA, yet there remains a lack of succinct and effective methods for modeling interactions between answer spans, resulting in underutilization of annotated answers. Therefore, we introduce a novel framework aimed at enhancing the model's capability for span interaction modeling. It is designed to integrates complete answer spans information into the [CLS] representation through two contrastive learning tasks during the continued pre-training phase. Consequently, during fine-tuning, the model can utilize self-attention layers to perform span interaction modeling via token interaction.

2.2   Span Modeling Methods

Previous work has focused on two key issues: 1) how to capture span boundaries and 2) how to represent of spans. Specifically, span modeling efforts have centered around information extraction fields such as named entity recognition and relation extraction, where their effectiveness has been widely validated. For instance, SpanNER (Fu et al., 2021) [11] highlights this focus. Recognizing that the representations at the beginning and end of entity spans are often most informative, Yu et al. (2020) [12] introduced a dual affine interaction operator to map the start and end markers of spans to a span-level feature space. Building on this understanding, Xu et al. (2021) [13]and Su et al. (2021) [14] employed multi-head additive attention and multi-head dot-product attention, respectively, to model the category features of entity spans. Zhang et al. (2023) [15] proposed the SpanKL, which further segregates the feature space during span modeling. Before scaling dot-product interactions, SpanKL uses a single-layer feedforward network (FFN) to model the start and end points, employing a total of 2K different FFNs, where K represents the number of span categories.

To achieve comprehensive span modeling, some researches have designed more intricate frameworks. For instance, Tan et al. (2020) [16] introduced a boundary detection task using a sequence tagging model to detect entity boundaries, aiming to capture the dependencies between entity boundaries and their category labels through multitask learning. While models such as BERT and RoBERTa are effective in token representations, relying solely on the representations of a span's start token and end token to model span features is insufficient, inevitably leading to the informational missing of intermediate tokens. To address this, Zheng et al. (2022) [17] proposed a triple-affine mechanism that includes triple-affine attention and scoring. This mechanism integrates boundaries, labels, internal tokens, and associated spans into a unified span representation, and this scoring interacts with boundary and span representations for classifying entity spans.

In summary, attention layers and linear layers have been widely used to model spans on tasks with formats similar MSQA, such as information extraction. It is appropriate to leverage the interactions between tokens to handle the interactions between spans, through attention mechanisms during fine-tuning. Before this, to ensure the model has access to global span information for interaction within the attention layers, we continue pre-training to enable the [CLS] token to act as a carrier of both global sequence semantics and global answer span information. Additionally, to address potential deficiencies in span representation, caused by BERT or RoBERTa, we use SpanBERT as the foundational encoder, as it offers more comprehensive span information in its token representations.

3 Approach

The primary goal of Multi-Span Extractive Question Answering (MSQA) tasks is to extract spans from a context C_i to answer a question Q_i and. These answer spans form a set $L_i = \{S_{i0}, S_{i1}, \ldots, S_{1k}\}$, where each span S_{ij} (for all $0 \leq j \leq k$) is a subsequence of the context and does not overlap with others. Our method aims to address 2 issues: 1) how to enable the model to access span information, and 2) how to handle interactions of span during modeling. We hope to develop an enhanced encoder that can naturally integrate span information into token representations, making it suitable for various MSQA architectures. To achieve this, we proposed a sentence-embedding-based span modeling approach that adjusts the [CLS] representation through two distinct contrastive learning tasks, turning it into a medium that carries complete answer spans' information. Consequently, all downstream models, such as TASE, can directly use the internal attention layers to inject the global answer spans' information from the [CLS] into other token representations.

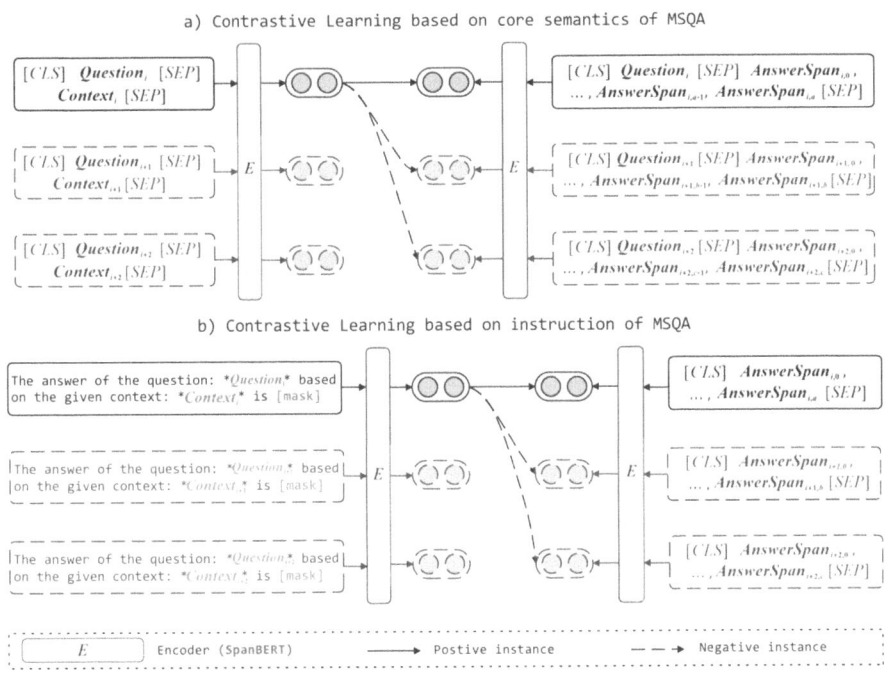

Fig. 1. An illustration of our framework architecture.

Under our framework, SpanBERT is an essential component for span representation. The SBO task enables token representations encoded by SpanBERT to carry extensive span information, allowing downstream models to achieve span interactions through attention interactions between tokens. This token-based span representation module, SpanBERT, ensures the effectiveness of token-based span interaction modules during the fine-tuning phase. Additionally, to activate the encoder's ability to process span interaction, as depicted in Fig. 1, we designed two complementary contrastive learning strategies during the continued pre-training phase: 1) We treat the sentence representations of "question-context" and "question-answer" sequences as positive pairs of contrast learning, termed "QC-QA" pairs. 2) We consider the [mask] representations in "question-context" sequences with template, and the sentence representations of answer sequences as another type of positive pairs of contrast learning, termed "PQC-A" pairs. These approach results in a sentence representation that carries global answer representations for downstream fine-tuning.

3.1 Contrastive Learning Based on Core Semantics of MSQA

We designed a template, $Temp_0$: :"$[X_0], [X_1], ..., [X_a]$", where each $[X_i]$ is a placeholder for an answer span. Assuming $A_i = \{S_{i0}, S_{i1}, ..., S_{1k}\}$ is the set of answer spans for question Q_i and context C_i, we use this template to map the set A_i to a natural language sentence PA_i. We then input the $< Q_i, C_i >$ and $< Q_i, PA_i >$ into the same SpanBERT respectively, obtaining the [CLS] representations for each sequence. Here, we suggest that in general question-answering task, the core semantics or focus of the sentence representation of input sequence $< Q_i, C_i >$, logically align with the answer spans in $< Q_i, C_i >$. Specifically, the function of the question extends beyond merely seeking information; it serves as an intent that channels the people's attention towards segments of the context that contain potential answers. Particularly, under the attention mechanism, the question in a QA can be seen as a volitional cue that directs the semantic focus to the tokens within the context that directly relevant to the query. Thus, the core semantics of the $< Q_i, C_i >$ can be viewed as $< Q_i, PA_i >$.

Based on this, for i^{th} example in batch, we treat each $< Q_i, C_i >$ and its semantically central counterpart $< Q_i, PA_i >$ as a positive pair of contrastive learning, with other examples and their positive pairs within the same batch serving as negatives. In essence, this task's objective is to integrate the comprehensive answer spans information within the overall semantics. By this way, encoder can easily connect various answer spans in context via interacting tokens within these spans during fine-tuning. Formally, let h_i^{qc} and h_i^{qa} respectively denote the sentence representations of $< Q_i, C_i >$ and $< Q_i, PL_i >$. For a batch size of N, and using τ as the temperature coefficient, the training objective for this task is defined as follows:

$$l_1 = -\log \frac{e^{\cos\left(h_i^{qc}, h_i^{qa}\right)/\tau}}{\sum_{j=0}^{N}\left(e^{\cos\left(h_i^{qc}, h_j^{qc}\right)/\tau} + e^{\cos\left(h_i^{qc}, h_j^{qa}\right)/\tau}\right)} \tag{1}$$

3.2 Contrastive Learning Based on Instructions of MSQA

To enhance the encoder's adaptability for answering question and alleviate the inadequate representation of [CLS], we have introduced another contrastive learning objective. Specifically, we have designed a new template, $Temp_1$: :"The answer of the question *QUESTION* based on the given context *CONTEXT* is [mask]". Here, "*QUESTION*" and "*CONTEXT*" serve as placeholders for the question and context sequences, respectively, while "[mask]" signifies the [MASK] token. Given a question Q_i and context C_i, along with a corresponding set of answer spans $A_i = \{S_{i0}, S_{i1}, \ldots, S_{1k}\}$, we use $Temp_0$ to map A_i into a natural language sentence PA_i. Similarly, $Temp_1$ maps $< Q_i, C_i >$ into another natural language sentence PQC_i.. [MASK] in PQC_i represents the complete answer inferred by the model, and should align with the gold answer sequence PA_i in semantic space. Based on this, we input PQC_i and PA_i into the same encoder respectively, using the last hidden state of [MASK] in PQC_i (denoted as $h_i^{[MASK]}$) and the last hidden state of [CLS] in PA_i (denoted as h_i^a) as an anther positive pair for contrastive learning. Other examples and their corresponding positive examples from the same batch serve as negatives for each example.

Additionally, to mitigate interference from the template within the inferred answer, for each PQC_i, we fill $Temp_1$ with [X] to ensure another template sequence $TempX_i$, that is exactly the same length as PQC_i. Furthermore, we also input $TempX_i$ into the encoder to obtain the representation of [MASK], denoted as $ht_i^{[MASK]}$. We consider $h_i^{[MASK]} - ht_i^{[MASK]}$ as the purified semantic of the answer, thereby refining the $h_i^{[MASK]}$. Formally, the training objective for this task is as follows:

$$l_2 = -\log \frac{e^{\frac{\cos\left(h_i^{[MASK]} - ht_i^{[MASK]}, h_i^a\right)}{\tau}}}{\sum_{j=0}^{N}\left(e^{\frac{\cos\left(h_i^{[MASK]} - ht_i^{[MASK]}, h_j^{[MASK]} - ht_j^{[MASK]}\right)}{\tau}} + e^{\frac{\cos\left(h_i^{[MASK]} - ht_i^{[MASK]}, h_j^a\right)}{\tau}}\right)} \quad (2)$$

Intuitively, this task requires the model to capture the complete information of answer span represented by [MASK], thereby enhancing its ability to answering in MSQA. Moreover, given that encoders from the BERT family generally perform well in token representation but are less effective at sentence representation, this objective attempt to bridge the semantic gap between the [MASK] token and the sentence embedding, thus improving the representation of [CLS]. Finally, the total loss function is as follows:

$$l = l_1 + l_2 \quad (3)$$

4 Experiment

In this section, we initially selected classical encoders with comparable model scale to implement several robust baselines for MSQA, in order to prove the effectiveness of our method. We begin by introducing the benchmark and experimental setup, followed by presenting and analyzing the experimental results.

4.1 Experiment Setting

We selected the MultiSpanQA dataset, a typical English multi-span question-answering dataset, as our benchmark. This dataset is specifically designed for questions requiring answers with two or more spans. The datasets were sourced from the Natural Questions and were subsequently re-annotated to highlight multi-span characteristics. The base version of this dataset comprises over 6,000 multi-span questions, while the expanded version adds more than 10,000 entries, including unanswerable questions and questions with single-span answers. Considering our study's focus on span interaction modeling, and since unanswerable and single-span questions do not require span interaction, we have chosen the base version of the MultiSpanQA dataset as our benchmark.

Secondly, to ensure a fair comparison among encoders, we selected the widely used $BERT_{base}$ as our baseline encoder, which is comparable in model scale to $SpanBERT_{base}$. Notably, several robust baselines for the MultiSpanQA benchmark have also been implemented on $BERT_{base}$ in previous studies. As described in the previous section, we use $SpanBERT_{base}$ as our primary encoder, and our continued pre-training tasks for span interaction modeling were conducted on this platform. Moreover, to analyze the effectiveness of each component within our framework, we implemented each robust baseline model on $SpanBERT_{base}$, and then compared their performance with those on $BERT_{base}$ and our enhanced encoder, SpanInteractor.

We selected four distinct models—TASE, LIQUID, Iterative Extractor, and SpanQualifier—as the baseline models for assess the effectiveness of our method. Additionally, we included a few-shot learning approach based on ChatGPT as another baseline model. The hyper-parameter settings for each baseline models were kept consistent with those reported in their papers, except for LIQUID. The hyper-parameters specified for the LIQUID in its paper do not adapt well to the SpanBERT and our framework. Given that the LIQUID approach focuses primarily on data augmentation without altering the original TASE architecture, we opted to fine-tune it with the hyper-parameter settings recommended for the TASE. And the parameter settings for the continued pre-training of our span interaction modeling are include a learning rate of 3e–5, a batch size of 64, gradient accumulation steps set at 8, a maximum sequence length of 512, a document stride of 128, a random seed of 42, and a total of 50 epochs.

Finally, in terms of evaluation metrics, following Li et al. (2022), we employ two types of scores: Exact Match (EM) and Partial Match (PM). We calculate the average precision, recall, and F1 score for these extraction matching metrics. An exact match occurs when the predicted span precisely corresponds with one of the actual answer spans. Partial match evaluates the overlap between the actual and predicted answers, determined by calculating the longest common substring between them.

4.2 Comparison Results

Table 2 presents the performance of various robust baseline models, including the current SOTA model, SpanQualifier, supported by $BERT_{base}$ and their performance on our encoder, SpanInteractor, which is optimized for span interaction modeling. The results indicate that all models achieve significant improvements in both exact match (EM) F1 and partial match (PM) F1 scores on SpanInteractor compared to $BERT_{base}$. Notably, despite SpanQualifier being specifically designed with modules for span representation and interaction, it still registers significant performance gains on SpanInteractor, thereby establishing a new SOTA at the $BERT_{base}$ model scale. Besides, with the support of our encoder, the simplest MSQA model, TASE, not only outperforms the top-performing model supported by $BERT_{base}$ but also exceeds the performance of few-shot learning strategies based on ChatGPT 3.5 for MultiSpanQA.

Table 2. Performance of All Competing Models Backed by BERT$_{base}$ and SpanInteractor

	Exact Match			Partial Match		
	F1(%)	P (%)	R (%)	F1(%)	P (%)	R (%)
BERT$_{base}$						
TASE	58.52	54.16	63.63	77.3	77.34	77.25
LIQUID	60.5	55.67	66.24	79.2	78.6	79.8
Iterative Extractor	61.97	62.25	61.7	79.47	80.53	78.43
SpanQualifier	67.49	62.57	79.09	79.43	79.09	79.43
ChatGPT	65.52	61.01	70.65	82.45	78.3	87.07
SpanInteractor						
TASE	**69.79**	**68.6**	**71.01**	**83.77**	**83.91**	**83.63**
LIQUID	**69.15**	**68.46**	**69.86**	**83.02**	**84.19**	**81.87**
Iterative Extractor	**68.32**	**67.48**	**69.18**	**83.06**	**83.10**	**83.02**
SpanQualifier	**70.35**	**72.19**	**68.6**	**82.11**	**85.37**	**79.09**

Specifically, all models consistently achieve higher exact match scores on SpanInteractor than on BERT$_{base}$. Supported by BERT$_{base}$, TASE, LIQUID, Iterative Extractor, and SpanQualifier achieved EM F1 scores on the MultiSpanQA benchmark of 58.52, 60.05, 61.97, and 67.49, respectively; whereas on SpanInteractor, these scores increased to 69.79, 69.15, 68.32, and 70.35. Compared to BERT$_{base}$, the adoption of SpanInteractor significantly elevated these models' EM F1 scores, with increases ranging from 2.88 to 11.27. Specifically, TASE improved by 11.27, LIQUID by 8.65, Iterative Extractor by 6.35, and SpanQualifier by 2.88.

The PM F1 results mirror the EM F1 trends: all models also saw substantial improvements in PM F1 scores on SpanInteractor, compared to BERT$_{base}$. Using BERT$_{base}$, TASE, LIQUID, Iterative Extractor, and SpanQualifier scored PM F1 results of 77.3, 79.2, 79.47, and 79.43, respectively; after employing SpanInteractor, these scores improved to 83.77, 83.02, 83.59, and 82.68, indicating improvements of 6.47, 3.82, 3.59, and 2.68 respectively. These results underscore the effectiveness of our span interaction modeling strategy, which combines various MSQA modeling paradigms, demonstrating robust generalization across different models' architectures and highlighting the importance of span interaction modeling for MSQA.

4.3 Ablation Study

To further analyze the effectiveness of each component within our framework, Table 3 presents ablation experiments detailing the performance of TASE, LIQUID, Iterative Extractor, and SpanQualifier on the SpanBERT$_{base}$. The results show that almost all models significantly improved their EM F1 and PM F1 scores on SpanBERT$_{base}$ compared to the BERT$_{base}$, highlighting the efficacy of our choice of span representation encoder. Moreover, the results for all models except the Iterative Extractor, on SpanBERT$_{base}$, are significantly lower than those on SpanInteractor, further underscoring the effectiveness of the continued pre-training component.

Table 3. Results from All Competing Models Using SpanBERT$_{base}$ as Backbones

	Exact Match			Partial Match		
	F1(%)	P (%)	R (%)	F1(%)	P (%)	R (%)
TASE	68.72	68.63	68.81	81.92	83.42	80.45
LIQUID	68.43	67.64	69.23	83.02	84.5	81.6
Iterative Extractor	70.23	70.34	70.12	83.57	84.39	82.75
SpanQualifier	69.79	67.89	71.79	82.62	82.08	82.16

Specifically, with SpanBERT$_{base}$, the EM F1 scores for TASE, LIQUID, Iterative Extractor, and SpanQualifier on MultiSpanQA dataset are 68.72, 68.43, 70.23, and 69.79, respectively; and their PM F1 scores are 81.92, 83.02, 83.57, and 82.6. In contrast, on the SpanInteractor, the objective of span interaction modeling led to declines in EM F1 scores for TASE, LIQUID, and SpanQualifier by 1.07, 0.72, and 0.56, respectively, while Iterative Extractor improved by 1.91. Unlike the other models, the Iterative Extractor uses an iterative querying approach to handle multi-span questions through single-span question answering, essentially a boundary recognition task. Hence, a model solely with robust single-span representation capabilities, such as SpanBERT$_{base}$, is well-suited to this model. It is noteworthy that although the Iterative Extractor performs better without the span interaction module, its EM F1 score based on SpanBERT$_{base}$ is still lower than our optimal results achieved on SpanInteractor.

Table 4. Results of Incrementally Adding Components to the TASE Architecture.

	Exact Match			Partial Match		
	F1(%)	P (%)	R (%)	F1(%)	P (%)	R (%)
TASE	58.52	54.16	63.63	77.3	77.34	77.25
+QC-QA	**62.68**	**61.03**	**61.42**	**76.49**	**77.39**	**75.61**
+QC-QA, PQC-A	**65.23**	**61.96**	**68.86**	**79.57**	**79.79**	**79.34**
+All	**69.79**	**68.6**	**71.01**	**83.77**	**83.91**	**83.63**

Additionally, Table 4 presents the ablation results of the TASE model on the MultiSpanQA with the gradual addition of each component. The results indicate that the standalone TASE model (merely utilizing BERT$_{base}$ as the encoder) achieved an EM F1 score of 58.52. This score increased to 62.68 after incorporating the contrastive learning strategy based on "QC-QA" pairs positive pairs, which activated the span information in the [CLS] representation. Building on this improvement, the score further increased to

65.23% with the subsequent addition of the contrastive learning strategy based on PQC-A positive examples, which strengthened the model's question-answering reasoning ability and adjusted the [CLS] representation capability. Finally, by replacing $BERT_{base}$ with $SpanBERT_{base}$ as the foundational encoder, and incorporating all previously mentioned strategies, the score reached 69.79. Similarly, the PM F1 score sequentially increased from 77.3 to 76.49, 79.57, and 83.77. These outcomes further demonstrate that our continued pre-training indeed enhance the span interactions modeling capabilities of model, thereby improving the performance of multi-span question answering models primarily based on sequence labeling and span classification paradigms, for which span interaction modeling is important.

5 Conclusion

In conclusion, we propose a concise and effective method for modeling span interactions, which primarily includes two components: 1) a span representation module that utilizes SpanBERT to enhance the span information within token representation, and 2) a span interaction module that employs 2 contrastive learning tasks to strengthen answer spans' interaction within token representation. This approach has resulted in a specific encoder, SpanInteractor, which enables our framework to be applicable across various MSQA models. Based on SpanInteractor, various models, during fine-tuning, can use the attention layers within the encoder to incorporate span information into token representations through interactions between the [CLS] token and other tokens. Experiments indicate that our method effectively addresses the limitations of existing models in span interaction modeling, with achieving the best performance, on MultiSpanQA, at comparable model scale.

References

1. Li, H., Tomko, M., Vasardani, M., et al.: MultiSpanQA: a dataset for multi-span question answering. In: NACAL-HLT 2022, pp. 1250–1260 (2022)
2. Luo, Z., Zhang, Y., Luo, S., et al.: A dataset of open-domain question answering with multiple-span answers. arXiv preprint arXiv:2402.09923 (2024)
3. Huang, Z., Zhou, J., Niu, C., et al.: Spans, not tokens: a span-centric model for multi-span reading comprehension. In: CIKM 2023, pp. 874–884 (2023)
4. Joshi, M., Chen, D., Liu, Y., et al.: Spanbert: improving pre-training by representing and predicting spans. In: TACL 2020, pp. 64–77 (2020)
5. Lee, S., Kim, H., Kang, J.: LIQUID: a framework for list question answering dataset generation. In: AAAI2023, pp. 13014–13024 (2023)
6. Segal, E., Efrat, A., Shoham, M., Globerson, A., et al.: A simple and effective model for answering multi-span questions. In: EMNLP 2019, pp. 3074–3080 (2019)
7. Luo, Z., Zhang, Y., Luo, S.: A Token-based transition-aware joint framework for multi-span question answering. Inf. Process. Manage. **61**(3), 103678 (2023)
8. Zhang, C., Lin, J., Liu, X., et al.: How many answers should i give? An empirical study of multi-answer reading comprehension. In: ACL 2023, pp. 5811–5827 (2023)
9. Ai, L., Hui, Z., Liu, Z., et al.: Enhancing pre-trained generative language models with question attended span extraction on machine reading comprehension. arXiv preprint arXiv:2404.17991(2024)

10. Huang, Z., Zhou, J., Xiao, G., et al.: Enhancing in-context learning with answer feedback for multi-span question answering. In: NLPCC 2023, pp. 744–756 (2023)
11. Fu, J., Huang, X., Liu, P.: SpanNER: named entity recognition as span prediction. In: ACL 2021, pp. 7183–7195 (2021)
12. Yu, J.; Bohnet, B., Poesio, M.: Named entity recognition as dependency parsing. In: ACL 2020, 6470–6476 (2020)
13. Xu, Y.; Huang, H., Feng, C., et al.: A SupFervised multi-head self-attention network for nested named entity recognition. In: AAAI 2021, pp. 14185–14193 (2021)
14. Su, J., Murtadha, A., Pan, S., et al.: Global pointer: novel efficient span-based approach for named entity recognition. arXiv preprint arXiv:2208.03054 (2022)
15. Zhang, Y., Chen, Q.: A neural span-based continual named entity recognition model. In: AAAI 2023, pp. 13993–14001 (2023)
16. Tan, C., Qiu, W., Chen, M., et al.: Boundary enhanced neural span classification for nested named entity recognition. In: AAAI 2020, pp. 9016–9023 (2020)
17. Zheng, Y., Tan, C., Huang, S., et al.: Fusing heterogeneous factors with triaffine mechanism for nested named entity recognition. In: ACL 2022, pp. 3174–3186 (2022)

FacGPT: An Effective and Efficient Method for Evaluating Knowledge-Based Visual Question Answering

Sirui Cheng, Siyu Zhang, Jiayi Wu, Muchen Lan, and Yaoru Sun[✉]

The Department of Computer Science and Technology, Tongji University,
Shanghai, China
{2332021,zsyzsy,2332019,2332020,yaoru}@tongji.edu.cn

Abstract. Enhancing the accuracy of model evaluation accelerates the subsequent optimization process of large visual language models (LVLMs). However, evaluating the diversity of LVLM outputs is challenging. The long-form responses provided by LVLM are susceptible to interference from visual facts, which mainly manifests as factual inaccuracies stemming from not following the given image instructions. This problem makes the traditional Exact Match evaluation method no longer satisfied with measuring the correct expression of LVLM. To this end, this paper proposes KVQA-Eval, a novel evaluation benchmark aiming to reflect the discriminative ability of LVLM in the knowledge VQA domain. We propose a dataset (40k) called K-VQA, which improves the evaluation of answer correctness by incorporating human annotations. Furthermore, we train a scalable and deterministic FacGPT evaluator model based on GPT2. FacGPT not only achieves better correlation with human evaluators and GPT4 but also improves evaluation efficiency by 300%. More encouragingly, this evaluation model will help promote the development of automated evaluation tools due to their data safety, cost-effectiveness, and reproducibility. Our open-source code, dataset, and model at https://github.com/Siri-2001/FacGPT.

Keywords: LVLM · Knowledge VQA · Evaluation benchmark

1 Introduction

Recently, Large Language Models (LLMs), such as ChatGPT, GPT-4 [1], and LLaMA [2], have made significant progress owing to their exceptional natural language processing capabilities. Given that much of human perception of the surrounding environment relies heavily on visual cues [3], it becomes imperative to integrate visual features into LLMs. Benefiting from the success of LLMs, many researchers have dedicated substantial efforts to extending them

---

S. Cheng and S. Zhang—Equal contribution.

© The Author(s), under exclusive license to Springer Nature Singapore Pte Ltd. 2025
D. F. Wong et al. (Eds.): NLPCC 2024, LNAI 15359, pp. 201–214, 2025.
https://doi.org/10.1007/978-981-97-9431-7_16

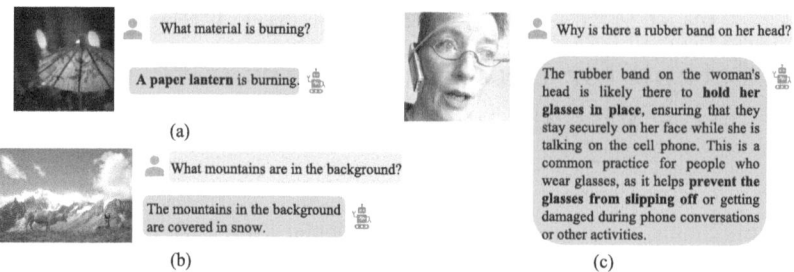

Fig. 1. Examples of visual information factual incorrectness generated by LVLMs. The factual incorrectness is indicated in **bold**.

into Large Visual Language Models (LVLMs) to enhance comprehension of real-world images, including Flamingo [4], LLaVA [5], and MiniGPT-4 [6].

While LVLMs have achieved commendable performance, evaluating the quality of their generation remains a challenge [7–11], primarily due to its long-form format and complex semantic information contained. On the one hand, the model is easy to make factual errors with visual inputs [12]. As shown in Fig. 1, the LVLM in both case (a) and case (c) generates incorrect descriptions and reasoning. In case (b), the LVLM only describes the content of the image without providing a direct answer. The above problems limit the practicality of LVLMs in different scenarios. However, it is difficult for commonly-used evaluation methods, such as Exact Match [13,14] and BERT-Score [15], to accurately evaluate the quality of model output. It is because of their lacking ability of understanding the complex semantic of the rich contexts. The traditional metric heavily relies on the lexical similarity between the golden answer and the generated answer. This limitation inherently hinders the method's ability to accommodate variability in answer descriptions when evaluating more advanced LVLMs. Some recent proposals [16,17] have adopted GPT-4 as an evaluation method, supplemented by meticulous human manual design. Although GPT-4 has the potential to be an evaluator, its closed-source nature limits transparent evaluation. In addition, frequent use of GPT-4 or other OpenAI Trans-former Agents may increase the risk of data leakage. Given this, employing high-quality human evaluations is critical to improving evaluation benchmarks. For visual question answering tasks in the open knowledge domain, human evaluation remains the most reliable discriminant method. However, biases, the number of evaluations, times, and the substantial computational costs associated with the human evaluation process hinder its large-scale use [18,19]. To effectively promote the development of automatic evaluation tools, we inherit the 'LM-as-a-Judge' paradigm [20–23] using language models (LMs) as evaluators and propose the KVQA-Eval evaluation benchmark.

Unlike previous evaluation methods that focus on understanding and reasoning of language content, we consider visual facts to comprehensively improve the comprehensive evaluation capabilities of multi-modal models. We construct the K-VQA dataset based on the currently popular LVLM generator, containing 40k augmented data that determines the correctness of facts based on specific rules. This dataset is designed to optimize implementation through guide generation and manual annotation. We also propose a visual fact-based evaluation model FacGPT based on GPT-2. The test set provided in the experiments shows that FacGPT correlates better with human judgment and is competitive with state-of-the-art evaluations. The contributions of this article can be summarized as follows:

– We propose the KVQA-Eval evaluation benchmark, which thoroughly analyzes the fine-grained performance of existing LVLMs in knowledge-based VQA tasks by emphasizing the impact of visual content on language comprehension.
– We design a novel K-VQA dataset, which is the first dataset for evaluating VQA tasks in open knowledge domains.
– We develop FacGPT by utilizing the K-VQA dataset as a foundation, a robust fact correctness discrimination model based on GPT2. It not only achieves 96.9% of the evaluation performance of GPT-4 but also improves evaluation speed by 300%. More importantly, this model will help promote the development of automatic evaluation tools due to its advantages of information security, low cost, and reproducibility.

2   Related Work

Evaluation for Large Visual Language Models. Recent methods such as MME [16] proposed an automatic evaluation strategy based on LVLM, which limits the model output to a binary type ("yes" or "no") to effectively judge the accuracy of the model. MMBench [24] adopted ChatGPT to match the model's prediction with a given choice. After that, MM-Vet [17] redefined VL capabilities, allowing the evaluation across different question types and answer choices. MLLM-Bench [32] introduced a benchmark for automatically evaluating the MLLMs' ability on open-ended queries. Furthermore, other researchers aimed at a comprehensive evaluation of models, concluding that the absolute performance of models was far from ideal.

Knowledge-Based VQA Datasets. Knowledge-based VQA requires knowledge of the world beyond the image content to correctly answer questions. Such knowledge can be retrieved from various resources, including Wikipedia articles, Internet search engines, and common concepts. KB-VQA [25] is the early exploration dataset, which contains 2,402 questions generated from templates for 700 images. Later on, F-VQA [26] is widely used as a knowledge-based VQA dataset focusing on multimodal reasoning. F-VQA consists of 5,826 questions, each referring to a fact triplet (*e.g.*, "peaches are fruits") retrieved from an external knowledge base. Specifically, "peaches" or "fruits" in this example are used as two nodes to infer the correct answer. The recent OK-VQA dataset [27] is designed on COCO images in the open domain. 14,055 questions are obtained from 14,031 images, each with 5 ground-truth answers.

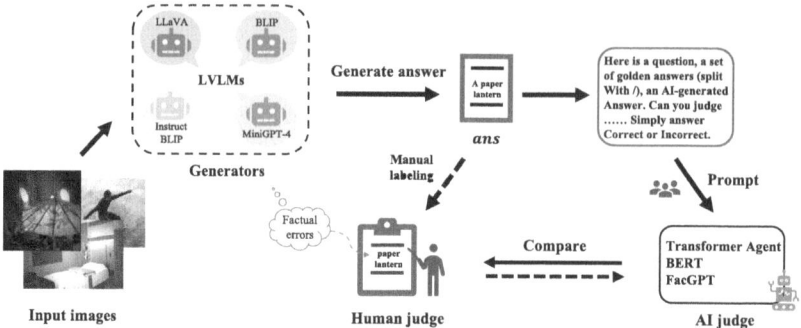

Fig. 2. An illustration of KVQA-Eval Framework.

3   Method

The incorporation of multimodal data has heralded a paradigm shift in artificial intelligence, but current evaluation benchmarks struggle to accurately capture changes in answer descriptions. Hence, evaluating the generalization ability of large models poses a significant challenge. There are two common ways to improve LVLM models, namely collecting and building higher quality data or designing a more general large model. Instead, we focus more on improving evaluation. For similar models, slight differences may swap the order of the models. However, it makes sense to improve the quality of evaluation by training on the right objects. In this section, we propose an evaluation benchmark VQA-Eval, which mainly involves three essential parts: generator evaluation, human evaluation guidelines, and evaluation method analysis. Here, the proposed KVQA-Eval benchmark aims to train LM as an automatic evaluator and compare it with human-evaluated standards. Considering the quantitative performance statistics, we designed a binary judgment prompt output for the model. The prompt design mainly includes two parts, *i.e.*, concise questions, and corresponding answers. The answers can be further divided into human-preferred gold standard answers and LVLM-generated answers. The illustration of this evaluation method is shown in Fig. 2.

3.1   LVLM-Based Generators

Since the proposed KVQA-Eval evaluation benchmark focuses more on evaluating the factual accuracy of the model. To this end, we studied the performance and error analysis of seven currently mainstream LVLM baselines, including LLaVA-v1.5 (7b & 13b) [7], InstructBLIP (7b) [8], MiniGPT-4 (7b) [6], MiniGPT-v2 (7b) [28], BLIP-2 (7b) [29], VisualGLM (8b) [30], and Open-Flamingo (9b) [31], in the domain of knowledge VQA. Furthermore, their output can be used to collect and build the K-VQA dataset.

Specifically, a given image I is first defined, and a natural language question Q within an open knowledge domain. Then, the LVLM-based model $\mathcal{M}$ is tasked with generating the corresponding answer ans, while the gold standard answer is denoted as Ans. Subsequently, the question $\mathcal{Q}$ is fed into the model $\mathcal{M}$ to obtain the generated answer ans, expressed as follows:

$$ans = \mathcal{M}_{LVLM}(\mathcal{Q}) \tag{1}$$

where $\mathcal{M}_{LVLM}$ represents the current LVLMs, which contains LLaVA-v1.5, InstructBLIP, MiniGPT-4, MiniGPT-v2, BLIP-2, VisualGLM, and Open-Flamingo.

3.2   Human Evaluation Guidelines

Compared with traditional VQA datasets, it is challenging to evaluate the LVLM output in knowledge-based VQA task scenarios. On the one hand, knowledge-based VQA involves obtaining information from external knowledge bases, which diversifies the output results. On the other hand, LVLM tends to output image-related long-form responses. Based on this broad evaluation perspective, it is necessary to construct an augmented K-VQA dataset (40k), which contains 2000 OK-VQA and 500 F-VQA. It is worth noting that OK-VQA and F-VQA are chosen for the following two reasons: *1)* They are larger in scale and can provide more knowledge-based questions and answers. *2)* Due to the current lack of available knowledge source lists for external knowledge, making them more open and challenging. To ensure the quality of the dataset collection, we conduct reliable human annotations to verify the answers Ans of the LVLM-based generator response obtained from Sect. 3.1.

Specifically, we collected four elements for each case in the K-VQA dataset, including the question $\mathcal{Q}$ based on the knowledge VQA dataset, the gold standard answer Ans, the LVLM-based generator response answer ans, and the human-assisted judgment $Judge$ (*i.e.*, the annotators are asked to determine whether it is correct or incorrect). Moreover, we employ the assistance of three human annotators to conduct manual evaluations, providing them with detailed guidance and examples beforehand to ensure the stability of the evaluation results by different human annotators. The specific guidelines are as follows:

Guideline 1: ans must correspond to at least one potential candidate in Ans (*i.e., ans* $\in Ans$). If there is an obvious answer and a detailed explanation in ans, you only care whether the obvious answer is correct.

Guideline 2: For years, if only specific years are involved in Ans, then Ans must be evaluated to the specific year. If Ans only includes fuzzy years, the year in ans must fall within the range of these fuzzy years. If both of the aforementioned situations occur simultaneously, ans must align with the fuzzy year specified in Ans. To determine ans to be a specific year, ans must match the specific year provided in Ans. If the input question explicitly inquires about the year or date, the corresponding ans must reference the specific year or date.

Guideline 3: For categories, it is similar to the year. If *Ans* only includes specific categories, the *ans* must pertain to specific categories. If there is a broad category in *Ans*, it may either encompass the broad category or a specific category consistent with the image description. If *Ans* contains both broad categories and specific categories, *ans* must correspond to either the broad category or the specific category in *Ans*.

Guideline 4: For the location, if the question only asks "*where*", the *ans* must be assessed by referring to the year and categories of questions. Here, the location simply needs to match that specified in *Ans*. Once the question is precise to a specific "*state*" or "*country*", then *ans* must provide a clear response accordingly.

3.3 Evaluators Analysis

To verify the ability of LM to evaluate knowledge-based VQA systems and the degree of matching human preferences, we used three representative evaluation methods, namely Exact Match, LLM, and BERT-Score methods. In addition, we also introduce the FacGPT evaluation model.

Exact Match: Traditional VQA evaluation method requires writing a text output given an image and a text question, which has been widely used to evaluate open-ended VQA systems. Here, we use the short-form answers from OK-VQA and F-VQA datasets as candidate answers in the input. Each question has ten free-response answers generated by different annotators, ensuring that the people who ask questions are not the same as those who provide answers. An accuracy metric to evaluate the generated answers for each test image is expressed as follows:

$$Accuracy = min(\frac{\#humans\ provided\ answer}{3}, 1) \tag{2}$$

where #humans provided answer means the number of humans that provided answers. If at least three people provided that exact answer, the corresponding score is deemed 100%.

Large Language Models: The current LLMs have evaluation potential due to their impressive generalization abilities. In this work, we incorporate human annotations and advanced LLMs as evaluators to enable automated evaluation. Concretely, we prompt an LLM to generate a question q, the AI-generated answer *ans*, and golden standard answers *Ans*. The prediction $\mathcal{Y}$ can be calculated by feeding the prompt into the LVLMs as follows:

$$\mathcal{Y} = \mathcal{M}_{LLM}(prompt) \tag{3}$$

where $\mathcal{M}$ denotes the LLM-based models. Here, we select Transformer Agents (GPT4).

BERT-Score: BERT-score is one of the typical methods that shows remarkable ability in QA result evaluation. This work chooses the BERT-score as the neural evaluation mechanism, which judges the similarity between the generated answer sequence and the gold standard answer sequence in a binary manner.

FacGPT: In this work, we propose a robust FacGPT evaluation model based on the K-VQA dataset. It mainly uses GPT-2 as the basic backbone model, and the training process adopts sequence classification. The input sequence will contain a fixed phrase "Judge", which helps prevent degradation during inference. It is worth noting that the hyperparameters set during training are the same as GPT-2.

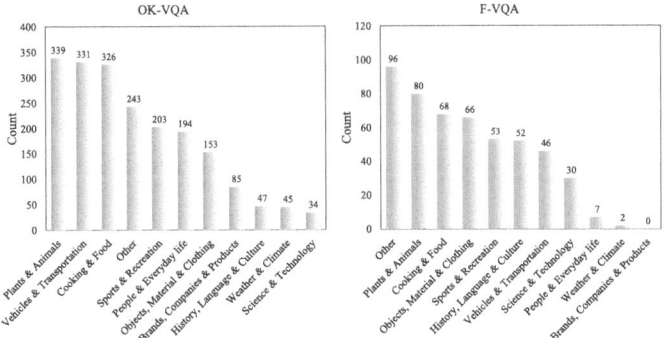

Fig. 3. Distribution statistics of knowledge question types in K-VQA dataset.

4   Experimental Results

4.1   Parameter Settings

In the development of the FacGPT model, we use DialogRPT as the backbone network. AdamW is selected as the optimizer, where the learning rate is set to 2×10^{-5} and the weight decay is set to 1×10^{-3}. Additionally, the batch size for model training is set to 2 and the number of training iterations is 5. It is worth noting that all programming tasks in this study are performed using Python 3.6 and PyTorch 1.7. All code runs use two NVIDIA A100 (40G) GPUs.

4.2   Dataset Analysis

Figure 3 presents the distribution of knowledge-based question types within the subsets of OK-VQA and F-VQA. Each question corresponds to the answers to 7 LVLM generator responses. Here we group them into eleven different categories, which helps to understand the range and diversity of the dataset fully. In Fig. 4,

Generators	Generated Answer *ans*	Human Judge
LLaVA(7b)	In the image, there is a hospital bed with a patient lying on it, surrounded by various medical equipment and supplies. A person might need to be in this place for medical reasons, such as receiving treatment, recovering from an illness or injury, or undergoing a medical procedure. The presence of the hospital bed, medical equipment, and supplies suggests that the patient is receiving care and attention from medical professionals to help them recover and improve their health.	incorrect
BLIP	Because it is a hospital room.	incorrect
InstructBLIP	Someone might need to be in the hospital room depicted in the photo for medical treatment or observation. The room features a hospital bed with a tray on it, a clock on the wall, and a chair near the bed. These elements suggest that the room serves as a patient's temporary living space during their hospital stay, where they can rest, receive medical care, and monitor their vital signs. Additionally, the presence of a clock on the wall allows patients to keep track of time, which can be an important aspect of maintaining their mental and emotional well-being during their hospitalization.	correct
MiniGPT-4	A hospital room for patients who need medical attention.	correct

Fig. 4. An illustrative example from the K-VQA dataset.

we provide examples of answers generated by different models to the same question. The question in focus is *"Why might someone need to be in the place of this photo?"*, with the golden answer being *"sick/they are sick"*. Human judges then provide corresponding judgments by analyzing the accuracy of each generated answer.

4.3 Human Annotator Evaluation

This work invited three annotators to collaborate to ensure consistency and accuracy among different annotators during the annotation process. Furthermore, we instruct annotators to go beyond evaluating the correctness of responses, enabling them to emphasize clarity, thoroughness, and compliance with instructions. Table 1 provides Cohen's Kappa index of different Inter-Annotator Agreements (IAA). For different model output results, partial subsets are randomly selected three times for labeling in OK-VQA for different annotators, and their average value is calculated. The average IAA scores of the three annotators are all above 90, as measured by Cohen's Kappa, indicating the relatively high reliability of using human annotations as the evaluation criterion.

Table 1. Inter-annotator agreement for OK-VQA dataset

Cohen 's Kappa	LLaVA (7b)	(13b)	Instruct BLIP	MiniGPT –4	BLIP	Visual GLM	Open Flamingo
Annotator 1 & 2	96.7	92.3	97.2	95.9	96.3	91.0	91.3
Annotator 1 & 3	95.9	96.5	96.2	98.0	97.2	89.2	93.5

4.4 Human Evaluation of K-VQA

Table 2 provides a performance comparison between human evaluation and Exact Match on OK- VQA and F-VQA. It is observed that there are significant differences between the Exact Match and human evaluation results in all models.

Table 2. Performance comparison of human evaluation and Exact Match

Generators	OK-VQA		F-VQA	
	Human score	Exact Match	Human score	Exact Match
LLaVA(7b)	77.30	70.85	78.40	78.00
LLaVA(13b)	78.20	72.95	76.80	77.20
InstructBLIP	80.20	67.55	80.00	68.40
MiniGPT-4	52.20	47.30	42.00	40.00
MiniGPT-2v	70.10	64.65	80.40	66.00
BLIP	48.40	20.50	68.80	57.60
VisualGLM	52.75	50.79	61.60	71.20
OpenFlamingo	47.00	40.00	56.00	44.00

For example, for LLaVA-13b and InstructBLIP, their average deviation amplitude is about 5%–10%, which inevitably affects the performance evaluation of the model. This experiment also reflects the weakness of the Exact Match evaluation metric, which shows that it is not suitable for evaluating LVLMs. In addition, the relative rankings between the two metrics differ for different models. However, even the best-performing models do not achieve perfect accuracy. For example, InstructBLIP has an accuracy of about 80% on OK-VQA, which shows that there is still room for improvement in model evaluation metrics.

Table 3. Performance comparison of different evaluation metrics

Generators	Accuracy	Precision	Recall	Macro-F1
LLaVA(7b)	85.65	97.17	84.79	90.56
LLaVA(13b)	88.95	95.95	89.62	92.68
InstructBLIP	84.15	98.66	81.67	89.37
MiniGPT-4	91.60	97.67	90.14	93.76
MiniGPT-2v	92.80	98.78	91.01	94.73
BLIP	93.00	91.95	77.89	84.34
VisualGLM	82.05	84.31	81.04	82.64
OpenFlamingo	85.80	91.00	77.44	83.67

Table 3 tests the performance comparison of Exact Match based on the OK-VQA subset on different indicators, in which the model is judged based on human annotation criteria. Specific performance indicators include TP, FN, FP, TN, accuracy, precision, recall, and Macro-F1. Although Exact Match achieves a precision of about 98% on most models, the overall performance of the recall rate is not ideal. This causes the overall performance of the Macro-F1 value to fluctuate between 74% and 85%, which cannot meet the needs of evaluating the model.

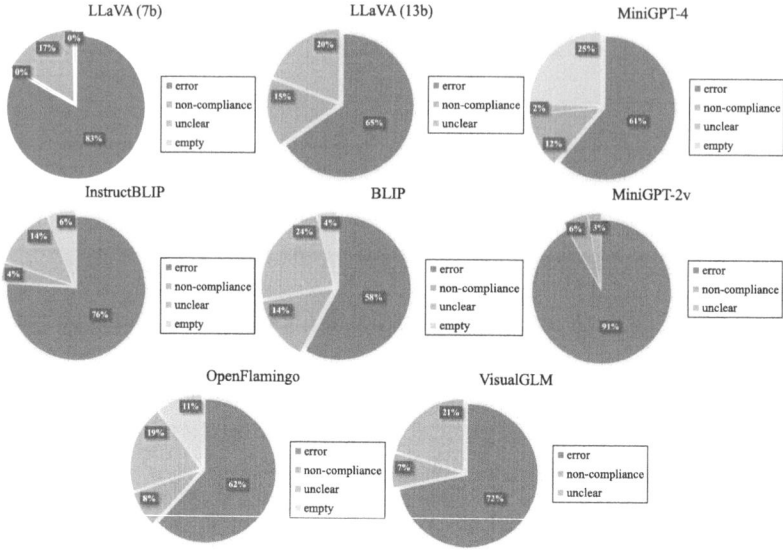

Fig. 5. Distribution of error answer categories provided by different generators.

4.5   Generator Performance Evaluation

To more accurately evaluate model performance, we perform the error categories analysis for each generator to explore their inherent limitations fully. The error categories mainly include four common cases: *1) "error"*, which means that the generator answered the question, but provided an answer that did not meet the gold standard answer. *2) "unclear"*, *i.e.*, the generator did not answer explicitly for some reason. *3) "empty"*, indicates that the answer content is NAN or empty. This is due to the generator having trouble understanding the input prompt and not responding with an answer. *4) "non-compliance"*, *i.e.*, the generator does not output the answer according to the requirements of the question, for example, it only describes the image content and other information. Figure 5 shows the performance effect of each generator and the categories for producing error answers. The category *"error"* generally accounts for a higher proportion, followed by the category *"unclear"*. For *"empty"*, MiniGPT-4 accounts for 25%, which indirectly shows that this model is weaker in understanding ability than other models.

4.6   Evaluator Analysis

In this work, we focused on testing and analyzing the performance of four evaluators on the K-VQA dataset, including our FacGPT and other three mainstream

Table 4. Various performance tests on the OK-VQA

Evaluators	Accuracy	Precision	Recall	Macro-F1	Times (cases\min)	Security	API Cost
Exact Match	87.05	93.29	82.96	87.77	≈10 million	Good	-
BERT-Score	68.80	85.40	74.30	79.40	≈170	Good	–
GPT-4	93.00	95.80	94.50	95.20	≈100	Bad	3.8\$ 1000\cases
FacGPT	89.00	92.34	92.08	92.21	≈3000	Good	–

evaluators. such as BERT-Score, Exact Match, and GPT-4. Note that BERT-Score and GPT-4 are only recognized by the generator model LLaVA-1.5(7b) that created them. Table 4 not only provides various evaluation metrics on the OK-VQA subset, but also tests the evaluation speed, API usage cost, and data security status. Next, we will discuss various evaluators in detail to provide a comprehensive in-depth analysis of their limitations.

Based on the above experimental observations, Exact Match achieves higher precision rates but lower recall rates, making it difficult to evaluate answers with diversity effectively. For BERT-Score, as shown in Table 4, both precision and recall are at lower scores. This is because once the model answers more complex questions, more representation information will be derived, resulting in a decrease in evaluation performance. Additionally, a response may be judged to be incorrect even if a correct answer appears in the response. GPT-4 remains the most powerful LLM estimator currently available. However, observing Table 4, we can find that GPT-4 has many problems, such as *1)* OpenAI has very high requirements for network environment configuration. Given that the servers used by some domestic research institutions cannot effectively connect to the network due to data privacy protection issues, this will pose a serious challenge to the OpenAI-based evaluation benchmark. *2)* The use of Transformer Agent will incur expensive API fees. When performing a large amount of evaluation work, the consumption introduced by the API can significantly increase the computational overhead. *3)* The Transformer Agent is rate-limited. The Tier-1 standard formulated on the official website is 500 cases\min, but in this work, the speed of network re-quest generation and the time the API request waits for the output to end can only reach about 50 cases\min. Our FacGPT model is trained on a GPT-2-based backbone. As shown in Table 4, FacGPT outperforms other evaluation benchmarks FacGPT not only achieves obvious advantages in speed but can also achieve 96% performance of GPT-4 while ensuring data privacy and security, effectively reducing API usage costs. Moreover, FacGPT is better suited to the evaluation of factual correctness due to its reproducibility.

5   Limitations

Our study has some limitations. First, our evaluation results come from OpenAI's API or webpage, and Transformer Agent is frequently updated, so they cannot be fully reproduced. Second, due to the constraints on OpenAI GPT-4V's API, we could not gather ample GPT-4V results for our KVQA-Eval experiments.

Finally, as the gold standard answers in the OK-VQA and F-VQA datasets occasionally contain inaccuracies, our dataset also carries the risk of inadvertently disseminating misinformation since we are not able to completely get rid of them.

6   Conclusion

We propose the KVQA-Eval evaluation benchmark, which aims to provide a powerful tool for a comprehensive review of open knowledge-based VQA models. Furthermore, we construct the K-VQA dataset combined with human annotations and propose a robust FacGPT model. We conducted an in-depth analysis of the results presented by different LVLMs on K-VQA to evaluate the strengths and weaknesses of each evaluator type. Experimental results show that the proposed FacGPT improves the evaluation capability of LVLMs and provides meaningful help for the subsequent optimization of model evaluators.

Acknowledgments. This study was funded by the National Natural Science Foundation of China (grant number 91748122).

Disclosure of Interests. The authors have no competing interests to declare that are relevant to the content of this article.

References

1. Bubeck, S., Chandrasekaran, V., Eldan, R.: Sparks of artificial general Intelligence: Early experiments with GPT-4.arXiv preprint arXiv:2303.12712 (2023)
2. Touvron, H., Lavril, T., Izacard, G.: LLaMA: open and efficient foundation language models. arXiv preprint arXiv:2302.13971 (2023)
3. Politzer, T.: Vision is our dominant sense. Brainline. https://www.brainline.org/article/vision-our-dominant-sense (2008)
4. Alayrac, J. B., Donahue, J., Luc, P.: Flamingo: a visual language model for few-shot learning. In: International Conference on Advances in Neural Information Processing Systems, vol. 35, pp. 23716–23736 (2022)
5. Liu, H., Li, C., Wu, Q.: Visual instruction tuning. In: International Conference on Advances in Neural Information Processing Systems, vol. 36 (2024)
6. Zhu, D., Chen, J., Shen, X.: Minigpt-4: Enhancing vision-language understanding with advanced large language models. In: The Twelfth International Conference on Learning Representations (2023)
7. Liu, H., Li, C., Li, Y., Lee, Y. J.: Improved baselines with visual instruction tuning. arXiv preprint arXiv: 2310.03744 (2023)
8. Dai, W., Li, J., Li, D.: Instructblip: towards general-purpose vision-language models with instruction tuning. In: International Conference on Advances in Neural Information Processing Systems, vol. 36 (2023)
9. Gao, P., Han, J., Zhang, R.: Llama-adapter v2: parameter-efficient visual instruction model. arXiv preprint arXiv: 2304.15010 (2023)
10. Ye, Q., Xu, H., Xu, G.: mplug-owl: modularization empowers large language models with multimodality. arXiv preprint arXiv: 2304.14178 (2023)

11. OpenAI GPT-4V(ision) system card. https://openai.com/research/gpt-4v-system-card (2023)

12. Lee, S., Kim, S., Park, S. H.: Prometheus-vision: vision-language model as a judge for fine-grained evaluation. arXiv preprint arXiv: 2401.06591 (2024)

13. Agrawal, A., Kajic, I., Bugliarello, E.: Reassessing evaluation practices in visual question answering: a case study on out-of-distribution generalization. Findings of the Association for Computational Linguistics: EACL, pp. 1201–1226 (2023)

14. Mañas, O., Krojer, B., Agrawal, A.: Improving automatic VQA evaluation using large language models. In: The AAAI Conference on Artificial Intelligence, vol. 38, no. 5, pp. 4171–4179 (2024)

15. Zhang, T., Kishore, V., Wu, F.: BERTScore: evaluating text generation with BERT. In: International Conference on Learning Representations (2019)

16. Yin, S., Fu, C., Zhao, S.: A survey on multimodal large language models. arXiv preprint arXiv:2306.13549 (2023)

17. Yu, W., Yang, Z., Li, L.: Mm-vet: evaluating large multimodal models for integrated capabilities. arXiv preprint arXiv:2308.02490 (2023)

18. Ye, S., Kim, D., Kim, S.: Flask: fine-grained language model evaluation based on alignment skill sets. arXiv preprint arXiv:2307.10928 (2023)

19. Kim, S., Joo, S. J., Jang, Y.: Cotever: chain of thought prompting annotation toolkit for explanation verification. In:17th Conference of the European Chapter of the Association for Computational Linguistics: System Demonstrations, pp. 195–208 (2023)

20. Kim, S., Shin, J., Cho, Y.: Prometheus: inducing fine-grained evaluation capability in language models. arXiv preprint arXiv:2310.08491 (2023)

21. Wu, Z., Hu, Y., Shi, W.: Finegrained human feedback gives better rewards for language model training. In: International Conference on Advances in Neural Information Processing Systems, vol. 36 (2023)

22. Jang, J., Kim, S., Lin, B. Y.: Personalized soups: personalized large language model alignment via post-hoc parameter merging. arXiv preprint arXiv:2310.11564 (2023)

23. Kim, T. S., Lee, T., Shin, J.: Evallm: interactive evaluation of large language model prompts on user-defined criteria. arXiv preprint arXiv:2309.13633 (2023)

24. Liu, Y., Duan, H., Zhang, Y.: MMBench: is your multi-modal model an all-around player? arXiv preprint arXiv:2307.06281(2023)

25. Wang, P., Wu, Q., Shen, C., Dick, A.: Explicit knowledge-based reasoning for visual question answering. In: 26th International Joint Conference on Artificial Intelligence, pp. 1290–1296 (2017)

26. Chen, Z., Chen, J., Geng, Y.: Zero-shot visual question answering using knowledge graph. In: 20th International Semantic Web Conference, pp. 146–162 (2021)

27. Marino, K., Rastegari, M., Farhadi, A., Mottaghi, R.: Ok-VQA: a visual question answering benchmark requiring external knowledge. In: the IEEE Conference on Computer Vision and Pattern Recognition, pp. 3195–3204 (2019)

28. Chen, J., Zhu, D., Shen, X.: Minigpt-v2: large language model as a unified interface for vision-language multi-task learning. arXiv preprint arXiv:2310.09478 (2023)

29. Li, J., Li, D., Savarese, S.: BLIP-2: bootstrapping language-image pre-training with frozen image encoders and large language models. In: 40th International Conference on Machine Learning, pp. 19730–19742 (2023)

30. Du, Z., Qian, Y., Liu, X.: GLM: general language model pretraining with autoregressive blank infilling. In: 60th Annual Meeting of the Association for Computational Linguistics, pp. 320–335 (2022)

31. Awadalla, A., Gao, I., Gardner, J.: OpenFlamingo: an open-source framework for training large autoregressive vision-language models. arXiv preprint arXiv:2310.09478 (2023)
32. Ge, W., Chen, S., Hardy Chen, G.: MLLM-Bench: evaluating multimodals LLMs with per-sample criteria. arXiv preprint arXiv:2311.13951 (2024)

PAPER: A Persona-Aware Chain-of-Thought Learning Framework for Personalized Dialogue Response Generation

Yameng Li, Shi Feng[✉], Daling Wang, Yifei Zhang, and Xiaocui Yang

Department of Computer Science, Northeastern University, Shenyang, China
{liyameng,yangxiaocui}@stumail.neu.edu.cn,
{fengshi,wangdaling,zhangyifei}@cse.neu.edu.cn

Abstract. Endowing chatbots with a consistent persona is particularly important to generate engaging dialogues. Existing models struggle to effectively perceive and comprehend persona, especially when confronted with persona tags that have unique and obscure meanings, presenting barriers to generating a consistent response. Besides, previous studies have not fully utilized the rich persona information implied in the dialogue history. In this paper, we propose a **P**ersona-**A**ware chain-of-thought (CoT) learning framework for **PE**rsonalized **R**esponse generation (PAPER), encompassing the persona understanding stage, the persona perception stage and the response generation stage. Specifically, we first leverage persona explanation data to train the model to interpret persona tags, equipping the model with ability to comprehend and interpret personas. Moreover, the model obtained during the persona understanding stage is also employed to extract persona information from the dialogue history and generate persona explanations to enhance persona traits. Subsequently, we utilize expanded persona information and dialogue history to generate consistent response. The generated persona explanations and the persona information extracted from the dialogue are regarded as intermediate persona CoT rationales. The response generation can leverage generated persona CoT rationales that are based on persona tags and dialogue history. Extensive experiments demonstrate that PAPER outperforms baselines and can effectively improve the quality and persona consistency of generated responses.

Keywords: Personalized Dialogue Systems · Persona Perception · Large Language Models · Chain of Thought

1 Introduction

Building a more human-like dialogue system has attracted an increasing amount of research interests, where one of the critical yet challenging problems is endowing them with a specific persona, and generating responses that are both natural

D. F. Wong et al. (Eds.): NLPCC 2024, LNAI 15359, pp. 215–227, 2025.
https://doi.org/10.1007/978-981-97-9431-7_17

and consistent with this persona, enhancing the user's sense of experience and interaction. Previous studies explore character personality through key-value persona pairs [11] or concise descriptive sentences [19]. Promising performance have been achieved on these 'well-defined' persona datasets [2,17]. However, this may significantly constrain the interactivity between human and agent, especially when the agent is expected to respond to query that go beyond predefined personas. Additionally, these personas, characterized by predefined categories or descriptive sentences, tend to encompass only specific facets of information, thereby failing to capture the entirety of the speaker's personality trait and style. Consequently, the responses generated by these systems may lack a certain level of persona consistency.

Recently, Ju et al. [7] introduce a novel personalized dialogue dataset, HLA-Chat++, which utilizes tags as persona information. The persona tags in this dataset are usually very unique and rare words representing the unique persona of the character. For models, comprehending and perceiving these tags can be arduous, presenting barriers to generating consistent responses. To tackle this issue, Ju et al. [7] propose the PersonaTKG with addressee selecting mechanism that integrates personas, dialogue utterances, and external text knowledge into a unified graph. Despite these efforts, challenges such as sparse personas and the model's limited capacity to perceive character persona information still persist.

As humans, when it comes to learning a new word or idiom, we often rely on the previous accumulation of vocabulary. We start by learning some words and their meanings, developing the ability to interpret word definitions. When we encounter similar words, we can make analogies and draw connections, enabling us to understand and use new words to some extent. However, most existing LLM-based studies directly feed the persona or dialogue context to the LLM for generating a response with a preceding prompt, making the responses inconsistent and tedious. In the contrary, LLMs have shown impressive performance on complex reasoning by leveraging chain-of-thought (CoT) prompting to generate intermediate reasoning chains as the rationale to infer the answer [20]. There are several ways to elicit CoT reasoning, and a recent interest is eliciting CoT reasoning by fine-tuning language models with CoT annotations.

Building upon the aforementioned ideas and inspired by Zhang et al. [20], we propose PAPER, a **P**ersona-**A**ware chain-of-thought learning framework for **PE**rsonalized **R**esponse generation which comprises the persona understanding stage, the persona perception stage and the response generation stage. Unlike previous studies that generate responses directly based on pre-defined persona and dialogue history, we decompose personalized response generation task into different consecutive steps while the final step is to generate responses according to previous reasoning outputs. We refer to this process as the persona CoT reasoning process illustrated in Fig. 1(b).

We observe that there are explanations about partial persona tags for our reference on TVTropes website, as shown in Fig. 1(a). During the persona understanding stage, we fine-tune a large language model using persona explanation as CoT annotations to enhance its ability to recognize and comprehend persona

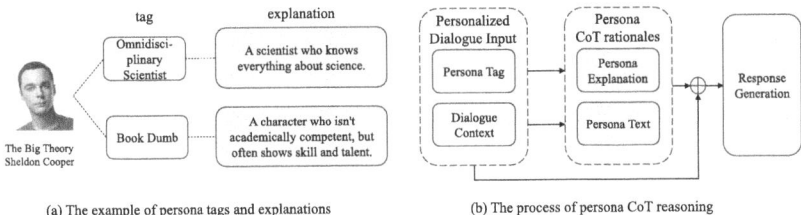

(a) The example of persona tags and explanations   (b) The process of persona CoT reasoning

Fig. 1. The example of persona tags and explanations, and the process of persona CoT reasoning.

tags, fostering an understanding of the underlying connections between persona tags and their explanations.

During the persona perception stage, we employ the model obtained during the persona understanding stage to generate persona CoT rationals to enhance persona traits. The model trained during the persona understanding stage possesses certain capabilities for recognizing personas, and it can better focus on as much conversational history as possible. Firstly, we leverage the model obtained during the persona understanding stage to interpret the speaker's persona tags in the dialogue, generating more comprehensible explanations of their persona. Additionally, to further enhance model consistency and its ability to effectively express one's persona, the model is also employed to extract persona information from the dialogue history. Specifically, we design a prompt template, employing prompt engineering to facilitate the model's extraction of personality information from the speaker's conversational history.

As shown in Fig. 1(b), we treat the persona explanations generated during the persona perception, along with the persona information extracted from the dialogue, as intermediate persona CoT rationales. In the response generation stage, we further fine-tune the model obtained in the previous stage by utilizing dialogue data and generated persona CoT rationals. Through this approach, we can enhance the model developed in the previous stage to enable it to generate responses maintaining persona consistency. Our model is intended to improve the overall performance of the dialogue system in comprehending and interpreting personas, and generating responses consistent with personas.

To summarize, our main contributions in this paper are as follows:

- We propose a chain-of-thought learning framework that enables the model to have persona-perception and persona-interpretive capabilities, while the model generates richer persona expanding information to generate responses consistent with persona.

- We design a persona enhancement method to assist personalized response generation by extracting speaker's personality information from rich dialogue history information leveraging a large language model trained during the persona understanding stage.

– We conduct extensive experiments, and automatic, human and LLM-based evaluations show that our proposed model can improve the quality and persona consistency of generated responses.

2   Related Work

2.1   Personalized Dialogue System

To improve persona consistency, many works explicitly use predefined persona descriptions or attributes as users' profile to generate personalized responses. Zhang et al. [19] constructed a new dataset Persona-Chat, where a pre-defined persona is a form of short descriptive sentences. Based on this setting, lots of work has taken long-term persona memory [17], persona order-insensitive [2], data manipulation [1], etc. into account to improve the quality of personalized response generations.

Other studies extracting implicit persona information from dialogue history to generate personalized responses. Zhong et al. [21] design an MSP model which consists of three personal information refiners and a personalized response generator. Although these models have achieved promising results, they all have limitations when the persona information is incomprehensible, and incapable to learn persona consistent expression effectively. Ju et al. [7] construct a new personalized dialogue dataset HLA-Chat++, which takes persona tags as the character's persona information, and propose Text Knowledge enhanced GCN with addressee selecting mechanism, but still suffers from the problem that the model is unable to perceive and interpret personality well, and at the same time, does not fully utilize the character personality embodied in the dialog history.

2.2   Large Language Models

Large language models demonstrate remarkable capabilities such as in-context learning, few-shot prompt, and instruction following. These LLMs are categorized into two distinct groups based on their specialization: general LLMs and specialized LLMs. Specialized LLMs also known as task-specific LLMs, are fine-tuned for specific tasks via task-specific architectures and knowledge, allowing them to achieve higher or comparable performance against general LLMs with fewer parameters. For example, Liu et al. [10] fine-tuned the Goat model to handle arithmetic tasks based on the LLaMA model. Some research scholars have guided personalized conversation generation by leveraging the power of LLMs. Wang et al. [16] build a personalized knowledge-grounded dialogue dataset, KBP and augment the dialogue system to plan and incorporate multiple sources of knowledge into responses. Different from the above-mentioned works, we aim to explore the potential of LLMs in persona understanding domain and take a further step towards personalized response generation.

3   Method

3.1   Problem Definition

In this paper, the personalized dialogue generation problem aims at endowing a dialogue system with a consistent persona, which can be formally defined as: given context $X = \{X_1, X_2, \ldots, X_m\}$, where X_i denotes the utterance of the speaker, and persona set $P = \{P_1, P_2, \ldots, P_k\}$, where k denotes k persona tags of responder. The goal is to generate response $Y = y_1 y_2 \ldots y_n$ based on context and persona set, where y_i denotes the word generated in each step.

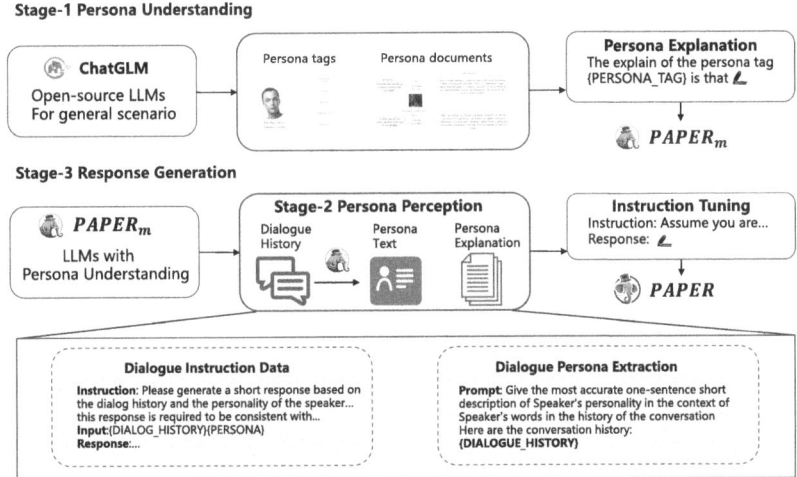

Fig. 2. The architecture overview of the proposed PAPER.

3.2   Three Stage Framework

The model consists of three stages: persona understanding, persona perception and response generation. Persona understanding and response generation share the same model architecture but differ in the input X and output Y. The overall framework is illustrated in Fig. 2.

Persona Understanding Stage. In the persona understanding stage, we feed the model with persona tag, which represents the speaker's original set of personas, where each persona tag is an obscure word. The goal is to learn a persona-aware interpretable model $P_{exp} = F(P_{tag})$, where P_{exp} deserves to be a more detailed and understandable interpretation of the persona tag [7].

We utilize supervised learning to fine-tune ChatGLM3 using a variety of annotated persona explanations data. The input of the Supervised Fine-Tuning(SFT) model is divided into two parts: instruction and context. The instruction, with M tokens, and the context, with N tokens, are encoded by ChatGLM3 to derive vector representations $x = [x_{i1}, \ldots, x_{iM}; x_{c1}, \ldots, x_{cN}] \in \mathbb{R}^{(M+N) \times D}$, where D represents the dimension of the embedding. The probability of generating each token is as follows:

$$p\left(y_i \mid x\right) = \frac{p\left(v\left(y_i\right) \mid c\left(x; y_{i-1}\right)\right)}{\sum_{y' \in \mathcal{V}} p\left(v\left(y'\right) \mid c\left(x; y_{i-1}\right)\right)} \qquad (1)$$

where $\mathcal{V}$ represents a vocabulary of 130,528 tokens. v is a MLP, and c is the decoder of ChatGLM3. The dimension of $p\left(y_i \mid x\right)$ is $\mathbb{R}^{|\mathcal{V}|}$. The objective function of SFT is to maximize the likelihood:

$$\mathcal{L}_{SFT} = \frac{1}{L} \sum_{i=0}^{L} CE\left(y_i, p\left(y_i \mid x\right)\right) \qquad (2)$$

where L represents the target sequence length. CE is the cross-entropy loss.

Persona Perception Stage. Following the persona understanding training stage of the language model, the model is capable of persona comprehension and interpretability. We utilize these persona aware language models for persona explanation inference tasks, represented as $PAPER_m$.

$$P_{\text{exp}} = PAPER_m\left(P_{\text{tag}}\right) \qquad (3)$$

where P_{tag} represents the persona tag as a role persona, $PAPER_m$ is an instruction fine-tuned ChatGLM model with persona perception ability, and P_{exp} represents a more understandable persona explanation generated by the trained ChatGLM model.

In addition, LLMs have shown increased capacity for understanding the context of given inputs and then generating contextually coherent responses, allowing users and system designers to easily customize LLM responses through prompt engineering. We extract the speaker's personality traits and persona information from the speaker's dialogue history through prompt engineering using the large language model fine-tuned during the persona perception stage. The final constructed prompt template is as follows.

Give the most accurate one-sentence short description of speaker's personality in the context of speaker's words in the history of the conversation.

The process of extract persona information from dialogue history can be summarized as follows.

$$P_{\text{text}} = PAPER_m(X) \qquad (4)$$

where P_{text} represents the persona information extracted from the dialogue history, and X denotes the dialogue context.

The generated persona explanations and the persona information extracted from the dialogue are treated as intermediate persona CoT rationales to assist in generating personalized response.

Response Generation Stage. Similar to the persona perception stage, in the response generation stage, we use supervised learning to instruction fine-tune the model obtained in the previous stage. The objective function is the same as in the previous stage. Overall, the process of the response generation stage is as follows.

The persona explanations generated during the persona perception stage, the initial persona tags, and the personality extracted from the dialogue history together serve as the final persona information.

$$P' = P_{\text{tag}} \cup P_{\text{exp}} \cup P_{\text{text}} \tag{5}$$

where P_{text} represents the personality extracted by the dialogue persona extraction module from the dialogue history.

Then the context and persona information are input into the model to generate consistent responses.

$$R = PAPER(X, P') \tag{6}$$

where R represents the generated response, $PAPER$ represents the model fine-tuned through three-stage CoT learning framework, and X denotes the dialogue context.

3.3 Training Method

We utilize Supervised Fine-Tuning(SFT) on tunable language models. We adopt LoRA-Tuning [6], which is a parameter-efficient fine-tuning method that modifies a pre-trained model by introducing low-rank updates to specific weight matrices. It allows for signifcant changes in the model's behavior while only training a small number of additional parameters. The idea behind LoRA is to update the weights of the model using low-rank matrices, which significantly reduces the number of parameters to be fine-tuned. For a weight matrix $W \in \mathbb{R}^{m \times n}$, the low-rank update is given by:

$$\Delta W = BA \tag{7}$$

where $B \in \mathbb{R}^{m \times r}$ and $A \in \mathbb{R}^{r \times n}$ are the low-rank matrices, and r is the rank which is much smaller than m and n.

In practice, LoRA is applied to specific layers of a neural network, such as the attention and feedforward layers in transformer models. The updated weight matrix is:

$$W' = W + \Delta W \tag{8}$$

where W' is the new weight matrix used during fine-tuning and inference.

4   Experiments

4.1   Dataset

We use the HLA-Chat++ dataset for our experiments, which has 823,204 conversations with character persona annotations. According to the statistics, HLA-Chat++ has 239 characters in the dataset, with an average of 3,444 dialogues per character, and an average of 27,440 dialogues per TV dramas.

For the initial dataset, we filter out 23,062 conversations using a specific filtering method transformed them into the instruction data format. Then the filtered dataset is divided into train/valid/test set according to the proportion of 80%, 10% and 10%.

4.2   Baselines and Comparison Models

We compare PAPER with the following strong models, and the baseline models are categorized into three main types: non-pre-trained baseline models, pre-trained baseline models, and large language models. For the large language model baselines, We conduct experiments under both zero-shot and few-shot settings. Specifically, we use the instructions from the constructed instruction data as prompts for the large language model baselines.

Seq2Seq: A Seq2Seq model with attention mechanism [13]. **DialogueGCN:** A dialogue emotion analysis algorithm with a graph neural network encoder. We implement the encoder and add a decoder for generation [5]. **SIRNN:** A multi-party dialogue model with addressee selecting mechanism. We implement the encoder and add a decoder for generation [18]. **PersonaTKG:** A graph convolution network model with addressee selecting mechanism that integrates personas, dialogue utterances and external text knowledge in a unified graph [7]. **GPT-2:** A unidirectional pre-trained language model. Following its primitive concatenation operation, all input sources and responses are concatenated with special token [SEP] as encoding input [12]. **BERT:** A bidirectional pre-trained language model [3]. Each token in the context discourse can focus on all tokens in the context discourse, but each token in the response cannot focus on future tokens in the discourse. **PersonaGKE:** A multi-party Personalized dialogue generation model based on Generative Knowledge Enhancement, which is an improved version of PersonaTKG, replacing the base model with BERT. **CLV:** A contrastive latent variable-based model that clusters the dense persona descriptions into sparse categories [14]. **RECAP:** a retrieval-enhanced approach for personalized response generation [9]. **ChatGLM3-6B:** ChatGLM-6B is an open-source conversational language model [4]. ChatGLM3-6B is a new generation of dialogue pre-training model based on ChatGLM-6B. **LLaMA2-7B:** LLaMA [15] takes a sequence of words as an input and predicts a next word to recursively generate text. **ChatGPT:** ChatGPT offers faster response times and lower costs compared to its counterparts. It introduces improvements such as enhanced instruction following, JSON patterns, repeatable output, and parallel function calls.

4.3   Implementation Details

We choose ChatGLM3-6B as backbone model for supervised setting. Considering the efficiency and effectiveness of Parameter-Efficient-Fine-Tuning (PEFT), we adopt LoRA-Tuning [6] and insert low-rank adapters after self-attention layers. For training, we set the batch size as 8, train models with 3 epochs and save the checkpoint with the lowest validation loss.

4.4   Automatic Evaluation

To highlight the quality of generation on both personality and contextual aspects, we utilize a variety of automatic evaluation metrics to comprehensively evaluate the performance of PAPER from many aspects.

BLEU-1/2: The word-overlap scores of calculating unigrams and bigrams against the ground truth. **Dist-1/2:** The proportions of distinct unigrams and bigrams in the generated responses. **Embedding-based metrics:** Emb E calculates the semantic similarity between the generated response and the ground truth by averaging word embeddings. Emb A and Emb G calculate the semantic similarity between the generated response and the ground truth based on average and greedy matching, respectively. **Per R/P/F1:** The uni-gram Recall/Precision/F1 scores between the generated response and the persona set with explanations [8]. **Rouge-l:** The word overlap-based metric for measuring the similarity between the generated response and the ground truth. **Ave_len:** The average length of generated response.

Table 1. Results of automatic evaluation. The best results among all models are highlighted in bold.

	BLEU-1/2%	Dist-1/2%	Emb E/A/G%	Per-R/P/F1%	Avg_len
Seq2Seq	9.51/10.57	0.79/2.53	36.05/46.65/41.64	0.02/0.14/0.04	4.90
DialogGCN	9.75/11.03	0.51/1.35	36.89/45.29/42.35	0.02/0.11/0.03	5.11
SIRNN	10.32/11.41	0.81/2.64	36.79/48.75/43.19	0.02/0.14/0.04	5.18
PersonaTKG	13.18/14.17	1.59/6.90	38.82/53.23/45.83	0.05/0.61/0.07	5.78
GPT-2	9.98/10.88	0.92/3.01	36.24/47.79/42.50	0.02/0.15/0.04	5.30
BERT	11.06/12.16	0.96/3.14	37.09/47.81/42.52	0.02/0.16/0.05	5.15
PersonaGKE	14.65/15.48	2.25/7.61	38.52/52.49/44.86	0.06/0.62/0.08	5.44
CLV	20.92/12.41	4.07/6.98	45.17/46.88/47.45	0.07/0.13/0.08	21.12
RECAP	16.12/8.67	4.29/10.27	38.31/46.17/43.72	0.06/0.51/0.11	6.53
ChatGLM3	40.31/25.69	13.52/47.20	49.67/59.96/51.48	0.11/0.39/0.17	72
LLaMA2	38.07/22.42	12.93/41.14	49.79/57.99/49.60	0.06/0.33/0.09	67
ChatGPT	41.29/28.35	**36.61/76.10**	53.81/60.64/**52.39**	0.12/0.57/0.20	15.45
PAPER	**44.16/29.23**	28.91/68.39	**54.48/61.03**/49.89	**0.15/0.62/0.23**	9.28
w/o PP	39.88/26.84	31.09/72.08	53.61/60.38/50.02	0.11/0.59/0.19	7.87
w/o DPE	43.30/28.29	27.56/65.79	53.98/60.56/49.73	0.14/0.61/0.23	8.85

For the large language model baselines, we conduct experiments under both zero-shot and few-shot settings and place the best results from both settings in the table.

The results of the automatic evaluation are shown in the Table 1, with the best results for each metric in bold. Overall, PAPER achieves the best results compared to the baseline models for the vast majority of evaluation metrics.

We find that compared with small models, large models will have a certain magnitude of improvement in the overall, which also proves that some existing large models already have good results in dialogue generation. However, existing large language models such as LLaMA tend to respond to query in conversations with long and complex sentences or paragraphs, which is not consistent with real-life human dialogues. In reality, each person has his own unique personality traits and habits, and in everyday life situations, people typically respond with shorter sentences rather than long speeches.

Comparing PAPER with large language model baselines such as ChatGLM3, we can find that through three-stage CoT learning framework, PAPER has shown effective improvements in various metrics, especially in personality-related metrics. The results prove that by using generated persona CoT rationals, we can improve the model's ability to understand and perceive the persona. The persona-aware CoT learning framework enables the model to generate responses that are consistent with the character's persona and real-life scenarios.

4.5   Human Evaluation

Due to the variability of human language, a response that differs from the ground-truth may also be appropriate. To better evaluate the quality of the generated responses, we conduct a human evaluation. We randomly sample 100 examples from the test set and hire 4 graduate students majoring in dialogue system, none of whom were authors of the paper and were unaware of which model the responses came from when evaluating. The evaluator carefully read the persona of the speaker in the dialogue before evaluating. We compare with two relatively strong baselines in automatic evaluation from the following three criteria:

Fluency: The quality of the response in terms of grammar, spelling, punctuation, word choice, and sentence structure. **Coherency:** The extent to which the response is consistent with the dialogue history. The response should build upon the information and context provided in the dialogue history. **Persona Consistency:** The extent to which the response is consistent with the persona of speaker.

For each aspect, the evaluator can choose Win, Tie, and Lose. Win outperformed the other, Lose instead, and Tie represents both tied.

Based on the results in Table 2, PAPER outperforms other baselines across Coherency and Persona Consistency, indicting that PAPER can comprehend persona effectively, exact precise persona from dialogue history, and express own persona more appropriately. For the fluency metric, PAPER is generally comparable to other large language model baselines. This is because large language

Table 2. Human evaluation results.

PAPER vs.	LLaMA2			ChatGPT		
	Win	Tie	Loss	Win	Tie	Loss
Fluency	28	48	24	21	54	25
Coherency	56	35	9	30	47	23
Persona Consistency	61	26	13	49	35	16

models have already performed well in the field of response generation. The responses produced by PAPER and other large language model baselines are usually smooth and natural, with no hesitations or disruptions, and rarely contain grammatical errors or semantic inconsistencies.

4.6 LLM-Based Evaluation

We intend to conduct a holistic evaluation of the agents, with a specific focus on their capability of dialogue and follow character's own persona. We ask GPT-4 to score performance on three main dimensions and calculate an average score to reflect the overall performance of the model. Specifically, we evaluate the quality of the generated text along the same three dimensions as the human evaluation.

Table 3. Results of the five-point evaluation of GPT-4 on different dimensions.

	Coherency	Fluency	Persona Consistency	Avg
ChatGLM3	3.13	3.73	3.08	3.31
LLaMA2	2.95	4.09	2.62	3.22
ChatGPT	3.68	**4.12**	3.34	3.71
PAPER	**3.76**	3.94	**3.67**	**3.79**

We require the LLM to individually assign a score on a scale from 1 to 5, where 1 is the lowest and 5 is the highest, based on three dimensions: fluency, coherency, and persona consistency.

As shown in the Table 3, PAPER surpasses other large language models in terms of average scores, particularly in aspects of coherency and persona consistency, which is consistent with the results of automatic and human evaluations. It is slightly inferior to ChatGPT in terms of fluency, but still demonstrates good performance.

4.7 Ablation Study

In order to investigate the effect of persona understanding stage and the influence of dialogue persona extraction module on response generation, ablation experiments are carried out on these two modules.

w/o PU: The persona understanding stage is removed and directly instruction tune ChatGLM3 with dialogue data.

w/o DPE: The operation of extracting personality from dialogue history is removed, only use dialogue history and the original persona tags, along with the generated persona explanations to generate responses.

As reported in Table 1, removing the persona understanding stage results in a significant decrease in most of the metrics such as BLEU and persona-related metrics, suggesting that the persona understanding stage plays a crucial role in enhancing response fluency and maintaining persona consistency. Notably, there is a slight increase in Distinct, which we attribute to the fact that with fewer persona constraints, the responses are less restricted, and accordingly the diversity is somewhat improved. After removing dialogue persona extraction module, all the metrics have a decrease, indicating that the module is able to fully utilize the character's persona information from the dialogue history. Meanwhile, the extracted persona information has a good impact on the coherency between the generated responses and the conversation history, as well as the consistency of the persona.

5   Conclusion

In this work, we propose a persona-aware chain-of-thought learning framework PAPER, which can perceive and understand complex and obscure persona tags, and generate explanations for persona tags to better generate responses that is consistent with persona. We construct instruction data for the persona understanding stage to instruction tune large language models. The model obtained during the persona understanding stage is employed to extract persona information from the dialogue history and generate persona explanations to enhance persona traits. Then we use dialogue instruction data to fine-tune the model obtained in the previous stage. Extensive experiments confirm the effectiveness in generating fluent, coherent, and personalized responses.

Acknowledgments. This work is supported by the National Natural Science Foundation of China (No. 62272092, No. 62172086) and the Fundamental Research Funds for the Central Universities of China (No. N2116008).

References

1. Cao, Y., Bi, W., Fang, M., Shi, S., Tao, D.: A model-agnostic data manipulation method for persona-based dialogue generation. In: ACL, pp. 7984–8002 (2022)
2. Chen, L., Wang, H., Deng, Y., Kwan, W.C., Wang, Z., Wong, K.F.: Towards robust personalized dialogue generation via order-insensitive representation regularization. In: ACL, pp. 7337–7345 (2023)
3. Devlin, J., Chang, M.W., Lee, K., Toutanova, K.: Bert: pre-training of deep bidirectional transformers for language understanding. arXiv preprint arXiv:1810.04805 (2018)

4. Du, Z., et al.: GLM: general language model pretraining with autoregressive blank infilling. In: Proceedings of the 60th Annual Meeting of the Association for Computational Linguistics (Volume 1: Long Papers), pp. 320–335 (2022)
5. Ghosal, D., Majumder, N., Poria, S., Chhaya, N., Gelbukh, A.: DialogueGCN: a graph convolutional neural network for emotion recognition in conversation. arXiv preprint arXiv:1908.11540 (2019)
6. Hu, E.J., et al.: Lora: low-rank adaptation of large language models. arXiv preprint arXiv:2106.09685 (2021)
7. Ju, D., Feng, S., Lv, P., Wang, D., Zhang, Y.: Learning to improve persona consistency in multi-party dialogue generation via text knowledge enhancement. In: Proceedings of the 29th International Conference on Computational Linguistics, pp. 298–309 (2022)
8. Lian, R., Xie, M., Wang, F., Peng, J., Wu, H.: Learning to select knowledge for response generation in dialog systems. arXiv preprint arXiv:1902.04911 (2019)
9. Liu, S., Cho, H., Freedman, M., Ma, X., May, J.: Recap: retrieval-enhanced context-aware prefix encoder for personalized dialogue response generation. In: ACL, pp. 8404–8419 (2023)
10. Liu, T., Low, B.K.H.: Goat: fine-tuned llama outperforms GPT-4 on arithmetic tasks. arXiv preprint arXiv:2305.14201 (2023)
11. Qian, Q., Huang, M., Zhao, H., Xu, J., Zhu, X.: Assigning personality/profile to a chatting machine for coherent conversation generation. arXiv:1706.02861 (2017)
12. Radford, A., Narasimhan, K., Salimans, T., Sutskever, I.: Improving language understanding by generative pre-training (2018)
13. Sutskever, I., Vinyals, O., Le, Q.V.: Sequence to sequence learning with neural networks. In: Advances in Neural Information Processing Systems, vol. 27 (2014)
14. Tang, Y., et al.: Enhancing personalized dialogue generation with contrastive latent variables: Combining sparse and dense persona. In: ACL, pp. 5456–5468 (2023)
15. Touvron, H., et al.: LLaMA: open and efficient foundation language models. arXiv preprint arXiv:2302.13971 (2023)
16. Wang, H., et al.: Large language models as source planner for personalized knowledge-grounded dialogues. In: EMNLP, pp. 9556–9569 (2023)
17. Xu, X., et al.: Long time no see! open-domain conversation with long-term persona memory. In: ACL, pp. 2639–2650 (2022)
18. Zhang, R., Lee, H., Polymenakos, L., Radev, D.: Addressee and response selection in multi-party conversations with speaker interaction RNNs. In: Proceedings of the AAAI Conference on Artificial Intelligence, vol. 32 (2018)
19. Zhang, S., Dinan, E., Urbanek, J., Szlam, A., Kiela, D., Weston, J.: Personalizing dialogue agents: I have a dog, do you have pets too? In: ACL, pp. 2204–2213 (2018)
20. Zhang, Z., Zhang, A., Li, M., Zhao, H., Karypis, G., Smola, A.: Multimodal chain-of-thought reasoning in language models. arXiv preprint arXiv:2302.00923 (2023)
21. Zhong, H., Dou, Z., Zhu, Y., Qian, H., Wen, J.R.: Less is more: learning to refine dialogue history for personalized dialogue generation. In: NAACL, pp. 5808–5820 (2022)

Towards Building a Robust Knowledge Intensive Question Answering Model with Large Language Models

Xingyun Hong[1], Yan Shao[1,2(✉)], Zhilin Wang[1], Manni Duan[1],
and Xiongnan Jin[1]

[1] Zhejiang Lab, Hangzhou, China
{xyhong,zlwang,mnduan,xnjin}@zhejianglab.com,
shaoyan@cmhi.chinamobile.com
[2] China Mobile, Hangzhou Research and Development Center, Hangzhou, China

Abstract. The development of LLMs has greatly enhanced the intelligence and fluency of question answering, while the emergence of retrieval enhancement has enabled models to better utilize external information. However, the presence of noise and errors in retrieved information poses challenges to the robustness of LLMs. In this work, to evaluate the model's performance under multiple interferences, we first construct a dataset based on machine reading comprehension datasets simulating various scenarios, including critical information absence, noise, and conflicts. To address the issue of model accuracy decline caused by noisy external information, we propose a data augmentation-based fine-tuning method to enhance LLM's robustness against noise. Additionally, contrastive learning approach is utilized to preserve the model's discrimination capability of external information. We have conducted experiments on both existing LLMs and our approach, the results are evaluated by GPT-4, which indicates that our proposed methods improve model robustness while strengthening the model's discrimination capability.

Keywords: Retrieval-augmented LLM · Question answering · Robustness

1 Introduction

With the development of deep learning and reinforcement learning, large language models (LLMs) have demonstrated significant potential in various natural language processing (NLP) applications [1]. As LLMs continue to evolve, concerns regarding the reliability have risen, such as outdated information and fabricated outputs [2]. Outdated information stems from static pre-training data, leading to model's lack of the latest knowledge. Moreover, the hallucination of model may mislead its user, undermining the credibility of LLMs. To address these issues, retrieval-augmented generation (RAG) [3] has been proposed and

D. F. Wong et al. (Eds.): NLPCC 2024, LNAI 15359, pp. 228–242, 2025.
https://doi.org/10.1007/978-981-97-9431-7_18

combined with LLMs. By incorporating external information, LLMs can adapt to dynamic contexts and provide more reliable and relevant results.

While retrieval-augmented enhancement proven to be helpful, it introduces its own set of challenges. External knowledge sources vary in terms of reliability, structure and quality. For example, knowledge from web search is updated more frequently, its format is relatively free and contains more noise; while knowledge from structured knowledge base like knowledge graph is more static and unified. The diversity of information may result in inconsistencies or conflicts. Figure 1 demonstrates the influence of external information on ChatGLM3-6B. When there is no external information, the model provides correct answer; however, when incorrect context or conflicting information is presented, the model tends to give incorrect answer. Previous studies also show that adding random or irrelevant context can decrease QA performance [5]. Therefore, how to enhance LLM's ability of utilizing various information is worth studying.

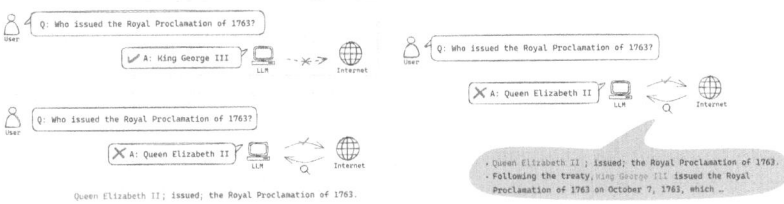

Fig. 1. An example of how external information impacts ChatGLM3-6B's performance.

Addressing concerns that adding certain question-related noise affects LLM's robustness, most of other work involves filtering of information in preliminary stages or controlling whether LLM should conduct additional retrieval. However, such prefixed processes do not always eliminate irrelevant information. Hence, we focus on strengthening LLM's discrimination ability to enhance its robustness.

In this work, to evaluate the robustness of LLM in retrieval scenarios, we first utilize datasets from machine reading comprehension (MRC) to create new datasets simulating various retrieval scenarios. Additionally, to effectively tackle challenges posed by critical information absence, noise and conflicts, we fine-tune LLM integrating data augmentation techniques including mask and swap to improve its performance on the question-answering task. Furthermore, to reinforce the model's ability to refrain from providing answers beyond its scope rather than generating inaccurate responses, we introduce a contrastive learning-based approach. By constructing training data based on whether the model knows the answer, this approach enhances model robustness while strengthening its discrimination capability.

The contributions of this paper can be summarized as follows:[1]

- We introduce a dataset construction method for evaluating model question answering accuracy under different interferences.
- We evaluate and analysis the performance of LLMs with various kinds of external information systematically.
- A data augmentation-based fine-tuning method for LLM is proposed to enhance its accuracy and robustness against various interferences.
- A contrastive learning-based method is proposed to enhance model's discrimination capability and utilization of both external information and its internal knowledge.

2   Related Work

2.1   Retrieval-Augmented LLMs

The role of retrieval enhancement encompasses enhancing inferential capabilities, elevating answer traceability, and alleviating model hallucination. External information can be obtained from web, knowledge base, database and other sources. [6] incorporates knowledge into prompts. [7] utilizes search and chain-of-thought, allowing models to follow logical sequences and retrieve information in a more contextually relevant manner. Some studies also teach LLMs to use external tools including retriever, calculator, and other foundation models [8]. In addition to merely use retriever, [9] collaboratively optimizes both retrieval models and language models.

While retrieval enhancement has demonstrated its efficiency, some studies indicate that the inclusion of irrelevant information can impact model performance. Consequently, the implementation of retrieval enhancement involves considerations such as when to invoke retrieval [4], the selection of external evidence [11], and post-evaluation of generated results [10]. These factors play crucial roles in fine-tuning the retrieval enhancement process and ensuring that the model leverages external knowledge judiciously to enhance its performance.

2.2   Robustness of LLMs

The robustness of LLMs is a crucial factor in application, typically evidenced by their performance under attack or disruptive inputs. Depending on where the perturbations occur, the study of model robustness can be classified into prompt robustness and task robustness.

PromptBench [12] constructs adversarial prompt datasets, perturbing prompts at multiple level to evaluate how slight deviations, such as spelling errors or synonyms, affect LLM results while maintaining semantic integrity. [13] is the work related to prompt injection attack.

Task robustness is to observe model performance by perturbing different tasks such as sentiment analysis, natural language inference, classification and so on

---

[1] https://github.com/sherryhongxy/Training-a-robust-QA-model-with-LLMs.

[14] with typos, grammatical errors, and insertions. Some datasets are designed to evaluate model robustness, including multi-task benchmark AdvGLUE [15], table-based question-answering dataset RobuT [16], and others focusing on code generation, math reasoning and dialogue generation.

3   Dataset Construction

In practical applications, deploying LLMs for knowledge-based question answering may encounter challenges when retrieving external knowledge through external searches. This is due to the potential presence of irrelevant or erroneous information, as well as variations in format among different knowledge sources.

To evaluate the performance of LLMs under such circumstances and enable them to better handle diverse scenarios, we first choose two MRC datasets, then we apply several data construct techniques to generate new datasets. The correctness of the generated samples is evaluated by rule-based methods and human review. According to the context type, the new constructed samples are categorized into five classes. Figure 2 illustrates the process of dataset construction.

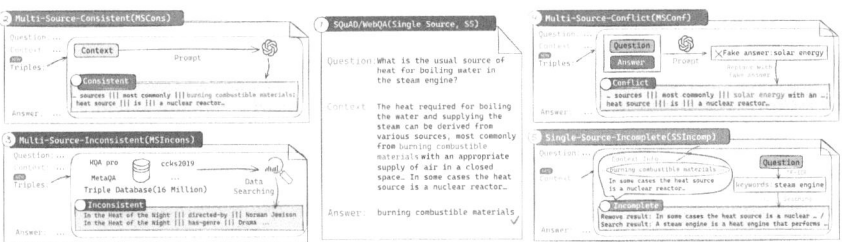

Fig. 2. Dataset construction: methods to create five kinds of samples.

Single Source (SS). The selection of MRC datasets serves various purposes in our work. These datasets typically comprise questions paired with corresponding contexts, from which the answers are extracted. This structure facilitates the addition of noise and the replacement of answers. Additionally, the datasets encompass a significant portion of questions that rely on common sense, which LLMs likely to have encountered during pre-training. As a result, these datasets allow us to examine models' discrimination ability under the impact of misleading external information.

SQuAD (in English) [17] and WebQA (in Chinese) [18] are chosen as our base datasets. SQuAD is a MRC dataset consisting of 100k+ questions posed by crowd workers on Wikipedia articles, where the answer to each question is a segment of text from the corresponding passage. WebQA is a large scale human annotated real-world QA dataset with more than 42k questions and 556k evidences.

We sample 500 instances from each dataset to form a development set and a test set respectively. The proportion of development and test set is 1:1. The original data contains question, question-related context and a corresponding answer. This dataset is referred as **SS** below.

Single-Source-Incomplete (SSIncomp). Incomplete text is designed for assessing LLMs' performance with relevant but insufficient data. In this case, the topic of context is partly relevant to the question, but the crucial information is absent from the context. Traditional MRC model can not handle such situation. As for the LLM, endowed with internal knowledge, is anticipated to determine whether the provided context sufficiently addresses the question, and leverage its internal knowledge to generate appropriate responses if the answer can not be inferred from the context.

In SQuAD, context originates from article paragraphs, our approach involves the removal of sentences containing answers, while retaining the remainder. However, context in WebQA is typically short and answer-centric, making the elimination process yield few information. Therefore, we employ TF-IDF to identify keywords in the question, leveraging them for online search.[2] Subsequently, the search result that devoid of the answer is retained as context.

Multi-source-Consistent (MSCons). When retrieving information, data from different sources may exhibit diverse formats and content variations. Our objective is to explore impact of multi-source information on model performance. Specifically, we aim to observe whether information with similar content but different formats affects the model's inference results. Since the original data is in natural language, we utilize GPT3.5-Turbo [19] to extract multiple sets of triples as an alternative data source. We retain those samples for which answers exist in the extracted triples.

Multi-source-Inconsistent (MSIncons). In addition to examining scenarios with consistent content across multiple sources, we anticipate the model to remain robust even if the retrieved results contain additional noise, which may be partially relevant or irrelevant to the question. Therefore, we build a triple database using several datasets, for instance, KQA pro, MetaQA dataset and so on, containing 163,776,434 triples in total. These triples are not necessarily related to the questions in WebQA and SQuAD. We utilize question or the head entities extracted by GPT3.5-Turbo as search terms, and ensure that the answers are not included in the retrieved results. The final selected triples are limited to 10 with respect to relevance.

Multi-source-Conflict (MSConf). Given the substantial variability in the quality of internet information, retrieval process occasionally yields erroneous or

---

[2] We utilize the SerpAPI service for Google search: https://serpapi.com/.

conflicting results. As such situations are often inevitable, it becomes imperative for LLMs to discriminate between correct and incorrect information when presented simultaneously. In this case, we have devised conflicting samples. First, we use GPT3.5-Turbo to generate a similar yet incorrect answer based on the question and original answer. Subsequently, the answer in the triples consistent with the context is substituted with the fabricated one.

Dataset Quality. Given the potential errors introduced by construction methods and tools, during dataset construction, we conduct multiple case-based optimizations of the prompt. For created samples, the unsatisfactory results are filtered out from our test set, ensuring the generated results align with our requirements. Specifically, for SSIncomp and MSIncons samples, we ensure that answers are not included in the deleted or retrieved results. For MSCons samples, triplets generated by GPT3.5-Turbo must contain corresponding answers. For MSConf samples, 100 instances are randomly sampled for human review. The plausibility of the generated false answers, considering the correspondences of the answer type (such as names, numbers, locations, times and so on), achieving an accuracy rate of 99%, guaranteeing that the generated samples meet the experimental requirements.

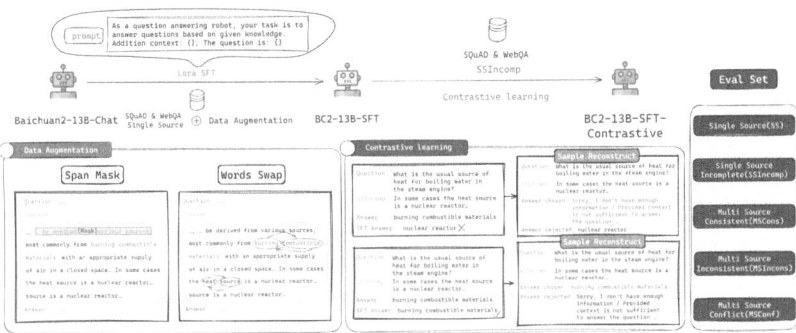

Fig. 3. Two-stage fine-tuning with the Baichuan2-13B-Chat model

4   Methods

4.1   Data Augmentation

To enhance the model's robustness under diverse contexts, we integrate data augmentation techniques during model fine-tuning. Original data in the SQuAD and WebQA dataset contains questions, context and answers. Typically, the answer is contained in the question-related context. Leveraging corresponding and comprehensive context to the question facilitates the task for LLMs, yet the presence of noise within the context may weaken the model's generalization ability. Consequently, we implement span masking and word swapping strategies to enhance the model's robustness.

Mask: We enhance the model's reasoning and generalization abilities by masking certain portions of the context. Even if the context does not explicitly contain the answer, LLM can leverage context related to the answer and its internal knowledge to improve accuracy. Masking is performed with spans, typically short sentences whose removal do not significantly affect semantic integrity.

Every span (usually delimited by two punctuation marks, using regex to separate) has equal possibility of being eliminated. The absence of answer motivates LLM to distinguish the relevance of information and stick to its own knowledge when confronted with inadequate context, whereas the removal of other span simulates the incompleteness of information.

Swap: As disorder of words between adjacent words dose not alter its overall meaning significantly, the switch of words can be regarded as adding noise to the context. In our approach, we randomly select a span from the context and a position within span, then interchange adjacent word sets.

Unlike methods involving open-ended searches or GPT generation, these approaches have comparatively low costs in constructing training data, thus are more practical for real-world applications.

4.2 Contrastive Learning

Through detailed case analysis (refer to Sect. 5.2), we discover that LLMs possess different levels of discrimination capabilities. When confronted with queries that cannot be answered with the given information, the model occasionally informs the user of the inadequacy of the provided knowledge. To strengthen model's discrimination ability, we employ contrastive learning after first stage fine-tuning.

As to find what does the model know and guide it to decline to the question beyond its knowledge, we create SSIncomp samples of each dataset as training data. For SQuAD, elimination of answer-contained sentence is applied. For WebQA, context relevant to question but does not include the answer is selected.

First, the fine-tuned model generates outputs for the aforementioned samples, subsequently assessed by GPT-4. To facilitate contrastive learning, we construct new dataset. Each question and context pair is accompanied by both an answer to accept and one to decline, as depicted in Fig. 3.

For correctly-inferred samples, the original sample label is designated as the chosen answer, while a specific expression is assigned as the rejected answer, such as "Provided context is not sufficient to answer the question/Sorry, I don't have enough information...". As for incorrect samples, the sentence indicating model's inability to respond constitutes the chosen answer, whereas the incorrect output from the fine-tuned model serves as the declined answer.

Throughout the training process, we aim to maximize the disparity in probability between accepted and declined answers through comparison.

Specifically, the loss function is defined as:

$$L = -\sum_{i=1}^{N} log\sigma(\frac{1}{C}\sum_{i=1}^{C} logp(y_{C_i}|x) - \frac{1}{R}\sum_{i=1}^{R} logp(y_{R_i}|x)) \qquad (1)$$

where N represents the sample numbers, σ is the sigmoid function. C and R stands for tokens of chosen label and rejected label respectively. $logp(y_{C_i}|x)$ is the log probability of the chosen token C_i when given x as input.

5   Experiment

5.1   Models

To examine the impact of various information on LLMs, we initially evaluate model performance using the dataset we construct. Subsequently, we select a base model to conduct further experiments. Below are the models utilized for our experimental evaluation.

GPT3.5-Turbo: GPT3.5-Turbo is a conversational artificial intelligence model developed by OpenAI, based on the GPT architecture.

Baichuan [21]: Generation of LLM from Baichuan Intelligence and supports both Chinese and English.

Llama [22]: A large language model released by Meta AI, which supports text completion and chat completion.

ChatGLM [23]: ChatGLM is an open bilingual language model (supports English and Chinese) based on General Language Model (GLM) framework.

5.2   Evaluation Metrics

Considering that the outputs of the original LLM are typically more comprehensive and long, whereas the labels in the MRC dataset are comparatively concise, utilizing n-gram metrics such as ROUGE and BLEU can not indicate real performance precisely. Therefore, for each sample, we employ recall and accuracy to evaluate. *Recall* assesses the percentage of overlapping words between the model outputs and labels, it's suitable for comparing model performance after fine-tuning, since the output format remains consistent.

While recall focuses on words matching, we utilize GPT-4 to determine whether the whole output aligns the key points of the label, even if in different ways of expression. In practical application, when querying LLM, it's preferable to receive a response indicating model's inability to answer rather than an incorrect one. Considering this scenario, GPT-4 is used to categorize the model's inferences into wrong (w), correct (c), or rejected (r, indicating the model declines to give answer directly due to lack of information or other reasons).

The standard accuracy metric (ACC) is defined as the proportion of the correct samples among all samples. Meanwhile, to further distinguish the model's ability to decline questions beyond its ability, correct, rejected and incorrect responses receive a score of 1, 0, and -1 respectively. The average score is then computed across all samples as the weighted score ($WSCORE$).

5.3 Experimental Setup

In the experiment, we commence by assessing the performance of several existing LLMs using our dataset. Among the open-source models, Baichuan2-13B-Chat demonstrates satisfactory performance, coupled with a relatively swift inference speed, thus making it a suitable candidate for further experiments.

Due to the resource limitation and the effectiveness of LoRA [24], we fine-tune LLMs based on LoRA framework. The rank of the adaptors is set as 8, maximum input length is 2048, and the learning rate is 1e-4 with a warm-up strategy. The experiment is accelerated using NVIDIA V100 GPUs with 32GB memory each.

During the first fine-tuning stage, approximately 40% of answer-located span are masked. In the second fine-tuning stage, we select 3,500 new samples, ensuring a balanced distribution of positive and negative instances at 1:1.

5.4 Results

Existing Model Performance Evaluation. As shown in Table 1, we observe that the accuracy of nearly every model (excluding Llama2-7B-Chat) surpasses 85% on the original single-source samples (SS). In this case, the context aligns perfectly with the question, apart from a few inference-based questions, which are challenging to answer.

However, for samples where the answer is absent in the context (SSIncomp), there is a notable decline in accuracy. This discrepancy can be attributed to certain questions heavily relying on contextual cues. To isolate this effect, we evaluate the accuracy solely based on the question using Baichuan2-13B-Chat. The accuracy is 52.2%, indicating that approximately half of the questions can be answered based on the internal knowledge of the Baichuan2-13B-Chat model alone. This figure surpasses Baichuan2-13B-Chat's accuracy on SSIncomp samples (48.8%), underscoring the disruptive impact of incomplete or irrelevant contextual information on the model's performance.

In scenarios involving multiple sources, even though the information extracted from triples corresponds to the context and contains answers (MSCons samples), its variability due to extraction still impacts model's robustness. While most models experience a slight decrease in accuracy, Llama models show improved performance, suggesting the proficiency in handling formally structured knowledge. If triples are retrieved from triple database (MSIncons samples), the accuracy further decreases. In such cases, the model becomes susceptible to unrelated triples, disregarding correct contextual information.

Table 1. Evaluation of different models on the test set: *ACC* stands for accuracy, *R* stands for rejection percentage, *WSCORE* is the weighted accuracy. Model name with * indicates it is a commercial model.

Model	SS		SSIncomp		MSCons		MSIncons		MSConf		Overall	
Metrics	ACC	R	ACC	R	ACC	R	ACC	R	ACC	R	ACC	WSCORE
GPT3.5-Turbo*	96.7	0.0	60.0	3.3	95.9	0.6	93.9	1.6	72.4	0.8	83.8	68.8
Llama2-7B-Chat	78.5	0.2	34.6	8.1	81.3	0.0	74.0	0.0	60.2	0.0	65.7	33.1
Llama2-13B-Chat	86.2	1.2	38.2	8.7	90.0	0.4	85.2	0.0	65.9	0.2	73.1	48.3
Baichuan2-7B-Chat	92.7	0.6	49.8	6.5	91.3	0.8	90.9	0.6	70.1	1.0	79.0	59.8
Baichuan2-13B-Chat	**93.9**	0.4	48.8	20.5	90.2	0.6	88.2	3.5	70.7	0.8	78.3	61.9
ChatGLM2-6B	85.8	1.2	33.3	15.4	85.4	0.6	83.9	1.4	75.4	0.2	72.8	49.3
ChatGLM3-6B	91.1	0.2	39.6	13.0	89.8	0.6	87.0	0.2	75.6	0.8	76.6	56.2
BC2-13B-SFT	93.7	0.0	**55.5**	0.0	**95.3**	0.0	**93.7**	0.0	77.8	0.0	**83.2**	66.4
BC2-13B-SFT-Contrastive	92.7	2.8	48.4	21.3	93.5	1.6	92.9	2.0	**78.5**	2.8	81.2	**68.5**

Finally, when we construct false answers which is similar to real ones and replace the information in the triples (MSConf samples), the model easily falls into hallucinations when faced with two conflicting contexts. Consequently, erroneous answers are generated, highlighting the vulnerability of the model in distinguishing between contradictory information.

From the perspective of how different model handles the situation of noise, GPT3.5-Turbo outperforms others in every scenarios except when confronted with conflicting contexts (MSConf). Despite ChatGLM's general inferiority to other models, its capability of managing conflict is surprisingly noteworthy.

Fine-Tuning Model Performance Evaluation. BC2-13B-SFT refers to the Baichuan2-13B-Chat model after fine-tuning utilizing data-augmentation strategies. As demonstrated in Table 1, compared to the original Baichuan2-13B-Chat, there are significant improvements in almost every scenarios. The overall accuracy increase by 6.3%, only slightly lower than GPT3.5-Turbo. Since GPT3.5-Turbo is a closed source model, the fine-tuned model offers the advantage of being more suitable for localized deployment.

The adopted training data is merely in single source format, however it still contributes to the improvement in every situation. This suggests that related but incomplete context motivates LLM to leverage its internal knowledge and thereby promoting its discrimination ability.

Evaluation of Model's Discrimination Ability. We further distinguish declined responses from incorrect responses to observe the proportion of rejection on SSIncomp and MSConf samples. Meanwhile, in other three scenarios, since the context contains the answer, though potentially with noise, we still anticipate correct responses from the model.

The metric r represents the proportion of declined responses. Each model demonstrates varying levels of discrimination capability, with Baichuan2-13B-

Chat and ChatGLM exhibiting relatively strong discrimination abilities. However, a higher rejection rate implies less informative responses. So it is necessary to assess this metric in conjunction with the correct answer proportion. In terms of the overall *WSCORE*, GPT3.5-Turbo remains the best. Despite its lower rejection rate, the proportion of correct answers significantly surpasses other models, followed by the Baichuan2-13B-Chat model.

As for the BC2-13B-SFT model, after fine-tuning with MRC samples, the model tends to provide answers even if they are incorrect. However, after second stage fine-tuning utilizing contrastive learning, model's discrimination capability is enhanced, transitioning from delivering an answer (regardless of correctness) to declining to the question beyond its capacity. Moreover, in the scenarios involving multi-source, the accuracy remains superior to that of original Baichuan2, maintaining robustness against noise. There is an increment of 10.7% in the overall

Table 2. Case study: The Mitchell Tower is designed to look like what Oxford tower? (Note the responses from some models are reduced to keywords for display purposes)

Sample	Additional context	Model response
SS	Text: ...Mitchell Tower, for example, is modeled after Oxford's **Magdalen Tower**, and the university Commons, Hutchinson Hall, replicates Christ Church Hall.	GPT3.5-Turbo: magdalen tower
		Baichuan2-13B-Chat: magdalen tower
		BC2-13B-SFT: magdalen tower
		BC2-13B-SFT-Contrast: magdalen tower
SS-Incomp	Text: The first buildings of the University of Chicago campus, which make up what is now known as the Main Quadrangles, ..., patterned on the colleges of the University of Oxford.	GPT3.5-Turbo: magdalen tower
		Baichuan2-13B-Chat: it is not meant to represent a specific tower
		BC2-13B-SFT: bodleian library
		BC2-13B-SFT-Contrast: sorry, I can't answer.
MsCons	Text: ...Mitchell Tower, for example, is modeled after Oxford's **Magdalen Tower**... Triples: ..., Mitchell Tower ||| modeled after ||| Oxford's **Magdalen Tower**, university Commons, ...	GPT3.5-Turbo: magdalen tower
		Baichuan2-13B-Chat: magdalen tower
		BC2-13B-SFT: magdalen tower
		BC2-13B-SFT-Contrast: magdalen tower
Ms-Incons	Text: ...Mitchell Tower, for example, is modeled after Oxford's **Magdalen Tower**... Triples: The Deadly Tower ||| directed by ||| Jerry Jameson, ...	GPT3.5-Turbo: magdalen tower
		Baichuan2-13B-Chat: magdalen tower
		BC2-13B-SFT: magdalen tower
		BC2-13B-SFT-Contrast: magdalen tower
MsConf	Text: ...Mitchell Tower, for example, is modeled after Oxford's **Magdalen Tower**... Triples: ... Mitchell Tower ||| modeled after ||| Oxford's **Radcliffe Camera**, university Commons, ...	GPT3.5-Turbo: oxford's Radcliffe Camera
		Baichuan2-13B-Chat: oxford's Radcliffe Camera
		BC2-13B-SFT: magdalen tower
		BC2-13B-SFT-Contrast: magdalen tower

weighted score of BC2-13B-SFT-Contrast compared to the original Baichuan2-13B-Chat model and approaching the performance of GPT3.5-Turbo. It is worth noting that despite the relatively small number of training samples, contrastive learning contributes to improving the model's discrimination capability.

Case Study. To give a more intuitive visualization, some qualitative comparison results are shown in Table 2. It is observed that for SS, MsCons and MsIncons samples, the listed models provide correct answers consistently. However, for SSIncomp sample, while GPT3.5-Turbo is capable of generating a correct response based on its internal knowledge, Baichuan2-13B-Chat fails to produce a specific answer. Although fine-tuning reinforces model's confidence on the incorrect answers, BC2-13B-SFT-Contrast, guided by further contrastive learning, appropriately declines to answer when lacking internal knowledge. As for MsConf sample, both Baichuan2-13B-Chat and GPT3.5-Turbo are misled by incorrect triples, whereas fine-tuned models exhibits robustness against such interference.

5.5   Ablation Study

Ablation Study of the First Stage Fine-Tuning. To validate the efficacy of data augmentation strategies, we conduct an ablation study using the dev set.

- **BC2-13B-SFT**: use both mask and swap strategies to process original data.
- **BC2-13B-SFT W/O SWAP**: use only mask to process original data.
- **BC2-13B-SFT W/O MASK & SWAP**: use original training data without any data augmentation strategy.

Table 3. Ablation study result on Baichuan2-Chat models.

Model ACC	SS	SSIncomp	MSCons	MSIncons	MSConf	Overall
Baichuan2-13B-Chat	93.7	46.9	91.3	87.6	67.7	77.4
BC2-13B-SFT	**96.9**	**56.5**	**98.4**	**95.9**	**79.1**	**85.4**
BC2-13B-SFT W/O SWAP	95.7	55.1	96.3	95.7	76.4	83.8
BC2-13B-SFT W/O MASK & SWAP	96.1	50.2	96.9	94.5	75.8	82.7

First, when compare BC2-13B-SFT with BC2-13B-SFT W/O SWAP, there is a notable improvement in MSConf samples, indicating the disorder of words motivates model's discrimination ability, facilitating more effective selection of the correct answer when faced with conflicting information from two sources (Table 3).

Second, when we further eliminate mask strategy in training samples, the performance of SSIncomp samples decreases. This decrease can be attributed to the model's training solely on samples exclusively containing context corresponding to the question, reinforcing the model's reliance on user-provided information, thereby diminishing its discrimination capabilities. As a result, when the provided text lacks essential information, the accuracy of the model decreases.

Finally, training with merely MRC dataset still improve the performance compared to the original Baichuan2 model, which demonstrates that the efficacy of aligning with the corresponding task format.

Effectiveness of Contrastive Learning. To validate the effectiveness of contrastive learning, we also compare the preference learning based on direct preference optimization (DPO) [20] and conventional fine-tuning methods.

In DPO, we utilize the same training samples as in the contrastive learning approach. While DPO yields further improvements in the model's accuracy in multi-source scenarios, it exhibits a relatively higher error rate with SSIncomp samples. This suggests a tendency of the model to provide answers indiscriminately, irrespective of their correctness.

Regarding conventional fine-tuning, the sample's label is determined by either retaining the original label or designating it as a rejected response (refer to sec 4.4), depends on whether the model accurately answers the question. While this fine-tuning approach effectively reduces the occurrence of erroneous outputs on SSIncomp samples, it concurrently impacts the model's discrimination ability in other scenarios severely. Consequently, a substantial portion of responses that could have been deemed correct are instead transformed into rejected outputs (Table 4).

Table 4. Evaluation of model's discrimination ability

Model	SS			SSIncomp			MSCons			MSIncons			MSConf			Overall
Metrics	W	C	R	W	C	R	W	C	R	W	C	R	W	C	R	WSCORE
Baichuan2-13B-Chat	3.7	93.9	2.4	29.3	46.9	23.8	7.7	91.3	1.0	9.6	87.6	2.8	31.5	67.7	0.8	61.1
BC2-13B-SFT-Contrast	3.3	93.9	2.8	30.9	44.7	24.4	2.4	96.1	1.6	3.5	93.7	2.8	18.9	78.3	2.8	**69.5**
BC2-13B-SFT-DPO	3.3	96.5	0.2	46.3	46.5	7.3	3.5	96.5	0.0	5.7	94.3	0.0	20.7	79.8	0.0	66.7
BC2-13B-SFT-SFT	8.3	68.7	23.0	16.5	32.9	50.6	7.9	76.4	15.8	9.8	67.5	22.6	22.4	59.7	17.9	48.0

6   Conclusions

In this paper, we first create dataset simulating various scenarios, including critical information absence, noise, and conflicts, based on MRC datasets to assess various model's performance under multiple interferences. To mitigate the decline in model accuracy attributed to noise, we introduce a data augmentation-based fine-tuning method to enhance LLM's robustness against noise. Additionally, we employ contrastive learning to strengthen the model's discrimination capability. Experimental results indicate that our proposed methods improve model robustness while strengthening the model's discrimination capability.

Acknowledgments. This study was funded by Independent Project of Zhejiang Lab (K2023NB0AC13), National Natural Science Foundation of China (Grant No.62306287), Zhejiang Provincial Natural Science Foundation of China (Grant No. LY23F020012), Joint R&D Project of Smart Home Intelligent Interaction Laboratory (R2411A77)

References

1. Kojima, T., Gu, S.S., Reid, M., Matsuo, Y., Iwasawa, Y.: Large language models are zero-shot reasoners. In: Advances in Neural Information Processing Systems, vol. 35, pp. 22199–22213 (2022)
2. Ji, Z., Lee, N., Frieske, R., et al.: Survey of hallucination in natural language generation. ACM Comput. Surv. **55**(12), 1–38 (2023)
3. Asai, A., Min, S., Zhong, Z., Chen, D.: Retrieval-based language models and applications. In: Proceedings of the 61st Annual Meeting of the Association for Computational Linguistics (Volume 6: Tutorial Abstracts), pp. 41–46 (2023)
4. Wang, Y., Li, P., Sun, M., Liu, Y.: Self-knowledge guided retrieval augmentation for large language models. In: Findings of the Association for Computational Linguistics: EMNLP, pp. 10303–10315 (2023)
5. Shi, F., et al.: Large language models can be easily distracted by irrelevant context. In: International Conference on Machine Learning, pp. 31210–31227. PMLR (2023)
6. Lazaridou, A., Gribovskaya, E., Stokowiec, W., Grigorev, N.: Internet-augmented language models through few-shot prompting for open-domain question answering. arXiv preprint arXiv:2203.05115 (2022)
7. Trivedi, H., Balasubramanian, N., Khot, T., Sabharwal, A.: Interleaving retrieval with chain-of-thought reasoning for knowledge-intensive multi-step questions. In: Proceedings of the 61st Annual Meeting of the Association for Computational Linguistics (2023)
8. Shen, Y., Song, K., Tan, X., Li, D., Lu, W., Zhuang, Y.: HuggingGPT: solving AI tasks with ChatGPT and its friends in hugging face. In: Advances in Neural Information Processing Systems, vol. 36 (2024)
9. Lewis, P., et al.: Retrieval-augmented generation for knowledge-intensive NLP tasks. In: Advances in Neural Information Processing Systems, vol. 33, pp. 9459–9474 (2020)
10. Asai, A., Wu, Z., Wang, Y., Sil, A., Hajishirzi, H.: Self-rag: learning to retrieve, generate, and critique through self-reflection. arXiv preprint arXiv:2310.11511 (2023)
11. Shi, W., et al.: REPLUG: retrieval-augmented black-box language models. In: Proceedings of the 2024 Conference of the North American Chapter of the Association for Computational Linguistics, pp. 8371–8384 (2024)
12. Zhu, K., et al.: PromptBench: towards evaluating the robustness of large language models on adversarial prompts. arXiv preprint arXiv:2306.04528 (2023)
13. Greshake, K., Abdelnabi, S., Mishra, S., Endres, C., Holz, T., Fritz, M.: More than you've asked for: a comprehensive analysis of novel prompt injection threats to application-integrated large language models. arXiv e-prints arXiv: 2302.12173 (2023)
14. Wang, J., et al.: On the robustness of ChatGPT: an adversarial and out-of-distribution perspective. arXiv preprint arXiv:2302.12095 (2023)
15. Wang, B., et al.: Adversarial glue: a multi-task benchmark for robustness evaluation of language models. In: Advances in Neural Information Processing Systems (2021)

16. Zhao, Y., et al.: RobuT: a systematic study of table QA robustness against human-annotated adversarial perturbations. In: Proceedings of the 61st Annual Meeting of the Association for Computational Linguistics, pp. 6064–6081 (2023)
17. Rajpurkar, P., Zhang, J., Lopyrev, K., Liang, P.: Squad: 100,000+ questions for machine comprehension of text. In: Proceedings of the 2016 Conference on Empirical Methods in Natural Language Processing, pp. 2383–2392 (2016)
18. Li, P., et al.: Dataset and neural recurrent sequence labeling model for open-domain factoid question answering. arXiv preprint arXiv:1607.06275 (2016)
19. Ouyang, L., et al.: Training language models to follow instructions with human feedback. In: Advances in Neural Information Processing Systems, pp. 27730–27744 (2022)
20. Rafailov, R., Sharma, A., Mitchell, E., Manning, C.D., Ermon, S., Finn, C.: Direct preference optimization: your language model is secretly a reward model. In: Advances in Neural Information Processing Systems, vol. 36 (2024)
21. Yang, A., et al.: Baichuan 2: open large-scale language models. arXiv preprint arXiv:2309.10305 (2023)
22. Touvron, H., et al.: LLaMA 2: open foundation and fine-tuned chat models. arXiv preprint arXiv:2307.09288 (2023)
23. Du, Z., et al.: GLM: general language model pretraining with autoregressive blank infilling. In: Proceedings of the 60th Annual Meeting of the Association for Computational Linguistics, pp. 320–335 (2022)
24. Hu, E.J., et al.: Lora: low-rank adaptation of large language models. In: International Conference on Learning Representations (2022)

Fundamentals of NLP

Model-Agnostic Knowledge Distillation Between Heterogeneous Models

Jiaxin Shen[1], Yanyao Liu[1], Yong Jiang[2], Yufeng Chen[1], and Wenjuan Han[1(✉)]

[1] Beijing Key Lab of Traffic Data Analysis and Mining, Beijing Jiaotong University, Beijing, China
{jiaxinshen,yanyaoliu,chenyf,wjhan}@bjtu.edu.cn
[2] Alibaba DAMO Academy, Hangzhou, China

Abstract. The goal of KD is to transfer valuable knowledge from a strong teacher model to a weaker student model in order to bridge the performance gap. However, the conventional teacher-student paradigm of KD can not be applied to the teacher model and student model with different output representations (referred to as heterogeneous models). To overcome this limitation, we propose a model-agnostic approach for KD called MAKD. MAKD consists of two stages: *informative sample generation* and *knowledge transfer*. The key idea is to generate informative samples that convey the discrepancy between the teacher model and student model, so that the generated samples are effective and efficient. We formulate two ways for *informative sample generation*: word substitution and text generation. After generating desired samples, we perform *knowledge transfer* by mixing the informative samples into the original training set and retraining the student model to improve its performance. We conducted experiments on two tasks, dependency parsing, and grammatical error correction, and the results demonstrate that MAKD successfully enhances the performance of the student model on both tasks. Our data and code are available at https://github.com/WinnieHAN/Model_Agnostic_Knowledge_Distillation.

Keywords: Knowledge Distillation · Data Augmentation · Model Agnostic

1 Introduction

Researchers have noted that excessively large models have strong generalization ability but learn redundant representations in the process [12], and they are difficult to deploy in an online setting. Therefore, knowledge distillation (KD) [14] – transferring valuable knowledge from deep and slow models to smaller and faster networks so as to close their potential performance gap – has been an active area of research.

The most popular teacher-student paradigm in KD implements knowledge transfer by training a weak student model by mimicking the output distributions

D. F. Wong et al. (Eds.): NLPCC 2024, LNAI 15359, pp. 245–257, 2025.
https://doi.org/10.1007/978-981-97-9431-7_19

of a teacher model [4–6]. In addition to the final output layer, some prior work focuses on the internal layers [2,3]. Besides them, prior arts, such as Abnar et al. [1], explore a more model-agnostic KD, allowing transfer knowledge from one model with a specific network architecture to another model with a different architecture.

Either work mentioned above has a flaw: KD can not be applied to the teacher model and student model with different output representations (referred to as heterogeneous models). Put simply, different output representations mean different formats, which prevent effective knowledge transfer from one format to another, *e.g.*, from tree to sequence. This heterogeneous issue limits KD from achieving full model-agnostic. Unfortunately, in effect, a model focusing on fast prediction and portable size often does not have the same output representation as a model focusing on expressive power. Thus, a fully model-agnostic KD technique is desired.

In this paper, we propose a **M**odel-**A**gnostic **KD** approach, called MAKD, which is specified for KD between heterogeneous models. Our focus is on heterogeneous scenarios where previous approaches cannot be applied. In effect, a model focusing on fast prediction and portable size often has a representation that is heterogeneous as a model focusing on expressive power, for example, dependency parsing task (Sect. 4.1), and grammatical error correction task (Sect. 4.2). MAKD is a two-stage process(Sect. 3): *informative sample generation* and *knowledge transfer*. We formulate two ways for *informative sample generation*: word substitution and text generation. Because we generate informative samples based on the discrepancy between the teacher's output and the student's output instead of using the original training data, the generated samples are effective and efficient for illustrating the potential gap. By collecting informative samples, we perform *knowledge transfer* by mixing the generated samples into the original training set to retrain the student model. Through this two-stage process, the whole process is guided by the final result of the teacher/student and places no constraint on the output representation. As such, it can be called fully model-agnostic. We evaluate MAKD on the aforementioned two typical tasks (*i.e.*, dependency parsing task and grammatical error correction task) to illustrate how MAKD can easily handle heterogeneous models. Experimental results show that MAKD successfully boosts the performance of the smaller and faster student model on both tasks (Sects. 4.1 and 4.2).

2   Background

2.1   Heterogeneous Models for Dependency Parsing Task: Graph-Based Model Vs. Action-Sequence-Based Model

Dependency parsing (DP) aims to extract from a sentence $\mathbf{x}$ a dependency parse $\mathbf{y}$ that represents its syntactic structure. $\mathbf{x} = [x_0, x_1, \ldots, x_n]$ is a sequence of words $x_1, \ldots, x_n$ while $ROOT$ is a pseudo token x_0 defined at the beginning of a sentence. The relationship between two words is defined from the head to the dependent, where the dependent modifies the head. For example, in Fig. 1,

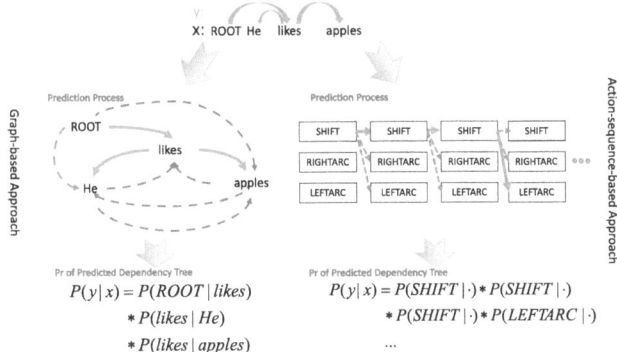

Fig. 1. Two typical paradigms for DP. For the graph-based model (LEFT), the dependency tree is regarded as a weighted directed graph and the prediction process is to find the maximum spanning tree. For the action-sequence-based model (RIGHT), the dependency tree is defined as a sequence of actions instead of a graph and the prediction process is a greedy search. We use "He likes apples" as an illustrating example. For the prediction process, we use gray dashed lines to represent the search space and blue solid lines to represent the prediction results. At the bottom, we show how to calculate the probability of the predicted dependency tree for the two models. (Color figure online)

"likes" modifies $ROOT$, and "He" and "apples" modify "likes". For DP, there are two typical models as shown in Fig. 1: the graph-based model [13] and the action-sequence-based model (commonly referred to as transition-based model) [10].

Graph-Based Model. The representation of the dependency tree is regarded as a directed graph and the prediction is to find the best tree $\hat{\mathbf{y}}$ with the highest probability from a fully connected graph as follows[1].

$$\hat{\mathbf{y}} = arg\max_{\mathbf{y}\in\mathcal{Y}} P(\mathbf{y}|\mathbf{x})$$
$$= arg\max_{\mathbf{y}\in\mathcal{Y}} \sum_{r\in\mathbf{y}} P(r|\mathbf{x})$$

where $\mathcal{Y}$ denotes all valid trees in the search space, a.k.a the fully connected graph. The probability of a tree $\mathbf{y}$ is determined by the probabilities of all the factorized edges r.

Action-Sequence-Based Model. The representation of action-sequence-based model[2], is defined as a sequence of actions instead of a tree or a graph.

---

[1] For simplicity, we use probabilities to weight the edges. In more general cases, edges are weighted by scores instead of probabilities and normalized globally.

[2] Action-sequence-based models (commonly referred to as transition-based model) is an action sequence and differs with respect to the configurations they use. We show the arc-standard configuration in Fig. 1, where three actions, SHIFT/RIGHTARC/LEFTARC, are used.

It is a sequence of classifications: predict the next action from SHIFT/ RIGHTARC/LEFTARC given the current configuration. The final probability of **y** is as follows.

$$\hat{\mathbf{y}} = arg \max_{\mathbf{y} \in \mathcal{Y}} \prod_t P(y_t | \mathbf{y}_{<t}) \tag{1}$$

where the probability of a sequence **y** is determined by the probabilities of all the actions y_t.

While the cost of rich feature computation of most current graph-based models [13] restricts parsing speed significantly, action-sequence-based models [10] can use greedy search which yields good gains in speed, even though there is no guarantee that the best parse tree is found. Therefore, transforming knowledge between these two models will take great advantage: the fast prediction from the transition-based model and the good performance from the graph-based model. However, there is a significant discrepancy in the representation of the parse tree, model architecture, and learning algorithm, which we refer to as **heterogeneity**. Basically, the dimension of the output for the graph-based model is the sentence length, while for the transition-based model, it is the action size (*i.e.*, three). Thus KD between these two models using current technologies is impossible.

2.2   Heterogeneous Models for Grammatical Error Correction Task: Word-Sequence-Based Model Vs. Action-Sequence-Based Model

A Grammatical error correction (GEC) system takes a potentially erroneous word sentence (with errors such as spelling, punctuation, grammatical, and word choice errors) as input and transforms it into a corrected version. For GEC, word-sequence-based models and action-sequence-based models [19] are often used. A dilemma exists in knowledge transfer between a well-designed action-sequence-based and a simple and fast word-sequence-based model: knowledge cannot be transferred by using cross-entropy loss [14] or mean squared error loss [21,22] since their token types (*i.e.*, word *vs.* action) are different and representations are **heterogeneous**.

More specifically, the word-sequence-based model generates words directly while the action-sequence-based generates the actions (*i.e.*, remove, add, *etc.*.).

It is beneficial if KD between these two models is possible. Action-sequence-based models (*e.g.*, GECToR [19] which is an ensemble model containing 3 sub-models) are well-performed, excessively large, and very hard to deploy on a device with limited resources or for many users in parallel. Compared to the action-sequence-based models with a complex pipeline including pre-processing and post-processing, the simple word-sequence-based model runs faster and is much easier to deploy.

3   Approach

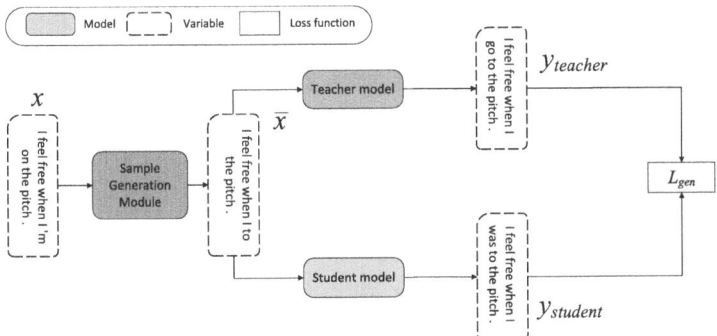

Fig. 2. Illustration of TG. The sample generation module takes a natural sentence as input and outputs a sentence that can reflect the discrepancy between the teacher's output and the student's output. While the WS approach does not have any parameters to be updated, the TG approach leverages a seq2seq model as the sample generation module and optimized with a reinforcement learning strategy guided by   . (Color figure online)

To eliminate the limitation of KD between heterogeneous models, we turn to leverage retraining approaches with informative samples to better bridge the gap between the teacher and student model, so that the process of retraining the student model is independent of the heterogeneous teacher model. We formulate MAKD as a two-stage process: *informative sample generation* and *knowledge transfer*

The idea underlying *informative sample generation* is that some samples are more informative than others for training the student model to get closer to the teacher model. We take an explicit approach to this generation problem: since the student model will be retrained using the generated samples to get closer to the teacher model, we will aim to generate informative samples that can reflect the discrepancy between the teacher and student models. To achieve this, we use **word substitution** (WS) to replace some words in the original samples to maximize the discrepancy between the student's and the teacher's output[3]. Furthermore, we propose a **text generation** (TG) approach to learning an additional model to generate the samples with sentence-level guidance from the student model and teacher model. Then the generated samples are mixed into the original training set as the transfer set to perform distillation so as to improve the performance of the student model.

---

[3] When calculating the discrepancy, there is an inconsistency in the output representation between the teacher and student models. To ensure that the final output of the teacher model matches that of the student model, we use mapping processing.

The transfer set drawn from WS and TG aims to illustrate the potential gap and can make rapid progress in training the student model. The two stages during the whole process are guided by the final result and make no assumption on the form of the output representations.

3.1 Informative Sample Generation

Word Substitution. The WS approach is inspired by adversarial machine learning [16,17] which aims at the victim model's vulnerabilities by generating samples to mislead the victim model to depart from the "ground truth". Here, the student model is to the teacher model as the victim model is to the "ground truth". We speculate that the student model using the generated samples as inputs would predict outputs that are different from the teacher model, so as to model the discrepancy between the teacher and the student model.

Formally, $\mathbf{x}$ denotes the input sentence[4]. We first obtain a strong teacher model and a weak student model through two loss functions $\mathcal{L}_t$ and $\mathcal{L}_s$, respectively. We do not place any constraint on the loss functions, but here we take the general cross-entropy loss as an example. For a student model with trained parameters Θ, the final output $\mathbf{y}$ given an input sentence $\mathbf{x}$ is computed by maximizing the log conditional probability: $\log P(\mathbf{y}|\mathbf{x};\Theta)$.

Inspired by [16], we leverage a sentence $\mathbf{x}$ as input and compute the vectorized representation $\mathbf{x}'$ of an informative sample by solving the following problem:

$$\mathbf{x}' = \rho + f(\mathbf{x})$$
$$\rho = \epsilon \nabla \mathcal{L}_s(\mathbf{x}, \mathbf{y}_t, \Theta)$$

where $\nabla \mathcal{L}_s(\mathbf{x}, \mathbf{y}_t, \Theta)$ computes the gradient of the "student" cost function around the current value of the model parameters Θ w.r.t. $\mathbf{y}_t$. Here, $\mathbf{y}_t$ is defined as the predicted output of the teacher model given the input sentence $\mathbf{x}$. ϵ is a hyperparameter that controls the strength. In most cases, ϵ is a small scalar value. $f(\mathbf{x})$ denotes a vectorized representation of sentence $\mathbf{x}$ in the student model. Both $\mathbf{x}'$ and ρ are vectors. $\mathcal{L}_s(\mathbf{x}, \mathbf{y}_t, \Theta)$ is defined as follows:

$$\mathcal{L}_s(\mathbf{x}, \mathbf{y}_t, \Theta) = -\log P(\mathbf{y}_t|\mathbf{x};\Theta)$$

In other words, the discrepancy between the predicted output of the student model and the teacher model is backpropagated to the original input sentence to obtain $\mathbf{x}'$ that leads to a different prediction from the teacher model. More specifically, we use $\mathbf{y}_t$ as the target instead of the ground truth and minimize the discrepancy between the output of the teacher model and the prediction of the student model. ρ in the direction of the gradient ensures that $\mathbf{x}$ is modified to increase the loss so that the model is less likely to predict a similar output as the teacher model.

---

[4] $\mathbf{y}^*$ denotes the corresponding ground truth output. But in this section, only the prediction $\mathbf{y}_t$ of the teacher is used.

To generate natural and legible samples, we follow the idea from [20] and use word-level manipulations to get tokenized representation $\bar{\mathbf{x}}$ from vectorized representation $\mathbf{x}'$. We simply search in the word embedding space and pick up words close to $\mathbf{x}'$.

Text Generation. The WS approach is a word-level approach and can only consider local information at each step when generating samples, thus it cannot take advantage of global information from the whole sentence. Ideally, we would like the student model to mimic the teacher's actions at the sentence level. To achieve this, we propose to use a seq2seq model [25] as the sample generation module, which has been widely used in machine translation, dialogue generation, *etc.*. We train the generation module by reinforcement learning guided by our designed criteria. We illustrate this stage in Fig. 2.

We represent a sample in the training dataset as $\mathbf{x}$ and the corresponding generated sample as $\bar{\mathbf{x}}$. Then TG models the distribution $P(\bar{\mathbf{x}}|\mathbf{x}; \Phi)$, where Φ is a set of parameters. Different from WS, TG has parameters to be updated during training. We define the objective function as the expected reward of sentences from the training corpus $\mathcal{X}$:

$$\mathcal{L}_{gen}(\Phi) = \sum_{\mathbf{x} \in \mathcal{X}} E_{\bar{\mathbf{x}} \sim P(\bar{\mathbf{x}}|\mathbf{x}; \Phi)} r(\bar{\mathbf{x}})$$

This objective function can be maximized using the REINFORCE algorithm [26]. The essential part of REINFORCE algorithm is to define the reward function $r(\bar{\mathbf{x}})$. The primary criterion is that the generated sentence should yield significantly different predictions between the teacher model and the student model. The reward $r(\bar{\mathbf{x}})$ is defined as the degree of discrepancy between teacher's output and the student's output. We explain the details of the degree of discrepancy according to the specific task (Sects. 4.1 and 4.2).

3.2 Knowledge Transfer

We represent the training data for knowledge transfer as $\mathcal{D} = \{\mathbf{x}^{(j)}, \mathbf{y}^{(j)} : j = 1, ..., M+N\}$, where $\mathbf{x}^{(j)}$ is the j-th sentence and $\mathbf{y}^{(j)}$ is the corresponding ground truth. The training data is used as the transfer set to train the student model. In our experiment, it is a mixed set including the set of M samples generated by WS or TG and the original training dataset including N samples. For the set of samples generated by WS or TG, we regard the outputs of the teacher model as the ground truth. The student model can be trained over $\mathcal{D}$ by minimizing the following function $\mathcal{L}_{kt}(\Theta)$, defined as a composition of two parts:

$$\mathcal{L}_{kt}(\Theta) = \mathcal{L}_{trans}(\Theta) + \mathcal{L}_s(\Theta)$$

$$= -\frac{1}{M}\sum_{j=1}^{M}\log P(\mathbf{y}_{teacher}^{(j)}|\bar{\mathbf{x}}^{(j)};\Theta)$$

$$-\frac{1}{N}\sum_{j=1}^{N}\log P(\mathbf{y}^{(j)}|\mathbf{x}^{(j)};\Theta)$$

where M is the number of generated samples and N is the number of samples in the original training dataset.

4   Experiments

4.1   Experiments on Dependency Parsing

We adopt two widely used parsers for KD: the graph-based model of Dozat et al. [13] and the action-sequence-based model of Chen et al. [10] to validate our MAKD. The former is a parser with high accuracy, while the latter gives the fastest speed in parsing.

    While the cost of rich feature computation of most current graph-based models restricts parsing speed significantly, action-sequence-based models can use greedy search which yields good gains in speed, even though there is no guarantee that the best parse tree is found. Therefore, transforming knowledge between these two models will take great advantage: the fast prediction from the transition-based model and the good performance from the graph-based model. However, there is a significant discrepancy in the output representation of the parse tree, model architecture, and learning algorithm, which we refer to as **heterogeneity**.

Data. Both the teacher and student model are trained on Penn Treebank 3.0 (PTB, [15]). Here, we choose to use PTB to train our sample generation module for simplicity. In order to verify the effectiveness of our informative samples, we compare them to an additional dataset, BLLIP[5], which comes from the same news sources as the PTB.

Setup. We conduct experiments on both the WS approach and TG approach. The WS approach uses a one-step gradient. According to the L2 norm distance in the word embedding space, the word that is closest to its vectorized representation is chosen. For the training of the teacher and student model, we follow most default hyper-parameter values as reported in the original article. For the TG

---

[5] Brown Laboratory for Linguistic Information Processing (BLLIP) 1987-89 WSJ Corpus Release 1.

Table 1. Comparison of UAS on PTB dev set and test set.

		Dev	Test
Student	*Without Retraining*	87.33	86.98
	ORIGINAL	87.37	87.01
	SYNONYM REPLACEMENT	87.33	87.05
	MAKD (WS)	87.76	87.21
	MAKD (TG)	**87.95**	**87.67**
Teacher	*Without Retraining*	94.01	95.7

approach, We utilize a three-layer attention-based BiLSTM with a hidden layer dimension of 1024 (32). We pre-train the sample generation module as a denoising autoencoder using samples. Then we use a reinforcement learning strategy to train the sample generation module. We evaluate performance via a commonly used metric from the CoNLL 2006-7 shared task [9]: unlabeled attachment score (UAS), which corresponds to the number of correctly predicted dependencies over the number of tokens.

Table 2. Comparison of the number of parameters and inference time on DP.

Model	#Parameters (Million)	Inference Time (Second)	Speed
Teacher	21.03	472.97	×1
Student	**2.46**	**125.06**	**×3.79**

Results. The results obtained by retraining the student model using the generated informative samples are summarized in Table 1. The number of informative samples is the same as the PTB training dataset. For both WS and TG, our model consistently outperforms the baseline model (**Student** *without retraining*). We also observe that sentence-level TG performs better than word-level WS. To verify if the performance gain is because of our generated informative samples or just the data augmentation, we conduct two experiments: (1) Further training the student model using samples in the original training data has not much different compared with the result in the "**Student** *Without Retraining*" row. (2) Further training using the original training data (**Student** *ORIGINAL*) which is labeled by the teacher model leads to a slight increase in performance 86.98 → 87.01. However, it still underperforms WS and TG (87.01 < 87.21, 87.01 < 87.67). Additionally, we compare our approach with the synonym replacement approach [29] (**Student** *SYNONYM REPLACEMENT*). The synonym replacement leads to a slight increase in performance. However, it still underperforms MAKD. Other text augmentation methods, *e.g.*, back translation, random insertion/deletion/swap, perform similarly compared with the synonym replacement. Next, we perform a significance test to measure the statistical significance of the advantage of our method. After 10 runs with different random seeds, the p-value is calculated as $0.031 < 0.05$ which is considered statistically significant.

Then we further investigate the speed/size trade-off on DP. We compare the number of parameters along with the inference time for the teacher and student models in Table 2. The inference time is computed by a full pass on the PTB development dataset on CPU (Intel(R) Xeon(R) CPU E5649) using one thread. The student model has far fewer parameters and is 3.79 times faster than the teacher model.

4.2   Experiments on Grammatical Error Correction

We adopt a transformer proposed by Vaswani et al. [24] as the word-sequence-based student model and GECToR proposed by Omelianchuk et al. [19] as the action-sequence-based teacher model.

Action-sequence-based models (*e.g.*, GECToR which is an ensemble model containing 3 sub-models) are well-performed, excessively large, and very hard to deploy on a device with limited resources or for many users in parallel. Compared to the action-sequence-based models with a complex pipeline including pre-processing and post-processing, the simple word-sequence-based model runs faster and is much easier to deploy. It would be advantageous if we transfer knowledge between these two models.

Data. We adopt the official shared task data[6] [8] of the BEA-2019 Workshop. We conduct experiments in the Restricted Track. Training for both the teacher and student model consists of pretraining on the synthetic training data and fine-tuning on the parallel training data. We use 9M parallel sentences with synthetically generated grammatical errors[7] [7]. And fine-tuning the model on data provided in the shared task: the FCE corpus [28], NUCLE [11], W&I+LOCNESS datasets [27], and a pre-processed version of the Lang-8 Corpus of Learner English [18]. We assemble the parallel training data from the corpus and filter out short and noisy data in the ensemble dataset.

Setup. We adopt GECToR [19] as the teacher model. It is an ensemble model and the final prediction is obtained by averaging output probabilities from three single models (*i.e.*, BERT, RoBERTa, and XLNet). For the student model, inspired by Sun et al., [23], we adopt the Transformer base architecture and train it using the data described in Sect. 4.2. Compared with the teacher model which is an ensemble model, the student model can speed up the inference and preserve the performance simultaneously.

---

[6] https://www.cl.cam.ac.uk/research/nl/bea2019st/.

[7] https://github.com/awasthiabhijeet/PIE/tree/master/errorify.

Table 3. Comparison of $F_{0.5}$ on the BEA-2019 test set.

		Pre.	Rec.	$F_{0.5}$
Student	*Without Retraining*	68.84	51.46	64.48
	ORIGINAL	70.26	51.00	65.32
	tiny-BERT	67.66	51.29	63.60
	MAKD (WS)	69.49	53.29	65.51
	MAKD (TG)	70.42	**53.67**	**66.28**
Teacher	*Without Retraining*	78.81	58.42	73.6

Table 4. Comparison of the number of parameters and inference time on GEC.

Model	#Parameters (Million)	Inference Time (Second)	Speed
Teacher	361.22	129.6	×1
Student	**73.65**	**34.7**	**×3.73**

Results. Table 3 reports the $F_{0.5}$ score of the student model on the test set, together with baselines and the teacher model for reference. To note, the original sample was integrated with the corresponding informative sample for the retraining model in the fine-tuning stage. In general, retraining using informative samples via WS or TG approach consistently outperforms the baseline without retraining. We additionally conduct a statistical significance test. Based on experiments of three runs, we obtain a p-value of 0.043 demonstrating that the improvement is statistically significant at the 0.05 level.

We further investigate the speed/size trade-off on GEC. We compare the number of parameters along with the inference time for the teacher and student model in Table 4. The inference time is computed by a full pass on the test dataset on NVIDIA 2080ti using a single thread. The student model has 4.9 times fewer parameters and is 3.73 times faster than the teacher model.

5   Conclusion

This work is the first to overcome the limitation faced by current KD techniques which can not be applied to two heterogeneous models. To overcome this limitation, we propose a model-agnostic approach for KD: MAKD. We evaluate our approach to two typical tasks that often have heterogeneous models due to varied deployment requirements: dependency parsing and grammatical error correction. Experimental results on these two tasks show that MAKD successfully makes KD possible in scenarios that previous approaches cannot handle. MAKD achieved an efficient and effective student model through knowledge transfer.

Acknowledgement. This work is supported by the Talent Fund of Beijing Jiaotong University (2023-XKRC006) and the Pattern Recognition Center, WeChat AI, Tencent Inc.

References

1. Abnar, S., Dehghani, M., Zuidema, W.: Transferring inductive biases through knowledge distillation. arXiv preprint arXiv:2006.00555 (2020)
2. Romero, A., Ballas, N., Kahou, S.E., Chassang, A., Gatta, C., Bengio, Y.: FitNets: hints for thin deep nets. arXiv preprint. arXiv:1412.6550 (2014)
3. Wu, Y., Rezagholizadeh, M., Ghaddar, A., Haidar, M.A., Ghodsi, A.: Universal-KD: attention-based output-grounded intermediate layer knowledge distillation. In: Proceedings of the 2021 Conference on Empirical Methods in Natural Language Processing, pp. 7649–7661. Association for Computational Linguistics, Punta Cana, Dominican Republic (2021)
4. Liu, C., Tao, C., Feng, J., Zhao, D.: Multi-granularity structural knowledge distillation for language model compression. In: Proceedings of the 60th Annual Meeting of the Association for Computational Linguistics (Volume 1: Long Papers), pp. 1001–1011 (2022)
5. Ge, L., Hu, C., Ma, G., Liu, J., Zhang, H.: Discrepancy and uncertainty aware denoising knowledge distillation for zero-shot cross-lingual named entity recognition. Proc. AAAI Conf. Artif. Intell. **38**(16), 18056–18064 (2024)
6. Tan, S., et al.: Are intermediate layers and labels really necessary? a general language model distillation method. In: Findings of the Association for Computational Linguistics: ACL 2023, pp. 9678–9696. Association for Computational Linguistics, Toronto, Canada (2023)
7. Awasthi, A., Sarawagi, S., Goyal, R., Ghosh, S., Piratla, V.: Parallel iterative edit models for local sequence transduction. In: Proceedings of the 2019 Conference on Empirical Methods in Natural Language Processing and the 9th International Joint Conference on Natural Language Processing (EMNLP-IJCNLP), pp. 4260–4270 (2019)
8. Bryant, C., Felice, M., Andersen, Ø.E., Briscoe, T.: The BEA-2019 shared task on grammatical error correction. In: Proceedings of the Fourteenth Workshop on Innovative Use of NLP for Building Educational Applications, pp. 52–75 (2019)
9. Buchholz, S., Marsi, E.: CoNLL-X shared task on multilingual dependency parsing. In: Proceedings of the CoNLL, pp. 149–164 (2006)
10. Chen, D., Manning, C.D: A fast and accurate dependency parser using neural networks. In: Proceedings of the EMNLP, pp. 740–750 (2014)
11. Dahlmeier, D., Ng, H.T., Wu, S.M.: Building a large annotated corpus of learner English: the NUS corpus of learner English. In: Proceedings of the Eighth Workshop on Innovative Use of NLP for Building Educational Applications, pp. 22–31 (2013)
12. Denil, M., Shakibi, B., Dinh, L., Ranzato, M.A., de Freitas, N.: Predicting parameters in deep learning. In: Advances in Neural Information Processing Systems (2013)
13. Dozat, T., Manning, C.D.: Deep biaffine attention for neural dependency parsing. In: Proceedings of the ICLR (2017)
14. Hinton, G., Vinyals, O., Dean, J.: Distilling the knowledge in a neural network. In: NIPS Deep Learning Workshop (2015)
15. Marcus, M., et al.: The penn treebank: annotating predicate argument structure. In: Proceedings of the Workshop on Human Language Technology, pp. 114–119 (1994)
16. Miyato, T., Dai, A.M., Goodfellow, I.: Adversarial training methods for semi-supervised text classification. In: Proceedings of the ICLR (2017

17. Han, W., Zhang, L., Jiang, Y., Tu, K.: Adversarial attack and defense of structured prediction models. In: Proceedings of the EMNLP, pp. 2327–2338 (2020)
18. Mizumoto, T., Komachi, M., Nagata, M., Matsumoto, Y.: Mining revision log of language learning SNS for automated Japanese error correction of second language learners. In: Proceedings of the IJCNLP, pp. 147–155 (2011)
19. Omelianchuk, K., Atrasevych, V., Chernodub, A., Skurzhanskyi, O.: GECToR – grammatical error correction: tag, not rewrite. In: Proceedings of the Fifteenth Workshop on Innovative Use of NLP for Building Educational Applications, pp. 163–170 (2020)
20. Papernot, N., McDaniel, P., Swami, A., Harang, R.: Crafting adversarial input sequences for recurrent neural networks. In: MILCOM 2016-2016 IEEE Military Communications Conference, pp. 49–54 (2016)
21. Sun, S., Cheng, Y., Gan, Z., Liu, J.: Patient knowledge distillation for BERT model compression. In: Proceedings of the EMNLP-IJCNLP, pp. 4314–4323 (2019)
22. Zagoruyko, S., Komodakis, N.: Paying more attention to attention: improving the performance of convolutional neural networks via attention transfer. arXiv preprintarXiv:1612.03928 (2016)
23. Sun, X., Ge, T., Wei, F., Wang, H.: Instantaneous grammatical error correction with shallow aggressive decoding. In: Proceedings of the 59th Annual Meeting of the Association for Computational Linguistics and the 11th International Joint Conference on Natural Language Processing (Volume 1: Long Papers), pp. 5937–5947 (2021)
24. Vaswani, A., et al.: Attention is all you need. In: Advances in Neural Information Processing Systems, pp. 5998–6008 (2017)
25. Wang, Y., Huang, M., Zhu, X., Zhao, L.: Attention-based LSTM for aspect-level sentiment classification. In: Proceedings of the EMNLP, pp. 606–615 (2016)
26. Williams, R.J.: Simple statistical gradient-following algorithms for connectionist reinforcement learning. Mach. Learn. **8**(3–4), 229–256 (1992)
27. Yannakoudakis, H., Andersen, Ø.E., Geranpayeh, A., Briscoe, T., Nicholls, D.: Developing an automated writing placement system for ESL learners. Appl. Measur. Educ. **31**(3), 251–267 (2018)
28. Yannakoudakis, H., Briscoe, T., Medlock, B.: A new dataset and method for automatically grading ESOL texts. In: Proceedings of the ACL, pp. 180–189 (2011)
29. Zhang, X., Zhao, J., LeCun, Y.: Character-level convolutional networks for text classification. In: Advances in Neural Information Processing Systems, vol. 28 (2015)

Exploring Multimodal Information Fusion in Spoken Off-Topic Degree Assessment

Fan Cong⬧, Guo Shen⬧, and Aishan Wumaier(✉)⬧

School of computer science and technology, Xinjiang University, Urumqi, China
hasan1479@xju.edu.cn

Abstract. Currently, most research methods for spoken off-topic detection are based on the results of upstream speech recognition tasks. However, upstream speech recognition tasks may introduce issues such as homophones, text recognition errors, and semantic confusion. Therefore, this study aims to explore the impact of integrating audio features into text information on off-topic degree assessment. To achieve this goal, we collected a dataset consisting of 2652 responses in question-answering scenarios from public competitions. The data was annotated according to the evaluation guidelines for farmers and herdsmen, creating a dataset named ASAG-TD for assessing off-topic degree in question-answering scenarios. In addition, we conducted research using the pre-trained language model RoBERTa, combined with commonly used neural network models, exploring two aspects: audio features and self-supervised pretrained acoustic model. Experimental results demonstrate the effectiveness of our method, with the mean absolute error (MAE) of off-topic degree in spoken responses reduced to 0.414 and a Pearson correlation coefficient of 0.95.

Keywords: off-topic degree assessment · cross-modal attention · semantic fusion · multimodal

1 Introduction

Off-topic detection is an important classification task that is commonly included in the preliminary scoring phase of essay automated scoring systems and in spoken language automated assessment systems.

Off-topic detection is crucial for automated scoring systems in both essay writing and spoken language assessment. It assesses the relevance of the content to the given topic before evaluating the linguistic and logical proficiency of the response [2]. When candidates fail to understand the topic or provide an unrelated response, their scores naturally lower, even if their answers are well-articulated. Therefore, the accuracy, practicality, and fairness of off-topic detection are essential for these systems.

Researchers have explored various methods for detecting off-topic content in written essays and spoken responses. Some employed vector space models to measure topic relevance [5], while others used text similarity approaches based on student-teacher answer correlation [10]. With the advancements in Deep Neural Networks (DNN) for Natural Language Processing (NLP), many DNN-based methods have been applied to off-topic response detection. For instance, Topic-Adaptive Recurrent Neural Network Language Models (RNN-LM) ranked answer sentences based on topic conditional probability [8]. However, these approaches have limitations in detecting off-topic answers prompted by new question cues not present in the training data.

Recent approaches have utilized similarity grids and deep CNNs [15] or combined hierarchical attention and similarity grids [12] to achieve better off-topic detection performance. Another approach involves using the Sentence-BERT model to detect off-topic essays [6]. This method first constructs an off-topic essay corpus with a large amount of high-quality data and then uses twin pretrained models for off-topic detection.

2   Contribution

Current research studies have used the speech recognition results of the test audio as input and explored the framework of essay off-topic detection. However, due to potential recognition errors and homophonic words in the transcribed text, the introduction of speech features has been proposed to reduce errors introduced by speech recognition. To enhance the accuracy of off-topic detection and the granularity of evaluation, off-topic degree scoring is conducted. This paper proposes two models for assessing the off-topic degree in spoken language: one based on RoBERTa [7] and cross-attention, and the other based on Wav2Vec2.0 [1] and multi-feature fusion. Experimental results on a self-built dataset demonstrate that both models effectively utilize the multimodal information of text and speech features, significantly improving the performance of spoken language off-topic degree assessment.

3   Model

3.1   Task Definition

This paper examines the extent to which spoken responses deviate from the topic by utilizing a regression model, as illustrated in Fig. 1. The specific definition is as follows: Given a question text comprising n characters and an answer audio consisting of m characters, along with the corresponding transcript text, the model generates a score representing the degree of off-topicness between the answer and the question. Notably, the scores range from 0 to 10, with six intervals established based on criteria devised by language experts. A score of 0 indicates no response or incomprehensibility within the allotted time. Scores between 2 and 4 indicate that the response is unrelated to the question. Scores between 4 and 6 suggest that the response is loosely connected to the question and lacks comprehensiveness in expression. Scores between 6 and 8 imply that the response generally aligns with the question, albeit with potential coherence issues. Scores above 8 indicate that the response is pertinent to the question, well-expressed, and exhibits a structured approach. Within a narrower range, further evaluation is conducted, taking into account various aspects of the user's response, including vocabulary appropriateness, fluency of expression, standard pronunciation, natural intonation, and grammatical accuracy. Each aspect incurs a deduction of 0.4 points. For instance, if a user's response falls within the 2-4 score range but exhibits deficiencies in all the aforementioned aspects, the final score will be 2 points. On the other hand, if the vocabulary is appropriate, the expression is fluent, albeit with slight pronunciation issues, unnatural intonation, and some grammatical inaccuracies, the score will be 2.8 points.

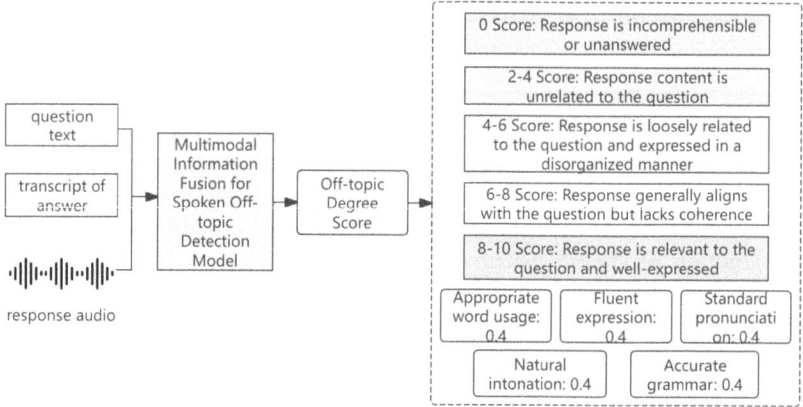

Fig. 1. Flowchart of Multimodal Information Fusion for Off-Topic Degree Assessment.

3.2   Spoken Off-Topic Degree Assessment Model Based on RoBERTa and Cross-Attention

The overall structure of the spoken language off-topic degree assessment model based on multimodal information fusion proposed in this chapter is shown below (Fig. 2).

The model contains the following parts: Considering the advancements in Automatic Speech Recognition (ASR) technology, it is assumed that the speech transcription can be extracted from audio signals with high accuracy [17]. To explore an alternative modality for predicting off-topic detection given a signal, this study attempts to utilize processed textual information. In order to leverage the textual information, the pre-trained language model RoBERTa is employed to extract text features. RoBERTa is trained on a larger scale of unsupervised data during the pre-training phase, including more text corpora and longer training time, compared to BERT [4]. This training approach enables RoBERTa to

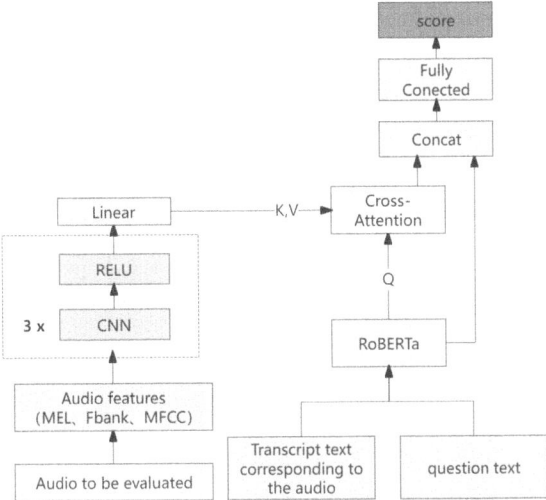

Fig. 2. Structural diagram of the Spoken Off-Topic Degree Assessment Model based on RoBERTa and Cross-Attention.

learn richer language representations and better capture the relationships and contextual information among words.

1. Text feature extraction: in order to obtain rich semantic representations of answer texts and question texts, the RoBERTa language model is used. For a question text with n characters and an answer text with m characters, the text feature vectors after fine-tuning the RoBERTa model are represented as Eq. (1).

$$E = RoBERTa(Q, A) = [w_{[CLS]}, w_1^q, w_2^q, ..., w_m^q, w_{[SEP]}, w_1^a, w_2^2, ..., w_n^a] \quad (1)$$

where [CLS] denotes a special marker in the RoBERTa model to indicate the beginning of a sentence or the representation of the overall sentence. [SEP] denotes a separator identifier between different sentences. RoBERTa denotes a fine-tuned pre-trained language model.

2. Speech feature extraction: this paper compares different speech features to understand their impact on rating prediction. Some commonly used frequency domain features are examined, including Mel spectrogram, MFCC and Fbank features. In the implementation, this paper uses the Librosa library to extract audio features [9].

3. Feature fusion layer: in order to fuse the text vectors and the acoustic features of the audio, a convolutional neural network is used to extract local key features. For the acoustic features of the audio, they are represented as Z and the Z are fed into a one-dimensional temporal convolutional layer separately to extract the temporal information. The filters in the convolution layer capture the features on different time scales, which helps in extracting the temporal information of the audio. The convolution process is shown in Eq. (2), where k corresponds to

the size of the convolution kernel used for different modes.

$$\hat{X}_Z = Conv1D(X_Z, k_Z) \in R^{T_Z \times d} \tag{2}$$

The convolved audio features $\hat{X}_Z$ and text features E are fed into the Cross-Attention module to calculate attention weights and determine the highly correlated time segments in the audio with the words or phrases in the text. The computation of Cross-Attention is as follows:

$$MH(Q_i, K_i, V_i) = Concat(head_1, head_2, ..., head_n)W^d \tag{3}$$

4. Output layer: By splicing the audio attention weights obtained from the cross-attention with the original text features, the key parts of the audio are associated with the semantic information of the text to better capture the semantic alignment between the audio and the text. The input is then fed into the full connectivity layer, which can yield a final score indicating the degree of digression. This output layer is able to map the fused features to the prediction result of the degree of off-topicness. Assume that the input feature after feature fusion is represented as F, with dimension D_f. The weight matrix of the output layer is W, with dimension $(D_f, 1)$, indicating the mapping of features to individual values. The bias term is b. The final formula for the degree of departure can be expressed as Eq. (4).

$$O = W^T F + b \tag{4}$$

3.3 Spoken Off-Topic Degree Assessment Model Based on Wav2Vec and Multi-feature Fusion

In this subsection, we enhance the performance of the spoken off-topic degree assessment by jointly fine-tuning the RoBERTa pretrained language model and the self-supervised pretraining acoustic model Wav2Vec2.0. The overall model architecture is illustrated in Fig. 3.

Wav2Vec2.0 is an unsupervised speech pre-training model. It constructs a self-supervised training target through vector quantisation and masking operations, and uses a contrast learning loss function for training. By optimising the contrast loss L (Eq. 5) required by the target model, the model is able to bring the distance between the contextual representation C and the corresponding discrete feature Q closer for the purpose of self-supervised learning.

$$L = \frac{\log exp\left(\frac{[c,q]}{\kappa}\right)}{\sum_{\tilde{q} \sim Q} exp\left(\frac{sim(C,\tilde{q})}{\kappa}\right)} \tag{5}$$

Here, Q represents discrete features that are derived from the frame feature sequence through a quantization module, serving as the self-supervised objective. C represents contextual representations obtained by feeding the masked frame feature sequence into the Transformer model. $\tilde{q}$ denotes the negative sample. The vectors input to the quantization module are not masked. [c, q] denotes the

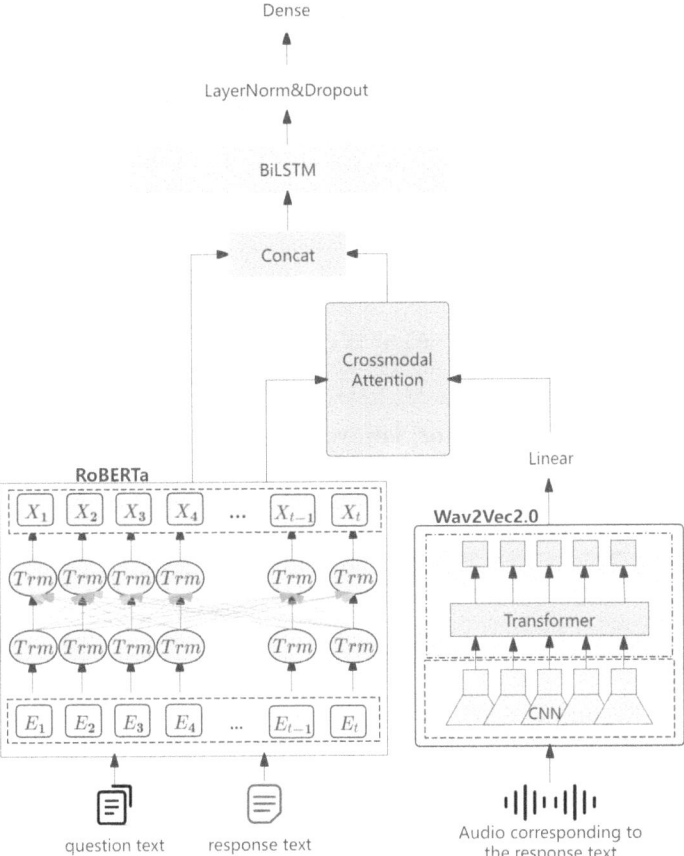

Fig. 3. Structural diagram of the Spoken Off-Topic Degree Assessment Model based on Wav2vec2.0 and Multi-Feature Fusion.

concatenation of input feature c and query feature q. κ represents the scaling factor used to control the weight of the loss function.

In this paper, the Wav2Vec2.0 model was utilized to extract embedded representations of answer audio corresponding to questions. These representations were then combined with rich textual semantic vectors for off-topic degree evaluation. In the proposed method, the audio files were fed into the model, and the final hidden layer output Z was obtained. This is illustrated in Eq. (6).

$$Z = Wav2Vec(L_a) = [k_1, k_2, ..., k_m] \in R^{m \times d} \tag{6}$$

L_a represents the original audio corresponding to the answer text. M denotes the length of the audio sequence, and d represents the dimensionality of the output vector. To facilitate better fusion of textual and audio data across different modalities, a cross-modal attention mechanism is introduced [13,14], enabling one modality to incorporate information from another modality. A detailed description of the cross-modal attention mechanism for the fusion of speech and text information.

First, taking the example of modality text (t) to each modality audio (a), denoted as t $\longrightarrow$ a, the vector representations are X_a and X_t. Similar to all attention mechanisms, it includes query vector Q, key-value pairs vectors K and V, which are obtained by applying different linear transformations W_q, W_k, and W_v to T for Q, and to A for K and V, as shown in Eqs. (7), (8), and (9).

$$Q_a = W_{Q_a} \cdot X_a \tag{7}$$

$$K_t = W_{K_t} \cdot X_t \tag{8}$$

$$V_t = W_{V_t} \cdot X_v \tag{9}$$

Next, the obtained query vector, key vectors, and value vectors are used to calculate attention scores, determining the correlation between different modalities. The value vectors (V) are weighted and fused onto the query vector (Q) based on the obtained attention scores, resulting in the final semantically fused representation. This process can be represented by Eq. (10).

$$CrossModal_{t \to a}(X_a, X_t) = softmax\left(\frac{Q_a K_t^T}{\sqrt{d_k}}\right) V_t \tag{10}$$

Here, Q_a, K_t, and $V_t \in R^T \times d_k$ represent the cross-modal attention module from modality t to modality a.

4   Experiment

4.1   Dataset

In this study, we constructed the off-topic dataset ASAG-TD by selecting 2652 data samples from the participating data of the 3rd National General Language and Writing Competition for Youth in Southern Xinjiang. These samples covered 54 question-and-answer types. We invited five Master's students from the School of Literature to rate the data, and the average ratings provided by these five evaluators were used as the labels.

4.2   Experimental Environment and Parameters

The experiments in this section were conducted on a 3090 GPU server for training and tuning, using the PyTorch [11] framework for model construction. The experimental parameter settings for the Spoken Off-Topic Degree Assessment Model based on RoBERTa and Cross-Attention are shown in Table 1. In this experiment, we utilized the RoBERTa-base pretrained language model and the self-supervised pretraining acoustic model Wav2Vec2.0, both implemented based on the Huggingface library [16].

The experimental setup parameters for the spoken off-topic evaluation model based on Wav2Vec and multi-feature fusion are shown in Table 2. In this experiment, the batch size was reduced from 64 to 2 to meet the training requirements of the Wav2Vec model. This sacrifice in training efficiency was made to ensure effective training of the model within the given resource constraints.

Table 1. Detailed Experimental Parameters of RoBERTa-CNN-CA.

Parameters	Settings
LSTM hidden layer units	768
learning rate	2e-5
Attention dimension	768
Fbank dimension	40
Window size in Short-Time Fourier Transform (STFT)	2048
MFCC dimension	13
maxlen	128
batch size	64
epoch	30
loss function	Mean Squared Error (MSE) loss function
RoBERTa-base	FacebookAI/roberta-base

Table 2. Detailed Experimental Parameters of Multi-Feature Fusion.

Parameters	Settings
BiLSTM hidden layer units	512
learning rate	2e-5
maxlen	128
batch size	2
epoch	30
loss function	Mean Squared Error (MSE) loss function
Wav2Vec2.0-large	Fjonatasgrosman/wav2vec2-large-xlsr-53-chinese-zh-cn

4.3   Evaluation Metrics

In addition to using RMSE [3] (Root Mean Square Error), MAE [3] (Mean Absolute Error), and Pearson's correlation coefficient, additional regression model metrics such as MSE [3] (Mean Squared Error) and R-Square (R^2) [3] have been introduced to comprehensively evaluate the performance of the model. MSE (Mean Squared Error) is one of the evaluation metrics for regression models. It calculates the average squared difference between the predicted values and the true values. The calculation process is shown in Eq. (11), where y_i represents the true value and $\hat{y}_i$ represents the predicted value.

$$MSE = \frac{1}{m}\sum_{i=1}^{m}(y_i - \hat{y}_i)^2 \tag{11}$$

The coefficient of determination (R^2) is a metric used to assess the goodness of fit of a regression model. It ranges from 0 to 1, where 1 indicates a perfect fit of the model to the data, and 0 indicates that the model cannot explain the variability of the target variable. The calculation formula is shown in Eq. (12), where SSR represents the sum of squares due to regression, SST is the total sum of squares, and $\bar{y}_i$ represents the mean value.

$$R^2 = 1 - \frac{SSR}{SST} = \frac{\sum_i (y_i - \hat{y}_i)}{\sum_i (y_i - \bar{y}_i)} \tag{12}$$

In summary, MSE and R^2 are metrics used to measure the performance of regression models. MSE provides the average squared value of prediction errors, while R2 is used to evaluate the goodness of fit of the model. By utilizing these metrics, the prediction ability and fitting performance of regression models can be more comprehensively assessed.

4.4   Experimental Results and Analysis of RoBERTa and Cross-Attention Model

When considering only text features, we employed the pre-trained language model RoBERTa and the Bert-based deep neural network [18] as the baseline models for spoken off-topic detection. This study compared them with other comparative models, including RoBERTa-CNN, RoBERTa-BiLSTM-CNN, RoBERTa-BiLSTM, and RoBERTa-BiLSTM-CNN-MultiHead-Attention. For audio features, commonly used frequency-based audio features such as Fbank, MFCC, and Mel spectrogram were considered, and their impact on spoken off-topic detection was investigated. The experimental results demonstrate that the RoBERTa-CrossAttention model for spoken off-topic detection achieved promising results on the ASAG-TD dataset, as shown in Table 3.

Based on the experimental results in Table 3, the following conclusions can be drawn. Firstly, in the single modality text experiment, when fine-tuning the pre-trained language model, a Pearson correlation coefficient of 80% was observed between the predicted scores of the text-only model and the human ratings. This indicates a linear correlation between the model's predicted scores and human ratings. Secondly, adding neural networks such as CNN and BiLSTM on top of the pre-trained language model further improved the model's performance. However, in the actual scoring process, evaluating only the transcribed text without considering fluency and pronunciation accuracy in spoken responses is not comprehensive enough.

Although significant progress has been made in automatic speech recognition technology, there is still room for improvement in speech recognition for second

Table 3. Experimental Results of the Spoken Off-Topic Detection Model based on RoBERTa-CrossAttention

	ASAG-TD Dataset				
	MSE	RMSE	MAE	R2	Pearson
Single modality: Text only					
RoBERTa(Baseline)	3.081	1.755	0.840	0.687	0.830
Bert-based-deep-neural-network(Baseline)	2.412	1.553	0.573	0.751	0.883
RoBERTa-CNN	2.029	1.424	0.834	0.787	0.888
RoBERTa -BiLSTM	3.014	1.736	1.010	0.693	0.848
RoBERTa -BiLSTM-CNN	2.386	1.544	0.756	0.753	0.873
RoBERTa -CNN-ATT	2.190	1.479	0.948	0.765	0.878
RoBERTa -BiLSTM-CNN-ATT	2.679	1.636	0.850	0.700	0.838
Multimodal: Text + 13-dimensional MFCC					
RoBERTa-CNN	2.684	1.638	0.745	0.740	0.866
RoBERTa-CNN-CA(our)	1.676	1.294	0.581	0.805	0.898
Multimodal: Text + 40-dimensional Fbank					
RoBERTa-CNN	2.114	1.454	0.703	0.798	0.894
RoBERTa-CNN-CA(our)	1.813	1.346	0.696	0.821	0.907
Multimodal: Text + Mel-Spectrogram					
RoBERTa-CNN	1.308	1.144	0.511	0.855	0.926
RoBERTa -CNN-CA(our)	**0.957**	**0.978**	**0.414**	**0.903**	**0.950**

language learners. In this context, this study explores the effect of introducing different audio features on model performance.

Mel-spectrogram, FBank and MFCC are chosen as audio features because they are widely used in speech processing and have unique advantages. The Mel-spectrogram is crafted in alignment with the frequency perception attributes of the human auditory system, facilitating a superior capture of speech signal spectral features and furnishing abundant frequency domain insights. Conversely, FBank encodes spectral details through a filter bank mechanism, enhancing the extraction of speech signal spectral traits and minimizing data redundancy. In parallel, MFCC diminishes feature dimensions, amplifies computational efficiency, and conserves crucial speech features through the Mel-frequency cepstrum transformation applied to spectral data. According to the experimental results in the continuation of Table 3, regardless of the introduced audio feature, evaluation metrics such as MSE, RMSE, and Pearson were superior to the baseline model. When comparing different audio features (such as MFCC, FBank, and Mel-spectrogram).

Compared to the best-performing model, RoBERTa-CNN, in the single modality, the introduction of Mel-spectrogram feature resulted in a decrease in MSE from 2.029 to 0.957, a 44.6% decrease in RMSE, a 42% decrease in

MAE, an increase in R2 from 0.787 to 0.903, and a Pearson correlation coefficient of 0.95. These results indicate that the introduction of Mel-spectrogram feature significantly improves the performance of off-topic detection, enhancing model fit and correlation.

4.5 Experimental Results and Analysis of the Wav2Vec and Multi-feature Fusion Model

Self-built supervised pretrained acoustic models have been widely used in tasks such as speech recognition and phoneme recognition, allowing for the extraction of high-dimensional representations directly from raw audio. Therefore, this study combines text features from pretrained language models with high-dimensional representations extracted from self-supervised pretrained acoustic models to enhance the performance of the spoken off-topic detection model. The experimental results of the spoken off-topic detection model based on Wav2Vec and multi-feature fusion are shown in Table 4. According to the experimental

Table 4. Experimental Results of the Spoken Off-Topic Detection Model based on Wav2Vec and Multi-Feature Fusion

	ASAG-TD Dataset				
	MSE	RMSE	MAE	R2	Pearson
Single modality: Text only					
RoBERTa(Baseline)	2.834	1.683	0.710	0.693	0.836
Bert-based-deep-neural-network(Baseline)	2.536	1.592	0.535	0.738	0.870
RoBERTa-CNN	2.430	1.559	0.761	0.767	0.879
RoBERTa -BiLSTM	3.326	1.823	0.879	0.636	0.800
RoBERTa -BiLSTM-CNN	2.514	1.585	0.775	0.744	0.869
RoBERTa -CNN-ATT	2.833	1.683	1.018	0.681	0.828
RoBERTa -BiLSTM-CNN-ATT	3.684	1.919	1.024	0.633	0.797
Multimodal: Text + Wav2Vec					
RoBERTa-Wav2vec-CNN	2.006	1.416	0.638	0.775	0.882
Wav2Vec-Feature-fusion(our)	1.700	1.303	0.618	0.805	0.897

results in Table 4, it can be observed that the two off-topic detection models utilizing the self-supervised pre-trained acoustic model Wav2Vec as the audio feature extractor show significant improvements over the baseline RoBERTa model across five evaluation metrics. This indicates that incorporating appropriate audio features can effectively enhance the performance of the spoken off-topic detection model. Comparing with the experiments in Table 3, it is found that introducing Mel-spectrogram feature achieves the maximum optimization of evaluation metrics. However, due to the potentially higher resource requirements of the Wav2Vec model, only a limited amount of data (2 batches per round) was used for training, which somewhat affected the training effectiveness of the model. In the model using text features alone, it was experimentally observed that the CNN neural network outperformed the LSTM network. This may be attributed to the fact that the answer texts are typically shorter, within 50 words, which falls into the category of short texts, and CNN is better at extracting local important information from the text.

5   Conclusion

This paper aims to address issues such as homophonic words and recognition errors that may arise in upstream speech recognition tasks, and proposes two multimodal information fusion models for spoken language off-topic detection and assessment. Experimental results indicate that simply concatenating the original speech features and textual information has little effect on improving model performance in Mandarin spoken language off-topic detection tasks. However, by introducing convolutional neural networks, attention mechanisms, and utilizing pre-trained acoustic models, both proposed models in this chapter outperform the baseline model in terms of performance improvement. Since there are very few datasets that contain both text, corresponding audio, and rating labels, there are limitations in validating the model's effectiveness only on a self-constructed dataset.

Acknowledgments. This research was funded by the Science and Technology Innovation Leading Talents Project - High-Level Leading Talents (2022TSYCLJ0036).

References

1. Baevski, A., Zhou, Y., Mohamed, A., Auli, M.: wav2vec 2.0: a framework for self-supervised learning of speech representations. In: Advances in Neural Information Processing Systems, vol. 33, pp. 12449–12460 (2020)
2. Chen, Z., Chen, W.: Off-topic essays detection based on document divergence. J. Chin. Inf. Process. **31**(1), 23–30 (2017)
3. Chicco, D., Warrens, M.J., Jurman, G.: The coefficient of determination r-squared is more informative than SMAPE, MAE, MAPE, MSE and RMSE in regression analysis evaluation. PeerJ Comput. Sci. **7**, e623 (2021)
4. Devlin, J., Chang, M.W., Lee, K., Toutanova, K.: Bert: pre-training of deep bidirectional transformers for language understanding. arXiv preprint arXiv:1810.04805 (2018)
5. Higgins, D., Burstein, J., Attali, Y.: Identifying off-topic student essays without topic-specific training data. Nat. Lang. Eng. **12**(2), 145–159 (2006)
6. Huang, P., Li, L., Wu, C., Zhang, X., Liu, Z.: A study of sentence-bert based essay off-topic detection. In: Proceedings of the 2023 4th International Conference on Computing, Networks and Internet of Things, pp. 515–519 (2023)
7. Liu, Y., et al.: RoBERTa: a robustly optimized BERT pretraining approach. arXiv preprint arXiv:1907.11692 (2019)

8. Malinin, A., Van Dalen, R., Knill, K., Wang, Y., Gales, M.: Off-topic response detection for spontaneous spoken English assessment. In: Proceedings of the 54th Annual Meeting of the Association for Computational Linguistics (Volume 1: Long Papers), pp. 1075–1084 (2016)
9. McFee, B., et al.: librosa: audio and music signal analysis in python. In: SciPy, pp. 18–24 (2015)
10. Mohler, M., Mihalcea, R.: Text-to-text semantic similarity for automatic short answer grading. In: Proceedings of the 12th Conference of the European Chapter of the ACL (EACL 2009), pp. 567–575 (2009)
11. Paszke, A., et al.: Automatic differentiation in pytorch. In: 31st Conference on Neural Information Processing Systems (NIPS 2017) (2017)
12. Raina, V., Gales, M.J., Knill, K.: Complementary systems for off-topic spoken response detection. In: Proceedings of the Fifteenth Workshop on Innovative Use of NLP for Building Educational Applications (2020)
13. Sahay, S., Okur, E., Kumar, S.H., Nachman, L.: Low rank fusion based transformers for multimodal sequences. arXiv preprint arXiv:2007.02038 (2020)
14. Tsai, Y.H.H., Bai, S., Liang, P.P., Kolter, J.Z., Morency, L.P., Salakhutdinov, R.: Multimodal transformer for unaligned multimodal language sequences. In: Proceedings of the Conference. Association for Computational Linguistics. Meeting, vol. 2019, p. 6558. NIH Public Access (2019)
15. Wang, X., Yoon, S.Y., Evanini, K., Zechner, K., Qian, Y.: Automatic detection of off-topic spoken responses using very deep convolutional neural networks. In: INTERSPEECH, pp. 4200–4204 (2019)
16. Wolf, T., et al.: HuggingFace's transformers: state-of-the-art natural language processing. arXiv preprint arXiv:1910.03771 (2019)
17. Yu, D., Deng, L.: Automatic Speech Recognition, vol. 1. Springer (2016). https://doi.org/10.1007/978-1-4471-5779-3
18. Zhu, X., Wu, H., Zhang, L.: Automatic short-answer grading via BERT-based deep neural networks. IEEE Trans. Learn. Technol. $15(3)$, 364–375 (2022)

Integrating Hierarchical Key Information and Semantic Difference Features for Long Text Matching

Chunnian Wang[⊠], Junliang Li, and Hu Zhang

School of Computer and Information Technology (School of Big Data),
Shanxi University, Taiyuan, China
{wangcn,zhanghu}@sxu.edu.cn, 202222404011@email.sxu.edu.cn

Abstract. Long text matching refers to the process of matching two pieces of text at the document level. Current methods struggle to effectively capture the key information scattered throughout long texts, and are insensitive to the semantic differences of identical words and the semantic similarities of different words. Therefore, this paper proposes the integrating hierarchical key information and semantic difference features for long text matching (HKIDF). Firstly, at the sentence level, we use information entropy to extract key sentences with a large amount of information, and then at the word level, we use an improved TextRank algorithm integrated with Transformer for word-level filtering of key sentences; Secondly, we use the improved Diff Transformer in BERT to learn difference features from the filtered key information; Finally, through a gate mechanism, we selectively fuse the semantic representations of key information and difference features to determine the matching relationship between long texts. Experimental results on the Chinese datasets CNSE and CNSS and the English dataset PAN demonstrate that our model outperforms existing baseline models.

Keywords: Long text matching · Information entropy · Difference feature

1 Introduction

Text matching is to analyze the semantics of text pairs and determine their matching relationship. It is widely applied in scenarios such as community question answering, information retrieval, and recommendation systems. Text matching is a key core task in natural language processing. Based on the length of the text, it can be categorized into short-text matching and long text matching tasks. Long text matching, in comparison to short-text matching, has numerous important applications and holds significant research and practical value. Consequently, it has garnered increasing attention.

Recent advancements in short text matching technology have been made. Traditional models like BM25 [1] and LDA [2] rank by calculating word correlations, but they fall short in handling sequence information and text interactions.

The introduction of deep learning has brought forth representation-based and interaction-based methods; the former extracts powerful feature vectors through the design of efficient text encoders [3–5], while the latter studies the deep semantic relationships between texts [6,7].

However, methods designed for short text matching cannot effectively handle long text. Long text matching faces more challenges due to its increased length and complexity of information. Firstly, long texts contain rich semantic information but key information is scattered, often mixed with noise, affecting the matching effect; Secondly, long text matching involves very long texts, but they are often truncated during computation, such as BERT limiting text length to 512, leading to information loss. Previous work such as Match-Ignition [8] attempted to solve these problems, but the PageRank algorithm lacks document set information when calculating node weights, and the weight information of words has no practical meaning, unable to distinguish the strength of connections. Moreover, in long texts, semantic differences may occur among words. For example, in Fig. 1, the words "五一" and "五月" have different literal meanings, but express similar semantics. This kind of difference may interfere with the model's semantic learning. Therefore, this semantic difference [9] is also a key difficulty in long text matching.

长文本 1：五一假期过后，8 个好消息让你"满血复活"......↵

Long Text 1: After the May Day holiday, 8 good news will bring you back to life with full health...↵

长文本 2：五月还有 8 个节日 8 个好消息，让你立马"满血复活"......↵

Long Text 2: There are 8 holidays and 8 good news in May, which will bring you back to life with full health immediately...↵

Fig. 1. Example of literal differences with same semantics.

Inspired by the aforementioned research, this paper proposes the integrating hierarchical key information and semantic difference features for long text matching (HKIDF), to improve the interference caused by noise and word semantic differences in long text matching. The main contributions of this paper are as follows:

- To effectively extract key information from long texts, we approach it from two levels: sentences and words. We use information entropy to extract key sentences, and an improved TextRank algorithm integrated into the Transformer to extract keywords.
- To enhance the model's sensitivity to semantic differences in words within long texts, we have introduced an improved Diff Transformer into BERT, which learns the difference features of key words through difference type discrimination and self-attention weights. A gate mechanism is used to fuse key information features and difference features.

– We conducted experiments on two Chinese long text news datasets (CNSE and CNSS) and an English plagiarism detection dataset (PAN), which demonstrate the effectiveness of the HKIDF.

2   Related Work

2.1   Short Text Matching

Traditional text matching methods, such as TF-IDF [10] and BM25 [1], calculate the semantic distance between text pairs through unsupervised learning. The development of deep learning has led to two types of text matching models: representational and interactive. Representational models, like DSSM [3] and CDSSM [4], use Siamese networks to learn sentence vectors and predict similarity, but they lack detailed interaction. Interactive models, such as ARC-II [6] and Match Pyramid [7], enhance matching effects through information interaction. Pre-trained models like BERT [11] improve representation capabilities through the Transformer [12]. Sentence-BERT [5] optimizes the application of Siamese networks. GSD [13] learns sentence difference features, and Diff [9] extracts contextual semantic differences between short texts, both enhancing matching performance through gate mechanisms.

2.2   Long Text Matching

In the field of long text matching, SMASH RNN [14] integrates multi-level document structure information to learn comprehensive semantics and infer similarity. SMITH [15] extends BERT's input to 2048 tokens to enhance semantic matching. Longformer [16] expand the Transformer to long texts through sliding window or memory strategies. CIG [17] employs a concept interaction graph and graph convolution to decompose the matching task. Match-Ignition [8] uses PageRank to eliminate noise. CoLDE [18] segments documents and trains using contrastive learning. FBC [19] combines Bi-Encoder and Cross-Encoder, using entity-driven extraction of key sentences to improve matching efficiency.

3   Method

In this section, we introduce the integrating hierarchical key information and semantic difference features for long text matching (HKIDF). The overall framework of HKIDF in Fig. 2. HKIDF consists of the following three main parts: (1) Key information extraction adopts a dual-layer filtering strategy for sentences and words; (2) Difference feature encoding uses the filtered key information features as input to learn the semantic difference features of words; (3) Gate mechanism is used to selectively fuse the key information features and difference features of long text, and then perform matching.

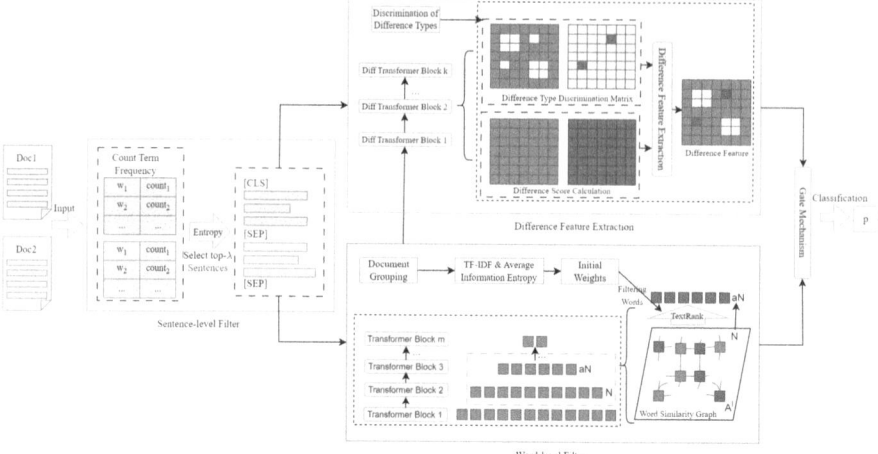

Fig. 2. The overall framework of HKIDF.

3.1 Key Information Extraction

Sentence-Level Filtering Layer. The sentence filtering layer selects key sentences from long texts to reduce the impact of noise. Information entropy, as an indicator of uncertainty, is used to evaluate the information content and importance of sentences. This stage can be formalized as follows: For a long text d_s, it is divided into a set of sentences $d_s = \{s_1, s_2, \ldots s_{L_1}\}$, where L_1 is the total number of sentences. Each sentence s_i is composed of a sequence of words $\{w_1, w_2, \ldots w_n\}$, with n being the number of words. We calculate the word frequency $count_k$ of word w_k in d_s, and subsequently obtain the information entropy of each sentence s_i:

$$H(s_i) = -\sum_{k=1}^{n} (p(w_k) \times \log(p(w_k))), \qquad (1)$$

where $p(w_k)$ represents the frequency of the k-th word in sentence s_i. After calculating the information entropy of all sentences, we sort the sentences based on their information entropy. To adapt to the input length of the BERT model and ensure matching effectiveness, we select the top five sentences with the highest information entropy as the key sentences. This approach not only achieves preliminary denoising but also ensures that the matching process focuses on the core information of the document.

Word-Level Filtering Layer. The sentence filtering layer removes some document noise, but word noise can still interfere with the model. The word filtering layer aims to select key words within key sentences, and preserve their semantics.

The TextRank algorithm is a graph-based ranking algorithm for keyword extraction, derived from the PageRank algorithm. It constructs relationships between words using a co-occurrence window and extracts keywords based on the co-occurrence information within a document.

In BERT, the attention weight matrix $\mathbf{A}^1$ of each Transformer layer forms a fully connected graph between words, which can serve as the word graph for node transition probabilities in the TextRank algorithm. By inserting the TextRank algorithm into the Transformer, treating words as nodes, and $\mathbf{A}^l$ as the weight of the edges between nodes, we calculate the importance scores of words for word filtering. Traditional TextRank does not fully utilize corpus information, resulting in word weights that lack practical significance and cannot distinguish the strength of connections [20]. Therefore, we combine TF-IDF and average information entropy to calculate the importance of each word. The TF-IDF weight is:

$$W_{TF-IDF}(w_i) = TF_{w_i} \times IDF_{w_i}, \tag{2}$$

$$IDF_i = \log\left(\frac{N}{DF_{w_i}}\right), \tag{3}$$

where TF_{w_i} represents the frequency of the word w_i in the document, N denotes the total number of documents in the corpus, DF_{w_i} indicates the number of documents containing the word w_i, and IDF_{w_i} reflects the topic representation ability of the word w_i. The average information entropy characterizes the uniformity of a word's distribution across the entire corpus, thereby measuring the word's capability to express the text's theme:

$$W_{Entropy}(w_i) = 1 - \frac{1}{logN}\sum_{k=1}^{N}\left(\frac{f_{w_ik}}{n_{w_i}}log\frac{n_{w_i}}{f_{w_ik}}\right), \tag{4}$$

where f_{w_ik} denotes the frequency of the word w_i in document k, n_{w_i} represents the frequency of the word w_i across the entire document set, and N signifies the total number of documents in the corpus. We consider the contributions of TF-IDF weight and average information entropy weight to the importance of words to be equal. Therefore, we use a weighted average as the initial weight $\mathbf{u}^0$ of the TextRank word nodes:

$$\mathbf{u}^0 = (W_{TF-IDF}(i) + W_{Entropy}(i))\ /\ 2. \tag{5}$$

To integrate TextRank with the Transformer, we use $\left(\mathbf{A}^l\right)^T$ as the state transition probability matrix. The tensor version of the TextRank algorithm [21] is utilized to calculate the importance scores of words:

$$\mathbf{u} = (1 - d) \cdot I + d \times \left(\mathbf{A}^l\right)^T \mathbf{u}^0, \tag{6}$$

where matrix I is an identity matrix with values of 1, used for tensor calculations. The computed $\mathbf{u}$ represents the TextRank score of each node in layer $l - 1$, indicating the importance of the nodes at layer $l - 1$. By using the attention matrix $\mathbf{A}^l$ as the weight matrix and multiplying it by $\mathbf{u}$, we obtain the score value $\mathbf{R}$ for each node at layer l, which can be represented as $\mathbf{R} = \mathbf{A}^l \mathbf{u}$. Based on $\mathbf{R}$, each layer filters out the bottom 10% of non-key nodes by score. After the final Transformer layer, the key information feature representation of the original sentence, denoted as O_h, is obtained.

3.2 Difference Feature Encoding Layer

Through the extraction of key information, noise within long texts is effectively reduced. However, within this key information, the same words may exhibit semantic differences, while different words may show semantic similarities, which can interfere with the model's semantic learning. Therefore, inspired by Diff [9], we introduce the difference feature learning method used for short texts into long texts to learn the semantic difference features of words within key information.

The difference feature encoding layer in BERT is parallelly modified as the Diff Transformer, which transforms the mask into a difference type discriminator. The self-attention weights are used as similarity scores, and difference scores are derived using 1 minus the similarity score. The difference type discrimination matrix is calculated in advance. Marking words as consistent or inconsistent only up to the cutoff position inputted into BERT.

When learning semantic difference features, the filtered key features of the original sentence O_h are input into the Diff Transformer to obtain similarity and dissimilarity scores. Since the difference type discrimination matrix is constructed based on the key sentence before word filtering, but the score matrix is based on the filtered key features O_h, direct calculation would result in mismatched dimensions and tokens between the score matrix and the discrimination matrix. Therefore, during the word filtering process, we prune the difference type discrimination matrix at the same positions as the word filtering to ensure consistency in dimensions and tokens with the original sentence key features O_h. According to the difference type discrimination matrix, for consistent words, the difference scores are retained, and for inconsistent words, the similarity scores are retained, resulting in the difference features of key information $Deff_h$.

3.3 Gate Mechanism

To effectively fuse key information features and difference features, we adopt the gate mechanism proposed by GSD [13] for selectively fusing the key information feature O_h and the difference feature $Deff_h$.

Firstly, we apply a non-linear function with the same parameters to transform O_h and $Deff_h$, resulting in transformed original sentence representation H_o and difference representation H_d:

$$H_o = \tanh\left(O_h \cdot W_n + b_n\right), \tag{7}$$

$$H_d = \tanh\left(Deff_h \cdot W_n + b_n\right). \tag{8}$$

Secondly, we use a non-linear function with different parameters to transform O_h and $Deff_h$, obtaining the gate vector G_{emb}. The use of different parameters ensures that O_h and $Deff_h$ retain their respective features:

$$G_{emb} = sigmoid\left(O_h \cdot W_{g1} + Deff_h \cdot W_{g2} + b_g\right). \tag{9}$$

Finally, we selectively fuse the original sentence representation H_o and the difference representation H_d using the gate vector G_{emb} to obtain the final joint semantic vector H:

$$H = H_o \cdot G_{emb} + H_d \cdot \left(1 - G_{emb}\right). \tag{10}$$

When the gate vector approaches 1, it indicates that more of the original sentence features are retained. Otherwise, the difference features are more preserved. After computing H in the BERT model, we fine-tune the model within BERT for the long text matching task. The objective function for long text matching is binary cross-entropy loss:

$$\mathcal{L} = -\sum_{i=1}^{N}\left(y_i \log\left(p_i\right) + \left(1 - y_i\right)\log\left(1 - p_i\right)\right), \tag{11}$$

where $y_i \in \{0, 1\}$ represents the label of the i-th training sample, and $p_i \in [0, 1]$ is the model's predicted result.

4   Experiments

4.1   Datasets

Our experiments utilized two Chinese datasets, CNSE and CNSS [17], which contain news on various topics annotated by experts. CNSE focuses on whether the same news event is reported, while CNSS concentrates on whether the same news hotspots are involved. Additionally, we conducted experiments on the English dataset PAN [22], which compiles English documents from the web representing various cases of plagiarism. For specific divisions refer to Table 1.[1]

---

[1] Datasets are available at https://github.com/BangLiu/ArticlePairMatching.

Table 1. The division of the dataset. AvgWPerD denotes the average number of words per document, AvgSPerD denotes the average number of sentences per document.

Dataset	Sample size				
	AvgWPerD	AvgSPerD	Train	Dev	Test
CNSE	982.7	20.1	17,438	5,813	5,812
CNSS	996.6	20.4	20,102	6,701	6,700
PAN	1569.7	47.4	17,968	2,908	2,906

4.2   Experimental Settings

Parameters Settings. We implemented all the models using pytorch. And we choose the fine-tuned BERT model bert-base-chinese and bert-base-uncased as the encoder of our model. The d for TextRank was set to 0.85. The number of documents N used for calculating initial weight was set to groups of 1000. The fine-tuning optimizer used was Adam [23], with a learning rate of 10^{-5}, $\beta_1 = 0.9$, $\beta_2 = 0.999$, $\epsilon = 10^{-8}$. Batch size is set to 8. The number of layers in the Diff Transformer is an adjustable parameter.

Evaluation Metrics. The evaluation metrics of the experiments use the widely used binary classification evaluation criteria in the field of long text matching, i.e., accuracy and F1 value to assess the performance of the text matching model.

4.3   Baselines

This paper compares the HKIDF model with several types of text matching baseline models, including (1)Traditional word-based models: BM25 [1], LDA [2], and SimNet [17]. (2)Deep learning models for short text matching: DSSM [3] and C-DSSM [4]. MatchPyramid [7]. RE2 [24]. BERT-Finetuning [11]. (3)Long text matching models: Longformer [16], BERT-OPT [25], FBC [19], the graph-based model CIG [17], and the filter-strategy-based Match-Ignition [8].

4.4   Experimental Results and Analysis

Table 2 presents the comparative results of our model HKIDF against baseline models on the dataset. The main conclusions are as follows:(1) Traditional models struggle with the details of long texts and perform poorly. BERT shows improvement but is limited by input length and noise processing, hindering further enhancement. (2) Models utilizing key information extraction, such as Match-Ignition, FBC, and HKIDF, exhibit superior performance, demonstrating the advantages of eliminating noise interference and extracting key information for long text matching. (3) Match-Ignition and FBC do not consider the difference information in the matching objects after filtering, leading to the models' inability to recognize interference caused by semantic differences in words.

Table 2. Comparing the results of the experiments, the best results are highlighted in bold

	Model	CNSE		CNSS		PAN	
		ACC	F1	ACC	F1	ACC	F1
I	BM25 [1]	69.63	66.60	67.77	70.40	61.59	62.47
	LDA [2]	63.81	62.44	64.37	65.92	60.75	60.51
	SimNet [17]	71.05	69.26	70.78	74.50	79.47	77.64
II	DSSM [3]	58.08	64.68	61.09	70.58	49.88	66.56
	C-DSSM [4]	60.17	48.57	52.96	56.75	71.21	74.57
	MatchPyramid [7]	66.36	54.01	54.01	62.52	64.02	71.14
	BERT-Finetuning [11]	81.30	79.20	86.64	87.08	59.11	69.66
	RE2 [24]	80.59	78.27	84.84	85.28	61.97	58.30
III	Longformer [16]	82.99	82.58	88.24	89.61	86.23	85.78
	CIG-S&Siam-GCN-Sg [17]	84.21	82.46	90.03	90.29	89.37	88.88
	Match-Ignition [8]	86.32	84.55	91.28	91.39	89.37	89.42
	BERT-OPT [25]	78.41	77.76	81.20	81.79	89.09	88.61
	FBC [19]	86.96	85.35	93.39	93.60	90.02	89.61
IV	**HKIDF**	**88.02**	**86.38**	**93.92**	**94.04**	**92.98**	**92.86**

HKIDF performs the best, proving the importance of addressing semantic differences in words during the matching process.

To explore the impact of the setting of the number of layers k in difference feature encoding on the extraction effect of difference features, we conducted experiments on the CNSE and CNSS datasets with different numbers of layers k. The results of the impact of different layers k on this experiment are shown in Fig. 3. When k=3, the effect is best on the CNSE dataset, and when k=5, the result is best on the CNSS dataset. When the number of layers is too small, the model's extraction capability is insufficient; when the number of layers is too large, gradient vanishing or overfitting may occur, leading to a decline in performance.

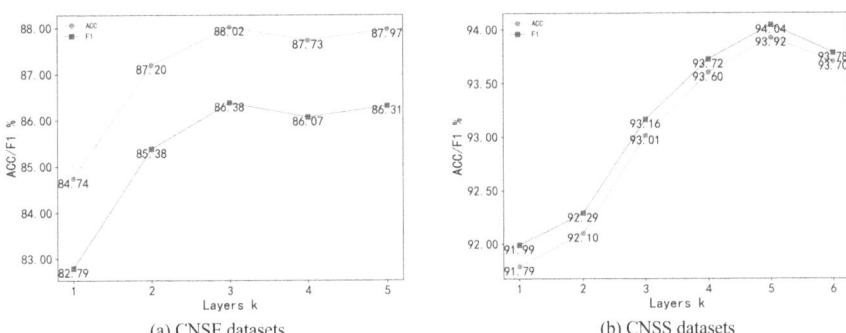

(a) CNSE datasets   (b) CNSS datasets

Fig. 3. In the CNSS and CNSE datasets, comparison result chart of different number layers of difference feature encoding.

To analyze the stability of the model, we validated the prediction accuracy on positive and negative samples using the CNSE and CNSS datasets. Additionally, we compared our model with BERT-Finetuning [11], BERT-OPT [25], CIG [17], and Match-Ignition [8], as shown in Table 3. The results indicate that the HKIDF model not only achieved better performance but also maintained a balanced accuracy on both positive and negative samples, demonstrating the stability of our model.

Table 3. Results of the model stability analysis. $|\Delta|$ represents the absolute difference between Acc_{pos} and Acc_{neg}.

Model	CNSE			CNSS		
	Acc_{pos}	Acc_{neg}	$|\Delta|$	Acc_{pos}	Acc_{neg}	$|\Delta|$
BERT-Finetuning	77.96	83.33	5.37	86.23	88.15	1.92
BERT-OPT	73.05	81.61	8.56	79.95	82.46	2.51
CIG	81.24	87.19	5.95	88.44	91.39	2.95
Match-Ignition	79.91	90.23	10.32	91.19	92.59	1.40
HKIDF	86.65	89.36	**2.71**	94.30	93.71	**0.59**

4.5   Ablation Study

Ablation experiments were conducted on the CNSE and CNSS datasets to validate the effectiveness of each module. The results, as shown in Table 4, are as follows: The absence of difference feature enhancement $(w/o - Deff)$ led to insensitivity to semantic differences in words, resulting in decreased performance. Training directly on the original data without using the filtering strategy $(w/o - Filter)$ resulted in worse outcomes, demonstrating the effectiveness of key information extraction in eliminating noise interference. However, $w/o - Filter$ performed better than BERT-Finetuning, further proving the effectiveness of the semantic difference encoding module. Simple feature fusion without the use of the gate mechanism $(w/o - Gate)$ reduced performance, highlighting the advantage of the gate mechanism in feature fusion.

Table 4. Results of the ablation experiment. w/o indicates that the corresponding module was deleted.

Model	CNSE		CNSS		PAN	
	ACC	F1	ACC	F1	ACC	F1
HKIDF	**88.02**	**86.38**	**93.92**	**94.04**	**92.98**	**92.86**
$w/o - Deff$	85.62	83.62	92.78	92.95	92.49	92.25
$w/o - Filter$	83.96	81.50	92.75	92.95	84.07	83.05
$w/o - Gate$	86.98	85.22	93.59	93.77	92.36	92.24
BERT-Finetuning	81.30	79.20	86.64	87.08	59.11	69.66

4.6   Case Analysis

To more intuitively verify the effectiveness of the proposed method in extracting key information for matching, we refer to the visualization method from the Match-Ignition paper [8] and provide an example from the CNSE dataset to visualize word importance, as shown in Fig. 4. The more layers a word retains, the darker its color, indicating higher importance. Keywords extracted by the HKIDF method, such as 'Changzhou', 'property market', 'rise' and 'rose' received higher importance scores, which are crucial for matching the two documents and are consistent with human judgment.

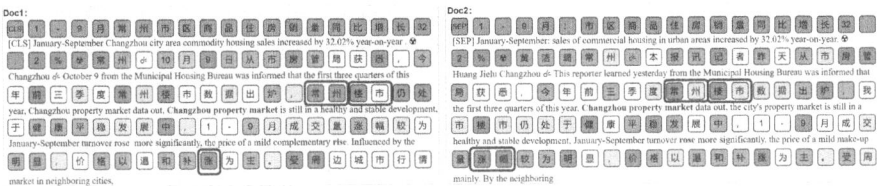

Fig. 4. Visualization of word importance in word filtering. Special characters represent separators.

To explore the impact of word semantic difference features on model predictions, Table 5 presents two cases comparing the predictions of HKIDF-NoDeff and HKIDF. In Case 1, despite the literal differences between "小年" (Minor Year) and "春运" (Chunyun), "抢光" (grab all) and "告急" (emergency), the semantics are similar. The HKIDF model can predict correctly, while HKIDF-NoDeff errs. In Case 2, the character "挺" (support/quite) is the same in appear-

Table 5. Sample analysis for difference feature validity. T represent correct label. P represent predent label. A represent HKIDF-NoDeff. B represent HKIDF.

	Content	T	P	
			A	B
1	Doc 1:小年火车票开售临沂-牡丹江方向10分钟**抢光**...... (Linyi - Mudanjiang direction 10 minutes to **grab all** the train tickets for the **Minor Year**) Doc 2:春运抢票迎节前高峰热门线路车票"**告急**"...... (**Chunyun** ticket rush to meet the pre-holiday peak popular line tickets "**emergency**")	1	0	1
2	Doc 1:火箭官推晒图力**挺**哈登MVP暗讽威少三双无用? ...... (The Rockets official tweeted a picture to **support** Harden's MVP insinuating that Westbrook's triple-double is useless?) Doc 2: ......三双只是数据剑指威少，威少**挺**好了。常规赛MVP之中...... (......triple-double just data sword Westbrook, Westbrook **quite**well. Among the regular season MVP ......)	0	1	0

ance, but its semantics differ between the two documents. HKIDF correctly handles this difference, whereas HKIDF-NoDeff does not. This demonstrates the importance of difference features in model training.

5 Conclusion

This paper proposes the integrating hierarchical key information and semantic difference features for long text matching (HKIDF) to optimize long text matching. The model extracts key information from two levels, sentences and words, through information entropy and an improved TextRank algorithm combined with BERT. It utilizes an improved Diff Transformer to learn the semantic difference features of words, thereby heightening sensitivity to semantic discrepancies. A gate mechanism is then applied to merge features for prediction. The method's effectiveness is proven by its superior performance over baseline models on the CNSE, CNSS, and PAN datasets. Despite its merits, the approach has limitations. Initially, during word filtering, the computation of initial weights led to the segmentation of the dataset, learning only from the documents within that segment rather than across the entire corpus. Furthermore, learning the semantic difference features of words has increased the model's training time. Future research will focus on addressing these shortcomings.

Disclosure of Interests. The authors have no competing interests to declare that are relevant to the content of this article.

References

1. Robertson, S., Zaragoza, H., Taylor, M.: Simple BM25 extension to multiple weighted fields. In: Proceedings of the thirteenth ACM international Conference on Information and Knowledge Management, pp. 42–49 (2004)
2. Blei, D.M., Ng, A.Y., Jordan, M.I.: Latent dirichlet allocation. J. Mach. Learn. Res. **3**, 993–1022 (2003)
3. Huang, P.S., He, X., Gao, J., Deng, L., Acero, A., Heck, L.: Learning deep structured semantic models for web search using clickthrough data. In: Proceedings of the 22nd ACM International Conference on Information & Knowledge Management, pp. 2333–2338 (2013)
4. Shen, Y., He, X., Gao, J., Deng, L., Mesnil, G.: A latent semantic model with convolutional-pooling structure for information retrieval. In: Proceedings of the 23rd ACM International Conference on Conference on Information and Knowledge Management, pp. 101–110 (2014)
5. Reimers, N., Gurevych, I.: Sentence-bert: sentence embeddings using siamese bert-networks. arXiv preprint arXiv:1908.10084 (2019)
6. Hu, B., Lu, Z., Li, H., Chen, Q.: Convolutional neural network architectures for matching natural language sentences. In: Advances in Neural Information Processing Systems, vol. 27 (2014)
7. Pang, L., Lan, Y., Guo, J., Xu, J., Wan, S., Cheng, X.: Text matching as image recognition. In: Proceedings of the AAAI Conference on Artificial Intelligence, vol. 30 (2016)

8. Pang, L., Lan, Y., Cheng, X.: Match-ignition: plugging PageRank into transformer for long-form text matching. In: Proceedings of the 30th ACM International Conference on Information and Knowledge Management, CIKM 2021 (2021)

9. Wenhui, Z., Meiling, W., Zhirong, H.: A short text matching model incorporating contextual semantic differences. Acta Scientiarum Naturalium Universitatis Pekinensis **59**(1), 30 (2023)

10. Aizawa, A.: An information-theoretic perspective of TF-IDF measures. Inf. Process. Manage. **39**(1), 45–65 (2003)

11. Devlin, J., Chang, M.W., Lee, K., Toutanova, K.: Bert: pre-training of deep bidirectional transformers for language understanding. arXiv preprint arXiv:1810.04805 (2018)

12. Vaswani, A., et al.: Attention is all you need. In: Advances in Neural Information Processing Systems, vol. 30 (2017)

13. Liu, X., et al.: Gated semantic difference based sentence semantic equivalence identification. IEEE/ACM Trans. Audio Speech Lang. Process. **28**, 2770–2780 (2020)

14. Jiang, J.Y., Zhang, M., Li, C., Bendersky, M., Golbandi, N., Najork, M.: Semantic text matching for long-form documents. In: The World Wide Web Conference, pp. 795–806 (2019)

15. Yang, L., Zhang, M., Li, C., Bendersky, M., Najork, M.: Beyond 512 tokens: siamese multi-depth transformer-based hierarchical encoder for long-form document matching. In: Proceedings of the 29th ACM International Conference on Information & Knowledge Management, pp. 1725–1734 (2020)

16. Beltagy, I., Peters, M.E., Cohan, A.: Longformer: the long-document transformer. arXiv preprint arXiv:2004.05150 (2020)

17. Liu, B., et al.: Matching article pairs with graphical decomposition and convolutions. arXiv preprint arXiv:1802.07459 (2018)

18. Jha, A., Rakesh, V., Chandrashekar, J., Samavedhi, A., Reddy, C.K.: Supervised contrastive learning for interpretable long-form document matching. ACM Trans. Knowl. Discov. Data **17**(2), 1–17 (2023)

19. Liao, J., Jia, M., Duan, J., Wang, J.: FBC: fusing Bi-encoder and cross-encoder for long-form text matching. In: European Conference on Artificial Intelligence (2023). https://api.semanticscholar.org/CorpusID:264290177

20. Dongju, Y., Chengfu, H.: Keyword extraction method for scientific text based on improved TextRank. J. Comput. Appl. **44**(6), 1720 (2023)

21. Mihalcea, R., Tarau, P.: Textrank: bringing order into text. In: Proceedings of the 2004 Conference on Empirical Methods in Natural Language Processing, pp. 404–411 (2004)

22. Potthast, M., et al.: Overview of the 5th international competition on plagiarism detection. In: CLEF Conference on Multilingual and Multimodal Information Access Evaluation, pp. 301–331. CELCT (2013)

23. Kingma, D.P., Ba, J.: Adam: a method for stochastic optimization. arXiv preprint arXiv:1412.6980 (2014)

24. Yang, R., Zhang, J., Gao, X., Ji, F., Chen, H.: Simple and effective text matching with richer alignment features. arXiv preprint arXiv:1908.00300 (2019)

25. Yu, W., Pang, L., Xu, J., Su, B., Dong, Z., Wen, J.R.: Optimal partial transport based sentence selection for long-form document matching. In: Proceedings of the 29th International Conference on Computational Linguistics, pp. 2363–2373 (2022)

CausalAPM: Generalizable Literal Disentanglement for NLU Debiasing

Shihan Dou[1] ⓘ, Songyang Gao[1] ⓘ, Tao Gui[2]([✉]) ⓘ, and Qi Zhang[1,3]

[1] School of Computer Science, Fudan University, Shanghai, China
shdou21@m.fudan.edu.cn
[2] Institute of Modern Languages and Linguistics, Fudan University, Shanghai, China
tgui@fudan.edu.cn
[3] Shanghai Collaborative Innovation Center of Intelligent Visual Computing, Shanghai, China

Abstract. Dataset bias, i.e., the over-reliance on dataset-specific literal heuristics, is getting increasing attention for its detrimental effect on the generalization ability of NLU models. Existing works focus on eliminating dataset bias by down-weighting problematic data in the training process, which induces the omission of valid feature information while mitigating bias. In this work, we analyze the causes of dataset bias from the perspective of causal inference and propose CausalAPM, a generalizable literal disentangling framework to ameliorate the bias problem from feature granularity. The proposed approach projects literal and semantic information into independent feature subspaces, and constrains the involvement of literal information in subsequent predictions. Extensive experiments on three NLP benchmarks (i.e., MNLI, FEVER, and QQP) demonstrate that our proposed framework significantly improves the OOD generalization performance while maintaining ID performance.

Keywords: Dataset Bias · NLU · Debiasing

1 Introduction

Natural Language Understanding (NLU) aims to train machines in comprehension of the structure and meaning of human language. Pre-trained language models, like BERT [6], have achieved remarkable performance on NLU benchmarks [28]. However, recent observations [12,14] show that, NLU models tend to over-rely on specific shallow heuristics instead of capturing underlying semantics, resulting in inadequate generalization capability in out-of-distribution (OOD) settings [20]. In addition, some researchers [16,21] have reported the insensitivity to word-order permutations among transformer-based models. When permuted randomly, both the original example and the out-of-order one elicit the same classification label, which contradicts the conventional understanding of semantics. These phenomena are referred to as dataset bias problems.

© The Author(s), under exclusive license to Springer Nature Singapore Pte Ltd. 2025
D. F. Wong et al. (Eds.): NLPCC 2024, LNAI 15359, pp. 284–297, 2025.
https://doi.org/10.1007/978-981-97-9431-7_22

Existing works tend to eliminate dataset bias by reducing the negative impact of problematic data. One strategy is identifying or constructing counterexamples to existing biases, and then focusing the main model on those hard minorities, such as learned-mixin [4], re-weighting [20], or confidence regularization [25]. The other strategy depends on the specific assumption that dataset biases can be known as a prior with limited capacity models [18,26] or early training [24]. However, these methods are not end-to-end, accompanied by a complicated training process. Furthermore, weak-weighted bias samples at data granularity simultaneously obstruct learning from their non-biased parts, resulting in a drop in the in-distribution (ID) datasets [29].

The abovementioned trade on ID and OOD tasks inspires us to study debiasing from a fine-grained perspective. Motivated by Predictability Minimization (PM) [19], we propose a novel learning framework-Causal Adversarial Predictability Minimization (CausalAPM). The proposed method trains an encoder to extract and weaken literal bias while maintaining semantic information by generalizable disentangled representation learning (DRL). Specifically, CausalAPM contains two adversarial learning objectives: 1) Literal information maximization, which aims to maximize the heuristic-related

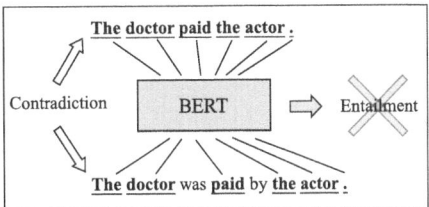

Fig. 1. An example indicating dataset bias. "The doctor paid the actor" is contradict to "The doctor was paid by the actor". However, with almost identical words employed in the two sentences, BERT predicts "Entailment" for the above sentence pair.

information extracted from sentence representations; 2) Dependence minimization, which prevents the model from separating excessive features, causing detriment to semantic information. Overall, our main contributions are summarized as follows:

- We analyze multiple existing generalization tasks to verify the wild existence of literal heuristics and propose a Structural Causal Model (SCM) to model this generalization hindrance during fine-tuning.
- We evaluate the disentanglement performance of the VAE-based model on generalization tasks, demonstrating the necessity for a more generalizable disentangle model.
- We propose CausalAPM, a causal-based adversarial disentangle framework. Extensive experiments validate the competitive effectiveness of our proposed approach for overcoming literal heuristics, while maintaining in-distribution performances.

2   Motivation

In this section, we present two preliminary experiments. We verify the universal existence of literal heuristics in discovered bias datasets and observe that existing VAE-based disentangle methods underperform on aforementioned generalizing tasks.

2.1   Literal Heuristics

We fine-tune the BERT-base model on MNLI [30], FEVER [23], and QQP[1] datasets and evaluate their performance on HANS, SYMM, and PAWS datasets. Figure 1 verifies the heuristic captured by the model during the training process. As positive samples increase with high lexical overlap, the model tends to predict the specific label for high overlap instances on OOD datasets, e.g., "Entailment" for HANS. While MNLI and QQP are constructed with higher overlap bias, FEVER is slightly more gentle with such defects, a positive correlation between the predicted label and overlap severity can still be observed. Overall, the over-reliance on literal heuristics is a universal detriment to the model's ability to generalize.

Table 1. β-VAE performance on MNLI, FEVER and QQP dataset, and their respective challenge test sets. S.v1 and S.v2 denote Symm.v1 and Symm.v1. respectively.

Dataset	MNLI	HANS	FEVER	S.v1	S.v2	QQP	PAWS dupl	PAWS ¬ dupl
BERT	84.3	61.1	85.4	55.2	63.1	91	96.9	9.8
β-**VAE**	84.7	65.6	85.5	58	64.8	90.7	81	24

2.2   Debiasing with β-VAE

Previous works have proposed that extracted disentangled representations can improve generalization and robustness across downstream tasks [1,9]. We evaluate the β-VAE disentangle method with consistent settings to current debiasing models on three NLU tasks with eight datasets. Table 1 shows the improvement in generalization by disentangling. The VAE-based method exhibits superior results to original models. However, the results on the OOD dataset are weaker relative to prior debiasing works. We argue that unsupervised disentanglement has indeed separated generative factors in the data representation, but failed to eliminate the abovementioned literal heuristics caused by unbalanced label distribution in datasets. Besides, while separated factors are independent of each other, they may consist of a combination of literal and semantic information, which induces a weaker bias.

---

[1] https://quoradata.quora.com/First-Quora-Dataset-Release-Question-Pairs.

3 Method

In this section, we first highlight the predictability minimization principle and analyze possible issues when applying it to literal disentanglement. Subsequently, we discuss how to train the CausalAPM model in order to learn the generalizable representation.

3.1 Predictability Minimization (PM)

PM principle originated in the unsupervised minimax game. It attempts to achieve a disentangled factorial code of given data without assumptions about the prior distribution of input data. The code components are statistically independent of each other, which facilitates subsequent downstream learning.

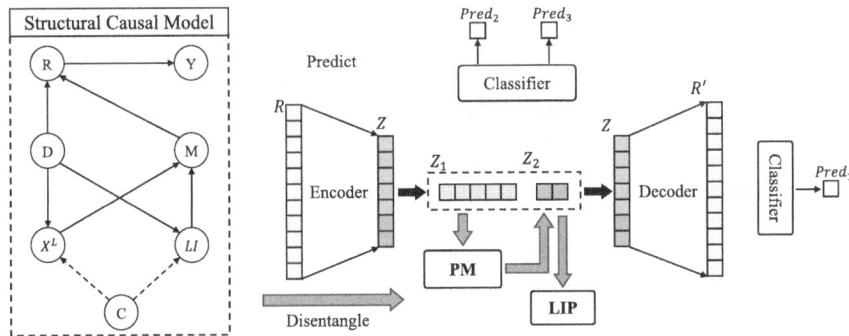

Fig. 2. Visualization of our structural causal model and CausalAPM framework. Under the guidance of SCM, we identify that dataset bias originated in the spurious correlations caused by backdoor paths. To tackle this problem, in CausalAPM, the input data is encoded into independent Z_1 and Z_2 with the Disentangle process, which consists of PM and LIP modules. Then the disentangled representation is fed into the classifier module for the Predict process. Detailed explanations can be found in Sect. 3.

Given an input data (X, Y), auto-encoder try to learn a reasonable low-dimensional embedding $P(Z_1, ..., Z_n|X)$ to reconstruct X, where $\{Z_1, ..., Z_n\}$ is the hidden representation of input data. Considering a subset of the feature vector $M = \{Z_1, ..., Z_k|k < n\}$, PM eliminates the correlation between M and it's complementary set M^Z by empirical estimating the distribution of $P(M|M^Z)$ and $P(M)$, which is equivalent to minimize the conditional entropy:

$$H(M|M^Z) = -\int_Z P(Z)log(P(M|M^Z)). \tag{1}$$

In this way, we can obtain the disentangled factors $P(Z|X)$ which can be written as $P(Z|X) = P(M|X)P(M^Z|X)$.

Unlike GAN or VAE methods which map the input data into an isotropic Gaussian distribution, PM loosens the constraints on hidden probability distribution. With more difficulties for generation tasks as a price, PM enhances its effectiveness in feature extraction and disentanglement. In reality, the decoder is usually omitted in several PM applications to focus on disentangling internal representations. Section 2.1 has suggested that directly applying unsupervised disentanglement can not bring obvious improvement. We argue that auto-encoder cannot guarantee well-generalizing representation without prior knowledge. In Sect. 3, we demonstrate how we extend adversarial PM training to debiasing tasks.

3.2   Structural Causal Model for NLU Debiasing

The left of Fig. 2 shows the structural causal model for NLU debiasing, containing 7 nodes in the debiasing procedure: D is the actual distribution of tasks corresponding to the dataset. C denotes the confounders introduced during the dataset construction. These confounders have been observed by previous work [12]. X^L denotes the distribution of the samples with different Literal Information. LI denotes the distribution of literal information. M denotes the embedding layer in the model. R denotes the representation of samples encoded by M. Y denotes the labels which the classifier predicts.

Defining these factors, the causal process of dataset bias is observed as follows:

- $D \to X^L \to M$ and $D \to LI \to M$ denote the training process of the model, which constructs the training data from the real data distribution.
- Accompany with the construction process of the data, a backdoor path $D \to X^L \to C \to LI \to M$ is created by confounders C, who introduces pseudo-correlation between the training data distribution X^L and literal information LI, leading to the dataset bias.

According to the backdoor criterion [15], we can block the path by intervention on node LI, which is processed with the calibration formula:

$$P(M|\text{do}(X^L = x)) = \sum_{Li} P(M|X^L = x, Li)P(Li), \tag{2}$$

where $\text{do}(X^L)$ denotes intervention on variable X^L to fix its value. Based on the above analysis, CausalAPM should remove the spurious correlations introduced by backdoor paths and capture the true semantic causal relations. To this end, we conduct causal interventions to debias from the literal factors. We disentangle confounder information from input representation to block the aforementioned backdoor paths in SCM, and then the literal heuristic introduced by the dataset confounder will be removed. Specifically, we conduct backdoor adjustment to learn debiased NLU models, i.e., we optimize the model based on the unbiased distribution, rather than from the dataset-specific distribution.

3.3   Causal Debiasing for Literal Disentangle

In this section, we introduce our framework for generalizable Literal Disentanglement. The right part of Fig. 2 exhibits our model architecture. Overall, we propose three training objectives: the basic task, APM learning, and disentangled prediction.

Basic Task. Our backbone shares a similar structure with normal works to introduce NLU task-related information to the trained model. Let (X, Y) indicate the input data and corresponding labels. We use BERT-base [6] as the embedding layer to get the representation of the input data. Then, we use two linear layers as encoder and decoder to get the low-dimensional representation of R, as follows:

$$R^{'} = \text{Decoder}(\text{Encoder}(\text{Embedding}(X))) \tag{3}$$

The hidden representation Z is separated into two pieces, Z_1 and Z_2, which are subsequently constrained to encode semantic and literal information, respectively. To obtain task-relevant information, the reconstructed $R^{'}$ is imported into classifier[2] to obtain the probability of its label Pred_1. Based on the prediction, the basic training objective is provided:

$$L_{\text{base}} = - \sum_{y^i \in Y} (\log(\text{pred}_1^T)y^i) + \text{score}(R, R^i), \tag{4}$$

where Y represents the label set, y^i represents a one-hot vector with one at the i-th position, and $\text{score}(\cdot, \cdot)$ represents the MSE loss function. The loss is subsequently back-propagated and only optimizes the backbone model (i.e., BERT-base).

APM Learning. The analysis in Sect. 3.2 demonstrates that the calibration operator on Li can block the backdoor path and prompt the model to fit the correct causality $P(M|\text{do}(X^L))$ with (2). To achieve this, an adversarial approach is introduced to train the disentangle encoder. Given the representation R of input data, we propose two training objectives to supervise the low-dimensional representation Z: 1) Literal information maximization and 2) Dependence minimization

Literal information maximization aims to extract complete literal-related information sentence representations which are named informativeness [3]. We measure the informativeness of a representation by its ability to predict the generative factor following previous work [7]. However, previous works are supervised by predicting the bag of words of the input, which introduces extra bias to encourage the model to predict high-frequency words [27]. In the LIP module, we design a weaker word-independent objective, constraining the encoder to disentangle the literal information. In summary, as each piece of training data for the debiasing task consists of a pair of sentences, we use the

---

[2] A single-layer FFN network with Softmax activation.

separated representation Z_2 to predict the sequence similarity of the sentence pairs instead of specific words. Let $X^1 = \{x_1^1, x_2^1..., x_n^1\}$ and $X^2 = \{x_1^2, x_2^2..., x_k^2\}$ denote the input pair, the sequence similarity S and loss function is computed like the following:

$$L_{\text{LIP}} = (\text{LIP}(Z_2) - \frac{\text{Card}(X^1 \cap X^2)}{\max(n,k)})^2, \tag{5}$$

where $\text{Card}(X)$ represents the element numbers of a collection, and $\text{LIP}(Z_2)$ represents the predicted similarity of sentence pairs.

Dependence minimization prevents the model from separating excessive features, which cause detriment to semantic information. In terms of disentangling, the representation of literal generating factors should lie in an independent vector space and invariant to a variation on other factors [8]. Therefore, we introduce the PM module shown in Fig. 2, which acts similarly to the discriminator in GAN [5], aiming to predict Z_2 by Z_1 as precise as possible. The prediction acts as a supervisory signal to guide the encoder. As a result, the encoder is instructed to encode complete literal information into Z_2, providing an accurate representation for LIP predictor and depositing residual information in Z_1 to maintain independence between two components. The training objectives for PM can be expressed as min $I(Z_1, Z_2)$, where $I(\cdot, \cdot)$ denotes the mutual information between two variables.

Specifically, the encoder has the opposite optimization objective to the PM module, which tries to output an independent representation to keep $P(Z_2|Z_1)$ close to $P(Z_2)$. The loss function is defined as follows:

$$L_{\text{PM}} = \beta * \text{Score}(\text{PM}(Z_1), Z_2), \tag{6}$$

where $Score()$ represents the MSE loss function. The PM module and the encoder are trained by setting β to 1 and -1, respectively.

Disentangled Prediction. The prediction is finally introduced after obtaining the disentangled representation. We complete the prediction by controlling the weight of literal information in the input. We feed Z_1 and Z_2 into the classifier to obtain the probabilities of labels from both semantic and literal perspectives. The two different outputs are then weighted for the final prediction. The training process can be represented as:

$$L_{\text{pred}} = - \sum_{y^i \in Y} (\log(\text{pred}_2^T + \delta * \text{pred}_3^T)y^i), \tag{7}$$

where δ represents the weighting parameter between semantic and literal information.

Combining Eqs. (4), (5), (6), and (7), we can get the following objective function, which tries to minimize:

$$L = L_{\text{base}} + \lambda * (L_{\text{PM}} + L_{\text{LIP}}) + L_{\text{pred}}, \tag{8}$$

where λ is the temperature parameter aiming to control learning objectives for different training periods. In short, the model primarily focuses on optimizing the basic task in the early stage of training and learning to disentangle representation afterwards.

4 Experiments

In this section, we illustrate datasets and implementation details. Then we evaluate CausalAPM on three widely used NLU tasks compared with nine SOTA methods.

4.1 Datasets

The experiments are conducted on three well-known NLU tasks: natural language inference, fact verification, and paraphrase identification. The datasets used for training on each task, as well as their corresponding challenge test sets, are briefly discussed below to evaluate the impact of our debiasing methods:

Natural Language Inference (NLI). NLI aims to infer the relationship between the premise and the hypothesis. Recent researchers [12,17] have revealed that the widely used NLI datasets contain a variety of biases. In this paper, we conduct experiments on the English Multi-Genre Natural Language Inference (MNLI) dataset [30] and Heuristic Analysis for NLI Systems (HANS) [12]. We train the model using the training set of MNLI, and choose MNLI-mm as the ID test set and HANS as the OOD test set.

Fact Verification. The task is to evaluate the validity of a claim sentence in the context of a given evidence sentence, which can be categorized as support, refutes, or not enough information. We use the training dataset provided by the FEVER [23] for this task. Also, we use the test set of FEVER as the ID dataset and FEVER Symmetric [20] as the OOD dataset for evaluation.

Paraphrase Identification. It aims to identify whether a pair of statements are semantically similar. We train the model using the Quora Question Pairs (QQP) dataset. We perform the evaluation using QQP as ID dataset and PAWS [33] as OOD dataset which consists of two types of data including *duplicate* if they are paraphrased, and *non-duplicate* otherwise.

4.2 Implementation Details

Similar to current debiasing methods, we apply our debiasing method on the BERT-base model [6]. For two sentences in a sample pair, we stitch them together and then feed them to the model. The hidden state at the [CLS] position will be used for the following downstream task. The hyperparameters of BERT are consistent with previous research papers (i.e., the learning rate is 5e-5 for MNLI and 2e-5 for FEVER and QQP, the batch size is 32 and the optimizer is AdamW with a weight decay of 0.01). For the implementation of CausalAPM, we chose 64 for the hidden dimension of the auto-encoder, 4 for literal information and 60 for semantic information. The values of β and δ are insensitive to specific tasks, empirically, 0.6 for β with 0.15 for δ can achieve promised results. λ is set to 0 for the first 2000 steps, and set to 0.6 for the rest training process.

Table 2. Performance on MNLI, Fever, QQP, and their respective challenge test sets. S.v1 and S.v2 denote Symm.v1 and Symm.v1. respectively.

Model	MNLI		FEVER			QQP		
	ID	HANS	ID	S.v1	S.v2	ID	PAWS dupl	PAWS ¬ dupl
BERT-base	84.3	61.1	85.4	55.2	63.1	91	96.9	9.8
DRiFt	80.2	69.1	84.2	62.3	65.9	–	–	–
Reweighting	83.5	69.2	84.6	61.7	66.5	85.5	49.7	51.2
Product-of-Experts	84.1	66.3	82.3	62.0	65.9	88.8	50.3	61.2
PoE$_{cross-entropy}$	83.6	67.3	85.7	57.7	61.4	–	–	–
PoE$_{self-debias}$	80.7	68.5	85.4	59.7	65.3	77.4	44.1	**69.4**
Learned-Mixin	84.2	64.0	83.3	60.4	64.9	86.6	69.7	51.7
Conf-reg	**84.3**	69.1	86.4	60.5	66.2	89.1	91.0	19.8
Conf $-$ reg$_{self-debias}$	84.3	67.1	87.6	59.8	66.0	85.0	48.8	28.7
MoCaD	82.3	70.7	87.1	65.9	69.1	–	–	–
CausalAPM(Ours)	84.2	**71.1**	**87.8**	**66.1**	**71.6**	**90.6**	79.1	31.3

4.3   Experimental Results and Discussions

To fully demonstrate the generalization ability of our proposed method, we conduct experiments on three different NLU tasks and compare the results with the other 9 SOTA methods. The evaluation results of all methods are illustrated in Table 2. Note that previous methods [11,18,31] have shown high variance in experiment results under different experimental settings, we evaluate the performance of our model by randomly choosing five random seeds and report the averaged result at last.

By analyzing the experiment results of Tables 2 and 3, it is obvious that our method achieves excellent performance on the OOD dataset of all three tasks. Also, compared with other SOTA methods, our method shows the best accuracy (i.e., 71.1%) on the HANS dataset. So our method has the best generalization on the NLI tasks among these SOTA methods. Moreover, our method is an end-to-end approach that does not rely on any prior knowledge of the dataset (i.e., it does not require the knowledge of the type of bias existing in the dataset in advance) compared to other methods and achieves better usability and scalability. It suggests that the majority of debiasing methods improve performance on OOD datasets by sacrificing the performance on ID datasets, which means current debiasing methods attempt to achieve a trade-off between ID datasets and OOD datasets. However, our method obtains the best performance on the HANS dataset compared to all other SOTA methods, with a 10% improvement compared to the baseline, without excessive performance degradation on ID datasets.

For the fact verification task, our method improves by 10.9% and 8.5% relative to the baseline on the Symm.v1 and Symm.v2, respectively, which contains the best accuracy compared with other SOTA methods. Moreover, other meth-

Table 3. Details of nine SOTA debiasing methods used to compare with CausalAPM.

Model	Requires prior knowledge	End-to-end
DRiFt	✔	✘
Reweighting	✔	✘
Product-of-Experts	✔	✘
PoE**cross-entropy**	✔	✘
PoE**self-debias**	✘	✘
Learned-Mixin	✔	✘
conf-reg	✔	✘
Conf-reg**self-debias**	✘	✘
MoCaD	✘	✘
CausalAPM(Ours)	✘	✔

ods are not end-to-end methods, so it has quite limited scalability, while our method can be easily expanded to other tasks. Our approach is designed to mitigate the damage to generalizable features while eliminating dataset bias, which can achieve better performance on both ID and OOD evaluation in the FEVER dataset. For the QQP dataset, we also obtain decent generalization in the PAWS dataset with a minimum loss on the ID dataset (Fig. 3).

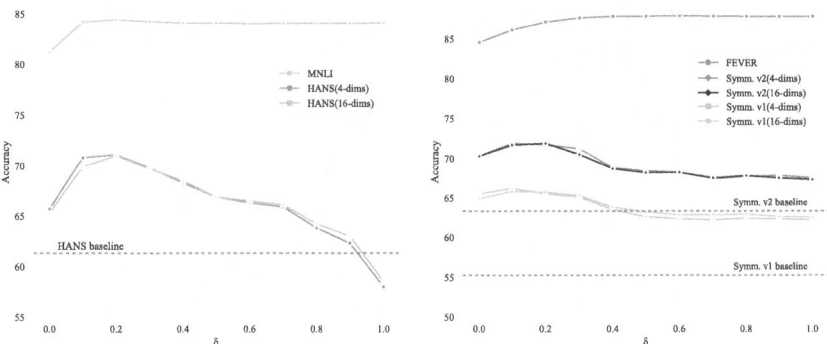

Fig. 3. Illustrate of accuracy in different δ values. Experiments were conducted on 4 and 16 dimensional Z_2 with $\lambda = 0.6$, the black dotted line donates accuracy when $\lambda = 0$.

4.4 Sensitivity Analysis of δ and Z_2

To illustrate the effect of the involvement of literal information in decoupling and prediction on the ability to generalize, we conduct sensitivity analysis of the δ and the size of Z_2, i.e., the hidden dimension for literal subspace. Figure 2 shows the performance change under different settings of the two coefficients. Accuracy at $\delta = 0$ represents model performance with only semantic information and accuracy at $\delta = 1$ represents model performance with full literal information. The black dotted line donates ablation results without APM objectives (with $\lambda = 0$).

We can observe that the performance is significantly enhanced with a literal rate between 0.1 and 0.3, and declines with greater weight on literal information, while ID datasets can maintain a stable accuracy. It proves the effectiveness of our proposed training objectives that extract and weaken literal bias while maintaining semantic information. In addition, with only semantic information, we can still achieve significant improvements on OOD datasets, while the ID performance shows a marked decline. This phenomenon validates the correlation between the model performance on ID datasets and the literal heuristics, which are analyzed by our SCM in Sect. 2.1.

5   Related Work

5.1   Disentangled Representation Learning

Disentangled Representation Learning (DRL) aims to find a low-dimensional representation that consists of multiple explanatory and generative factors of the observational data. Some methods [1,9] have proposed that extracted disentangled representations can improve generalization and robustness across downstream tasks. However, unsupervised disentangle methods only perform well in the simplest settings but struggle in more difficult ones [34]. The separated factors may consist of a combination of valid and invalid information, which hinders its performance on debiasing tasks.

5.2   Causal Inference for Disentanglement

Recently, the community has raised interest in introducing causality as supervisory signals to explain disentangled latent representations, thereby improving the generalization and Interpretability of disentangling learning [22]. For instance, CausalGAN [10] supports "do-operation" on images with a causal graph given as a prior. Instead of catching independent latent factors, CGM [2] introduces a layer containing disentangled nodes representing outputs of mutually independent causal mechanisms [13]. CausalVAE [32] introduces causally structured layers to disentangle factors, which enable automatic causality discovery to construct the SCM. Causal inference helps to analyze important factors of the task and provides reasonable objectives for disentangled learning.

6   Conclusion

In this paper, we analyze how to introduce generalizable disentanglement to eliminate dataset bias based on recent studies on generalization and disentanglement. Subsequently, we propose a novel and flexible method - CausalAPM, to tackle the spurious correlation caused by literal heuristics. CausalAPM provides a new generalizable disentangling method that separates literal and semantic information from feature granularity. It effectively retains generalizable features, while eliminating dataset bias. Experiments on various datasets demonstrate that CausalAPM obtains a better performance on both ID and OOD datasets than comparative works.

References

1. Bengio, Y., Courville, A., Vincent, P.: Representation learning: a review and new perspectives. IEEE Trans. Pattern Anal. Mach. Intell. **35**(8), 1798–1828 (2013)
2. Besserve, M., Mehrjou, A., Sun, R., Schölkopf, B.: Counterfactuals uncover the modular structure of deep generative models. In: 8th International Conference on Learning Representations, ICLR 2020 (2020)
3. Cheng, P., Min, M.R., Shen, D., Malon, C., Zhang, Y., Li, Y., Carin, L.: Improving disentangled text representation learning with information-theoretic guidance. In: Proceedings of the 58th Annual Meeting of the Association for Computational Linguistics, ACL 2020 (2020)
4. Clark, C., Yatskar, M., Zettlemoyer, L.: Learning to model and ignore dataset bias with mixed capacity ensembles. Findings of the Association for Computational Linguistics: EMNLP 2020, Online Event, 16-20 November 2020 (2020)
5. Creswell, A., White, T., Dumoulin, V., Arulkumaran, K., Sengupta, B., Bharath, A.A.: Generative adversarial networks: an overview. IEEE Signal Process. Mag. **35**(1), 53–65 (2018)
6. Devlin, J., Chang, M.W., Lee, K., Toutanova, K.: BERT: pre-training of deep bidirectional transformers for language understanding. In: NAACL, pp. 4171–4186. Association for Computational Linguistics, Minneapolis, Minnesota, June 2019
7. Eastwood, C., Williams, C.K.: A framework for the quantitative evaluation of disentangled representations. In: International Conference on Learning Representations (2018)
8. Higgins, I., et al.: Towards a definition of disentangled representations. arXiv preprint arXiv:1812.02230 (2018)
9. Higgins, I., et al.: beta-vae: learning basic visual concepts with a constrained variational framework. In: International conference on learning representations (2017)
10. Kocaoglu, M., Snyder, C., Dimakis, A.G., Vishwanath, S.: CausalGAN: learning causal implicit generative models with adversarial training. In: 6th International Conference on Learning Representations, ICLR 2018, Vancouver, BC, Canada, April 30–May 3, 2018, Conference Track Proceedings (2018)
11. Mahabadi, R.K., Belinkov, Y., Henderson, J.: End-to-end bias mitigation by modelling biases in corpora. In: Proceedings of the 58th Annual Meeting of the Association for Computational Linguistics, ACL 2020, 5-10 July 2020 (2020)
12. McCoy, R.T., Pavlick, E., Linzen, T.: Right for the wrong reasons: diagnosing syntactic heuristics in natural language inference. Proceedings of the 57th Conference of the Association for Computational Linguistics, ACL 2019, Florence, Italy, July 28- August 2, 2019, Volume 1: Long Papers (2019)
13. Mitrovic, J., McWilliams, B., Walker, J., Buesing, L., Blundell, C.: Representation learning via invariant causal mechanisms. In: 9th International Conference on Learning Representations, ICLR 2021 (2021)

14. Naik, A., Ravichander, A., Sadeh, N., Rose, C., Neubig, G.: Stress test evaluation for natural language inference. In: Proceedings of the 27th International Conference on Computational Linguistics, COLING 2018, Santa Fe, New Mexico, USA, 20-26 August 2018 (2018)

15. Pearl, J.: Bayesian analysis in expert systems: comment: graphical models, causality and intervention. Stat. Sci. **8**(3), 266–269 (1993)

16. Pham, T.M., Bui, T., Mai, L., Nguyen, A.: Out of order: how important is the sequential order of words in a sentence in natural language understanding tasks? In: Findings of the Association for Computational Linguistics: ACL/IJCNLP 2021, Online Event, 1–6 August 2021 (2021)

17. Poliak, A., Naradowsky, J., Haldar, A., Rudinger, R., Van Durme, B.: Hypothesis only baselines in natural language inference. In: Proceedings of the Seventh Joint Conference on Lexical and Computational Semantics, pp. 180–191. Association for Computational Linguistics, New Orleans, Louisiana, June 2018

18. Sanh, V., Wolf, T., Belinkov, Y., Rush, A.M.: Learning from others' mistakes: avoiding dataset biases without modeling them. In: 9th International Conference on Learning Representations, ICLR 2021, Virtual Event, Austria, 3-7 May 2021 (2020)

19. Schmidhuber, J.: Generative adversarial networks are special cases of artificial curiosity (1990) and also closely related to predictability minimization (1991). Neural Netw. **127**, 58–66 (2020)

20. Schuster, T., Shah, D., Yeo, Y.J.S., Roberto Filizzola Ortiz, D., Santus, E., Barzilay, R.: Towards debiasing fact verification models. In: EMNLP-IJCNLP, pp. 3419–3425. Association for Computational Linguistics, Hong Kong, China, November 2019

21. Sinha, K., Parthasarathi, P., Pineau, J., Williams, A.: Unnatural language inference. In: ACL/IJCNLP 2021 (2021)

22. Suter, R., Miladinovic, D., Schölkopf, B., Bauer, S.: Robustly disentangled causal mechanisms: validating deep representations for interventional robustness. In: International Conference on Machine Learning, pp. 6056–6065. PMLR (2019)

23. Thorne, J., Vlachos, A., Cocarascu, O., Christodoulopoulos, C., Mittal, A.: The fact extraction and VERification (FEVER) shared task. In: Proceedings of the First Workshop on Fact Extraction and VERification (FEVER), pp. 1–9. Association for Computational Linguistics, Brussels, Belgium, November 2018

24. Tu, L., Lalwani, G., Gella, S., He, H.: An empirical study on robustness to spurious correlations using pre-trained language models. Trans. Assoc. Comput. Linguist. **8**, 621–633 (2020)

25. Utama, P.A., Moosavi, N.S., Gurevych, I.: Mind the trade-off: Debiasing NLU models without degrading the in-distribution performance. In: ACL 202 (2020)

26. Utama, P.A., Moosavi, N.S., Gurevych, I.: Towards debiasing NLU models from unknown biases. In: EMNLP 2020 (2020)

27. Vasilakes, J., Zerva, C., Miwa, M., Ananiadou, S.: Learning disentangled representations of negation and uncertainty. In: ACL 2022 (2022)

28. Wang, A., Singh, A., Michael, J., Hill, F., Levy, O., Bowman, S.R.: Glue: a multitask benchmark and analysis platform for natural language understanding. In: ICLR 2019 (2019)

29. Wen, Z., Xu, G., Tan, M., Wu, Q., Wu, Q.: Debiased visual question answering from feature and sample perspectives. In: Advances in Neural Information Processing Systems, vol. 34 (2021)

30. Williams, A., Nangia, N., Bowman, S.: A broad-coverage challenge corpus for sentence understanding through inference. In: NAACL, pp. 1112–1122. Association for Computational Linguistics (2018)
31. Xiong, R., Chen, Y., Pang, L., Cheng, X., Ma, Z.M., Lan, Y.: Uncertainty calibration for ensemble-based debiasing methods. In: Advances in Neural Information Processing Systems, vol. 34 (2021)
32. Yang, M., Liu, F., Chen, Z., Shen, X., Hao, J., Wang, J.: Causalvae: disentangled representation learning via neural structural causal models. In: CVPR, pp. 9593–9602 (2021)
33. Zhang, Y., Baldridge, J., He, L.: PAWS: paraphrase adversaries from word scrambling. In: NAACL, pp. 1298–1308. Association for Computational Linguistics, Minneapolis, Minnesota, Jun 2019
34. Zhao, S., Ren, H., Yuan, A., Song, J., Goodman, N., Ermon, S.: Bias and generalization in deep generative models: an empirical study. In: Advances in Neural Information Processing Systems, vol. 31 (2018)

W2CL: A Multi-task Learning Approach to Improve Domain-Specific Sentence Classification Through Word Classification and Contrastive Learning

Sirui Yan, Zhiyi Luo[(✉)], Shuyun Luo, and Ying Qiu

Zhejiang Sci-Tech University, Hangzhou, China
{luozhiyi,shuyunluo,qiuying}@zstu.edu.cn

Abstract. Sentence classification task plays a crucial role in various NLP tasks. Recent studies have shown that contrastive learning can enhance the representational capability of Pre-trained Language Models (PLMs) and that different methods for constructing positive and negative samples can be applied to various downstream application scenarios. Therefore, in this study, we propose **W2CL**, a novel multi-task learning framework based on **W**ord **C**lassification and **C**ontrastive **L**earning, aimed at integrating domain knowledge extracted by ChatGPT from raw corporas into PLMs and improving the performance of PLMs in domain-specific sentence classification tasks. Contrastive learning assists the model in gradually learning the semantic similarity and contextual relevance between words during the training process to enhance its ability to understand text. Word classification provides additional contextual understanding, thereby improving the model's ability to differentiate between different classes within the specific domain. Experiments demonstrate that our multi-task approach significantly outperforms other methods, leading to substantial improvements in domain-specific sentence classification performance. This framework offers a robust solution for adapting general-purpose language models to specialized domains, ensuring better performance and generalization in various domain applications.

Keywords: Sentence Classification · Contrastive Learning · Multi-task Learning

1 Introduction

In recent years, mainstream sentence classification tasks have largely relied on deep representation learning methods, especially PLMs such as BERT [3], RoBERTa [11], and T5 [18]. Although the vector representations from these models capture richer textual features compared to traditional methods, simple fine-tuning is insufficient for integrating domain-specific knowledge into language

D. F. Wong et al. (Eds.): NLPCC 2024, LNAI 15359, pp. 298–310, 2025.
https://doi.org/10.1007/978-981-97-9431-7_23

models for domain-specific sentence classification tasks. Therefore, we propose the W2CL framework to effectively incorporate domain knowledge into the language models to improve the performance of these models in domain-specific tasks.

Numerous studies have demonstrated that integrating effective knowledge with PLMs can enhance the performance of PLMs on certain downstream tasks. LIBERT [8] adds a lexical relationship classification task to the original BERT pre-training tasks to help the model acquire richer semantic information. Sense-BERT [9] adds a part-of-speech layer to the BERT model, that is, it adds part-of-speech information of words (such as noun.food and noun.state, etc.) to the original input, and uses the representation vector after integrating part-of-speech information for masking tasks and part-of-speech classification tasks. SKEP [22] integrates sentiment knowledge (sentiment words, sentiment polarity, and aspect-sentiment pairs) into the model by designing three types of sentiment analysis tasks. Sentiprompt [10] integrates sentiment knowledge by constructing different paradigm templates and masking aspects, polarities, and opinions in the templates, and designing tasks to predict the masked tokens. LET [13] integrates all classification definitions of HowNet entities into the input, uses the original input and classification information for masking tasks, and finally integrates the knowledge contained in HowNet into the model. KEAR [27] directly faces the multiple-choice task, integrates the knowledge relationship of questions and options, the dictionary's definition knowledge of questions and options, and the knowledge of annotated training samples into the model, improving the model's performance in the commonsense knowledge question answering task.

The aforementioned methods can enhance the performance of models in various downstream tasks. However, these methods have two issues: First, knowledge cannot be extracted from the raw corporas, which means that acquiring knowledge is challenging; Second, the training frameworks of the aforementioned methods are complex, requiring intricate training procedures to match the corresponding forms of knowledge.

With the development of large language models (LLMs) [3,5,7,11,19,21,23, 29], particularly ChatGPT [17], which has attracted significant attention from NLP researchers, some studies [12,14–16,20] have shown that ChatGPT has demonstrated impressive performance, outperforming many models even in zero-shot settings. As a result, for issue 1, we utilize ChatGPT to acquire domain knowledge from raw corporas, a process that is both simple and results in high-quality knowledge.

Meanwhile, some studies have demonstrated that contrastive learning has superior capabilities in the field of NLP. SimCSE [4] uses the randomness of the dropout layer to construct positive samples, treating other samples in the same batch as negative samples. Building on SimCSE, ESimCSE [24] uses random word repetition to construct positive samples. PromptBERT [6] applies multiple templates that do not affect semantics within the same sample, treating samples reconstructed with different templates as positive samples. BGE [26] treats the question and its corresponding answer as positive samples, and other samples in the same batch as negative samples. For domain-specific tasks, domain vocabulary contains more domain-specific information compared to sentences. Therefore, for issue 2, we propose word-level contrastive learning and word classification, which together form the proposed W2CL framework.

To better validate the effectiveness of our proposed method, we need to test it on datasets from multiple domains. However, sentence classification datasets in the Chinese domain are not sufficiently abundant. Therefore, we will contribute our proprietary domain-specific datasets for future research and development, which include text retrieval datasets from four domains and sentence classification datasets from two domains.

Overall, our contributions can be summarized from four perspectives. 1) We propose a novel framework called W2CL, which can better transfer general models to specific domains. 2) We propose a novel and simple general method for knowledge extraction and integration. The knowledge extraction method based on ChatGPT and the knowledge integration method based on word-level contrastive learning and word classification are both effective and scalable. 3) Our experimental results demonstrate that the proposed method can enhance the performance of various language models across multiple domains and tasks, indicating that the W2CL framework is both effective and generalizable. 4) For domain-specific tasks, we contribute six task datasets to support future research and development.

2   The Proposed Method

This section introduces the detailed methodology of the our proposed W2CL framework, which mainly consists of two parts: domain knowledge extraction with ChatGPT and knowledge integration based on multi-task learning.

2.1   Domain Knowledge Extraction with ChatGPT

In the domain knowledge acquisition phase, we use ChatGPT as a knowledge extractor to extract the necessary domain knowledge for multi-task learning from raw text corporas which can be easily obtained from online resources like Baidu Zhidao. This step can be divided into three stages, as shown in Fig. 1.

In Step 1, we first use the Jieba tool to segment the raw text corpus and then compile a list of frequently occurring words. ChatGPT is then employed to filter out domain-specific vocabulary from this list, as illustrated in Fig. 1a, and the prompt1 shown in the Fig. 1 is "I currently have several terms. You will categorize all the terms I provide into levels of relevance: high, medium, and low. This relevance level pertains to the XX domain". Finally, extract the terms with high relevance to compile the final domain-specific vocabulary list.

In Step 2, ChatGPT is used to categorize the domain-specific vocabulary obtained in Step 1 into relevant categories within the domain, and the prompt2 is "Assume you are now an expert in the XX domain. Please classify the terms I provide within the subcategories of this domain.". This step allows us to obtain the initial version of domain-specific classification knowledge.

In Step 3, we manually consolidate all categories obtained in Step 2 to create a final comprehensive category list that covers all terms. Finally, we provide ChatGPT with this finalized category list to reclassify the vocabulary, producing the ultimate domain knowledge, and the prompt3 is "Assume you are an expert in the XX domain. I will provide you with several terms related to this domain, along with a list of categories: [Categories]. I need you to assign each of my terms to a category from the provided list. If a term cannot be assigned to any of the existing categories, please mark it as None. The required format for the response is 'Term: Category'.".

Finally, we applied this knowledge extraction framework across four domains: automotive, medical, financial, and legal. In the automotive domain, we identified 22 subcategories: brands, models, parts, equipment, design, technology, companies, specifications, materials, accessories, services, traffic management, manufacturers, types, exhibitions, driving behavior, legal documents, performance, safety measures, craftsmanship, competitions, environmental protection. In the medical domain, we identified 17 subcategories: internal medicine, surgery, pediatrics, obstetrics and gynecology, psychiatry, dermatology and venereology, traditional Chinese medicine, infectious diseases, plastic surgery, nutrition, reproductive medicine, anesthesiology, otorhinolaryngology, medical imaging, andrology, medical terminology, non-medical terms. In the financial domain, we identified 13 subcategories: stocks, funds, financial and tax management, venture capital, banking, foreign exchange, industry information, personal finance, trade, insurance, business documents, corporate management, economic research. In the legal domain, we identified 13 subcategories: criminal law, civil law, administrative law, economic law, labor and social security law, intellectual property law, environmental law, land and real estate law, industry-specific law, international and foreign-related law, constitutional law, military law, criminal and civil procedure law.

2.2   Domain Knowledge Integration

Our proposed knowledge integration method is based on Whole Word Masking(WWM) [2] and incorporates two additional training tasks: Word Classification and Contrastive Learning. The details about WWM will be introduced in the BASELINES section of Sect. 3. The following sections will introduce other two tasks individually.

Word Classification. Given a sentence $\{x_1, x_2, x_3, [MASK], x_5, [MASK], x_7\}$ where x_i means one word which may cover several tokens and a list of categories for the masked words $\{C_1, C_2\}$. Word Classification adds a classification layer to the original model architecture. The classification loss function is then computed

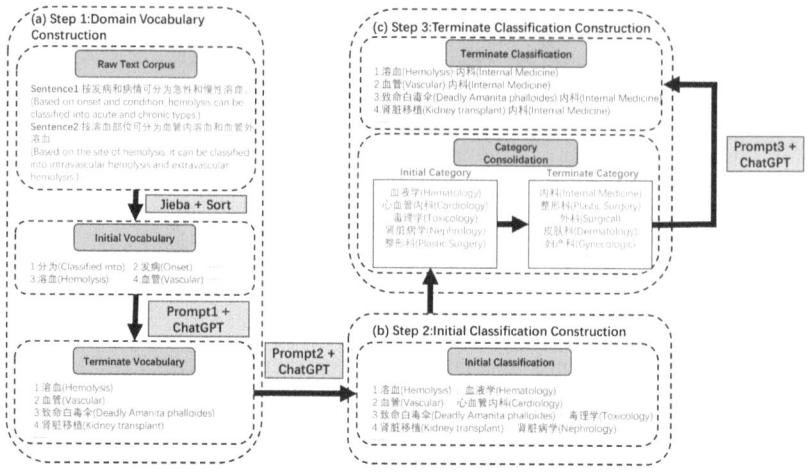

Fig. 1. Knowledge Extraction Framework

as shown in Eq. 1:

$$L(\mathbf{y}, \hat{\mathbf{y}}) = -\sum_{i=1}^{C}\left(y_i \log(\hat{y}_i) + (1 - y_i)\log(1 - \hat{y}_i)\right) \tag{1}$$

- $\mathbf{y} = [y_1, y_2, \ldots, y_C]$: The multi-label binary vector of true labels, where C is the number of classes. Each y_i represents the true label for class i (1 indicates the presence of the class, 0 indicates the absence of the class).
- $\hat{\mathbf{y}} = [\hat{y}_1, \hat{y}_2, \ldots, \hat{y}_C]$: The predicted probability distribution vector from the model, where each $\hat{y}_i$ represents the predicted probability for class i, with values in the range $[0, 1]$.
- $L(\mathbf{y}, \hat{\mathbf{y}})$: The loss function value for the multi-label classification task.

Contrastive Learning. Given a sentence $\{x_1, x_2, x_3, [MASK], x_5, [MASK], x_7\}$ where x_i means one word which may cover several tokens, and the actual words masked by [MASK] $\{x_4, x_6\}$. Our proposed contrastive learning method uses the actual word corresponding to the current [MASK] position as the positive sample for the current [MASK]. All the positive samples of other [MASK] tokens from other sentences in the same batch are used as the negative samples for the current [MASK]. The specific calculation method is shown in Eq. 2:

$$L(\mathbf{t}, \mathbf{t}') = -\frac{1}{N}\sum_{i=1}^{N}\log\frac{e^{sim(f(\mathbf{t}_i)\cdot f(\mathbf{t}'_i))/\tau}}{\sum_{j=1}^{N}e^{sim(f(\mathbf{t}_i)\cdot f(\mathbf{t}'_j))/\tau}} \tag{2}$$

- $\mathbf{t} = [t_1, t_2, \ldots, t_N]$: N is the number of [MASK] in one batch. Each $f(t_i)$ represents the representation of i_{st} [MASK] token in the batch.

- $\mathbf{t}' = [t_1', t_2', \ldots, t_N']$: $f(t_i')$ represents the representation of the true label t_i' corresponding to the i_{st} [MASK] token, which is the positive sample for $f(t_i)$.
- $L(\mathbf{t}, \mathbf{t}')$: The loss function value for the contrastive learning task.
- $sim(\mathbf{h1} \cdot \mathbf{h2})$: $sim(\mathbf{h1} \cdot \mathbf{h2})$ is the cosine similarity $\frac{\mathbf{h1}^T\mathbf{h2}}{\|\mathbf{h1}\|\cdot\|\mathbf{h2}\|}$.
- τ: is a temperature hyperparameter, with a default value of 0.01.

Training Framework. The overall training objective comprises three parts:

$$L_{overall} = L_{WWM} + L_{WC} + L_{CL} \tag{3}$$

where L_{WWM} is the loss of the WWM task, L_{WC} is calculated by Eq. 1, and L_{CL} is calculated by Eq. 2.

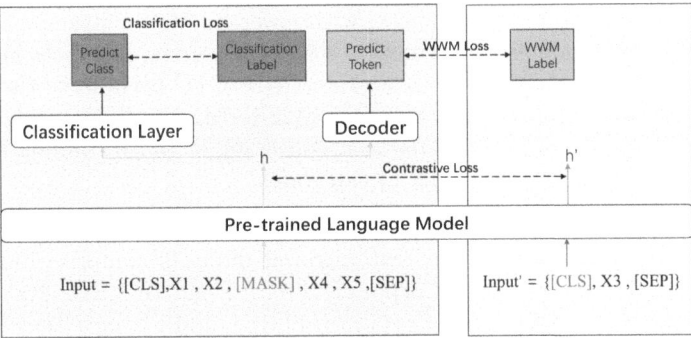

Fig. 2. Training Framework

The training framework is depicted in Fig. 2. Firstly, we obtain the loss(L_{WWM}) for the WWM task, which aims to help the model learn the meanings, usage, and contextual relationships of vocabulary, facilitating the model's adaptation to the specific domain context. Secondly, the loss(L_{CL}) from contrastive learning can assist the model in gradually learning the semantic similarity and contextual relevance between words during the training process, thereby enhancing its ability to understand text. Finally, the loss(L_{WC}) from word classification provides additional contextual understanding and domain knowledge, thereby improving the model's ability to differentiate between different classes within the specific domain.

3 Experiments

In this chapter, we validate the proposed W2CL method on sentence classification tasks across four domains. Additionally, we demonstrate the effectiveness of this method in domain transfer tasks.

3.1   Dataset and Experiment Details

We evaluated the proposed multi-task learning method on four sentence classification datasets, covering the domains of automotive, legal, finance, and medicine. For the transfer learning tasks, we assessed the method on four text retrieval datasets from the same domains. For the sentence classification task datasets, the automotive and financial domains are the datasets we contributed, while the legal and medical domains use public datasets. The text retrieval task datasets are all contributed by us. Below, we provide a brief introduction to these datasets.

Sentence Classification Dataset. The evaluation sets for sentence classification task consist of four datasets: Automatic Sentence Classification Corpora (ASCC), CAIL [25], CHIP-CTC [28], and Finance Sentence Classification Corpora (FSCC). ASCC pertains to the automotive domain and includes 6174 training instances and 1000 test instances, with coverage of 10 categories. CAIL is related to the legal domain and comprises 154592 training instances and 49639 test instances, encompassing 134 categories. CHIP-CTC pertains to the medical domain, with 24516 training instances and 6128 test instances, covering 44 categories. FSCC is a finance-related dataset, consisting of 10346 training instances and 3332 test instances, and spans 14 categories.

Text Retrieval Dataset. The text retrieval datasets comprise four collections: Automatic Text Retrieval Corpora (ATRC), Legal Text Retrieval Corpora (LTRC), Medical Text Retrieval Corpora (MTRC), and Finance Text Retrieval Corpora (FTRC). These datasets correspond to the automotive, legal, medical, and financial domains, respectively. Each dataset contains 1000, 232, 3520, and 1953 retrieval test texts, with a retrieval text space of 7175, 5232, 15000, and 12000 texts accordingly.

Experiment Details. Our model begins with the checkpoint of BERT/ RoBERTa model, and we utilize the [CLS] token representation as the sentence representation. During training, we employ an Adam optimizer with a batch size of 16. The learning rate for the sentence representation model is set to 5e-5. During the fine-tuning stage, we modified the learning rate to 3e-5 based on the training hyperparameters. Additionally, we set the seed to 0, 1, and 2, respectively, and calculated the average experimental data metrics for these three scenarios.

3.2   BASELINES

We validated the effectiveness of our proposed method by comparing it against three baseline approaches: Whole Word Masking(WWM), SimCSE, and SSCL [1], using BERT and RoBERTa as basic models.

WWM. WWM modifies the random masking task by changing the masking unit from token to whole word, leveraging contextual information to predict the masked word. For instance, in WWM, both "play" and "#ing" would be masked together. We selected WWM as a baseline method instead of random masking because, for domain-specific tasks, domain-specific word tends to contain more domain-relevant information.

SimCSE. SimCSE constructs positive samples based on the randomness of dropout and uses in-batch sampling to create negative samples. The model is trained by generating a loss value through the contrast between the original samples and the positive and negative samples.

SSCL. SSCL enhances the construction of negative samples by leveraging the principles of SimCSE. Specifically, SSCL employs hidden representations from intermediate layers of PLMs as negative samples. The objective is to ensure that the final sentence representations are distinctly separated from these intermediate representations.

3.3   Experiment Results

In this chapter, we will present the experimental results for the sentence classification and retrieval tasks. F1 score and Mean Reciprocal Rank(MRR) are used as evaluation metrics for these two tasks, respectively.

Sentence Classification Task. Table 1 presents the performance of various methods on the sentence classification task, with F1 score as the evaluation metric. From the experimental results, it can be observed that the proposed W2CL method outperforms other methods. Compared to the WWM method, W2CL incorporates contrastive learning task and word classification task on top of WWM. In comparison to SimCSE and SSCL methods, W2CL modifies the construction of positive and negative samples for contrastive learning and introduces word classification task. Based on the experimental results, the following conclusions can be drawn: 1) Domain knowledge constructed based on Chat-GPT is effective; 2) The proposed W2CL method effectively integrates domain knowledge into the model; 3) The proposed W2CL method outperforms other methods across different baseline models and domains. This indicates that W2CL can serve as a universal method, adaptable to any model as the basic model and transferable across various domains.

Transfer Task. In this section, we evaluate the generalization ability of the proposed W2CL method on text retrieval tasks across four domains. The objective of this task is to rank the candidate retrieval texts based on their similarity to the given retrieval text. For this task, we directly utilize the representation vector of the [CLS] token, without the need for fine-tuning.

Table 1. Evaluation performance on the sentence classification tasks. The evaluation metric is F1 score(%).

Model	ASCC	CAIL	CHIP-CTC	FSCC	Avg.
BERT Version					
BERT	92.48	65.58	82.91	85.82	81.70
WWM-BERT	94.08	66.62	83.52	85.91	82.53
SimCSE-BERT	93.70	66.68	83.64	85.81	82.46
SSCL-BERT	93.76	66.43	83.56	85.67	82.36
W2CL-BERT(Ours)	**94.93**	**66.83**	**84.06**	**86.08**	**82.98**
RoBERTa Version					
RoBERTa	93.93	67.38	83.91	86.10	82.83
WWM-RoBERTa	94.26	67.46	83.59	86.11	82.86
SimCSE-RoBERTa	94.14	67.43	83.92	85.83	82.83
SSCL-RoBERTa	94.41	67.18	83.56	86.27	82.86
W2CL-RoBERTa(Ours)	**94.84**	**67.71**	83.98	**86.53**	**83.27**

The experimental results are shown in Table 2. From the table, it can be observed that the proposed W2CL method achieves superior MRR scores on most datasets. This result indicates that the W2CL method exhibits better generalization ability compared to other methods in the study. When using RoBERTa as the basic model, the average MRR of WWM and SimCSE is lower than that of RoBERTa. As shown in the table, this is mainly because the MRR of WWM and SimCSE is lower than RoBERTa on the automotive domain dataset, leading to a lower average MRR. Since there is no fine-tuning phase in this task, we guess that this is primarily due to the randomness of the dataset and pre-training.

4   Analysis

4.1   Ablation Study

To evaluate the effectiveness of the two modules in the proposed method-the contrastive learning module and the word classification module, we conducted an ablation study. The experimental results are shown in Table 3. From the experimental results, it can be seen that removing the contrastive learning module leads to an average F1 score decrease of 0.37%, and removing the word classification module results in an average F1 score decrease of 0.34%. These findings indicate that the removal of either module results in a decline in the model's performance.

Table 2. Evaluation performance on the text retrieval tasks. The evaluation metric is MRR score(%).

Model	ATRC	LTRC	MTRC	FTRC	Avg.
BERT Version					
BERT	5.22	63.36	53.86	48.91	42.84
WWM-BERT	63.33	76.93	78.14	62.81	70.30
SimCSE-BERT	68.48	84.49	86.90	66.48	76.59
SSCL-BERT	32.91	85.85	79.70	79.44	69.48
W2CL-BERT(Ours)	**72.30**	**93.54**	**87.45**	**83.12**	**84.10**
RoBERTa Version					
RoBERTa	87.40	93.19	89.17	86.50	89.07
WWM-RoBERTa	80.36	95.69	91.77	88.19	89.00
SimCSE-RoBERTa	76.65	96.20	88.58	89.49	87.73
SSCL-RoBERTa	80.71	**97.61**	92.50	**90.86**	90.42
W2CL-RoBERTa(Ours)	**90.20**	97.01	**94.81**	87.95	**92.49**

Table 3. Ablation study for several methods evaluated on the sentence classification tasks. The evaluation metric is F1 score(%). CL: Contrastive Learning Module. WC: Word Classification Module.

Model	ASCC	CAIL	CHIP-CTC	FSCC	Avg.
W2CL-BERT	94.93	66.83	84.06	86.08	82.98
w/o CL	94.55(-0.38)	66.53(-0.30)	83.25(-0.81)	85.96(-0.12)	82.57(-0.41)
w/o WC	94.39(-0.54)	66.76(-0.07)	83.28(-0.78)	85.87(-0.21)	82.58(-0.40)
W2CL-RoBERTa	94.84	67.71	83.98	86.53	83.27
w/o CL	94.70(-0.14)	67.33(-0.38)	83.35(-0.63)	86.38(-0.15)	82.94(-0.33)
w/o WC	94.55(-0.29)	67.56(-0.15)	83.48(-0.50)	86.39(-0.14)	83.00(-0.27)

4.2   Influence of Batch Size

During the training phase, the impact of batch size on the model's final performance is illustrated in Table 4. As shown in the table, the model performs best when the batch size is set to 16. For the proposed W2CL method, a larger batch size not only increases the sample diversity within each batch during training but also provides more negative samples for contrastive learning. Additionally, some studies [24,26] have demonstrated that the larger batch size enhances the effectiveness of contrastive learning.

Table 4. The model's performance under different batch size

Model	ASCC	CAIL(Wait)	CHIP-CTC	FSCC	Avg.
W2CL-BERT	94.93	66.83	84.06	86.08	82.98
bs=4	93.89(-1.04)	66.29(-0.54)	83.15(-0.91)	85.31(-0.77)	82.16(-0.82)
bs=8	94.42(-0.51)	66.45(-0.38)	83.42(-0.64)	85.83(-0.25)	82.53(-0.45)
W2CL-RoBERTa	94.84	67.71	83.98	86.53	83.27
bs=4	94.10(-0.74)	67.01(-0.70)	83.35(-0.63)	85.60(-0.93)	82.52(-0.75)
bs=8	94.55(-0.29)	67.26(-0.45)	83.56(-0.42)	86.13(-0.40)	82.88(-0.39)

5   Conclusion

This study proposes a novel framework called W2CL, which aims to better trans-fer general-purpose PLMs such as BERT and RoBERTa to specific domains, thereby improving the performance of the model in sentence classification tasks. First, we propose a domain knowledge extraction method based on ChatGPT. This method can extract high-quality domain knowledge from raw texts easily in different domains. Next, we introduce a multi-task learning approach that includes three tasks: WWM, contrastive learning, and word classification. This approach allows better integration of domain knowledge into the model. Our experimental results demonstrate that our proposed W2CL method outperforms other methods in sentence classification tasks across four domains, regardless of whether BERT or RoBERTa is used as the basic model. This also indicates that the W2CL method proposed in this study has general applicability.

Acknowledgements. This work was supported by the Natural Science Foundation of Zhejiang Province, China (Grant No. LQ22F020027), the Key Research and Development Program of Zhejiang Province, China (Grant No. 2024SJCZX0026) and Fundamental Research Funds of Zhejiang Sci-Tech University (Grant No. 23232138-Y).

References

1. Chen, N., et al.: Alleviating over-smoothing for unsupervised sentence representation. arXiv preprint arXiv:2305.06154 (2023)
2. Cui, Y., Che, W., Liu, T., Qin, B., Yang, Z.: Pre-training with whole word masking for Chinese BERT. IEEE/ACM Trans. Audio Speech Lang. Process. **29**, 3504–3514 (2021)
3. Devlin, J., Chang, M., Lee, K., Toutanova, K.: BERT: pre-training of deep bidirectional transformers for language understanding. In: Proceedings of the 2019 Conference of the North American Chapter of the Association for Computational Linguistics: Human Language Technologies, NAACL-HLT 2019, Minneapolis, MN, USA, June 2–7, 2019, Volume 1 (Long and Short Papers), pp. 4171–4186 (2019)
4. Gao, T., Yao, X., Chen, D.: SimCSE: simple contrastive learning of sentence embeddings. In: Proceedings of the 2021 Conference on Empirical Methods in Natural Language Processing, EMNLP 2021, Virtual Event / Punta Cana, Dominican Republic, 7–11 November, 2021, pp. 6894–6910 (2021)

5. He, P., Liu, X., Gao, J., Chen, W.: DeBERTa: decoding-enhanced BERT with disentangled attention. arXiv preprint arXiv:2006.03654 (2020)

6. Jiang, T., et al.: PromptBERT: improving BERT sentence embeddings with prompts. In: Proceedings of the 2022 Conference on Empirical Methods in Natural Language Processing, EMNLP 2022, Abu Dhabi, United Arab Emirates, December 7–11, 2022, pp. 8826–8837 (2022)

7. Johnson, R., Zhang, T.: Supervised and semi-supervised text categorization using LSTM for region embeddings. In: International Conference on Machine Learning, pp. 526–534. PMLR (2016)

8. Lauscher, A., Vulic, I., Ponti, E.M., Korhonen, A., Glavas, G.: Specializing unsupervised pretraining models for word-level semantic similarity. In: Proceedings of the 28th International Conference on Computational Linguistics, COLING 2020, Barcelona, Spain (Online), December 8–13, 2020, pp. 1371–1383 (2020)

9. Levine, Y., et al.: SenseBERT: driving some sense into BERT. In: Proceedings of the 58th Annual Meeting of the Association for Computational Linguistics, ACL 2020, Online, July 5–10, 2020, pp. 4656–4667 (2020)

10. Li, C., et al.: SentiPrompt: sentiment knowledge enhanced prompt-tuning for aspect-based sentiment analysis. CoRR arXiv:2109.08306 (2021)

11. Liu, Y., et al.: RoBERTa: a robustly optimized BERT pretraining approach. arXiv preprint arXiv:1907.11692 (2019)

12. Liu, Z., et al.: DeID-GPT: zero-shot medical text de-identification by GPT-4. arXiv preprint arXiv:2303.11032 (2023)

13. Lyu, B., Chen, L., Zhu, S., Yu, K.: LET: linguistic knowledge enhanced graph transformer for Chinese short text matching. In: Thirty-Fifth AAAI Conference on Artificial Intelligence, AAAI 2021, Thirty-Third Conference on Innovative Applications of Artificial Intelligence, IAAI 2021, The Eleventh Symposium on Educational Advances in Artificial Intelligence, EAAI 2021, Virtual Event, February 2–9, 2021, pp. 13498–13506 (2021)

14. Nov, O., Singh, N., Mann, D.M.: Putting ChatGPT's medical advice to the (turing) test. medrxiv. Preprint posted online January 24 (2023)

15. Peng, K., et al.: Towards making the most of ChatGPT for machine translation. arXiv preprint arXiv:2303.13780 (2023)

16. Qin, C., Zhang, A., Zhang, Z., Chen, J., Yasunaga, M., Yang, D.: Is ChatGPT a general-purpose natural language processing task solver? arXiv preprint arXiv:2302.06476 (2023)

17. Radford, A., Narasimhan, K., Salimans, T., Sutskever, I.: Improving language understanding by generative pre-training (2018)

18. Raffel, C., et al.: Exploring the limits of transfer learning with a unified text-to-text transformer. J. Mach. Learn. Res. **21**(140), 1–67 (2020)

19. Sanh, V., Debut, L., Chaumond, J., Wolf, T.: DistilBERT, a distilled version of BERT: smaller, faster, cheaper and lighter. arXiv preprint arXiv:1910.01108 (2019)

20. Shen, Y., Song, K., Tan, X., Li, D., Lu, W., Zhuang, Y.: HuggingGPT: Solving AI tasks with ChatGPT and its friends in hugging face. In: Advances in Neural Information Processing Systems, vol. 36 (2024)

21. Tai, K.S., Socher, R., Manning, C.D.: Improved semantic representations from tree-structured long short-term memory networks. arXiv preprint arXiv:1503.00075 (2015)

22. Tian, H., et al.: SKEP: sentiment knowledge enhanced pre-training for sentiment analysis. In: Proceedings of the 58th Annual Meeting of the Association for Computational Linguistics, ACL 2020, Online, July 5–10, 2020, pp. 4067–4076 (2020)

23. Vaswani, A., et al.: Attention is all you need. In: Advances in Neural Information Processing Systems, vol. 30 (2017)

24. Wu, X., Gao, C., Zang, L., Han, J., Wang, Z., Hu, S.: ESimCSE: enhanced sample building method for contrastive learning of unsupervised sentence embedding. In: Proceedings of the 29th International Conference on Computational Linguistics, COLING 2022, Gyeongju, Republic of Korea, October 12–17, 2022, pp. 3898–3907 (2022)

25. Xiao, C., et al.: Cail2018: a large-scale legal dataset for judgment prediction. arXiv preprint arXiv:1807.02478 (2018)

26. Xiao, S., Liu, Z., Zhang, P., Muennighof, N.: C-Pack: packaged resources to advance general Chinese embedding. CoRR arXiv:2309.07597 (2023)

27. Xu, Y., et al.: Human parity on commonsenseqa: augmenting self-attention with external attention. In: Proceedings of the Thirty-First International Joint Conference on Artificial Intelligence, IJCAI 2022, Vienna, Austria, 23–29 July 2022, pp. 2762–2768 (2022)

28. Zhang, N., et al.: CBLUE: a Chinese biomedical language understanding evaluation benchmark. arXiv preprint arXiv:2106.08087 (2021)

29. Zhu, X., Sobihani, P., Guo, H.: Long short-term memory over recursive structures. In: International Conference on Machine Learning, pp. 1604–1612. PMLR (2015)

Outperforming Larger Models on Text Classification Through Continued Pre-training

Yu Zheng[1] , Ming Liu[2,3] , Zou Ao[1] , Wenning Hao[1] , Hui Zhang[2,3] ,
and Yi Sun[2,3]([⊠])

[1] College of Command and Control Engineering, Army Engineering University of
PLA, Nanjing 210007, China
{zhengyu,zouao,hwnbox}@aeu.edu.cn
[2] The Sixty-Third Research Institute, National University of Defense Technology,
Nanjing 210007, China
{liuming20,zhanghui82,sunyi_gfkd}@nudt.edu.cn
[3] Laboratory for Big Data and Decision, National University of Defense Technology,
Changsha 410073, China

Abstract. Generative large language models (LLMs), such as GPT-4, have demonstrated remarkable performance across a wide range of NLP tasks. The increased number of LLMs' parameters enhances their generalization capabilities, but it also results in a higher computational burden and slower inference speed. Addressing these concern, through continued pre-training, we have enhanced the BERT model (based on MLM and NSP pre-training tasks) to achieve performance comparable to that of the large Qwen-1.5 series models in zero-shot and few-shot text classification tasks, demonstrating that non-generative pre-trained models like BERT are still relevant. Additionally, by using LLMs to expand topic words related to downstream tasks and employing word density methods to retrieve corresponding subsets from large corpora, we have obtained better pre-training results.

Keywords: PLMs · Continued Pre-training · Corpus

1 Introduction

In recent times, generative LLMs like GPT-4 [1] have achieved remarkable performance in natural language processing tasks. They have acquired capabilities such as zero-shot and in-context few-shot learning [2], instruction following [3], and chain-of-thought reasoning [4], and have been applied in intelligent agents [5–7] and embodied AI [8]. Following scaling laws, the pre-training corpora and parameter sizes of various models are continuously expanding, leading to breakthroughs in task performance and domain knowledge. However, this also requires immense computational resources, making their application to "simple" tasks like text classification somewhat impractical. Although generative LLMs can address

D. F. Wong et al. (Eds.): NLPCC 2024, LNAI 15359, pp. 311–323, 2025.
https://doi.org/10.1007/978-981-97-9431-7_24

various NLP tasks, it does not imply that pre-training tasks like masked language model (MLM) and next sentence prediction (NSP) are rendered meaningless. In this paper, we attempt to further enhance the performance of pre-trained language models (PLMs) like BERT [9] model on zero-shot and few-shot text classification tasks through continued pre-training. Additionally, we aim to improve the specificity of pre-training by retrieving subsets from large pre-training corpora. The contributions of this paper are mainly as follows:

- By continuing to pre-train the original Google BERT models in both Base and Large versions, we have significantly enhanced the text classification capabilities of the BERT model in zero-shot and few-shot scenarios (based on MLM and NSP prompt learning). On 7 typical text classification tasks, the performance of our BERT is now comparable to that of the Qwen-1.5 series LLMs.
- We have also identified the instability of model checkpoints during pre-training when dealing with zero-shot text classification scenarios.
- We propose the use of JS divergence to analyze the differences between corpora and downstream tasks, which does not rely on manually defined empirical parameters such as vocabulary size.
- We suggest using LLMs for multi-round reflection to expand the task-related topic vocabulary, and then employing topic word density to retrieve subsets from large corpora, thereby improving the efficiency and effectiveness of pre-training.

2   Related Work

Expanding Corpora. The continual expansion of pre-training corpora has emerged as a prominent trend in the era of PLMs, epitomized by BERT [9]. Various PLMs have explored diverse pre-training tasks. However, under comparable parameter scales, expanding pre-training corpora and engaging in continuous pre-training have demonstrated greater efficacy. The original BERT model was pre-trained on 16 GB of data. RoBERTa [10] expanded this to 160GB. The GPT-1 [11] model was pre-trained on approximately 5GB of data, GPT-2 [12] utilized 40GB, and GPT-3 [2] was pre-trained on about 570GB. LLAMA-1 [13] employed 1T tokens for pre-training, LLAMA-2 [13] increased this by 40%, and LLAMA-3[1] achieved 15T.

Optimizing Corpus Quality. Beyond merely increasing the quantity of pre-training corpora, enhancing their quality and specificity is also a potent strategy. Yao et al. [14] employ BM25 for retrieval to gather task-related pre-training corpora for each example in the task data. Xie et al. [15] introduce the DSIR framework, which estimates importance weights in a reduced feature space for tractability and selects data through importance resampling based on these weights. Kaddour, in creating MiniPile [16], infers embeddings for all documents in the Pile [17], utilizes k-means clustering in the embedding space, and filters

---

[1] https://github.com/meta-llama/llama3.

out low-quality clusters. Fei et al. [18] propose the Query of CC approach, which bootstraps seed information via an LLM, retrieves related data from public corpora, and curates a high-quality dataset named KNOWLEDGE PILE.

3   Methods

3.1   Pre-training Corpora Construction and Analysis

Pre-training Corpora. In this study, we focus on examining the corpora utilized by BERT [9] and RoBERTa [10]. The original BERT model is trained on Wikipedia and BooksCorpus [19], while RoBERTa extends this by incorporating OpenWebText [20], CC-News, and Stories [21]. However, due to copyright concerns, CC-News and Stories are not publicly accessible. As a result, we replace CC-News with Newsroom [22]. To compensate for the absence of Stories, we adopt the approach suggested by Trinh and Le [21], selecting content from the CC-100 [23] corpus. Specifically, we choose the 1% of articles most akin to the WSC-273 [24] dataset for our analysis. We refer to the corpora used by BERT and RoBERTa as $\mathcal{C}_B$ and $\mathcal{C}_R$, respectively. Furthermore, we introduce domain-specific corpora from Amazon [25] and Yelp for analysis.

Document Slicing. In the BooksCorpus and OpenWebText corpora, original articles tend to be quite lengthy. Since the BERT model's pre-training task involves sampling from diverse articles, it is essential to segment these extensive texts into shorter pieces. To ensure the segments' lengths appear more natural, we employ the NLTK tool to divide the long text into sub-sentences. Then, we create a new article by concatenating every l sentences. We use a gamma distribution $L \sim \Gamma(k, \theta)$ to model l, with the density function $\frac{1}{\Gamma(k)\theta^k} l^{k-1} e^{-\frac{l}{\theta}}$. Here, the shape parameter k is set to 3.6, and the scale parameter θ is set to 1.4. To avoid excessively short segments, we set $l \geqslant 3$. The expected value $E(L) = k\theta \approx 5$, indicating that each new segment, on average, comprises 5 sentences.

Analyzing Corpus Similarity. Gururangan et al. [26] utilized overlap as a straightforward metric to quantify discrepancies between corpora $\mathcal{C}_S$ and datasets $\mathcal{C}_T$. This was achieved by examining the vocabulary consisting of the top 10,000 most prevalent unigrams, with a specific focus on nouns. These unigrams were derived from a randomly sampled subset of 50,000 articles within the corpus.

Regarding the selection of the vocabulary size, the authors did not elaborate on their rationale. It is presumed that this value is based on empirical observations, as the similarity between diverse source and target domains tends to stabilize when the vocabulary size is augmented further. To facilitate a more rigorous analysis, we suggest employing the Jensen-Shannon divergence [27] as a measure to compute the similarity between vocabularies.

$$\text{Sim}_{JS}(\mathcal{C}_T, \mathcal{C}_S) = \frac{1}{2}\text{KL}(P_{\mathcal{C}_T} \| \frac{P_{\mathcal{C}_T} + P_{\mathcal{C}_S}}{2}) + \frac{1}{2}\text{KL}(P_{\mathcal{C}_S} \| \frac{P_{\mathcal{C}_T} + P_{\mathcal{C}_S}}{2}) \qquad (1)$$

$$\mathrm{KL}(\mathrm{P}_{\mathcal{C}_S}||\frac{\mathrm{P}_{\mathcal{C}_T}+\mathrm{P}_{\mathcal{C}_S}}{2}) = \frac{1}{2}\sum_{w_i\in\mathcal{V}_{\mathcal{C}_T}} pc_S(w_i)\log(\frac{pc_S(w_i)}{\frac{pc_T(w_i)+pc_S(w_i)}{2}}) \qquad (2)$$

$p(w_i)$ represents the probability of a word w_i, $p(w_i) = \frac{freq(w_i)}{\sum_{w_j\in\mathcal{V}} freq(w_j)}$, when $w_i \notin \mathcal{V}_{\mathcal{C}_S}$, $p(w_i) = 0$. A smaller value of $\mathrm{Sim_{JS}}$ indicates a higher dissimilarity between the corpus and the dataset's vocabulary.

The results are depicted in Fig. 1. It is evident that even corpora within the same general domain exhibit significant variations in vocabulary similarity with downstream tasks.

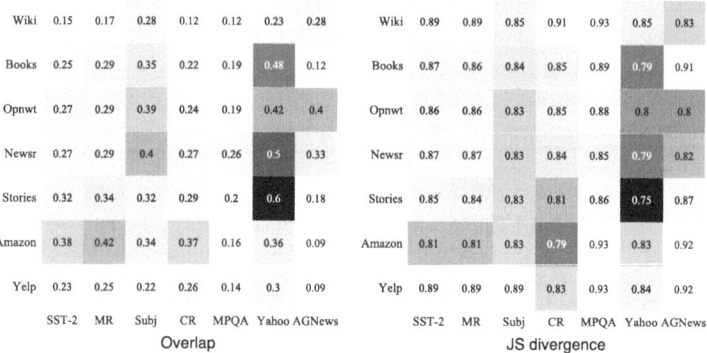

Fig. 1. Vocabulary overlap [26] and word frequency Jensen-Shannon divergence [27] between corpora and downstream task datasets.

3.2   Using Topic Words to Retrieve Corpus

Utilizing a large corpus such as $\mathcal{C}_R$ for the training of a PLM is computationally intensive and time-consuming. To address this, it is essential to extract subsets of $\mathcal{C}_R$ that are particularly pertinent to the subsequent tasks for focused pre-training. Zhang et al. [28] implemented the BM25 algorithm to select the Top-200 most analogous sentences from $\mathcal{C}_R$ for each test set sample, which were then utilized to continue pre-training. This method, however, depends on the availability of test set samples. In many scenarios, direct access to sample data for downstream tasks is not feasible, we only possess knowledge about the domain and topic of these tasks. Given this constraint, we introduce a retrieval method based on topic word density. This method effectively identifies more relevant corpora for pre-training in alignment with the downstream tasks.

Building Topic Words Vocabulary with LLMs. For a specific downstream task, we describe the domain with a few seed words, such as *movie* and *actor*. Using these seed words and a simple description of the target domain, we employ LLMs (like GLM-4 [29], etc.) with the instruction *"Please expand the topic words*

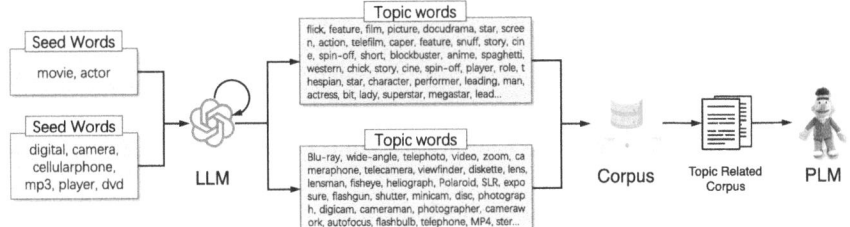

Fig. 2. The pipeline of expanding the topic words based on LLMs then retrieving corpus to pre-train PLMs.

based on the domain description." to extend the topic words vocabulary. Due to the limitation of output sequence length, the number of topic words output by the LLM at one time is limited. Therefore, we use the instruction "*Please continue to add more!*" to continuously expand the vocabulary until a certain number of rounds. In addition, following [30, 31], we also attempted to use labels as seed words (such as *great* and *terrible*) for retrieval.

Retrieving Corpus by Topic Words Density. We propose the word density (WD) retrieval method, where for a document d_i and our topic words vocabulary $\mathcal{V}$, we traverse the words w_j in the document, then calculate the ratio of the number of words in the vocabulary $\mathcal{V}$ to the number of sentences in the document.

Table 1. Seed words and topic words expanded by LLMs. The seed words are mainly generated according to the source of the dataset and the description in the paper.

Dataset	Seed words	Topic words expanded by LLMs
SST-2 MR Subj	movie, actor	flick, feature, film, picture, docudrama, star, screen, action, telefilm, caper, feature, snuff, story, cine, spin-off, short, blockbuster, anime, spaghetti, western, chick, story, cine, spin-off, player, role, thespian, star, character, performer, leading, man, actress, bit, lady, superstar, megastar, lead, supporting, stand-in, tragedian, trouper, artist, cameo, double, playback, singler...
CR	digital, camera, cellularphone, mp3, player, dvd	Blu-ray, wide-angle, telephoto, video, zoom, cameraphone, telecamera, viewfinder, diskette, lens, lensman, fisheye, heliograph, Polaroid, SLR, exposure, flashgun, shutter, minicam, disc, photograph, digicam, cameraman, photographer, camerawork, autofocus, flashbulb, telephone, MP4, ster, podcast, beatbox, minidisc, cassette, WAV, CD, CD-ROM, VCR, CD-R, DVR, PVR ...

$$\mathrm{Sim_{WD}}(d_i, \mathcal{V}) = \frac{1}{|\{s_k\}_{s_k \in d_i}|} \sum_{w_j \in d_i} \mathbb{I}_{w_j \in \mathcal{V}} \tag{3}$$

Then, we will sort the documents according to their word density $\mathrm{Sim_{WD}}$ and select the top-N documents with the highest $\mathrm{Sim_{WD}}$ as the pre-training corpus. When using the topic vocabulary for retrieval, we represent the retrieval corpus as $\mathcal{C}_{\mathrm{R_{TD}}}$. And when using the label vocabulary, we represent it as $\mathcal{C}_{\mathrm{R_{LD}}}$.

3.3   Zero and Few-Shot Methods

Prompt-learning for PLMs. To investigate the influence of pre-training on PLMs, we selected two fundamental zero/few-shot learning approaches that are compatible with the standard BERT [9]: PET [32], which utilizes the masked language model (MLM), and NSP-BERT [33], based on the next sentence prediction (NSP) task.

Instruction-learning for LLMs. For the Qwen series of LLMs, we utilize the foundational task of generative language model (LM), employing instruction-learning method for zero-shot text classification.

4   Experimental Setting

PLMs and Pre-training Settings. We choose Google's BERT-Large-cased (BERT$_{\mathrm{LARGE}}$, 0.3B) and BERT-Base-cased[2] (BERT$_{\mathrm{BASE}}$, 0.1B) as the main PLMs in our paper cause they can be used by both PET and NSP-BERT. All our continued pre-trainings are based on these models. We still use the same training objective as BERT [9], which is MLM+NSP. We set the sequence length to 128, then pre-training can be performed on a single 24G GPU such as RTX4090 or A5000. The learning rate is 2e-5 and duplicate factor is 2. For BERT$_{\mathrm{LARGE}}$, we trained for a total of 15M steps over 80 days with batch size 24. For BERT$_{\mathrm{BASE}}$, we trained for 5M steps, which took about 30 days with batch size 96.

LLMs. We utilized the Qwen-1.5 series [34] of LLMs for comparing, which includes 4 differently sizes - 0.5B, 1.8B, 4B, and 7B - in their Chat versions, which have been calibrated based on human preferences[3].

---

[2] https://github.com/google-research/bert.
[3] https://github.com/QwenLM/Qwen1.5.

Table 2. Pre-training details of Google's vanilla BERT $\mathcal{C}_{\mathrm{B}}$ and our BERT $\mathcal{C}_{\mathrm{R}}$. †: We made our own Stories corpus.

Models	Pre-train Corpora	Model Size	Corpora Size	Seq. Length	#Steps	Batch size	#Total Samples
BERT $\mathcal{C}_{\mathrm{B}}$	Wikipedia, BooksCorpus	0.1B/0.3B	16GB	512	1M	256	256M
BERT $\mathcal{C}_{\mathrm{R}}$ (Ours)	Wikipedia, BooksCorpus, Newsroom, OpenWebText, Stories†	0.1B 0.3B	23.6GB	128	5M 15M	96 24	480M 360M

Retrieval Corpus. Following [28], we use the BM25 algorithm to retrieve the Top-200 most similar sentences in $\mathcal{C}_{\mathrm{R}}$ for each sample in the test set, and then use the retrieved corpus ($\mathcal{C}_{\mathrm{R_{BM25}}}$) to train for 200K steps. To ensure fairness, the total number of samples retrieved by our LD and TD methods (Top-N) is consistent with the number of samples obtained by the BM25.

Datasets. We selected 7 widely utilized text classification evaluation tasks [30, 35] [36–38], encompassing 5 binary classification tasks: SST-2 [39], MR [40], Subj [41], CR [42] and MPQA [43], along with 2 multi-class tasks: Yahoo! and AGNews [44].

Evaluation Protocol. For all datasets, we employ the accuracy method (Acc.) for result evaluation. In particular, for few-shot results, following [35], for each dataset, we use random seeds to generate 5 K-shot sub training sets (K=16), then run 5 experiments for each sub set and report the average accuracy and standard deviations.

Hyper-parameters for Few-shot Learning. For PET and NSP-BERT, our hyper-parameters are the same, the batch size is 8, the learning rate is 2e-5, and the number of training epochs is 10.

Prompt and Instruction. For the prompts of PET and NSP-BERT, we used the same as Sun et al. [33]. For the instructions of the Qwen series, we designed templates such as the following: "You are a helpful assistant. Please judge whether the following text is positive or negative, reply 'Positive' or 'Negative', do not reply with any other content!"

5   Results and Analysis

Smaller Models Outperform Larger Models. We use $\mathcal{C}_{\mathrm{R}}$ to continue pre-training $\mathrm{BERT}_{\mathrm{BASE}}$(0.1B) until 5M steps and $\mathrm{BERT}_{\mathrm{LARGE}}$(0.3B) until 15M steps, and its effect on 7 datasets is shown in Table 3 and Figure 3. In almost all downstream tasks, the performance improvement is very significant. In the zero-shot scenario, the accuracy of NSP-BERT has been increased by 7.6%-17.9% in all 7 datasets, and the accuracy of PET is also greatly improved.

In addition, the performance of the $\mathrm{BERT}_{\mathrm{BASE}}$(0.1B) after continued pre-training is now comparable to that of the $\mathrm{BERT}_{\mathrm{LARGE}}$(0.3B) without continued pre-training. Moreover, both the $\mathrm{BERT}_{\mathrm{BASE}}$ and $\mathrm{BERT}_{\mathrm{LARGE}}$ have achieved performance on par with the generative LLMs of the Qwen series in zero-shot text classification tasks.

Table 3. The Acc. of the Qwen series (using LM-based method) and the BERT series (using MLM-based [32] and NSP-based [33] method) on 7 text classification tasks. The BERT $\mathcal{C}_R$ with a blue background is the result of our continued pre-training. **Zero** means no in-context samples are used.

Shot	Model	Size	Method	Corpus	Binary					Multi-Class		Average
					SST-2	MR	Subj	CR	MPQA	Yahoo!	AGNews	
Zero	Qwen1.5	0.5B	LM	-	74.3	70.4	50.7	73.6	72.8	15.4	55.4	58.9
		1.8B		-	89.8	85.2	57.0	87.5	84.4	24.3	**72.7**	71.6
		4B		-	93.8	89.3	52.3	90.9	80.9	23.4	57.5	69.7
		7B		-	<u>94.8</u>	<u>89.9</u>	63.7	<u>91.7</u>	**86.6**	45.9	56.9	**75.6**
	BERT	0.1B	MLM	$\mathcal{C}_B$	62.2	60.6	**51.8**	63.9	68.1	20.6	52.5	54.2
				$\mathcal{C}_R$	64.9	63.1	50.5	63.1	63.6	35.5	70.6	58.8
			NSP	$\mathcal{C}_B$	73.1	68.1	51.1	79.1	72.8	42.4	75.0	65.9
				$\mathcal{C}_R$	80.7	76.6	<u>76.4</u>	80.4	71.7	56.0	67.7	**72.8**
		0.3B	MLM	$\mathcal{C}_B$	67.6	65.3	**61.0**	61.2	63.9	25.6	54.5	56.6
				$\mathcal{C}_R$	80.7	76.6	57.3	68.9	68.4	39.8	56.2	**64.0**
			NSP	$\mathcal{C}_B$	75.6	74.4	53.9	59.4	59.9	47.0	77.5	63.9
				$\mathcal{C}_R$	87.6	83.6	71.8	75.5	74.1	<u>59.5</u>	<u>85.1</u>	<u>76.7</u>

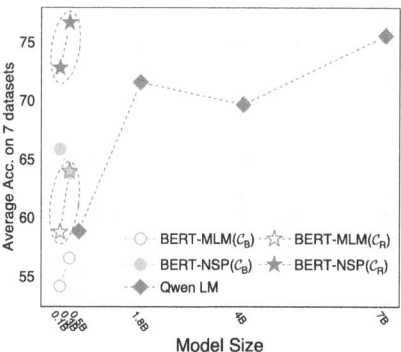

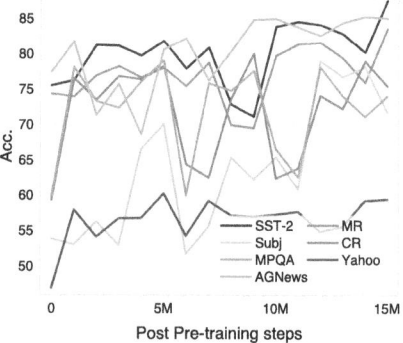

Fig. 3. Average Zero-shot Acc. of various-sized LLMs and PLMs across 7 text classification tasks. BERT-MLM/NSP ($\mathcal{C}_R$) signifying the BERT we developed. The x-coordinate is the model size.

Fig. 4. Zero-shot Acc. of checkpoints during pre-training BERT$_{LARGE}$ $\mathcal{C}_R$. The x-coordinate is the number of continued pre-training steps, and the y-coordinate is the zero-shot accuracy of NSP-BERT.

Instability of the Checkpoints' Performance. Although the final results of continued pre-training are satisfactory, the zero-shot learning performance of pre-trained checkpoints is very unstable. As shown in Fig. 4, we saved the checkpoint every 1M steps and verified its zero-shot performance using the NSP-BERT algorithm. On 7 datasets, the performance does not show a steady improvement. This phenomenon may be caused by catastrophic forgetting in small pre-trained language models (PLMs), such as $BERT_{BASE}$ and $BERT_{LARGE}$, which are not large enough to retain knowledge in a steady state.

How Many Data Points is the Continued Pre-training Worth. Following Le Scao et al. [45], to clarify how many labeled task data samples can bridge the gap brought by pre-training, we employ the PET [32] (MLM) method for few-shot learning. We continuously increase the number of prompt-tuning samples for $BERT_{BASE}$ $\mathcal{C}_B$ and $BERT_{LARGE}$ $\mathcal{C}_B$ (K-shot), aiming to achieve performance parity with $BERT_{BASE}$ $\mathcal{C}_R$ and $BERT_{LARGE}$ $\mathcal{C}_R$ (16-shot) on text classification tasks. The numbers are shown in Table 4, and the performance changes of different models with the increase of training data are illustrated in Fig. 5.

Table 4. The number of labeled data points that can bridge the continued pre-training gap between vanilla BERT $\mathcal{C}_B$ (K-shot) and our BERT $\mathcal{C}_R$ (16-shot). We select K from $\{32, 64, 128, 256, 512, 1024, 2048\}$. The data points number is calculated as $(K - 16) \times |\mathcal{Y}|$.

Shot	Model	Method	Size	Binary					Multi-class	
				SST-2	MR	Subj	CR	MPQA	Yahoo!	AGNews
Few	BERT	MLM	0.1B	480	224	32	480	32	1,120	192
			0.3B	2,016	992	96	224	96	2,400	64

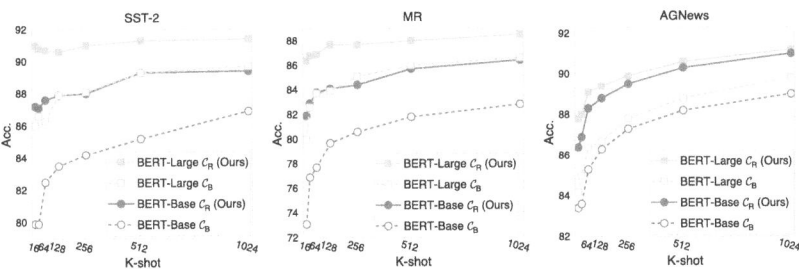

Fig. 5. Acc. of our $BERT_{BASE/LARGE}$ $\mathcal{C}_R$ and Google's vanilla $BERT_{BASE/LARGE}$ $\mathcal{C}_B$, based on few-shot PET (MLM) [32], during increasing the number of training samples (K-shot).

Different Corpora have Different Impacts. We conducted continued pre-training on BERT using three diverse corpora: OpenWebText, Newsroom, and

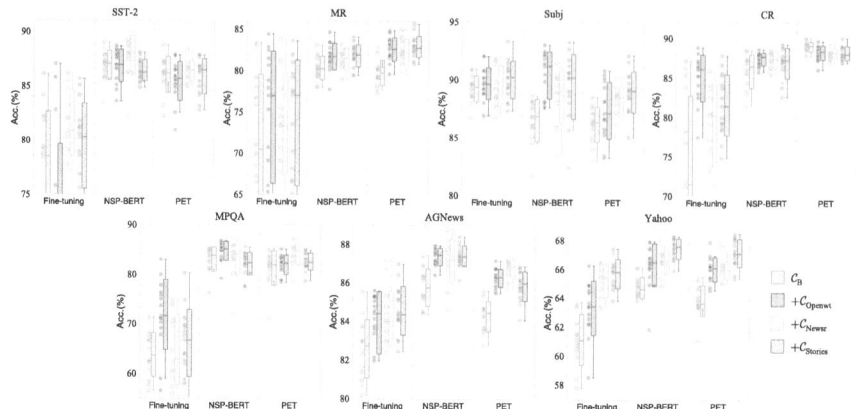

Fig. 6. The results of multiple runs under different few-shot training sets generated by random seeds. $+\mathcal{C}_{\mathrm{Openwt}}$, $+\mathcal{C}_{\mathrm{Newsr}}$ and $+\mathcal{C}_{\mathrm{Stories}}$ represent continuing to pre-train BERT $\mathcal{C}_{\mathrm{B}}$ with these corpora.

Table 5. Applying original $\mathcal{C}_{\mathrm{R}}$ and different methods to retrieve corpus from $\mathcal{C}_{\mathrm{R}}$ ($\mathcal{C}_{\mathrm{R_{BM25}}}$, $\mathcal{C}_{\mathrm{R_{LD}}}$ and $\mathcal{C}_{\mathrm{R_{TD}}}$) to continue pre-training vanilla BERT$_{\mathrm{LARGE}}$(0.3B) for 200K steps individually, the result is on few-shot (16-shot) settings.

Shot	Model	Method	Corpus	SST-2	MR	Subj	CR
Few	BERT (0.3B)	MLM	$\mathcal{C}_{\mathrm{B}}$	85.3±1.7	80.3±2.1	85.4±1.9	88.9±0.6
			$+\mathcal{C}_{\mathrm{R}}$	86.0±0.8	82.6±0.5	88.1±1.2	88.1±0.9
			$+\mathcal{C}_{\mathrm{R_{BM25}}}$	86.9±1.8	81.5±1.9	87.3±1.8	88.8±1.0
			$+\mathcal{C}_{\mathrm{R_{LD}}}$	**87.3±0.8**	82.8±1.2	88.1±1.5	88.7±0.6
			$+\mathcal{C}_{\mathrm{R_{TD}}}$	86.6±1.6	**83.3±1.1**	88.4±0.7	89.5±0.5
		NSP	$\mathcal{C}_{\mathrm{B}}$	86.7±2.1	80.3±1.8	86.6±0.9	86.7±1.7
			$+\mathcal{C}_{\mathrm{R}}$	87.0±0.6	81.6±0.7	89.4±2.5	87.2±1.0
			$+\mathcal{C}_{\mathrm{R_{BM25}}}$	87.2±1.1	84.1±1.4	91.8±1.4	86.8±1.7
			$+\mathcal{C}_{\mathrm{R_{LD}}}$	88.5±1.0	81.4±1.6	91.9±1.6	86.6±2.0
			$+\mathcal{C}_{\mathrm{R_{TD}}}$	**89.0±0.9**	**84.4±1.3**	**92.2±1.6**	**88.5±1.0**

Stories, for a total of 200,000 steps. Subsequently, we evaluated their impact on seven text classification tasks in few-shot settings (fine-tuning, NSP-BERT and PET). The results are presented in Fig. 6. Continued pre-training with these corpora demonstrated enhanced performance on downstream tasks, albeit with varying degrees of effectiveness. In comparison with Fig. 1, which illustrates the discrepancies among different corpora and downstream tasks, the most pronounced improvement was observed with the Stories corpus on the Yahoo! task.

Topic Related Corpus is Important. As shown in Table 5, using the same amount of data and the same number of training steps, the model trained on the corpus $\mathcal{C}_{R_{TD}}$ retrieved by our topic word density method significantly outperforms those trained on randomly selected subset $\mathcal{C}_R$, $\mathcal{C}_{R_{BM25}}$ retrieved using BM25, and$\mathcal{C}_{R_{LD}}$ using label word density. This indicates that corpus related to the downstream task's topic is more beneficial for the task. The experimental results also suggest that, for the purpose of retrieving task-related corpora, the data samples may not be essential, keywords alone can be adequate.

6   Conclusion

To illustrate that PLMs maintain competitiveness with LLMs in text classification tasks, we continued pre-trained the original BERT model, substantially augmenting its capabilities. Furthermore, we introduced a novel method for topic words density retrieval, which leverages LLMs to enrich a limited set of topic seed words without relying on any task-specific samples. This approach allows the model to extract a more advantageous subset of the corpus for downstream datasets.

References

1. Achiam, J., et al.: Gpt-4 technical report. arXiv preprint arXiv:2303.08774 (2023)
2. Brown, T.B., et al.: Language models are few-shot learners. In: Advances in Neural Information Processing Systems, vol. 33, pp. 1877–1901 (2020)
3. Ouyang, L., et al.: Training language models to follow instructions with human feedback. Adv. Neural. Inf. Process. Syst. **35**, 27730–27744 (2022)
4. Wei, J., et al.: Chain-of-thought prompting elicits reasoning in large language models. Adv. Neural. Inf. Process. Syst. **35**, 24824–24837 (2022)
5. Liang, T., et al.: Encouraging divergent thinking in large language models through multi-agent debate. arXiv preprint arXiv:2305.19118 (2023)
6. Park, J.S., O'Brien, J., Cai, C.J., Morris, M.R., Liang, P., Bernstein, M.S.: Generative agents: interactive simulacra of human behavior. In: Proceedings of the 36th Annual ACM Symposium on User Interface Software and Technology, pp. 1–22 (2023)
7. Li, G., Hammoud, H., Itani, H., Khizbullin, D., Ghanem, B.: Camel: communicative agents for "mind" exploration of large language model society. In: Advances in Neural Information Processing Systems, vol. 36 (2024)
8. Rana, K., Haviland, J., Garg, S., Abou-Chakra, J., Reid, I., Suenderhauf, N.: SayPlan: grounding large language models using 3d scene graphs for scalable task planning. arXiv preprint arXiv:2307.06135 (2023)
9. Devlin, J., Chang, M.W., Lee, K., Toutanova, K.: BERT: pre-training of deep bidirectional transformers for language understanding. In: Proceedings of the 2019 Conference of the North American Chapter of the Association for Computational Linguistics: Human Language Technologies, Volume 1 (Long and Short Papers), pp. 4171–4186. Association for Computational Linguistics, Minneapolis, Minnesota, June 2019. https://doi.org/10.18653/v1/N19-1423, https://aclanthology.org/N19-1423
10. Liu, Y., et al.: Roberta: a robustly optimized bert pretraining approach. arXiv preprint arXiv:1907.11692 (2019)

11. Radford, A., Narasimhan, K., Salimans, T., Sutskever, I.: Improving language understanding by generative pre-training (2018)
12. Radford, A., Wu, J., Child, R., Luan, D., Amodei, D., Sutskever, I., et al.: Language models are unsupervised multitask learners. OpenAI Blog **1**(8), 9 (2019)
13. Touvron, H., et al.: Llama 2: open foundation and fine-tuned chat models. arXiv preprint arXiv:2307.09288 (2023)
14. Yao, X., Zheng, Y., Yang, X., Yang, Z.: NLP from scratch without large-scale pre-training: a simple and efficient framework. In: International Conference on Machine Learning, pp. 25438–25451. PMLR (2022)
15. Xie, S.M., Santurkar, S., Ma, T., Liang, P.S.: Data selection for language models via importance resampling. Adv. Neural. Inf. Process. Syst. **36**, 34201–34227 (2023)
16. Kaddour, J.: The minipile challenge for data-efficient language models. arXiv preprint arXiv:2304.08442 (2023)
17. Gao, L., et al.: The pile: an 800gb dataset of diverse text for language modeling. arXiv preprint arXiv:2101.00027 (2020)
18. Fei, Z., et al.: Query of cc: unearthing large scale domain-specific knowledge from public corpora. arXiv preprint arXiv:2401.14624 (2024)
19. Zhu, Y., et al.: Aligning books and movies: towards story-like visual explanations by watching movies and reading books. In: 2015 IEEE International Conference on Computer Vision (ICCV), pp. 19–27 (2015)
20. Gokaslan, A., Cohen, V.: Openwebtext corpus (2019)
21. Trinh, T.H., Le, Q.V.: A simple method for commonsense reasoning. ArXiv **abs/1806.02847** (2018)
22. Grusky, M., Naaman, M., Artzi, Y.: Newsroom: A dataset of 1.3 million summaries with diverse extractive strategies. In: Proceedings of the 2018 Conference of the North American Chapter of the Association for Computational Linguistics: Human Language Technologies (2018)
23. Conneau, A., et al.: Unsupervised cross-lingual representation learning at scale. In: Proceedings of the 58th Annual Meeting of the Association for Computational Linguistics, pp. 8440–8451. Association for Computational Linguistics, July 2020. https://doi.org/10.18653/v1/2020.acl-main.747, https://aclanthology.org/2020.acl-main.747
24. Levesque, H., Davis, E., Morgenstern, L.: The winograd schema challenge. In: Thirteenth international conference on the principles of knowledge representation and reasoning (2012)
25. McAuley, J., Leskovec, J.: Hidden factors and hidden topics: understanding rating dimensions with review text. In: Proceedings of the 7th ACM Conference on Recommender Systems (2013)
26. Gururangan, S., et al.: Don't stop pretraining: adapt language models to domains and tasks. In: Proceedings of the 58th Annual Meeting of the Association for Computational Linguistics, ACL 2020, 5–10 July 2020, pp. 8342–8360. Association for Computational Linguistics (2020). https://doi.org/10.18653/v1/2020.acl-main.740, https://doi.org/10.18653/v1/2020.acl-main.740
27. Menéndez, M., Pardo, J., Pardo, L., Pardo, M.: The jensen-shannon divergence. J. Franklin Inst. **334**(2), 307–318 (1997)
28. Yao, X., Zheng, Y., Yang, X., Yang, Z.: NLP from scratch without large-scale pretraining: a simple and efficient framework. ArXiv **abs/2111.04130** (2021)
29. Zeng, A., et al.: GLM-130b: an open bilingual pre-trained model. In: The Eleventh International Conference on Learning Representations (2022)
30. Chen, Y., et al.: Adaprompt: adaptive model training for prompt-based NLP. ArXiv **abs/2202.04824** (2022)

31. Chen, X., et al.: Decoupling knowledge from memorization: retrieval-augmented prompt learning. Adv. Neural. Inf. Process. Syst. **35**, 23908–23922 (2022)

32. Schick, T., Schütze, H.: Exploiting cloze-questions for few-shot text classification and natural language inference. In: Proceedings of the 16th Conference of the European Chapter of the Association for Computational Linguistics: Main Volume, pp. 255–269 (2021)

33. Sun, Y., Zheng, Y., Hao, C., Qiu, H.: NSP-BERT: a prompt-based few-shot learner through an original pre-training task —— next sentence prediction. In: Proceedings of the 29th International Conference on Computational Linguistics, pp. 3233–3250. International Committee on Computational Linguistics, Gyeongju, Republic of Korea, October 2022. https://aclanthology.org/2022.coling-1.286

34. Bai, J., et al.: Qwen technical report. arXiv preprint arXiv:2309.16609 (2023)

35. Gao, T., Fisch, A., Chen, D.: Making pre-trained language models better few-shot learners. In: ACL 2021: 59th annual meeting of the Association for Computational Linguistics, pp. 3816–3830 (2021)

36. Wang, S., Fang, H., Khabsa, M., Mao, H., Ma, H.: Entailment as few-shot learner. ArXiv **abs/2104.14690** (2021)

37. Liang, X., et al.: Contrastive demonstration tuning for pre-trained language models. ArXiv **abs/2204.04392** (2022)

38. Hu, S., Ding, N., Wang, H., Liu, Z., Li, J.Z., Sun, M.: Knowledgeable prompt-tuning: incorporating knowledge into prompt verbalizer for text classification. In: ACL (2022)

39. Socher, R., et al.: Recursive deep models for semantic compositionality over a sentiment treebank. In: Proceedings of EMNLP (2013)

40. PANG, B.: Seeing stars: Exploiting class relationships for sentiment categorization with respect to rating scales. In: Proceedings of ACL (2005)

41. Pang, B., Lee, L.: A sentimental education: sentiment analysis using subjectivity summarization based on minimum cuts. In: Proceedings of ACL (2004)

42. Hu, M., Liu, B.: Mining and summarizing customer reviews. In: Proceedings of KDD (2004)

43. Wiebe, J., Wilson, T., Cardie, C.: Annotating expressions of opinions and emotions in language. Language resources and evaluation (2005)

44. Zhang, X., Zhao, J., LeCun, Y.: Character-level convolutional networks for text classification. In: Advances in Neural Information Processing Systems, vol. 28 (2015)

45. Le Scao, T., Rush, A.M.: How many data points is a prompt worth? In: Proceedings of the 2021 Conference of the North American Chapter of the Association for Computational Linguistics: Human Language Technologies, pp. 2627–2636 (2021)

Semantic Knowledge Enhanced and Global Pointer Optimized Method for Medical Nested Entity Recognition

Yilin Song⬤ and Fang Kong(✉)⬤

Laboratory for Natural Language Processing, Soochow University, Suzhou, China
20225227119@stu.suda.edu.cn, kongfang@suda.edu.cn

Abstract. In the medical field, unstructured medical text holds rich medical knowledge. Identifying medical entities in this text accurately is crucial for structured medical databases, knowledge graphs, and intelligent diagnostic systems. Medical text has unique features, making it hard for traditional NER methods to identify complex medical entities. In particular, the recognition of nested entities within medical text poses a significant challenge, as it requires systems to recognize and understand the complex hierarchical relationships between entities, placing higher demands on traditional entity recognition systems. To overcome the challenges of nested entity recognition in medical text, we propose a method that combines semantic knowledge enhancement and global pointer optimization. Initially, we incorporate semantic prior knowledge of entity categories, capturing the interplay between labels and text by integrating label relationships. This allows us to obtain candidate entity information enriched with integrated label details. Following this, we establish a classification module to evaluate and score these candidate entities along with their labels, enabling entity prediction. To address nested entities, we introduce a Efficient GlobalPointer module that computes the likelihood of each text span being a specific entity type, thus bolstering nested entity recognition. By merging the outputs from both modules, we arrive at the final predicted entities. Experimental results indicate that our method excels on two flat entity datasets, CMedQANER and CCKS2017, as well as on the nested entity dataset CMeEE. Compared to baseline models, our approach demonstrates notable performance enhancements.

Keywords: Named Entity Recognition · Nested Entity Recognition · Medical Named Entity Recognition

1 Introduction

Named Entity Recognition (NER) is an important branch of natural language processing, aiming to identify entities such as persons, locations, and organizations from text. This technology serves as a key foundation for many downstream NLP tasks, including machine translation [1], text understanding [24],

© The Author(s), under exclusive license to Springer Nature Singapore Pte Ltd. 2025
D. F. Wong et al. (Eds.): NLPCC 2024, LNAI 15359, pp. 324–336, 2025.
https://doi.org/10.1007/978-981-97-9431-7_25

information retrieval [6,14], and more. In the medical field, vast amounts of unstructured medical texts contain a wealth of medical knowledge. Accurately identifying medical entities such as diseases, symptoms, anatomical sites, and medications from these texts holds profound significance for accumulating medical knowledge, improving healthcare quality, and advancing the medical industry. NER technology can extract these specific entities with meaning from complex medical texts, providing strong support for constructing structured medical text data, medical knowledge graphs, and intelligent medical diagnostic systems. In comparison to general domains, NER in the biomedical field possesses the following characteristics. Firstly, medical texts exhibit strong domain specificity, with their unique text structures and word distributions making it challenging for traditional sequence labeling NER methods to accurately identify complex medical entities. Secondly, medical texts often have nested structures. As shown in Fig. 1, in the first half of the sentence, "brain parenchyma and meninges edema, congestion" are categorized as symptoms entities, containing nested "brain parenchyma" and "meninges" body parts entities. In the second half of the sentence, "minor hemorrhages in the microvasculature" symptoms entity contains the "microvasculature" body parts entity.

主要病理改变为[脑实质　　和 脑膜　　水肿、充血]$_{sym}$，[微小血管　　出血]$_{sym}$。
The primary pathological changes consist of brain parenchymal and meninges edema, congestion, and minor hemorrhages in the microvasculature.

Fig. 1. The differences between three templates.

In the medical domain, Zhang et al. [23] proposed a medical pre-training model called SMedBERT, which was trained on a large-scale medical corpus containing deep structured semantic knowledge from linked entity neighbors. Experiments demonstrated that SMedBERT significantly outperformed strong baseline systems in various knowledge-intensive Chinese medical tasks. Chen et al. [2] introduced a hybrid neural network model based on medical MC-BERT, namely MC-BERT+BiLSTM+CNN+MHA+CRF, to enhance named entity recognition performance in Chinese electronic medical records.

For nested entities, current methods can be categorized into the following four types: For nested entities, current methods can be categorized into the following four types: Sequence labeling methods [7,8,10] aim to identify nested entities by improving traditional sequence labeling models. However, this approach is prone to error propagation, where misidentification of one entity may affect the recognition of subsequent entities, especially when dealing with closely adjacent or nested entities. Sequence-to-sequence methods [4,16,19] directly generate entity sequences, bypassing the traditional label prediction process. However, the decoding process is less efficient, and these models are susceptible to common issues associated with sequence-to-sequence models, such as exposure bias. Span-based methods [15,20,21] enumerate all possible spans in a sentence and classify them to identify entities. Relying solely on boundary information may not effectively detect complex nested entity structures. While this method focuses on the scope of entities, it lacks sufficient consideration of internal entity structures and context, thus not providing comprehensive recognition for certain nested cases. Hypergraph-based methods [12,18] represent all entity spans as graph nodes and combine them to form a hypergraph. However, this approach may introduce structural errors and ambiguities during the inference process.

In response to the nested entities in medical texts and the domain-specific characteristics of medical literature, we propose the following methods. Firstly, we introduce semantic prior knowledge of entity categories to capture the interaction between labels and text by integrating label relationships, thereby obtaining candidate entity information fused with label information. Subsequently, we establish a candidate entity classification module to score the candidate entity information and label information, thereby predicting entities. Furthermore, to enhance the recognition capability of nested entities, we introduce a Efficient GlobalPointer module to calculate the probability score of each span in the text as an entity of a certain type. Finally, we combine the results of the two modules to obtain the final predicted entities.

To demonstrate the effectiveness of our approach, we conducted experiments on three datasets: CCKS2017, CMedQANER, and CMcEE. Among these, CMeEE is a medical nested entity dataset, while CCKS2017 and CMedQANER are medical flat entity datasets. The experimental results indicate that our method outperforms other baseline models. Our contributions can be summarized as follows:

- Integration of semantic prior knowledge, such as medical label information, to enhance semantic information and predict potential entity types of the text.
- Introduction of a Efficient GlobalPointer method to enhance the recognition of nested entities.
- Experimental validation on three datasets: CCKS2017, cMedQANER, and CMeEE. The experimental results demonstrate that our current method outperforms the current state-of-the-art baseline models, whether on flat entity datasets or nested entity datasets.

2   Related Work

2.1   Nested NER

Sequence Labeling Methods. The traditional approach [7,8,10] treats Named Entity Recognition (NER) as a sequence labeling task, where each word or character in the sentence is assigned a specific label. While the sequence labeling framework has achieved good performance in flat NER, it encounters difficulties when dealing with nested NER.

Hypergraph-Based Methods. Lu et al. (2015) [12] first proposed a hypergraph-based approach to address nested entity problems. Wang et al. (2018) [18] introduced a segmented hypergraph model for identifying nested entities. This method requires a significant amount of manual construction of hypergraph structures and careful inspection to avoid structural errors and ambiguities in the hypergraph.

Sequence-to-Sequence Methods. Gillick et al. (2016) [4] first proposed a Seq2Seq model where the input is the original sentence, and the output is the starting position, length, and type of the entity. Strakova et al. (2019) [16] employed the Seq2Seq architecture to handle nested entities. Yan et al. (2021) [19] combined the Seq2Seq model with a BART-based pointer network to address unified NER. Unfortunately, the Seq2Seq architecture suffers from potential decoding efficiency issues and exposure bias.

Span-Based Methods. This approach predicts the entity type of spans by enumerating all potential spans in the sentence. Research in this area has mainly focused on span sampling and span representation methods. Yu et al. (2020) [20] employed a dual-attention model to assign scores to all potential spans and achieved state-of-the-art performance on both flat and nested English NER datasets. Shen et al. (2021) [15] divided the entity recognition process into two stages: entity extraction and entity classification, further utilizing span boundary information. Yuan et al. (2022) [21] proposed three affine mechanisms to integrate all useful information in different formats, including tokens, labels, boundaries, and relevant spans, to enhance span representation. However, this method needs to strike a balance between the sample candidate range and span attention. A smaller sample candidate range may risk missing entities, while a larger sample size often renders span attention ineffective due to involving too many low-quality samples and requiring substantial computational resources.

2.2 NER in the Medical Field

Chen et al. (2022) [2] proposed a hybrid neural network model based on medical MC-BERT, namely MC-BERT+BiLSTM+CNN+MHA+CRF [4], to enhance named entity recognition performance in Chinese electronic medical records. Duan et al. (2022) [11] introduced the FLR-MRC model, which utilizes a graph attention network to model label relationships and trains/predicts using label information and text to address the issue of multiple nested entities in medical texts. Cong et al. (2023) [3] presented a Chinese medical nested named entity recognition model based on feature fusion and bidirectional lattice embeddings. They introduced medical vocabularies and phonetic information to enhance the model's ability to capture Chinese medical NER functionality. They also considered the similarity between different types of entities to improve the model's effectiveness. Chen et al. (2022) [5] proposed a new method for studying the regularity of entity spans in Chinese NER, called the Regularity-Inspired Cognitive Network (RICON), to address flat and nested entities.

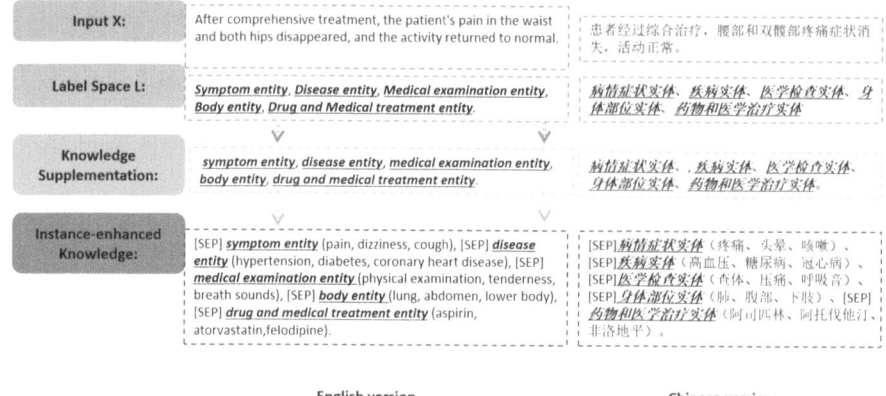

Fig. 2. The differences between three templates.

3   Task Formulation

For the task of medical named entity recognition, the goal is to identify predefined medical entities in medical texts, which are typically domain-specific. In this paper, we integrate label knowledge to capture the interaction between labels and text, obtaining text embeddings that contain semantic information from the labels, aiming to improve the accuracy of entity recognition.

For each sample (X, P, Y), $X = \{x_i\}_{i=1}^{L}$ represents an input sentence X with L tokens. $P = \{(i_t, j_t)\}_{t=1}^{M}$ means that the sentence X contains M entities, and the boundary index of the t-th entity is located by i_t and j_t. $Y = \{y_{i_t, j_t}\}_{t=1}^{M}$ is the entity type set corresponding to the entity span set P.

4   Method

In this section, we will provide a detailed description of our method from two aspects: semantic knowledge augmentation and model structure.

4.1   Semantic Knowledge Augmentation

The process of selecting semantic knowledge is crucial, as integrating label relationships can capture the interaction between labels and text, aiding in the subsequent recognition of entities. In this paper, we choose to use category information described in natural language, as well as partial examples, as supplementary semantic knowledge. As shown in the Fig. 2, based on its ability to better assist our model in improving domain adaptation, we ultimately select Instance-enhanced Knowledge as our final knowledge supplementation.

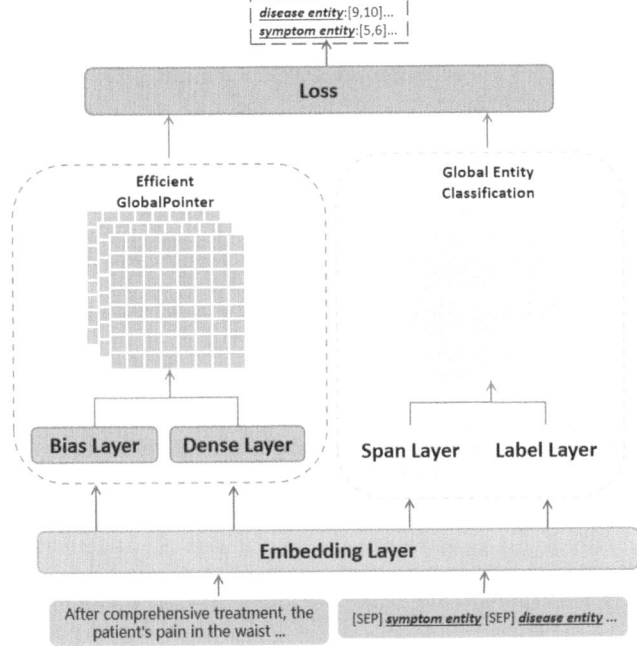

Fig. 3. Overall model architecture.

4.2 Model Structure

Figure 3 depicts the overall framework of our model, which is composed of three parts: encoder module, global entity classification and Efficient GlobalPointer.

Encoder Module. For an input sentence $X = \{x_i\}_{i=1}^{L}$ with L tokens, we first concatenate a template "[SEP]μ_1[SEP]μ_2..." to the end of it. Note that μ_t is the description of entity class t. As a result, a concatenated sentence $\mathcal{X} = \{x_1, ..., x_L, [SEP], \mu_1, ...\}$ can be obtained.

Then, we employ the pre-trained language model BERT for contextualized representation $H = \{h_1, ..., h_L, h_{SEP}, h_{\mu_1}, h_{SEP}, h_{\mu_2}, ...\}$. Afterwards, we concatenate the start token and end token of each span, and then use a multi-layer perceptron(MLP) to obtain the corresponding span representation. The final span representation $p_{i,j}$ can be computed as follows:

$$H = PLM(\mathcal{X}) \tag{1}$$

$$p_{i,j} = MLP([h_i; h_j]) \tag{2}$$

where $[;]$ denotes concatenation operation.

Efficient GlobalPointer. This module decomposes named entity recognition into two steps: extraction and classification. Extraction involves retrieving segments of entities, while classification involves determining the type of each entity. Firstly, the extraction operation is achieved through a scoring matrix $(W_q h_i)^T$ $(W_k h_j)$; secondly, through feature concatenation and a dense layer, specifically $\omega_\alpha^T [h_i; h_j]$, classification is implemented. The combination of the two serves as the new scoring function:

$$s_\alpha(i, j) = (W_q h_i)^T (W_k h_j) + \omega_\alpha^T [h_i; h_j] \tag{3}$$

Furthermore, by defining $q_i = W_q h_i$, $k_i = W_k h_i$, and replacing $[q_i; k_i]$ with h_i, we have:

$$s_\alpha(i, j) = q_i^T k_j + \omega_\alpha^T [q_i; k_i; q_j; k_j] \tag{4}$$

To further enhance the model's capability of capturing entity length and span information, we explicitly introduce Rotary Position Embedding, RoPE [17], into the scoring function. RoPE is a design that, in conjunction with the Attention mechanism, achieves "relative position encoding through absolute position encoding." Essentially, it is a transformation matrix $\mathcal{R}_i$ that satisfies the relationship $\mathcal{R}_i^T \mathcal{R}_j = \mathcal{R}_{j-i}$. When applied to q and k, we obtain:

$$s_\alpha(i, j) = q_i^T \mathcal{R}_{j-i} k_j + \omega_\alpha^T [q_i; k_i; q_j; k_j] \tag{5}$$

The loss function for this module is:

$$\mathcal{L}_{gp} = \log \left(1 + \sum_{(i,j) \in P_\alpha} e^{-s_\alpha(i,j)} \right) + \log \left(1 + \sum_{(i,j) \in Q_\alpha} e^{s_\alpha(i,j)} \right) \tag{6}$$

Global Entity Classification. The candidate entity classification module calculates the score for each span by directly computing the dot product between the entity description span and the input sentence span. Each span's score can be expressed as a formula:

$$s_t(i, j) = p(i, j)^T p(\mu_t^s, \mu_t^e) \tag{7}$$

where μ_t^s and μ_t^e respectively stand for the starting and ending tokens of the entity description for entity type t. The loss function of candidate entity classification module can be formulated as:

$$\mathcal{L}_{span} = \log \left(1 + \sum_{t \in T} \sum_{(i,j) \in Pos} e^{-s_t(i,j)} \right) + \log \left(1 + \sum_{t \in T} \sum_{(i,j) \in Neg} e^{s_t(i,j)} \right) \tag{8}$$

where, Pos and Neg denote the entity set and the non-entity set, T represents the class set. The total loss of our model is a weighted sum of the two losses:

$$\mathcal{L} = \mathcal{L}_{gp} + \gamma \mathcal{L}_{span} \tag{9}$$

where, γ is hyper-parameter.

Inference. During the inference stage, we take the union of $s_t(i,j) \geq 0$ and $s_\alpha(i,j) \geq 0$ as the predicted set of entities.

5   Experiment

5.1   Datasets

We evaluate our method using three medical named entity recognition datasets: CMedQANER, CCKS2017 and CMeEE [22]. CMedQANER and CCKS2017 are flat entity recognition datasets, while CMeEE is a nested entity recognition dataset.

Furthermore, CMeEE is one of the largest and most comprehensive datasets for Chinese biomedical entity recognition tasks, widely used as a benchmark for evaluating the performance of various NER models on Chinese biomedical texts. This dataset comprises 15,000 training samples, 5,000 validation samples, and 3,000 test samples. The annotated data contains a total of 2.2 million characters, composed of 47,194 sentences and 938 files. On average, each file contains 2,355 characters. The dataset encompasses nine different types of medical entities, labeled as diseases (dis), clinical symptoms (sym), drugs (dru), medical equipment (equ), medical procedures (pro), body parts (bod), medical laboratory test items (ite), microorganisms (mic), and departments (dep).

5.2   Baselines

To validate the effectiveness of the method proposed in this paper, we compared it with the following baselines. The baselines include models that perform well in medical text mining tasks such as SMedBERT [23] and MC-BERT+BiLSTM+C-NN+MHA+CRF [2], and models that excel in nested entity recognition tasks such as BERT-Biaffine [20], UIE [13], W2NER [9], and RICON [5].

5.3   Implementation Details

Parameter Settings. To ensure fairness, baselines and our method all employ RoBERTa-wwm-large-ext-Chinese as the encoder. Moreover, we use AdamW as our optimizer with a warm up rate of 0.1. We set the dropout ratio to 0.1, batch size to 4, max sequence length to 256 and train all models for 50 epochs. Additionally, we determine the weight of global entity classification module loss α to 0.1 after conducting a series of experiments.

5.4   Main Results

The results presented in Table 1 demonstrate the comparison between our approach and other baseline methods across three medical NER datasets. From these findings, we can infer that our approach exhibits a slightly superior performance compared to previous methods in the field of medical NER.

In comparison with the top results of the publicly available baselines Bert-Biaffine, UIE, RICON, and W2NER, our method achieved improvements of 0.94%, 0.6%, and 1.38% on the three datasets, respectively. Furthermore, when compared with the best results of baselines pre-trained on medical domain data, specifically SMedBERT (Zhang et al., 2021) and MC-BERT+BiLSTM+CNN+M- HA+CRF (Chen et al., 2022), our method demonstrated enhancements of 1.02% and 0.16% on the cMeDQANER and CCKS2017 datasets, respectively.

Table 1. F1 scores on three datasets. The best results are in **bold**.

Model	cMedQANER	CCKS2017	CMeEE
Bert-Biaffine	83.82	92.65	62.29
RICON	–	–	65.57
W2NER	84.25	93.92	64.86
UIE	84.83	93.71	64.95
SMedBERT	84.75	–	–
MC-BERT+BiLSTM+CNN+MHA+CRF	–	94.22	–
Ours	**85.77**	**94.38**	**66.95**

6   Analysis

6.1   Ablation Study

In order to verify the effectiveness of each component in our proposed approach, we conduct ablation experiments with the following variants:

1. w/o instance augmentation: we omit the instance augmentation operation and directly use general entity description in the template.
2. w/o global entity classification: we remove the auxiliary task of global entity classification and directly utilize Efficient GlobalPointer as the decoder and treat NER as a span classification task.
3. w/o efficient globalpointer: we removed the auxiliary task of Efficient GlobalPointer and only scored the candidate entity information and label information to obtain the predicted entities.

Table 2 provides evidence for the necessity of each component in our proposed approach. In summary, we can conclude that:

1. The introduction of instance enhancement is also effective, as this method can enhance the semantic information of entity descriptions.
2. Integrating semantic prior knowledge such as medical knowledge label information can enhance semantic information and improve overall effectiveness.
3. The introduction of the global pointer method can enhance the recognition ability of nested entities.

Table 2. The average F1 scores of ablation study on cMedQANER, CCKS2017 and CMeEE.

Model	cMedQANER	CCKS2017	CMeEE
Ours	**85.77**	**94.38**	**66.95**
w/o instance augmentation	85.19	93.67	66.32
w/o global entity classification	84.12	93.11	64.43
w/o efficient globalpointer	84.75	93.53	65.16

6.2 Instance Selection Strategies: Random or High-Frequency?

To delve deeper into how to effectively enhance the semantic representation of entity descriptions through instances, we conducted a comparative analysis between two selection strategies: random selection and high-frequency selection. Our investigation, as presented in Table 3, reveals that the high-frequency selection strategy consistently outperforms the random selection strategy. This superior performance can be attributed to several key factors.

Firstly, the high-frequency selection process involves identifying instances that occur frequently in the context of a given entity. These instances are more likely to capture the defining characteristics and salient features of the entity. By focusing on these high-frequency instances, we can enrich the semantic representation of the entity description with information that is both relevant and representative.

Secondly, random selection, while covering a broader range of instances, may inadvertently include examples that are less relevant or informative to the entity in question. These non-representative instances can dilute the effectiveness of the semantic enhancement process. In contrast, high-frequency selection ensures that the selected instances are tightly coupled with the entity and contribute meaningfully to its representation.

To summarize, our study emphasizes the importance of selecting instances carefully when enhancing the semantic representation of entity descriptions. The results indicate that high-frequency selection, which focuses on the most representative and relevant instances, is a highly effective strategy in most cases. Nevertheless, the optimal approach may vary depending on the specific characteristics of the dataset and the goals of the enhancement process.

Table 3. The F1 scores of different instance selection strategies on cMedQANER, CCKS2017 and CMeEE.

Model	cMedQANER	CCKS2017	CMeEE
w/o instance	85.19	93.67	66.32
Random selection	85.28	93.96	66.57
High-frequency selection	**85.77**	**94.38**	**66.95**

7 Conclusion

In this paper, we propose a method based on semantic knowledge enhancement and global pointer optimization to address the issue of nested entities in the medical domain. Our approach outperforms other baseline models in the field of medical named entity recognition. Firstly, our method introduces semantic prior knowledge of entity categories, capturing the interaction between labels and text through the fusion of label relationships to obtain candidate entity information with integrated label information. Subsequently, we establish a candidate entity classification module to score the candidate entity information and label information, resulting in the prediction of entities. Furthermore, to enhance the recognition capacity for nested entities, we introduce a global pointer module to compute the probability scores of each span in the text as an entity of a certain type. Finally, we integrate the results from both modules to obtain the ultimate predicted entities. Experimental results demonstrate that our approach achieves superior performance on both medical flat entity datasets and nested entity datasets compared to baseline models. In the future, our model can be extended to general domain NER and diverse scenarios such as relation extraction and event extraction. This work represents a significant step forward in the field of medical entity recognition and holds promise for broader applications across various domains.

Acknowledgments. This work was supported by the Project 62276178 under the National Natural Science Foundation of China, the Key Project 23KJA520012 under the Natural Science Foundation of Jiangsu Higher Education Institutions and the Priority Academic Program Development of Jiangsu Higher Education Institutions.

Disclosure of Interests. The authors have no competing interests to declare that are relevant to the content of this article.

References

1. Babych, B., Hartley, A.: Improving machine translation quality with automatic named entity recognition. In: Proceedings of the 7th International EAMT workshop on MT and other language technology tools, Improving MT through other language technology tools, Resource and tools for building MT at EACL 2003 (2003)
2. Chen, P., Zhang, M., Yu, X., Li, S.: Named entity recognition of Chinese electronic medical records based on a hybrid neural network and medical mc-bert. BMC Med. Inform. Decis. Mak. **22**(1), 315 (2022)
3. Cong, Q., Feng, Z., Rao, G., Zhang, L.: Chinese medical nested named entity recognition model based on feature fusion and bidirectional lattice embedding graph. In: International Conference on Database Systems for Advanced Applications, pp. 314–324. Springer (2023). https://doi.org/10.1007/978-3-031-30678-5_24
4. Gillick, D., Brunk, C., Vinyals, O., Subramanya, A.: Multilingual language processing from bytes. In: Proceedings of NAACL-HLT, pp. 1296–1306 (2016)

5. Gu, Y., Qu, X., Wang, Z., Zheng, Y., Huai, B., Yuan, N.J.: Delving deep into regularity: a simple but effective method for chinese named entity recognition. In: Findings of the Association for Computational Linguistics: NAACL 2022, pp. 1863–1873 (2022)
6. Guo, J., Xu, G., Cheng, X., Li, H.: Named entity recognition in query. In: Proceedings of the 32nd international ACM SIGIR Conference on Research and Development in Information Retrieval, pp. 267–274 (2009)
7. Huang, Z., Xu, W., Yu, K.: Bidirectional lstm-crf models for sequence tagging. arXiv preprint arXiv:1508.01991 (2015)
8. Lample, G., Ballesteros, M., Subramanian, S., Kawakami, K., Dyer, C.: Neural architectures for named entity recognition. In: Proceedings of the 2016 Conference of the North American Chapter of the Association for Computational Linguistics: Human Language Technologies, pp. 260–270 (2016)
9. Li, J., Fei, H., Liu, J., Wu, S., Zhang, M., Teng, C., Ji, D., Li, F.: Unified named entity recognition as word-word relation classification. In: Proceedings of the AAAI Conference on Artificial Intelligence, vol. 36, pp. 10965–10973 (2022)
10. Li, X., Yan, H., Qiu, X., Huang, X.J.: Flat: Chinese ner using flat-lattice transformer. In: Proceedings of the 58th Annual Meeting of the Association for Computational Linguistics, pp. 6836–6842 (2020)
11. Liu, S., Duan, J., Gong, F., Yue, H., Wang, J.: Fusing label relations for Chinese EMR named entity recognition with machine reading comprehension. In: International Symposium on Bioinformatics Research and Applications, pp. 41–51. Springer (2022). https://doi.org/10.1007/978-3-031-23198-8_5
12. Lu, W., Roth, D.: Joint mention extraction and classification with mention hypergraphs. In: Proceedings of the 2015 Conference on Empirical Methods in Natural Language Processing, pp. 857–867 (2015)
13. Lu, Y., Liu, Q., Dai, D., Xiao, X., Lin, H., Han, X., Sun, L., Wu, H.: Unified structure generation for universal information extraction. In: Proceedings of the 60th Annual Meeting of the Association for Computational Linguistics (Volume 1: Long Papers), pp. 5755–5772 (2022)
14. Petkova, D., Croft, W.B.: Proximity-based document representation for named entity retrieval. In: Proceedings of the sixteenth ACM Conference on Conference on Information and Knowledge Management, pp. 731–740 (2007)
15. Shen, Y., Ma, X., Tan, Z., Zhang, S., Wang, W., Lu, W.: Locate and label: a two-stage identifier for nested named entity recognition. In: Proceedings of the 59th Annual Meeting of the Association for Computational Linguistics and the 11th International Joint Conference on Natural Language Processing (Volume 1: Long Papers), pp. 2782–2794 (2021)
16. Straková, J., Straka, M., Hajic, J.: Neural architectures for nested ner through linearization. In: Proceedings of the 57th Annual Meeting of the Association for Computational Linguistics, pp. 5326–5331 (2019)
17. Su, J., Ahmed, M., Lu, Y., Pan, S., Bo, W., Liu, Y.: Roformer: enhanced transformer with rotary position embedding. neurocomputing **568**, 127063 (2024)
18. Wang, B., Lu, W.: Neural segmental hypergraphs for overlapping mention recognition. In: Proceedings of the 2018 Conference on Empirical Methods in Natural Language Processing, pp. 204–214 (2018)
19. Yan, H., Gui, T., Dai, J., Guo, Q., Zhang, Z., Qiu, X.: A unified generative framework for various ner subtasks. In: Proceedings of the 59th Annual Meeting of the Association for Computational Linguistics and the 11th International Joint Conference on Natural Language Processing (Volume 1: Long Papers), pp. 5808–5822 (2021)

20. Yu, J., Bohnet, B., Poesio, M.: Named entity recognition as dependency parsing. In: Proceedings of the 58th Annual Meeting of the Association for Computational Linguistics, pp. 6470–6476 (2020)
21. Yuan, Z., Tan, C., Huang, S., Huang, F.: Fusing heterogeneous factors with triaffine mechanism for nested named entity recognition. In: Findings of the Association for Computational Linguistics: ACL 2022, pp. 3174–3186 (2022)
22. Zhang, N., et al.: Cblue: a Chinese biomedical language understanding evaluation benchmark. In: Proceedings of the 60th Annual Meeting of the Association for Computational Linguistics (Volume 1: Long Papers), pp. 7888–7915 (2022)
23. Zhang, T., Cai, Z., Wang, C., Qiu, M., Yang, B., He, X.: Smedbert: a knowledge-enhanced pre-trained language model with structured semantics for medical text mining. In: Proceedings of the 59th Annual Meeting of the Association for Computational Linguistics and the 11th International Joint Conference on Natural Language Processing (Volume 1: Long Papers), pp. 5882–5893 (2021)
24. Zhang, Z., Han, X., Liu, Z., Jiang, X., Sun, M., Liu, Q.: Ernie: Enhanced language representation with informative entities. arXiv preprint arXiv:1905.07129 (2019)

Information Extraction and Knowledge Graph

CSLAN: A Novel Lexicon Attention Network for Chinese NER

Rongsheng Lin[1], Shubin Cai[1,2(✉)], and Zhong Ming[2,3]

[1] College of Computer Science and Software Engineering, Shenzhen University,
Shenzhen, China
[2] Laboratory of Artificial Intelligence and Digital Economy (Shenzhen),
Shenzhen, China
shubin@szu.edu.cn, mingz@szu.edu.cn
[3] College of Big Data and Internet, Shenzhen Technology University,
Shenzhen, China

Abstract. Recently, many studies have employed lexicon-based models to integrate lexicon information into character repersentation for Chinese Named Entity Recognition(NER) tasks, and these models have demonstrated high effectiveness. However, previous approaches to incorporate lexicon information into character representations calculate the correlation solely between the current character and the matching words. They neglect the words matched by neighboring characters, leading to an underutilization of lexicon information in character sequences. To address this issue, we introduce a novel lexical attention network (CSLAN). This network improves character representation by incorporating a new lexical attention mechanism. This mechanism enables the current character to consider the lexicon information from neighboring characters when fusing it into the character representation, thereby regulating attention between the character and the associated vocabulary. We conduct extensive experiments, and results show that our proposed CSLAN achieves competitive results on four publicly available datasets.

Keywords: Chinese Named Entity Recognition · Lexicon Enhancement · Attention Mechanism

1 Introduction

As a critical task in the field of information extraction, Named Entity Recognition (NER) aims to automatically identify and classify entities such as persons, locations, and organizations from the original corpus. It plays a pivotal role in downstream natural language processing tasks like relationship extraction and knowledge graph construction.

Chinese NER differs significantly from its English counterpart due to the natural word boundaries in English sentences. In Chinese NER, some intuitive approaches involve initially segmenting sentences into words using Chinese word segmentation tools, followed by employing a word-based approach

[8,10] for entity recognition. However, this approach has a significant drawback-segmentation errors inevitably arise during word segmentation. Consequently, many studies [4,13] treat sentences as sequences of characters and employ character-level inputs for Chinese NER, thereby benefiting from reduced ambiguity. Nevertheless, the trade-off is evident: the absence of word-level information, including potential word boundaries, can render the model less effective.

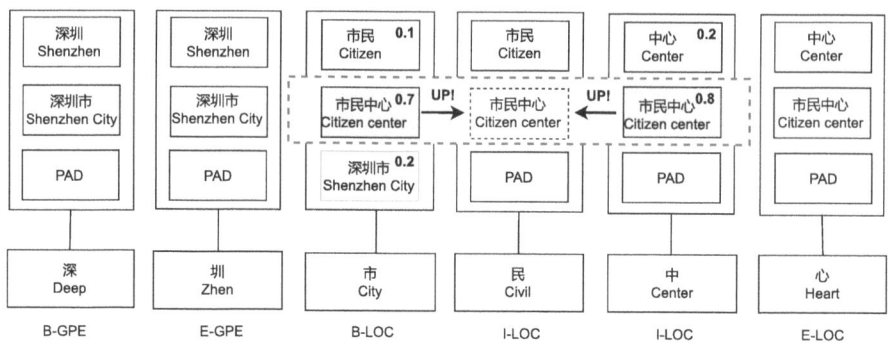

Fig. 1. An example of words matched by neighboring characters improving their own attention to the matched word. The upper right corner of the rectangle indicates the attention level of the word.

To enhance model performance by leveraging hidden boundary information within sentences, Zhang and Yang [25] proposed Lattice LSTM, which utilizes the lattice structure to incorporate lexicon information into the LSTM model. However, constructing the lattice structure consumes significant resources, and the model cannot undergo batch training. Ma et al. [16] introduced the SoftLexicon structure, which merges words matched by characters into the character representation at the embedding layer based on their frequency of occurrence. This simplifies the model structure and significantly enhances training efficiency. In recent studies [9,15], researchers have used BERT combined with lexicon information for the task of Chinese NER. Jia et al. [9] introduced Entity Enhanced BERT, incorporating a domain-specific lexicon into the BERT pre-training process. LEBERT [15] innovatively introduced the Adapter structure, designed to incorporate lexical information into the BERT model at a lower depth, enhancing its adaptability.

Nevertheless, the methods mentioned above have certain limitations. They fail to consider the word information associated with neighboring characters when integrating the lexicon data into the character representation. For example, let's consider the matching words in Fig. 1 from the character sequence "深圳市民中心(Shenzhen Citizen Park)". In this scenario, we have observed that when the character "民(Civil)" calculates the attention for "市民中心(Citizen Park)', if the attention score for "市民中心(Citizen Park)" within the words matched by the character "市(City)" is high, then the attention for the word "市民中

心(Citizen Park)" matched by the character "民(Civil)" should naturally be elevated. This is due to the fact that location entity '市民中心(Citizen Park)' comprises the four characters '市(City)', '民(Civil)', '中(Center)' and '心(Heart)' and the attention levels assigned by these characters to '市民中心(Citizen Park' should be consistent.

To overcome these challenges, we introduce CSLAN, a novel Chinese NER model. In CSLAN, we initially employ BERT to convert characters into character embeddings. Subsequently, to incorporate lexicon information into character representation, we have devised a new lexicon attention layer. This layer can efficiently utilize the word information of neighboring character matches to help establish attention between the current character and the matched word. Specifically, we first compute Self-words Attention between characters and their matched words, and then combining the words information from neighboring characters with our own matched words to compute Cross-words attention. These two types of attention are then weighted and fused to derive the ultimate lexicon attention, then fusing the word information into the character representation based on the attention information. After acquiring character representations with fused lexicon information, we input them into the BiLSTM encoder. Finally, we employ the standard CRF [11] decoder for the ultimate prediction.

In conclusion, our contributions in this study can be summarized as follows:

– We introduce a novel Chinese NER model (CSLAN) that can efficiently utilize lexicon information to capture boundary information in sentence.
– We design a novel Lexicon Attention Mechanism, allowing the current character to perceive the words matched by neighboring characters and leveraging this insight to enhance attention towards its own matching words.
– The results show that our proposed CSLAN achieves competitive results on all four publicly available datasets.

2   Related Work

Lexicon-Base Model: Recent research has shown an increased focus on the integration of lexicon information into character-based models in Chinese NER tasks. Zhang and Yang [25] initially proposed integrating lexicon information into character-based models using lattice structures to capture potential sentence boundary information. Gui et al. [6] introduced LR-CNN models that incorporated lexicon via a rethinking mechanism, improving training efficiency and addressing vocabulary conflicts. Gui et al. [7] and Sui et al. [19] made the model more efficient by converting the lattice structure into a corresponding graph structure and integrating the lexicon information through a graph neural network. Li et al. [14] designed a FLAT structure by first transforming the lattice structure into a flat structure consisting of spans, and subsequently encoding the FLAT structure with a Transformer, which was used to improve the shortcomings of the Lattice structure. Wu et al. [24] introduced the Multivariate Data Embedding-based CrossTransformer (MECT), which enhances the performance of Chinese NER through the integration of structural information from Chinese characters. RICONNER [5] employed a straightforward yet effective approach to investigate the principles governing entity spans in Chinese NER, leading to notable performance improvements.

Lexicon Attention Mechanism: In the Chinese NER model based on Lexicon information, characters must assign varying weights to matched words based on their significance when integrating lexicon information. Sui et al. [19] developed a collaborative graph network to capture the relationship between character and matched words. Ma et al. [16] introduced SoftLexicon (LSTM), which incorporates lexicon information into character representations based on the frequency of occurrence of words. Liu et al. [15] introduced LEBERT, which models the bidirectional relationship between characters and words using a bilinear attention mechanism, and incorporates Lexicon information into BERT at a lower level. Shan et al. [26] utilize dynamic cross-attention and a self-lattice attention network to capture fine-grained character-to-words relationships, fully harnessing lexicon information to enhance model performance. Wang et al. [22] introduced PGAT, a novel network that leverages the Lattice structure to create four distinct subgraphs: B, M, E, and S. Subsequently, it dynamically computes attention scores for words on each of these subgraphs using the graph attention mechanism.

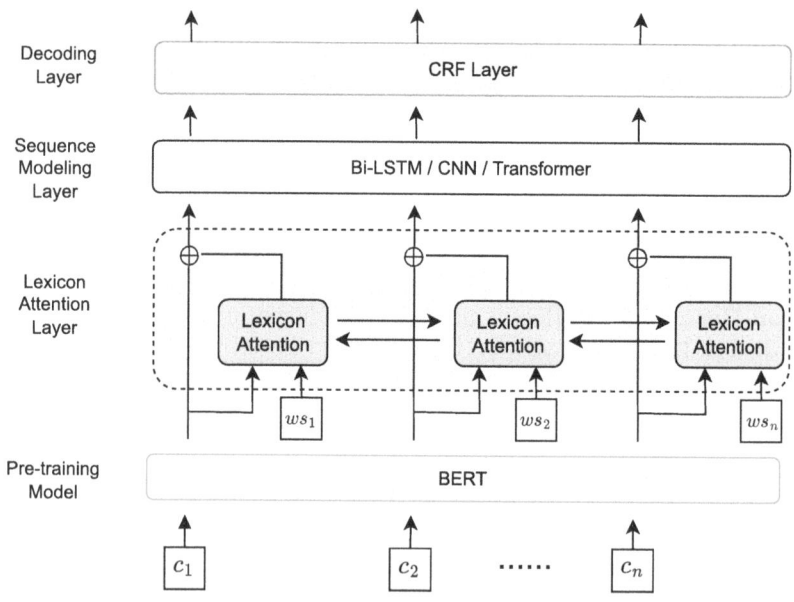

Fig. 2. Framework of the proposed CSLAN. Our network mainly consists of four components, i.e., BERT layer, lexicon attention layer, sequence modeling layer and CRF layer.

3   Methodology

In this section, we provide a comprehensive overview of CSLAN. The model's overall structure, as depicted in Fig. 2, comprises several key modules. Initially, character-word pairs are established by associating character sequences with their matched words. Subsequently, the character sequences are transformed into character embeddings through the BERT. These character representations are further enriched with lexicon information at the Lexicon Attention layer. Following this, the hidden state of the amalgamated character sequences is fully encoded using the BiLSTM layer. Ultimately, the CRF Layer is employed for the decoding and prediction process.

3.1   Char-Words Pair Sequence

We denoted a Chinese sentence as $S_c = \{c_1, c_2, ..., c_n\}$ which comprising n characters. To harness the potential word information for aiding the model in recognizing word boundaries, we extend the sentence into character-words sequence, following the approach of LEBERT [15]. Given a lexicon $\mathbf{D}$, for each character c_i, we match m words $ws_i = \{w_1, w_2, ..., w_m\}$ in the lexicon. As illustrated in Fig. 1, in the Chinese sentence "深圳市民中心(Shenzhen Citizen Park)", the character "深(Deep)" can match two different words, "深圳(Shenzhen)" and "深圳市(Shenzhen City)" in the lexicon $\mathbf{D}$. Subsequently, we create binary pair (c_i, ws_i) that correspond to matched words and their respective character. Finally, we pair all characters with the words they match, forming the character-words binary sequence $s_{cw} = \{(c_1, ws_1), (c_2, ws_2), ..., (c_n, ws_n)\}$. Here, c_i represents the i-th character in the character sequence, and ws_i denotes all words matched by c_i in lexicon $\mathbf{D}$. Subsequently, we employ BERT to encode the character sequence c, in order to capture the contextual relationships among characters, as follows:

$$H = BERT(S_c) \qquad (1)$$

where $H = \{h_1, h_2, ..., h_n\}$ represents the sequence of character embeddings after encoding the character sequence.

3.2   Lexicon Attention Layer

To leverage lexicon information for the enhancement of our model, we have designed the Lexicon Attention Layer to integrate lexicon information into the model. Our Lexicon Attention Layer receives two kinds of inputs, the hidden vector representation of the character and the vector representation of all words matched by the character, denote as (h_i, x_i^{ws}). Where h_i denotes the character hidden state, which is the vector output from the L-th layer Transformer in BERT, $x_i^{ws} = \{x_{i1}^w, x_{i2}^w, ..., x_{im}^w\}$ is a set of word embeddings, and the i-th word in x_i^{ws} is represented as follows:

$$x_{i,j}^w = e^w(w_{i,j}) \qquad (2)$$

where e^w is a pre-trained embedding lookup table and $w_{i,j}$ denotes the j-th word in the sequence of words ws_i matched by character c_i.

To align these two different inputs, we need to do a nonlinear transformation of the word vectors:

$$v_{i,j}^w = W_2(tanh(W_1 x_{i,j}^w + b_1)) + b_2 \tag{3}$$

where W_1 is a $d_c \times d_w$ matrix, W_2 is a $d_c \times d_c$ matrix, and b_1 and b_2 are the bias values. d_w and d_c represents the dimension of the word embedding and the dimension of BERT hidden layer size respectively.

Lexicon Attention Mechanism: Since each matched word holds a distinct level of significance for the character, we have devised a novel lexicon attention mechanism to compute the attention score for each word. Initially, we calculate the Self-words Attention , which measures the interaction between the character and the matched word. Subsequently, we calculate the Cross-words Attention by merging the information from words matched by neighboring characters with the information from words matched by the character itself. Lastly, we determine the ultimate Lexicon Attention through a weighted fusion of these two attentions.

Initially, we compute the Self-Words Attention. We represent the hidden state of all words matched by character c_i after the nonlinear mapping as $V_i = \{v_{i,1}^w, v_{i,2}^w, ..., v_{i,m}^w\}$, with m denoting the number of matched words, and d_c representing the dimension of the BERT hidden layer. The size of V_i is $m \times d_c$. To calculate the Self-words Attention a_i^1 between the current character and the matched words, we employ a bilinear attention formula as follows:

$$a_i^1 = softmax(h_i W_{attn} V_i^T) \tag{4}$$

where $W_{attn} \in \mathbb{R}^{d_c \times d_c}$ is a trainable bilinear attention weight matrix, and h_i^L represents the hidden vector representation of character c_i following BERT coding. Subsequently, we leverage the Self-words Attention score to integrate information from all matched words using the following operation:

$$z_i^w = \sum_{j=1}^{m} a_{i,j}^1 v_{i,j}^w \tag{5}$$

where $a_{i,j}^1$ represents the Self-words Attention of the j-th word matched by character c_i, and $v_{i,j}^w$ corresponds to the j-th vector in V_i.

To obtain information from words matched by neighboring characters, we directly concatenate the word information vectors matched by the current character with those matched by the neighboring characters. Subsequently, we apply a nonlinear transformation, as depicted in the following steps:

$$q_i = tanh(W_z[z_i^w; z_{i-1}^w; z_{i+1}^w])) \tag{6}$$

where $W_z \in \mathbb{R}^{d_c \times 3d_c}$. Subsequently we utilize the obtained q_i to compute the Cross-words Attention score a_i^2 of character c_i for the matched word with the following formula:

$$a_i^2 = softmax(q_i W_{attn} V_i^T) \tag{7}$$

Now we have obtained Self-Words Attention and Cross-Words Attention scores, we assign distinct weights to these two attentions in the calculation of the final lexicon attention. We designate the weight of the Self-words Attention score as p and the weight of the Cross-words Attention score as $(1 - p)$. The combination of these two attention score components is performed as follows:

$$a_i = p \times a_i^1 + (1 - p) \times a_i^2 \tag{8}$$

Finally, we employ the calculated lexicon attention score in the last fusion operation of word information using the following formula:

$$\tilde{z}_i^w = \sum_{j=1}^{m} a_{i,j} v_{i,j} \tag{9}$$

Char-Words Fusion: Finally, in order to retain as much information as possible, we connect h_i^L to the word hideen vector z_i^w, which operates as follows:

$$\tilde{h}_i = [h_i^L \oplus \tilde{z}_i^w] \tag{10}$$

where $\oplus$ represents concat operation. After obtaining $\tilde{h}_i$, we need to feed it into the dropout layer and layer normalization to help the model converge faster.

3.3 Bi-LSTM

After integrating the lexicon information into the character representation, the character representation is fed into the next encoding layer for further capturing the dependencies between characters. Common architectures for this layer include Bidirectional Long Short-Term Memory Network (BiLSTM), Convolutional Neural Networks (CNNs) and Transformer. In this study, we adopt BiLSTM for this layer:

$$[\overrightarrow{H}, \overleftarrow{H}] = BiLSTM(\tilde{H}) \tag{11}$$

where $\tilde{H} = \{\tilde{h}_1, \tilde{h}_2, ..., \tilde{h}_n\}$ represents the hidden vectors produced by the Lexicon Attention Layer, $BiLSTM$ represents Bidirectional Long Short-Term Memory Network. Subsequently, we combine the BiLSTM forward hidden vector output $\overrightarrow{h}_i$ with the reverse hidden vector $\overleftarrow{h}_i$ output into $\hat{h}_i = [\overrightarrow{h}_i; \overleftarrow{h}_i]$ to denote the final hidden vector representation of the i-th character.

3.4 Training and Decoding

Considering the correlation between labels, we use CRF Layer for final decoding after BiLSTM coding layer. Given the final output of BiLSTM layer $\hat{H} = \{\hat{h}_1, \hat{h}_2, ..., \hat{h}_n\}$, the probability of label sequence $y = \{y_1, y_2, ..., y_n\}$ can be denoted as:

$$p(y|s) = \frac{\exp(\sum_{i=1}^{n} \Phi(y_{i-1}, y_i, \hat{h}_i))}{\sum_{y' \in Y(s)} \exp\left(\sum_{i=1}^{n} \Phi(y'_{i-1}, y'_i, \hat{h}_i)\right)} \tag{12}$$

where $\Phi(y_{i-1}, y_i, c_i^T) = W_{(y_{i-1}, y_i)} c_i^T + b_{(y_{i-1}, y_i)}$ is the scoring function, and $W_{(y_{i-1}, y_i)} c_i^T$ and $b_{(y_{i-1}, y_i)}$ are the weight vector and bias, $Y(s)$ is the set of all arbitrary label sequences.

Given N manually labeled data, we train the model by minimizing the log-likelihood loss at the sentence level:

$$L_{ner} = -\sum_{i=1}^{n} \log\left(p(y_i|s_i)\right) \qquad (13)$$

4   Experiments

In this section, we evaluate our method on four publicly available datasets. We use the Micro-F1 score (F1) to evaluate the performance of the model.

4.1   Experimental Settings

Datasets: We conduct experiments on four datasets including Weibo [17], Resume [25], Ontonotes [23], and MSRA [12]. The Weibo dataset is obtained from social media, the Resume dataset is collected from Sina Finance, and Ontonotes and MSRA are data from the news domain.

Baselines: To comprehensively evaluate the performance of our proposed model, we compare our method with the following baseline methods. These can be categorized into two main types of models: those not using the Transformer architecture, including Lattice-LSTM [25] and SoftLexicon [16], and those using the Transformer architecture, including BERT [3], FLAT [14], ERNIE [20], ChineseBERT [21], MECT [24], LEBERT [15], and MCL [27]. All these models have demonstrated strong performance in various Chinese language tasks in recent years.

Implementation Details: We initialize our BERT pre-training model using the chinese-bert-wwm-ext [1] checkpoint downloaded from Huggingface[1], which is a BERT model pre-trained on a Chinese corpus using the Whole Word Masking [2] technique. The pre-trained lexicon **D** uses the embedding corpus published by Tencent AI Lab [18], where each word has an embedding dimension of 200. The initial learning rate for BERT is set to 1e-5, with epsilon in the Adam optimizer set to 1e-8. In the Lexicon Attention Layer and BiLSTM layer, we maintain an initial learning rate of 1e-4. Training is conducted for 50 epochs across all datasets, with a fixed sequence length of 256. The number of matched words per character is set to 4. The value of hyperparameter p varies: 0.7 for Weibo, 0.1 for Resume, 0.5 for OntoNotes, and 0.7 for MSRA. The training batch size is 8 for the MSRA dataset and 4 for the other datasets. Finally, all the weights in the BERT model are fine-tuned during training.

---

[1] https://huggingface.co.

4.2   Overall Performance

Table 1 illustrates our model's superior performance compared to other lexicon-based models across four Chinese NER datasets. Our model demonstrates competitive performance, achieving F1 scores of 72.78, 96.81, 82.96, and 96.58 on the Weibo, Resume, OntoNotes, and MSRA datasets, respectively. In comparison with various baseline models, our method achieved significant F1 score improvements on two datasets: Resume (+0.36%) and MSRA (+0.35%). Additionally, it achieved competitive results on the Weibo and Resume datasets. These results indicate that CSLAN can utilize lexicon information more efficiently than other lexicon-based models, enhancing Chinese NER performance. Therefore, we conclude that our approach provides a feasible method to improve the performance of Chinese NER models.

Table 1. Main results on Weibo,Resume,Ontonotes and MSRA datasets.The best F1 score is highlighted in bold.

Models	Weibo	Resume	Ontonotes	MSRA
Lattice-LSTM(2018) [25]	58.79	94.46	73.88	93.18
SoftLexicon(2019) [16]	61.42	95.53	75.64	93.66
BERT(2018) [3]	67.27	95.29	79.93	94.71
FLAT(2020) [14]	60.32	95.45	76.45	94.12
ENRIE(2019) [20]	67.96	94.82	77.65	95.08
ChineseBERT(2021) [21]	69.02	95.89	81.65	95.39
MECT(2021) [24]	70.50	95.98	82.57	96.24
LEBERT(2021) [15]	70.75	96.08	82.08	95.70
MCL(2023) [27]	**73.08**	96.46	**82.96**	96.11
CSLAN(Ours)	72.78	**96.81**	**82.96**	**96.58**

4.3   Discussion

Impact of Hyperparameter P: To investigate the impact of different p values on model performance, we conducted experiments on both the Weibo and Resume datasets. The range of p in the experiments was set between 0 and 1 with a step size of 0.1. We measured the F1 score to determine the optimal p value. For the Weibo dataset, as shown in Fig. 3, the optimal performance is observed at $p=0.7$. This outcome can be attributed to the limited presence of entities within the Weibo dataset, which reduces the necessity for frequent lexicon analysis of adjacent character matches. Consequently, the model benefits more from focusing on Self-words Attention. Conversely, for the Resume dataset, as shown in Fig. 4, the model attains peak performance at $p=0.1$. This significant deviation from the Weibo dataset's performance is due to the higher density of entities in the Resume dataset. Here, the model requires frequent analysis of lexicon information from neighboring character matches to accurately capture boundary information, making Cross-words Attention more crucial.

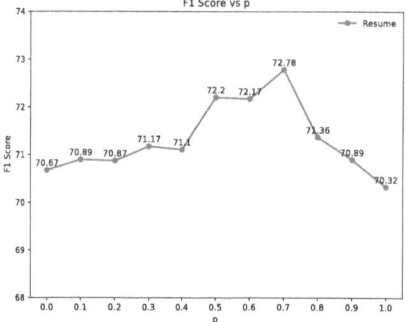
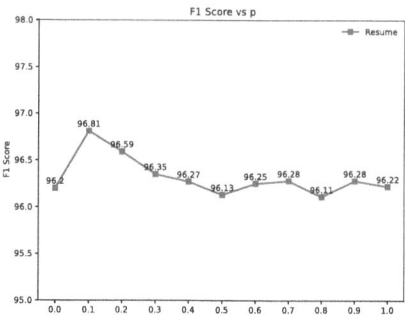

Fig. 3. Influence of p value on Weibo   **Fig. 4.** Influence of p value on Resume

Table 2. The impact of different BERT checkpoints on model performance.

Models	Weibo	Resume	Ontonotes	MSRA
CSLAN w/ bert-base-chinese	72.13	96.44	82.22	96.17
CSLAN w/ chinese-bert-wwm	72.32	96.52	82.30	96.11
CSLAN(Ours)	**72.78**	**96.81**	**82.96**	**96.58**

Impact of BERT Checkpoints: We examined the effects of three distinct BERT checkpoints on CSLAN: bert-base-chinese [3], chinese-bert-wwm [1], and chinese-bert-wwm-ext [1], all of which were directly downloaded from Huggingface. Experiments were conducted on both the Weibo and Resume datasets, and the results are shown in Table 2. The results indicate that different checkpoints have varying degrees of influence on the performance of CSLAN. Among them, the chinese-bert-wwm-ext checkpoint demonstrated the best performance for Chinese NER, leading us to choose it for our experiments.

4.4   Case Study

To visualize the performance of our proposed CSLAN, we compare it with LEBERT, a model that uses a traditional attention mechanism that focuses

Table 3. Example of Weibo test set, where red colors represent the wrong labels.

Case1:	Example of Chinese NER
Sentence	悟智乐园位于台南市安南区
	Wuzhi Park is located in Anan District, Tainan City
Matched Words	悟, 智乐, 乐园, 位于, 台南, 台南市, 南市, 安南, 南区
	Realize, Wisdom and Happiness, Disneyland, Located in, Tainan, Tainan City,
	South City, Annan, Southern District
Character	悟 智 乐 园 位 于 台 南 市 安 南 区
Gold Labels	B-LOC I-LOC I-LOC E-LOC O O B-GPE I-GPE E-GPE B-GPE I-GPE E-GPE
LEBERT	B-LOC I-LOC I-LOC E-LOC O O B-GPE I-GPE E-GPE B-GPE I-LOC E-LOC
CSLAN(our)	B-LOC I-LOC I-LOC E-LOC O O B-GPE I-GPE E-GPE B-GPE I-GPE E-GPE

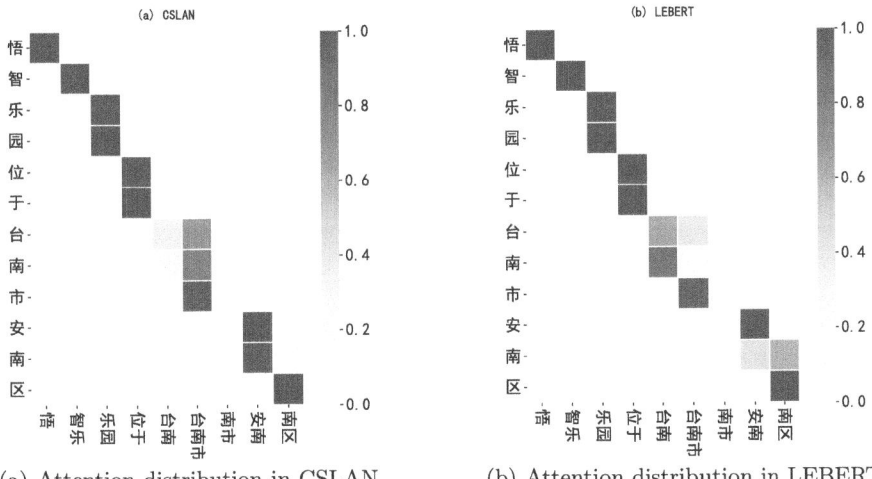

(a) Attention distribution in CSLAN   (b) Attention distribution in LEBERT

Fig. 5. The distribution of attention for words matched by characters in the example.

only on the intrinsic relationship between the current character and the matching word, and the results are shown in Table 3.

In the case, LEBERT made an incorrect classified "南区(South District)" as a location(LOC) entity. Conversely, CSLAN correctly classifying "安南区(Annan District)" as a geopolitical(GPE) entity. We speculate that the accurate boundary information was not captured because the attention calculation for the character "南(South)" in relation to the matching words "南区(South District)" and "安南(Anan)" overlooked the fact that the adjacent character "安(An)" also corresponds to the term "安南(Anan)".

We visualized the attention information between each character and its matched words in the above case. The results are presented in Fig. 5. We use a heatmap to illustrate the intensity of attention, where yellow signifies low attention, and red indicates high attention. In Fig. 5(a), it is evident that the allocation of attention for "南(South)" towards the matching terms "安南(Annan)" and "南区(South District)" in CSLAN is logically consistent. In Fig. 5(b), however, the allocation of attention to the two terms in LEBERT appears notably less logical. This demonstrates that CSLAN can utilize the information of adjacent characters to improve its attention and capture the correct boundary information.

5   Conclusion

In this paper, we propose CSLAN, a novel lexicon attention network. CSLAN allows the current character to perceive the lexicon information of neighboring character matches when fusing the lexicon information into the model, which significantly improves the attention to its own matched lexicon to help the model better capture boundary information. Extensive experiments show that CSLAN achieves competitive performance on four benchmark Chinese NER datasets. In future work, we will adapt CSLAN to different NLP tasks, such as Chinese POS Tagging and Chinese Segmentation tasks.

Acknowledgements. This research is supported by the Guangdong Province Key Laboratory of Popular High Performance Computers (Grant No. 2017B030314073).

References

1. Cui, Y., Che, W., Liu, T., Qin, B., Wang, S., Hu, G.: Revisiting pre-trained models for Chinese natural language processing. In: Proceedings of the 2020 Conference on Empirical Methods in Natural Language Processing: Findings, pp. 657–668. Association for Computational Linguistics, Online (Nov 2020)
2. Cui, Y., Che, W., Liu, T., Qin, B., Yang, Z.: Pre-training with whole word masking for Chinese BERT. IEEE/ACM Trans. Audio Speech Lang. Process. **29**, 3504–3514 (2021). https://doi.org/10.1109/TASLP.2021.3124365
3. Devlin, J., Chang, M.W., Lee, K., Toutanova, K.: BERT: pre-training of deep bidirectional transformers for language understanding. In: Proceedings of the 2019 Conference of the North American Chapter of the Association for Computational Linguistics: Human Language Technologies, Volume 1 (Long and Short Papers), pp. 4171–4186 (2019)
4. Ding, R., Xie, P., Zhang, X., Lu, W., Li, L., Si, L.: A neural multi-digraph model for Chinese NER with gazetteers. In: Proceedings of the 57th Annual Meeting of the Association for Computational Linguistics, pp. 1462–1467 (2019)
5. Gu, Y., Qu, X., Wang, Z., Zheng, Y., Huai, B., Yuan, N.J.: Delving deep into regularity: a simple but effective method for Chinese named entity recognition. In: Findings of the Association for Computational Linguistics: NAACL 2022, pp. 1863–1873 (2022)
6. Gui, T., Ma, R., Zhang, Q., Zhao, L., Jiang, Y.G., Huang, X.: CNN-based Chinese NER with lexicon rethinking. In: IJCAI, vol. 2019 (2019)
7. Gui, T., Zou, Y., Zhang, Q., Peng, M., Fu, J., Wei, Z., Huang, X.J.: A lexicon-based graph neural network for Chinese NER. In: Proceedings of the 2019 Conference on Empirical Methods in Natural Language Processing and the 9th International Joint Conference on Natural Language Processing (EMNLP-IJCNLP), pp. 1040–1050 (2019)

8. He, H., Sun, X.: A unified model for cross-domain and semi-supervised named entity recognition in Chinese social media. In: Proceedings of the AAAI Conference on Artificial Intelligence, vol. 31 (2017)
9. Jia, C., Shi, Y., Yang, Q., Zhang, Y.: Entity enhanced BERT pre-training for Chinese NER. In: Proceedings of the 2020 Conference on Empirical Methods in Natural Language Processing (EMNLP), pp. 6384–6396 (2020)
10. Jie, Y., Zhiyang, T., Meishan, Z., Yue, Z.: Combining discrete and neural features for sequence labeling. In: International Conference on Computational Linguistics and Intelligent Text Processing, pp. 140–154 (2016)
11. Lafferty, J., McCallum, A., Pereira, F.C.: Conditional random fields: Probabilistic models for segmenting and labeling sequence data (2001)
12. Levow, G.A.: The third international Chinese language processing bakeoff: word segmentation and named entity recognition. In: Proceedings of the Fifth SIGHAN Workshop on Chinese Language Processing, pp. 108–117 (2006)
13. Li, H., Hagiwara, M., Li, Q., Ji, H.: Comparison of the impact of word segmentation on name tagging for Chinese and japanese. In: LREC, vol. 2014, pp. 2532–2536 (2014)
14. Li, X., Yan, H., Qiu, X., Huang, X.J.: Flat: Chinese NER using flat-lattice transformer. In: Proceedings of the 58th Annual Meeting of the Association for Computational Linguistics, pp. 6836–6842 (2020)
15. Liu, W., Fu, X., Zhang, Y., Xiao, W.: Lexicon enhanced Chinese sequence labeling using BERT adapter. In: Proceedings of the 59th Annual Meeting of the Association for Computational Linguistics and the 11th International Joint Conference on Natural Language Processing (Volume 1: Long Papers), pp. 5847–5858 (2021)
16. Ma, R., Peng, M., Zhang, Q., Wei, Z., Huang, X.J.: Simplify the usage of lexicon in Chinese NER. In: Proceedings of the 58th Annual Meeting of the Association for Computational Linguistics, pp. 5951–5960 (2020)
17. Peng, N., Dredze, M.: Named entity recognition for Chinese social media with jointly trained embeddings. In: Proceedings of the 2015 Conference on Empirical Methods in Natural Language Processing, pp. 548–554 (2015)
18. Song, Y., Shi, S., Li, J., Zhang, H.: Directional skip-gram: explicitly distinguishing left and right context for word embeddings. In: Proceedings of the 2018 Conference of the North American Chapter of the Association for Computational Linguistics: Human Language Technologies, Volume 2 (Short Papers), pp. 175–180 (2018)
19. Sui, D., Chen, Y., Liu, K., Zhao, J., Liu, S.: Leverage lexical knowledge for Chinese named entity recognition via collaborative graph network. In: Proceedings of the 2019 Conference on Empirical Methods in Natural Language Processing and the 9th International Joint Conference on Natural Language Processing (EMNLP-IJCNLP), pp. 3830–3840 (2019)
20. Sun, Y., et al.: Ernie: Enhanced representation through knowledge integration. arXiv preprint arXiv:1904.09223 (2019)
21. Sun, Z., et al.: ChineseBERT: Chinese pretraining enhanced by glyph and pinyin information. In: Proceedings of the 59th Annual Meeting of the Association for Computational Linguistics and the 11th International Joint Conference on Natural Language Processing (Volume 1: Long Papers), pp. 2065–2075 (2021)
22. Wang, Y., Lu, L., Wu, Y., Chen, Y.: Polymorphic graph attention network for Chinese NER. Expert Syst. Appl. **203**, 117467 (2022)
23. Weischedel, R., et al.: Ontonotes release 4.0. LDC2011T03, Philadelphia, Penn.: Linguistic Data Consortium (2011)

24. Wu, S., Song, X., Feng, Z.: Mect: multi-metadata embedding based cross-transformer for Chinese named entity recognition. In: Proceedings of the 59th Annual Meeting of the Association for Computational Linguistics and the 11th International Joint Conference on Natural Language Processing (Volume 1: Long Papers), pp. 1529–1539 (2021)
25. Zhang, Y., Yang, J.: Chinese NER using lattice LSTM. In: Proceedings of the 56th Annual Meeting of the Association for Computational Linguistics (Volume 1: Long Papers). pp. 1554–1564. Association for Computational Linguistics, Melbourne, Australia (Jul 2018). https://doi.org/10.18653/v1/P18-1144
26. Zhao, S., Hu, M., Cai, Z., Chen, H., Liu, F.: Dynamic modeling cross-and self-lattice attention network for Chinese NER. In: Proceedings of the AAAI Conference on Artificial Intelligence, vol. 35, pp. 14515–14523 (2021)
27. Zhao, S., Wang, C., Hu, M., Yan, T., Wang, M.: Mcl: multi-granularity contrastive learning framework for Chinese NER. In: Proceedings of the AAAI Conference on Artificial Intelligence, vol. 37, pp. 14011–14019 (2023)

S2D: Enhancing Zero-Shot Cross-Lingual Event Argument Extraction with Semantic Knowledge

Zongkai Zhao[1], Xiuhua Li[1(✉)], and Kaiwen Wei[2(✉)]

[1] School of Big Data and Software Engineering, Chongqing University,
Chongqing, China
`zhaozongkai@stu.cqu.edu.cn, lixiuhua@cqu.edu.cn`
[2] College of Computer Science, Chongqing University, Chongqing, China
`weikaiwen@cqu.edu.cn`

Abstract. Zero-shot Cross-lingual EAE has garnered significant interests from the community because it could minimize the need for extensive data annotation to identify the roles of the arguments within a specific event. Some prior works point out that syntactic structures could be regarded as the language-independent features and those methods have achieved promising performance. However, sometimes even the sentences in different languages express the same meaning, the syntactic parsing results are quite different. To alleviate this problem, we find the semantic information is rarely considered, which could be considered as another language-independent features and provides more consistent parsing results across languages. To this end, in this paper, we propose the Semantic-Syntactic Driven framework (S2D) for incorporating the semantic and syntactic information simultaneously. Specifically, we design a language-independent dual-prefix constructor module to handle the semantic and syntactic discrepancies between source and target languages. Besides, we introduce a semantic role labeling source generator module to expand the source language dataset with semantic features. The experimental results illustrate that S2D surpasses the state-of-the-art methods by 3.4% and 5.3% in terms of average F1-score on the ACE-2005 and ERE datasets, respectively.

Keywords: Event Extraction · Cross Lingual · Semantic Knowledge

1 Introduction

Event Argument Extraction (EAE) focuses on identifying the entities serving as event arguments and determining their specific roles within that event. For example, given a sentence "The criminal was arrested by policemen yesterday" and its trigger word "arrested", an EAE system is required to recognize event arguments "the criminal", "policemen", and "yesterday", and then categorizes them as "Target", "Arrester", and "Time", respectively. Zero-shot Cross-lingual EAE (ZCEAE)

© The Author(s), under exclusive license to Springer Nature Singapore Pte Ltd. 2025
D. F. Wong et al. (Eds.): NLPCC 2024, LNAI 15359, pp. 353–365, 2025.
https://doi.org/10.1007/978-981-97-9431-7_27

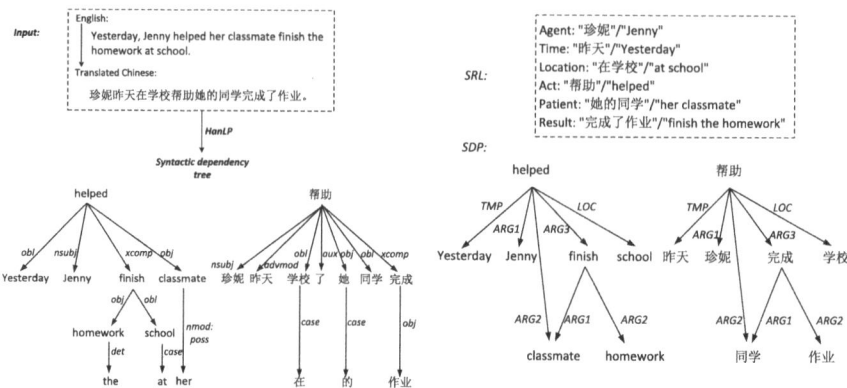

(a) Syntactic dependency trees.   (b) Semantic role labeling and semantic dependency trees.

Fig. 1. The (a) syntactic parsing results and (b) semantic parsing results. It can be seen that even though the sentences in different languages express the same meaning, their syntactic dependency trees are different, which may introduce noises. However, the semantic information remains similar.

is a pioneering approach aiming at overcoming the challenge of data scarcity in languages with limited resources for traditional EAE. By training an EAE model on annotated data from the source language, this task seeks to find the event arguments without necessitating any annotated data in different target languages. ZCEAE is crucial for various downstream applications, such as timeline generation [10], conversational AI [21] and recommendation engines [9].

Previous studies typically leverage syntactic information as the *language-independent feature* and model ZCEAE as a classification task [14] or a sequence generation task [11]. For example, Cao et al. [4] devise a language-oriented syntactic prefix to overcome the syntactic differences among languages. Besides, there have been a study proposing a unique template [8] from a syntactic point of view, which prevents the model from over-fitting to the source language's vocabulary and facilitates cross-lingual transfer with its language compatibility.

However, existing methods typically ignore the necessity of semantic information, which can also be used as language-independent feature. Semantic information consists of two crucial components: the Semantic Role Labeling (SRL) and the Semantic Dependency Parsing (SDP). As shown in Fig. 1 (a), we give an English and a translated Chinese sentence as examples, and the trees obtained from the syntactic dependency analysis of the two are different. However, as shown in Fig. 1 (b), the SRL and SDP results of the two sentences in different languages are strikingly similar. This suggests that syntactic knowledge sometimes could introduce error, and the semantic information could be regarded as another language independent feature. As for the reasons, SRL extracts predicate argument structures using broader frame ontologies, benefiting from rich resources like FrameNet [2], closely resembling EAE in identifying semantic frames triggered by predicates and finding participating role arguments. Moreover, with the development of large-scale annotated corpora [3], SDP aims to build a semantic dependency graph that captures a more comprehensive picture of the sentence's meaning by identifying various semantic relations.

To incorporate the semantic information, we propose the Semantic-Syntactic Driven framework (S2D). Specifically, we devise a *Semantic Role Labeling Source Generator* module to incorporate the SRL knowledge. The module first processes the SRL datasets into a language-agnostic template and spliced into the EAE training set. Besides, we design a *Language-independent Dual-prefix Constructor* module to handle the discrepancies between source and target languages. The module first obtains the language-universal dependency structure of the input sentence with stanza [17], and then utilizes trigger-centric neighbor information to initialize continuous syntactic prefix vectors. Extensive experiments on ACE-2005 and ERE datasets demonstrate that S2D substantially outperforms previous state-of-the-art ZCEAE methods. Specially, for the ACE-2005 dataset, S2D improves over the best past method LAPIN [4] by 5.9% about the average F1-score on the mT5-base backbone.

Overall, the contributions of this work can be summarized as follows: (1) We observe that the semantic information can serve as another valuable feature for ZCEAE task. To this end, we propose the Semantic-Syntactic Driven framework (S2D) to fuse the syntactic and semantic information. (2) We devise the Semantic Role Labeling Source Generator to incorporate the training dataset for the EAE task with the classical dataset for the SRL task. Besides, the SDP prefix is introduced to incorporate semantic dependencies with the design of Language-independent Dual-prefix Constructor. (3) Experimental results indicate that S2D significantly outperforms previous state-of-the-art methods, achieving 3.4% and 5.3% improvements of average F1-score on the ACE-2005 and ERE datasets.

2   Related Work

Zero-shot Cross-Lingual Event Argument Extraction. This task attracts increasing attention [8,20] as a solution to meet the need for more annotated training data in traditional EAE, aiming to overcome linguistic resource constraints. With the influence of the great results of the generation-based models of monolingual EAE, Huang et al. [8] construct language-agnostic template to the ZCEAE task. Moreover, Language-oriented prefix-tuning network (LAPIN) [4] was proposed to address the linguistic differences between the source and target languages by generating language-oriented syntactic prefix, which achieves the state-of-the-art result for ZCEAE. Nevertheless, the actual semantic relationships among words are often ignored though the method performs syntactic dependency analysis.

Semantic Analysis. There are two main ways serving as semantic information: the Semantic Role Labeling (SRL) and the Semantic Dependency Parsing (SDP). For the SRL, transfer learning from SRL to EAE demonstrates SRL's potential as a direct training resource [22] but its application to expand EAE resources in ZCEAE contexts remains limited. And then for the SDP, Dozat and Manning

[6] introduced a graph-based neural model for SDP that has indirectly benefited EAE through more accurate semantic mappings. This underscores the growing recognition of SDP as a valuable tool for improving ZCEAE. It is noteworthy that there has been little work investigating ZCEAE with extended SRL training annotations enhanced by semantic dependency parsing. As far as we know, this could be the first time to apply semantic dependency parsing explicitly and enrich training data with SRL annotations in ZCEAE task.

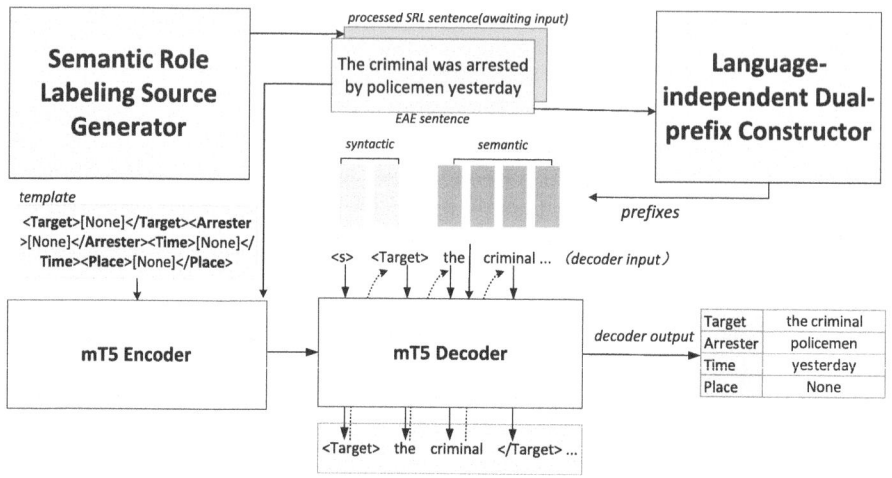

Fig. 2. The architecture of S2D model for ZCEAE task.

3   Method

Figure 2 shows the overall architecture of S2D, which consists of two components: 1) Semantic Role Labeling Source Generator, which converts SRL annotations into the form of the templates to incorporate semantic information in the training data; 2) Language-independent Dual-prefix Constructor, which initializes syntactic and semantic prefixes using language-universal dependency structure to enhance the extraction of syntactic and semantic knowledge in Pretrained Language Models (PLMs).

3.1   Semantic Role Labeling Source Generator

The semantic role labeling source generator first processes the data into SRL template, and then transforms the data into the language-independent template, which is directly spliced into the EAE resources of the training set. Specifically, it is devised as follows:

SRL Templates. We utilize PropBank [15], NomBank [13], and FrameNet [2] as the SRL resources. First, we map NomBank frames to corresponding Prop-Bank frames using the "source" attribute and focus on non-core roles essential for the target EAE task. Role names are adopted from FrameNet. Besides, we train a role label classifier using FrameNet data and then apply this classifier to the PropBank data. Role orders in templates are based on average relative distances and frequently used prepositions are retained. Then templates are created by ordering and concatenating these elements. For instance, the "buy.01" PropBank frame is represented by the template "buyer **buy** goods for recipient from seller for money in place." For Arabic and Chinese, we use PropBank data from OntoNotes and apply the same methodology to determine role names.

Language-independent EAE Template. Following Huang et al. [8] and Cao et al. [4], we employ a distinctive HTML-tag-style template, which is language-independent. For the example in Fig. 2, the output template for *Attack* events is "<Target>The criminal </Target> <Arrester>policemen </Arrester><Time>yesterday </Time><Place>[None] </Place>." where "The criminal", "policemen", "yesterday" and [None] are the ground truth value. Those special tokens (e.g., ⟨Target⟩, ⟨/Target⟩), unseen by PLMs during pre-training, render the template language-agnostic. For roles with multiple arguments, these are sorted by spans and linked via [and]. Lastly, SRL templates were manually adapted to language-independent EAE formats and integrated into their respective EAE training datasets.

3.2   Encoder-Decoder Architecture

Given the input sentence S, the template T_e (for the event type e) is designed using the above template construction strategy. Our method S2D generates the output sequence Y via multilingual generative PLMs (i.e., mT5). Concretely, our method first encodes the input sequence and obtains corresponding representations:

$$E_X = \text{Encoder}(X), \quad X = [S; [SEP]; T_e], \tag{1}$$

where $\text{Encoder}(\cdot)$ is a multi-layer transformer encoder. X denotes the input sequence that is concatenated by the sentence S and template T_e. [SEP] denotes the separate marker in the PLMs. $[;]$ indicates the sequence concatenation operation. $E_X \in \mathbb{R}^{|X| \times d}$ denote the hidden representations for each token in the input sequence.

After obtaining hidden representations of the input sequence, we feed them into the decoder for generating the output sequence Y in an auto-regressive style (i.e., token-by-token). At step t, the decoder generates the t-th token y_t and decoder state h_t^d as follows:

$$y_t, e_t^d = \text{Decoder}(E_X, E_{<t}^d, y_{t-1}), \tag{2}$$

where $\text{Decoder}(\cdot)$ is a multi-layer transformer decoder. $E_{<t}^d \in \mathbb{R}^{(t-1) \times d}$ are past states of the decoder during decoding. The conditional probability of the entire output sequence, denoted as $p(Y|X)$, can be computed as follows:

$$p(Y|X) = \prod_{t=1}^{|Y|} p(y_t|y_{<t}, X), \tag{3}$$

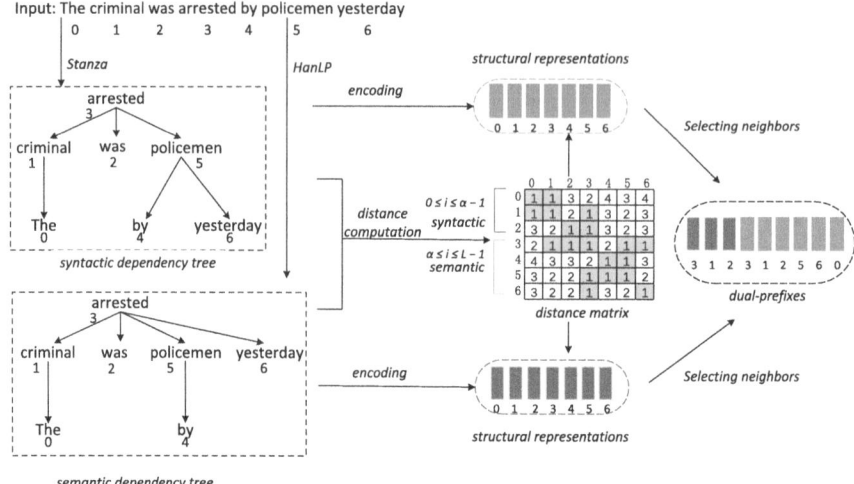

Fig. 3. An illustration of language-independent dual-prefix constructor. In the example, the distance δ is 1 and the length of the prefix is 9 where the length of the syntactic prefix α is 3. For the distance matrix, green means visible (i.e., $\boldsymbol{B}_{ij}=0$), and white means invisible.

where $p(y_t|y_{<t})$ is the probability of predicting token y_t, given the previous generated tokens $y_{<t}$ and the encoder input X.

3.3   Language-Independent Dual-Prefix Constructor

In this section, we introduce the language-independent dual-prefix constructor (Fig. 3) that enables incorporating both syntactic and semantic dependencies across languages. Explicitly, it is devised as follows:

Encoding of Dependency Structure. We utilize Stanza [17] for syntactic and HanLP [7] for semantic dependency parsing to construct dependency trees and calculate distances between token pairs. This process yields a distance matrix $\boldsymbol{H} \in \mathbb{R}^{|K| \times |K|}$ for a input sentence of length K. A hyper-parameter α determines the split between syntactic (α) and semantic ($L - \alpha$) prefix lengths in the total prefix length L, with H_{ij} indicating syntactic (if $0 \leq i \leq \alpha - 1$) or semantic (if $\alpha \leq i \leq L - 1$) distances. We use the mT5 encoder for token mapping into a cross-language semantic space, followed by employing a transformer as the structural encoder. Tokens attend to others within a distance δ, represented by a mask matrix:

$$\boldsymbol{B}_{ij} = \begin{cases} 0, & \text{if } \boldsymbol{H}_{ij} \leq \delta \\ -\infty, & \text{otherwise,} \end{cases} \tag{4}$$

where δ is a hyper-parameter. This approach incorporates the syntactic and semantic structure into the mask matrix. For the l-th transformer layer, the self-attention distribution P^l is calculated in the following manner:

$$P^l = \text{softmax}\left(\frac{QK^T}{\sqrt{d_k}} + B\right)V, \qquad (5)$$

where Q, K and V are queries, keys and values of the l-th layer, respectively, whose hidden size is d_k. P^l_{ij} signifies the attention from token i to token j. Leveraging syntactic and semantic distances' value between triggers and arguments [1], we refine self-attention using these distances, inspired by Cao et al. [4]:

$$A^l_{ij} = \frac{P^l_{ij}}{F_i H_{ij}}, \qquad (6)$$

where $F_i = \sum_j \frac{P_{ij}}{H_{ij}}$ is the normalization factor. $A^l \in \mathbb{R}^{|K| \times |K|}$ is the revised self-attention matrix, which is used to compute the l-th layer output of the transformer.

How to Select Neighbors. After encoding, we transform syntactic and semantic dependency trees from Stanza and HanLP into undirected graphs, using breadth-first search from triggers to select neighbors, which indicates trigger positions and dependencies. This process forms a trainable matrix $U \in \mathbb{R}^{L \times d}$ for syntactic (U_{sy}) and semantic (U_{se}) prefixes, appended to sequences in both encoder and decoder layers. With the injection of prefixes U, the computation of decoder state e^d_t in Eq. (2) is modified as follows:

$$e^d_t = \begin{cases} U^t_{sy} = U[t,:], & \text{if } 0 \le t \le \alpha - 1 \\ U^t_{se} = U[t,:], & \text{if } \alpha \le t \le L - 1 \\ \text{Decoder}(E_x, E^d_{<t}, y_{t-1}), & \text{otherwise,} \end{cases} \qquad (7)$$

Similarly, the computation of encoder states follows a comparable process.

3.4   Training and Inference

S2D's trainable parameters encompass both the encoder-decoder model parameters and the generated prefixes. To optimize the model, we employ the negative log-likelihood function. Following Cao et al. [4], to enhance adaptability to cross-lingual scenarios, we enhance multilingual generative PLMs with a copy mechanism, as proposed by See, Liu, and Manning [18]. This augmentation allows our S2D method to better handle situations where most tokens in the target output sequence are also present in the input sequence.

4   Experiment

4.1   Datasets and Evaluation Metrics

S2D undergoes evaluation on ACE-2005 [5] and ERE [19] datasets. The ACE-2005 dataset are annotated in three languages: English (en), Chinese (zh), and

Arabic (ar). As for the ERE dataset, annotations are available in two languages: English and Spanish (es). We adhere to the same dataset split and pre-processing methodologies as prior research [4,8]. Dataset statistics are shown in Table 1. Moreover, the EAE dataset is enriched with four SRL datasets: PropBank, Nom-Bank, FrameNet, and OntoNotes. Specifically, after converting the first three datasets into 1200 desired EAE task pieces according to §3.1, they are added to the English EAE training set. For Arabic and Chinese, we utilize PropBank annotations from OntoNotes.

Table 1. Statistics of the ACE 2005 and ERE datasets.

Dataset	Task	Language	# of train samples	# of dev samples	# of test samples
ACE2005	EAE	en	4202	450	403
		zh	2895	217	190
		ar	1743	117	198
ERE	EAE	en	6204	525	551
		es	3109	190	255

We use the F1-score for argument classification and select the closest matching string to the predicted trigger for fair evaluation.

Table 2. Experimental results (F1-score, %) of different models on the ACE-2005 dataset. The languages on left and right of → denote the source language and target language, respectively. "avg" denotes the average performance of all the combinations of the source language and the target language.

Models	PLMs	en→en	En→zh	en→ar	ar→ar	ar→en	ar→zh	zh→zh	zh→en	zh→ar	avg
Classification-based Methods											
OneIE	XLM-R-large	63.6	42.5	37.5	57.8	27.5	31.2	69.6	51.5	31.1	45.8
CL-GCN	XLM-R-large	59.8	29.4	25.0	47.5	25.4	19.4	62.2	40.8	23.3	37.0
GATE	XLM-R-large	67.0	49.2	44.5	59.6	27.6	26.3	70.6	46.7	37.3	47.6
GATE	mBART-50-large	65.5	43.0	38.9	58.5	27.5	26.1	65.9	45.3	30.2	44.5
GATE	mT5-base	59.8	47.7	32.6	45.4	20.7	21.0	64.0	35.3	22.8	38.8
Generation-based Methods											
TANL	mT5-base	59.1	38.6	29.7	50.1	18.3	16.9	65.2	33.3	18.3	36.6
X-GEAR	mT5-base	67.9	53.1	42.0	66.2	27.6	30.5	69.4	52.8	32.0	49.1
X-GEAR	mT5-large	71.2	54.0	44.8	68.9	32.1	33.3	68.9	55.8	33.1	51.3
LAPIN	mT5-base	69.0	57.1	41.8	67.0	29.5	36.0	68.0	55.3	36.2	51.1
LAPIN	mT5-large	74.4	59.3	52.0	69.4	36.8	44.3	72.5	59.1	37.4	56.1
S2D											
S2D	mT5-base	74.7	62.6	48.4	73.7	36.7	40.7	72.6	64.6	39.0	57.0
S2D	mT5-large	**77.1**	**63.0**	**52.9**	**74.8**	**38.7**	**45.6**	**73.3**	**68.3**	**41.7**	**59.5**

Table 3. Experimental results of different models on the ERE dataset.

Models	PLMs	en→en	en→es	avg
Classification-based Methods				
OneIE	XLM-R-large	64.4	56.8	60.6
CL-GCN	XLM-R-large	61.9	51.9	56.9
GATE	XLM-R-large	66.4	61.5	64.0
Generation-based Methods				
TANL	mT5-base	65.9	40.3	53.1
X-GEAR	mT5-base	69.8	57.9	63.9
X-GEAR	mT5-large	72.9	59.7	66.3
LAPIN	mT5-base	71.6	59.8	65.7
LAPIN	mT5-large	73.1	64.6	68.9
S2D				
S2D	mT5-base	76.8	66.2	71.5
S2D	mT5-large	**78.8**	**69.5**	**74.2**

4.2 Hyper-Parameters Setting

We employ *mT5-base* and *mT5-large* as encoder-decoder backbones. To embed dependency structure tokens into vectors, we use another raw mT5 encoder. The learning rate is initialized as $3e - 5$ or $1e - 4$ with a linear decay for mT5-base or mT5-large models, respectively. The batch size is 8. S2D employs beam search with a beam size of 4 for output generation. The length of total prefix L is set to 30. Semantic and syntactic prefix lengths are set to 20 and 10, respectively with the distance hyper-parameter δ at 2. The number of processed SRL data added to ACE05 English, Arabic, and Chinese training datasets are: 1200, 400, and 700, respectively. SRL data with arguments exceeding two words are removed. The number of training epochs is 100. All experiments are conducted on NVIDIA RTX A800 GPUs.

4.3 Baselines

We compare S2D with the following methods: 1) **OneIE** [12] employs XLM-R-large for monolingual EAE and adapts to cross-lingual settings via token embeddings. 2) **CL-GCN** [20], a graph-based model for EARL, integrates a named entity recognition component due to its dependency on pre-defined entities. 3) **GATE** [1], similar to CL-GCN but utilizing transformers for EARL, employs multilingual PLMs for token representation. 4) **TANL** [16], initially a monolingual EAE model, is adapted for cross-lingual tasks by using mT5-base. 5) **X-GEAR** [8] and 6) **LAPIN** [4] are template-based generative methods.

4.4 Main Experiment

We conduct experiments on ACE-2005 and ERE datasets. From Tables 2 and 3, we could find that: S2D sets new benchmarks on the ACE-2005 and ERE datasets, surpassing previous bests like LAPIN with increases of 3.4% and 5.3% in F1-score, respectively, which demonstrates its strength in ZCEAE. Besides, It significantly outperforms classification models like GATE(XLM-R-large) by up to 11.9%, thanks to leveraging argument dependencies and semantic knowledge. Compared to the generation model TANL, S2D shows superior results. This benefits from larger PLMs and the effective use of semantic information, including SRL and SDP, which highlights the value of semantic insights in enhancing cross-lingual EAE performance.

4.5   Ablation Study

To evaluate S2D's core SDP and SRL modules, we performed an ablation study: 1) w/o SDP, removing S2D's SDP component; 2) w/o SRL, excluding SRL external resources. Results are shown in Table 4. In the study, we find that removing SDP from S2D significantly lowers performance across all scenarios, particularly in cross-lingual contexts compared to monolingual ones, which highlights SDP's

Table 4. Ablation study of S2D on the ACE-2005 dataset. "avg_M" indicates the average of monolingual settings . "avg_C" indicates the average of cross-lingual settings. "avg_A" indicates the average of all the combinations of the source language and the target language. The average F1-score is followed by the drop (↓) compared with the method S2D.

Models	en→en	ar→ar	zh→zh	avg_M	en→ar	en→zh	ar→en	ar→zh	zh→ar	zh→en	avg_C	avg_A
S2D(mT5-base)	74.7	73.7	72.6	73.7	48.4	62.6	36.7	40.7	39.0	64.6	48.7	57.0
w/o SDP	74.0	71.7	72.1	72.6(↓1.1)	46.6	60.5	34.4	39.5	37.3	62.1	46.7(↓2.0)	55.4(↓1.6)
w/o SRL	73.8	71.1	72.0	72.3(↓1.4)	45.3	60.7	36.6	40.2	38.9	63.3	47.5(↓1.2)	55.8(↓1.2)
S2D(mT5-large)	77.1	74.8	73.3	75.1	52.9	63.0	38.7	45.6	41.7	68.3	51.7	59.5
w/o SDP	76.5	72.7	72.6	73.9(↓1.2)	50.9	60.3	36.0	44.2	40.1	65.5	49.5(↓2.2)	57.6(↓1.9)
w/o SRL	76.2	72.9	72.8	74.0(↓1.1)	52.4	62.6	37.2	45.3	41.2	66.5	50.9(↓0.8)	58.6(↓0.9)

Table 5. F1-score on the ACE-2005 dataset with different distance spans between triggers and arguments. Instances with distance spans exceeding 40 were scarce and therefore omitted from our analysis. "en → xx" denotes the average performance across "en → en", "en → zh", and "en → ar" settings. S2D and LAPIN, both leverage the mT5-base model.

Models	(0,5]	(5,10]	(10,15]	(15,20]	(20,30]	(30,40]
en → xx						
LAPIN	62.9	56.5	52.5	53.7	60.8	28.2
S2D	**67.8**	**62.4**	**58.3**	56.9	**65.0**	**32.5**
ar → xx						
LAPIN	47.2	43.7	41.7	41.4	10.6	**26.7**
S2D	**53.1**	**49.9**	**47.5**	**47.6**	**16.2**	25.4
zh → xx						
LAPIN	57.2	52.9	53.5	53.6	**60.5**	37.8
S2D	**62.0**	**58.4**	53.7	**59.1**	57.2	**42.6**

crucial role in ZCEAE. Similarly, removing SRL resources decreases performance in both contexts, with average F1-scores(i.e., avg_A) dropping up to 1.2%. This suggests that SRL effectively expands the training set, acting as data augmentation and thereby improving task performance. Notably, SDP's absence has a greater impact than SRL's removal, underscoring its significance in the model's effectiveness.

4.6   Sensitivity to the Distance Between Triggers and Arguments

The trigger-argument distance disparity across languages, with English at 9.8 and Chinese at 21.7 [4], suggests that a less sensitive EAE model towards these distance variations could reduce overfitting to the source language. Table 5 shows ACE-2005 results, with S2D outperforming LAPIN in nearly all distance distributions and notably over X-GEAR as distance increases, which indicates its ability to handle language-specific differences and mitigate overfitting.

4.7   Impact of Semantic Dependency Parsing Prefix Length

Table 6. F1-scores of S2D with different SDP prefix length on the ACE-2005. The top row of numbers represents the SDP prefix length. The "en" indicates the performance average of "en → en", "en → zh", and "en → ar".

Settings	5	10	15	20	25	30
en	61.1	60.5	60.9	61.9	60.8	61.1
zh	60.0	57.7	58.6	58.7	58.9	58.1
ar	49.1	50.6	49.7	50.4	48.7	50.4

We conduct experiments to explore the impact of semantic dependency parsing prefix length. As shown in Table 6, we can observe that for English and Chinese as the training languages, the performance of S2D decreases, then increases and decreases again. The initial decline may be due to the small number of SDP prefixes, leading to duplicates with syntactic dependency prefixes. For example, in the example we gave in Fig. 3, the first three syntactic dependency prefixes and SDP prefixes are same, which are 3, 1, and 2. As SDP prefix length grows, PLMs begin to absorb useful semantic knowledge, but performance plateaus or declines when the prefix becomes overly long.

5   Conclusion

In this paper, we propose the Semantic-Syntactic Driven framework (S2D) for the ZCEAE task. To incorporate the language-independent semantic information, we consider both semantic dependency parsing and semantic role labeling. Specifically, we devise a semantic role labeling source generator module to expand the source language dataset. Besides, we design a language-independent dual-prefix constructor module to obtain semantic and syntactic prefixes based on language-universal dependency structures. Experiments demonstrates that S2D achieves superior performance compared to previous state-of-the-art methods on two datasets.

Acknowledgement. This work is supported in part by National Key R & D Program of China (Grants No. 2022YFE0125400), National NSFC (Grants No. 62372072, 62102053, 62072060, 92067206 and 61972222), the General Program of Chongqing Science & Technology Commission (Grant No. CSTB2023TIAD-STX0035, CSTB2022TIAD-GPX0017, CSTB2022TIAD-STX0006), Chongqing Research Program of Basic Research and Frontier Technology (Grant No. cstc2022 ycjhbgzxm0058), Haihe Lab of ITAI (Grant No. 22HHXCJC00002), the Natural Science Foundation of Chongqing, China (Grant No. CSTB2022NSCQ-MSX1104), Key Laboratory of Big Data Intelligent Computing, Chongqing University of Posts and Telecommunications (Grant No. BDIC-2023-B-003), Regional Innovation Cooperation Project of Sichuan Province (Grants No. 2023YFQ 0028, 24QYCX0019), and Regional Science and Technology Innovation Cooperation Project of Chengdu City (Grant No. 2023-YF11-00023-HZ), Fundamental Research Funds for the Central Universities (Grant No. 2024CDJGF-003).

References

1. Ahmad, W.U., Peng, N., Chang, K.W.: Gate: graph attention transformer encoder for cross-lingual relation and event extraction. In: Proceedings of the AAAI Conference on Artificial Intelligence, vol. 35, pp. 12462–12470 (2021)
2. Baker, C.F., Fillmore, C.J., Lowe, J.B.: The berkeley framenet project. In: COLING 1998 Volume 1: The 17th International Conference on Computational Linguistics (1998)
3. Bies, A., Mott, J., Warner, C., Kulick, S.: English web treebank. Linguistic Data Consortium, Philadelphia, PA (2012)
4. Cao, P., Jin, Z., Chen, Y., Liu, K., Zhao, J.: Zero-shot cross-lingual event argument extraction with language-oriented prefix-tuning. In: Proceedings of the AAAI Conference on Artificial Intelligence, vol. 37, pp. 12589–12597 (2023)
5. Doddington, G.R., Mitchell, A., Przybocki, M.A., Ramshaw, L.A., Strassel, S.M., Weischedel, R.M.: The automatic content extraction (ace) program-tasks, data, and evaluation. In: Lrec, vol. 2, pp. 837–840. Lisbon (2004)
6. Dozat, T., Manning, C.D.: Simpler but more accurate semantic dependency parsing. arXiv preprint arXiv:1807.01396 (2018)
7. He, H.: Hanlp: Han language processing (2014). https://github.com/hankcs/HanLP
8. Huang, K.H., Hsu, I., Natarajan, P., Chang, K.W., Peng, N., et al.: Multilingual generative language models for zero-shot cross-lingual event argument extraction. arXiv preprint arXiv:2203.08308 (2022)
9. Li, H., Sanner, S., Luo, K., Wu, G.: A ranking optimization approach to latent linear critiquing for conversational recommender systems. In: Proceedings of the 14th ACM Conference on Recommender Systems, pp. 13–22 (2020)

10. Li, M., et al.: Timeline summarization based on event graph compression via time-aware optimal transport. In: Proceedings of the 2021 Conference on Empirical Methods in Natural Language Processing, pp. 6443–6456 (2021)

11. Li, S., Ji, H., Han, J.: Document-level event argument extraction by conditional generation. arXiv preprint arXiv:2104.05919 (2021)

12. Lin, Y., Ji, H., Huang, F., Wu, L.: A joint neural model for information extraction with global features. In: Proceedings of the 58th Annual Meeting of the Association for Computational Linguistics, pp. 7999–8009 (2020)

13. Meyers, A., et al.: The nombank project: An interim report. In: Proceedings of the Workshop Frontiers in Corpus Annotation at HLT-NAACL 2004, pp. 24–31 (2004)

14. Nguyen, T.H., Cho, K., Grishman, R.: Joint event extraction via recurrent neural networks. In: Proceedings of the 2016 conference of the North American Chapter of the Association for Computational Linguistics: Human Language Technologies, pp. 300–309 (2016)

15. Palmer, M., Gildea, D., Kingsbury, P.: The proposition bank: an annotated corpus of semantic roles. Comput. Linguist. **31**(1), 71–106 (2005)

16. Paolini, G., et al.: Structured prediction as translation between augmented natural languages. arXiv preprint arXiv:2101.05779 (2021)

17. Qi, P., Zhang, Y., Zhang, Y., Bolton, J., Manning, C.D.: Stanza: A python natural language processing toolkit for many human languages. arXiv preprint arXiv:2003.07082 (2020)

18. See, A., Liu, P.J., Manning, C.D.: Get to the point: Summarization with pointer-generator networks. arXiv preprint arXiv:1704.04368 (2017)

19. Song, Z., et al.: From light to rich ere: annotation of entities, relations, and events. In: Proceedings of the the 3rd Workshop on EVENTS: Definition, Detection, Coreference, and Representation, pp. 89–98 (2015)

20. Subburathinam, A., et al.: Cross-lingual structure transfer for relation and event extraction. In: Proceedings of the 2019 conference on empirical methods in natural language processing and the 9th International Joint Conference on Natural Language Processing (EMNLP-IJCNLP), pp. 313–325 (2019)

21. Zhang, T., Chen, M., Bui, A.A.T.: Diagnostic prediction with sequence-of-sets representation learning for clinical events. In: Michalowski, M., Moskovitch, R. (eds.) AIME 2020. LNCS (LNAI), vol. 12299, pp. 348–358. Springer, Cham (2020). https://doi.org/10.1007/978-3-030-59137-3_31

22. Zhang, Z., Strubell, E., Hovy, E.: Transfer learning from semantic role labeling to event argument extraction with template-based slot querying. In: Proceedings of the 2022 Conference on Empirical Methods in Natural Language Processing, pp. 2627–2647 (2022)

Bias-Rectified Multi-way Learning with Data Augmentation for Implicit Discourse Relation Recognition

Ziwei Zheng[1], Chao Liang[1], Wei Xiang[1,2], and Bang Wang[1(✉)]

[1] Hubei Key Laboratory of Smart Internet Technology, School of Electronic Information and Communications, Huazhong University of Science and Technology, Luoyu Road 1037, Wuhan 430074, Hubei, China
{ziwei_zheng,liangchao111,xiangwei,wangbang}@hust.edu.cn
[2] Faculty of Artificial Intelligence in Education, Central China Normal University, Wuhan, China

Abstract. Implicit Discourse Relation Recognition (IDRR) is a challenging but vital task in discourse analysis that focuses on identifying and classifying the relation between two arguments without explicit connectives. Previous research has focused on constructing sophisticated argument representations or utilizing labels' hierarchical information while neglecting the intrinsic prior relational bias, where some relation categories are significantly less frequent than others due to inherent linguistic properties. Furthermore, some works amalgamate Explicit Discourse Relation Recognition (EDRR) data with IDRR data to achieve data augmentation; however, the linguistic discrepancies between EDRR and IDRR data may mislead the relation recognition process. To address the prior relation bias and misleading from linguistic discrepancies, we propose a novel **B**ias-**RE**ctified **M**ulti-way Learning (BREM) model, which incorporates prior probability knowledge to assist in understanding the discourse relations and employs a PLM-based method for pretraining on the EDRR dataset to achieve data augmentation without introducing misleading effects. Experiments on the PDTB 3.0 corpus show that BREM outperforms previous models, especially in identifying less frequent relation senses, highlighting the effectiveness of our proposed model. The source code of our proposed model is publicly available at https://github.com/zzzziwy/NLPCC2024-BREM_for_IDRR.

Keywords: Implicit Discourse Relation Recognition · prior relation bias · Data Augmentation

1 Introduction

Implicit discourse relation recognition(IDRR) aims to classify the latent logical relation between two arguments(two clauses or sentences, denoted as Arg_1 and

---

Z. Zheng and C. Liang—Co-authors.

Arg_2 respectively) without explicit connectives [24,25]. IDRR is considered the essential step for many downstream Natural Language Process (NLP) applications, such as question answering [9], text generation [1], and summarization [4]. As illustrated in Fig. 1, implicit connective "so" does not exist between Arg_1 and Arg_2, but is inserted by annotators. The relation sense is annotated as *Contingency. Cause*, where *Contingency* is one of the four classes obtained by roughly dividing the relation sense(so-called top level), while *Cause* is a type obtained by dividing relation sense at a finer level of granularity(so-called second level).

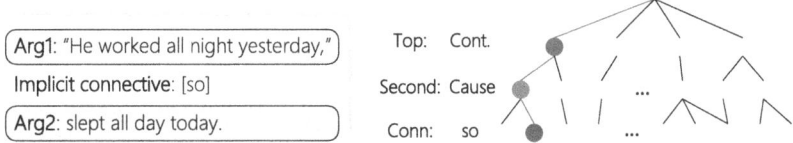

Fig. 1. An IDRR example in PDTB 3.0 corpus

The current IDRR task faces two primary challenges: the prior relation bias and the scarcity of data. Firstly, due to the inherent characteristics of natural language, there is a significant disparity in the frequency of occurrence among various relation senses, especially at the fine-grained level of categorization, which is called prior relation bias. However, previous research has exclusively focused on extracting information from individual samples, thereby overlooking the prior relation bias in the IDRR task, resulting in these models exhibiting generally poor performance on the relation senses with limited occurrence. Secondly, annotated IDRR data is scarce, and previous work has achieved data augmentation by extending the explicit discourse relation recognition (EDRR) dataset to the IDRR dataset. The distinction between the EDRR and IDRR datasets lies in the source of the connectives: in EDRR, they are present within the raw text, while in IDRR, inserted by the annotators. Due to the linguistic dissimilarity between explicit and implicit samples, researchers propose a variety of methods [6,7,18,20] to select the most suitable explicit samples from the EDRR dataset, thereby augmenting the IDRR dataset. However, regardless of the selection method employed, the semantic and categorical distribution gap between EDRR and IDRR datasets remains an unbridgeable divide.

Consequently, to maintain the model awareness of the prior relation bias throughout the training phase, we propose an adapted version of the focal loss [10], and apply Naive Bayes to comprehensively consider the relation sense within individual samples and the prior probability knowledge of relation senses. Furthermore, we train on the EDRR data leveraging Pre-trained Language Models (PLMs), which possess language comprehension capabilities, to learn the discourse relation paradigm without confounding the subsequent training of the IDRR task.

Motivated by such considerations, we propose the BREM model, which conducts both coarse-grained and fine-grained classification of relation senses at the top and second levels, respectively. Additionally, we incorporates the concept of connective node similarity to facilitate the training of the model, and integrates the information from the hierarchical structure of labels to perform joint probability prediction and to enforce structured hard constraints. Experiment results show that our proposed BREM model outperforms previous models for IDRR and achieves new state-of-the-art performance on the latest PDTB 3.0 corpus [21].

2   Related Work

2.1   Prompt Learning in IDRR

With the advent of large-scale PLMs such as RoBERTa [13], DeBERTa [3], and T5 [16], the paradigm of prompt learning has emerged as a novel and prevalent approach to IDRR task [11,22,23,26]. For example, [26] transforms the IDRR as a connective-cloze task to predict an answer word and map it to a relation sense. [22] instruct large-scale PLMs to mine the latent correlations between connectives and discourse relations via knowledge distillation. [11] is inspired by the annotation process of PDTB [21] to design a prompt-based model to explicitly generate discourse connectives and then insert them between the arguments, realizing the transition from an IDRR task to a simpler EDRR task. These works grounded in the paradigm of prompt learning, by transforming the IDRR task into the Masked Language Model (MLM) task that PLM excels at, fully exploit the latent knowledge of PLM from large-scale corpora, thereby enhancing the performance of the IDRR task. Consequently, the model we propose also adopts this prompt learning paradigm.

2.2   Hierarchy-Aware Multi-level IDRR

Recently, studies increasingly utilize annotated relation senses' hierarchical information [2,8,27]. For instance, [8] integrates global and local hierarchy-aware contrastive learning to fully leverage the hierarchical structure information of discourse relation labels, thereby enhancing the performance of implicit discourse relation recognition. [27] aggregates semantics from lower-level labels upward, dynamically updating the verbalizer to capture hierarchical connections between discourse relations. [2] propose a prompt-based path prediction method to utilize the interactive information and intrinsic senses among the hierarchy in IDRR. The aforementioned works has improved the predictive performance at various levels by integrating hierarchical information of labels.

2.3   Data Augmentation in IDRR

Researchers propose various methods to select suitable explicit samples in the EDRR dataset into an IDRR dataset [7,18]. For example, [18] proposes metrics for assessing the omittable degree of EDRR connectives and their contextual divergence across implicit and explicit discourse relations. Samples with highly omittable connectives and minimal contextual variance are candidates for selection. [7] utilized a teacher-student framework, in which a teacher model was trained on both EDRR and IDRR data, then transferred the learned feature to the student model through knowledge distillation. However, these researchers did not use a base model with strong linguistic understanding, which led to models being partially misrepresented by the EDRR data, which our BREM model circumvents.

3   Our Model: BREM

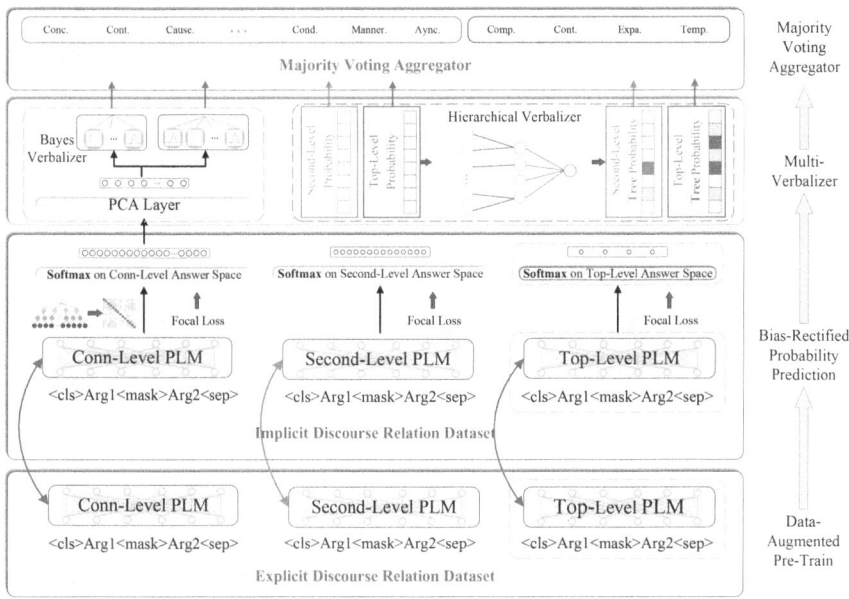

Fig. 2. Illustration of our BREM framework. It mainly contains four modules of the data-augmented pre-train, bias-rectified probability prediction, multi-verbalizer, and majority voting aggregator for the three levels' PLMs(conn-level, second-level, and top-level PLMs)

As Fig. 2 presents, our BREM model includes four modules of the data-augmented pre-train, bias-rectified probability prediction, multi-verbalizer, and majority voting aggregator. Firstly, our BREM model pre-trains three PLMs on the EDRR dataset for learning the conn-level, second-level and top-level discourse relation paradigm, respectively. Secondly, we train the model on the IDRR dataset to enhance the understanding of implicit discourse relations and model's capability to represent information related to connectives. Subsequently, we channel the probability predictions of discourse relations from the PLM through three verbalizers with distinct focuses to obtain three sets of answers. Ultimately, our BREM model applies majority voting decisions to the three sets of answers at the top level and second level, respectively, to obtain the final prediction results.

Task Formulation. Given an input argument pair $x_i = (Arg_1, Arg_2)$ and M hierarchical levels of labels $\mathbb{L} = \{\mathbb{L}^1, \mathbb{L}^2, \mathbb{L}^3\}$, where $\mathbb{L}^m$ is the set of labels at the m-th hierarchical level, the target label sequence is $y_i = (y_i^1, y_i^2, y_i^3)$, where $y_i^m \in \mathbb{L}^m$. Here, y_i^1, y_i^2 and y_i^3 represent the labels of top-level, second level and conn-level for the argument pair x_i, respectively.

3.1   Data-Augmented Pre-train

We pre-train three PLMs on the EDRR dataset. The first conn-level PLM predicts connectives from 77 options, which constitute the answer space V_3 of the conn-level PLM. Meanwhile, the second-level and top-level PLMs are endowed with virtual answer vocabularies that accommodate their respective relation sense labels. Namely, the answer space of second-level PLM is V_2 ={[Conc.], [Contr.], ..., [Sync.]}, while that of top-level PLM is V_1 ={[Comp.], [Conti.], [Expa.], [Temp.]}

Firstly, We reformulated $x = (Arg_1, Arg_2)$ into a prompt template

$$T(x) = <cls> +Arg_1 + <mask> +Arg_2 + <sep>, \tag{1}$$

where <cls>, <sep> and <mask> are special PLM tokens. The <cls> and <sep> denote the beginning and end of the sequence, respectively, while the <mask> signifies the position at which PLMs predict the answer word score. Then, we use PLMs to encode $T(x)$ and extract the hidden states of <mask> to obtain answer word scores at <mask> positions through the Masked Language Model (MLM) head. Finally, the prediction scores are normalized via a softmax layer in the pre-defined answer space into probabilities as follows:

$$P(v \in V | T(x)) = \frac{e^{p_{v_i}}}{\sum_{j=1}^{n} e^{p_{v_j}}}, \tag{2}$$

In the pre-train phase, we tune the PLMs' parameters based on the probability predictions via cross entropy loss as follows:

$$J(\theta) = -\frac{1}{K} \sum_{k=1}^{K} \mathbf{y}^{(k)} \log \mathbf{p}^{(k)} + \lambda \|\theta\|^2, \tag{3}$$

where $\mathbf{y}^{(k)}$ and $\mathbf{p}^{(k)}$ are the gold label and probability prediction of the k-th training instance respectively. θ are the regularized parameters and the λ is the regularization hyper-parameter.

3.2   Bias-Rectified Probability Prediction

We proceed to train the pre-trained PLMs on IDRR data. The training regimen closely mirrors the pre-training phase, (i.e. reformulation, encoding, prediction, and normalization) with the principal distinction residing in the loss functions. We have applied a modified focal loss [10] in the training phase as follows:

$$FL(\theta|\mathbf{y}, \mathbf{p}) = -\frac{1}{K} \sum_{k=1}^{K} \alpha \cdot (1 - \mathbf{p}^{(k)})^\gamma \cdot \mathbf{y}^{(k)} \cdot \log \mathbf{p}^{(k)} + \lambda \|\theta\|^2, \qquad (4)$$

$$\alpha_i = \log \frac{K}{K_i}, \qquad (5)$$

where $\alpha \in \mathbb{R}^{\|V\|}$ is weight factor. γ is a modulation factor. Equation 5 represents our innovatively proposed scheme for weight allocation, where K_i is the number of instances of the i-th class in the training set, which facilitates the model's adaptive rectification of the prior relation bias. By employing the modified focal loss, we intend to orient the model's focus towards infrequent discourse relations during the training process, thereby rectifying the prior relation bias.

Additionally, we design a similarity matrix $M_{simi} \in \mathbb{R}^{\|V_3\| \times \|V_3\|}$, in which the element $M_{simi}^{i,j}$ is determined by the similarity of the i-th connective to the j-th connective. We denote the set of connectives under the i-th label $L_i^1 \in \mathbb{L}^1$ as $\mathbb{C}_i^1$ and the set of connectives under the j-th label $L_j^2 \in \mathbb{L}^2$ as $\mathbb{C}_j^2$. Then $M_{simi}^{i,j}$ is specifically determined as follows:

$$M_{simi}^{i,j} = \begin{cases} \beta_0, conn_i = conn_j \\ \beta_1, conn_i \in \mathbb{C}_k^2 \quad and \quad conn_j \in \mathbb{C}_k^2 \\ \beta_2, conn_i \in \mathbb{C}_k^1, conn_i \in \mathbb{C}_n^2 \quad and \quad conn_j \in \mathbb{C}_k^1, conn_j \notin \mathbb{C}_n^2 \\ \beta_3, conn_i \in \mathbb{C}_k^1, conn_i \in \mathbb{C}_n^2 \quad and \quad conn_j \notin \mathbb{C}_k^1, conn_j \notin \mathbb{C}_n^2 \end{cases} \qquad (6)$$

where β_i is the similarity score of i-degree sibling nodes. When training the conn-level PLM, we select focal loss as the loss function, where the gold labels of connectives are transitioned from hard targets to soft targets based on M_{simi}. The comprehensive formulation of the loss function is delineated as follows:

$$Loss_x = FL(\theta|\mathbf{y}, \mathbf{p}), \qquad x \in \{PLM_1, PLM_2\} \qquad (7)$$

$$Loss_x = FL(\theta|\mathbf{y}', \mathbf{p}), \qquad x \in \{PLM_3\} \qquad (8)$$

$$\mathbf{y}' = \mathbf{y} \times M_{simi}, \qquad (9)$$

where PLM_1, PLM_2, and PLM_3 denote the top-level, second-level, and conn-level PLMs, respectively.

3.3   Multi-verbalizer

In this module, we have architected three verbalizers, each with a distinct focus, to amalgamate the probabilistic predictions across three levels, thereby yielding three sets of discourse relation recognition results.

The first verbalizer, designated as the Direct Verbalizer, focuses on considering the semantic features of individual samples. It maps the maximum values from the probability predictions to their corresponding relation senses.

For the second verbalizer, called the Hierarchical Verbalizer, the focus lies in integrating label hierarchical structure information into the prediction process. The top-level output is derived by correlating the second-level output of Direct Verbalizer to their respective parent labels. For the second-level result:

$$\mathbf{p}_{i,j}^{s'} = \mathbf{p}_i^t \cdot \mathbf{p}_{i,j}^s, \tag{10}$$

where $\mathbf{p}_i^t$ denotes the probability prediction of the i-th relation in the top level, $\mathbf{p}_{i,j}^s$ signifies the prediction of the second-level label which is the j-th label at the subset of the i-th top-level label. Then we map the maximum of the adjusted probability prediction to the corresponding second-level relation.

In the third verbalizer, called Bayes Verbalizer, we design a PCA layer [19] to reduce the dimension of probability prediction of connectives, and then input it into two Gaussian Naive Bayesian models constructed for top and second level, respectively, as follows:

$$P(C_j|X^{(k)}) = \frac{\prod_n^N P\left(X_n^{(k)}|C_j\right) \cdot P(C_j)}{P(X)}, \tag{11}$$

$$P(X_n|C_j) = \frac{1}{\sigma_{n,j}\sqrt{2\pi}} \exp\left(-\frac{(x - \mu_{n,j})^2}{2\sigma_{n,j}^2}\right), \tag{12}$$

where $X_n^{(k)}$ denotes the n-th feature value of k-th sample, $P(C_j)$ denotes the frequency of j-th class. Parameters $\sigma_{n,j}$ and $\mu_{n,j}$ are estimated using the Bayesian algorithm based on the feature distribution. In Eq. 11, we integrate the prior knowledge of the relation senses' probability $P(C)$ into the predictive process, enabling the model to consider both the individual sample features and the prior probability knowledge.

3.4 Majority Voting Aggregator

We implement a consensus-based aggregation strategy using a majority vote mechanism for the ultimate determination of relation sense. If two or more verbalizers agree on a relation sense, it is recognized as the final prediction. In cases where each verbalizer yields a distinct prediction, the prediction emanating from the verbalizer that exhibits the highest F1 score in the validation dataset is selected as the definitive choice.

4 Experiments

4.1 The PDTB Dataset

Our experiments are conducted on the Penn Discourse TreeBank(PDTB) 3.0 [21] corpus annotated on Wall Street Journal (WSJ) articles. It contains both the EDRR dataset and the IDRR dataset, and we use its EDRR dataset for pre-training after removing connectives, and its IDRR dataset for training and testing. Following previous work [11,22,27], we perform 4-way classifications at the top level and 14-way classifications at the second level, and we adopt PDTB-Ji data partition [5]: taking sections 2–20 as training set, sections 0–1 as dev set, sections 21–22 as test set.

4.2 Parameter Setting

We use the Pytorch library to implement the BREM model and choose RoBERTa-base [13] PLM and AdamW [14] optimizer. We set the mini-batch size to 8, the learning rate to 5e-6, 5e-6, and 1e-5 for conn-level, second-level, and top-level PLM, respectively, the similarity score space β to $(1, 0.2, 0.05, 0)$ All experiments are performed with CUDA on NVIDIA GTX 3090 Ti GPUs.

4.3 Baselines

- NNMA [12] merges the representations of two arguments for successive inter-active attention mechanisms.
- IPAL [17]: propagates self-attention into interactive attention by a cross-coupled network.
- TEPROMPT [23] introduces two auxiliary tasks, integrating the features learned from them into the primary task to inspire its performance in IDRR.
- GOLF [8] leverages contrastive learning to model the hierarchical structure of labels, thereby enhancing the representation of relation senses
- CPKG [22] guides large-scale PLM to mine the latent correlations between connectives and discourse relations via knowledge distillation.
- ADCG [11] proposes an end-to-end neural network model that predicts discourse relations by explicitly generating and integrating discourse connectives.
- ChatGPT [15] is a versatile large-scale language model(LLM), for which we have meticulously crafted user instructions to ensure its comprehension of the IDRR task definition and to facilitate the resolution of IDRR tasks.

4.4 Result and Analysis

Table 1 compares the overall performance of our BREM model with the baselines. We perform 4-way and 14-way classification on top-level and second-level relation sense on PDTB 3.0 corpus. Macro-F1 and accuracy are chosen to be metrics.

Our BREM model demonstrates superior performance over all preceding models when evaluated by the macro F1 score metric, especially in the second level. We attribute the excellent performance of the BREM model to its rectification of prior relation bias and the data augmentation achieved by introducing the EDRR dataset into the IDRR task. This will be further analyzed in our ablation study. Moreover, it can be observed from Table 1 that models utilizing dynamic encoding with PLMs, such as BERT and RoBERTa, outperform models like NNMA that are based on static language encoding. This is attributed to

Table 1. Comparison models on PDTB 3.0

Model	PLM	Top Level		Second Level	
		Acc	F1	Acc	F1
NNMA	GloVe	46.13	57.67	–	–
IPAL	BERT	49.45	58.01	–	–
TEPROMPT	RoBERTa	75.51	72.26	63.03	54.93
GOLF	RoBERTa	75.03	70.88	63.57	55.30
CPKG	RoBERTa	**77.00**	72.07	**66.21**	50.12
ADCG	RoBERTa	76.23	71.15	65.51	54.92
ChatGPT	–	36.97	31.93	20.74	14.05
OUR BREM	RoBERTa	76.26	**72.92**	63.90	**59.29**

the context sensitivity of dynamic encoding, which enables the models to adjust word representations dynamically based on the entire sentences. In contrast, GloVe embeddings are context-independent and incapable of capturing contextual information. Furthermore, we conducted experiments utilizing ChatGPT to address the IDRR task. The experimental results indicate that the performance of ChatGPT is significantly inferior to that of other models, suggesting that ChatGPT's capacity for understanding discourse relations, especially fine-grained discourse relations, is limited, and there remains a necessity for further research in the IDRR task.

Table 2. Second Level Label-wise F1(%)

type	label-wise F1			number of
	OURS	PEMI	TEpropmt	samples
Comparison.Concession	61.32($\downarrow$3.36)	**64.68**	58.31	1165
Comparison.Contrast	51.85($\downarrow$1.09)	**52.94**	52.73	742
Contingency.Cause	67.67($\downarrow$1.65)	69.04	**69.32**	4484
Contingency.Cause+Belief	0.00($\uparrow$0)	0.00	0.00	159
Contingency.Condition	**83.87**($\uparrow$8.87)	68.97	75.00	152
Contingency.Purpose	92.17($\downarrow$2.74)	91.49	**94.91**	1105
Expansion.Conjunction	**61.07**($\uparrow$2.25)	58.82	58.39	3586
Expansion.Equivalence	**39.29**($\uparrow$13.21)	0.00	26.08	254
Expansion.Instantiation	**72.20**($\uparrow$1.78)	70.42	67.83	1163
Expansion.Level-of-detail	**58.71**($\uparrow$3.24)	54.25	55.47	2601
Expansion.Manner	**63.16**($\uparrow$3.90)	59.26	59.26	673
Expansion.Substitution	**65.38**($\uparrow$16.4)	48.98	48.28	342
Temporal.Asynchronous	**69.27**($\uparrow$1.09)	66.67	68.18	1011
Temporal.Synchronous	**44.07**($\uparrow$8.59)	32.73	35.48	436

We can observe in Table 2 that the BREM model generally performs much better than the comparison model on relation sense with less occurrence (e.g., Cont. Condition, Expa. Substitution, etc.). Moreover, it has also yielded satisfactory outcomes in categories (e.g., Expa.Equivalence) where the predictive performance of other models was zero. It is attributed to the fact that BREM's use of modified focal loss prevents the model from leaning towards relation with more occurrence during training. Once again, this confirms the importance of considering the prior relation bias on the IDRR task. Furthermore, the performance of all three models in predicting the Cont.Cause+Belief category is notably poor. This is attributed to the fact that this category is not only exceedingly rare but also highly confusable with the Cont.Cause category.

4.5 Abalation Study

Table 3. Abalation study

Model	Top Level		Second Level	
	Acc	F1	Acc	F1
BREM w/o FL	75.77	71.86	**65.12**	56.54
BREM w/o HV	74.70	70.84	62.19	57.23
BREM w/o PT	74.98	70.97	63.12	57.58
BREM w/o FT	63.05	58.95	41.88	38.44
FULL MODEL	**76.26**	**72.92**	63.90	**59.29**

To examine the effectiveness of different modules, we design the following ablation studies.

1. BREM w/o FL is the BREM model where the PLMs are trained without modified focal loss but with Cross-Entropy loss.
2. BREM w/o HV is the BREM model without the Hierarchical Verbalizer.
3. BREM w/o PT is the BREM model without pre-training on EDRR dataset.
4. BREM w/o FT is the BREM model without fine-tuning on IDRR dataset.

We can observe that the BREM model, with the modified FL, achieves an F1 score improvement of 2.75% compared to the BREM w/o FL, which substantiates the significance of rectifying the prior relational bias in the IDRR task, thereby enhancing the capability of PLM to model discourse relations. However, in comparison to the full model, the BREM model w/o FL exhibits superior performance in terms of accuracy. This is attributed to the high proportion of negative samples, where the absence of FL leads to the correct prediction of a greater number of negative instances. Nevertheless, the incorporation of FL results in a higher F1 score, which is the primary metric of our concern. Furthermore, the F1 score of BREM outperforms that of BREM w/o HV by 2.06%, which is attributed to the incorporation of label hierarchy information into the BREM's predictive process. Ultimately, the 1.71% improvement on the F1 score of BREM over BREM w/o PT is attributed to the BREM's additional learning of implicit discourse relation paradigms on the EDRR dataset. Additionally, the phenomenon that BREM w/o FT outperforms NNMA and IPAL as depicted in Table 1, thereby corroborating this point.

4.6   Few Shot Learning

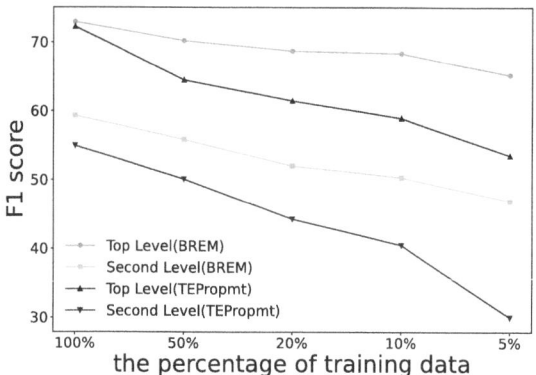

Fig. 3. Performance comparison of few shot learning on the PDTB corpus

It can be observed in Fig. 3 that the BREM model outperforms TEPrompt at the same percentage of training data. It can still maintain excellent performance in scenarios with scarce training data, which is due to the fact that the model fully exploits the implicit knowledge of PLM and realizes the alignment of PLM and IDRR tasks on the EDRR dataset.

5   Conclusion

In this paper, we argue that rectifying the prior relation bias and data augmentation from the EDRR dataset can improve performance on the IDRR task. We propose the BREM model, which realizes our ideas through voting decisions of three verbalizers with different focuses. Experimental results and ablation studies confirm the validity of our viewpoint and design goals. In future work, we will explore the applicability of this viewpoint on other NLP tasks. We have realized the BREM model to operationalize our idea, which adopts a specialized loss function to rectify prior relation bias and incorporates EDRR data into the pre-train phase. Experimental results have demonstrated the efficacy of our proposed methodology. Additionally, we conducted ablation studies to evaluate the contributions of individual modules and demonstrated the robustness of the model under low-resource scenarios. In the future, we will explore superior integration strategies among various language models to combine their respective strengths and enhance overall performance.

Acknowledgment. This work is supported by National Natural Science Foundation of China (No. 62172167).

References

1. Bosselut, A., Celikyilmaz, A., He, X., Gao, J., Huang, P.S., Choi, Y.: Discourse-aware neural rewards for coherent text generation. arXiv preprint arXiv:1805.03766 (2018)
2. Chan, C., et al.: Discoprompt: Path prediction prompt tuning for implicit discourse relation recognition. arXiv preprint arXiv:2305.03973 (2023)
3. He, P., Liu, X., Gao, J., Chen, W.: Deberta: Decoding-enhanced bert with disentangled attention. arXiv preprint arXiv:2006.03654 (2020)
4. Huang, Y.J., Kurohashi, S.: Extractive summarization considering discourse and coreference relations based on heterogeneous graph. In: Proceedings of the 16th Conference of the European Chapter of the Association for Computational Linguistics: Main Volume, pp. 3046–3052 (2021)
5. Ji, Y., Eisenstein, J.: One vector is not enough: Entity-augmented distributed semantics for discourse relations. Trans. Assoc. Comput. Linguist. **3**, 329–344 (2015)
6. Ji, Y., Zhang, G., Eisenstein, J.: Closing the gap: domain adaptation from explicit to implicit discourse relations. In: Proceedings of the 2015 Conference on Empirical Methods in Natural Language Processing, pp. 2219–2224 (2015)
7. Jiang, C., Qian, T., Liu, B.: Knowledge distillation for discourse relation analysis. In: Companion Proceedings of the Web Conference 2022, pp. 210–214 (2022)
8. Jiang, Y., Zhang, L., Wang, W.: Global and local hierarchy-aware contrastive framework for implicit discourse relation recognition. arXiv preprint arXiv:2211.13873 (2022)
9. Liakata, M., Dobnik, S., Saha, S., Batchelor, C., Schuhmann, D.R.: A discourse-driven content model for summarising scientific articles evaluated in a complex question answering task. In: Proceedings of the 2013 Conference on Empirical Methods in Natural Language Processing, pp. 747–757 (2013)
10. Lin, T.Y., Goyal, P., Girshick, R., He, K., Dollár, P.: Focal loss for dense object detection. In: Proceedings of the IEEE International Conference on Computer Vision, pp. 2980–2988 (2017)
11. Liu, W., Strube, M.: Annotation-inspired implicit discourse relation classification with auxiliary discourse connective generation. arXiv preprint arXiv:2306.06480 (2023)
12. Liu, Y., Li, S.: Recognizing implicit discourse relations via repeated reading: Neural networks with multi-level attention. arXiv preprint arXiv:1609.06380 (2016)
13. Liu, Y., et al.: Roberta: A robustly optimized bert pretraining approach. arXiv preprint arXiv:1907.11692 (2019)
14. Loshchilov, I., Hutter, F.: Decoupled weight decay regularization. arXiv preprint arXiv:1711.05101 (2017)
15. Ouyang, L., et al.: Training language models to follow instructions with human feedback. Adv. Neural. Inf. Process. Syst. **35**, 27730–27744 (2022)

16. Raffel, C., et al.: Exploring the limits of transfer learning with a unified text-to-text transformer. J. Mach. Learn. Res. **21**(140), 1–67 (2020)

17. Ruan, H., Hong, Y., Xu, Y., Huang, Z., Zhou, G., Zhang, M.: Interactively-propagative attention learning for implicit discourse relation recognition. In: Proceedings of the 28th International Conference on Computational Linguistics, pp. 3168–3178 (2020)

18. Rutherford, A., Xue, N.: Improving the inference of implicit discourse relations via classifying explicit discourse connectives. In: Proceedings of the 2015 Conference of the North American Chapter of the Association for Computational Linguistics: Human Language Technologies, pp. 799–808 (2015)

19. Shlens, J.: A tutorial on principal component analysis. arXiv preprint arXiv:1404.1100 (2014)

20. Wang, X., Li, S., Li, J., Li, W.: Implicit discourse relation recognition by selecting typical training examples. In: Proceedings of COLING 2012, pp. 2757–2772 (2012)

21. Webber, B., Prasad, R., Lee, A., Joshi, A.: The penn discourse treebank 3.0 annotation manual. Philadelphia, University of Pennsylvania **35**, 108 (2019)

22. Wu, H., Zhou, H., Lan, M., Wu, Y., Zhang, Y.: Connective prediction for implicit discourse relation recognition via knowledge distillation. In: Proceedings of the 61st Annual Meeting of the Association for Computational Linguistics (Volume 1: Long Papers), pp. 5908–5923 (2023)

23. Xiang, W., Liang, C., Wang, B.: Teprompt: Task enlightenment prompt learning for implicit discourse relation recognition. arXiv preprint arXiv:2305.10866 (2023)

24. Xiang, W., Wang, B.: A survey of implicit discourse relation recognition. ACM Comput. Surv. **55**(12), 1–34 (2023)

25. Xiang, W., Wang, B., Dai, L., Mo, Y.: Encoding and fusing semantic connection and linguistic evidence for implicit discourse relation recognition. In: Findings of the Association for Computational Linguistics: ACL 2022. pp. 3247–3257 (2022)

26. Xiang, W., Wang, Z., Dai, L., Wang, B.: Connprompt: connective-cloze prompt learning for implicit discourse relation recognition. In: Proceedings of the 29th International Conference on Computational Linguistics, pp. 902–911 (2022)

27. Zhao, H., He, R., Xiao, M., Xu, J.: Infusing hierarchical guidance into prompt tuning: A parameter-efficient framework for multi-level implicit discourse relation recognition. arXiv preprint arXiv:2402.15080 (2024)

Retrieval-Enhanced Template Generation for Template Extraction

Renyu Wang[1], Wei Xiang[1,2], Zhenhua Wang[1], and Bang Wang[1(✉)]

[1] School of Electronic Information and Communications, Huazhong University
of Science and Technology (HUST), Wuhan, China
{wry2021,xiangwei,u202013820,wangbang}@hust.edu.cn
[2] Faculty of Artificial Intelligence in Education, Central China Normal University,
Wuhan, China

Abstract. Template extraction tasks, such as role-filler entity extraction (REE) and template filling (TF), are classic problems in information extraction. Previous works usually simplify the TF task and focus only on the REE task. Few works attempt to tackle the more challenging template filling task. However, they design sophisticated models for individual REE or TF that can hardly tackle those two tasks concurrently. In this work, we formulate those two tasks as a template sequence generation problem, which can be solved by a unified generation framework. Specifically, we leverage the template to guide the model to extract event entities from a document and fill them into the predefined template. Furthermore, to enhance the model's understanding of the input document and capture the dependency between similar templates, we employ a retrieval-enhanced approach. The most semantically similar template is retrieved from the training data and augments the current context with similar structures and semantic information captured in the retrieved demonstration. Extensive experiments on the MUC-4 dataset demonstrate the generality and effectiveness of our proposed model. (The source code is available at https://github.com/luwry/RTG4TE).

Keywords: Template filling · Role-filler entity extraction · Retrieval-enhanced template generation

1 Introduction

Template extraction requires extracting event-based templates across an entire document, and is beneficial for various downstream tasks, including knowledge graph construction [27] and relation extraction [15,26]. In this work, we study two template extraction tasks: document-level role-filler entity extraction (REE) task and template filling (TF) task. REE aims to extract all event-relevant entities from a document and identify the role type for each extracted entity. Template filling is a more challenging task, it further determines the number of templates in a document and corresponding template types, as well as assigning each of the candidate entities to the event template it participates in. An

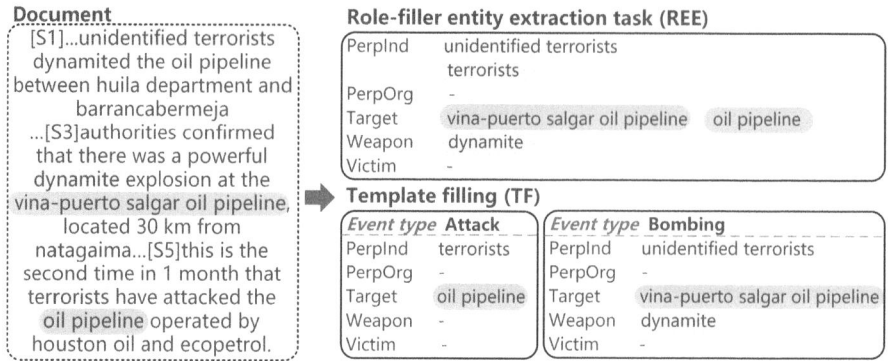

Fig. 1. An example of template extraction. A generic template is extracted for document-level REE task. Two event templates including an **Attack** event template and a **Bombing** event template are extracted for TF task.

example of template extraction is shown in Fig. 1. In the REE task, only a single event template is extracted from the entire document. In the TF task, multiple event templates are extracted from the document and the type of each extracted event template is also identified.

Prior works usually simplify the TF task assuming that there is a generic template and focus only on REE task [5,6,9]. Few works attempt to tackle the more challenging template filling task which requires extracting multiple event templates along with their corresponding template types. However, they design sophisticated models for each task independently and can hardly tackle those two tasks concurrently. Considering the issue, we use a generalized template extraction framework to extract one or multiple event templates from the document, unifying REE and TF in a generation paradigm. In this paper, we propose a unified retrieval-enhanced template generation framework for REE and TF, named RTG4TE, which takes a document and a retrieved demonstration as input and follows the predefined event template to fill event entities into slots in the event template. The template type and slot filling entities can then be extracted from the generated event template. In particular, we design the output template in HTML-tag style with special slot-type tokens that are more flexible and easily decoded. Moreover, RTG4TE retrieve the most semantically similar training example for the current input document and transform it into a demonstration style to enhance the input context learing. Through the retrieved demonstration, RTG4TE can fully leverage the annotated training data and enable our model to better understand the output process, so as to improve the performance.

Our contributions can be summarized as follows:

We propose a generalized template generative method to unify REE and TF in a generation paradigm. The design prompt template is in HTML-tag style with special slot-type tokens that are more flexible and easily decoded.

We retrieve the most semantically similar example to enable our model to learn the output template process explicitly. The retrieved example not only makes full use of the semantic information of event templates but also provides rich information in low-resource scenarios.

We demonstrate state-of-the-art results on the MUC-4. Ablation studies and the impact analysis of similarity-based retrieval further justify our design.

2   Related Work

Template Extraction. Document-level template extraction tasks, such as REE task and template filling task have a long history which were originally proposed in the Message Understanding Conferences [20]. Previous works usually focus on REE task and use hand-crafted discrete features with pipeline-based methods to extract role-filler mentions into corresponding slots for one event template [10]. Recently, following renewed interest in document-level information extraction, researchers revisit MUC with an end-to-end nernal network method to automatically learn feature representations [5,8,25], and propose new evaluations such as CEAF-REE metric [6]. For example, [6] proposes a generative Transformer-based encoder-decoder framework (GRIT) to model contexts at document-level and capture cross-role dependencies in the template structure. [9] incorporates label semantics into the template to help a pre-trained language model (PLM) in correctly identifying entities. While fewer works have explored the complete template filling task. To our knowledge, [7] firstly revisits this full task recently, they build an end-to-end generative transformers for template filling, where carefully-designed event templates are used to capture cross-event dependencies. [4] utilizes Markov decision process to iteratively generate templates without the pre-defined template orders. Different from the work above, we not only explored the simplified REE task but also further considered the more complex template filling task with a generalized template generation framework to tackle those two tasks concurrently. There are also works on unsupervised template schema induction [2,3] and open-domain event extraction from documents [17]. Without predefined event types and semantic roles, event schemas are learned through event clustering, and event information are extracted from event schemas.

Demonstration-Based Learning. The demonstration term is originally proposed by the GPT3, where the demonstrations are randomly sampled from training data [1]. Recent studies have shown leveraging a retrieval module to augment neural networks is simple-yet-effective [19,21,23]. For example, [16] proposes a semantically-similar retrieval strategy to retrieve examples that are semantically-similar to a test query sample to formulate its corresponding prompt. [13] constructs task demonstrations and let the input be prefaced by task demonstrations for Named Entity Recognition (NER). [28] designs pathological demonstrations to take a deep dive of the robustness of demonstration-based sequence labeling for NER task. Our method differs from these studies from: (1) the demonstration-enhanced paradigm is designed specifically for template extraction task. (2) Our proposed generative method is more reliable since the prediction space can be alignment with the demonstrations.

3   A Unified Formulation of Template Extraction

Given a tokenized input document $D = [w_1, w_2, ..., w_i]$ where each w_i is a token, the unified template extraction aims to extract a collection of structured templates $\{(t_1, S_1), ..., (t_n, S_n)\}$ where n represents the number of templates that exist in the document, t is template type and S represents all slot types corresponding to the template t.

For TF task, we defined a template ontology as a set of template types $\mathcal{T}$, where each template type $t \in \mathcal{T}$ corresponds to a set of slot types S_t. A template instance consists of $(s_k : V_k)$ pairs, where $s_k \in S_t$, $V_k \in V$ presents a subset of all extracted slot values for filling slot type s_k. $V_k = \emptyset$ indicates that there is no slot for filling slot type s_k. For the example in Fig. 1, the slot values for slot type Target are vina-puerto salgar oil pipeline and oil pipeline.

We reduce the template extraction to extract a single template for the REE task. The target is to extract multiple $(s_k : V_k)$ pairs for pre-defined slot types. $V = \emptyset$ indicates an empty template exists in the current document.

4   Methods

In this section, we describe the retrieval-enhanced template generation approach including (1) the template construction and the output template format; (2) how to construct the demonstration; (3) training and inference details.

4.1   Retrieval-Enhanced Template Generation

As illustrated in Fig. 2, given an input document $D = [w_1, w_2, ..., w_i]$ and a queried template type Q_t, RTG4TE first constructs retrieved demonstration R_t and the gold output template O. Then RTG4TE concatenates R_t, Q_t and D via the separation token <SEP>, and feeds them into BART-Encoder to gain the demonstration-enhanced input representation X_i. RTG4TE further feeds X_i and O into BART-Decoder and generates event templates $Y_i = \{y_{im}\}_{m=1}^{|Y_i|}$.

$$X_i = Encoder([Q_t; R_t; D]) \tag{1}$$

$$Y_i = Decoder([X_i; O]) \tag{2}$$

where Y_i denotes the annotated output template representation. Through iterating generation Y_i process for all template types $\mathcal{T}$, then the complete event templates $Y = \{Y_i\}_{i=1}^{|\mathcal{T}|}$ are obtained.

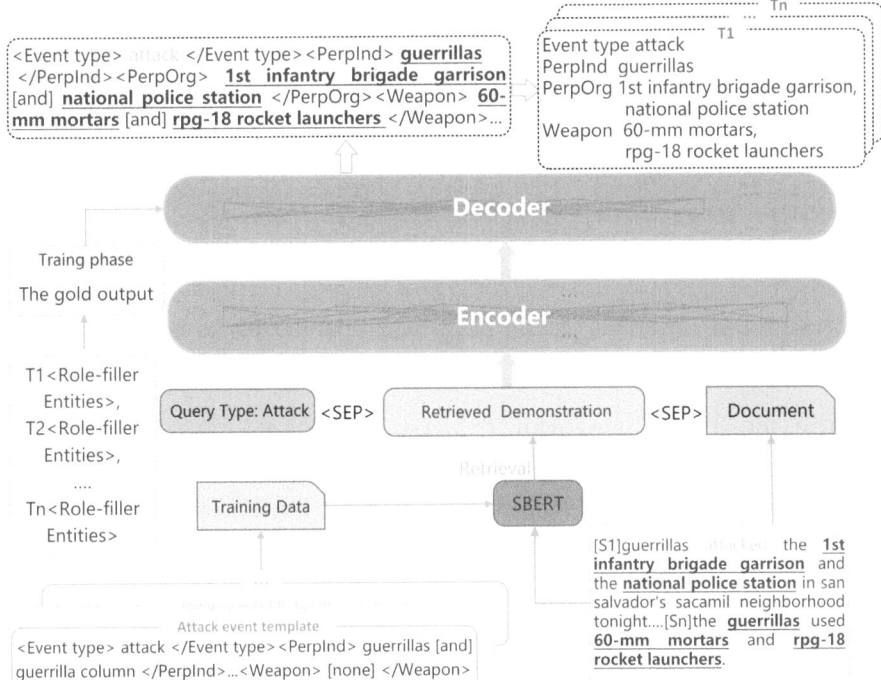

Fig. 2. An illustration of RTG4TE for predicting `Attack` event templates. The input consists of a given document, a query event type text and the retrieval demonstration which is retrieved from the annotated training data. RTG4TE is trained to generate output templates, each of output templates is filled with the event type and role-filler entities (underlined words). The event information is then decoded from the output template.

4.2   Template Construction

We create two templates for TF and REE tasks respectively as shown in Table 1. The template consists of special slot type tokens and the special placeholder token [none]. The template is pre-defined in the ontology. The pre-defined template defines the output template format and guides the model to explicitly learn the output template process.

The decoder input is constructed as slotted templates. Considering the example in Fig. 2, there is an `attack` event, then the decoder input is `<Event type>` attack `</Event type>` `<PerpInd>` guerrillas `</PerpInd><PerpOrg>` 1st infantry brigade garrison [and] national police station `</PerpO rg><Target>` [none] `</Target><Victim>` [None] `</Victim><Weapon>` 60-mm mortars [and] rpg-18 rocket launchers `</Weapon>`. The underlined strings are slot-filling entities corresponding to a slot type. For instance, the slot type is `Weapon` and the corresponding slots are 60-mm mortars and rpg-18 rocket launchers. Multiple slots for the same slot type are concatenated with

Table 1. Pre-defined Templates for TF and REE tasks.

Task	Template
TF	$\langle Event\ type\rangle[none]\langle/Event\ type\rangle\langle PerpInd\rangle[none]\langle/PerpInd\rangle$ $\langle PerpOrg\rangle[none]\langle/PerpOrg\langle Target\rangle[none]\langle/Target\rangle\langle Victim\rangle$ $[none]\langle/Victim\rangle\langle Weapon\rangle[none]\langle/Weapon\rangle$
REE	$\langle PerpInd\rangle[none]\langle/PerpInd\rangle\langle PerpOrg\rangle[none]\langle/PerpOrg\rangle\langle Target\rangle$ $[none]\langle/Target\rangle\langle Victim\rangle[none]\langle/Victim\rangle\langle Weapon\rangle[none]\langle/Weapon\rangle$

the special token [and]. So the output template is flexible to decode multiple slots.

4.3   Retrieved Demonstration Construction

To facilitate the model to better understand the input document and learn the template generation paradigm, we provide a retrieved demonstration in the model input. Specifically, the demonstration is constructed with an example from training set that is most semantically similar to the input document. We first employ the S-BERT [22] to encode all documents in training set. For an input document, we rank other candidate documents based on the cosine similarity scores with current input:

$$cos\_sim(D_i, D_r) = (D_i^{emb})^T \cdot D_r^{emd} \tag{3}$$

where D_i^{emb} and D_r^{emd} represent the input and candidate document embeddings encoded by S-BERT[1], respectively. Next, the top-ranked candidate is retrieved and transformed to an annotation slotted template.Note that we use the unified annotation template for both demonstrations and model predictions, which can enhance the interaction between them.

4.4   Training and Inference

The training objective is to generate output templates which are filled with the gold labels. For the example in Fig. 2, each template is expected to replace the placeholder [none] with the gold event type and gold role-filler entities. If there are multiple entities for the same slot type, they are concatenated by the special token [and]; if there is no predicted entity for one slot type, the corresponding placeholder [none] is retained in the predicted template. For the case where there are multiple event templates for the same event type, the output consists of multiple event templates, and each template contains an event type and corresponding entities.

The generation probability of output template Y_i is computed by the encoder input and the previous generated tokens across all the time steps.

$$P(Y_i|R_t, Q_t, D_i) = \prod_{m=1}^{|Y_i|} P(y_m|y_{<m}, R_t, Q_t, D) \tag{4}$$

---

[1] https://www.sbert.net/docs/quickstart.html.

The model is trained by minimizing the negative log-likelihood across all instances in the dataset E. The θ represents the model parameters.

$$\mathcal{L}(E) - -\sum_{i=1}^{|E|} \log P(Y_i|R_t, Q_t, D_i, \theta) \tag{5}$$

During the inference phase, the model iteratively generates event templates for each event type through enumerating all event types. Then we apply string matching between the generated event template and the pre-defined output template to obtain the slots values including event types and slotted entities.

5   Experiments

Experimental Setup. We evaluate the RTG4TE on the MUC-4 dataset[2] [20] for the document-level role-filler entity extraction (REE) and template filling (TF). MUC-4 contains 1,700 English documents concerning geopolitical conflict and terrorism in Latin America. Documents are annotated with six template types including `attack, arson, bombing, murder, robbery, forced work stoppage`. Each document may contain multiple templates or no template. All templates share the same five slot types - `PerpInd` (an individual perpetrator), `PerpOrg` (a group or organizational perpetrator), `Target` (physical objects targeted by the incident), `Victim` (victims of the incident), and `Weapon` (weapons employed by the perpetrators). Each slot is filled with zero or more entities (role-filler). As the previous work [6,9], we use the same dataset pre-processing procedure and split the dataset into training/validation/testing set with 13:2:2.

We fine-tune the pre-trained BART models [14], and consider AdamW optimizer [18] with learning rate as 1e-5 and weight decay as 1e-05. We set the batch size as 8 for base models and 1 for large models. The maximum length of our proposed model is 512 and 1024 for base and large models respectively. During test time, our model applied beam search with beam width 4 to generate tokens. All experiments are run on NVIDIA GeForce RTX 3090.

Evaluation Metrics. Following [6], we use CEAF-REE metric for the TF and REE. The CEAF-REE metric computes an optimal alignment between predicted and gold templates by using Kuhn Munkres algorithm [11,12]. CEAF-REE selects the template alignment that yields the highest micro-F1 over all slots including *template type* in the template. Recently, [4] proposes the CEAF-RME which is different from CEAF-REE, it treats the template type individually and elides *template type* from the F1 calculation.

  Baselines

- **ITERX** [4], which treats the template filling task as a Markov decision process (MDP), where an action corresponds to a single template generation, and states are sets of predicted templates.

---

[2] https://www-nlpir.nist.gov/related_projects/muc/muc_data/muc_data_index. html.

- **GTT** [7], is the recent first attempt to build an end-to-end learning framework for the TF task. It can extract multiple events from a document and substantially outperforms pipeline-based approaches.
- **GRIT** [6], a generative transformer-based encoder-decoder framework. The model is evaluated by a CEAF-REE metric on the MUC-4 REE task.
- **TEMPGEN** [9], that formulate the REE task as a template generation problem, allowing model to exploit label semantics.
- **NST** [5] is a end-to-end neural sequence tagging model for document-level role-filler entity extraction. To dynamically aggregate information captured by neural representations learned at sentence-level and paragraph-level.
- **DYGIE++** [24] is a span enumeration based multitask framework for three information extraction tasks: named entity recognition, relation extraction and event extraction.

Table 2. Performance (%) evaluated by CEAF-REE and CEAF-RME merics for template filling task. The highest scores are highlighted in bold and the second-highest scores are underlined.

	CEAF-REE			CEAF-RME		
	P	R	F1	P	R	F1
GTT (BERT-base)	61.7	42.4	50.2	55.0	36.8	44.1
TEMPGEN (BART-base)	55.7	40.0	46.4	58.3	31.0	40.5
TEMPGEN (BART-large)	63.7	37.4	47.2	61.3	32.9	42.8
ITERX (BERT-base)	52.3	51.1	51.7	47.2	45.0	46.1
ITERX (BART-base)	49.8	45.7	47.6	44.8	40.1	42.3
ITERX (T5-large)	60.9	46.9	53.0	55.8	42.4	48.2
RTG4TE (BART-base)	57.0	51.7	54.2	52.3	45.7	48.8
RTG4TE (BART-large)	**70.3**	**53.0**	**60.4**	**65.5**	**46.5**	**54.4**

Overall Results. Table 2 presents the overall results of our proposed model and baselines. We can observe that:

(1) Our proposed model significantly outperforms the baseline methods under two metrics. Comparing the highest baseline for base pre-trained language models (PLMs), it achieves a +2.5%/+2.7% improvement in CEAF-REE F1 and CEAF-RME F1 respectively. These results demonstrate the effectiveness of our design.
(2) While using large versions of PLMs, RTG4TE gains an even further improvement of +7.4%/+6.2% on CEAF-REE F1 and CEAF-RME F1 respectively. These observations suggest using larger pre-trained language models are better.
(3) Futhermore, there is a significant gap between CEAF-REE and CEAF-RME, we conjecture that the CEAF-RME meric excludes the template type score from the F1 calculation. The template type score is higher than slot type scores, which leads to a higher CEAF-REE F1.

Table 3. Performance (%) evaluated by CEAF-REE meric for REE task. The highest scores are highlighted in bold and the second-highest scores are underlined.

	CEAF-REE		
	P	R	F1
DYGIE++	57.0	46.8	51.4
NST	56.8	48.9	52.6
GRIT (BERT-base)	<u>64.2</u>	47.4	54.5
TEMPGEN (BART-base)	**68.6**	<u>49.9</u>	<u>57.8</u>
RTG4TE (BART-base)	63.6	**57.5**	**60.4**

Table 4. Ablation study for the components of RTG4TE on TF and REE.

	TF task			REE task		
	P	R	F1	P	R	F1
RTG4TE (BART-base)	<u>57.0</u>	51.7	**54.2**	63.6	**57.5**	60.4
w/o retrieval	51.9	51.2	51.5	62.0	55.6	58.6
w random retrieval	51.7	<u>52.9</u>	52.3	62.8	54.8	58.5
w multiple retrieval	**58.8**	45.2	51.1	62.2	52.5	56.9
w random order 1	49.5	**58.0**	<u>53.4</u>	63.4	<u>56.0</u>	<u>59.5</u>
w random order 2	56.2	49.9	52.9	<u>67.0</u>	52.1	58.6
w random order 3	54.7	51.3	53.0	**67.5**	52.1	58.8

As shown in Table 3, we additionally study the performance of the REE task. (1) RAG4REE outperforms all baselines in CEAF-REE F1 score and surpasses the highest baseline by +2.6% for the base PLMs. These results provide compelling evidence for the effectiveness of our proposed model. (2) Comparing the experimental results of the TF task in Table 2, template filling is a more challenging task than the REE task. (3) Moreover, our proposed method shows a more significant improvement in the TF task compared to in REE task, indicating that the retrieval module plays a more prominent role in extracting multiple types of templates, and the diversity of demonstrations for the TF task which contain different types of templates can facilitate the improvement of model performance.

Ablation Studies. Table 4 demonstrates how different components of RTG4TE affects the performance of template filling and role-filler entity extraction. We observe that: (1) removing `retrieval` results in performance drops, which validates the necessary of the retrieval component. (2) Replacing `the similarity retrieval` with `random retrieval`, the CEAF-REE F1 also drops on both two tasks, indicating that the introduction of similarity retrieval examples enhances the ability of RTG4TE to generate correct entities. (3) In addition, the perfor-

Table 5. Performance of RTG4TE under the CEAF-REE evaluation with a similarity score > 0.7 or ≤ 0.7.

	> 0.7			≤ 0.7		
	P	R	F1	P	R	F1
Template filling task: TF task						
RTG4TE (BART-base)	60.7	**50.1**	**54.9**	51.9	**54.4**	**53.1**
w/o retrieval	**61.7**	44.0	51.4	**53.0**	48.2	50.5
w random retrieval	58.3	47.3	52.2	47.6	49.8	48.7
Role filling Entity Extraction task: REE task						
RTG4TE (BART-base)	66.3	**56.8**	**61.2**	56.6	**58.9**	**57.7**
w/o retrieval	68.7	49.9	57.8	54.0	52.4	53.2
w random retrieval	**69.4**	51.6	59.2	**56.7**	57.7	57.2

mance of `retrieving multiple templates` drops 3.1% and 2.8% of CEAF-REE F1-scores for TF and REE tasks. This can be explained by multiple retrieved examples are bounded by the model's maximum input length and the long contexts make it difficult for RTG4TE to learn from. (4) We also study the influence of slot/role order in the template. RTG4TE with random orders still achieve good performance but slightly worse than the original order. This suggests that RTG4TE is not very sensitive to different templates while providing appropriate order of roles can lead to a small improvement.

Influence of Similarity-Based Retrieval. In Table 5, we study the impact of the similarity score between retrieval documents and input documents on both TF and REE tasks. We divide the original test dataset into two subsets according to a similarity score > 0.7 or ≤ 0.7. Comparing with the method RTG4TE, the performance of RTG4TE without retrieval is substantially dropped on both subsets. While with a random retrieval, there is also a drop of the performance. It is interesting that the performance of RTG4TE slightly improves with random retrieval compared to not applying retrieval for REE task. This is consistent with findings in other areas of NLP, exploring how random retrieval of samples can lead to performance improvements, especially in the few-shot learning setting [21]. Furthermore, we notice that the F1-score on the subset for a similarity score > 0.7 is higher than that ≤ 0.7, indicating the retrieval information with higher similarity scores is effective.

Since the retrieval examples can effect the performance for TF and REE, we randomly drop 40% of retrieval examples during the training or inference phases to explore the robustness of retrieval-based method. `Test Drop 40%` performs dropping 40% during the inference phase only, while `Train-test Drop 40%` applies dropping during both training and inference phases. From Fig. 3, we can observe that dropping 40% retrieval examples leading to a performance reduction for both TF and REE task, particularly 4.9% and 1.6% for CEAF-

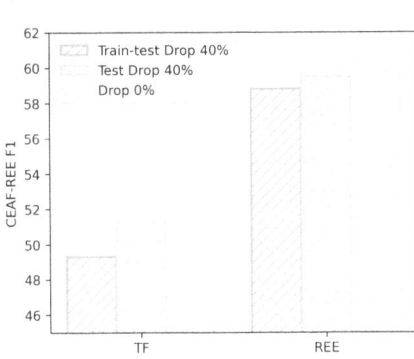

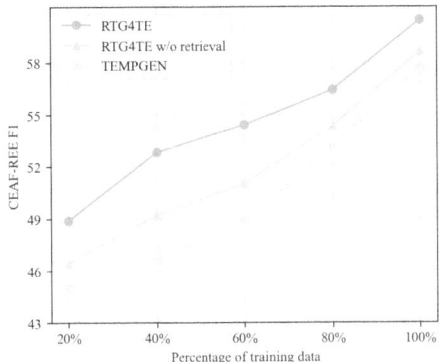

Fig. 3. Experiment result of the robustness of retrieved demonstrations.

Fig. 4. REE test set performance with different proportions of training data.

Table 6. Types of errors made by RTG4TE for REE task.

	PerpInd	PerpOrg	Target	Victim	Weapon	All
Misidentified	46(39.3%)	32(46.4%)	44(39.3%)	21(47.7%)	25(58.1%)	168(43.6%)
Missing	71(60.7%)	37(53.6%)	68(60.7%)	23(52.3%)	18(41.9%)	217(56.4%)

REE F1 during both training and inference phases. This shows that the number of demonstrations affects the model performance. While dropping demonstrations during the inference phases only leads to a recovery of 2.0% and 0.7% for TF and REE tasks respectively, compared to dropping during both training and inference phases. These results further demonstrating that more retrieved demonstrations boost the model performance.

Low-Resource Settings. To verify the effectiveness of RTG4TE without sufficient annotations, we conduct low-resource experiments on the REE task using different proportions (20%, 40%, 60%, and 80%) of training data. As seen in Fig. 4, both RTG4TE and RTG4TE w/o retrieval outperform TEMPGEN across all settings. These results validate the data efficiency of our proposed model. And RTG4TE is always better than RTG4TE w/o retrieval, which confirms the effectiveness of retrieved demonstrations for low-resource settings.

Error Analysis. Table 6 categorizes types of role-filler entity extraction errors made by RTG4TE. The majority of errors are due to missing entities, around 56.4% of errors are caused by the failure to extract entities from the documents. Moreover, for the role PerpInd and Target, the percentages of missing entities are higher than other roles, indicating that human names are difficult to be extracted and the number of Target entities is large and more Target entities need to be generated.

6   Concluding Remarks

In this paper, we have introduced a Retrieval enhanced Template Generation for Template Extraction (RTG4TE) which frames TF and REE tasks as a unified template extraction framework. Demonstrations are used to help RTG4TE explicitly learn the output process and augment the PLM for understanding different tasks. Experiment results show that RTG4TE outperforms the current state-of-the-art methods on TF and REE tasks. Under different proportions of training data, RTG4TE demonstrates robustness across all settings, showing the effectiveness of RTG4TE in low-resource scenarios. In the future, we are interesting in extending our method to multi-slot relation extraction tasks.

Acknowledgments. This work is supported by National Natural Science Foundation of China (No. 62172167).

References

1. Brown, T., et al.: Language models are few-shot learners. Adv. Neural. Inf. Process. Syst. **33**, 1877–1901 (2020)
2. Chambers, N.: Event schema induction with a probabilistic entity-driven model. In: EMNLP, pp. 1797–1807 (2013)
3. Chambers, N., Jurafsky, D.: Template-based information extraction without the templates. In: ACL, pp. 976–986 (2011)
4. Chen, Y., Gantt, W., Gu, W., Chen, T., White, A., Van Durme, B.: Iterative document-level information extraction via imitation learning. In: EACL, pp. 1858–1874 (2023)
5. Du, X., Cardie, C.: Document-level event role filler extraction using multi-granularity contextualized encoding. In: ACL, pp. 8010–8020 (2020)
6. Du, X., Rush, A., Cardie, C.: GRIT: generative role-filler transformers for document-level event entity extraction. In: EACL, pp. 634–644 (2021)
7. Du, X., Rush, A., Cardie, C.: Template filling with generative transformers. In: NAACL, pp. 909–914 (2021)
8. Gantt, W., Kriz, R., Chen, Y., Vashishtha, S., White, A.: On event individuation for document-level information extraction. In: Findings of EMNLP, pp. 12938–12958 (2023)
9. Huang, K.H., Tang, S., Peng, N.: Document-level entity-based extraction as template generation. In: EMNLP, pp. 5257–5269 (2021)
10. Huang, R., Riloff, E.: Peeling back the layers: detecting event role fillers in secondary contexts. In: ACL, pp. 1137–1147 (2011)
11. Kronenfeld, D.B.: Scripts, plans, goals, and understanding: an inquiry into human knowledge structures by roger c. schank and robert p. abelson. Language **54**(3), 779–779 (1978)
12. Kuhn, H.W.: The Hungarian method for the assignment problem. Naval Res. Logist. Q. **2**(1–2), 83–97 (1955)
13. Lee, D.H., et al.: Good examples make a faster learner: simple demonstration-based learning for low-resource NER. In: ACL, pp. 2687–2700 (2022)
14. Lewis, M., et al.: BART: denoising sequence-to-sequence pre-training for natural language generation, translation, and comprehension. In: ACL, pp. 7871–7880 (2020)

15. Liu, C., Xiang, W., Wang, B.: Identifying while learning for document event causality identification. In: ACL, pp. 3815–3827 (2024)
16. Liu, J., Shen, D., Zhang, Y., Dolan, B., Carin, L., Chen, W.: What makes good in-context examples for gpt-3? In: DeeLIO, pp. 100–114 (2022)
17. Liu, X., Huang, H., Zhang, Y.: Open domain event extraction using neural latent variable models. In: ACL, pp. 2860–2871 (2019)
18. Loshchilov, I., Hutter, F.: Decoupled weight decay regularization. In: International Conference on Learning Representations (2019)
19. Lu, Y., Bartolo, M., Moore, A., Riedel, S., Stenetorp, P.: Fantastically ordered prompts and where to find them: Overcoming few-shot prompt order sensitivity. In: ACL, pp. 8086–8098 (2022)
20. McLean, V.: Fourth message understanding conference (muc-4). In: MUC-4 (1992)
21. Min, S., et al.: Rethinking the role of demonstrations: what makes in-context learning work? In: EMNLP, pp. 11048–11064 (2022)
22. Reimers, N., Gurevych, I.: Sentence-BERT: sentence embeddings using Siamese BERT-networks. In: EMNLP-IJCNLP, pp. 3982–3992 (2019)
23. Rubin, O., Herzig, J., Berant, J.: Learning to retrieve prompts for in-context learning. In: NAACL, pp. 2655–2671 (2022)
24. Wadden, D., Wennberg, U., Luan, Y., Hajishirzi, H.: Entity, relation, and event extraction with contextualized span representations. In: Inui, K., Jiang, J., Ng, V., Wan, X. (eds.) EMNLP-IJCNLP, pp. 5784–5789 (2019)
25. Wang, B., Du, X., Cardie, C.: Probing representations for document-level event extraction. In: Findings of EMNLP, pp. 12675–12683 (2023)
26. Xiang, W., Wang, B.: A survey of implicit discourse relation recognition. ACM Comput. Surv. **55**(12), 1–34 (2023)
27. Zhang, H., Liu, X., Pan, H., Song, Y., Leung, W.: Aser: a large-scale eventuality knowledge graph. In: WWW, pp. 201–211 (2020)
28. Zhang, H., Zhang, Y., Zhang, R., Yang, D.: Robustness of demonstration-based learning under limited data scenario. In: EMNLP, pp. 1769–1782 (2022)

Chinese Named Entity Recognition Based on Template and Contrastive Learning

Jingjing Zhu, Tianyu Cai, Zhenyu Zhao, and Shenggen Ju[✉]

College of Computer Science, Sichuan University, Chengdu 610065, China
`2022223045242@stu.scu.edu.cn, jsg@scu.edu.cn`

Abstract. Introducing lexicon knowledge into character-level models enhances their ability to discern word boundaries, thus boosting the model's performance. Although the above methods have significantly improved the performance of the model, there are still the following issues. The existing character-level models can only obtain word boundary information from potential lexicon generated from text, and special word information that does not appear in the lexicon cannot be perceived and obtained. Therefore, the problem of out-of-vocabulary words in the lexicon will reduce the performance of the model. To address this, we propose a Chinese Named Entity Recognition Based on Template and Contrastive Learning model(TBCL). This model segments input sentences into n-gram spans and constructs prompt templates to capture comprehensive word information. Leveraging contrastive learning, we designed a triplet loss function to efficiently utilize prompt templates for learning word boundary information. The model is tested on three Chinese named entity recognition datasets: Resume, MSRA and OntoNotes, and the experiment results obtained are superior to the baseline models, which fully prove the effectiveness of the proposed model.

Keywords: Chinese named entity recognition · Prompt learning · Contrastive learning

1 Introduction

Named entity recognition (NER) is a fundamental task in the field of natural language processing (NLP). It aims to extract the words that have special meaning in the text such as person, location, organization etc. NER is commonly viewed as a sequence labeling task, which identifies words with special meanings in the text by using specified entity labels. Because Chinese text is presented in characters and there is a lack of separators between words in Chinese sentences, word information needs to be obtained through other methods. In order to enable the model to perceive word boundary information, existing methods can be divided into two categories: word-based methods and character-based methods.

The word-based method starts by segmenting Chinese text into words using a segmentation algorithm. It then identifies whether each word corresponds to a specific entity type and categorizes potential entity accordingly. He et al. [5]

© The Author(s), under exclusive license to Springer Nature Singapore Pte Ltd. 2025
D. F. Wong et al. (Eds.): NLPCC 2024, LNAI 15359, pp. 392–405, 2025.
https://doi.org/10.1007/978-981-97-9431-7_30

utilized CRF network for text segmentation and entity type prediction. Whereas Peng et al. [15] employed recurrent neural network for segmentation and word-based sequence labeling method to predict entity labels. Although this method conforms to the processing flow of Chinese text, excessive reliance on word segmentation algorithms can make word-based methods susceptible to error propagation, and therefore have been replaced by character-based methods.The character-based method involves dividing the entire sentence into independent character units and inputting them into the model. This eliminates the error propagation caused by operations such as word segmentation, thereby improving the overall performance of the model. However, while character-based methods circumvent error propagation, they cannot directly utilize word boundary information in sentences. To overcome this limitation, Zhang et al. [20] proposed integrating lexicon knowledge into the model, enhancing its ability to perceive word boundary information. However, this way of introducing lexicon knowledge comes from the lexicon information derived from the current sentence. Due to the size of the lexicon, the model cannot perceive the information of certain specific or special entities that may not exist in the lexicon, that is, out-of-vocabulary (OOV). To mitigate this, this article introduces a Chinese Named Entity Recognition Based on Template and Contrastive Learning model (TBCL) that expands the lexicon, enabling the model to perceive complete word boundary information.

The main contributions of this article include three aspects: 1) We extract segments from sentences as latent word information in the form of n-gram, and then construct an anchor sample template, a positive sample template, and a negative sample template for each sentence segment based on prompt learning method. By incorporating latent word information into the model in the form of templates, we obtain complete lexicon knowledge; 2) Based on the idea of contrastive learning, we designed a triplet loss function to make the distance between the positive sample template and the anchor sample template closer in space, and to increase the distance between the negative sample and the anchor sample, in order to better improve the performance of the model; 3) The experiment results on the Resume, MSRA, and OntoNotes datasets show that our proposed TBCL model can effectively improve the performance of the model.

2   Related Work

2.1   Character-Based Methods

To enable character-level models to detect word boundaries, researchers match characters in input text with an external lexicon to derive word information for the current text. Zhang et al. [20] introduced a lattice-based recurrent neural network (RNN) model, integrating word information into the final character representation by adding an extra memory unit to the conventional character-level model. Gui et al. [3] proposed a multi-layer convolutional neural network (CNN) architecture with a reflective mechanism that adjusts weights between character-related word information through feedback on high-level features. Xue et al. [18] proposed a porous mechanism for lattice-aware self-attention, enhancing NER systems' performance by utilizing adjacent character information. Li et al. [10] proposed the FLAT model, leveraging a self-attention network with four relative position encodings to enhance the model's capacity to learn from each node in a word lattice. Ma et al. [13]introduced the SoftLexicon model, categorizing each character's associated words into four sets based on the "BMES" relation pattern, and calculating fusion weights through the model to integrate word information into character representation. Hu et al. [6] categorized word-related character information into two types and designed different fusion strategies to link word information with character representations.Wu et al. [17] introduced the MECT model, computing structural information for each character, constructing a cross-attention network, and ultimately fusing information for NER. Li et al. [9] framed the Chinese NER task as a word classification task, proposing a novel neural framework, significantly enhancing model performance with 2D grids corresponding to words. Guo et al. [4] integrated external lexicon knowledge into the BERT [2] via a lexicon adapter mechanism and utilized a pointer network to extract global semantic features. Zhang et al. . [19] proposed the Visphone model, efficiently utilizing character features by integrating phonetic and visual features into the Transformer encoder. Long et al. [12] proposed a multi embedding fusion model that improves the performance of the model by fusing four types of feature information. However, despite introducing lexicon knowledge to address the inability of character-level models to perceive word boundaries, limitations arise from the incompleteness of the lexicon derived from the input text, thus restricting model performance.

2.2 Prompt Learning

Prompt learning simplifies template creation for guiding models in specific tasks during pre-training, boosting their ability to comprehend text context. The construction of prompt templates involves manual and automatic methods. Manual construction relies on designers creating task-specific templates based on experience, while automatic construction, a popular approach, minimizes labor costs [11]. In English NER tasks, Cui et al. [1] transformed NER into a language model sorting problem, employing hard prompt templates to enhance model performance. Ma et al. [14] replaced the method of constructing templates for each latent word with predicting the central word, reducing the number of inefficient templates and improving the efficiency and performance of the prompt method.

2.3 Contrastive Learning

Contrastive learning is a self-supervised method, whose basic idea is to design positive and negative samples, so that positive samples are closer to the source sample in the feature space and farther away from negative samples, so that the model can better distinguish different samples and learn richer information representations. The main goal of contrastive learning is to construct a contrastive loss function, so that the score of positive samples far exceeds that of negative samples, which can be expressed as:

$$\text{Score}(f(x), f(x^+)) \gg \text{Score}(f(x), f(x^-)). \tag{1}$$

where x represents a sample, x^+ is a positive sample similar to the sample feature, x^- is a negative sample different from the sample feature, and $Score(\cdot)$ is a similarity calculation function between samples. $f(\cdot)$ is a learning goal, which makes the gap between the source sample and the positive sample as small as possible, and the gap between the negative sample as large as possible.

3   Templated-Based and Contrastive Learning Model

3.1   Model Introduction

The overall architecture of the TBCL model is shown in Fig. 1, which can be divided into three modules: the coding layer, template calculation layer, and entity prediction layer. Rather than directly introducing an external lexicon for unknown words, the TBCL model utilizes n-gram to extract sentence spans, constructing the entity lexicon manually to expand its scope. Subsequently, to optimize the utilization of word information, the model generates three types of prompt templates for each word, facilitating the selection of semantically relevant word information. The coding layer encodes input sentences using the BART encoder [8], feeding embedded character information and sentence context into subsequent decoding processes. Treating Chinese NER as a language model ranking problem within the Seq2Seq framework, the template calculation layer scores prompt templates based on coding layer outputs. Utilizing a triplet loss function, the template computing layer adjusts distances between positive and negative sample templates and anchor sample templates. Finally, the entity prediction layer employs a fully connected neural network and *softmax* function to predict the entity label for each potential word.

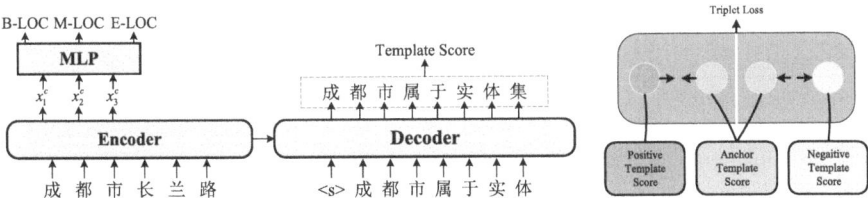

Fig. 1. TBCL model architecture   Fig. 2. Triplet loss

3.2   Prompt Template

Label the given input text as $S = (c_1, c_2, \ldots, c_n)$, where n is the length of the text and c_i represents the i-th character in the text. The words extracted in n-gram form from sentence S are denoted as $W = \{w_1, w_2, \ldots, w_m\}$, where m is the number of words and w_j is the j-th word, which can also be represented as a character sequence between the first and last characters. If the first character of the k-th word is c_i and the last character is c_j, then the word $w_k = \{c_i, c_{i+1}, \ldots, c_{j-1}, c_j\}$, abbreviated as $w_k = S_{i:j}$. The prompt template generated by the input text S

is represented as $T^f = (t_1, t_2, \ldots, t_m)$, the number of templates is the same as the number of words, and the i-th prompt template t_i is constructed from the i-th word w_i. f represents the type of prompt template, where $f \in [A, P, N]$ represents anchor sample template, positive sample template and negative sample template respectively.

In the TBCL model, we manually created three types of templates, namely anchor, positive and negative sample template: A, P, N respectively, each of which is composed of a candidate word slot and prompt information. Each type of template contains two specific forms based on the entity labels of candidate words, as described below. (1) Anchor sample template: according to whether the candidate word w_i formed by the selected span is an entity, it can be divided into two forms. When the candidate word belongs to the entity set, the anchor sample template is T_1: "w_i 属于实体集", and otherwise denoted as T_2: "w_i 不属于实体集". (2) Positive sample template: when the candidate word w_i belongs to the entity set, its positive sample template is T_3: "w_i 是一个实体". Otherwise, T_4: "w_i 不是一个实体". (3) Negative sample template: when the candidate word w_i does not belong to the entity set, its positive sample template is T_5: "w_i 不是一个实体". Otherwise, T_6: "w_i 是一个实体". We give an example, if the input text is "成都市长兰路". When the candidate word is "成都市" and it is an entity, so anchor sample template T_1 is "<成都市>属于实体集", positive sample template T_3 is "<成都市>是一个实体", negative sample template T_5 is "<成都市>不是一个实体". Conversely, when the candidate word is "<兰路>" and it is not an entity, so T_2 is "<兰路>不属于实体集", T_4 is "<兰路>不是一个实体" and T_6 is "<兰路>是一个实体". In summary, candidate words generate prompt templates information according to whether they belong to real entities, as described in Table 1.

Table 1. Prompt template detail

Template type	Whether the candidate word is an entity	Prompt template
Anchor sample template	Yes	T_1: "<词语>属于实体集"
Positive sample template	Yes	T_3: "<词语>是一个实体"
Negative sample template	Yes	T_5: "<词语>不是一个实体"
Anchor sample template	No	T_2: "<词语>不属于实体集"
Positive sample template	No	T_4: "<词语>不是一个实体"
Negative sample template	No	T_6: "<词语>是一个实体"

3.3　Model Inference

First, we list all possible spans in sentence S and extract word information from them. Then, we fill these words into the prepared three types of templates. Next, we use BART to calculate scores for each prompt template. The input data of the BART encoder is text S, and the input data of the BART decoder is three types of template information: T^f, denoted as $X = (S, T)$. The specific calculation method is as follows: The encoder based on BART obtains the hidden representation h^{enc} of the sentence. The input of the decoder consists of h^{enc} and the output of the template information before the decoder. At time c, the output calculation method of the decoder is:

$$h^{enc} = Encoder(S), \tag{2}$$

$$h_c^{dec} = Decoder(h^{enc}, x_{1:c-1}). \tag{3}$$

where $x_{1:c-1}$ represents the output data of the decoder before time c.

Then calculate the score for the prompt template. The probability of the character predicted by the decoder at time c is:

$$p(x_c|x_{1:c-1}, S) = \sigma(h_c^{dec} W_{lm} + b_{lm}). \tag{4}$$

where, W_{lm} and b_{lm} are learnable matrix parameters and bias parameters respectively, and σ are *softmax* activation functions. At this time, for the prompt template $t \in T^f$, its score is calculated as follows:

$$f(t|S) = \sum_{c=1}^{|t|} \log p(x_c|x_{1:c-1}, S). \tag{5}$$

3.4   Triplet Loss Function

The anchor sample template is the core of the three types of prompt templates used in the TBCL model. The TBCL model uses a triplet loss function [16] to train and optimize the prompt template information. Ultimately, the distance between the anchor sample template and the positive sample template in space is closer, and the distance between the anchor sample template and the negative sample template is farther. The triplet loss function is shown in Fig. 2. The application form of the triplet loss function in the TBCL model is as follows:

$$L_{Triplet} = \max(Dist(f(T^A), f(T^P)) - Dist(f(T^A), f(T^N)) + \alpha, 0), \tag{6}$$

$$Dist(f_1, f_2) = exp(-|f_1 - f_2|). \tag{7}$$

where, $f(T^A)$ is the anchor sample template score, $f(T^P)$ is the positive sample template score, $f(T^N)$ is the negative sample template score, α is the margin parameter, and $Dist(\cdot, \cdot)$ is the similarity measurement function. In the process of minimizing the loss $L_{Triplet}$, the value of the first term in the maximum function is required to be as small as possible, which is equivalent to making the difference between the similarity $Dist(f(T^A), f(T^P))$ between the anchor sample and the positive sample and the similarity $Dist(f(T^A), f(T^N))$ between the anchor sample and the negative sample larger than the margin α.

The example is shown in Fig. 3. When the candidate word belongs to the entity set, the anchor, positive and negative sample template generated by the word are T_1, T_3 and T_5, respectively. Conversely, when the candidate word does not belong to the entity set, the anchor, positive and negative sample template are T_2, T_4 and T_6, respectively. When the candidate word belongs to the entity set, the similarity between T_1 and T_3 is higher and the distance is closer; the similarity between T_1 and T_5 will be lower and the distance between them will be greatert. On the contrary, when the candidate word does not belong to the entity set, the similarity between T_2 and T_4 is higher and the distance is closer; the similarity between T_2 and T_6 will be lower and the distance will be higher.

3.5 Entity Prediction

In the prediction stage, we use fully connected neural network and $softmax$ to annotate entities. Specifically, the input text S is first obtained by the BART encoder to obtain the hidden representation of each character. For each word, the hidden representation of its first character and last character is concatenated and input into the fully connected neural network to predict the entity label, the specific calculation method is as follows:

$$h_i^{enc} = Encoder(S), \tag{8}$$

$$h_{w_k}^{ffn} = ReLU(W_{ffn}h_{w_k} + b_{ffn}), \tag{9}$$

$$\hat{y}_{w_k} = softmax(W_{out}h_{w_k}^{ffn} + b_{out}), \tag{10}$$

$$h_{w_k} = [h_i^{enc}; h_j^{enc}]. \tag{11}$$

where W and b are learnable matrix parameters and bias parameters respectively, $ReLU$ is the activation function, and i and j are the first and last character positions of the word w_k respectively. $\hat{y}_{w_k} = \{\hat{y}_{w_k}^1, \hat{y}_{w_k}^2, \ldots, \hat{y}_{w_k}^l\}$ represents the prediction probability of all entity labels for the current word w_k, and l is the number of entity labels. For a word w_k, if it is a candidate entity, its true entity label is calculated as:

$$y_{w_k} = argmax \ \hat{y}_{w_k}. \tag{12}$$

Otherwise, if it does not belong to the candidate entity, as shown in Fig. 4, TBCL will eventually mask the entity label information output by its fully connected neural network and directly label its entity label as "O".

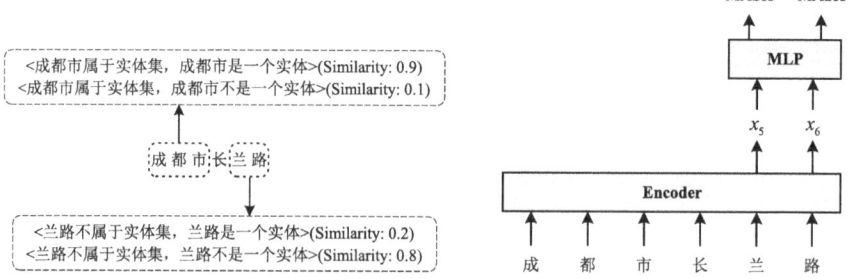

Fig. 3. Template similarity   **Fig. 4.** Non-candidate word label output

3.6   Model Optimization

The TBCL model uses triplet loss and cross-entropy loss as joint loss when updating parameters, as shown below:

$$L = \beta^1 L_{Triplet} + \beta^2 L_{CEL}, \tag{13}$$

$$L_{CEL} = -\frac{1}{m} \sum_{i=1}^{m} \sum_{c=1}^{l} y_{ic} \log(p_{ic}). \tag{14}$$

where m is the number of words, l is the number of entity labels; y_{ic} is an indicator function. The i-th sample obtained by p_{ic} in the prediction stage belongs to the prediction probability of label c. β^1 and β^2 are hyper-parameters, we set both parameters to 0.5 in this experiment.

4   Experiments

4.1   Experiments Settings and Baselines

The TBCL model proposed in this article is tested on three Chinese NER benchmark datasets: Resume [20], MSRA [7], and OntoNotes. The evaluation metrics used in this experiment are Precision(P), Recall(R) and F1 score. The experiment parameter settings for each module of the TBCL model and experiment environment details are shown in Tables 2 and 3, respectively.

The TBCL model proposed in this article selects the following models as baseline models:(1)BERT [2](2018); (2)PLTE [18](2020): It proposes a lattice-aware porous attention network encoder to capture dependency information between nodes in word lattices; (3)SoftLexicon [13](2020): It divides the word information related to characters into four sets based on the matching relation between words, and uses different weights to fuse the information of the four word sets into the character representation; (4)FLAT [10](2020): It incorporates four types of relative position encoding into the self-attention network to obtain information about each node in the word lattice; (5)MECT [17](2021): It constructs a cross-attention network between character structure information and word lattice information to separately calculate the feature representations of these two parts of data, and finally fuses these two parts of information; (6)W^{2}NER [9](2022): It models the Chinese NER task as a word-word classification task, using 2D grids corresponding to words to learn word information; (7)Guo et al. [4](2022): It proposes a new BERT-based lexicon enhancement adapter model, which fuses external lexicon features into the deep representation of BERT; (8)VisPhone [19](2023): It combines the phonetic and visual features of characters and inputs them into the Transformer encoder. Among them, baseline models (2)–(8) were compared with experiment results combined with pre-training language models. The specific experiment details are presented in Sect. 4.2.

Table 2. TBCL model experiment hyper-parameter

Hyper-parameter	Resume	MSRA	OntoNotes
Optimizer	Adam	Adam	Adam
Learning rate	$1e-5$	$1e-5$	$5e-3$
BART learning rate	$1e-6$	$1e-6$	$1e-7$
FCNN dimension	1024	1024	1500
α	0.2	0.2	0.2
Dropout	0.3	0.5	0.2
N-gram	12	7	9
Gradient clipping	$[-5.0, 5.0]$	$[-5.0, 5.0]$	$[-5.0, 5.0]$

Table 3. TBCL model experiment environment detail

Experiment environment	Detail
Operating system	Ubuntu 22.04.3 LTS
Memory	128 GB
CPU	13th Gen Intel® CoreTM i9-13900K
GPU	NVIDIA GeForce RTXTM 4090
CUDA	12.2
Python	3.9.18
Pytorch	2.3.0.dev20240115+cu121

4.2 Results

Table 4 provides a detailed description of the experiment comparison results between the TBCL model proposed in this chapter and other baseline models. Compared with BERT, the TBCL model shows an increase of 1.7%, 2.92%, and 5.53% in F1 score on Resume, MSRA, and OntoNotes datasets, respectively. BERT is based on character context information to predict character label information, so it cannot obtain word boundary information, but TBCL model can effectively utilize word boundary information to improve its performance. PLTE and FLAT model both obtain word boundary information from lexicon, while SoftLexicon model uses the matching relation between characters and words to integrate word information. Compared with these three models, The performance improvements of TBCL model in Resume, MSRA, and OntoNotes datasets are 0.93%, 1.52%, 1.27%; 2.79%, 0.59%, 1.9%; 2.86%, 1.0%, 0.65%, respectively. TBCL can mine OOV words and obtain more complete words information. The MECT and VisPhone model respectively incorporate character radical information and character phonetic, visual features to explore the internal potential information of characters and words. The core of Chinese NER lies in mining richer and more comprehensive word boundary information. Therefore, the TBCL model has more advantages compared to these two models.

W^2NER transforms NER tasks into a word-word classification task, which integrates multiple features containing characters and words through joint training. The model proposed by Guo et al. can better integrate lexical information with semantic information to improve the performance of the model. Compared with these two models, the TBCL model relies on prompt templates and triplet loss function to achieve stronger learning ability in Chinese NER tasks, with performance improvements of 0.73%, 0.65%, 0.58%; 0.3%, 0.38%, 0.58% on three datasets respectively.

Table 4. TBCL model experiment result

Model	Resume			MSRA			OntoNotes		
	P(%)	R(%)	F1(%)	P(%)	R(%)	F1(%)	P(%)	R(%)	F1(%)
BERT	94.87	96.50	95.68	93.40	94.12	93.76	76.01	79.96	77.93
PLTE	96.16	96.75	96.45	94.91	94.15	94.53	79.62	81.82	80.60
SoftLexicon	96.08	96.13	96.11	95.75	95.10	95.42	83.41	82.21	82.81
FLAT	–	–	95.86	–	–	96.09	–	–	81.82
MECT	–	–	95.98	–	–	96.24	–	–	82.57
W^2NER	96.96	96.35	96.65	96.12	96.08	96.10	82.31	83.36	83.08
Guo et al.	97.87	95.62	96.73	97.56	95.23	96.38	95.46	76.54	84.96
VisPhone	–	–	96.26	96.31	95.83	96.07	–	–	82.36
TBCL	96.41	98.37	97.38	96.95	96.40	96.68	83.22	87.99	85.54

4.3 Ablation Study

To verify the effectiveness of the prompt template and triplet loss function used in the TBCL model, we conducted two ablation experiments as follows: (1) W/o Template: Since no prompt template was added, word boundary information could not be obtained. Instead, a cross-entropy loss function was used. (2) W/o Triple Loss: Only construct positive and negative sample templates for the model to learn word information, without using anchor sample templates. Replace the loss function with a binary loss function between the positive and negative sample templates.

The results of the above two ablation experiments are shown in Table 5. After removing the prompt template, the model was unable to perceive word boundary information, and the final result of the model was lower than that of the TBCL model. When the triplet loss function is not used, the model constructs a binary loss function to learn word information through positive and negative sample templates during the experiment, and the utilization rate of templates is relatively low. Therefore, after using binary loss, the output of the model is also inferior to that of the TBCL model.

Table 5. TBCL model ablation experiment result

Model	Resume F1(%)	MSRA F1(%)	OntoNotes F1(%)
TBCL	97.38	96.68	85.54
w/o Template	95.51	94.83	81.82
w/o Triplet loss	96.06	95.37	82.85

4.4 Triplet Loss Function Margin Parameter Experiment

We explore the effect of margin parameters α in triplet loss functions on model performance. We set the α of 0.1, 0.2 and 0.3 respectively in the experiment, and the specific experiment results are shown in Fig. 5. When the α is 0.2, the TBCL model can achieve better performance. When the α is 0.1, the margin value is small, and the loss value is easy to approach 0, which makes it difficult to effectively learn the sample template. When the α is 0.3, the margin value is large, and the loss value is not easy to approach 0. As a result, the network does not converge.

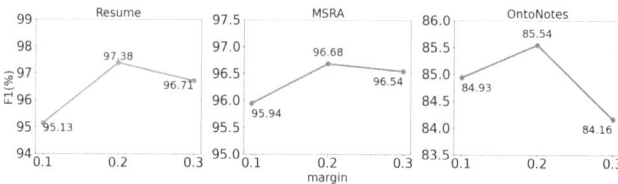

Fig. 5. Margin parameter experiment result

4.5 N-Gram Parameter Experiment

From Fig. 6, it can be concluded that as the n-gram increases, more spans can be extracted, leading to an increase in the number of potential words. Due to the use of three types of prompt templates in the TBCL model, for every additional potential word added during the training phase, the model needs to add three prompt templates, resulting in a larger number of templates and a slower training speed, as shown in Fig. 7. The performance of the TBCL model is basically similar under different n-gram, as shown in Fig. 8. Taking into account the GPU's capabilities and model training time, selecting n-gram of 12, 7, and 9 respectively can achieve ideal performance and training time for the TBCL model.

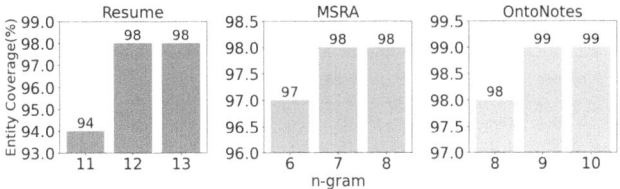

Fig. 6. Coverage of different n-gram

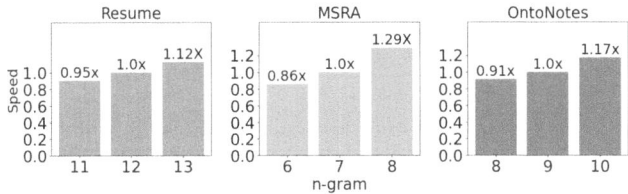

Fig. 7. Training speed of different n-gram

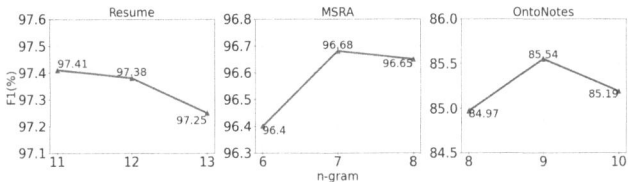

Fig. 8. Model performance of different n-gram

4.6   Case Study

In this section, this article conducts a case study. We use "四川省石油集团董事" as the input sentence, which should include: organization entity - "四川省石油集团" and title entity - "董事". For the segmentation algorithm, it will segment the sentence based on the frequency of each potential word in the corpus, and cannot consider the semantic information of the sentence, resulting in an incorrect segmentation result: "四川省/石油集团/董事". For the model based on character matching to generate a lexicon, it provides more word boundary information compared to the segmentation model. However, "四川省石油集团" as a special word does not appear in the lexicon, thus incorrectly detecting the three entities: location entity - "四川省", organization entity - "石油集团" and the title entity - "董事". For the TBCL model proposed in this chapter, it extracts spans from sentences in the form of n-gram to manually expand the lexicon, using prompt templates, the TBCL model can learn the most accurate word boundary information and output correct entity recognition results. The details of the case study are shown in Fig. 9.

Sentence	四川省石油集团董事								
Segment	四川省 / 石油集团 / 董事								
True Entity Label	四 B-ORG	川 M-ORG	省 M-ORG	石 M-ORG	油 M-ORG	集 M-ORG	团 E-ORG	董 B-TITLE	事 E-TITLE
Entity Lexicon	四川、四川省、石油、石油集团、集团、集团董事、董事								
Entity Lexicon Model	四 B-LOC	川 M-LOC	省 E-LOC	石 B-ORG	油 M-ORG	集 M-ORG	团 E-ORG	董 B-TITLE	事 E-TITLE
Template Lexicon	四川、四川省、四川省石、四川省石油、四川省石油集、四川省石油集团、四川省石油集团董、四川省石油集团董事、···、集团董事、团董事、董事								
TBCL	四 B-ORG	川 M-ORG	省 M-ORG	石 M-ORG	油 M-ORG	集 M-ORG	团 E-ORG	董 B-TITLE	事 E-TITLE

Fig. 9. Case study

5   Summary

This article introduces a novel Chinese NER model TBCL, which aims to solve the problem of OOV words faced by existing character-level methods based on lexicon knowledge. Specifically, the TBCL model manually extracts latent words from input sentences in the form of n-gram, and then constructs three types of entity templates (anchor, positive and negative sample template) for latent words based on prompt learning. Based on contrastive learning method, a triplet loss function is designed to reduce the distance between anchor template and positive template, and increase the distance between negative template, thereby improving the performance of the model and ultimately solving the problem of OOV words. The experiment results on three Chinese NER benchmark datasets: Resume, MSRA and OntoNotes, further demonstrate the efficiency of the TBCL model.

Acknowledgments. This work is supported by grant from National Natural Science Foundation of China (NO. 62137001), the Science and Technology Innovation Foundation of Sichuan(2023YFG0265).

Disclosure of Interests. The authors have no competing interests to declare that are relevant to the content of this article.

References

1. Cui, L., Wu, Y., Liu, J., Yang, S., Zhang, Y.: Template-based named entity recognition using BART. In: ACL/IJCNLP (Findings). Findings of ACL, vol. ACL/IJCNLP 2021, pp. 1835–1845. Association for Computational Linguistics (2021)

2. Devlin, J., Chang, M., Lee, K., Toutanova, K.: BERT: pre-training of deep bidirectional transformers for language understanding. In: NAACL-HLT (1), pp. 4171–4186. Association for Computational Linguistics (2019)
3. Gui, T., Ma, R., Zhang, Q., Zhao, L., Jiang, Y., Huang, X.: CNN-based Chinese NER with lexicon rethinking. In: IJCAI, pp. 4982–4988. ijcai.org (2019)
4. Guo, Q., Guo, Y.: Lexicon enhanced Chinese named entity recognition with pointer network. Neural Comput. Appl. **34**(17), 14535–14555 (2022)
5. He, J., Wang, H.: Chinese named entity recognition and word segmentation based on character. In: IJCNLP, pp. 128–132. The Association for Computer Linguistics (2008)
6. Hu, J., Ouyang, Y., Li, C., Wang, C., Rong, W., Xiong, Z.: Hierarchical lexicon embedding architecture for Chinese named entity recognition. In: Farkaš, I., Masulli, P., Otte, S., Wermter, S. (eds.) ICANN 2021. LNCS, vol. 12895, pp. 345–356. Springer, Cham (2021). https://doi.org/10.1007/978-3-030-86383-8_28
7. Levow, G.: The third international Chinese language processing bakeoff: word segmentation and named entity recognition. In: SIGHAN@COLING/ACL, pp. 108–117. Association for Computational Linguistics (2006)
8. Lewis, M., et al.: BART: denoising sequence-to-sequence pre-training for natural language generation, translation, and comprehension. In: ACL, pp. 7871–7880. Association for Computational Linguistics (2020)
9. Li, J., et al.: Unified named entity recognition as word-word relation classification. In: AAAI, pp. 10965–10973. AAAI Press (2022)
10. Li, X., Yan, H., Qiu, X., Huang, X.: FLAT: Chinese NER using flat-lattice transformer. In: ACL, pp. 6836–6842. Association for Computational Linguistics (2020)
11. Liu, P., Yuan, W., Fu, J., Jiang, Z., Hayashi, H., Neubig, G.: Pre-train, prompt, and predict: a systematic survey of prompting methods in natural language processing. ACM Comput. Surv. **55**(9), 195:1–195:35 (2023)
12. Long, K., et al.: Deep neural network with embedding fusion for Chinese named entity recognition. ACM Trans. Asian Low Resour. Lang. Inf. Process. **22**(3), 91:1–91:16 (2023)
13. Ma, R., Peng, M., Zhang, Q., Wei, Z., Huang, X.: Simplify the usage of lexicon in Chinese NER. In: ACL, pp. 5951–5960. Association for Computational Linguistics (2020)
14. Ma, R., et al.: Template-free prompt tuning for few-shot NER. In: NAACL-HLT, pp. 5721–5732. Association for Computational Linguistics (2022)
15. Peng, N., Dredze, M.: Improving named entity recognition for Chinese social media with word segmentation representation learning. In: ACL (2). The Association for Computer Linguistics (2016)
16. Schroff, F., Kalenichenko, D., Philbin, J.: Facenet: a unified embedding for face recognition and clustering. In: CVPR, pp. 815–823. IEEE Computer Society (2015)
17. Wu, S., Song, X., Feng, Z.: MECT: multi-metadata embedding based cross-transformer for Chinese named entity recognition. In: ACL/IJCNLP (1), pp. 1529–1539. Association for Computational Linguistics (2021)
18. Xue, M., Yu, B., Liu, T., Zhang, Y., Meng, E., Wang, B.: Porous lattice transformer encoder for Chinese NER. In: COLING, pp. 3831–3841. International Committee on Computational Linguistics (2020)
19. Zhang, B., Cai, J., Zhang, H., Shang, J.: Visphone: Chinese named entity recognition model enhanced by visual and phonetic features. Inf. Process. Manag. **60**(3), 103314 (2023)
20. Zhang, Y., Yang, J.: Chinese NER using lattice LSTM. In: ACL (1), pp. 1554–1564. Association for Computational Linguistics (2018)

Enhancing Logical Rules Based on Self-Distillation for Document-Level Relation Extraction

Yanxu Mao[1(✉)], Tiehan Cui[1], and Ying Ding[2]

[1] School of Software, Henan University, Kaifeng, China
{maoyanxu,cuitiehan}@henu.edu.cn
[2] School of Computer Science and Technology, Henan Institute of Science and Technology, Xinxiang, China

Abstract. Document-level Relation Extraction (DocRE) aims to identify and extract relations between entities from entire documents. Unlike sentence-level relation extraction, document-level relation extraction requires considering cross-sentence contextual information to capture complex relations expressed across multiple sentences or paragraphs. Previous research has shown that the application of Logical Rules (LR) can improve the efficiency of relation extraction. However, identifying and extracting these logical rules require significant memory consumption, and the obtained logical rules lack specificity. To address this issue, we propose a novel approach in this paper (ELRSD (The implementation code for ELRSD can be obtained from the GitHub link: https://github.com/maoxuxu/elrsd.)), Based on the Self-Distillation (SD) training process, utilize Multi-head Graph Convolution Networks and Transformer synergistic learning to improve the extraction of logical rules, thereby enhancing the extraction of entity relations. We conduct comprehensive experiments on three popular benchmark datasets. The results obtained under the same experimental settings indicate that our method achieved state-of-the-art performance.

Keywords: DocRE · LR · Graph Convolution Networks · Self-Distillation

1 Introduction

Document-level Relation Extraction (DocRE) is a crucial task in Natural Language Processing (NLP) aimed at revealing the relations between entities throughout an entire document [1,8,10,30]. The initial research primarily focused on sentence-level relation extraction, where each sentence is regarded as an independent analytical unit [4,13]. However, with the increase in text data, there is a growing emphasis on the importance of document-level relation extraction, which can extract entity pair relations from the entire document. Figure 1

Y. Mao and T. Cui—Contributed equally.

© The Author(s), under exclusive license to Springer Nature Singapore Pte Ltd. 2025
D. F. Wong et al. (Eds.): NLPCC 2024, LNAI 15359, pp. 406–418, 2025.
https://doi.org/10.1007/978-981-97-9431-7_31

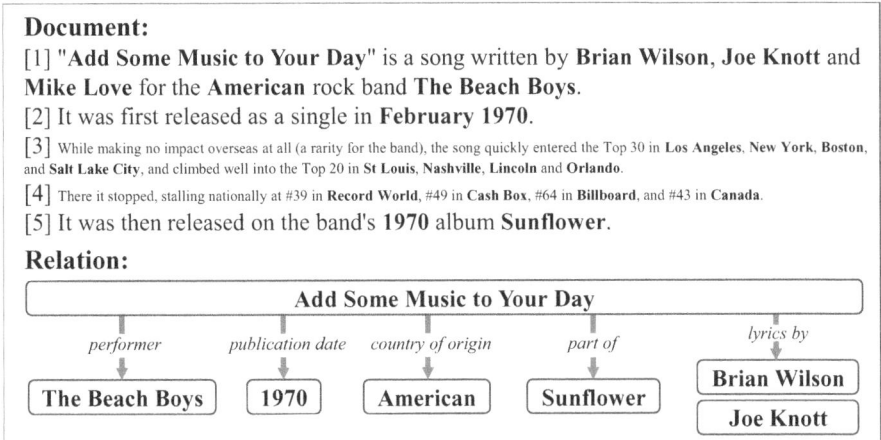

Document:
[1] **"Add Some Music to Your Day"** is a song written by **Brian Wilson**, **Joe Knott** and **Mike Love** for the **American** rock band **The Beach Boys**.
[2] It was first released as a single in **February 1970**.
[3] While making no impact overseas at all (a rarity for the band), the song quickly entered the Top 30 in **Los Angeles**, **New York**, **Boston**, and **Salt Lake City**, and climbed well into the Top 20 in **St Louis**, **Nashville**, **Lincoln** and **Orlando**.
[4] There it stopped, stalling nationally at #39 in **Record World**, #49 in **Cash Box**, #64 in **Billboard**, and #43 in **Canada**.
[5] It was then released on the band's **1970** album **Sunflower**.

Relation:

Fig. 1. An example in the DocRED dataset presents all relation triples with "Add Some Music to Your Day" as the head entity.

shows an example of a DocRED dataset. Unlike traditional sentence-level relation extraction, DocRE needs to consider cross-sentence contextual information to capture complex relations spanning multiple sentences or even paragraphs [16, 22, 24]. This necessitates models capable of capturing remote dependencies and subtle differences in a wide context.

Recent research has focused more on the role of local information in document extraction tasks, transforming triples $< entity_1, relation, entity_2 >$ in DocRE datasets into quadruples $< entity_1, relation, entity_2, evidence_{[1,2,3]} > [6,17,22]$ where a list of sentences providing evidence for the relation between two entities is added. We can directly perform relation extraction based on the potential logical rules in the sentence list of the quadruplet, without relying on the content of the entire document. However, in the new benchmark datasets, there is no evidence information in the distant supervision data. This necessitates us to retrieve evidence information from the document and then use the logical rules in the evidence information to predict the relation between entities.

Previous methods can be broadly categorized into two main types: Graph-based and Transformer-based. Graph-based methods typically employ Graph Neural Networks (GNNs) to construct sentence-level or document-level dependency graphs for inferring relations between entity pairs [10,11,25,28] . Transformer-based methods typically utilize pre-trained models to encode entire documents and integrate attention mechanisms to capture complex relations between entities within the document, thereby achieving precise classification and extraction of entity relations [5,19–21,30].

Existing models based on the above two types of relation extraction methods suffer from two limitations. Firstly, previous systems introduced neural networks to jointly learn Relation Extraction (RE) and Logic Rules (LR) [3,15], leading to both being treated as independent tasks. This not only increases model complexity but also escalates memory overhead. Secondly, the evidence obtained through logical rule reasoning is not sufficiently explicit and lacks specificity for particular relation triple, resulting in poor performance when extracting relations involving complex cross-entity pairs.

To address the two aforementioned limitations, we propose a novel model for document-level relation extraction: ELRSD. We adopt a supervised learning approach, first performing standard training on a dataset annotated with logical rules to obtain an initial model. Subsequently, we use the initial model to generate logical rule labels on a distant supervision dataset, and then utilize these logical rule labels to further train the model itself.

Compared with existing work, our contributions can be summarized as follows:

1. We propose a novel approach that utilizes Self-Distillation (SD) training methods to integrate Transformer and Graph neural networks, enhancing logical rule inference capabilities and improving relation extraction performance.
2. We parallelize the extraction of logical rules and entity relation extraction, significantly improving computational efficiency without requiring additional computational resources.
3. Our approach is evaluated on three benchmark datasets, achieved advanced performance under the same experimental settings. The evaluation of the test set in DocRED has been submitted to the rating leaderboard[1].

2   Task Formulation for DocRE

In a document D, consisting of entities $E = \{e_1, e_2, \ldots, e_n\}$, each entity e_i at position p_i may have relations with other entities. The task of DocRE is to extract relations $R = \{r_1, r_2, \ldots, r_m\}$ from D. Each relation r_i is represented as (e_i, e_j, r_{ij}), where r_{ij} is the predicted relation label between entities e_i and e_j, and $i \neq j$.

3   Proposed Method

As illustrated in Fig. 2, Our proposed model is mainly divided into three parts: Bert Encoder Layer, Multi-Scale Convolutional (MC) Layer and Joint Classification Layer.

3.1   The Bert Encoder

For document encoding, we follow the method described by [16]. First, we use the special marker "*" to denote the beginning and end of mentions in the input document D. Then, we use a BERT encoder to encode the document to obtain the contextual feature representation $H, A = \text{BERT}([\,D\,]) \in R^{|D| \times d}$

---

[1] Please refer to ELRSD: https://codalab.lisn.upsaclay.fr/competitions/365#results.

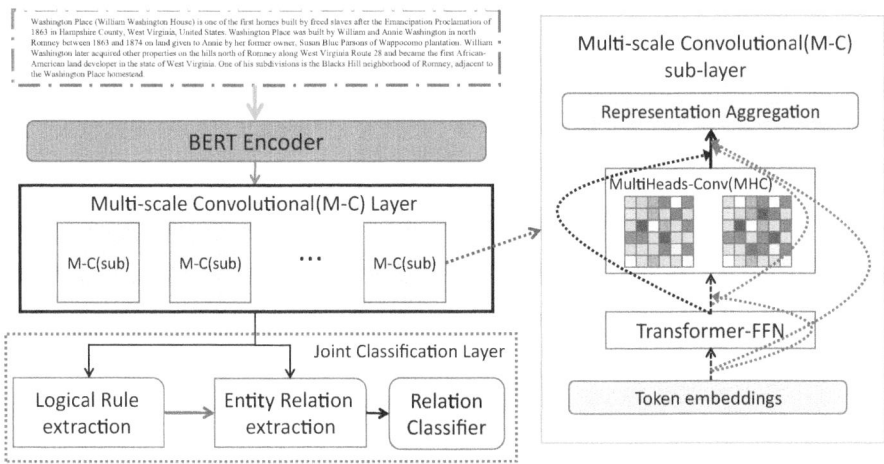

Fig. 2. Illustrations of our ELRSD.

tokens, where d is the dimension of the BERT encoder's hidden states. Finally, the embedded representation $\boldsymbol{h}_e \in R^d$ of the entity is calculated through the *logsumexp* [7] pooling operation, can be calculated as follows:

$$h_e = \log \sum_{i=1}^{|\mathcal{M}_e|} \exp\left(\mathbf{BERT}([\ D\ ])_{m_i}\right), \tag{1}$$

3.2 The Multi-scale Convolutional (MC) Layer

The Multi-Scale Convolutional (MC) Layer consists of multiple sub-layers, each containing the following three components: Transformer-FNN, MultiHeads-Conv, and Representation Aggregation. Multi-Scale Convolutional (MC) Layer.

Transformer-FNN (TransFNN). First, we calculate the localized context embedding of entity pairs through the attention weight matrix (A_s, A_o) obtained from the last layer output of Bert encoder: $Con_{s,o} = H^\top \frac{A_s \circ A_o}{(A_s \circ A_o)}$, where $\circ$ refers to matrix multiplication.

Then, the embedding representations of the relational entity pairs and the localized context embeddings are concatenated and processed through a Transformer Feed-forward Neural Network (TransFNN) to compute the feature vectors F_s and F_o for the entity pair (e_s, e_o):

$$\begin{aligned}
F_s &= \text{TransFNN}\left(\left(\left[tanh\left(W_s\left[h\left(e_s\right);Con_{s,o}\right]\right)\right)\right., \\
F_o &= \text{TransFNN}\left(\left(\left[tanh\left(W_o\left[h\left(e_o\right);Con_{s,o}\right]\right)\right)\right.,
\end{aligned} \tag{2}$$

where W_s and W_o are the weight parameters, $tanh$ is the hyperbolic tangent activation function.

The MultiHeads-Conv (MHC). GCNs [9] stands for Graph Convolutional Network. It is a type of neural network designed to operate on graph-structured data. GCNs generalize the concept of convolution from traditional grid data (such as images) to graph data, enabling the processing of nodes, edges, and their features. GCNs are widely used in various applications such as social network analysis, recommendation systems, and molecular biology, where data can be naturally represented as graphs. In this module, we use MultiHeads-Conv(MHC) to process the entity pair feature vectors generated by TransFNN. Each MHC will produce an attention weight matrix, calculated as follows:

$$MHC(F^{(l)}) = softmax\left(\frac{\left((F_s : F_o)^{(l)}W^Q\right)\left((F_s : F_o)^{(l)}W^K\right)^\top}{\sqrt{d}}\right), \quad (3)$$

where W^Q and W^K are learnable weight parameter matrices, and ":" denotes the concatenation operation.

When dealing with all feature matrices, we use the normalization technology layer normalization (LayerNorm) commonly used in neural networks to make the input features of each layer have similar mean and variance, accelerate the training and improve the generalization ability of the model.

$$V^{(l)} = LayerNorm(F^{(l-1)} + MHC(F^{(l)})), \quad (4)$$

The Representation Aggregation. In the final stage of this module, we aggregate multiple feature representations into a single one. To reduce the spatial dimensions of the feature maps, thereby reducing the number of parameters and computational complexity, we adopt Average pooling to preserve the overall trends of the feature matrices and enhance the model's translational invariance. Where the input feature matrix V has a size of $m \times n$ and the pooling window size is $p \times q$, the output feature map Y will have a size of $\lceil\frac{m}{p}\rceil \times \lceil\frac{n}{q}\rceil$. The computation of each element $Y_{i,j}$ in the output feature map is as follows:

$$Y_{i,j}^{(1)} = \frac{1}{p \times q} \sum_{u=0}^{p-1}\sum_{v=0}^{q-1} V_{i \times p+u, j \times q+v}, \quad (5)$$

where i and j respectively represent the row and column indices in the output features, and u and v represent the row and column indices within the pooling window. $V_{i \times p+u, j \times q+v}$ denotes the value at the corresponding position in the input feature matrix.

$$\tilde{H}^{(Multi)} = Concat\left(Y^{(1)}, \ldots, Y^{(l)}\right)W^H, \quad (6)$$

where $W^H \in R^{ld \times d}$ is the weight parameter of the linear transformation applied to the ultimate output.

3.3 The Joint Classification

We utilize the obtained feature representations $\tilde{H}^{(\text{Multi})}$ for both logical rule extraction and relation extraction, training them in parallel. We first use the manually labeled data to train a teacher model, then use the teacher model to extract the logical rules from the distantly-supervised data, and then use the logical rules and distantly-supervised data to train a student model, and finally use the manually labeled data set to self train and fine tune the student model. When the results of logical rule extraction are used as input for relation extraction, the relation extraction process can solely rely on logical rules to predict relations between entity pairs. We use a single-layer classifier to predict the relation probability distribution of entity pairs (e_s, e_o):

$$p\left(r \mid e_s, e_o\right) = \sigma\left(W_h \tilde{H}^{(\text{Multi})}_{(s,o)} + b_h\right), \tag{7}$$

where W_h are learnable parameters, b_h is the offset term.

3.4 Loss

When calculating the loss of the model, we follow the Adaptive Thresholding Loss proposed in ATLOP [30]. Firstly, we calculate the score $s = F_o^\top W_h F_s + b_h$ for relation classification, and then generate a threshold class ATL through training. The positive and negative instances of the relation will generate scores higher and lower than the threshold (TH), and the threshold loss $\mathcal{L}$ can be calculated as:

$$\mathcal{L}_{\text{positive}} = -\sum_{s_i \neq o_i} \sum_{r \in \mathcal{R}_P} \frac{\exp\left(s_r^{(s,o)}\right)}{\sum_{r' \in \mathcal{R}_P \cup \{\text{TH}\}} \exp\left(s_{r'}^{(s,o)}\right)}, \tag{8}$$

$$\mathcal{L}_{\text{negative}} = -\sum_{s_i \neq o_i} \frac{\exp\left(s_{\text{TH}}^{(s,o)}\right)}{\sum_{r' \in \mathcal{R}_N \cup \{\text{TH}\}} \exp\left(s_{r'}^{(s,o)}\right)}, \tag{9}$$

$$\mathcal{L} = \mathcal{L}_{\text{positive}} + \mathcal{L}_{\text{negative}} \tag{10}$$

4 Experiment

4.1 Datasets and Settings

To evaluate the performance of ELRSD model, we conducted experiments on three different datasets: DocRED, Re-DocRED, and DWIE. Our model was implemented using the PyTorch framework, and we employed five different random seeds to ensure the robustness of the experimental results.

DocRED [22] is a dataset constructed from Wikipedia and Wikidata, annotated for named entities and relations. It is the largest human-annotated dataset for document-level relation extraction from raw text. In addition to the manually annotated data, it also provides large-scale distant supervision data, allowing us to perform both fully supervised and weakly supervised training using DocRED.

Re-DocRED [17] is the data set after correcting the false negative example (incomplete annotation) of the DocRED data set. A large number of relational triples are added to correct the problems of logical inconsistency and coreferential errors.

DWIE [24] is regarded as an entity centric dataset, which describes the interaction and attributes of conceptual entities at the level of complete documents. For relation extraction, it has 65 multi label relation types and 21749 relation entity pairs.

4.2   Baseline

We divide existing models into two categories: (1) Graph based: LSR [11], GAIN [25], MRN [10], DocuNet [28]. (2) Transformer based: SSAN [21], ATLOP [30], E2GRE [5], EIDER [20], SAIS [19], KD-DocRE [16]. To ensure a fair comparison of performance differences among various methods, we adopted BERT as the pretrained model premise and compared the scores obtained by different methods.

Table 1. The experimental results of ELRSD on the DocRED development and test sets. All methods' scores were derived based on BERT-base as the pre-trained language model (PLM).

Category	Model (With BERT$_{base}$)	Dev			Test		
		Ign-$F1$	$F1$	LR-$F1$	Ign-$F1$	$F1$	LR-$F1$
Graph(G)	LSR [11]	52.43	59.00	–	56.97	59.05	–
	GAIN [25]	59.14	61.22	–	59.00	61.24	–
	MRN [10]	59.74	61.61	–	59.52	61.74	–
	DocuNet [28]	59.86	61.83	–	59.93	61.86	–
Tranformer(T)	SSAN [21]	57.03	59.19	–	55.84	58.16	–
	ATLOP [30]	59.22	61.09	–	59.31	61.30	–
	E2GRE [5]	55.22	58.72	47.12	–	–	–
	CFER [2]	59.23	61.41	–	59.16	61.28	–
	EIDER [20]	60.51	62.48	50.71	60.42	62.47	51.27
	SAIS [19]	59.98	62.96	53.70	60.96	62.77	52.88
G+T	ELRSD (Ours)	**61.52**	**63.58**	**54.30**	**61.33**	**63.40**	**54.01**

4.3   Main Results of DocRED

As shown in Table 1, our model outperforms previous state-of-the-art methods, achieving an $F1$ score of 63.40% and an $Ign-F1$ score of 61.33% on the DocRED test set, representing improvements of 0.63% and 0.37%, respectively, over the previous best model, SAIS [19]. $LR - F1$ is a new benchmark for evaluating the quality of evidence extracted by logical rule extraction models and for assessing the effectiveness of relation extraction models. Our ELRSD model outperforms EIDER [20] on the development set and test set by 1.10% and 0.93%, respectively.

4.4   Main Results of Re-DocRED and DWIE

The experimental results on Re-DocRED and DWIE are presented in Table 2, where the best performance scores are highlighted in bold. GTN is a document level RE model with Graph-Transformer Network (GTN), which has achieved advanced scores in this field. It includes two cores: 1) graph attention, which models both the global and local context of nodes in the document graph; 2) Cross attention enables GTN to capture non entity clue information from the document encoder. We observe that ELRSD achieves $F1$ scores on the development and test sets of Re-DocRED, respectively, outperforming GTN-BERT [26] by 1.57% and 0.94%. Meanwhile, the $IgnF1$ scores have also increased by 1.06% and 0.44% compared to GTN-BERT, respectively. Additionally, ELRSD exhibits a slight improvement in performance on the DWIE dataset, achieving a 0.60% increase in $F1$ score and a 0.94% increase in $Ign - F1$ score compared to GTN-BERT on the test set.

Table 2. The experimental results on the Re-DocRED and DWIE dataset and the rest scores refer to the academic papers of [26]

Model (With BERT$_{base}$)	Re-DocRED				DWIE			
	Dev		Test		Dev		Test	
	Ign-$F1$	$F1$	Ign-$F1$	$F1$	Ign-$F1$	$F1$	Ign-$F1$	$F1$
GAIN-BERT [25]	71.99	73.49	71.88	73.44	58.63	62.55	62.37	67.57
DocuNet-BERT [28]	73.68	74.65	73.60	74.49	65.65	71.52	70.04	76.79
KMGRE-BERT [8]	73.33	74.44	73.39	74.46	65.56	71.40	69.94	76.71
ATLOP-BERT [30]	73.35	74.22	73.22	74.02	63.57	69.96	67.56	74.36
KD-DocRE-BERT [16]	73.76	74.69	73.67	74.55	65.84	71.78	70.27	77.01
GTN-BERT [26]	75.03	75.85	74.85	75.77	67.42	**73.45**	71.90	78.55
ELRSD (Ours)	**76.09**	**77.42**	**75.29**	**76.71**	**68.85**	73.42	**72.84**	**79.15**

5   Analysis

5.1   Ablation Study

We conducted ablation experiments on each layer of ELRSD to explore the impact of each layer on the overall performance of the model. From Table 3, we

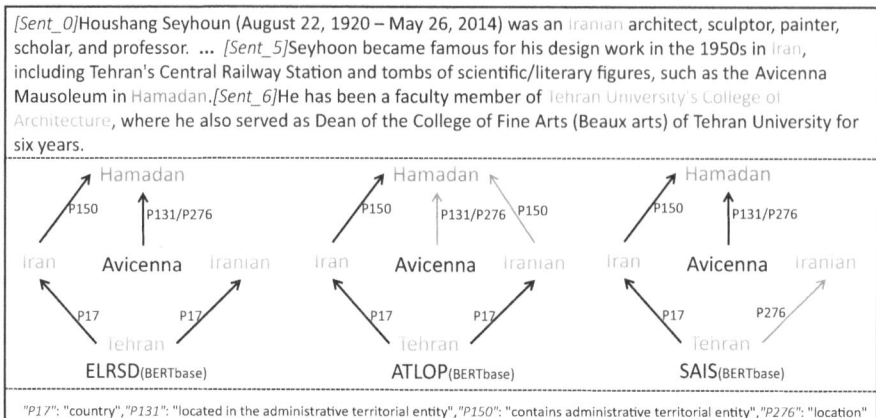

Fig. 3. The comparison results of a case on three advanced models show that the entity is marked with special color, P_{number} is the relation label, and the red arrow is the prediction error. (Color figure online)

can see that when the TransFNN layer is removed first, there is a slight decline in performance scores, which we suspect is related to the use of a pre-trained BERT model. Subsequently, removing the MHC layer results in a severe drop in scores, and similarly, there is a substantial decrease in scores when feature fusion is not performed. Finally, when both the MHC and TransFNN layers are simultaneously ablated, the performance scores show the most noticeable decline, with Ign-F1 decreasing by 2.71% and F1 decreasing by 3.7%.

Table 3. Statistics of ablation experiment results for ELRSD

Model(With BERT)	Re-DocRED-Test	
	Ign-$F1$	$F1$
• Model layer ablation		
ELRSD(ours)	**75.29**	**76.71**
w/o Transformer-FFN (TransFNN) Layer	75.01	76.21
w/o MultiHeads-Conv (MHC) SubLayer	72.94	73.32
w/o Representation Aggregation	73.87	74.61
w/o MHC and TransFNN	72.58	73.01
w/o Both	72.88	73.21

5.2   Case Study

To further demonstrate the excellent performance of ELRSD, we extract a case from the DocRED dataset and compare it with two other state-of-the-art methods. From Fig. 3, we understand that there are four types of relations among five entities. ATLOP only identifies 3 types of relations, ignoring the relation *"located in the administrative territorial entity"* between *"Avicenna"* and *"Hamadan"*, and erroneously identifying a relation *"contains administrative territorial entity"* between *"Iranian"* and *"Hamadan"*. SAIS incorrectly identifies the relation *"country"* between *"Tehran"* and *"Iranian"* as *"location"*. In contrast, ELRSD perfectly extracts the correct relation network in this case.

5.3   Effect Analysis of MC and LR

MC: MC utilize parallel operations across multiple subspaces to capture various types of relations and contextual information, integrating multiple scales and reducing the bias of a single viewpoint, thereby providing richer feature representations. This also assists the model in understanding relations between distant sentences within a document, enabling more accurate relation extraction. Additionally, we employ parallel computation without adding extra computational burden to the model, thereby maintaining low computational overhead.

LR: Evidence sentences provide critical information sources, and through logical rules, this information can be effectively integrated and correlated, thereby enhancing the accuracy and robustness of relation extraction. At the same time, logical rules help the model understand the relations and context between sentences, allowing for more accurate identification and extraction of relations in complex documents. Moreover, reasonable logical rules can reduce noise and misjudgment, improving the model's ability to handle long texts and diverse sentences, ensuring the reliability and consistency of extraction results. Therefore, the extraction of logical rules is an indispensable subtask in the DocRE task.

6   Related Work

6.1   DocRE

Relation Extraction (RE) is a critical task in information extraction and serves as the foundation for many advanced NLP tasks [22]. In recent years, numerous RE methods have utilized pre-extracted named entities and established links between them using heuristic or machine learning-based algorithms [12].

Graph-Based: Graph-based methods convert sentences in a document into dependency graphs and then perform relation reasoning. [29] proposed a pruning technique centered around dependency paths to remove irrelevant information for extracting correct relations. [4] employed graph convolutional networks to guide attention, generating a fully connected attention matrix instead of pruning dependency trees, which is also regarded as a form of soft pruning capable of capturing multi-hop dependency information. Building upon this, [11] introduced the Latent Structure Refinement model, primarily utilizing a new iterative refinement strategy for incrementally learning document-level structures and making predictions in an end-to-end manner. Meanwhile, [25] proposed the Graph Aggregation-and-Inference Network, aiming to construct a heterogeneous mention-level graph and then build an entity-level graph, followed by explicit inference through a reasoning network. Subsequently, [14] used heuristics to generate reasoning paths and incorporated them into subgraphs.

Transformer-Based: The research by [18] indicates that using Transformer-based models can significantly improve performance. [23] designed Mention Reference Prediction (MRP) based on a masking strategy, which can capture coreferential relations in documents. Recently, [21] proposed integrating structural dependency relations with PLM to enhance performance. Additionally, [30] introduced techniques such as local context pooling and adaptive threshold loss to enhance relation extraction. [27] proposed a self-distillation training framework with a dual-branch structure. This framework explicitly models the relation reasoning process and integrates it into conventional supervised training.

6.2   DocLR

In recent years, an increasing number of scholars have started to pay attention to the logical rule extraction capability of relation extraction models [6,19,20]. Utilizing logical rule retrieval as a subtask can capture more evidence information for relation extraction [19,20,26]. [5] introduced a module for predicting supporting evidence sentences and serialized document texts to simplify the task of PLM. [19] posited that there exists an intermediate reasoning stage from inputting documents with determined entities to outputting relation extraction, and proposed improving relation extraction by quantifying and supervising key reasoning stages. [20] employed multi-task learning to jointly extract relations and evidence, utilizing the extracted evidence for logical reasoning. [26] expanded the patterns of logical reasoning by improving the previous self-attention reasoning module and introducing a self-distillation training framework. Compared to previous methods, we enhance the specificity of logical rule extraction by leveraging a collaborative learning approach that integrates MultiHeads-Conv and Transformer-FNN, while simultaneously reducing memory overhead through the parallel operation of Logical Reasoning (LR) and Relation Extraction (RE).

7   Conclusion

To address the issues of unclear logical rules in document-level relation extraction and inefficient extraction of logical rules from evidence information, we propose ELRSD, a DocRE model that integrates transformer and multi-head graph convolution through self-distillation. ELRSD achieves state-of-the-art scores on three authoritative benchmarks. In the future, we plan to conduct experiments on more datasets and leverage ELRSD's excellent scalability to apply it to fields such as entity recognition and text classification.

References

1. Choi, M., Lim, H., Choo, J.: Prism: enhancing low-resource document-level relation extraction with relation-aware score calibration. In: ACL-IJCNLP, pp. 39–47 (2023)
2. Dai, D., Ren, J., Zeng, S., Chang, B., Sui, Z.: Coarse-to-fine entity representations for document-level relation extraction. In: NLPCC, pp. 185–197 (2023)
3. Fan, S., Mo, S., Niu, J.: Boosting document-level relation extraction by mining and injecting logical rules. In: Proceedings of the 2022 Conference on Empirical Methods in Natural Language Processing, pp. 10311–10323 (2022)
4. Guo, Z., Zhang, Y., Lu, W.: Attention guided graph convolutional networks for relation extraction. In: ACL, pp. 241–251 (2019)
5. Huang, K., Qi, P., Wang, G., Ma, T., Huang, J.: Entity and evidence guided document-level relation extraction. In: ACL(RepL4NLP-2021), pp. 307–315 (2021)
6. Huang, Q., Hao, S., Ye, Y., Zhu, S., Feng, Y., Zhao, D.: Does recommend-revise produce reliable annotations? an analysis on missing instances in docred. In: ACL, pp. 6241–6252 (2022)
7. Jia, R., Wong, C., Poon, H.: Document-level n-ary relation extraction with multi-scale representation learning. In: NAACL-HLT, pp. 3693–3704 (2019)
8. Jiang, F., Niu, J., Mo, S., Fan, S.: Key mention pairs guided document-level relation extraction. In: COLING, pp. 1904–1914 (2022)
9. Kipf, T.N., Welling, M.: Semi-supervised classification with graph convolutional networks. In: ICLR (2016)
10. Li, J., Xu, K., Li, F., Fei, H., Ren, Y., Ji, D.: Mrn: a locally and globally mention-based reasoning network for document-level relation extraction. In: ACL-IJCNLP, pp. 1359–1370 (2021)
11. Nan, G., Guo, Z., Sekulić, I., Lu, W.: Reasoning with latent structure refinement for document-level relation extraction. In: ACL, pp. 1546–1557 (2020)
12. Nasar, Z., Jaffry, S.W., Malik, M.K.: Named entity recognition and relation extraction: state-of-the-art. ACM Comput. Surv. (CSUR) **54**(1), 1–39 (2021)
13. Peng, N., Poon, H., Quirk, C., Toutanova, K., Yih, W.T.: Cross-sentence n-ary relation extraction with graph lstms. TACL **5**, 101–115 (2017)
14. Peng, X., Zhang, C., Xu, K.: Document-level relation extraction via subgraph reasoning. In: IJCAI, pp. 4331–4337 (2022)
15. Ru, D., et al.: Learning logic rules for document-level relation extraction. In: Proceedings of the 2021 Conference on Empirical Methods in Natural Language Processing, pp. 1239–1250 (2021)
16. Tan, Q., He, R., Bing, L., Ng, H.T.: Document-level relation extraction with adaptive focal loss and knowledge distillation. In: ACL, pp. 1672–1681 (2022)

17. Tan, Q., Xu, L., Bing, L., Ng, H.T., Aljunied, S.M.: Revisiting docred-addressing the false negative problem in relation extraction. In: EMNLP, pp. 8472–8487 (2022)
18. Wang, H., Focke, C., Sylvester, R., Mishra, N., Wang, W.: Fine-tune bert for docred with two-step process. arXiv preprint arXiv:1909.11898 (2019)
19. Xiao, Y., Zhang, Z., Mao, Y., Yang, C., Han, J.: Sais: supervising and augmenting intermediate steps for document-level relation extraction. In: NAACL, pp. 2395–2409 (2022)
20. Xie, Y., Shen, J., Li, S., Mao, Y., Han, J.: Eider: empowering document-level relation extraction with efficient evidence extraction and inference-stage fusion. In: ACL, pp. 257–268 (2022)
21. Xu, B., Wang, Q., Lyu, Y., Zhu, Y., Mao, Z.: Entity structure within and throughout: modeling mention dependencies for document-level relation extraction. In: AAAI, pp. 14149–14157 (2021)
22. Yao, Y., et al.: Docred: a large-scale document-level relation extraction dataset. In: ACL, pp. 764–777 (2019)
23. Ye, D., et al.: Coreferential reasoning learning for language representation. In: EMNLP, pp. 7170–7186 (2020)
24. Zaporojets, K., Deleu, J., Develder, C., Demeester, T.: Dwie: an entity-centric dataset for multi-task document-level information extraction. Inf. Process. Manag. **58**(4), 102563 (2021)
25. Zeng, S., Xu, R., Chang, B., Li, L.: Double graph based reasoning for document-level relation extraction. In: EMNLP, pp. 1630–1640 (2020)
26. Zhang, L., Min, Z., Su, J., Yu, P., Wang, A., Chen, Y.: Exploring effective inter-encoder semantic interaction for document-level relation extraction. In: IJCAI, pp. 5278–5286 (2023)
27. Zhang, L., et al.: Exploring self-distillation based relational reasoning training for document-level relation extraction. In: AAAI, pp. 13967–13975 (2023)
28. Zhang, N., et al.: Document-level relation extraction as semantic segmentation. In: IJCAI, pp. 3999–4006 (2021)
29. Zhang, Y., Qi, P., Manning, C.D.: Graph convolution over pruned dependency trees improves relation extraction. In: EMNLP, pp. 2205–2215 (2018)
30. Zhou, W., Huang, K., Ma, T., Huang, J.: Document-level relation extraction with adaptive thresholding and localized context pooling. In: AAAI, pp. 14612–14620 (2021)

Prompt-Based Joint Contrastive Learning for Zero-Shot Relation Extraction

Jianjian Zou[1], Yuhui Xiao[1], Sichi Zhou[1], Wei Li[2], and Qun Yang[1(✉)]

[1] College of Computer Science and Technology, Nanjing University of Aeronautics
and Astronautics, Nanjing, China
{jj.zou,xiaoyuhui,zhousichi,qun.yang}@nuaa.edu.cn
[2] Nari Group Corporation (State Grid Electric Power Research Institute),
Nanjing, China
liwei@sgepri.sgcc.com.cn

Abstract. Zero-shot relation extraction is proposed to address the issue that the model performance drops dramatically when identifying novel relations that cannot be observed at the training stage. Existing works focus more on the pattern of matching between instances and relation descriptions, however, they ignore the capabilities of pre-trained model in zero-shot scenarios. In this paper, we propose a novel prompt-based joint contrastive learning framework (PCL) to enhance zero-shot relation extraction. Specifically, we construct a prompt template to leverage prior knowledge in PLMs for better representation of the relation. In order to learn more effective features, we design two contrastive learning modules to jointly optimize the obtained representations. Experimental results on two publicly available datasets show that PCL outperforms the previous methods.

Keywords: zero-shot relation extraction · prompt learning · contrastive learning

1 Introduction

Relation extraction (RE) aims to identify the relation between a pair of entities mentioned in unstructured text. Since the supervised paradigm requires a large amount of labeled data, which is costly and impractical in real-life scenarios, zero-shot relation extraction (ZSRE) is proposed to address the above limitations. It learns the semantic features of seen classes in order to generalize to unseen classes. Some works reformulate ZSRE as other natural language processing tasks, such as slot-filling [12] and text entailment [15,18]. However, they all require additional manual annotation, which is expensive and time-consuming. RelationPrompt [4] utilizes generative models to generate pseudo-samples for unseen classes. ZS-BERT [2] and RE-Matching [24] propose to match instances with corresponding relation descriptions in order to enhance the performance of ZSRE. Despite they achieve promising results, the gap between pre-training and fine-tuning of pre-trained language models (PLMs) hinders better performance.

Recently, prompt-based learning [19] has attracted a lot of attention. The core idea of prompt learning is to reformulate the downstream task as a cloze-style task by wrapping the input text with a task-specific template, thereby facilitating the transfer and adaptation of knowledge from PLMs to downstream tasks. Taking the relation extraction as an example, given the sentence *"The capital of France is Paris"*, the template *"The relationship between head entity and tail entity is* [MASK]*"* is used to wrap the input as *"The capital of France is Paris. The relation between France and Paris is* [MASK]*"*. Then PLMs are asked to infer the word to fill in [MASK], and the word is further mapped to corresponding label through a verbalizer. Moreover, some studies [13,23] investigate the potential of large language models (LLMs) to address ZSRE. However, these approaches require domain knowledge and well-designed prompts.

In this work, we propose a novel **P**rompt-based joint **C**ontrastive **L**earning framework (PCL) to address aforementioned issues. Specifically, to take advantage of the prior knowledge in PLMs, we guide PLMs to output the relation representation by constructing a simple prompt template. Next, we decompose the matching module into three fine-grained interactions, namely head entity, tail entity and relation, and design two contrastive learning modules to optimize the resulting representations. One of the contrastive modules encourages the model to push similar instances closer together and dissimilar instances further away in the feature space, so as to better distinguish the differences between instances. Another contrastive learning module projects and aligns relation representations and relation description representations into the same embedding space. By jointly optimizing the two contrastive modules, PCL can not only learn subtle differences between instances, but also establish an effective mapping of instances to relation descriptions. When testing, we can utilize PCL to generate entity representation and relation representation of new-coming sentence, and then predict its relation label by using nearest neighbor search.

In summary, our contributions are as follows:

- We propose a prompt-based zero-shot relation extraction framework to leverage prior knowledge in PLMs to obtain better representations of relation;
- To optimize the entity representation and the relation representation, we design two contrastive learning modules. These modules are modeled based on instances-instances and instances-relation descriptions, respectively, which improve the performance of the model.;
- We conduct experiments on two well-known datasets, and experimental results show that PCL outperforms previous baselines and achieves new state-of-the-art.

2   Related Work

2.1   Zero-Shot Relation Extraction

The potential of zero-shot relation extraction to address the limitations of conventional supervised paradigm has attracted increasing attention in recent years.

ESIM [12] turns zero-shot relation extraction into a question answering task. PromptMatch [18] treat zero-shot relation extraction as a text entailment task. RelationPrompt [4] leverages the semantics of relation labels to generate samples for unseen classes that will be used during training. ZS-BERT [2] proposes representation matching-based approach that encodes relation and instance into the same semantic space, respectively, and generates the prediction of unseen relation for new sentence by nearest neighbor search. RCL [21] enhances the representation of hard examples through contrastive learning. RE-Matching [24] introduces a fine-grained semantic matching method to enhance the performance of ZSRE. Despite their impressive results, they fail to focus on the gap between the pre-training phase of the PLMs and the downstream task to further take advantage of the potential capabilities of PLMs to enhance the matching process.

2.2 Prompt-Based Learning

Influenced by GPT-3 [1], prompt-based learning has recently gained a lot of attention. PET [19] uses manual-designed templates and verbalizers for prompting text classification tasks. PTR [8] applies several sub-prompts constructed by logical rules to prompt-tuning pre-trained model. KnowPrompt [3] injects knowledge into prompt template and answer construction, thereby encoding rich semantic knowledge between entity types and relation. Since constructing templates manually requires domain knowledge and can be challenging to achieve optimal performance, several works explore automatic designing and optimizing prompts [6,10,20]. However, without any data to optimize the verbalizer under the zero-shot setting, it is difficult to apply prompt-tuning directly. To solve the above problems, we combine prompt-based learning with matching-based methods to deal with zero-shot relation extraction.

3 Methodology

3.1 Task Formulation

In zero-shot relation extraction, let $Y_s = \{y_1^s, y_2^s, \ldots, y_n^s\}$ and $Y_u = \{y_1^u, y_2^u, \ldots, y_m^u\}$ denote the labels of seen and unseen classes, respectively. Such two sets are disjoint, i.e., $Y_s \cap Y_u = \varnothing$, and only Y_s is available during training. Given the training set $D = \{x, e_1, e_2, y, d\}$ with N samples, consisting of input instance x, two entities (e_1, e_2) mentioned in x, relation label $y \in Y_s$ and its corresponding relation description d. Our objective is to train a model $\mathcal{M}$ that can align input sentence with its corresponding relation description. During testing, $\mathcal{M}$ should have the ability to accurately predict the label of new sentence.

3.2 Method Overview

An overview of our proposed PCL is shown in Fig. 1. First, input sentence x is wrapped with prompt template $T(\cdot)$ and then $T(x)$ is encoded with BERT [5].

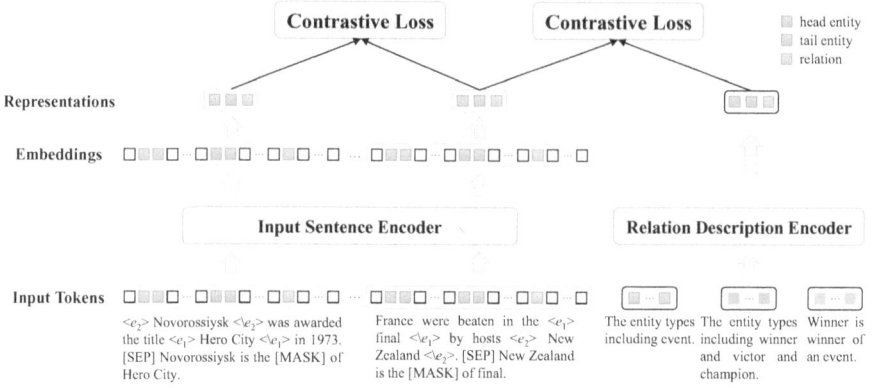

Fig. 1. Overview of the proposed PCL.

Next, we decompose the matching module into three fine-grained interactions, including head entity, tail entity, and relation. In order to learn the distinctions between instances and the alignment of instances with relation descriptions, we then design two contrastive learning modules. One of them expects similar instances to be closer in feature space than dissimilar ones, while the other aligns each instance to its relation description and differentiates it from other relation descriptions. Jointly optimizing two contrastive learning modules can effectively enhance entity representation and relation representation. In the test phase, we use cosine similarity to calculate the matching score between the new sentence and the unseen label, and obtain the maximum score as the prediction result. The details are described in the following sections.

3.3   Input Sentence Encoder

Given an input sentence $x = \{x_1, x_2, \ldots, x_L\}$, where L is the length of the sentence. Before encoding x, we insert four special tokens $\langle e_1 \rangle$, $\langle \backslash e_1 \rangle$, $\langle e_2 \rangle$, $\langle \backslash e_2 \rangle$ to explicitly mark entity position. Then we construct the prompt template $T(\cdot)$ to wrap x. The final input x_{prompt} can be formalized as:

$$x = x_1, \ldots, \langle e_1 \rangle, x_{e_1}, \langle \backslash e_1 \rangle, \ldots, \langle e_2 \rangle, x_{e_2}, \langle \backslash e_2 \rangle, \ldots, x_L \qquad (1)$$

$$x_{\text{prompt}} = \texttt{[CLS]}\ x\ \texttt{[SEP]}\ T(x)\ \texttt{[SEP]} \qquad (2)$$

where [CLS] and [SEP] are predefined in PLMs, x_{e_1}, x_{e_2} denote the span of the head entity and tail entity, respectively. Next, we utilize BERT [5] to encode x_{prompt}, and take the hidden state of the [MASK] token as the relation representation. The entity representation is obtained by maxpooling the hidden state of the entity tokens.

$$\mathbf{h}_1, \ldots, \mathbf{h}_n = \text{BERT}(x_{\text{prompt}}) \qquad (3)$$

$$\mathbf{h}_r = \mathbf{h}_{\texttt{[MASK]}} \tag{4}$$

$$\mathbf{h}_{e_1/e_2} = \text{MaxPooling}\left(\mathbf{h}_{b_h/b_t}, \ldots, \mathbf{h}_{e_h/e_t}\right) \tag{5}$$

where $\mathbf{h}_{\texttt{[MASK]}}$ represents the hidden states of [MASK]. b_h, e_h, b_t, e_t denote the beginning and end position indexes of the head and tail entities, respectively.

3.4   Relation Description Encoder

For each relation label, its semantic representation can be learned based on its relation description $d \in \left\{d_{y_i^s} | i = 1, 2, \ldots, n\right\}$. Following [24], we also separate the head entity d_{e_1} and tail entity d_{e_2} from the relation description d and augment the entity descriptions with synonyms and rule-based template filling to obtain entity representations. Then we use Sentence-BERT [17] as the encoder to obtain the relation description representation $\hat{d}$, and entity descriptions representation $\hat{d}_{e_1}$ and $\hat{d}_{e_2}$, respectively.

3.5   Contrastive Learning Module

Sentences expressing the same relation should have similar entity representations and relation representations. Therefore, we utilize supervised contrastive loss to enhance ability of PCL to distinguish differences between instances. In other words, this module pushes instances with the same relational semantics closer and instances with different relational semantics farther away. Specifically, for a mini-batch with N samples, sample pairs with the same label are considered positive pairs, and sample pairs with different labels are considered negative pairs. The training objective [11] can be formalized as:

$$\mathcal{L}_{ins} = \frac{1}{M_{y_i} - 1} \sum_{j=1}^{N} l_{i \neq j} l_{y_i = y_j} \log \frac{e^{\text{sim}(\mathbf{h}_i, \mathbf{h}_j)/\tau}}{e^{\text{sim}(\mathbf{h}_i, \mathbf{h}_j)/\tau} + \sum_{k=1}^{N} l_{y_i \neq y_k} e^{\text{sim}(\mathbf{h}_i, \mathbf{h}_k)/\tau}} \tag{6}$$

where y_i and y_j represent the label of the i-th sample and the j-th sample, respectively. M_{y_i} represents the number of samples whose label is y_i in a mini-batch. $l_{i \neq j}$, $l_{y_i = y_j}$ and $l_{y_i \neq y_k}$ are similar indicator functions. Taking $l_{i \neq j}$ as an example, $l_{i \neq j} = 1$ if $i \neq j$, otherwise $l_{i \neq j} = 0$. $\mathbf{h}_i \in \left\{\mathbf{h}_r^i, \mathbf{h}_{e_1}^i, \mathbf{h}_{e_2}^i\right\}$, where $\mathbf{h}_r^i$ denotes the relation representation, $\mathbf{h}_{e_1}^i$ and $\mathbf{h}_{e_2}^i$ denote the head and tail entity representation, respectively. $\text{sim}(a, b)$ denotes the cosine similarity $\frac{a^\top b}{\|a\| \cdot \|b\|}$, and τ is temperature hyperparameter.

Besides modeling relational semantics through interactions between sentences pairs, the relation descriptions are also beneficial for obtaining better relation representation. To establish an effective mapping of instances to labels, we further add a contrastive module between instances and relation descriptions. Specifically, we regard instance and its corresponding relation description as positive pair, and relation descriptions of other seen classes as negative samples. We use InfoNCE [16] to optimize the training process:

$$\mathcal{L}_{rel} = \log \frac{e^{\text{sim}(\mathbf{h}_i, \hat{d}_{y_i})/\tau}}{\sum_{j=1}^{|Y_s|} e^{\text{sim}(\mathbf{h}_i, \hat{d}_{y_j})/\tau}} \tag{7}$$

where $|Y_s|$ is the number of seen classes during training. Similar to $\mathbf{h}_i$, $\hat{d}_{y_i} \in \left\{ \hat{d}_r^{y_i}, \hat{d}_{e_1}^{y_i}, \hat{d}_{e_2}^{y_i} \right\}$ is attribute triplet of relation description.

3.6 Training and Test

The training objective of PCL is to make instance as close to its relation description as possible and as far away as possible from other relation descriptions. Furthermore, we utilize cross-entropy loss to train PCL to predict the [MASK] token as an appropriate relation label.

$$\mathcal{L}_{CE} = y_i \log p\left(y|x_{\text{prompt}}\right) \tag{8}$$

The overall training objective is as follows:

$$\mathcal{L} = \frac{1}{N} \sum_{i=1}^{N} \left(\mathcal{L}_{CE} + \mathcal{L}_{ins} + \mathcal{L}_{rel}\right) \tag{9}$$

After training the model, we can generate the relation attribute triples $(\mathbf{h}_r, \mathbf{h}_{e_1}, \mathbf{h}_{e_2})$ of the new-coming sentence, then calculate the cosine similarity score with each label $y_i \in Y_u$ and choose the label $\hat{r}$ with the highest score as the prediction result. It can be formulated as follows:

$$\text{score}\left(x, y_i\right) = \text{cosine}\left(\mathbf{h}_r, \hat{d}_i\right) + \text{cosine}\left(\mathbf{h}_{e_1}, \hat{d}_{e_1}^i\right) + \text{cosine}\left(\mathbf{h}_{e_2}, \hat{d}_{e_2}^i\right) \tag{10}$$

$$\hat{r} = \arg\max_i \text{score}\left(x, y_i\right) \tag{11}$$

4 Experiment

4.1 Datasets

To ensure a fair comparison, we maintain the same setup as in the previous work, we evaluate PCL on FewRel [9] and Wiki-ZSL [2]. Following [24], we use $m \in \{5, 10, 15\}$ relations as unseen classes for test set, and the remaining relations as seen classes for training set, so as to ensure that $Y_s \cap Y_u = \varnothing$. For each setting, we repeat the experiment five times and take the average value as the result. We use precision (Prec.), recall (Rec.), and Macro F1 (F_1) as evaluation metrics to verify the performance of PCL in different zero-shot scenarios.

4.2 Implementation Details

Following [24], we adopt bert-base-uncased as the input instance encoder and Sentence-Bert [17] stsb-bert-base as the relation description encoder. The prompt template is constructed as *"tail entity is the* [MASK] *of head entity"*. We choose AdamW [14] as the optimizer. The learning rate is 2e-6, the batch size is 64 and the temperature $\tau = 0.01$. All experiments are conducted using an NVIDIA TITAN Xp.

4.3 Baseline Methods

We compare PCL with previous methods consisting of a classic supervised method, state-of-the-art matching-based ZeroRE methods, a seq2seq-based ZeroRE method and LLMs-based methods. For supervised method, we choose **R-BERT** [22]. For ZeroRE methods, **ESIM** [12], **PromptMatch** [18], **ZS-BERT** [2] and **RE-Matching** [24] are selected to compare with PCL. For seq2seq-based ZeroRE method, we choose **PromptMatch** [18]. For LLMs-based methods, we investigate simple prompting strategies **VANILLA** and state-of-the-art prompting strategies **SUMASK** [13].

4.4 Experimental Results

Main Results. The experimental results on FewRel and Wiki-ZSL datasets are shown in Table 1. Compared with the previous methods, PCL achieves the best performance when targeting at a different number of unseen relations. These results demonstrate the superiority of PCL in zero-shot relation extraction. Notably, when the unseen label set size m are 5 and 15, PCL has a significant improvement over the previous methods on the Wiki-ZSL dataset, increasing by 5.58% and 2.27%, respectively. It demonstrates that the proposed two contrastive modules in PCL can better deal with the noise in Wiki-ZSL as it is generated by distant supervision.

Ablation Study. We conduct ablation experiments on the two datasets to verify the effectiveness of each component in the PCL, and the results are shown in Table 2. As can be seen from the results, combining the prompt template and the two contrastive modules can significantly improve the performance of the two datasets. When we use the hidden state of the [CLS] token as the relation representation instead of using the [MASK] token in the prompt template, the results on the two datasets drop by 9.93% and 7.33%, respectively. This demonstrates that the prompt template can steer the PLMs in generating more effective representation of relation. For the two contrastive learning modules, the prediction results will drop regardless of which module is removed. It is worth noting that relation descriptions plays a crucial role in the matching process, as the model relies on this information to align instances with relation descriptions. After removing the ins-to-rel contrastive module, the model performance drops dramatically, with drops of 15.2% and 21.75% on both datasets,

Table 1. Main results on two relation extraction datasets. The results of the baselines are retrieved from [24] and [13].

Unseen Labels	Method	Wiki-ZSL			FewRel		
		Prec.	Rec.	F_1	Prec.	Rec.	F_1
m = 5	R-BERT	39.22	43.27	41.15	42.19	48.61	45.17
	ESIM	48.58	47.74	48.16	56.27	58.44	57.33
	ZS-BERT	71.54	72.39	71.96	76.96	78.86	77.90
	PromptMatch	77.39	75.90	76.63	91.14	90.86	91.00
	RelationPrompt$_{\text{NoGen}}$	51.78	46.76	48.93	72.36	58.61	64.57
	RelationPrompt	70.66	**83.75**	76.63	90.15	88.50	89.30
	RE-Matching	78.19	78.41	78.30	92.82	92.34	92.58
	VANILLA	64.47	70.83	67.50	67.41	72.97	70.08
	SUMASK	75.64	70.96	73.23	78.27	72.55	75.30
	PCL	**84.80**	82.97	**83.88**	**93.30**	**92.97**	**93.02**
m = 10	R-BERT	26.18	29.69	27.82	25.52	33.02	28.20
	ESIM	44.12	45.46	44.78	42.89	44.17	43.52
	ZS-BERT	60.51	60.98	60.74	56.92	57.59	57.25
	PromptMatch	71.86	71.14	71.50	83.05	82.55	82.80
	RelationPrompt$_{\text{NoGen}}$	54.87	36.52	43.80	66.47	48.28	55.61
	RelationPrompt	68.51	**74.76**	71.50	80.33	79.62	79.96
	RE-Matching	74.39	73.54	73.96	83.21	82.64	82.93
	VANILLA	41.83	46.22	43.92	42.48	46.26	44.29
	SUMASK	62.31	61.08	61.69	64.77	60.94	62.80
	PCL	**75.22**	74.14	**74.68**	**83.92**	**83.22**	**83.57**
m = 15	R-BERT	17.31	18.82	18.03	16.95	19.37	18.08
	ESIM	27.31	29.62	28.42	29.15	31.59	30.32
	ZS-BERT	34.12	34.38	34.25	35.54	38.19	36.82
	PromptMatch	62.13	61.76	61.95	72.83	72.10	72.46
	RelationPrompt$_{\text{NoGen}}$	54.45	29.43	37.45	66.49	40.05	49.38
	RelationPrompt	63.69	67.93	65.74	74.33	72.51	73.40
	RE-Matching	67.31	67.33	67.32	73.80	**73.52**	73.66
	VANILLA	23.17	27.82	25.28	25.71	27.77	26.70
	SUMASK	43.55	40.27	41.85	44.76	41.13	42.87
	PCL	**70.03**	**69.15**	**69.59**	**74.97**	72.76	**73.85**

respectively. When both modules are discarded, model performance is seriously affected, which demonstrates the effectiveness of both modules. When all components are removed, the matching performance will be severely hurt.

4.5   Hyper-Parameter Analysis

Effect of Different Temperature. Temperature τ is an important hyper-parameter in the optimization objective. By fixing m = 10 and varying τ, the results in terms of F1 scores on two datasets are exhibited on Fig. 2. Tempera-

Table 2. Ablation study about the impact of individual components in PCL on the downstream task performance (m=10). "ins-to-ins" indicates the contrastive module between instances and instances (Eq. 6). "ins-to-rel" indicates the contrastive module between instances and relation descriptions (Eq. 7).

Method	prompt template	ins-to-ins	ins-to-rel	FewRel			Wiki-ZSL		
				Prec.	Rec.	F_1	Prec.	Rec.	F_1
PCL		✓	✓	76.51	70.61	73.44	69.28	65.52	67.35
	✓		✓	82.29	81.32	81.80	72.61	71.96	72.28
	✓	✓		73.06	63.89	68.17	58.28	48.48	52.93
	✓			65.72	62.77	64.21	45.94	45.20	45.57
				54.18	56.17	55.16	34.66	36.82	35.71
	✓	✓	✓	83.92	83.22	83.57	75.22	74.14	74.68

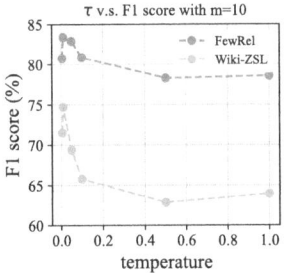

Fig. 2. Experimental results with different temperature τ (m=10)

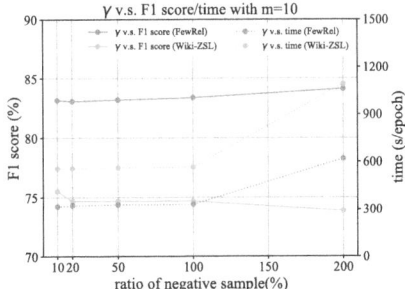

Fig. 3. Experimental results with different ratio γ of negative samples (m=10).

ture τ has a huge impact on performance because it controls how smooth the probability distribution of the final output is, i.e., how much attention is paid to hard instances. Small τ makes the model give more penalty to the closer negative samples. Nevertheless, not always the smaller values of τ lead to better performance. Too small τ will cause numerical instability. We would suggest setting τ = 0.01 to achieve satisfactory results on both datasets.

Effect of Different Ratio of Negative Samples. We further discuss the effect of the ratio of negative samples. γ is defined as the ratio of the number of negative samples to the batch size. In particular, when $\gamma = 2.0$, we use data augmentation to amplify the semantic difference between similar instances without breaking the semantic of relation representations. Specifically, we augment sentence embeddings by feeding the same input sentence to BERT again [7]. The experimental results are displayed in Fig. 3. When $\gamma \leq 1.0$, the performance of the model is not significantly affected by changes in γ. When $\gamma = 2.0$, inconsistent results are exhibited on the two datasets. Although the results improve

Table 3. Experimental results with different prompt template on FewRel (m = 10). h indicates *head entity*, t indicates *tail entity*.

Template	Prec.	Rec.	F_1
h, [MASK], t	80.59	81.84	81.21
t *is* h's [MASK]	82.91	82.71	82.81
t *is the* [MASK] *of* h	83.92	83.22	83.57

when using data augmentation on the FewRel dataset, the time cost is almost doubled. A more compromised approach is to lose a little accuracy in exchange for an increase in efficiency. In contrast, using data augmentation on the Wiki-ZSL dataset results in performance degradation, possibly because the Wiki-ZSL dataset contains more noise, which is amplified with data augmentation and thus causing interference. We believe that considering all available data as negative samples (i.e., $\gamma = 1.0$) is beneficial for the model to measure semantics globally.

Effect of Different Prompt Template. In the proposed PCL, the prompt template is used to guide PLMs to output the relation representation of input sentence. In order to explore the impact of different prompt templates, we construct three simple prompt templates. The experimental results are shown in Table 3. The prompt template "h, [MASK], t" has the worst performance compared with other templates, which indicates that abstract prompt template is not conducive to PLMs understanding semantics. In other words, prompt templates that follow human natural language descriptions can better guide PLMs to output the correct relation representation. We believe that a well-designed prompt template can further enhance the final matching results. However, this is not the focus of this paper. PCL demonstrates impressive results with a simple prompt template. We leave this as future work.

5   Limitations and Future Work

Our model and experiments show that the prompt learning and contrastive learning can effectively optimize the relation embeddings to enhance the performance of zero-shot relation extraction. However, this work still has the following limitations: (1) Existing work including PCL focuses only on conventional zero-shot learning, where the test set only contains data from the unseen classes. In real-world scenarios, a more common condition is generalized zero-shot learning, where the test set contains data from both seen and unseen classes, making it more challenging. (2) As described in Sect. 4.5, we believe that a more efficient method of constructing prompt templates could provide more robust improvements to our approach. We leave these as future work for further exploration.

6   Conclusion

In this paper, we propose a prompt-based joint contrastive learning approach to tackle the zero-shot relation extraction. We leverage the prior knowledge of PLMs by constructing prompt templates to obtain better relation representations. Embedding quality is significantly enhanced by the joint optimization of the two contrastive modules. We demonstrate the effectiveness of our framework on two datasets, and our method can steadily outperform previous studies.

References

1. Brown, T., et al.: Language models are few-shot learners. In: Larochelle, H., Ranzato, M., Hadsell, R., Balcan, M., Lin, H. (eds.) Advances in Neural Information Processing Systems, vol. 33, pp. 1877–1901. Curran Associates, Inc. (2020). https://proceedings.neurips.cc/paper_files/paper/2020/file/1457c0d6bfcb4967418bfb8ac142f64a-Paper.pdf

2. Chen, C.Y., Li, C.T.: ZS-BERT: towards zero-shot relation extraction with attribute representation learning. In: Toutanova, K., et al. (eds.) Proceedings of the 2021 Conference of the North American Chapter of the Association for Computational Linguistics: Human Language Technologies, pp. 3470–3479. Association for Computational Linguistics (2021). https://aclanthology.org/2021.naacl-main.272

3. Chen, X., et al.: Knowprompt: knowledge-aware prompt-tuning with synergistic optimization for relation extraction. In: Proceedings of the ACM Web Conference 2022, WWW 2022, pp. 2778–2788. Association for Computing Machinery, New York (2022). https://doi.org/10.1145/3485447.3511998

4. Chia, Y.K., Bing, L., Poria, S., Si, L.: RelationPrompt: leveraging prompts to generate synthetic data for zero-shot relation triplet extraction. In: Muresan, S., Nakov, P., Villavicencio, A. (eds.) Findings of the Association for Computational Linguistics: ACL 2022, pp. 45–57. Association for Computational Linguistics, Dublin (2022). https://aclanthology.org/2022.findings-acl.5

5. Devlin, J., Chang, M.W., Lee, K., Toutanova, K.: BERT: pre-training of deep bidirectional transformers for language understanding. In: Burstein, J., Doran, C., Solorio, T. (eds.) Proceedings of the 2019 Conference of the North American Chapter of the Association for Computational Linguistics: Human Language Technologies, vol. 1 (Long and Short Papers), pp. 4171–4186. Association for Computational Linguistics, Minneapolis (2019). https://aclanthology.org/N19-1423

6. Gao, T., Fisch, A., Chen, D.: Making pre-trained language models better few-shot learners. In: Zong, C., Xia, F., Li, W., Navigli, R. (eds.) Proceedings of the 59th Annual Meeting of the Association for Computational Linguistics and the 11th International Joint Conference on Natural Language Processing, vol. 1: Long Papers, pp. 3816–3830. Association for Computational Linguistics (2021). https://aclanthology.org/2021.acl-long.295

7. Gao, T., Yao, X., Chen, D.: SimCSE: simple contrastive learning of sentence embeddings. In: Moens, M.F., Huang, X., Specia, L., Yih, S.W.t. (eds.) Proceedings of the 2021 Conference on Empirical Methods in Natural Language Processing, pp. 6894–6910. Association for Computational Linguistics, Online and Punta Cana (2021). https://aclanthology.org/2021.emnlp-main.552

8. Han, X., Zhao, W., Ding, N., Liu, Z., Sun, M.: Ptr: prompt tuning with rules for text classification (2021)

9. Han, X., et al.: FewRel: a large-scale supervised few-shot relation classification dataset with state-of-the-art evaluation. In: Riloff, E., Chiang, D., Hockenmaier, J., Tsujii, J. (eds.) Proceedings of the 2018 Conference on Empirical Methods in Natural Language Processing, pp. 4803–4809. Association for Computational Linguistics, Brussels (2018). https://aclanthology.org/D18-1514

10. Jiang, Z., Xu, F.F., Araki, J., Neubig, G.: How can we know what language models know? Trans. Assoc. Comput. Linguist. **8**, 423–438 (2020). https://aclanthology.org/2020.tacl-1.28

11. Khosla, P., et al.: Supervised contrastive learning. In: Larochelle, H., Ranzato, M., Hadsell, R., Balcan, M., Lin, H. (eds.) Advances in Neural Information Processing Systems, vol. 33, pp. 18661–18673. Curran Associates, Inc. (2020). https://proceedings.neurips.cc/paper_files/paper/2020/file/d89a66c7c80a29b1bdbab0f2a1a94af8-Paper.pdf

12. Levy, O., Seo, M., Choi, E., Zettlemoyer, L.: Zero-shot relation extraction via reading comprehension. In: Levy, R., Specia, L. (eds.) Proceedings of the 21st Conference on Computational Natural Language Learning (CoNLL 2017), pp. 333–342. Association for Computational Linguistics, Vancouver (2017). https://aclanthology.org/K17-1034

13. Li, G., Wang, P., Ke, W.: Revisiting large language models as zero-shot relation extractors. In: Bouamor, H., Pino, J., Bali, K. (eds.) Findings of the Association for Computational Linguistics: EMNLP 2023, pp. 6877–6892. Association for Computational Linguistics, Singapore (2023). https://aclanthology.org/2023.findings-emnlp.459

14. Loshchilov, I., Hutter, F.: Decoupled weight decay regularization. In: International Conference on Learning Representations (2019). https://openreview.net/forum?id=Bkg6RiCqY7

15. Obamuyide, A., Vlachos, A.: Zero-shot relation classification as textual entailment. In: Thorne, J., Vlachos, A., Cocarascu, O., Christodoulopoulos, C., Mittal, A. (eds.) Proceedings of the First Workshop on Fact Extraction and VERification (FEVER), pp. 72–78. Association for Computational Linguistics, Brussels (2018). https://aclanthology.org/W18-5511

16. van den Oord, A., Li, Y., Vinyals, O.: Representation learning with contrastive predictive coding (2019)

17. Reimers, N., Gurevych, I.: Sentence-BERT: sentence embeddings using Siamese BERT-networks. In: Inui, K., Jiang, J., Ng, V., Wan, X. (eds.) Proceedings of the 2019 Conference on Empirical Methods in Natural Language Processing and the 9th International Joint Conference on Natural Language Processing (EMNLP-IJCNLP), pp. 3982–3992. Association for Computational Linguistics, Hong Kong (2019). https://aclanthology.org/D19-1410

18. Sainz, O., Lopez de Lacalle, O., Labaka, G., Barrena, A., Agirre, E.: Label verbalization and entailment for effective zero and few-shot relation extraction. In: Moens, M.F., Huang, X., Specia, L., Yih, S.W.t. (eds.) Proceedings of the 2021 Conference on Empirical Methods in Natural Language Processing, pp. 1199–1212. Association for Computational Linguistics, Online and Punta Cana (2021). https://aclanthology.org/2021.emnlp-main.92

19. Schick, T., Schütze, H.: Exploiting cloze-questions for few-shot text classification and natural language inference. In: Merlo, P., Tiedemann, J., Tsarfaty, R. (eds.) Proceedings of the 16th Conference of the European Chapter of the Association for Computational Linguistics: Main Volume, pp. 255–269. Association for Computational Linguistics, Online (2021). https://aclanthology.org/2021.eacl-main.20

20. Shin, T., Razeghi, Y., Logan IV, R.L., Wallace, E., Singh, S.: AutoPrompt: eliciting knowledge from language models with automatically generated prompts. In: Webber, B., Cohn, T., He, Y., Liu, Y. (eds.) Proceedings of the 2020 Conference on Empirical Methods in Natural Language Processing (EMNLP), pp. 4222–4235. Association for Computational Linguistics (2020). https://aclanthology.org/2020.emnlp-main.346

21. Wang, S., Zhang, B., Xu, Y., Wu, Y., Xiao, B.: RCL: relation contrastive learning for zero-shot relation extraction. In: Carpuat, M., de Marneffe, M.C., Meza Ruiz, I.V. (eds.) Findings of the Association for Computational Linguistics: NAACL 2022, pp. 2456–2468. Association for Computational Linguistics, Seattle (2022). https://aclanthology.org/2022.findings-naacl.188

22. Wu, S., He, Y.: Enriching pre-trained language model with entity information for relation classification. In: Proceedings of the 28th ACM International Conference on Information and Knowledge Management, CIKM '19, pp. 2361-2364. Association for Computing Machinery, New York (2019). https://doi.org/10.1145/3357384.3358119

23. Zhang, K., Jimenez Gutierrez, B., Su, Y.: Aligning instruction tasks unlocks large language models as zero-shot relation extractors. In: Rogers, A., Boyd-Graber, J., Okazaki, N. (eds.) Findings of the Association for Computational Linguistics: ACL 2023, pp. 794–812. Association for Computational Linguistics, Toronto (2023). https://aclanthology.org/2023.findings-acl.50

24. Zhao, J., et al.: RE-matching: a fine-grained semantic matching method for zero-shot relation extraction. In: Rogers, A., Boyd-Graber, J., Okazaki, N. (eds.) Proceedings of the 61st Annual Meeting of the Association for Computational Linguistics, vol. 1: Long Papers, pp. 6680–6691. Association for Computational Linguistics, Toronto (2023). https://aclanthology.org/2023.acl-long.369

Low-Resource Event Causality Identification With Global Consistency Constraints

Kangyun Ning, Jian Liu[✉], and Jinan Xu

Beijing Key Lab of Traffic Data Analysis and Mining, Beijing Jiaotong University, Beijing, China
{22120409,jianliu,jaxu}@bjtu.edu.cn

Abstract. Event causality identification (ECI) primarily involves discerning causal relations between pairs of events within sentences. However, previous methods heavily rely on large volumes of high-quality annotated data, making them impractical in low-resource scenarios. Moreover, traditional methods often make independent predictions about event pairs, ignoring the influence between these relations, leading to incorrect predictions. We propose a low-resource ECI method with global consistency constraints to address these challenges. Our approach consists of two strategies: first, we efficiently utilize high-quality data through combined domain adaptation adversarial training and semi-supervised methods with external data sources. Second, we incorporate global consistency constraints into the training process, enhancing the model's ability to learn chain causal relations. Our method significantly improves the F1 score on the 10% Event Storyline Corpus (ESC) and 5% ESC extending the manually annotated relations within document event co-reference chains with external Causal News Corpus (CNC) and noisy causal data from Wikipedia (WNC) compared to the baseline. The addition of global consistency constraints further increases the model's prediction consistency.

Keywords: Event Causality Identification · Low Resources · Consistency Constraints

1 Introduction

Event causality identification (ECI) is crucial in natural language understanding, offering vital semantic information that enhances common sense reasoning [1] and reading comprehension tasks [2]. It primarily involves discerning whether causal relations exist between pairs of events within sentences, as illustrated in Fig. 1.

However, previous works [3,4,14] rely on large volumes of high-quality annotated data to learn event causality, making it impractical in low-resource scenarios. Besides, traditional causal identification methods often make independent

Ex1: Non-causal Relation
(1) Rath (*e1: interacted*) with the affected farmers who were yet to get compensation despite (*e2: repeated*) agitation over the issue.   *(e1, e2, not cause)*

Ex2: Causal Relation
(2) Emerging from a crowd, Chiu suddenly *(e1: threw)* a blue, plastic water bottle which *(e2: hit)* Lee's right thigh.   *(e1, e2, cause)*

Ex3: Causal Chain Relation
(3) A general *(e1: strike)* was staged as a *(e2: protest)* against a new round of draconian austerity measures. Authorities said as many as 20,000 people took to the streets of Athens as *(e3: rallies)* all around the country kicked off.

Event Pairs	Relation	Prediction
(e2, e1)	*cause*	*cause*
(e1, e3)	*cause*	*cause*
(e2, e3)	*cause*	*not cause*

Fig. 1. Illustration of non-causal, causal relation and causal chain relation.

predictions about the relations between pairs of events, potentially leading to prediction errors. Consider Ex3 in Fig. 1. Given that **e1: strike** was caused by **e2: protest** and **e1: strike** caused **e3: rallies**, the learning process should enforce that **e2: protest** caused **e3: rallies** by taking into account the conjunctive constraints in causal relations. We refer to this type of relation as a chain relation. However, traditional methods do not enforce these constraints, resulting in the relation **e2: protest** causing **e3: rallies** not being identified.

To address the above two issues, we propose a low-resource ECI method with global consistency verification. Our approach consists of two strategies: first, efficiently utilizing high-quality data to solve the low-resource problem through combined domain adaptation adversarial training and semi-supervised methods with external data sources. We use domain adaptation adversarial training to alleviate discrepancies between external resources and in-domain data annotations. Additionally, we employ semi-supervised methods to continuously filter and add high-quality data from external sources into the in-domain data, ensuring that the model benefits from an expanded and more relevant dataset. Second, we incorporate global consistency constraints into the training process to enhance the model's learning of chain causal relations. Specifically, we add conjunctive constraints for chain relations, enabling the model to simultaneously learn the three sets of relations between chain events, as shown in Fig. 1. On the 10% Event Storyline Corpus (ESC) [7] and 5% ESC extending the manually annotated relations within document event co-reference chains, our method significantly improves the F1 score compared to the baseline, and the addition of global consistency constraints further increases the model's prediction consistency.

Our contributions are as follows:

1. **Novel Low-Resource ECI Method**: We propose a low-resource ECI method that effectively utilizes domain adaptation adversarial training and semi-supervised learning to address the challenge of data scarcity and annotation discrepancies.
2. **Global Consistency Constraints**: We introduce global consistency constraints into the training process, enhancing the model's ability to learn and predict chain causal relations, which significantly improves the model's performance and prediction consistency.
3. **Empirical Validation**: Our method demonstrates substantial improvements in F1 score and prediction consistency on the ESC.

2   Related Works

2.1   Event Causality Identification

ECI tasks can be categorized based on the granularity of data into sentence-level and document-level. Recently, some approaches have introduced the integration of external knowledge bases [15,17] and weakly supervised methods [16] to address the challenges of data scarcity and implicit causal relation [18]. ECIFF [5] integrates contextual, semantic, and syntactic features to deepen causality detection, while Verbalizer [6] redefines the task as a masked language modeling challenge via prompt learning. However, most existing studies rely on large volumes of high-quality data and there is no attempt to leverage existing external data sources to solve the problem of low resources.

2.2   Global Consistency Constraints

To ensure the robustness of information extraction, an effective approach is to capture the logical constraints between labels, ensuring logical consistency during inference. [10] enforces logical constraints within and across multiple temporal and subevent relations. Li and Srikumar [11] demonstrated how to enhance existing neural network architectures by incorporating domain knowledge through the Lukasiewicz t-norm. Xu et al. [12] introduced a general framework for creating a semantically informed loss function that constrains a complex output space without relying on t-norms. Similarly, Fischer et al. [13] proposed a framework for designing loss functions using logic, albeit with a different approach.

3   Method

3.1   Overall

In Fig. 2, we demonstrate the main method in this paper. Specifically, we consider data from low-resource scenarios as the source corpus (in-domain data) and use external data sources as the target corpus (out-domain data) for domain adaptation adversarial training. The trained model is then used to predict out-domain

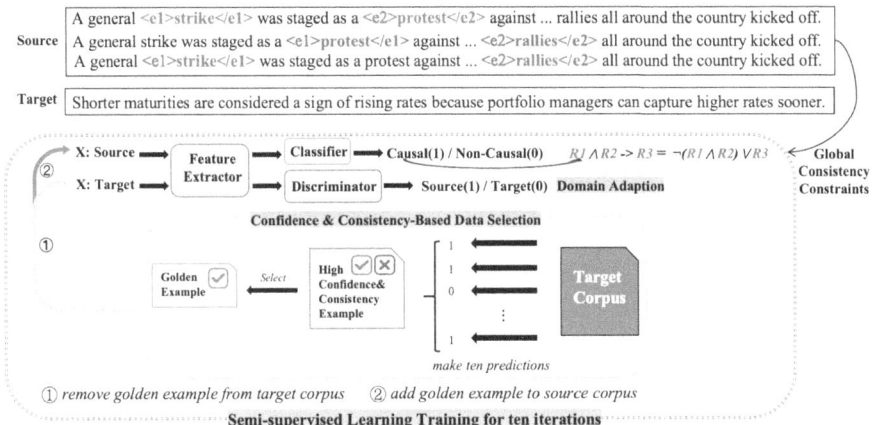

Fig. 2. Pipeline of our method. Source data represents the low-resource data while target data represents external data.

data. We add correctly predicted data to the in-domain corpus and remove this portion from the out-domain corpus before proceeding to the next round of semi-supervised iterative training. To ensure the higher quality of the data added to the in-domain corpus, we introduce a confidence consistency check method. Data with high consistency is added to the in-domain corpus. This approach allows for more efficient utilization of the out-domain data. Additionally, for potential chain causal relation data within the in-domain corpus, we introduce first-order logic rules as global consistency constraints. These constraints are incorporated into the training of the causality identification model, enabling the model to learn the interactions between causal event pairs.

3.2   Domain-Adaptive semi-supervised Learning

External Data Sources. We use two types of external data. The first type is high-quality annotated data with annotation rules different from in-domain data. The second type is noisy data from Wikipedia, called Wikipedia Noisy Causal corpus (WNC). The steps for collecting Wikipedia noisy data are as follows: First, we parse the Wikipedia dumps data into sentences and clean the sentences by removing web links. Next, we use the causal relation markers provided in the Penn Discourse TreeBank (all markers under the Contingency) to match sentences. The matched sentences are considered to have causal relations. This process introduces two types of noise into the collected sentences:

- **Polysemy of Causal Connectives:** The causal connectives such as "to" can have various meanings in different contexts, not all of which imply a causal relation. This polysemy introduces annotation noise.

- **Omission of Implicit Causal Relations:** Additionally, the dataset may contain sentences with implicit causal relations that lack explicit causal connectives, typically being annotated as non-causal. This omission further contributes to the data noise.

Domain-Adaptive Adversarial Training. In ECI, employing domain adaptation is a proven method to effectively utilize annotated data, which may vary significantly across datasets due to different annotation protocols or human factors [14]. To enhance performance on low-resource data and fully utilize these out-domain resources, we employ domain-adaptive adversarial training, integrating gradient reversal technology to improve the model's generalization between source domain and target domain.

The model includes a BERT-based feature extractor f and a domain classifier D. The feature extractor maps input data X into a feature space, while the domain classifier determines the domain origin of the input features. The Gradient Reversal Layer (GRL) plays a pivotal role by inverting the gradients during backpropagation, encouraging the learning of domain-invariant features.

During each training epoch, the model processes data from both the source and target domains:

- **Feature Extraction**: Model f extracts features from both low-resource data (source) and external data (target).
- **Domain Classification Task**: Enhanced by the GRL, the domain classifier D attempts to classify features as originating from either the source or the target domain. This task is essential as it forces the model to minimize the differences in feature distributions between the source and target data.

The overall training loss L combines the classification loss L_y and the domain classification loss L_d:

$$L_y = -\sum_{i=1}^{N} y_i \log(\hat{y}_i) \tag{1}$$

$$L_d = -\sum_{i=1}^{N} d_i \log(\hat{d}_i) + (1 - d_i) \log(1 - \hat{d}_i) \tag{2}$$

$$L = L_y - \lambda L_d \tag{3}$$

Here, λ serves as a crucial parameter within the GRL to adjust the degree of gradient reversal during backpropagation, modulating the model's focus on minimizing domain distinguishability.

By minimizing L, our model reduces reliance on specific annotation protocols while improving its adaptability across different annotation styles of external data sources.

Semi-Supervised Learning. Semi-supervised learning [9] leverages both a large volume of unlabeled data and a small set of labeled data to train models. For the semi-supervised approach, we train initially on low-resource data and then apply the trained model to predict external data. Correct predictions are integrated back into the low-resource training set, allowing iterative expansion and enhancement of the model's performance.

Confidence and Consistency Verification. In our semi-supervised learning framework, we implement a Confidence and Consistency Verification method based on entropy to assess the reliability of predictions over multiple iterations, which is shown in Fig. 2.

Predictions are made ten times for each data point in the external dataset, and the entropy of these predictions is calculated to quantify the uncertainty. Entropy, a measure of prediction dispersion, is computed as follows:

$$\text{Entropy}(x) = - \sum_i p_i(x) \log_2 p_i(x) \tag{4}$$

where $p_i(x)$ represents the proportion of times class i is predicted across ten predictions. A lower entropy value indicates higher consistency and reliability in predictions.

To enhance the quality of data incorporated into the training set, we introduce a confidence threshold τ. A sample x is added to the training set if:

$$\text{Entropy}(x) <= \tau \tag{5}$$

3.3   Global Consistency Constraints

T-norms. Symbolic knowledge can provide crucial logical biases for training neural networks in low-resource scenarios. Well-studied t-norms can relax first-order logic rules to define sub-differentiable functions for neural network training. Gödel fuzzy logic is a special form of many-valued logic that allows the truth values of propositions to vary continuously between [0, 1]. The corresponding basic logical operations' functions are shown in Table 1.

Table 1. S-Gödel Fuzzy Logic Operations

Operation	S-Gödel
Disjunction ($\vee$)	$\max(x, y)$
Conjunction ($\wedge$)	$\min(x, y)$
Negation ($\neg$)	$1 - x$
Implication ($\rightarrow$)	$\max(1 - x, y)$

Chain Causal Relation with Logical Constraints. Observing the chain causal relations mentioned in Fig. 1, we define the rule for such higher-order event relations as follows: (protest $\xrightarrow{\text{cause}}$ strike) $\wedge$ (strike $\xrightarrow{\text{cause}}$ rallies) $\rightarrow$ (protest $\xrightarrow{\text{cause}}$ rallies)

Each relation score is calculated by our causality identification model and defined as R_i, where i denotes the event pair, X_i denotes the sentence containing the i-th event pair, and $\sigma(x)$ is the sigmoid function:

$$R_i = \sigma(\text{Linear}(\text{BERT}(X_i, \text{attention\_mask})[1])) \qquad (6)$$

Then we can convert the rule mentioned forward to $R_1 \wedge R_2 \xrightarrow{R} 3$. Using S-Gödel logical operations' functions in Table 1, we transform the rewrite rule into an optimizable objective function:

$$L_o = -\max(1 - \min(R_1, R_2), R_3) \qquad (7)$$

4   Experiments

4.1   Experiment Settings

Datasets. Our experiments are conducted on three benchmark datasets, including a) ESC v0.9, which contains 2265 causal event pairs (ESC_ori) and 5519 causal event pairs (ESC_corf) by extending the manually annotated relations within document event co-reference chains. For the low-resource setting, we randomly sample 10% and 5% from ESC_ori and ESC_corf train set with five-fold cross-validation; b) CNC (Subtask 1) train set [14], which contains 1603 causal sentences and 1322 non-causal sentence; and c) WNC, which we discuss in Sect. 3.2, and contains 10000 sentences.

Evaluation Metrics. Our evaluation metrics include Precision, Recall, F1-Score, and C (the ratio of the number of predicted relations for all three pairs to the number of correctly predicted pairs of relations for the first two pairs).

Parameter Settings. We use BERT-Base architecture as the base model, which has 12 layers, 768 hidden, and 12 heads. We set the learning rate of the pretraining model as 1e-5, 1e-6, and 1e-7 respectively, and we apply Adam to optimize all models and discriminators. In discriminator training, we set λ as 1. For the epoch of semi-supervised learning techniques, we set 10 epochs.

4.2   Main Experiments and Results

Baseline. We conduct experiments with BERT in a) 10% ESC_ori, b) 5% ESC_corf; c) 10% ESC_ori combines with CNC; d) 5% ESC_corf combines with CNC; e) 10% ESC_ori combines with Wikipedia Noisy Corpus and f) 5% ESC_corf combines with Wikipedia Noisy Corpus; Since previous works [15–18] utilize the entire ESC relations instead of focusing on low-resource scenarios, we do not compare our results with theirs.

Table 2. Performance comparison of baseline and our methods. For metrics, P: Precision, R: Recall, and F1: F1-scores. For train set, ESC_ori: 10% ESC_ori, ESC_corf: 5% ESC_corf. The best results are highlighted in **bold**.

Method	Train	External Data	P	R	F1
Baseline	ESC_ori	–	0.543	0.252	0.344
	ESC_corf	–	0.632	0.238	0.346
	ESC_ori	CNC	0.489	0.298	0.370
	ESC_corf	CNC	0.584	0.298	0.395
	ESC_ori	Wikipedia	0.750	0.228	0.350
	ESC_corf	Wikipedia	0.746	0.242	0.366
Ours	ESC_ori	CNC	0.802	0.376	0.512 (+0.142)
	ESC_corf	CNC	0.807	0.387	**0.523** (+0.128)
	ESC_ori	Wikipedia	0.711	0.360	0.478 (+0.128)
	ESC_corf	Wikipedia	0.756	0.355	0.483 (+0.117)

Results of Domain-Adaptive Semi-Supervised Learning Method. We use ESC_ori and ESC_corf as source data, CNC and WNC as target data to conduct domain-adaptive semi-supervised learning training. As shown in Table 2, our method in 5% ESC_corf by using CNC achieves the best performance and improves 0.128 compared with the baseline, which proves the effectiveness of our method. Compared with the other settings, it is observed that ESC_corf, which includes event coreference relations, enables a better understanding of event causality for the model than ESC_ori. WNC, due to the inclusion of noisy data, performs worse than the high-quality manually annotated CNC.

In Fig. 3, we demonstrate the F1-Score trends across ten iterations. It is observed that the models generally peak around the 7th and 8th epochs, after which the performance stabilizes. Table 2 reports these peak values.

Results of Global Consistency Constraints. Due to the chain causal relation being scarce in 10%ESC_ori and 5%ESC_corf, we collect 928 groups of chain relations from ESC_ori and 1851 groups of chain relations from ESC_corf. As shown in Table 3, the consistency has improved by 12.8% in ESC_ori and 16.2% in ESC_corf. ESC_corf, having extended the causal relationships with event coreference, demonstrates better consistency in causal relationships than ESC_ori.

4.3 Ablation Experiments

As shown in Table 4, it is observed that the domain adaption is effective in improving the model's performance. Each component enables models to use external data efficiently by comparing with a simple combination of ESC and external data in the baseline.

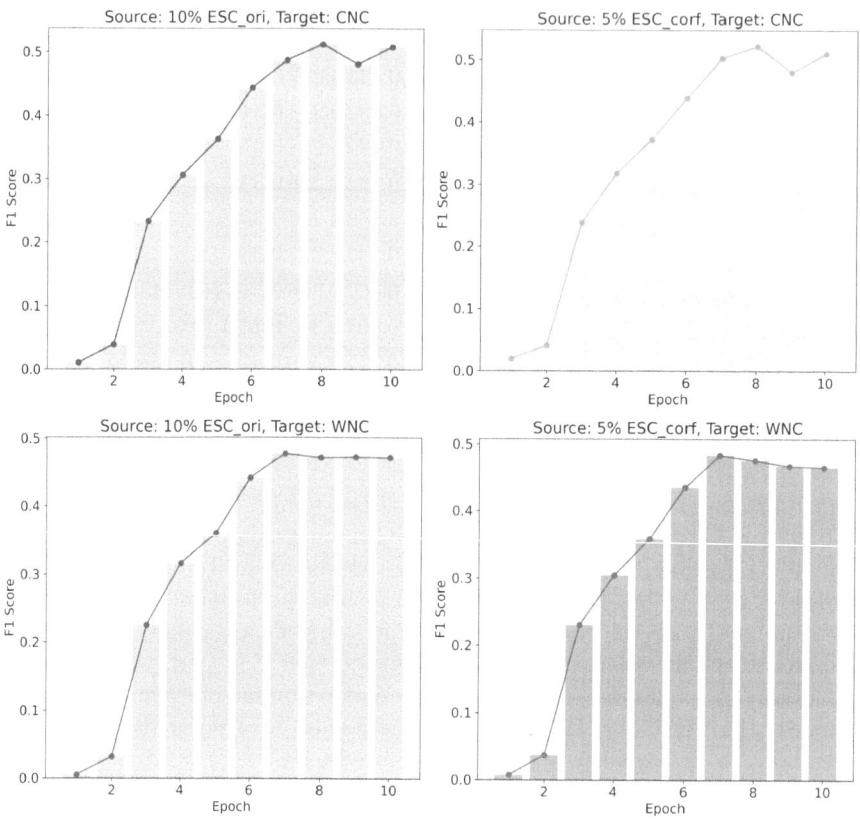

Fig. 3. F1-Score Trends across Ten Iterations on Domain-Adaptive Semi-Supervised Learning with Confidence and Consistency Validation

Table 3. Results of baseline and global consistency constraint. *Ours* means global consistency constraint. A group contains $e_1 \rightarrow e_2 \wedge e_2 \rightarrow e_3 \wedge e_1 \rightarrow e_3$.

Train Set	Method	First Two Pairs	Three Pairs	Consistency	Test Size/Group
ESC_ori	Baseline	70	30	0.428	186
	Ours	81	45	0.556	186
ESC_corf	Baseline	167	79	0.473	370
	Ours	170	108	0.635	370

Table 4. Results on Our Methods with Different Settings. For Methods, *domain*: only the domain adaptive training, *semi*: only the semi-supervised learning, *semi-ccv*: the semi-supervised learning training with confidence and consistency validation, *domain-semi*: domain adaptive and semi-supervised learning training, and *domain-semi-ccv*: domain adaptive and semi-supervised learning training with confidence and consistency validation.

(a) Source: 10% ESC_ori, Target: CNC

Method	P	R	F1
Baseline	0.489	0.298	0.370
domain	0.707	0.365	0.482
semi	0.632	0.364	0.462
semi-ccv	0.524	0.431	0.473
domain-semi	0.510	0.497	0.503
domain-semi-ccv	0.802	0.376	0.512

(b) Source: 5% ESC_corf, Target: CNC

Method	P	R	F1
Baseline	0.584	0.298	0.395
domain	0.664	0.399	0.498
semi	0.700	0.354	0.470
semi-ccv	0.710	0.371	0.487
domain-semi	0.710	0.399	0.511
domain-semi-ccv	0.807	0.387	0.523

(c) Source: 10%ESC_ori, Target: WNC

Method	P	R	F1
Baseline	0.750	0.228	0.350
domain	0.646	0.348	0.453
semi	0.514	0.378	0.435
semi-ccv	0.680	0.335	0.449
domain-semi	0.721	0.339	0.461
domain-semi-ccv	0.711	0.360	0.478

(d) Source: 5% ESC_corf, Target: WNC

Method	P	R	F1
Baseline	0.746	0.242	0.366
domain	0.524	0.431	0.473
semi	0.504	0.391	0.440
semi-ccv	0.521	0.411	0.459
domain-semi	0.684	0.365	0.476
domain-semi-ccv	0.756	0.355	0.483

5   Discussion

5.1   Event Temporal Relation with Global Consistency Constraints

In temporal relations, there are also many chain relations. For example, $e_1 \xrightarrow{\text{before}} e_2 \wedge e_2 \xrightarrow{\text{before}} e_3 \rightarrow e_1 \xrightarrow{\text{before}} e_3$. We also conduct the same experiment on TimeLine [8], a temporal relation corpus. In Table 5, our method has improved consistency by 11.9%. This indicates that our method can also be transferred to temporal relations.

Table 5. Results of baseline and our global consistency constraints on TimeLine.

Method	First Two Pairs	Three Pairs	Consistency	Test Set (Group)
Baseline	36	20	0.556	81
Ours	37	25	0.675	81

6 Conclusion

In this paper, we propose a low-resource ECI method that incorporates global consistency constraints and effectively uses the data. Our approach involves two main strategies: first, we efficiently leverage external data through a combination of domain adaptation adversarial training and semi-supervised learning using external data sources. Second, we integrate global consistency constraints into the training process to enhance the model's ability to learn chain causal relations.

Our method shows significant improvement in the F1 score on the ESC when combined with external data from the CNC and WNC compared to the baseline. Furthermore, the addition of global consistency constraints increases the model's prediction consistency. These results demonstrate that our approach effectively improves event causality identification performance in low-resource settings while enhancing the global consistency of predictions.

Acknowledgments. The research work described in this paper has been supported by the National Nature Science Foundation of China (No.62376019, 61976015, 61976016, 61876198, and 61370130). The authors thank the anonymous reviewers for their valuable comments and suggestions for improving this paper.

References

1. Rottman, B.M., Hastie, R.: Reasoning about causal relationships: inferences on causal networks. Psychol. Bull. **140**(1), 109 (2014)
2. Sun, Y., Cheng, G., Qu, Y.: Reading comprehension with graph-based temporal-causal reasoning. In: Proceedings of the 27th International Conference on Computational Linguistics, pp. 806–817 (2018)
3. Lai, V.D., Veyseh, A.P.B., Van Nguyen, M., Dernoncourt, F., Nguyen, T.H.: MECI: a multilingual dataset for event causality identification. In: Proceedings of the 29th International Conference on Computational Linguistics, pp. 2346–2356 (2022)
4. Zhao, K., Ji, D., He, F., Liu, Y., Ren, Y.: Document-level event causality identification via graph inference mechanism. Inf. Sci. **561**, 115–129 (2021)
5. Ding, S., Mao, Y., Cheng, Y., Pang, T., Shen, L., Qi, R.: ECIFF: event causality identification based on feature fusion. In: 2023 IEEE 35th International Conference on Tools with Artificial Intelligence (ICTAI), pp. 646–653 (2023)
6. Zhang, W., Hu, L., Wei, Y., Wu, B.: Verbalizer or classifier? a new prompt learning model for event causality identification. In: 2023 International Joint Conference on Neural Networks (IJCNN), pp. 1–7 (2023)
7. Caselli, T., Vossen, P.: The event storyline corpus: a new benchmark for causal and temporal relation extraction. In: Caselli, T., et al. (eds.) Proceedings of the Events and Stories in the News Workshop, pp. 77–86. Association for Computational Linguistics, Vancouver (2017). https://doi.org/10.18653/v1/W17-2711
8. Alsayyahi, S., Batista-Navarro, R.: TIMELINE: exhaustive annotation of temporal relations supporting the automatic ordering of events in news articles. In: Bouamor, H., Pino, J., Bali, K. (eds.) Proceedings of the 2023 Conference on Empirical Methods in Natural Language Processing, pp. 16336–16348. Association for Computational Linguistics, Singapore (2023). https://doi.org/10.18653/v1/2023.emnlp-main.1016

9. van Engelen, J.E., Hoos, H.H.: A survey on semi-supervised learning. Mach. Learn. **109**(2), 373–440 (2019). https://doi.org/10.1007/s10994-019-05855-6

10. Wang, H., Chen, M., Zhang, H., Roth, D.: Joint constrained learning for event-event relation extraction. In: Webber, B., Cohn, T., He, Y., Liu, Y. (eds.) Proceedings of the 2020 Conference on Empirical Methods in Natural Language Processing (EMNLP), pp. 696–706. Association for Computational Linguistics, Online (2020). https://doi.org/10.18653/v1/2020.emnlp-main.51

11. Li, T., Srikumar, V.: Augmenting neural networks with first-order logic. arXiv preprint arXiv:1906.06298 (2019)

12. Xu, J., Zhang, Z., Friedman, T., Liang, Y., Van den Broeck, G.: A semantic loss function for deep learning with symbolic knowledge. In: International Conference on Machine Learning, pp. 5502–5511. PMLR (2018)

13. Fischer, M., Balunovic, M., Drachsler-Cohen, D., Gehr, T., Zhang, C., Vechev, M.: DL2: training and querying neural networks with logic. In: International Conference on Machine Learning, pp. 1931–1941. PMLR (2019)

14. Tan, F.A., et al.: The causal news corpus: annotating causal relations in event sentences from news. In: Proceedings of the Thirteenth Language Resources and Evaluation Conference, pp. 2298–2310. European Language Resources Association, Marseille (2022)

15. Zuo, X., et al.: LearnDA: learnable knowledge-guided data augmentation for event causality identification. In: Proceedings of the 59th Annual Meeting of the Association for Computational Linguistics and the 11th International Joint Conference on Natural Language Processing, vol. 1: Long Papers, pp. 3558–3571. Association for Computational Linguistics, Online (2021)

16. Zuo, X., et al.: Improving event causality identification via self-supervised representation learning on external causal statement. In: Findings of the Association for Computational Linguistics: ACL-IJCNLP 2021, pp. 2162–2172. Association for Computational Linguistics, Online (2021)

17. Liu, J., Chen, Y., Zhao, J.: Knowledge enhanced event causality identification with mention masking generalizations. In: Proceedings of the Twenty-Ninth International Conference on International Joint Conferences on Artificial Intelligence, pp. 3608–3614 (2021)

18. Cao, P., et al.: Knowledge-enriched event causality identification via latent structure induction networks. In: Proceedings of the 59th Annual Meeting of the Association for Computational Linguistics and the 11th International Joint Conference on Natural Language Processing, vol. 1: Long Papers, pp. 4862–4872 (2021)

19. Man, H., Nguyen, M.V., Nguyen, T.H.: Event causality identification via generation of important context words. In: Proceedings of the 11th Joint Conference on Lexical and Computational Semantics (* SEM) at NAACL 2022 (2022)

20. Liu, J., et al.: KEPT: Knowledge enhanced prompt tuning for event causality identification. Knowl.-Based Syst. **259**, 110064 (2023)

Only One Relation Possible? Modeling the Ambiguity in Temporal Relation Extraction

Yutong Hu[1,2] , Quzhe Huang[1,2] , and Yansong Feng[1,2(✉)]

[1] Wangxuan Institute of Computer Technology, Peking University, Beijing, China
{huyutong,huangquzhe,fengyansong}@pku.edu.cn
[2] State Key Laboratory of General Artificial Intelligence, Beijing, China

Abstract. Event Temporal Relation Extraction (ETRE) aims to identify the temporal relationship between two events. Most previous works
follow a single-label classification paradigm, classifying an event pair into
either a well-defined temporal relation (e.g., *Before*, *After*) when its temporal relation is clear and unique, or a special relation *Vague* when there
are multiple possible temporal relations. This paradigm treats *Vague*
independently, ignoring that the instances labeled as *Vague* also convey
temporal information about well-defined relations. To better handle the
special relation Vague, we propose **M**ulti-label **E**vent **T**emporal **R**elation
Extraction (METRE), a new method treating the ETRE as a multi-label
classification task. METRE predicts the probability of each well-defined
relation separately and infers the relation *Vague* if there is more than
one relation possible for an event pair, instead of directly predicting the
probability of *Vague*. Considering the gold composition of *Vague* is not
available, we design a speculation mechanism to explore the possible
relations contributing to *Vague* in each case, which enables the latent
information to be used efficiently. Experiments on TB-Dense, MATRES
and UDS-T show that our method can make better use of the relation
Vague and outperform state-of-the-art methods.

Keywords: temporal relation extraction · multi-label classification

1 Introduction

Event Temporal Relation Extraction (ETRE) is a task to determine the temporal
relationship between two events in a given text, which could benefit many downstream tasks, like summarization, generation and question answering [16,19,25].

In previous studies, most benchmarks [1,18] categorize the temporal relationship between events into two types: the well-defined relations [1] and *Vague*.

D. F. Wong et al. (Eds.): NLPCC 2024, LNAI 15359, pp. 444–456, 2025.
https://doi.org/10.1007/978-981-97-9431-7_34

Well-defined relations indicate the temporal relation of the event pair is clear and unique based on the given context, like *Before* and *After*. As for the special relation *Vague*, it indicates ambiguous cases when there are multiple possible temporal relations based on the currently available context. For example, given text *"My son has fallen asleep, so I have some free time to read for a while."*, there could be two possible scenarios. If the son woke up before the mother finished her reading, the temporal relation between event "asleep" and event "read" is *Before*, while if the son did not wake up until the mother finished reading the book, then the temporal relation is *Include*. Since there is more than one possibility, the temporal relation should be determined as *Vague*.

Most previous studies on ETRE ignore such underlying meaning of *Vague*, and formulate ETRE as a single-label classification task by treating *Vague* independently and equally as other well-defined relations [9,24]. However, such a single-label classification paradigm will cause the model's confusion between *Vague* and other potentially related well-defined relations. Back to the example mentioned above, since the instance is labeled as *Vague*, a single-label classification based model will punish label *Before* and *Include*. Unfortunately, this will confuse the model, as the text contains the information that the event "asleep" may happen *before* or *during (include)* the event "read", which is also the reason that annotators label it as *Vague*.

To address the confusion brought by the underlying connections between *Vague* and other temporal relations, we can infer the possibility of *Vague* based on other well-defined temporal relations. Specifically, following the definition of *Vague*, we consider it as the situation when there is more than one possible temporal relation between an event pair. To better handle the special relation *Vague*, we propose a **M**ulti-label **E**vent **T**emporal **R**elation **E**xtraction (METRE) method that transforms the task into a multi-label classification framework and makes predictions on every temporal relation about its possibility for the given event pair. If more than one temporal relation is of high possibility, we consider the relation between the event pair as *Vague*. By doing so, the intrinsic composition of *Vague* can be captured and make it distinguishable from other well-defined relations. In addition, it reduces the model's confusion between *Vague* and well-defined relations, and understand all well-defined temporal relations better. Since the temporal relation composition in each case of *Vague* is unknown from the training corpus, we propose an effective speculation mechanism that dynamically infers the most possible temporal relations. With this mechanism, our model can fully explore the complex temporal relation compositions, and comprehend the intrinsic meaning of *Vague*.

Recent studies also pay attention to modeling the ambiguity of *Vague*. [22] treats *Vague* as out-of-distribution (OOD) cases that the probability distribution over the well-defined relations is flat, i.e., all relations have equal probabilities. However, since *Vague* mostly indicates a few, but not all, well-defined relations are of high probability based on the text, the probability distribution can be sharp, where the potential relations behind *Vague* have higher probabilities than others. [8] propose a unified framework to model the ambiguity of *Vague*. They treat *Vague* as the cases when both events in that event pair are possible to occur before the other one. Although this method can simulate the ambiguity of *Vague* to a certain extent, some kinds of cases, such as *Vague* caused by possible relations *Before* and *Equal*, can not be properly formulated. Different from previous works, our multi-label classification framework can model all kinds of temporal compositions of *Vague*. In this way, our model can better understand the meaning of *Vague* and reduce its confusion with well-defined relations.

We conduct experiments on three temporal relation extraction datasets: TB-Dense [1], MATRES [18] and UDS-T [20]. Experimental results show METRE outperforms previous state-of-the-art methods, indicating the effectiveness of our method in characterizing *Vague* and making full use of its underlying temporal information. Besides, consistent improvement in low-data scenarios and minority relations demonstrates that we can efficiently use the information hidden behind *Vague* to better understand well-defined temporal relations. We also show that our method could correctly find the possible temporal relations that cause the ambiguity of *Vague*, providing further interpretability for the ETRE task.

2   Related Work

Previous studies on temporal relation extraction often neglect the ambiguity of *Vague*. They mainly formulate ETRE as a single-label classification task, overlooking the intrinsic complexity of *Vague* and treating every relation equally. They pay attention to the essential context information extraction and are looking forward to obtaining a better event pair representation. For example, [2,15,26] notice the importance of syntactic features, e.g., Part-Of-Speech tags, dependency parses, etc., and incorporate them into the model. [24] predict the relative timestamp in the timeline, and [9] express the temporal information through box embeddings using the symmetry and conjunctive properties.

Nevertheless, the complex information in *Vague* can not be well represented only as a single label. [17] model the ambiguity of *Vague* by calculating the Kullback-Leibler divergence. [22] regard *Vague* as a source of distributional uncertainty and incorporate Dirichlet Prior [11,12] to provide the predictive uncertainty estimation. However, they both neglect the underlying meaning of *Vague*, and treat it as the case that the probabilities of all well-defined relations are similar. [8] represents *Vague* when both the time point of one event pair could occur earlier than another one's, but this method also fails to model some of the temporal relation compositions of *Vague*, bringing the confusion between *Vague* and other relations when training. Different from previous studies, we scrutinize the definition of *Vague* and employ a multi-label classification-based approach to capture its intrinsic ambiguity among all possible temporal relation compositions, thereby enhancing our model's comprehension of all temporal relations.

3   Our Approach

Given an input text sequence $\mathbf{S} = [w_1, w_2, ..., w_n]$ and an event pair (e_1, e_2), where both $e_1, e_2 \in S$. The task of temporal relation extraction is to predict the temporal relation $r \in \tilde{R} = R \cup \{Vague\}$ between e_1 and e_2, where R is the set of well-defined temporal relations. As shown in Fig. 1, METRE includes an encoder to get event representations, a classifier to obtain the probability distribution $P(R)$ and the threshold value T. Then the model will make the final prediction based on $P(R)$ and T. If more than one label or no label is chosen, our model will output *Vague*, otherwise, the well-defined relation. To train the model, we propose a speculation mechanism to construct the Composition Set of *Vague* that consists of the two most possible temporal relations behind *Vague*, and use it to train our model.

3.1   Encoder Module

In our work, we adopt pretrained language models BERT [5] and RoBERTa [10] as the encoder module. Taking the text sequence $\mathbf{S}$ and an event pair (e_1, e_2) as input, it computes the contextualized representation for the event pair. Following [27], we insert typed markers to highlight two event mentions in the given text at the input layer, i.e., <E1:L> e_1 <E1:R>, and <E2:L> e_2

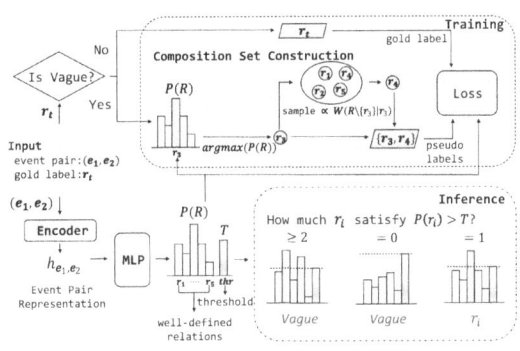

Fig. 1. The overview of METRE.

<E2:R>. Additionally, inspired by [21], we add cross-sentence context, i.e., one sentence before and after the given text, expecting models to capture more comprehensive information. We feed the new sequence $\tilde{\mathbf{S}}$ into the encoder and obtain the event pair representation: $\mathbf{h}_{e_1, e_2} = MLP_1([\mathbf{x}_{\hat{e}_1} || \mathbf{x}_{\hat{e}_2}])$. Here $\mathbf{x}$ is the output representation of the encoder, $\hat{e}_i$ is the index of e_i in $\tilde{\mathbf{S}}$, $[\cdot || \cdot]$ is the concatenation operator, and MLP_1 is a multilayer perceptron.

3.2   Multi-label Classifier

Different from the single-label classification paradigm, which directly chooses the relation of the highest probability from $\tilde{R}$, we adopt a multi-label classifier to better characterize *Vague*. Taking the event pair representation $\mathbf{h}_{e_1,e_2}$ as input, our classifier calculates the probability distribution over temporal relation set R.

Since most modern neural networks are poorly calibrated, a label's predicted probability can not reflect its ground truth correctness likelihood [6]. This perspective leads us to surmise that, in accordance with the given text, each instance needs its own optimal threshold as a calibrated confidence for the determination of the possible temporal relations. Benefit from [29] that it is effective to use an adaptive threshold in entity relation extraction task, we make our threshold learnable and dynamic for our classifier to make decisions. Specifically, we obtain the probability distribution $P(R|e_1, e_2) = MLP_2(\mathbf{h}_{e_1,e_2})$ and threshold $T_{e_1,e_2} = MLP_3(\mathbf{h}_{e_1,e_2})$, where $P(R|e_1, e_2) \in \mathbb{R}^{|R|}$ and $T_{e_1,e_2} \in \mathbb{R}$.

Therefore, the temporal relationship of event pair (e_1, e_2) can be deduced from $P(R|e_1, e_2)$ and T_{e_1,e_2}. If only one temporal relation whose probability is higher than the threshold, we consider it as the final prediction. If more than one temporal relation's probability is higher than the threshold, we think the temporal relation of the event pair is *Vague*, and we can provide detailed information on exactly what temporal relations cause the ambiguity. There are also a few cases that all relations' probabilities are lower than the threshold, and we map it to *Vague* as well, which can be explained as the model does not have enough confidence in any temporal relation for the event pair.

3.3   Composition Set Construction

During training, for each event pair, we need its labels over R to calculate the loss. However, this is not trivial in our case. For the instances labeled as *Vague*, we do not exactly know their possible temporal relation compositions, e.g., *Before* and *Include* for the example sentence in Sect. 1. To solve this problem, we need a new speculation mechanism to identify a set of the most likely temporal relations between the event pair. Here we denote the set as **Composition Set *CS***. Then the relations in CS can be regarded as the pseudo labels of *Vague* at the current stage to instruct the learning.

To formulate *Vague*, we think there could be two sources to build a dynamic CS: 1) TOP1 Relation: the relation r_{fir} which the model predicts as the most possible one to be the temporal relation between the given event pair. 2) Top1's Confusion Relation: the relation r_{sec} which may be more likely to be confused with r_{fir} as the cause of *Vague*.

Top1 Relation. As our model has the basic ability to provide a relatively accurate probability distribution over the well-defined relations for an event pair, the relation with the highest probability is most likely to be the temporal relation between the given event pair. Therefore, we adopt the top one temporal relation r_{fir}, ranked by $P(R)$, as a possible temporal relation between the event pair.

Top1's Confusion Relation. Since *Vague* indicates that there are at least two temporal relations possible for an event pair, we need to determine the second possible temporal relation r_{sec}. [18] claims that some temporal relation pairs are more difficult to distinguish than others, which can be attributed to the ambiguity of expressing and perceiving the duration of events [4]. Inspired by this, we believe that some temporal relation pairs, such as *Before* and *Include*, may occur more frequently than some other pairs like *After* and *Include*, as the compositions of *Vague*. Therefore, rather than deciding r_{sec} randomly, we choose the most possible one according to r_{fir}. Thanks to UDS-T [20], a temporal relation extraction corpus that reserves the detailed annotation results from three annotators, we treat the frequency of each temporal relation pair in the training set of UDS-T as prior knowledge, and decide r_{sec} based on it. We calculate the possibility of each temporal relation to be chosen with the following equation:

$$H(r_i|r_{fir}) = \frac{exp(freq_{i,fir})}{exp(freq_i) + exp(freq_{fir})}, i \in R \backslash \{r_{fir}\} \tag{1}$$

$$W(R \backslash \{r_{fir}\}|r_{fir}) = \frac{exp(H(r_i|r_{fir})/t)}{\sum_{r_j \in R \backslash \{r_{fir}\}} exp(H(r_j|r_{fir})/t)} \tag{2}$$

where $freq_{i,fir}$ (or $freq_i$) is the frequency of relation pair (r_i, r_{fir}) (or relation r_i) annotated in the training set of UDS-T, t is the temperature used to control the smoothing degree of the probability distribution. Then we sample r_{sec}, named as the confusion relation of r_{fir}, according to weight $P(W \backslash \{r_{fir}\}|r_{fir})$.

In summary, when the classifier outputs a probability distribution over temporal relations for a *Vague* instance, we speculate that the top-ranked relation r_{fir} along with its confusion counterpart r_{sec} are most likely to cause *Vague*'s ambiguity. Therefore, we use these two relations as the pseudo labels of *Vague*, and obtain the composition set $CS = \{r_{fir}, r_{sec}\}$.

We do not choose a third temporal relation into CS. Since we have selected two of the most possible relations, the third selection may involve less certainty and accuracy, which is more likely to bring noise into our model.

3.4   Training Objective

For the instance labeled as a well-defined relation $r \in R$, r is the only possible relation between the given event pair. Therefore, we encourage the gold label r

and penalize the probability of other temporal relations, respectively. The loss functions are formulated as:

$$L_1 = -log(\frac{exp(P(r))}{exp(P(r)) + exp(T)}) \tag{3}$$

$$L_2 = -log(\frac{exp(T)}{\sum_{r_i \in R \backslash \{r\}} exp(P(r_i)) + exp(T)}) \tag{4}$$

While for *Vague*, considering that some potential temporal relations may be ignored and not to be considered into CS, we avoid penalty mechanism that penalizes the probability of relations not in CS. Besides, as a warmed-up classifier, the model provides nearly random probability distribution at the first few steps of the training process, so we set a linear increasing weight w to control the effect of the loss from *Vague*. Thus we have:

$$L_3 = -w * \sum_{o_i \in CS} log(\frac{exp(P(r_i))}{\sum_{r'_i \in CS} exp(P(r'_i)) + exp(T)}) \tag{5}$$

where $w = MIN(\alpha * t * \bar{w}, \bar{w})$. α is the increasing rate and t is the training step. w will not exceed $\bar{w}$ due to the uncertainty in CS. Both $\bar{w}$ and α are hyperparameters. The final loss function is: $L = L_1 + L_2 + L_3$

4   Experiments

4.1   Dataset and Evaluation Metrics

We evaluate our model in three temporal relation extraction datasets: TB-Dense, MATRES and UDS-T. Event pairs in UDS-T's validation and test set are labeled by 3 annotators, so we determine the temporal relation by majority voting.

Following [26], we utilize the symmetry property of temporal relations to expand our training set for data enhancement. For example, if the temporal relation of an event pair (e_1, e_2) is *Before*, we add the event pair (e_2, e_1) with relation *After* into the training set. We do not expand the validation set and test set for a fair comparison. We use micro-F1 score as the metric following [14,26].

4.2   Baseline Model

We implement a single-label classification-based model as a baseline. Both METRE and the baseline model adopt the same encoder architecture to obtain the event pair representation. Then the baseline uses a MLP and a softmax layer to calculate the probability distribution over $\tilde{R}$: $P_{base}(\tilde{R}|e_1, e_2) = MLP_4(\mathbf{h}_{e_1, e_2})$. The relation with the highest probability is viewed as final prediction.

4.3 Main Results

Table 1 compares the performance of our approach with previous works and our baseline model. METRE makes a significant improvement based on the baseline model on all three benchmarks, and outperforms current state-of-the-art models. By modeling the latent composition of *Vague*, METRE can effectively use the hidden information about well-defined relations, leading to an enhanced understanding of temporal relations.

As *Vague* accounts for nearly half of the training set of TB-Dense, which is far more than the proportions in MATRES and UDS-T, METRE can explore more information from *Vague* when trained on TB-Dense. Therefore, compared to the baseline model, METRE shows

Table 1. F1 score(%). *: trained with additional resources. †: We re-run the code and report our results. ‡: We reproduce the model since the code is not publicly available. For RSGT, we do not add the post-processing when reproducing.

PLM	Model	TB-Dense	MATRES	UDST
Base	HNP [7]	64.5	75.5	–
	Syntactic [26]*	66.7	79.3	–
	Unified [8]	66.4	79.3	–
	Baseline Model	63.1	78.2	50.9
	METRE(Ours)	67.2	79.2	52.0
Large	Syntactic [26]*	67.1	80.3	–
	Time-Enhanced [24]	–	81.7	-
	SCS-EERE [13]†	–	81.6	-
	TIMERS [14]	67.8	82.3	-
	DCT [23]†	66.1	–	-
	RSGT [28]‡	–	78.9	-
	TCR-QA [3]‡	66.4	80.5	–
	Unified [8]	68.1	82.6	–
	Baseline Model	64.9	81.5	51.9
	METRE(Ours)	**68.5**	**82.9**	**52.8**

the largest improvement by 4.1% F1 score on TB-Dense with BERT-Base as encoder, while 1.0% and 1.1% F1 improvements on MATRES and UDS-T, respectively. Experiments with RoBERTa-Large also show a similar trend, which indicates the efficacy of METRE in extracting concealed information from *Vague* to facilitate temporal relation prediction.

Our approach is still effective when provided with better event pair representations. As the encoder is changed from BERT-Base to RoBERTa-Large, METRE shows a stable improvement on all benchmarks compared to the baseline. Due to our approach's exclusive focus on the classifier module, independent from most previous works that concentrate on enhancing the encoder to acquire superior event pair representations, we believe that our approach can be effortlessly integrated with a stronger encoder, and achieve better performance.

5 Analysis

5.1 Effectiveness of Speculation Mechanism

The key of our approach is how we speculate the possible temporal relations behind *Vague* for the design of CS. To assess the effectiveness of our speculation mechanism, we compare METRE with several model variants with different rules in determining the elements in CS: 1) METRE w. Top2. We simply choose the top two temporal relations with the highest probability. 2) METRE w. B&A. We fix $CS = \{Before, After\}$ as these two relations occur between event pairs most frequently, so they may be more likely to cause the ambiguity of *Vague*. 3) METRE w. >Thr. We set $CS = \{r_i | P(r_i | e_1, e_2) > T_{e_1,e_2}\}$ based on the hypothesis that every relation with a probability higher than the threshold is more likely to be the potential temporal relation. Besides, since CS can not exactly represent the gold potential relations, we avoid the penalty on the temporal relations $r \notin CS$. To evaluate the negative effect of the penalty mechanism, we implement another model variant METRE w. Pnt, where we penalize every relation $r \notin CS$. Experimental results are shown in Table 2.

***CS* Explores Potential Relations:** As mentioned in Sect. 3.3, CS is a set that represents the inferred composition of *Vague* based on the given text. Encouraging all relations in CS to have higher probabilities is built on the assumption that the context contains the relevant information about these relations. To evaluate the effectiveness of the speculation mechanism of CS, we experiment on the model variants METRE w. Top2, METRE w. >Thr and METRE w. B&A.

Compared to model variants, METRE delivers much better results on all datasets, demonstrating CS can effectively assist the model in exploring accurate latent temporal information behind *Vague* to better understand every temporal relation. For example, if the temporal relation of an event pair is *Vague* due to the ambiguity between *Before* and *Include*, after successfully predicting *Before*, METRE is likely to choose

Table 2. F1 scores of METRE and model variants.

	TB-Dense	MATRES	UDST
METRE	67.2	79.2	52.0
w. Top2	65.2	78.8	51.3
w. >Thr	61.2	78.2	51.7
w. B&A	66.9	79.2	51.8
w. Pnt	65.5	78.9	51.8

Include into CS as the confusion relation, and learn something about both relations simultaneously. Therefore, by exploring potential temporal relations and encouraging them to have higher possibilities, METRE can efficiently use such information and achieve better performance.

METRE w. B&A achieves the best performance among all model variants, indicating that relations *Before* and *After* are more likely to cause the ambiguity of *Vague*. In our approach, we also tend to choose *Before* or *After* into CS as r_{fir} because of their high frequency in the corpus. Moreover, our speculation mechanism provides the opportunity for other well-defined relations to be reasonably chosen into CS. In this way, METRE can fully explore the potential relations according to the given text, and learn the meaning of *Vague* more accurately.

Besides, we notice that there is only a slight gap between the performance of METRE and its variants on MATRES. We attribute this to the limited types of well-defined relations in MATRES, so the variants do not differ much from METRE. In addition, compared to MATRES and UDS-T, METRE w. >Thr delivers a much inferior performance on TB-Dense. It is because, after the model's warming up with well-defined relations, there is always only one element in $CS = \{r_i | P(r_i | e_1, e_2) > T_{e_1,e_2}\}$, which contradicts to the definition of *Vague*. After incorrectly learning the meaning of *Vague*, the model will predict *Vague* as other well-defined relations, leading to its lower recall. Since *Vague* accounts for nearly half of the proportion in TB-Dense, the performance of METRE w. >Thr on TB-Dense is most severely affected.

Incorrect Penalty is Reduced: In our approach, we do not penalize any relation $r \notin CS$ since they may be the potential temporal relations between the event pair. To evaluate the negative effect of the penalty on *Vague*, we add an extra loss L_4 in METRE w. Pnt: $L_4 = -log(\frac{exp(T)}{\sum_{r_i \in R \setminus CS} exp(P(r_i)) + exp(T)})$.

Experiment results show that the extra penalty on *Vague* leads to consistent drops of F1 score on all datasets. We attribute this negative effect to the incorrect penalty on the potential relations between the event pair. For example, when both *Before* and *Simultaneous* could possibly be the temporal relations between an event pair, and *Simultaneous* fails to be predicted into CS, the incorrect penalty may cause the model to misunderstand the meaning of *Simultaneous*. We hypothesize that this situation may be more serious in single-label classification-based methods, since they inevitably penalize every temporal relation when faced with *Vague*. However, our approach can easily avoid such a situation, and reduce the incorrect penalty on potential temporal relations.

5.2   Benefiting Minority Relations

Due to the imbalance among the label distributions of different relations, most previous models, e.g., single-label classification ones, learn more knowledge about the majority relations like *Before* and *After*, while the minority relations, i.e., *Include*, *Is_Included* and *Simultaneous*, often receive less attention during training. In contrast, our method can explore extra information regarding minority relations by speculating the potential relations behind *Vague*. Specifically, when a minority relation is selected as the potential relation $r \in CS$, it will provide the model with more opportunities to understand this minority relation.

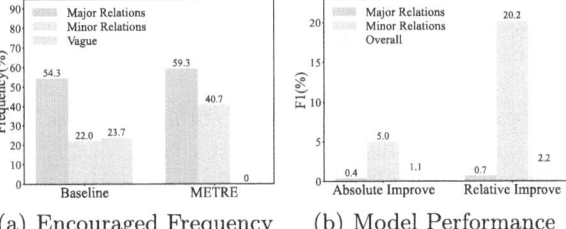

(a) Encouraged Frequency   (b) Model Performance

Fig. 2. Comparison of majority and minority relations.

To examine how much we can benefit from exploring CS, we calculate the frequency of each relation being encouraged to have a higher probability during training. We also compare the F1 score between majority and minority relations to demonstrate the improvement in the performance of minority relations. We calculate the value of the absolute and relative improvement compared to the baseline, which is shown in Fig. 2(a) and 2(b), respectively.

Compared to the baseline model, METRE delivers a 5.0% increase in the encouraged frequency for those majority relations but an 18.7% increase for the minority relations. By exploring the underlying compositions behind *Vague*, METRE achieves improvement in both types, especially for the minority ones, with greater absolute and relative improvement of 5.0% and 20.2%. We think the relations selected in the CS can help METER understand those minority relations better and alleviates the imbalanced label distribution issue.

5.3   Efficiently Using Latent Information

Since event pairs with temporal relation *Vague* contain sufficient information about the possible temporal relations, they can be used as supplementary resources to help METRE understand well-defined relations. In our approach, by treating *Vague* as the case when there are multiple possible well-defined relations, METRE can capture such latent information about these relations and learn more about their meaning. The importance of the supplementary information could be more obvious when the training resources are limited. Therefore, to eval-

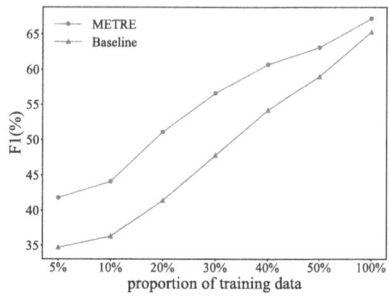

Fig. 3. Comparison of baseline and METRE in the few shot settings.

uate METRE's capability in effectively exploring sufficient information from training data, we conduct experiments with variable amounts of training data, ranging from 5% to 50%, while keeping the test set unchanged. In low resources scenarios, METRE outperforms the baseline model by 7.8% on average F1 score. Figure 3 illustrates the F1 scores of the baseline model and METRE on TB-Dense.

We can observe that, METRE stably outperforms baseline in every portion of the training set. This result indicates that METRE is more capable of capturing the information in *Vague* efficiently and making full use of it. When the smaller size of the training set is used, such as 5% to 30%, METRE shows a larger difference from the baseline. This phenomenon mainly results from the different amounts of information models can obtain. Since there are only a few well-defined relations in the small training set, single-label classification-based models are struggling to recognize them correctly. However, METRE's capability in leveraging *Vague* to learn knowledge of well-defined relations plays an important role, which helps to capture effective information from the limited training set more comprehensively and efficiently.

5.4   Interpretability of *Vague*

Treated as a multi-label classification task, METRE can predict the relation composition of *Vague*. To better evaluate the capability of METRE in interpreting the temporal relation composition of *Vague*, we check the consistency between our prediction of *Vague* and the annotation results from

Table 3. Absolute precision and relative precision on Top$K$ prediction of *Vague*.

Accuracy	Absolute Value			Relative Improve		
	Top1	Top2	Top3	Top1	Top2	Top3
Random	60.0	30.0	10.0	0.0	0.0	0.0
Baseline	70.8	47.7	19.9	18.0	59.0	99.0
METRE	80.5	63.8	33.6	34.2	112.7	236.0
Improve.	+9.7	+16.1	+13.7	×1.90	×1.91	×2.38

humans. As we mentioned in Sect. 4.1, for every event pair in UDS-T, its relation is determined by 3 annotators, so we can calculate the overlap of the prediction of METRE with the 3 different annotation results. Specifically, if we make a correct prediction on *Vague*, we choose the K relations with the highest probabilities and judge whether these Top$K$ relations all conform to the annotation results. The accuracy scores are shown in Table 3.

METRE outperforms baseline by 9.7%, 16.1% and 13.7% in Top1/2/3 accuracy respectively, demonstrating a greater capability of METRE in predicting the intrinsic temporal relation composition of *Vague*. Given the accuracy of random ranking, we calculate the relative accuracy improvement as $(Pr_{ours} - Pr_{random})/Pr_{random}$ and $(Pr_{base} - Pr_{random})/Pr_{random}$. The larger K is, the more we need to predict information about *Vague* comprehensively and accurately. As K increases, METRE shows a greater improvement in relative accuracy than baseline, from 1.90 times to 2.38 times, which indicates our stronger capability in predicting full latent information of *Vague*.

6   Conclusion

In this work, we investigate the underlying meaning of the special relation *Vague* in the temporal relation extraction task. A novel approach is proposed to effectively use the latent information behind *Vague*, helping our model understand the meaning of *Vague* and all well-defined relations more accurately. Experiments show that our model outperforms previous state-of-the-art methods on three benchmarks, indicating the effectiveness of our approach. Extensive analyses further demonstrate our model's advantage in using training data more comprehensively and making our predictions more interpretable.

Acknowledgments. This work is supported in part by NSFC (62161160339) and Beijing Science and Technology Program (Z231100007423011). We thank the anonymous reviewers for their valuable comments and suggestions. For any correspondence, please contact Yansong Feng.

References

1. Cassidy, T., McDowell, B., Chambers, N., Bethard, S.: An annotation framework for dense event ordering. In: ACL (2014)
2. Cheng, F., Miyao, Y.: Classifying temporal relations by bidirectional LSTM over dependency paths. In: ACL (2017)
3. Cohen, O., Bar, K.: Temporal relation classification using Boolean question answering. In: Findings of ACL (2023)
4. Coll-Florit, M., Gennari, S.P.: Time in language: event duration in language comprehension. Cogn. Psychol. **62**(1), 41–79 (2011)
5. Devlin, J., Chang, M.W., Lee, K., Toutanova, K.: BERT: pre-training of deep bidirectional transformers for language understanding. In: ACL (2019)
6. Guo, C., Pleiss, G., Sun, Y., Weinberger, K.Q.: On calibration of modern neural networks. In: ICML (2017)

7. Han, R., Ning, Q., Peng, N.: Joint event and temporal relation extraction with shared representations and structured prediction. In: EMNLP (2019)
8. Huang, Q., Hu, Y., Zhu, S., Feng, Y., Liu, C., Zhao, D.: More than classification: a unified framework for event temporal relation extraction. In: ACL (2023)
9. Hwang, E., Lee, J.Y., Yang, T., Patel, D., Zhang, D., McCallum, A.: Event-event relation extraction using probabilistic box embedding. In: ACL (2022)
10. Liu, Y., et al.: Roberta: a robustly optimized bert pretraining approach. arXiv preprint arXiv:1907.11692 (2019)
11. Malinin, A., Gales, M.: Predictive uncertainty estimation via prior networks (2018)
12. Malinin, A., Gales, M.: Reverse kl-divergence training of prior networks: Improved uncertainty and adversarial robustness (2019)
13. Man, H., Ngo, N.T., Van, L.N., Nguyen, T.H.: Selecting optimal context sentences for event-event relation extraction. In: AAAI, vol. 36 (2022)
14. Mathur, P., Jain, R., Dernoncourt, F., Morariu, V., Tran, Q.H., Manocha, D.: TIMERS: document-level temporal relation extraction. In: ACL (2021)
15. Meng, Y., Rumshisky, A., Romanov, A.: Temporal information extraction for question answering using syntactic dependencies in an LSTM-based architecture. In: EMNLP (2017)
16. Ng, J.P., Chen, Y., Kan, M.Y., Li, Z.: Exploiting timelines to enhance multi-document summarization. In: Proceedings of ACL (2014)
17. Ning, Q., Feng, Z., Roth, D.: A structured learning approach to temporal relation extraction (2019)
18. Ning, Q., Wu, H., Roth, D.: A multi-axis annotation scheme for event temporal relations. In: ACL (2018)
19. Shi, W., Zhao, T., Yu, Z.: Unsupervised dialog structure learning. In: NAACL (2019)
20. Vashishtha, S., Van Durme, B., White, A.S.: Fine-grained temporal relation extraction. In: ACL (2019)
21. Wadden, D., Wennberg, U., Luan, Y., Hajishirzi, H.: Entity, relation, and event extraction with contextualized span representations. In: EMNLP (2019)
22. Wang, H., Zhang, H., Deng, Y., Gardner, J., Roth, D., Chen, M.: Extracting or guessing? improving faithfulness of event temporal relation extraction. In: EACL (2023)
23. Wang, L., Li, P., Xu, S.: DCT-centered temporal relation extraction. In: COLING (2022)
24. Wen, H., Ji, H.: Utilizing relative event time to enhance event-event temporal relation extraction. In: EMNLP (2021)
25. Yu, M., Yin, W., Hasan, K.S., dos Santos, C., Xiang, B., Zhou, B.: Improved neural relation detection for knowledge base question answering. In: ACL (2017)
26. Zhang, S., Ning, Q., Huang, L.: Extracting temporal event relation with syntactic-guided temporal graph transformer. In: NAACL (2022)
27. Zhong, Z., Chen, D.: A frustratingly easy approach for entity and relation extraction. In: NAACL (2021)
28. Zhou, J., Dong, S., Tu, H., Wang, X., Dou, Y.: RSGT: relational structure guided temporal relation extraction. In: COLING (2022)
29. Zhou, W., Huang, K., Ma, T., Huang, J.: Document-level relation extraction with adaptive thresholding and localized context pooling (2020)

Empowering LLMs for Long-Text Information Extraction in Chinese Legal Documents

Chenchen Shen[1], Chengwei Ji[1], Shengbin Yue[2], Xiaoyu Shen[3], Yun Song[4], Xuanjing Huang[5], and Zhongyu Wei[1(✉)]

[1] School of Data Science, Fudan University, Shanghai, China
{ccshen22,cwji21}@m.fudan.edu.cn, zywei@fudan.edu.cn
[2] Shanghai Center for Mathematical Sciences, Fudan University, Shanghai, China
sbyue23@m.fudan.edu.cn
[3] Eastern Institute of Technology, Ningbo, China
xyshen@eitech.edu.cn
[4] Northwest University of Political and Law, Xi'an, China
1171991@s.hlju.edu.cn
[5] School of Computer Science, Fudan University, Shanghai, China
xjhuang@fudan.edu.cn

Abstract. Existing large language models(LLMs) in the legal domain typically only handle text within a limited context window size, making it challenging to fully meet the requirements of long legal texts. In this paper, we propose to achieve long-text information extraction for Chinese judgement documents by training on short-text models with low fine-tuning costs. Through training on short-text data and improving the rotational positional encoding method, we achieve a model capable of directly inferring on long texts with relatively low fine-tuning costs. Overall experimental results demonstrate that the our model for long judgement documents information extraction outperforms all compared LLMs.

Keywords: Information extraction · Large Language Model · Instruction Tuning · Intelligent Law

1 Introduction

Information extraction in the domain of Intelligent Law has garnered significant interest among researchers. To better utilize the specificity of legal texts, researchers have attempted to apply ontology [6,42] or global consistency [39] for named entity recognition [1,19] in Intelligent Law. For extracting relations and events [8,24,25,41] from legal documents, researchers have explored different NLP techniques, including manual rules [31] and joint models [33] to achieve satisfactory results.

C. Shen and C. Ji—Contribute equally to this paper.

© The Author(s), under exclusive license to Springer Nature Singapore Pte Ltd. 2025
D. F. Wong et al. (Eds.): NLPCC 2024, LNAI 15359, pp. 457–469, 2025.
https://doi.org/10.1007/978-981-97-9431-7_35

Figure 1 (left) shows an example of information extraction for Chinese judgment document. Judges and other legal professionals need to extract and classify key information from these texts. In practical applications, legal texts such as judgement documents are often lengthy or even super lengthy. Figure 1 (right) shows length distribution of 10,000 randomly sampled Chinese judgment documents, it can be seen that most documents have more than 5,000 words. Researchers have proposed methods such as paragraph selection strategies [32], long text encoders [23], and key segment learning [37] for processing long texts in the legal domain.

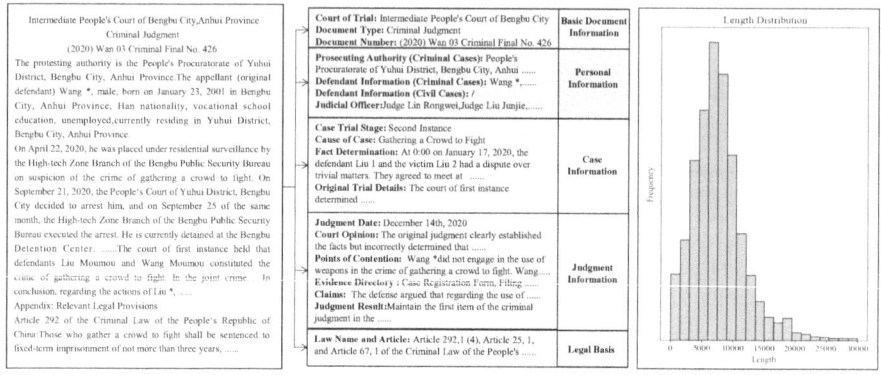

Fig. 1. Left: an example of information extraction for chinese judgment documents. Right: length distribution of chinese judgment documents (based on 10,000 randomly sampled documents).

In recent years, large language models have demonstrated outstanding performance across multiple traditional NLP tasks, including information extraction tasks in general domain [15,36]. Existing large language models in the legal domain, despite their good performance in various legal tasks [40], are typically limited to handling text within the context window size, making it challenging to fully meet the requirements of long legal texts. Although there are already open-source long-text foundation models with competitive advantages in processing long Chinese texts [3], fine-tuning on long-text training data directly incurs high costs. This paper proposes to achieve information extraction for long legal texts by training on short-text models with low fine-tuning costs. Specifically, the model is trained on short texts and then improves the model's positional encoding from RoPE to NTK-RoPE for inference on long texts, thus enabling processing of long texts while saving computational resources.

Our contributions are three-fold: (1) We propose a method to improve positional encoding after training on short-text models, enabling inference on long texts. This method achieves better results than all compared LLMs while saving resources. (2) We construct a large-scale dataset for judgement documents information extraction. (3) Experimental results demonstrate that our model for long judgement documents information extraction outperforms all compared Large Language Models.

2   Related Work

Due to limitations in the Transformer [34] architecture, training large language models directly on long texts requires substantial computational resources and often yields suboptimal performance. As a result, there are few open-source models specifically designed for processing lengthy texts. The main reasons for this scarcity include: (1) Model Training. The use of GPU memory scales quadratically with sequence length, sharply increasing training requirements. (2) Model Structure. Longer sequences result in more dispersed attention within the model, increasing the likelihood of forgetting earlier content. (3) Inference Speed. Longer sequences significantly reduce model inference speed.

Methods based on the Transformer architecture for handling long texts [17] include efficient attention mechanisms, long-term memory, extrapolated positional encoding, and context processing, as detailed below:

Efficient Attention: These methods aim to achieve efficient attention mechanisms with reduced computational demands, even achieving linear complexity. The attention mechanism serves as the core bottleneck module in Transformer. Optimizing attention mechanisms involves directly increasing hyperparameter $L_{\max}$ during pre-training, thus expanding the effective context length boundaries for large language models during inference. Strategies for these methods include local attention [4,9], hierarchical attention [30,38], sparse attention [10,27], approximated attention [22,35], and IO-aware attention [12,18].

Long-Term Memory: Large language models lack an explicit memory mechanism and solely rely on Key-Value (KV) caches to store representations of all previous tokens in a sequence. This design means that once a query is completed in one call, the Transformer architecture does not retain or remember any previous states or sequences in subsequent calls unless the entire history is individually reloaded into the KV cache. To address the limitations of working memory context, some methods aim to design explicit memory mechanisms, optimizing for KV caching to compensate for the lack of efficient and effective long-term memory in large language models [11,13].

Improved Positional Encoding: Enhancing the extrapolation performance of existing positional encoding schemes to improve the length scalability of large language models. The original Transformer architecture introduced Sinusoidal Position Encoding (SinPE) [34]. Many current large language models employ Rotary Position Embedding (RoPE) [29], such as LLaMA, ChatGLM, Baichuan-7B, etc. Common approaches to extend context length through optimizing positional encoding include extrapolation and interpolation [7]. Extrapolation involves directly applying the original encoding method to larger positions, while interpolation scales target positions proportionally to supported model positions.

Context Processing: In addition to modifying Transformer modules, some methods combine existing large language models with additional context preproc-essing/postprocessing [16,26]. These methods treat pre-trained large language models as black-box or gray-box models,addressing the handling of contexts exceeding model length limitations by invoking the model multiple times.It ensures that each call's actual input consistently meets the maximum length requirement $L_{\max}$, breaking the context window restriction by introducing overheads of multiple call.

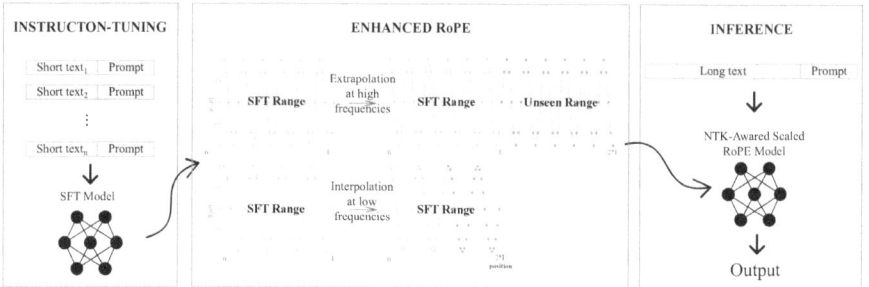

Fig. 2. Overview of our proposed approach for long-text information extraction.After training the model on short texts, the position encoding of the model is changed from RoPE to NTK-RoPE, allowing for inference on long texts while conserving computational resources.

Considering that efficient attention mechanisms and long-term memory involve model pre-training, which typically consumes more computational resources and training time than fine-tuning, and context processing requires longer inference time overhead, this paper primarily focuses on the method of improving positional encoding.

3   Method

3.1   Model

The average length of judgement documents often exceeds 10,000 words, far surpassing the processing length limit of most Chinese foundation models, which typically handle sequences up to 4096 tokens. While existing Chinese long-text foundation models such as ChatGLM2-6B-32K [14] and Qwen-7B-32K [2], fine-tuning these models directly with long-text training data is costly. This paper proposes achieving information extraction for lengthy judgement documents using short-text models with lower fine-tuning costs.

Figure 2 shows our proposed approach for long-text information extraction. After training the model on short texts, the position encoding of the model is changed from RoPE to NTK-RoPE, allowing for inference on long texts while conserving computational resources. Specifically, after fine-tuning a foundation model which can only handle 4k tokens with short-text dataset constructed in 3.2, we obtained a SFT model. Then, by modifying the positional encoding of this model, we developed the LawLongIE-NTK model proposed in this paper.

Rotary Position Embedding (RoPE) [29] is a positional encoding method adopted by many foundation models (e.g., LLaMA, ChatGLM, Baichuan-7B.). Unlike traditional positional encodings applied at the input layer of embeddings, RoPE operates within the computations of attention. In 2023, Su et al. [29] demonstrated:

$$f_{\{q,k\}}(x_m, m) = R^d_{\Theta,m} W_{\{q,k\}} x_m, \tag{1}$$

where the RoPE matrix $R^d_{\Theta,m}$ is:

$$R^d_{\Theta,m} = \begin{pmatrix} \cos(m\theta_1) & -\sin(m\theta_1) & 0 & 0 & \dots & 0 & 0 \\ \sin(m\theta_1) & \cos(m\theta_1) & 0 & 0 & \dots & 0 & 0 \\ \vdots & \vdots & \vdots & \vdots & \ddots & \vdots & \vdots \\ 0 & 0 & 0 & 0 & \dots & \cos(m\theta_{d/2}) & -\sin(m\theta_{d/2}) \\ 0 & 0 & 0 & 0 & \dots & \sin(m\theta_{d/2}) & \cos(m\theta_{d/2}) \end{pmatrix}, \tag{2}$$

$$\Theta = \{\theta_i = b^{-2i/d} \mid i \in [0, 1, \dots, d/2 - 1]\} \tag{3}$$

By applying Eq. 1 in the self-attention computation process, we can obtain self-attention that incorporates relative positional information. Equation 4 represents the inner product calculation between query and key:

$$q_m^T k_n = (R^d_{\Theta,m} W_q x_m)^T (R^d_{\Theta,n} W_k x_n) = x_m^T W_q R^d_{\Theta,n-m} W_k x_n. \tag{4}$$

RoPE effectively preserves the relative positional relationships. In theory, generating position encodings beyond the pretraining length using rotation matrices can achieve extrapolation of position encoding. However, when the text length exceeds a certain threshold, the model's performance significantly deteriorates, manifested by metrics like perplexity exhibiting notable increases [21].

The NTK-RoPE involves nonlinear interpolation by modifying the base of RoPE rather than the scale, thereby changing the "rotation" speed of each RoPE dimension vector with respect to the next vector. This modification of the base enables high-frequency extrapolation and low-frequency interpolation. The following function is a change of basis from b in Equation 3 to new base b', where α is a scale factor:

$$b' = b * \alpha^{d/(d-2)}. \tag{5}$$

Experiments have shown that NTK-Aware Scaled RoPE achieves good extrapolation results without fine-tuning [5, 28].

3.2   Dataset Construction

This dataset is sourced from authentic judgement documents in the real world, collecting from China Judgments Online[1], which provides civil and criminal judgments for various years. The original documents typically contain informations of basic document, personal, case, judgment, and legal statutes. Table 1 shows details of the specific items for information extraction. The data construction process consists of three stages: obtaining extraction results for various items, segmenting the original text into chunks, and data construction based on instructions.Figure 3 shows the data construction process.

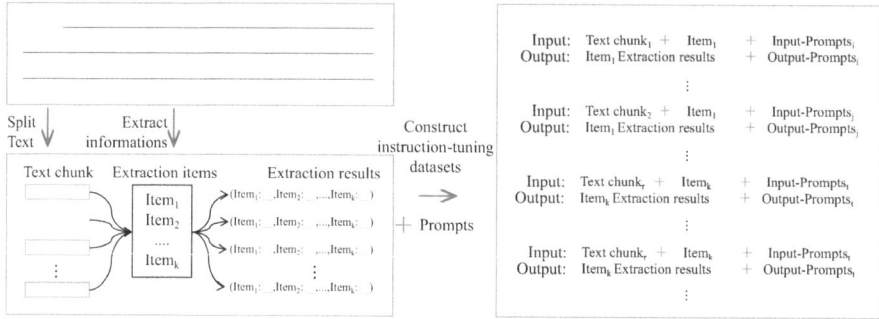

Fig. 3. Overview of dataset construction process.

Obtaining Extraction Results for Various Items: Content from the original judgement documents is extracted based on the fields listed in Table 1. The method involves a combination of regular expression matching and manual verification. There are five major categories comprising 18 specific items.

Segmenting the Original Text: Based on the model design described in Sect. 3.1, training data for the model are short texts. Therefore, the original judgement documents need to be segmented into text chunks, with chunk lengths set at 1-2k, 2-3k, 3-4k words respectively. The corresponding overlap between chunks is set at 50, 100, 150 words. The text segmentation algorithm is implemented using the open-source framework Langchain[2].

Data Construction Based on Instructions: After obtaining the text chunks and combining them with the extraction results for specific fields, data pairs $< textchunk - extractionresults >$ are generated. These data pairs are further combined with pre-designed prompts to produce instruction-tuning data pairs for this task $< input - output >$.

The training dataset consists of 9,832 judgement documents, yielding approximately 99,000 instruction-tuning pairs. The instruction-tuning data utilizes text

---

[1] https://wenshu.court.gov.cn/.
[2] https://www.langchain.com/.

chunks from the judgement documents, with an average input length of 1,988 words. Negative examples constitute about 10% of the positive examples, negative examples refer to data within the text chunks that do not contain corresponding field information. Table 1 provides a detailed analysis of training set, including extraction items, corresponding data sizes, number of negative samples, and average input length.

Table 1. Categories, question IDs, corresponding specific items for extracting judgement documents information, and statistical analysis of training dataset (including data scale, number of negative samples, average input length).

Category	Question ID	Extraction Item	Data Scale	Negative Samples	Average Input Length
Basic Document Information	1-1	Court of Trial	5.5k	500	2004
	1-2	Document Type	5.5k	500	1960
	1-3	Document Number	5.5k	500	2023
Personal Information	2-1	Prosecuting Authority (Criminal Cases)	5.5k	500	1893
	2-2	Defendant Information (Criminal Cases)	5.5k	500	2024
	2-3	Defendant Information (Civil Cases)	5.5k	500	1965
	2-4	Judicial Officer	5.5k	500	2005
Case Information	3-1	Case Trial Stage	5.5k	500	1969
	3-2	Cause of Case	5.5k	500	2032
	3-3	Fact Determination	5.5k	500	2025
	3-4	Original Trial Details	5.5k	500	1868
Judgment Information	4-1	Judgment Date	5.5k	500	2013
	4-2	Court Opinion	5.5k	500	1994
	4-3	Points of Contention	4.9k	446	1911
	4-4	Evidence Directory	5.5k	500	2043
	4-5	Claims	5.5k	500	1971
	4-6	Judgment Result	5.5k	500	2177
Legal Basis	5-1	Law Name and Article	5.5k	500	1914
Total			98k	8946	1988 (average)

The test dataset consists of 320 judgement documents, with document lengths distributed as follows: 0-4k, 4-8k, 8-16k, and 16k+, with 80 documents in each category. Each judgement document in the test set is subjected to extraction of the items listed in Table 1, totaling 5,760 test queries. The test set does not include judgement documents that overlap with those in the training set, and the test queries directly use the original judgement documents.

4   Experiments

4.1   Implementation Details

The comparison models, evaluation metrics, and settings for this experiment are as follows:

Comparison Models: In addition to the LawLongIE-NTK model proposed in Sect. 3.1 for judgement documents extraction, this experiment also compares other baseline models and general large language models. The models included are:

General large language models not fine-tuned for this task: Baichuan2-7B-Chat, Baichuan2-7B-Chat-NTK, ChatGLM2-6B-32K, ChatGLM3-6B-32K, GPT-3.5-Turbo-0125,GPT-4-0125-preview.

Models fine-tuned for this task: LawLongIE (Original PE), LawLongIE-NTK (modified PE).

Evaluation Metrics: ROUGE-L, this metric calculates the similarity score between predicted and reference texts based on tokenized processing, focusing on the overlap between predicted and reference texts.

F1 Score, this metric computes the similarity between predicted and reference texts based on tokenization and normalization, emphasizing the exact matching of each word between predicted and reference texts.

Settings for the Training and Testing Processes: We use 4 V100 GPUs to train our model on top of the Baichuan2-7B-Chat model with LoRA fine-tuning. The model is trained for 2 epochs with a batch size of 32, learning rate of 5e-5. We set the maximum token length to be 4096. For texts exceeding the model's processing length capacity, truncation is applied at the middle of the text to preserve information from both the beginning and end. This approach is based on a study which indicates minimal impact on model performance with this truncation method [20].

4.2   Experiments Results

Overall Experimental Results and Analysis. Table 2 presents the comprehensive experimental results for judgement documents information extraction. From Table 2, it is evident that LawLongIE-NTK achieved the highest scores across both evaluation metrics, ROUGE-L and F1, surpassing all other comparison models. Specifically, LawLongIE-NTK outperformed the GPT-4-0125-preview model with context length of 128k by 3.12% in ROUGE-L and 2.43% in F1, outperformed the GPT-3.5-turbo-0125 model with context length of 16k by 12.45% in ROUGE-L and 7.84% in F1.

Comparing LawLongIE, a model trained solely on this task using Baichuan2-7B-Chat without length expansion, with Baichuan2-7B-Chat-NTK, which is Baichuan2-7B-Chat extended without training specifically for this task, Law-LongIE showed a 2.09% improvement in ROUGE-L but a 0.89% decrease in F1. LawLongIE-NTK, the extended version of LawLongIE designed in Sect. 3.1, outperformed Baichuan2-7B-Chat-NTK by 14.23% in ROUGE-L and 11.49% in F1. This improvement is likely due to LawLongIE's enhanced ability after task-specific training. However, during inference, it was limited by length constraints, resulting in information loss. After NTK-Aware RoPE extension, LawLongIE-NTK's ability to handle increased context length improved, demonstrating the feasibility of training on short texts and directly inferring on long texts. This approach also conserves computational resources compared to directly fine-tuning long-context large language models.

Experimental Results and Analysis on Texts of Different Lengths.
Table 3 presents the overall experimental results for the judgement documents

Table 2. Overall experimental results for judgement documents information extraction (ROUGE-L and F1, %), where bold indicates the best result.

Model	Context Length	ROUGE-L	F1
Baichuan2-7B-Chat	4k	35.50	38.45
Baichuan2-7B-Chat-NTK	8k	40.75	44.04
ChatGLM2-6B-32K	32k	24.33	27.51
ChatGLM3-6B-32K	32k	28.43	32.07
GPT-3.5-Turbo-0125	16k	42.53	47.69
GPT-4-0125-preview	128k	51.86	53.10
LawLongIE	4k	42.84	43.15
LawLongIE-NTK	8k	**54.98**	**55.53**

information extraction task across texts of varying lengths. It is evident from Table 3 that LawLongIE-NTK nearly achieved the highest scores across both evaluation metrics, ROUGE-L and F1, surpassing almost all other comparison models. However, its performance for lengths exceeding 8k was inferior to the GPT-4-0125-preview model with 128k context length. Furthermore, nearly all models exhibited a gradual decline in performance as the length of the test texts increased. Notably, LawLongIE-NTK, extended with NTK-Aware techniques in this paper, demonstrated superior performance even on texts exceeding 8k in length compared to some models with 16k or 32k context lengths, including GPT-3.5-turbo-0125, GPT-4-0125-preview and the ChatGLM 32k series models. This highlights the effectiveness of LawLongIE-NTK in handling longer texts after extension, showcasing better performance than models with longer specified context lengths.

Table 3. Experimental results of judgement documents information extraction across texts of different lengths (%), where bold indicates the best result.

Model	Context Length	0-4k		4-8k		8-16k		16k+	
		ROUGE-L	F1	ROUGE-L	F1	ROUGE-L	F1	ROUGE-L	F1
Baichuan2-7B-Chat	4k	44.88	47.85	35.30	38.47	31.15	33.83	30.28	33.31
Baichuan2-7B-Chat-NTK	8k	48.35	51.39	43.60	46.97	36.92	40.16	33.35	36.93
ChatGLM2-6B-32K	32k	28.16	31.5	24.74	28.11	23.11	26.32	20.96	23.67
ChatGLM3-6B-32K	32k	33.06	36.65	29.70	33.39	26.14	29.88	24.41	27.95
GPT-3.5-Turbo-0125	16k	47.14	52.46	42.78	48.14	40.62	45.41	39.26	44.47
GPT-4-0125-preview	128k	53.98	55.18	51.79	52.86	**51.11**	**52.48**	**50.55**	**51.90**
LawLongIE	4k	52.89	53.14	39.83	40.17	39.56	39.82	38.82	39.20
LawLongIE-NTK	8k	**69.69**	**70.11**	**59.73**	**60.51**	46.78	47.18	42.61	43.20

Experimental Results and Analysis on Different Extraction Questions.
Table 4 present the overall experimental results for the judgement documents information extraction task across different extraction questions, evaluated using

the F1. From Table 4, it is observed that LawLongIE-NTK achieved the best F1 scores for 7 out of 18 extraction questions. LawLongIE-NTK performed less satisfactorily on two specific questions: "Evidence Directory" (4-4) and "Claims" (4-5). The GPT-4-0125-preview achieved the best results for those two questions. This difference in performance could be attributed to the fact that these questions require not only the ability to perform extractive reading comprehension but also the capability to summarize and synthesize extracted content.

Table 4. Experimental results of judgement documents information extraction task across different extraction questions (F1, %), where bold indicates the best result and underline indicates the second-best result.

Question ID	LawLongIE-NTK	LawLongIE	GPT-4-0125-preview	GPT-3.5-Turbo-0125	Baichuan2-7B-Chat	Baichuan2-7B-Chat-NTK	ChatGLM2-6B-32K	ChatGLM3-6B-32K
Average	**55.53**	43.15	53.10	47.69	38.45	44.04	27.51	32.07
1-1	**82.99**	60.86	81.05	71.78	60.34	69.45	66.55	39.41
1-2	**82.90**	71.40	71.09	68.54	54.55	55.91	37.02	35.66
1-3	74.84	47.52	**92.20**	80.64	46.11	67.98	42.79	53.90
2-1	**75.77**	68.51	38.99	40.82	48.19	55.44	43.26	18.90
2-2	71.65	60.47	**76.41**	75.65	52.20	62.65	53.76	48.36
2-3	**53.62**	31.95	44.49	50.71	24.44	26.97	14.76	29.94
2-4	36.08	**39.84**	37.12	27.36	19.87	19.54	8.48	12.28
3-1	71.27	57.09	70.81	72.57	69.27	**74.08**	56.09	50.36
3-2	74.56	**85.38**	80.26	68.90	70.81	71.89	33.30	27.47
3-3	34.08	18.69	**38.13**	29.83	30.96	36.75	17.22	32.61
3-4	**27.08**	18.54	24.80	13.87	10.77	14.67	8.30	24.32
4-1	**96.47**	81.71	59.91	79.25	49.89	57.90	23.76	25.67
4-2	42.67	10.33	**67.71**	33.15	30.42	40.11	7.55	63.57
4-3	39.32	**42.86**	14.22	12.80	17.71	17.23	17.66	11.42
4-4	16.00	8.33	**26.25**	17.23	18.47	21.93	8.85	21.05
4-5	26.86	16.27	**43.99**	34.78	23.49	31.30	20.91	34.90
4-6	30.51	9.03	**45.00**	26.69	19.08	25.30	6.81	27.57
5-1	**62.84**	47.85	43.43	53.86	45.57	43.68	28.16	19.85

5   Conclusion

In this paper, we 4propose to achieve long-text information extraction for Chinese judgement documents by training on short-text models with low fine-tuning costs. Through training on short-text data and improving the rotational positional encoding method, we achieve a model capable of directly inferring on long texts with relatively low fine-tuning costs. Overall experimental results demonstrate that the our model for long judgement documents information extraction outperforms all compared large language models.

References

1. Akbik, A., Bergmann, T., Vollgraf, R.: Pooled contextualized embeddings for named entity recognition. In: Proceedings of the 2019 Conference of the North American Chapter of the Association for Computational Linguistics: Human Language Technologies, Volume 1 (Long and Short Papers), pp. 724–728 (2019)
2. Bai, J., et al.: Qwen technical report. arXiv preprint arXiv:2309.16609 (2023)
3. Bai, Y., et al.: Longbench: a bilingual, multitask benchmark for long context understanding. arXiv preprint arXiv:2308.14508 (2023)
4. Beltagy, I., Peters, M.E., Cohan, A.: Longformer: the long-document transformer. arXiv preprint arXiv:2004.05150 (2020)
5. bloc97: Ntk-aware scaled rope allows llama models to have extended (8k+) context size without any fine-tuning and minimal perplexity degradation. https://www.reddit.com/r/LocalLLaMA/comments/14lz7j5/ntkaware_scaled_rope_allows_llama_models_to_have/
6. Bruckschen, M., et al.: Named entity recognition in the legal domain for ontology population. In: Workshop Programme, p. 16 (2010)
7. Chen, S., Wong, S., Chen, L., Tian, Y.: Extending context window of large language models via positional interpolation. arXiv preprint arXiv:2306.15595 (2023)
8. Chen, Y., Xu, L., Liu, K., Zeng, D., Zhao, J.: Event extraction via dynamic multi-pooling convolutional neural networks. In: Proceedings of the 53rd Annual Meeting of the Association for Computational Linguistics and the 7th International Joint Conference on Natural Language Processing (Volume 1: Long Papers), pp. 167–176 (2015)
9. Chen, Y., et al.: Longlora: efficient fine-tuning of long-context large language models. arXiv preprint arXiv:2309.12307 (2023)
10. Child, R., Gray, S., Radford, A., Sutskever, I.: Generating long sequences with sparse transformers. arXiv preprint arXiv:1904.10509 (2019)
11. Dai, Z., Yang, Z., Yang, Y., Carbonell, J., Le, Q.V., Salakhutdinov, R.: Transformer-xl: attentive language models beyond a fixed-length context. arXiv preprint arXiv:1901.02860 (2019)
12. Dao, T.: Flashattention-2: faster attention with better parallelism and work partitioning. arXiv preprint arXiv:2307.08691 (2023)
13. Ding, S., et al.: Ernie-doc: a retrospective long-document modeling transformer. arXiv preprint arXiv:2012.15688 (2020)
14. Du, Z., et al.: GLM: general language model pretraining with autoregressive blank infilling. In: Proceedings of the 60th Annual Meeting of the Association for Computational Linguistics (Volume 1: Long Papers), pp. 320–335 (2022)
15. Gui, H., Zhang, J., Ye, H., Zhang, N.: Instructie: a Chinese instruction-based information extraction dataset. arXiv preprint arXiv:2305.11527 (2023)
16. Hao, Y., Sun, Y., Dong, L., Han, Z., Gu, Y., Wei, F.: Structured prompting: scaling in-context learning to 1,000 examples. arXiv preprint arXiv:2212.06713 (2022)
17. Huang, Y., et al.: Advancing transformer architecture in long-context large language models: a comprehensive survey (2023)
18. Kwon, W., et al.: Efficient memory management for large language model serving with pagedattention. In: Proceedings of the 29th Symposium on Operating Systems Principles, pp. 611–626 (2023)
19. Lample, G., Ballesteros, M., Subramanian, S., Kawakami, K., Dyer, C.: Neural architectures for named entity recognition. arXiv preprint arXiv:1603.01360 (2016)

20. Liu, N.F., et al.: Lost in the middle: how language models use long contexts. Trans. Assoc. Comput. Linguist. **12**, 157–173 (2024)
21. Liu, X., Yan, H., Zhang, S., An, C., Qiu, X., Lin, D.: Scaling laws of rope-based extrapolation. arXiv preprint arXiv:2310.05209 (2023)
22. Ma, X., et al.: Luna: linear unified nested attention. Adv. Neural. Inf. Process. Syst. **34**, 2441–2453 (2021)
23. Masala, M., Rebedea, T., Velicu, H.: Improving legal judgement prediction in Romanian with long text encoders. In: Melero, M., Sakti, S., Soria, C. (eds.) Proceedings of the 3rd Annual Meeting of the Special Interest Group on Under-resourced Languages @ LREC-COLING 2024, pp. 126–132. ELRA and ICCL, Torino, Italia (2024). https://aclanthology.org/2024.sigul-1.16
24. Miwa, M., Bansal, M.: End-to-end relation extraction using LSTMs on sequences and tree structures. arXiv preprint arXiv:1601.00770 (2016)
25. Nguyen, T.H., Cho, K., Grishman, R.: Joint event extraction via recurrent neural networks. In: Proceedings of the 2016 Conference of the North American Chapter of the Association for Computational Linguistics: Human Language Technologies, pp. 300–309 (2016)
26. Ratner, N., et al.: Parallel context windows for large language models. arXiv preprint arXiv:2212.10947 (2022)
27. Roy, A., Saffar, M., Vaswani, A., Grangier, D.: Efficient content-based sparse attention with routing transformers. Trans. Assoc. Comput. Linguist. **9**, 53–68 (2021)
28. Su, J.: Upgrade road of transformer:10.rope is a β-base encoding. https://spaces.ac.cn/archives/9675
29. Su, J., Lu, Y., Pan, S., Murtadha, A., Wen, B., Liu, Y.: Roformer: enhanced transformer with rotary position embedding (2023)
30. Sukhbaatar, S., Grave, E., Bojanowski, P., Joulin, A.: Adaptive attention span in transformers. arXiv preprint arXiv:1905.07799 (2019)
31. Truyens, M., Van Eecke, P.: Legal aspects of text mining. Comput. Law Secur. Rev. **30**(2), 153–170 (2014)
32. Tuteja, M., González Juclà, D.: Long text classification using transformers with paragraph selection strategies. In: Preotiuc-Pietro, D., Goanta, C., Chalkidis, I., Barrett, L., Spanakis, G., Aletras, N. (eds.) Proceedings of the Natural Legal Language Processing Workshop 2023, pp. 17–24. Association for Computational Linguistics, Singapore (2023). https://doi.org/10.18653/v1/2023.nllp-1.3, https://aclanthology.org/2023.nllp-1.3
33. Vacek, T., Teo, R., Song, D., Nugent, T., Cowling, C., Schilder, F.: Litigation analytics: Case outcomes extracted from us federal court dockets. In: Proceedings of the Natural Legal Language Processing Workshop 2019, pp. 45–54 (2019)
34. Vaswani, A., et al.: Attention is all you need. CoRR abs/1706.03762 (2017). http://arxiv.org/abs/1706.03762
35. Wang, S., Li, B.Z., Khabsa, M., Fang, H., Ma, H.: Linformer: self-attention with linear complexity. arXiv preprint arXiv:2006.04768 (2020)
36. Wang, X., et al.: Instructuie: multi-task instruction tuning for unified information extraction. arXiv preprint arXiv:2304.08085 (2023)
37. Xie, S., Li, L., Yuan, J., Xie, Q., Tao, X.: Long legal article question answering via cascaded key segment learning (student abstract). In: Proceedings of the Thirty-Seventh AAAI Conference on Artificial Intelligence and Thirty-Fifth Conference on Innovative Applications of Artificial Intelligence and Thirteenth Symposium on Educational Advances in Artificial Intelligence. AAAI'23/IAAI'23/EAAI'23, AAAI Press (2023). https://doi.org/10.1609/aaai.v37i13.27042, https://doi.org/10.1609/aaai.v37i13.27042

38. Yang, Z., Yang, D., Dyer, C., He, X., Smola, A., Hovy, E.: Hierarchical attention networks for document classification. In: Proceedings of the 2016 Conference of the North American Chapter of the Association for Computational Linguistics: Human Language Technologies, pp. 1480–1489 (2016)
39. Yin, X., Zheng, D., Lu, Z., Liu, R.: Neural entity reasoner for global consistency in NER. arXiv preprint arXiv:1810.00347 (2018)
40. Yue, S., et al.: Disc-lawllm: fine-tuning large language models for intelligent legal services (2023)
41. Zeng, D., Liu, K., Chen, Y., Zhao, J.: Distant supervision for relation extraction via piecewise convolutional neural networks. In: Proceedings of the 2015 Conference on Empirical Methods in Natural Language Processing, pp. 1753–1762 (2015)
42. Zhang, N., Pu, Y.F., Yang, S.Q., Zhou, J.L., Gao, J.K.: An ontological Chinese legal consultation system. IEEE Access **5**, 18250–18261 (2017)

LLMADR: A Novel Method for Adverse Drug Reaction Extraction Based on Style Aligned Large Language Models Fine-Tuning

Huazi Yin, Jintao Tang$^{(\boxtimes)}$, Shasha Li, and Ting Wang

College of Computer Science and Technology, National University of Defense Technology, Changsha 410073, China
{huaziyin,tangjintao,shashali,tingwang}@nudt.edu.cn

Abstract. Adverse drug reaction (ADR) is a serious medical issue, so early ADR extraction from Electronic Medical Records (EMRs) is necessary. The majority of current researches on ADR extraction from EMRs are mainly oriented to sentence-level, non-real and single-source data, leading a gap in research and practice. To solve this problem, we propose a novel method LLMADR based on style aligned large language models (LLMs) fine-tuning for ADR extraction from document-level and real multi-source Chinese EMRs. We utilize the comprehension and generation capability of LLMs to accomplish ADR extraction from document-level EMRs where irrelevant information interference and long-distance ADR exist, and we craft prompts to guide LLMs in aligning multi-source EMRs with varying styles before training and reasoning, thereby enhancing the generalization capability of our model. Furthermore, We construct a document-level Chinese ADR dataset CADR from two medical organizations without simplification of EMRs to training and evaluating. Comparative experiments on CADR illustrate that from classification and extraction perspectives, LLMADR performs better than several mainstream models and has better generalization capability.

Keywords: Adverse drug reaction · Large language models · Style alignment

1 Introduction

Drugs are becoming more and more effective in treating a wider range of illnesses as medical science advances. Nevertheless, using medications can also come with some health risks, such as adverse drug reaction (ADR), which may hurt patients to some extent. ADR is defined as the harm that patients experience from medication-related medical procedures, including side effects. As an important global public health concern, ADR causes nearly 800,000 injuries or deaths per year, accounting for 3.6% of all hospital admissions globally [4]. Therefore, it is necessary to discover and record ADR in advance, avoiding the adverse effects of drugs on patients. According to statistics, the China National Center for ADR Monitoring had received a total of 2.419 million ADR reports in the year 2023. Additionally, since 1999, the number of ADR reports received annually has increased due to the increasing appearance of new drugs and the gradual increase in the identification of adverse reaction. Although quite a lot of ADR has been reported, this still represents only a small percentage, with more unknown ADR still in urgent need of detection [8]. Furthermore, even though clinical studies are carried out throughout the drug development process, traditional clinical trials are costly and ineffective, which makes it challenging to totally find out all potential adverse reaction. Electronic Medical Records (EMRs) are computerized case systems or computer-based patient records, which record a large amount of medical information of patients in hospitals, including much clinically detected ADR, for example, cytarabine may cause skin rash with itching. So it is extremely important to extract ADR in EMRs. Since manual analysis is time-consuming and labor-intensive, it is worthwhile to investigate how computers, especially Natural Language Processing (NLP) technology, can be utilized to automate the discovery of ADR in EMRs.

Most of the previous studies about extracting ADR from EMRs were oriented to English language [19]. In contrast, ADR extraction from Chinese EMRs begins later, has less study, but is more difficult because the Chinese language is more complex. Since there are plenty of ADR reports every year in China, it is worthwhile to explore how to extract ADR in Chinese context. Currently, the majority of studies on ADR extraction from Chinese EMRs are oriented to sentence-level [2,8] texts, making it difficult to handle more complex extraction in document-level EMRs where there are more interference information and ADR may be long-distance distribution. What's more, current studies tend to conduct their methods on non-real EMRs [3] from single source, i.e., the data used does not come directly from real clinic scenarios but is often simplified from real EMRs, and the training set and the testing set originate from merely one source. On one hand, without using real EMRs in research, the models obtained lack the ability to cope with the real EMRs with more complex structure in practice. On the other hand, the absence of multi-source data leads to doubtful generalization capacity of the models when facing with various EMRs with different writing styles. Therefore, in this paper we focus on ADR extraction from document-level and real multi-source Chinese EMRs, in order to fill in the blank of document-level ADR extraction and bridge the gap between research and practice.

Document-level EMRs often have hundreds or even thousands of words, which not only have a large amount of interference from irrelevant information other than ADR descriptions, but also have cross-sentence distribution of ADR, so the widely used miniaturisation models cannot be used directly due to the restricted input length, and the integrity of cross-sentence distribution of ADR will be destroyed if the EMRs are segmented and then given to the miniaturisation models for processing. Large language models (LLMs) has evolved rapidly in recent years and has demonstrated strong language comprehension and reasoning capabilities with larger input length. Therefore, we propose to apply LLMs into document-level ADR extraction from EMRs, using LLMs' excellent language comprehension ability to deal with interference information and long-distance ADR problem. We also apply some fine-tuning methods to enhance LLMs' instruction following ability. To deal with different writing styles of real multi-source Chinese EMRs, we also use LLMs' comprehension and generation ability to align the various styles of EMRs before LLMs fine-tuning and reasoning, in order to improve the generalization capability of our model. Furthermore, to study document-level ADR extraction from real multi-source EMRs, we collect complete EMRs from two medical organizations and construct a document-level Chinese ADR dataset CADR which can be used to evaluate the efficiency and generalization ability of models. In comparative experiments, we migrate several mainstream models to CADR and the experiment results indicate that our model has good performance and generalization capability. The contributions of our work are as follows:

- We propose a novel method LLMADR based on style aligned LLMs fine-tuning for ADR extraction from document-level and real multi-source Chinese EMRs. We use the long text comprehension capability of LLMs to exclude irrelevant information interference and to identify long-distance ADR in document-level EMRs, and we use the comprehension and generation capability of LLMs to style-align real multi-source EMRs with varying styles before LLMs fine-tuning and reasoning to improve the generalization capability of our model.
- We construct a document-level Chinese ADR dataset CADR from two medical organizations without simplification of EMRs, which contains various linguistic phenomena like long-distance ADR and can be used to evaluate the ability of models to generalize over different styles of real EMRs.
- A series of experiments are conducted and the model's performance is evaluated from two perspectives, classification and extraction of ADR. The experimental results indicate that LLMADR performs better than mainstream models and has relatively good generalization capability.

2   Related Work

2.1   ADR Datasets

The majority of earlier researches on extracting ADR from EMRs were conducted in English. The Informatics for Integrating Biology and the Bedside (I2B2) issued a challenge in 2010 that involved extracting medical entity relationships based on English EMRs. The I2B2 2010 dataset [19] then became a classic English dataset in ADR extraction. Chinese ADR extraction studies now tend to extract ADR from simplified EMRs, such as parts of EMRs, from single source, which are quite different from real EMRs. For example, Chen et al. [3] extracted ADR from the ADR description section of Chinese ADR reports, which is mostly a simplification of a complete EMR, leading to poor utility in real-world healthcare scenarios. CMeIE [9] and CMedCausal [15] are both Chinese medical entity relation extraction datasets, but most of the data is parts of EMRs, which is more simple than real EMRs.

2.2 ADR Extraction Methods

ADR extraction methods can be divided into co-occurrence based method, pattern matching based method, traditional machine learning method and deep learning method. The co-occurrence based method [10] counts the frequency of occurrence of drug and adverse reaction entities and considers that they have relation if both are often found in a single sentence. Hadzi-Puric et al. [10] used co-occurrence based method to find out the adverse reaction about children's medications from parenting websites. The disadvantage of the co-occurrence-based method is the difficulty in dealing with negative words when they appear in a sentence. Pattern matching based method [7,21] pre-constructs rules for ADR extraction, such as regular expressions, and then match ADR according to the rules. Federer et al. [7] used regular expressions and a pattern-based approach to extract ADR from a US clinical trials database. This method relies on expertise and has poor generalization ability. Traditional machine learning method [2,16,24] and deep learning method [8,13,14,18,23] automate the learning of useful features, but current studies mostly conduct sentence-level ADR extraction, rather than document-level. For example, Chee et al. [2] used support vector machine (SVM) and Bayesian network to discover ADR from user comments in online health forums. Feng et al. [8] performed ADR extraction based on deep learning models combined with a knowledge graph from sentence-level EMRs. Besides, LLMs have shown great performance in medical field. Xiong et al. [22] fine-tuned ChatGLM-6B [25] using medical dialogues in Chinese collected with ChatGPT's help and gained a medical LLM for medical Q&A. Other medical LLMs such as HuaTuo [20] and DISC-MedLLM [1] are both mainly generated by fine-tuning LLMs. What's more, Nori et al. [17] explored using special few-shot prompting methods to unlock LLMs' deeper specialist capabilities. Nevertheless, these medical LLMs are mostly designed for conversation scenarios, with few studies about ADR extraction.

3   Method

3.1   Framework of LLMADR

The framework of LLMADR is illustrated in Fig. 1. There are two main modules in LLMADR, the LLMs fine-tuning module and the style alignment module. To improve the generalization capability of our model, we align the style of EMRs to single medical event in both training and reasoning process. In training process, we first analyze whether an input EMR contains more than one medical events, and if it does, we align it according to its style into single medical events. After that, we input all EMRs containing only one medical event and all medical

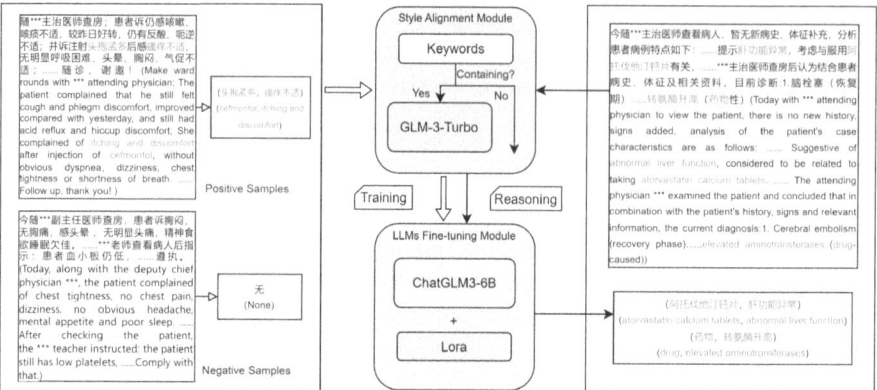

Fig. 1. Framework of LLMADR.

events generated from style alignment into LLMs fine-tuning module for LLMs fine-tuning. Using the same approach as in the training set, we analyze and style-align EMRs in the reasoning process. For the EMRs that have only one medical event, we obtain the ADR extraction results directly from the fine-tuned LLM, and for the EMRs that do not, their medical events will be input into the model independently and their outputs are combined to be the final answers.

3.2   Style Alignment Module

The writing style of EMRs varies depending on the hospitals from which the EMRs originate or the writing habits of the physicians, therefore, the performance of the model may degrade when the model with fixed parameters is used directly on EMRs with styles that differ significantly from those of the training set. Therefore, we propose a style alignment method to standardize all EMRs into a certain style called single medical event, in order to improve our model's generalization capability. Due to the generally long and complex structure of the EMRs and the lack of obvious medical event marker words, it is difficult for models with small scale to align the style. Therefore, we use the excellent capability of LLMs to help align all EMRs to single medical events.

Through analysis of a large number of EMRs, we find that the standard structure of EMRs should include only one medical event, consisting of two main parts, "current patient status or examination results" part and "physician's instructions or treatment plan" part, where the former one describes the patient's current self-reported symptoms, status or examination results returned after the current medical examination, and the latter one refers to the doctor's diagnosis or next treatment plan based on the patient's status or test results. In contrast to the standard structure, a few EMRs also include a "description of patient characteristics or review of past medical history" part that describes the patient's features or records the previous medical treatment the patient has got. This part

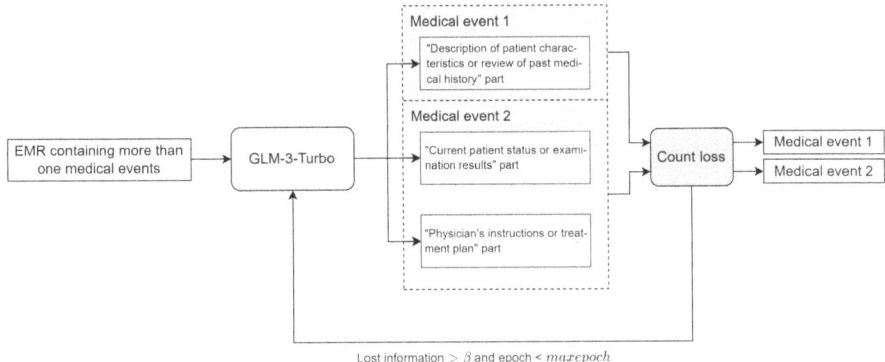

Fig. 2. The process of style alignment towards the EMRs containing more than one medical events.

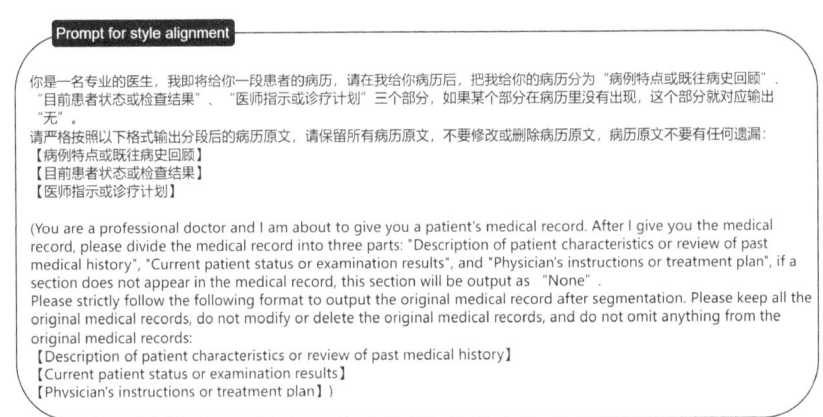

Fig. 3. The prompt used in style alignment module.

also includes the previous two main parts, and thus can be regarded as another medical event embedded in the original EMR. Therefore, we propose to split the EMRs containing "description of patient characteristics or review of past medical history" part into two separate medical events, so as to style-align all EMRs to single medical events. In addition, since the drugs used by the patient and the corresponding adverse reaction basically originate from one medical experience, the distribution of ADR in an EMR basically does not exceed the span of the medical events, which can improve the generalization of our model and lose as little document-level ADR as possible.

In our style alignment module, we first analyze whether an EMR contains more than one medical events using a rule-based method, in which we use the keywords "既往(past)", "病史(history)", "分析(analysis)", and "总结(summary)" to match the EMRs and consider the EMRs containing at least one of these keywords as the EMRs that have more than one medical events and need to be split. What's more, we merely split the EMRs whose lengths exceed a threshold value α that we set in advance, in order to avoid from splitting too short EMRs and destroying some ADR in them.

Since the structure of the EMRs is complex and obvious structural separating signals are lacked, we use LLMs prompt approach to split the proposed split EMRs. As shown in Fig. 2, GLM-3-Turbo that has large-scale parameters and can perform well under zero-shot prompting, splits the EMRs into "description of patient characteristics or review of past medical history" part and not this part. The prompt we use is illustrated in Fig. 3. These obtained two parts then serve as two medical events. Since some texts from the original EMRs may be lost throughout LLMs' output, we count the length of the lost texts in each epoch until the maximum epoch restriction $maxepoch$ is reached or no more than a threshold value β of the texts are lost.

Instruction for fine-tuning

你是一名专业的医生，请从我即将给你的病历里面抽取出"药物或治疗手段"导致患者"不良反应"的二元组，如果没有这样的二元组就输出无。
(You are a professional doctor, please extract from the medical records I am about to give you the dichotomy of "drug or treatment" that caused the patient's "adverse reaction", if there is no such dichotomy then output none.)

Fig. 4. The instruction used in LLMs fine-tuning module.

3.3   LLMs Fine-Tuning Module

Accurate feature learning for machine learning and small-scale deep learning models is challenging in document-level EMRs which have complicated structures, large amounts of useless information, and complex ADR phenomena such as long-distance ADR. Therefore we take LLMs as the foundation of our method, leveraging their excellent linguistic comprehension ability. Since ADR extraction requires medical expertise and command-following ability for LLMs, and our attempts to directly apply large-scale LLMs like GPT-3.5-Turbo using zero-shot prompt did not work well, we choose to fine-tune a medium-scale LLM considerately. ChatGLM3-6B is an open bilingual LLM based on the General Language Model (GLM) framework [6]. It was trained by diverse Chinese and English training data and reasonable training strategies, with further supervised fine-tuning, reinforcement learning using human feedback, and feedback bootstrap. On various LLM benchmarks, ChatGLM3-6B has the strongest performance of any LLMs under 10B scale. LoRA [11], or Low-Rank Adaptation, is a technique used in NLP to fine-tune LLMs with minimal parameter updates. It works by adding a low-rank matrix to the model's weights, which allows for efficient adaptation to new tasks without altering the majority of the model's parameters. To increase medical expertise, enhance the instruction-following capability and

Table 1. Statistics of CADR.

	Number	Positive samples	Negative samples
Internal dataset	3787	1713(45.23%)	2074(54.77%)
External testing set	974	119(12.22%)	855(87.78%)

Table 2. Samples of CADR.

EMR	ADR
今随***副主任医师查房，患者诉胸闷，无胸痛，感头晕......***查看病人后指示：患者血小板仍低，继续予预约血小板预防出血，余治疗暂不变，密观病情变化。遵执。(Today with *** deputy chief physician checkup, the patient complained of chest tightness, no chest pain, feeling dizziness......After checking the patient, *** instructions: the patient's platelets are still low, continue to book platelets to prevent bleeding, the rest of the treatment will remain unchanged for the time being, and closely observe changes in the condition. Compliance.)	无 (None)
今随***主治医师查房，患者神志清，精神可，诉有腹胀、呕吐1次，呕吐物为胃内容物，无咖啡色物质，睡眠可，食欲可，小便正常；今晨空腹血糖为6.9mmol/l，昨日早餐后为12.9mmol/l，中餐后8.2mmol/l，晚餐后5.7mmol/l；***查房指示：患者上诉症状，考虑"二甲双胍"药物副作用，嘱给予停药，患者晚餐血糖可，嘱晚餐前胰岛素减2IU,其他治疗同前，遵执，继观。(Today with *** attending physician checkup, the patient is clear, spirit can, complained of abdominal distension, vomiting once, vomit for the stomach contents, no coffee-coloured substances, sleep can be, appetite can be, normal urine; this morning fasting blood glucose is 6.9mmol/l, yesterday after breakfast is 12.9mmol/l, after the Chinese meal 8.2mmol/l, after dinner 5.7mmol/l; *** checkup instructions: Patient appeal symptoms, consider the 'metformin' drug side effects, asked to be given to stop the drug, the patient's dinner blood glucose can be asked before dinner insulin reduction of 2IU, other treatments with the previous, comply with the implementation of the following view.)	（二甲双胍，腹胀）(metformin, abdominal distension) （二甲双胍，呕吐）(metformin, vomiting)

standardize the output format of ChatGLM3-6B, we adapt LoRA to instruction tuning ChatGLM3-6B, balancing performance and training cost. The instruction we use is shown in Fig. 4.

4 Experiment

4.1 Dataset Construction

To construct a document-level Chinese ADR dataset close to real multi-source usage scenarios, we collect 3,787 EMRs from a tertiary medical institution A, containing 1,713 EMRs of patients who, between 2009 and 2019, reported ADR to the Hunan Province Adverse Drug Reaction monitoring center, in order to guarantee that adequate positive samples are involved. And we collect 974 EMRs from another tertiary medical institution B serving as the external testing set. Based on this, we pre-process the data by first de-privatizing information such as patient and physician names, and then cleaning irrelevant information such as time, title and signature at the beginning and end of the EMRs to avoid irrelevant information from interfering with automatically feature learning. In data annotation process, detailed labeling requirements are set in advance and there are 9 trained medical students participating in annotating all ADR from EMRs. To ensure objectivity, each sample is independently annotated by two students, and when their annotations differ, the third student is responsible for making a judge. Table 1 gives the statistics of our document-level Chinese ADR dataset CADR.

Some samples in CADR are shown in Table 2. Since EMRs in CADR are all document-level and from real-world scenarios, we find there is a complex linguistic phenomena which may be challenging for models to deal with but is worthwhile to focus on. Long-distance ADR means that the drug and the relative adverse reaction are not located in the same sentence. For instance, there are numerous sentences placed between metformin and its adverse reaction in Table 2. Current studies about ADR extraction are mostly sentence-level, so it is hard for these methods to handle long-distance ADR problem. What's more, the high proportion of irrelevant information in document-level EMRs also makes it challenging for models to understand.

We divide the internal dataset with the ratio 4:1 into the training set and the internal testing set and use the external testing set to evaluate the generalization ability of the models.

4.2 Experiment Setup

In LLMs fine-tuning module, we set the hyper-parameters in the training process as follows: a maximum input length of 1024, the maximum output length of 256, the batch size of 1, and the LoRA rank of 8. We conduct this fine-tuning process on a V100 GPU. In style alignment module, we set the threshold value α as 550 and β as 40%. The maximum epoch restriction $maxepoch$ is 11.

4.3 Experiment Results

Comparative Models. Since ADR may or may not be present in EMRs, we evaluate the performance and generalization ability of the models in terms of both classification of whether an EMR contains ADR and ADR extraction from the EMRs that truly contain ADR. For classification, we migrate **1**. BERT+Bi-LSTM: a model using BERT [5] as encoder and fine-tuning in downstream tasks using bi-directional long-short term memory (Bi-LSTM) [12] network. **2**. ChatGLM2-6B: a previous version of ChatGLM3-6B used by few-shot prompting in our comparative experiments. **3**. GPT-3.5-Turbo: a larger-scale parameter LLM also used by few-shot prompting for contrast. **4**. ChatGLM3-6B+LoRA:

ChatGLM3-6B that is fine-tuned by LoRA method. This method can also be considered as LLMADR without style alignment module. For ADR extraction, we mainly compare our model with ChatGLM3-6B+LoRA model, in order to compare the generalization capability.

Classification Results. The classification results shown in Table 3 illustrate that ChatGLM3-6B+LoRA method outperforms other models in accuracy and F1 value on both internal and external testing set, which proves that LLMs can better understand the document-level ADR and have better capability at excluding irrelevant information. Though with style alignment, the performance of LLMADR decreases slightly in accuracy and F1 value, LLMADR still exceeds other three models and achieves the best precision. We believe that the slight decline is owing to the lost context when splitting EMRs, and can be avoided by decreasing the threshold β. We can also notice that although Bert+Bi-LSTM achieves high recall, it has quite poor accuracy and F1 value on external testing set. The possible reason for its worst performance on external testing set is that Bert+Bi-LSTM cannot understand the complex document-level EMRs and learns some useless features when fine-tuning on the training set, leading to bad generalization ability. The results of ChatGLM2-6B and GPT-3.5-Turbo also show that without fine-tuning, it is difficult for LLMs to understand what the instruction forces them to do and the difference between the few-shot examples from the training set and the external testing set leads to a huge performance decline.

Table 3. Classification results on CADR. ChatGLM2-6B and GPT-3.5-Turbo are under few-shot setting and their undetermined outputs are ignored. ChatGLM3-6B+LoRA and LLMADR are under zero-shot setting.

	Internal testing set				External testing set			
	Acc(%)	Pre(%)	Rec(%)	F1(%)	Acc(%)	Pre(%)	Rec(%)	F1(%)
BERT+Bi-LSTM	83.11	74.08	97.72	84.28	22.59	14.02	**95.31**	24.45
ChatGLM2-6B	69.50	66.57	71.02	68.72	69.08	20.46	57.05	30.07
GPT-3.5-Turbo	73.64	64.02	**98.86**	77.72	54.72	21.39	91.41	34.67
ChatGLM3-6B+LoRA	**96.78**	98.63	94.36	**96.45**	**94.28**	77.29	80.00	**78.62**
LLMADR	96.44	**99.27**	92.99	96.03	94.26	**79.39**	76.09	77.70

ADR Extraction Results. Table 4 demonstrates the ADR extraction results of the EMRs that truly contain ADR. It can be seen that ChatGLM3-6B+LoRA performs well on the internal testing set without style alignment, but when applied to the external testing set, there is an obvious decline in micro-F1 value. After adding style alignment module, the micro-F1 value on external testing

Table 4. ADR Extraction results on CADR under zero-shot setting.

	Internal testing set			External testing set		
	Pre(%)	Rec(%)	F1(%)	Pre(%)	Rec(%)	F1(%)
ChatGLM3-6B+LoRA	**68.93**	52.13	**59.36**	**63.32**	39.50	48.63
LLMADR	65.24	**52.80**	58.35	57.74	**42.63**	**49.02**

set is improved, which confirms that the style alignment method can improve the generalization ability. What's more, though there is a slight decline on the internal testing set, it can be explained that after style alignment, the number of input samples is increased, leading to more possible errors statistically.

5   Conclusion

In order to reduce the gap between research and practice, in this paper we propose a novel method LLMADR based on style aligned LLMs fine-tuning for document-level ADR extraction from real multi-source EMRs. We leverage LLMs' excellent language comprehension and generation ability to understand the document-level complex EMRs, and help style-align EMRs in different writing styles to single medical events to improve generalization capability of our model. For training and evaluating, we construct a document-level Chinese ADR dataset CADR from two different medical organizations, in which various linguistic phenomena like long-distance ADR exists. Based on this, comparative experiments illustrate that from classification and ADR extraction, our model can achieve comparatively good performance and generalization capability. In the future, we will explore style alignment methods that lose less information and further improve the model's performance and generalization capability.

Acknowledgments. This work was supported by the National Key Research and Development Project of China (No. 2021ZD0110700) and Hunan Provincial Natural Science Foundation (Grant Nos. 2022JJ30668). The authors would like to thank the anonymous reviewers for their valuable comments and suggestions to improve this paper.

References

1. Bao, Z., et al.: Disc-medllm: bridging general large language models and real-world medical consultation. arXiv preprint arXiv:2308.14346 (2023)
2. Chee, B.W., Berlin, R., Schatz, B.: Predicting adverse drug events from personal health messages. In: AMIA Annual Symposium Proceedings, vol. 2011, p. 217. American Medical Informatics Association (2011)
3. Chen, Y., Wu, H., Ge, W.H., Zhang, H.X., Liao, J.: Research on entity relation extraction of Chinese adverse drug reaction reports based on deep learning method. Journal of China Pharmaceutical University **50**(6), 753–759 (2019). https://doi.org/10.11665/j.issn.1000-5048.20190617, https://jcpu.cpu.edu.cn/cn/article/doi/10.11665/j.issn.1000-5048.20190617

4. Cocos, A., Fiks, A.G., Masino, A.J.: Deep learning for pharmacovigilance: recurrent neural network architectures for labeling adverse drug reactions in Twitter posts. J. Am. Med. Inf. Assoc. **24**(4), 813–821 (2017). https://doi.org/10.1093/jamia/ocw180, https://doi.org/10.1093/jamia/ocw180

5. Devlin, J., Chang, M.W., Lee, K., Toutanova, K.: Bert: pre-training of deep bidirectional transformers for language understanding. arXiv preprint arXiv:1810.04805 (2018)

6. Du, Z., et al.: GLM: general language model pretraining with autoregressive blank infilling. In: Proceedings of the 60th Annual Meeting of the Association for Computational Linguistics (Volume 1: Long Papers), pp. 320–335 (2022)

7. Federer, C., Yoo, M., Tan, A.C.: Big data mining and adverse event pattern analysis in clinical drug trials. Assay Drug Dev. Technol. **14**(10), 557–566 (2016)

8. Feng, Z.Y., et al.: DKADE: a novel framework based on deep learning and knowledge graph for identifying adverse drug events and related medications. Briefings in Bioinformatics **24**(4), bbad228 (2023). https://doi.org/10.1093/bib/bbad228, https://doi.org/10.1093/bib/bbad228

9. Guan, T., Zan, H., Zhou, X., Xu, H., Zhang, K.: CMeIE: construction and Evaluation of Chinese Medical Information Extraction Dataset. Natural Language Processing and Chinese Computing, 9th CCF International Conference, NLPCC 2020, Zhengzhou, China, October 14-18, 2020, Proceedings, Part I (2020)

10. Hadzi-Puric, J., Grmusa, J.: Automatic drug adverse reaction discovery from parenting websites using disproportionality methods. In: 2012 IEEE/ACM International Conference on Advances in Social Networks Analysis and Mining, pp. 792–797. IEEE (2012)

11. Hu, E.J., et al.: Lora: low-rank adaptation of large language models (2021)

12. Huang, Z., Xu, W., Yu, K.: Bidirectional LSTM-CRF models for sequence tagging. arXiv preprint arXiv:1508.01991 (2015)

13. Li, F., Zhang, M., Fu, G., Ji, D.: A neural joint model for entity and relation extraction from biomedical text. BMC Bioinform. **18**, 1–11 (2017)

14. Li, F., Zhang, Y., Zhang, M., Ji, D.: Joint models for extracting adverse drug events from biomedical text. In: IJCAI, vol. 2016, pp. 2838–2844 (2016)

15. Li, Z.H., et al.: Cmedcausal: Chinese medical causal relationship extraction dataset. J. Med. Inform. **43**(12), 23–27 (2022)

16. Nikfarjam, A., Gonzalez, G.H.: Pattern mining for extraction of mentions of adverse drug reactions from user comments. In: AMIA Annual Symposium Proceedings, vol. 2011, p. 1019. American Medical Informatics Association (2011)

17. Nori, H., et al.: Can generalist foundation models outcompete special-purpose tuning? case study in medicine. ArXiv **abs/2311.16452** (2023). https://api.semanticscholar.org/CorpusID:265466787

18. Spandana, S., Prakash, R.V.: Multiple features-based adverse drug reaction detection from social media using deep convolutional neural networks (DCNN). Multimedia Tools Appl. 1–15 (2024)

19. Uzuner, , South, B.R., Shen, S., DuVall, S.L.: 2010 i2b2/VA challenge on concepts, assertions, and relations in clinical text. J. Am. Med. Inform. Assoc. **18**(5), 552–556 (2011). https://doi.org/10.1136/amiajnl-2011-000203

20. Wang, H., et al.: Huatuo: tuning llama model with Chinese medical knowledge. arXiv preprint arXiv:2304.06975 (2023)

21. Wang, X.Y., Cui, L.: Extract semantic relations between biomedical entities applied hybrid method. Data Anal. Knowl. Discov. **3**, 77–82 (2013)

22. Xiong, H., et al.: Doctorglm: fine-tuning your Chinese doctor is not a herculean task. arXiv preprint arXiv:2304.01097 (2023)

23. Yang, X., Bian, J., Gong, Y., Hogan, W.R., Wu, Y.: Madex: a system for detecting medications, adverse drug events, and their relations from clinical notes. Drug Saf. **42**, 123–133 (2019)
24. Yildirim, P., Majnarić, L., Ekmekci, O.I., Holzinger, A.: Knowledge discovery of drug data on the example of adverse reaction prediction. BMC Bioinform. **15**, 1–11 (2014)
25. Zeng, A., et al.: GLM-130b: an open bilingual pre-trained model. arXiv preprint arXiv:2210.02414 (2022)

Research on Named Entity Recognition in Ancient Chinese Based on Incremental Pre-training and Domain Lexicon

Wenjun Kang[1,2], Jiali Zuo[1(✉)], Qili Dai[1], Yiyu Hu[3], and Mingwen Wang[1]

[1] School of Computer and Information Engineering, Jiangxi Normal University,
Nanchang, China
{zjl,mwwang}@jxnu.edu.cn
[2] School of Computer Information Engineering, Nanchang Institute of Technology,
Nanchang, China
[3] School of Computer Science and Engineering, Guangzhou Institute of Science and
Technology, Guangzhou, China

Abstract. Currently, there is limited research on ancient Chinese named entity recognition, primarily due to the scarcity of publicly available datasets for model training. We constructed a CMAG-NER dataset based on the "Comprehensive Mirror for Aid in Government". Addressing the challenges faced by existing models in identifying person entities with omitted surnames and determining entity boundaries in ancient Chinese texts, we integrated the LEBERT-CRF model with a general domain lexicon and the "Comprehensive Mirror for Aid in Government Dictionary" to fuse external statistical information and rule-based knowledge, thereby enhancing the performance of ancient Chinese named entity recognition. Additionally, to improve the model's comprehension of ancient Chinese, we have compiled a substantial corpus of ancient Chinese literature for incremental pre-training of BERT-Ancient-Chinese. Experimental results demonstrate that the proposed method effectively mitigates the aforementioned challenges, but the performance of large models on this task still requires improvement.

Keywords: Chinese Named Entity Recognition · Data Annotation · Domain Knowledge · Large Language Models

1 Introduction

Named Entity Recognition (NER) is a task that involves identifying and classifying named entities within unstructured text into predefined categories such as person names, location names, and organization names [1]. It is crucial for various downstream natural language processing tasks, including relationship extraction, machine translation, and the construction of knowledge graphs.

Traditional NER tasks mostly focus on English and Chinese datasets. Compared to English NER, Chinese NER faces a unique challenge: there is no obvious word segmentation boundary between Chinese characters, requiring pre-segmentation. However, this can lead to the propagation of word segmentation

D. F. Wong et al. (Eds.): NLPCC 2024, LNAI 15359, pp. 483–503, 2025.
https://doi.org/10.1007/978-981-97-9431-7_37

errors, which in turn affects recognition performance. Therefore, early Chinese NER research usually adopted a character-based approach, but this method cannot effectively utilize lexical and boundary information [2]. In response to this issue, some studies have begun to explore how to integrate external lexicon information into the model to improve performance on benchmark datasets. Specifically, some researchers have improved the basic neural network model to better integrate external lexicon information [3–5]. In addition, some researchers choose to directly introduce external lexicon information into the embedding layer, combining it with the input character vectors, and then inputting them together into the encoding layer for feature extraction [6–8].

In recent years, several studies have focused on the task of NER in ancient Chinese texts, particularly within the domains of historical records, local chronicles, and traditional Chinese medicine. NER in ancient Chinese serves as a crucial initial step in the accurate analysis and processing of these texts, and it is essential for the deep mining and organization of humanistic knowledge. Despite its significance, the task of NER in ancient Chinese confronts numerous challenges [9]: (1) the scarcity of high-quality, publicly available datasets for ancient Chinese NER; (2) the inherent characteristics of ancient Chinese, such as the use of single characters to convey meaning, widespread abbreviation practices, and the complexities of word segmentation and sentence boundary determination, pose difficulties for existing mainstream Chinese NER models in accurately identifying personal name entities with frequently omitted surnames and delineating entity boundaries. In light of these challenges, we have undertaken research aimed at addressing the task of NER in ancient Chinese:

(1) In response to the lack of ancient Chinese NER datasets, we selected "Comprehensive Mirror for Aid in Government(资治通鉴)" as the basic corpus and combined the "Twenty-Four Histories(二十四史)" NER dataset published by Tianjin University to study the annotation rules of named entities in ancient Chinese. On this basis, we have annotated 4,335 sentences of ancient Chinese texts, 245,000 characters, and a total of 27,213 entities of five types. Through entity coverage analysis and fat-head entity analysis, we have confirmed that the dataset we have constructed can support the research of NER tasks in ancient Chinese.

(2) In response to the challenges faced by existing models in identifying personal name entities with omitted surnames in ancient Chinese texts and determining entity boundaries, we integrated the LEBERT-CRF model with a general domain lexicon and the "Comprehensive Mirror for Aid in Government Dictionary" to improve the performance of NER in ancient Chinese. At the same time, we have compiled a large amount of ancient Chinese literature for further pre-training BERT-Ancient-Chinese and training word vectors in the field of ancient Chinese. In addition, we also used the prompt method to evaluate the performance of ChatGLM3-6B [10], BaiChuan2-13B [11],

ChatGPT-3.5[1], and Xunzi[2] Ancient Books Large Model on ancient Chinese NER tasks.

2   Related Work

2.1   Chinese Named Entity Recognition

Traditional research in NER mostly uses rule-based and statistical machine learning-based methods, but they usually require researchers to design appropriate features in advance and have knowledge in related fields. With the development of deep learning, deep neural network-based NER models have almost overcome the limitations of these methods. Hammerton et al. [12] first attempted to use a neural network model to study the task of NER in 2003. Huang et al. [13] used the BiLSTM-CRF model in 2015 to improve the performance of Chinese sequence labelling tasks, including NER. Since 2018, companies such as Google have successively released various models such as BERT [14], which perform well in almost all natural language processing tasks, including NER. In 2019, Beltagy et al. [15] incrementally pre-trained BERT with unlabelled datasets from the scientific domain to mitigate the problem of poor performance in related domains due to the lack of labelled datasets.

In recent years, some researchers have improved the performance of Chinese NER models by introducing external dictionaries, and have achieved good results on several benchmark datasets. Zhang et al. [2] proposed the Lattice LATM network structure in 2018 to dynamically introduce lexicon-matched words in the input sentence into the character-level NER model. Gui et al. [16] proposed the LR-CNN model in 2019, which uses CNN to fuse lexicon information and introduces the Rethinking mechanism to realise the feedback of high-level semantic information to the lower layer, thereby updating the weight allocation ratio of potential words. Nie et al. [17] proposed an attention-based integrated model in 2020, which encodes and fuses multiple syntactic information including part-of-speech to help the model correctly identify entities. In this paper, by combining general domain dictionaries and "Comprehensive Mirror for Aid in Government dictionary", external statistical information and rule knowledge are integrated to improve the performance of ancient Chinese NER tasks.

2.2   Classical Chinese Named Entity Recognition

Research on NER in ancient Chinese also follows the three technical routes introduced earlier. Huangfu Jing and others [18] used "Records of the Three Kingdoms · Shu Book(三国志·蜀书)" as their research corpus in 2013. By analysing the types of ancient names and designing appropriate rules, they extracted personal name entities from it. Li Zhangchao et al. [19] used conditional random fields in 2020 to extract seven types of entities, including war places and war

---

[1] https://openai.com/chatgpt.

[2] https://github.com/Xunzi-LLM-of-Chinese-classics/XunziALLM.

results, from "Zuo Zhuan(左传)". Yu et al. [20] proposed a BERT-BiLSTM-CRF model combined with transfer learning in 2020 to extract personal and place names from the "Twenty-Four Histories(二十四史)".

Inspired by the idea of domain-adaptive training, some researchers have considered using electronic resources of ancient books to continue pre-training the model, improving the processing capabilities of pre-trained language models, and achieving a series of outstanding results. For example, SikuBERT [21], BERT-Ancient-Chinese [22], etc., have greatly promoted the development of intelligent ancient books. In this paper, we have compiled ancient Chinese literature, including "Comprehensive Mirror for Aid in Government(资治通鉴)", totalling about 970,000 ancient Chinese texts, and used this text to conduct incremental pre-training of BERT-Ancient-Chinese.

2.3 Large Language Models

Large Language Models (LLMs) are language models built with deep neural networks containing hundreds of billions of parameters or more, trained using self-supervised learning methods on a large amount of unlabelled text. In November 2022, OpenAI released a large-scale language model capable of multi-round dialogue, called ChatGPT (Chat Generative Pre-trained Transformer). This model can create content based on user input prompts, enabling various tasks from understanding to generation, including question answering, code generation and mathematical reasoning, etc. Currently, major companies and research institutions have also successively released such large language models, such as Zhipu ChatGLM, Bai Chuan Large Model, and the ancient Chinese domain large model Xunzi. Large language models have demonstrated strong mastery of world knowledge and language understanding abilities.

However, in certain specific vertical domain tasks, such as ancient Chinese NER tasks, few researchers have evaluated the performance of large language models in this task. Since large language models are essentially generative models, and NER tasks belong to sequence labelling tasks, the prompt method needs to be used to transform this task into a generative task. Subsequently, the prompt is fed into the large language model to generate predicted entity recognition results. In addition, these results can also be used to optimise manually written prompts, thereby improving the performance of large language models in ancient Chinese NER tasks. The large language model NER evaluation process is shown in Fig. 1.

3   Data Preparation

Currently, widely used benchmark datasets in the Chinese NER field include Ontonotes 4.0, MSRA, Weibo, Resume, and Cluener, etc. However, resources for NER datasets in ancient Chinese are relatively scarce. In view of this, we start with "Comprehensive Mirror for Aid in Government(资治通鉴)" and construct an ancient Chinese NER dataset. The annotation process of the dataset is shown in Fig. 2.

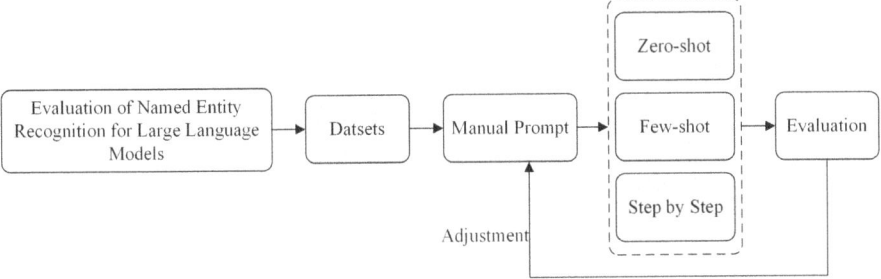

Fig. 1. Flowchart of Large Language Model Named Entity Recognition Evaluation.

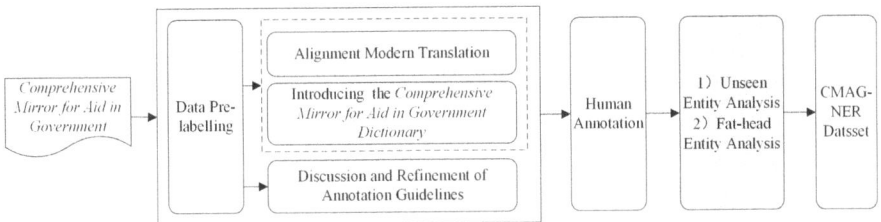

Fig. 2. CMAG-NER Dataset Annotation Process.

3.1 Data Selection

In order to construct an ancient Chinese NER dataset, we selected the simplified version of "Comprehensive Mirror for Aid in Government(资治通鉴)" included in the Ancient Poetry Network as the corpus source. By processing the text into sentences and manually proofreading the translation of classical Chinese and vernacular Chinese, we carried out and completed the entity annotation work on this corpus.

The reasons for choosing "Comprehensive Mirror for Aid in Government(资治通鉴)" as the annotated corpus in this paper are mainly as follows: (1) **Literary status**: "Comprehensive Mirror for Aid in Government(资治通鉴)" is a multi-volume chronological history book edited by Sima Guang, a historian of the Northern Song Dynasty, covering 1,362 years of history from the Zhou Dynasty to the Later Zhou Dynasty, with extremely high literary and historical value. (2) **Providing modern Chinese translations**: The Ancient Poetry Network provides modern Chinese translations of the original text of "Comprehensive Mirror for Aid in Government(资治通鉴)". We proofread and aligned these translations to reduce the difficulty of annotators' understanding of ancient Chinese and improve annotation efficiency. (3) **"Comprehensive Mirror for Aid in Government Dictionary"**: This dictionary is based on "Comprehensive Mirror for Aid in Government(资治通鉴)" and contains nearly 28,000 entity entries, including characters, official positions, classics, ethnic groups, and geography. When constructing the dataset, we introduced rule knowledge from the "Comprehensive Mirror for Aid in Government Dictionary" for entity pre-annotation to ensure the accuracy of annotation.

3.2 Annotation Guidelines

In this paper, we utilized the "Twenty-Four Histories(二十四史)" NER dataset published by Ji et al. [23] and formulated annotation specifications for personal names, place names, official titles, organization names, and time in "Comprehensive Mirror for Aid in Government(资治通鉴)". In the early stage of annotation, we continuously updated and improved the annotation specifications to ensure their accuracy.

Contextual and Semantic Prioty. During the annotation process, we combined contextual information to determine and annotate the entity categories, in order to resolve ambiguities caused by the same entity name potentially referring to different categories. For example, in example sentences (1) and (2), "韩王(King Han)" as a title refers to "韩成(Han Cheng)". However, based on the context, we can determine that in example sentence (1), "韩王(King Han)" is more likely to be an official position, while in example sentence (2), it is more likely to be a personal name.

(1) 项王以张良从汉王，韩王成又无功，故不遣之国，与俱至彭城，废以为穰侯。

(Xiangwang appointed Zhang Liang to follow the Hanwang, and Hanwang Cheng had no merit, so he was not sent to his country, but was taken to Pengcheng together and deposed as the Rang Hou.)

(2) 张良曰："臣为韩王送沛公。沛公今有急，亡去不义，不可不语。"

(Zhang Liang said, "I am escorting the King of Han to see the Duke of Pei. The Duke of Pei is now in a hurry and it is not right to leave without saying anything.")

Coarse-Grained Annotation. In addition, we adopted the principle of coarse-grained annotation to handle some special combinations of entities, such as the "扬州刺史(Yangzhou Cishi)" and "九江太守(Jiujiang Taishou)" in example sentence (3). For such combinations of place names and official positions, we annotate them as a whole as official positions.

(3) 扬州刺史尹耀、九江太守邓显讨范容等于历阳，败殁。

(Yangzhou Cishi Yin Yao and Jiujiang Taishou Deng Xian attacked Fan Rong and others at Liyang, and were defeated and killed.)

3.3 Data Distribution

Based on the "Comprehensive Mirror for Aid in Government(资治通鉴)", we selected chapters such as the Han Ji(汉纪), Jin Ji(晋纪), and Tang Ji(唐纪)

for annotation, resulting in a total of 4,335 sentences of classical Chinese text, 245,000 characters, and a total of 27,213 entities across five categories. Additionally, the dataset is divided into training, validation, and test sets in an 8:1:1 ratio, with the number of entities in each set shown in Table 1.

Table 1. Statistical analysis of the number of entities in the CMAG-NER dataset.

Entity Types	Train	Valid	Test
Person (PER)	10915	1271	1377
Location (LOC)	3250	437	423
Official (OFI)	4802	429	403
Organization (ORG)	1421	296	276
Time (TIME)	1743	74	96
Total	22131	2507	2575

3.4 Data Analysis

To ensure the quality of annotation, we adopted a multi-iteration correction model to refine the annotation specifications and execute the annotation tasks. Each classical Chinese text undergoes independent annotation by two annotators. In case of disagreement during the annotation process, the annotators will discuss together and seek guidance from senior annotation experts to formulate solutions and improve the annotation specifications. Finally, the annotation results are reviewed through cross-checking to ensure the accuracy of the annotation results.

In addition, we also conducted a quantitative evaluation of the quality of the annotated dataset from the perspectives of unseen entity analysis and fat-head entity analysis.

(1) **Unseen entity analysis.** We calculated the proportion of entities that appear in the training set among the validation set and test set. A higher proportion indicates that the model's performance on predicting unseen entities will be affected. The results show that in the CMAG-NER dataset, 43.6% and 42.5% of the entities in the validation set and test set have appeared in the training set, respectively. Compared with the Chinese benchmark datasets calculated by Liang et al. [24], where the entity coverage rate of the validation set is between 49.8% ∼ 61.5%, and the entity coverage rate of the test set is between 42.9% ∼ 70.9%, the entity coverage rate of the dataset divided in this paper is relatively low.

(2) **Fat-head entity analysis.** We used the kurtosis coefficient to measure the fat-head entities in the CMAG-NER dataset, that is, entities with high frequency of occurrence. A high kurtosis coefficient indicates that there are more outliers in the dataset, while a low kurtosis coefficient indicates fewer outliers.

As shown in Table 2, there are more fat-head entities in person names, official positions, and organization entities. This is mainly because the types of official positions and organization entities are relatively limited, while the person name entities have a higher frequency of occurrence due to some main characters. To alleviate this problem, we will consider increasing the scale of the dataset or using an entity replacement algorithm in the future.

Table 2. The kurtosis coefficients of different entity categories.

Entity Types	Train	Valid	Test
Person (PER)	113.6	21.0	91.8
Location (LOC)	58.4	15.2	8.5
Official (OFI)	183.9	42.2	59.3
Organization (ORG)	87.3	12.9	15.0
Time (TIME)	14.0	7.6	4.5

4   Model

4.1   Task Definition

According to task classification, NER can be divided into three subtasks: flat NER, nested NER, and discontinuous NER. We mainly focuses on the task of flat NER in ancient Chinese. In neural network models, this task is treated as a sequence labelling task, which assigns a corresponding label to each character in the sequence. For example, given an unlabeled text sequence $X = (x_1, x_2, ..., x_n)$, where x_i, i = 1, 2, ..., n represents character-level ancient text, the model recognizes and outputs the corresponding label sequence $Y = (y_1, y_2, ..., y_n)$, where y_i, i = 1, 2, ..., n represents the output sequence labels.

4.2   IPDL-LEBERT-CRF

To enhance the model's understanding and processing capabilities of ancient Chinese grammar and semantics, we integrate an **LEBERT-CRF** based on Incremental **P**re-training and **D**omain-specific **L**exicon(IPDL-LEBERT-CRF), aiming to improve the performance of NER tasks in ancient texts. The Diagram of the IPDL-LEBERT-CRF Model is shown in Fig. 3.

(1) **Character-word pair sequence** To integrate external Lexicon information, IPDL-LEBERT-CRF converted the original character sequence into a character-word pair sequence. For example, for a character sequence sc consisting of n characters, c_1, c_2, ..., c_n, we initially constructed a Trie tree structure using a general lexicon and domain-specific lexicon, such as the

"Comprehensive Mirror to Aid in Government Grand Dictionary." Subsequently, by traversing the entire character sequence, we retrieved all relevant words that match those in the dictionaries, giving priority to words from the domain-specific dictionaries. For instance, for the sentence "屯卫将军(Tunwei General)," possible relevant words include "屯卫(Tunwei)", "将军(General)", and "卫将军(Wei General)". Each character is paired with the words matched in the lexicon, and any insufficient number of words is filled with a special symbol <PAD>. Consequently, we obtained a character-word pair sequence $s_cw = (c_1, ws_1), (c_2, ws_2), ..., (c_n, ws_n)$. After incorporating the corresponding character-level and lexical features at each position in the sentence, we integrated this information into the lexicon adaptation layer of BERT, which is detailed in Sect. 4.3.

(2) **BERT with Lexicon Enhancement** After the character sequence input is embedded, information about tokens, segments, and positions is incorporated, and the resulting vector representation is fed into the Transformer layers:

$$G = \text{LN}(H^{(l-1)} + \text{HMAttn}(H^{(l-1)})) \tag{1}$$

$$H^l = \text{LN}(G + \text{FFN}(G)) \tag{2}$$

where $H^{(l-1)}$ is the output of the $(l-1)$-th hidden layer, H^l is the output of the l-th hidden layer, LN is the normalization layer, HMAttn is the multi-head attention mechanism, FFN is a two-layer feed-forward network with ReLU activation function. Then, lexicon information is added between the k-th and $(k+1)$-th Transformer layers:

$$\hat{h}_i^k = \text{LA}(h_i^k, x_i^{ws}) \tag{3}$$

Finally, the modified output $\hat{H}^k = \{\hat{h}_1^k, \hat{h}_2^k, \ldots, \hat{h}_n^k\}$ is fed into the remaining $(L-K)$ Transformer layers.

(3) **Training and Decoding Phase** Considering the dependency between labels, a CRF layer is added on top of the final output layer for label decoding. First, the output H^L of the last hidden layer of BERT is transformed through a linear layer and then fed into the CRF layer:

$$O = W_o H^L + b_o \tag{4}$$

Then, the output is fed into the CRF model to calculate the probability p of the label y:

$$p(y \mid s) = \frac{\exp\left(\sum_i \left(o_{i,y_i} + T_{y_{i-1},y_i}\right)\right)}{\sum_{\tilde{y}} \exp\left(\sum_i \left(o_{i,\tilde{y}_i} + T_{\tilde{y}_{i-1},\tilde{y}_i}\right)\right)} \tag{5}$$

During training, given a sentence S and its label Y, the negative log-likelihood of the entire sentence is calculated as the loss:

$$L = -\sum_j log(p(y|s)) \tag{6}$$

Finally, during the decoding phase, the Viterbi algorithm is used to compute the sequence with the highest score.

4.3   Lexicon Adapter

The lexicon adapter layer receives two inputs: a pair of characters and words, i.e., h_i^c and x_i^{ws}. Here, h_i^c is the character vector output from the previous Transformer layer, and x_i^{ws} is the word embedding composed of the words that may contain the character:

$$x_{ij}^w = e^w(w_{ij}) \tag{7}$$

where j is the j-th word in n, and e^w is a pre-trained word vector mapping table.
To handle sequences of varying lengths, we apply a nonlinear transformation to the word vectors:

$$v_{ij}^w = W_2(\tanh(W_1 x_{ij}^w + b_1)) + b_2 \tag{8}$$

where W_1 is a matrix of size $d_c \times d_w$, W_2 is a matrix of size $d_c \times d_c$, b_1 and b_2 are biases, d_c is the dimension of the hidden layer, and dw is the dimension of the word vector.
Considering that a character may correspond to multiple words, to identify the most relevant words, we introduced an attention mechanism from characters to words, calculated as follows:

$$a_i = \mathrm{softmax}(h_i^c W_{\mathrm{attn}} V_i^T) \tag{9}$$

where W_{attn} is the attention weight matrix, and V_i^T represents all the word vectors corresponding to the i-th character.
Next, we multiplied each word by its weight and sum them up to obtain the word representation at position i:

$$z_i^w = \sum_{j=1}^{m} a_{ij} v_{ij}^w \tag{10}$$

Finally, we added the lexicon information to the character vector to obtain the new vector at that position:

$$\hat{h}_j = h_i^c + z_i^w \tag{11}$$

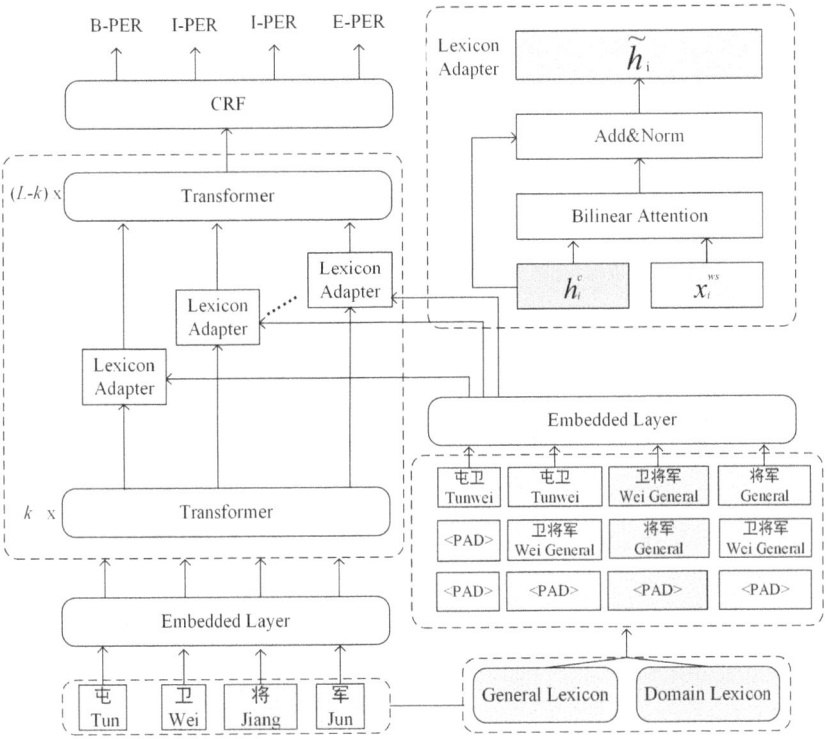

Fig. 3. Diagram of the IPDL-LEBERT-CRF Model.

4.4   Incremental Pre-Training

To ensure that the model fully understands the expression and cultural connotation of ancient Chinese, we continued to pre-train BERT-Ancient-Chinese based on the "Twenty-Four Histories(二十四史)" and "Comprehensive Mirror for

Aid in Government(资治通鉴)" published by Northeastern University[3], totaling 972,467 ancient Chinese text entries. During incremental pre-training, we
adopted the masking mechanism used in BERT pre-training methods, randomly
masking 15% of the characters in ancient Chinese sentences, with 80% of the
characters replaced by "[MASK]", 10% replaced by an arbitrary word from the
vocabulary, and the remaining 10% left unchanged. The batch_size is set to 64,
the maximum text length is 128, and the epoch is 300.

Moreover, we also utilized Fasttext[4] and jiayan[5]tools for training ancient
Chinese word vectors, with the word vector dimension set to 300, the epoch also
being 300, and the minimum and maximum character counts for n-grams being
1 and 4 respectively, the process of incremental pre-training is shown in Fig. 4.

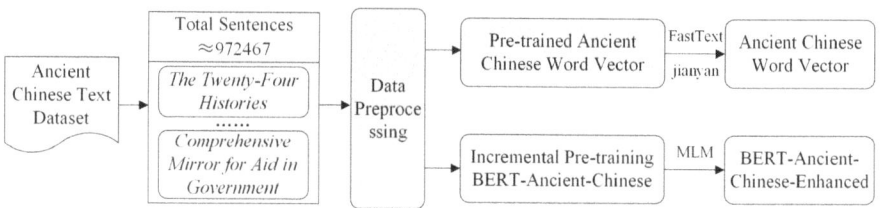

Fig. 4. Incremental Pre-training Process Diagram.

5   Experimental Results and Analysis

5.1   Datasets

In the experiments, we selected the CMAG-NER, C-CLUE, and GuNER2023
datasets as research objects. Among them, the CMAG-NER dataset has been
introduced earlier. C-CLUE is a "Twenty-Four Histories(二十四史)" NER dataset
based on a crowdsourcing annotation system released by Tianjin University in
2021, which annotates 2378 sentences of ancient Chinese texts, over 200,000 characters, and a total of 22,367 entities of five types. GuNER2023 is a "Twenty-Four
Histories(二十四史)" NER dataset provided by Peking University for evaluation
in the CCL2023 ancient book NER task, which annotates 2347 sentences of
ancient Chinese texts, over 150,000 characters, and a total of 10,246 entities of
three types. The detailed statistics of entity quantities are shown in Table 3.

---

[3] https://github.com/NiuTrans/Classical-Modern.
[4] https://github.com/facebookresearch/fastText.
[5] https://github.com/jiaeyan/Jiayan.

Table 3. Statistical analysis of the number of entities in C-CLUE and GuNER2023.

Entity Types	C-CLUE			GuNER2023		
	Train	Valid	Test	Train	Valid	Test
Person(PER)	11532	756	756	5408	594	668
Location(LOC)	3625	220	236	–	–	–
Offical(OFI)	2252	448	349	2717	307	339
Organization(ORG)	2041	4	45	–	–	–
BOOK(BOOK)	119	0	16	162	27	24
Total	19450	1428	1489	8287	928	1031

5.2 Experimental Setup and Evaluation Indicators

Experimental Setup: The experimental environment in this paper employs Ubuntu 18.04, Python 3.6, CUDA version 11.3, and an RTX 3060 graphics card. Additionally, the maximum input text length is set to 128, the batch size is configured as 4, the number of epochs is set to 50, and the learning rate is established at 1×10^{-5}.

Evaluation Indicators: We employ micro-averaged Precision, Recall, and F1-score to comprehensively evaluate the performance of the five entity categories across various models.

5.3 Comparative Model

(1) **BiLSTM-CRF** and **BERT-CRF**: These models incorporate a CRF layer at the end of the original BiLSTM and BERT architectures, respectively, to enhance performance on NER tasks.

(2) **TENER** [25]: This model significantly improves the performance of the original Transformer on NER tasks by introducing relative position encoding and modifying the attention scoring function.

(3) **Lattice-LSTM** [2]: This model features a lattice structure that incorporates all words within a sentence that match entries in a lexicon into character-level NER models, thereby assisting the model in addressing the issue of uncertain word boundaries.

(4) **FLAT** [26]: This model introduces a flat-lattice Transformer structure to integrate lexicon information, addressing the inability of the Lattice-LSTM model to utilize GPU parallel processing capabilities.

(5) **NFLAT** [27]: This model employs the InterFormer module to fuse word boundary and semantic information, and uses a Transformer encoder to model the fused information, effectively avoiding the high computational and memory costs of the FLAT model, enabling it to handle longer input texts.

(6) **LEBERT-CRF** [6]: This model integrates lexicon information into the underlying layers of BERT, leveraging BERT's language representation capabilities to learn deeper knowledge of vocabulary.

(7) **External Dictionaries**: "YJ" is a pre-trained word vector trained using Word2Vec on the Chinese Giga-Word corpus by Zhang et al. [2], containing approximately 700,000 vocabulary entries with 50-dimensional word vectors. "LS" is a Chinese pre-trained word vector trained on dozens of domain-specific corpora by Li et al. [28], encompassing nearly 1.29 million vocabulary entries with 300-dimensional word vectors. "TX" is a Chinese pre-trained word vector studied by Song et al. [29], comprising over 12 million vocabulary entries with 200-dimensional word vectors.

(8) **Pre-trained Models**: BERT-Base-Chinese is a pre-trained model tailored for the general Chinese domain, while SikuBERT and BERT-Ancient-Chinese are pre-trained models specifically designed for the Classical Chinese domain. BERT-Ancient-Chinese-Enhanced is a pre-trained model obtained in this paper through incremental pre-training based on BERT-Ancient-Chinese.

5.4   Examination on the C-CLUE and GuNER2023 Datasets

To validate the effectiveness of the proposed method for Classical Chinese NER tasks, we select BERT-CRF, LEBERT-CRF, and IPDL-LEBERT-CRF as benchmark models. The first two models employ BERT-Ancient-Chinese as the pre-trained model and conduct experiments on the C-CLUE and GuNER2023 datasets.

As shown in Table 4, the incorporation of lexicon information and pre-trained models specific to the Classical Chinese domain can significantly enhance the recognition performance of the models, particularly the model proposed in this paper, which demonstrates superior performance. Meanwhile, we identifies some discrepancies in entity annotation standards between C-CLUE and GuNER2023. For instance, entities combining place names and official titles, such as "九江太守(Jiujiang Taishou)", are annotated as two separate entities in GuNER2023, i.e., {九江(Jiujiang)|LOC}{太守(Taishou)|JOB}, whereas C-CLUE treats them as a single entity and uniformly annotates them as an official title. In the future, we will refine the annotation standards for various entity types in the CMAG-NER dataset based on the latest entity annotation specifications released by GuNER2023.

Table 4. The experimental results on the C-CLUE and GuNER2023 datasets(%).

Models	C-CLUE			GuNER2023		
	P	R	F1	P	R	F1
BERT-CRF	59.73	77.95	67.64	89.17	93.40	91.24
LEBERT-CRF	60.94	77.08	68.07	90.73	93.99	92.33
Ours	63.48	75.13	68.82	91.84	94.96	93.37

5.5 Research on the CMAG-NER Dataset

In order to compare the performance of different models incorporating lexicon information in ancient Chinese NER tasks, we conducted three groups of experiments. The first group of experiments selected benchmark models without any external information, including BiLSTM-CRF, TENER, and BERT-CRF; the second group of experiments selected traditional models that incorporate lexicon information, such as Lattice-LSTM, FLAT, and NFLAT; the third group of experiments selected models that integrate lexicon information into pre-trained language models, such as LEBERT-CRF. Additionally, BERT-CRF and LEBERT-CRF adopted BERT-Ancient-Chinese as the pre-training model.

As shown in Table 5, compared to the benchmark models, incorporating lexicon information helps improve the performance of basic neural network models in ancient Chinese NER. Without using a pre-trained model, the NFLAT model performed the best with an F1 score of 72.39%. Since the pre-trained model BERT usually focuses on character-level input when processing Chinese texts, the model's performance in ancient Chinese text NER is further enhanced when word-level information is added, with an F1 score of 84.07%. However, Our IPDL-LEBERT-CRF model based on incremental pre-training and domain dictionaries in this paper performs even better, with an F1 score as high as 85.13%.

Table 5. The experimental results on the CMAG-NER dataset(%).

Models	P	R	F1
BiLSTM-CRF	68.82	62.20	65.34
TENER	71.22	65.36	68.17
BERT-CRF	81.55	82.21	81.88
Lattice-LSTM	72.25	65.51	68.72
FLAT	75.62	68.65	71.96
NFLAT	75.24	69.75	72.39
LEBERT-CRF	83.69	84.47	84.07
Ours	85.54	84.74	85.13

5.6 Ablation Experiment

(1) Different External Dictionaries

Currently, models that incorporate external lexicons often use "YJ", "LS", and "TX" as pre-trained word vectors. Based on this, we selected IPDL-LEBERT-CRF as the benchmark model and used BERT-Base-Chinese as the pre-trained model to explore the impact of different external dictionaries on ancient Chinese NER tasks.

As shown in Table 6, when using "LS" pre-trained word vectors as the external lexicon, the model's F1 score reaches 81.63%, which is 0.67 higher than using "TX" pre-trained word vectors as the external lexicon. The reason for this is that compared to the other two pre-trained word vectors, "LS" includes character vectors pre-trained on the "Complete Library of the Four Branches of Literature" corpus, which to some extent enhances the model's performance in recognizing ancient Chinese named entities. Furthermore, when introducing the "Comprehensive Mirror in Aid of Governance Dictionary" as external rule knowledge, the model's F1 score is further improved.

Table 6. The experimental results of IPDL-LEBERT-CRF with different external dictionaries (%).

External Dictionaries	P	R	F1
TX	80.60	81.32	80.96
YJ	80.72	81.94	81.33
LS	81.55	81.71	81.63
Ours	81.85	81.94	81.89

(2) Different pre-trained models

To investigate the performance of different pre-trained models in ancient Chinese NER tasks, we selected IPDL-LEBERT-CRF as the benchmark model and uses BERT-Base-Chinese, SikuBERT, BERT-Ancient-Chinese, and BERT-Ancient-Chinese-Enhanced as pre-trained models for comparative experiments.

As shown in Table 7, compared to the Chinese pre-trained model BERT-Base-Chinese, the ancient Chinese pre-trained models exhibit superior performance in ancient Chinese NER tasks. In particular, the BERT-Ancient-Chinese-Enhanced obtained through incremental pre-training in this paper achieves the best results, with an F1 value of 85.13%. Additionally, in terms of indicators for various types of entities, the model shows the most significant performance improvement in recognizing person and place names. This phenomenon indicates that, compared to other types of entities, person and place names, due to their diverse composition and differences from modern usage, require more domain-specific information to assist the model in accurate identification.

6 Performance of Large Models in Ancient Chinese NER

In this paper, we adopted a method based on zero-shot, 1-shot, and 3-shot prompts to quantitatively evaluate the performance of ChatGLM3-6B, BaiChuan2-13B, and Xunzi (Qwen-7B) in ancient Chinese NER tasks. Furthermore, the form of the zero-shot prompt we used is as follows: "你是一

Table 7. Performance metrics of different models on various entity categories (%).

Models	PER	LOC	OFI	ORG	TIME	F1
BERT-Base-Chinese	85.69	81.12	81.58	66.30	77.78	81.89
SikuBERT	87.46	85.29	79.63	68.02	76.34	83.38
BERT-Ancient-Chinese	89.89	84.61	79.13	67.27	78.65	84.4
BERT-Ancient-Chinese-Enhanced	89.84	85.55	80.90	69.17	79.33	85.13

个古汉语命名实体识别专家，请在以下古汉语文本中识别人名、地名、官职名、组织名和时间名，并以{实体|类别}的格式返回结果，其中类别分别用PER、LOC、JOB、ORG和TIME表示。(You are an expert in ancient Chinese NER. Please identify person names, place names, official titles, organization names, and time names in the following ancient Chinese text and return the results in the format of {entity|category}, where the categories are represented by PER, LOC, JOB, ORG, and TIME respectively.)"

As shown in Table 8, compared to the large Chinese domain models ChatGLM3-6B and BaiChuan2-13B, the large model specifically designed for the ancient Chinese domain, Xunzi (Qwen7B), performs better. In particular, when using the 3-shot prompt method, the performance of Xunzi (Qwen7B) is further improved, indicating that adding a certain number of homologous examples can effectively enhance the performance of large models in ancient Chinese NER tasks.

Table 8. The experimental results of large models on ancient Chinese NER (%).

Models	zero-shot			1-shot			3-shot		
	P	R	F1	P	R	F1	P	R	F1
ChatGLM3-6B	24.33	28.24	26.14	23.86	24.16	24.01	23.41	32.44	27.19
BaiChuan2-13B	21.58	17.02	19.03	36.70	47.51	41.42	42.66	55.67	48.31
Xunzi(Qwen7B)	29.48	54.23	38.20	58.33	50.58	54.18	59.80	57.61	58.69

7   Case Analysis

In this paper, we selected the predicted results of ChatGPT-3.5, Xunzi (Qwen-7B), and IPDL-LEBERT-CRF models to qualitatively examine their performance in identifying omitted surname person name entities and entity boundaries.

As shown in Tables 9 and 10, compared to specialized small models, large models still have a certain gap in identifying omitted surname person name entities and entity boundaries. Additionally, the ancient Chinese large model

Xunzi performs better than the general domain large model ChatGPT-3.5 in identifying these two aspects. In the future, we will fine-tune the large models using the constructed dataset to improve their performance on this task.

Table 9. The model's performance in identifying personal name entities with omitted surnames

Input	长史崔俊肃固争，护儿不可，曰：贼势破矣，独以相任，自足办之。(Changshi Cui Junsu insisted on fighting, but Hu Er refused, saying: "The enemy's situation has been broken, and I alone am responsible for dealing with it.")
Ground Truth	{长史(Zhangshi)|OFI}、{崔俊肃(Cui Junsu)|PER}、{护儿(Hu Er)|PER}
ChatGPT-3.5	{史(Shi)|OFI}、{崔俊肃固(Cui Junsu Gu)|PER}
Xunzi(Qwen-7B)	{长史(Zhangshi)|OFI}、{崔俊肃(Cui Junsu)|PER}、{护儿(Hu Er)|PER}、{贼(Zei)|PER}
Ours	{长史(Zhangshi)|OFI}、{崔俊肃(Cui Junsu)|PER}、{护儿(Hu Er)|PER}

Table 10. The model's performance in identifying entity boundaries

Input	乃将十馀骑与封隆之子子绘潜谒欢于滏口，说欢曰：尔朱酷逆，痛结人神，凡曰有知，莫不思奋。(So he led more than a dozen riders and Fang Long's son Zihui to secretly visit Huan at the mouth of the Fu River, saying to Huan: "Erzhu is extremely rebellious, causing pain to both man and god. Everyone who knows this cannot help but want to fight.")
Ground Truth	{封隆之(Feng Longzhi)|PER}、{子绘(Zihui)|PER}、{欢(Huan)|PER}、{滏口(Fukou)| LOC }、{欢(Huan)|PER }、{尔朱(Erzhu)|ORG}
ChatGPT-3.5	{封隆(Feng Long)|PER}、{子绘Zihui)|PER}、{欢(Huan)|PER}、{滏口(Fukou)|LOC}
Xunzi(Qwen-7B)	{封隆之(Feng Longzhi)|PER}、{子绘(Zihui)|PER}、{欢(Huan)|PER}、{欢(Huan)|PER}
Ours	{封隆之(Feng Longzhi)|PER}、{子绘(Zihui)|PER}、{欢(Huan)|PER}、{滏口(Fukou)| LOC}、{欢(Huan)|PER }、{尔朱(Erzhu)|ORG}

8   Summary and Future Work

In this paper, we explore the challenges associated with current NER tasks in ancient Chinese texts. To address these challenges, we have developed the

CMAG-NER dataset specifically for ancient Chinese NER. Furthermore, we propose an NER model that incorporates incremental pre-training and domain-specific dictionaries, utilizing the newly constructed dataset. Additionally, we assess the efficacy of large language models in this context through the application of prompt-based methods. The findings indicate that our approach is effective for ancient Chinese NER; however, when compared to baseline models employing supervised learning strategies, the performance of large models in this domain requires further enhancement.

For future research, we aim to incorporate a broader range of external knowledge sources, including passage-level information and modern Chinese translations, with the goal of advancing the performance of ancient Chinese NER tasks. Concurrently, we intend to fine-tune large language models to bolster their effectiveness in this specialized area of NER.

Acknowledgments. The authors would like to thank the anonymous reviewers for their constructive feedback. This work was supported by the National Natural Science Foundation of China (Grant No. 61866018,62266023).

References

1. Liu, P., Guo, Y., Wang, F., Li, G.: Chinese named entity recognition: the state of the art. Neurocomputing **473**, 37–53 (2022)
2. Zhang, Y., and Yang, J.: Chinese NER using lattice LSTM. In: Proceedings of the 56th Annual Meeting of the Association for Computational Linguistics, pp. 1554–1564 (2018)
3. Liu, W., Xu, T., Xu, Q., Song, J., Zu, Y.: An encoding strategy based word-character LSTM for Chinese NER. In: Proceedings of the 2019 Conference of the North American Chapter of the Association for Computational Linguistics: Human Language Technologies, pp. 2379–2389 (2019)
4. Mengge, X., Yu, B., Liu, T., Zhang, Y., Meng, E., Wang, B.: Porous lattice transformer encoder for Chinese NER. In: Proceedings of the 28th International Conference on Computational Linguistics, pp. 3831–3841 (2020)
5. Gui, T., et al.: A lexicon-based graph neural network for Chinese NER. In: Proceedings of the 2019 Conference on Empirical Methods in Natural Language Processing and the 9th International Joint Conference on Natural Language Processing, pp. 1040–1050 (2019)
6. Liu, W., Fu, X., Zhang, Y. and Xiao, W.: Lexicon enhanced Chinese sequence labelling using Bert adapter. In: Proceedings of the 59th Annual Meeting of the Association for Computational Linguistics and the 11th International Joint Conference on Natural Language Processing, pp. 5847–5858 (2021)
7. Ding, R., Xie, P., Zhang, X., Lu, W., Li, L., Si, L.: A neural multi-digraph model for Chinese NER with gazetteers. In: Proceedings of the 57th Annual Meeting of the Association for Computational Linguistics, pp. 1462–1467 (2019)
8. Ma, R., Peng, M., Zhang, Q., Huang, X.: Simplify the usage of lexicon in Chinese NER. In: Proceedings of the 58th Annual Meeting of the Association for Computational Linguistics, pp. 5951–5960 (2020)
9. Su, Q., Wang, Y., Deng, Z., Yang, H., Wang, J.: Overview of CCL23-Eval Task 1: named entity recognition in ancient Chinese books. In: Proceedings of the 22nd Chinese National Conference on Computational Linguistics, pp. 34–40 (2023)

10. Du, Z., et al..: GLM: general language model pretraining with autoregressive blank infilling. In: Proceedings of the 60th Annual Meeting of the Association for Computational Linguistics, pp. 320–335 (2022)

11. Yang, A., et al.: Baichuan 2: open large-scale language models. arXiv preprint arXiv:2309.10305 (2023)

12. Hammerton, J.: Named entity recognition with long short-term memory. In: Proceedings of the Seventh Conference on Natural Language Learning at HLT-NAACL 2003, pp. 172–175 (2003)

13. Huang, Z., Xu, W., and Yu, K.: Bidirectional LSTM-CRF models for sequence tagging. arXiv preprint arXiv:1508.01991 (2015)

14. Devlin, J., Chang, M. W., Lee, K., Toutanova, K. BERT: pre-training of deep bidirectional transformers for language understanding. In: Proceedings of the 2019 Conference of the North American Chapter of the Association for Computational Linguistics: Human Language Technologies, pp. 4171–4186(2019)

15. Beltagy, I., Lo, K., Cohan, A.: SciBERT: a pretrained language model for scientific text. arXiv preprint arXiv:1903.10676 (2019)

16. Gui, T., Ma, R., Zhang, Q., Zhao, L., Jiang, Y.G., Huang, X.: CNN-Based Chinese NER with lexicon rethinking. In: Proceedings of the 28th International Joint Conference on Artificial Intelligence, pp. 4982–4988 (2019)

17. Nie, Y., Tian, Y., Song, Y., Ao, X., Wan, X.: Improving named entity recognition with attentive ensemble of syntactic information. In: Findings of the Association for Computational Linguistics, pp. 4231–4245 (2020)

18. Huang, F., Wang, L.: Rule-based Chinese person names identification in ancient Chinese literature of annals-biography (jizhuan) style. Library Inf. Serv. **57**(03), 120–124 (2013)

19. Li, Z., Li, Z., He, L.: Study on the extraction method of war events in Zuo Zhuan. Lib. Inf. Serv. **64**(7), 20–29 (2020)

20. Yu, P., Wang, X.: BERT-based named entity recognition in Chinese twenty-four histories. In: Wang, G., Lin, X., Hendler, J., Song, W., Xu, Z., Liu, G. (eds.) WISA 2020. LNCS, vol. 12432, pp. 289–301. Springer, Cham (2020). https://doi.org/10.1007/978-3-030-60029-7_27

21. Wang, D., et al.: Construction and application of pre-trained models of Siku Quanshu in orientation to digital humanities. Lib. Tribune **42**(06), 31–43 (2022)

22. Wang, P., and Ren, Z.: The uncertainty-based retrieval framework for ancient Chinese CWS AND POS. In: Proceedings of the Second Workshop on Language Technologies for Historical and Ancient Languages, pp. 164–168 (2022)

23. Ji, Z., Shen, Y., Sun, Y., Yu, T., Wang, X.: C-CLUE: a benchmark of classical Chinese based on a crowdsourcing system for knowledge graph construction. In: Knowledge Graph and Semantic Computing: Knowledge Graph Empowers New Infrastructure Construction, pp. 295–301 (2021)

24. Liang, G., Leung, C W K.: Improving model generalization: a Chinese named entity recognition case study. In: Proceedings of the 59th Annual Meeting of the Association for Computational Linguistics and the 11th International Joint Conference on Natural Language Processing, pp. 992–997 (2021)

25. Yan, H., Deng, B., Li, X., Qiu, X.: TENER: adapting transformer encoder for named entity recognition. arXiv preprint arXiv:1911.04474 (2019)

26. Li, X., Yan, H., Qiu, X., Huang, X.: FLAT: Chinese NER using flat-lattice transformer. In: Proceedings of the 58th Annual Meeting of the Association for Computational Linguistics, pp. 6836–6842 (2020)

27. Wu, S., Song, X., Feng, Z., Wu, X.J.: Nflat: non-flat-lattice transformer for Chinese named entity recognition. arXiv preprint arXiv:2205.05832 (2022)

28. Li, S., Zhao, Z., Hu, R., Li, W., Liu, T., Du, X.: Analogical reasoning on Chinese morphological and semantic relations. In: Proceedings of the 56th Annual Meeting of the Association for Computational Linguistics, pp. 138–143 (2018)
29. Song, Y., Shi, S., Li, J., Zhang, H.: Directional skip-gram: explicitly distinguishing left and right context for word embeddings. In: Proceedings of the 2018 Conference of the North American Chapter of the Association for Computational Linguistics: Human Language Technologies, pp. 175–180 (2018)

MCKRL: A Multi-channel Based Multi-graph Knowledge Representation Learning Model

Zihao Tang[1], Xiang Zhang[2(✉)], and Xiaoyu Shang[2]

[1] School of Software Engineering, Southeast University, Nanjing, China
zh.tang@seu.edu.cn
[2] School of Computer Science and Engineering, Southeast University, Nanjing, China
x.zhang@seu.edu.cn, 220201930@aa.seu.edu.cn

Abstract. Knowledge representation learning (KRL) aims to encode entities and relationships from the real world into low-dimensional, real-valued vectors. However, knowledge in specific domains is often distributed across multiple graphs, each complementing the others, posing challenges to current mainstream methods, which often fail to fully exploit the heterogeneity and complementarity of information across graphs. To address this issue, We propose MCKRL for multi-graph KRL, including two components to address the heterogeneity and complementarity of knowledge, respectively: (1) A hierarchical attention mechanism to convert diverse attributes into uniform-dimensional vectors, fusing them with attention from both attribute and source levels. (2) Introducing three channels (*single graph*, *sub-graph*, and *combined graph*), employing graph auto-encoders to learn entity embeddings in each channel, and combining them with graph-level attention for link prediction evaluation. Extensive experiments conducted on two representative knowledge graphs in biomedical research demonstrate the superior performance of MCKRL over the state-of-the-arts. The implementations areavailable at: https://github.com/wds-seu/MCKRL.

Keywords: Knowledge Graphs · Representation Learning · Graph Neural Networks · Link Prediction

1 Introduction

In many fields, knowledge graphs (KGs) serve as indispensable tools, serving pivotal roles in information retrieval systems [4], recommendation systems [1], and intelligent question-answering [3]. The advancement of knowledge representation learning (KRL) techniques [11] has led to the development of numerous methods for mapping KG nodes to low-dimensional vector spaces [10]. Such vector representations typically contain rich network information and are computationally efficient, making them suitable for various downstream tasks.

© The Author(s), under exclusive license to Springer Nature Singapore Pte Ltd. 2025
D. F. Wong et al. (Eds.): NLPCC 2024, LNAI 15359, pp. 504–516, 2025.
https://doi.org/10.1007/978-981-97-9431-7_38

Following the introduction of word2vec, numerous knowledge representation learning methods have surfaced, yielding positive outcomes. However, the field encounters two key challenges: **(1) Knowledge Heterogeneity**, as entities and relations within KGs feature a range of attributes, leading to high variability. For instance, medical KGs like DrugBank include drugs with attributes like *average dosage* and *drug category*, where each attribute type contributes uniquely to the entity descriptions. **(2) Knowledge Complementarity**, as knowledge spread across different KGs can enhance each other. In biomedicine, DrugBank and UniProtKB contain drugs and proteins, such as DB00002 (Cetuximab[1]) and P00533 (Epidermal growth factor receptor[2]), where the interaction between these entities is captured by triples. The connection through P00533 to more extensive protein data in UniProtKB, including interactions like (P00533, interacts_with, P00519), illustrates how disparate KGs can complement one another.

Existing KRL methods from multiple knowledge graphs often handle attributes in isolation [8] and are limited to single KG settings [7], leading to redundancy and failing to capture complex relationships between KGs [12].

We propose MCKRL, a novel model that addresses knowledge heterogeneity and complementarity in multi-KG embedding. MCKRL uses a hierarchical attention mechanism to unify diverse attribute types and fuse entity attributes from various sources. It also categorizes KGs into different channels, enabling feature learning across graphs and capturing comprehensive graph information using graph autoencoders and graph-level attention. Experiments on link prediction show MCKRL outperforms previous methods.

To sum up, our contributions are as follow:

– A multi-channel graph attention network for handling the complementarity of knowledge.
– A hierarchical attention-based mechanism for handling the heterogeneity of attributes.

2 Related Works

In recent years, researchers have proposed various Graph Neural Network (GNN) methods [18] for graph representation learning. GNN-based approaches [5], unlike conventional methods, iteratively aggregate neighborhood information of nodes using deep neural networks, resulting in more intricate graph representations [15]. The R-GCN algorithm introduced by Schlichtkrull et al. [13] addresses multiple relational features in knowledge graphs by maintaining distinct weight matrices for each edge type. The HetGNN model by Zhang et al. [20] employs a hierarchical aggregation strategy with Recurrent Neural Networks (RNNs) to encode neighboring node features for each type and aggregate embeddings of different node types using second-order RNNs. This hierarchical approach aims to mitigate the loss of node feature distribution information within individual

---

[1] https://go.drugbank.com/drugs/DB00002.
[2] https://go.drugbank.com/polypeptides/P00533.

graphs when merging graphs with different feature distributions. Additionally, considering the feature distribution of original graphs is crucial in multi-graph scenarios [14].

The AM-GCN model by Wang et al. [17] underscores the importance of integrating node attribute features and topological structures, leveraging k-nearest neighbor graphs and convolutional and attention mechanisms for computation. As entity attribute types diversify, attribute enhancement must consider topology, attribute information, and heterogeneity [19]. Chen et al. [2] enhance Het-GNN by introducing variance-based filters for feature selection and accounting for attribute importance discrepancies.

In multi-knowledge graph representation learning, current methods often aggregate knowledge directly from various sources under a single graph assumption, potentially losing original knowledge features. To optimize knowledge complementarity, there is a pressing need to simultaneously consider features from both individual and aggregated graphs. Furthermore, the nuances of semantic types and attribute origins are frequently disregarded in multi-graph. A unified strategy is needed to address this diversity, ensuring semantic preservation and feature balance for attribute processing and embedding.

3   Metholodogy

3.1   Perliminary

Task 1. Multi-Graph Heterogeneous Attribute Encoding. This task aims to transform diverse entity attributes across multiple knowledge graphs into a vector space. For a set of graphs $G = G_1, G_2, \ldots, G_K$, each with uniquely attributed entities, the objective is to translate these attributes into corresponding feature vectors, yielding a set of vectors $x_1, x_2, \ldots, x_N$, with N representing the number of entities, and x_i corresponding to the feature vector of the i-th entity.

Task 2. Multi-Graph Knowledge Representation Learning. This task aims to learn a mapping function $f : (V, E, X) \to Z$ for multiple interconnected graphs, where V is the set of nodes in the knowledge graph, E is the set of relations in the knowledge graph, X is the set of attribute embeddings and Z is the final entity embedding vector matrix. The goal is to produce an entity embedding matrix $Z \in \mathbb{R}^{n \times d}$, preserving both structural and attribute information. Evaluating Z on downstream tasks assesses the effectiveness of f.

3.2   Hierarchical Attention-Based Mechanism

Specific Type Attribute Content Encoding. We classify entity attributes into three data types: *numerical*, *categorical*, and *textual*. *Numerical* attributes are discretized into equal-width bins, *categorical* attributes are encoded using one-hot encoding, and *textual* attributes are embedded using Doc2Vec [9].

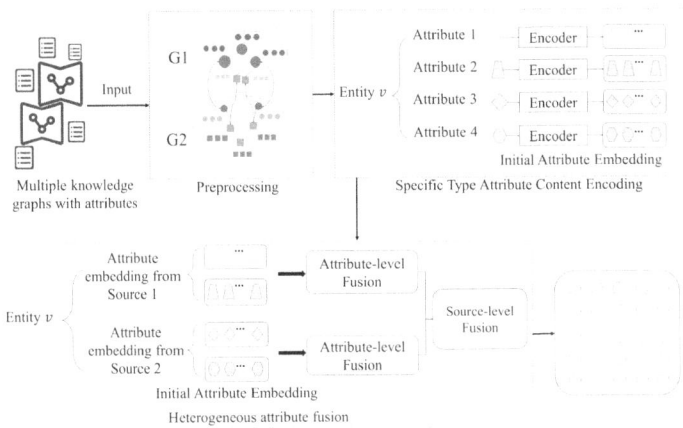

Fig. 1. The framework of Hierarchical Attention-based Mechanism (the first part of MCKRL).

Attribute-Level Fusion. First, we focus on attributes within a single source. In graph G_k, we have P different attribute semantic types, represented as $\mathcal{T}_k = \{\tau_1, \tau_2, \ldots, \tau_P\}$. Using a deep neural network $\text{att}_{atr}(\cdot)$ to compute the attention weights $\{\beta_k^{\tau_1}, \beta_k^{\tau_2}, \ldots, \beta_k^{\tau_P}\}$ for attribute vectors under each semantic type:

$$(\beta_k^{\tau_1}, \beta_k^{\tau_2}, \ldots, \beta_k^{\tau_P}) = \text{att}_{atr}(\mathbf{C}_k^{\tau_1}, \mathbf{C}_k^{\tau_2}, \ldots, \mathbf{C}_k^{\tau_P}) \qquad (1)$$

To find the attention distribution for all attribute vectors related to entity v, we use a query vector $\mathbf{q}_{atr} \in \mathbb{R}^{N_{atr} \times 1}$ at the attribute level. An additive model computes the relevance score $s(\mathbf{q}_{atr}, \mathbf{c}_{k,v}^{\tau_p})$ between entity v and attribute vectors of specific semantic type τ_p, determining the weight of attribute vectors associated with entity v:

$$\omega_{\tau_p}^{atr} = \frac{1}{|V|} \sum_{v \in V} \mathbf{q}_{atr}^\top \cdot \tanh(\mathbf{W}_{atr}^{att}(\mathbf{c}_{k,v}^{\tau_p})^\top + \mathbf{b}_{atr}^{att}) \qquad (2)$$

where $\omega_{\tau_p}^{atr}$ represents the average attention weight across all entities $\mathbf{v} \in V$ and $|V|$ represents the number of elements in the set of all entities with attributes of semantic type τ_p. The weight matrix $\mathbf{W}_{atr}^{att} \in \mathbb{R}^{N_{atr} \times N_c}$ and bias vector $\mathbf{b}_{atr}^{att} \in \mathbb{R}^{N_c \times 1}$ are shared by attribute embeddings of all semantic types and specific semantic types, respectively. And N_{atr} is the dimension of attribute vectors after attribute-level attention fusion.

The softmax function is used for normalization to obtain the attention distribution $\beta_k^{\tau_p}$ for different semantic type.

$$\beta_k^{\tau_p} = \text{softmax}(\omega_{\tau_p}^{atr}) \qquad (3)$$

The learned attribute semantic type weights serve as coefficients to linearly combine the attribute embeddings of entity v for each specific semantic category, resulting in the integrated attribute embedding $\mathbf{x}_{k,v}$:

$$\mathbf{x}_{k,v} = \sigma \left(\sum_{\tau_p \in \mathcal{T}} \omega_{\tau_p}^{atr} \cdot \mathbf{c}_{k,v}^{\tau_p} \right) \tag{4}$$

where $\mathbf{x}_{k,v} \in \mathbb{R}^{1 \times N_{atr}}$ represents the attribute embedding vector of entity v in the k-th source, applying this method to all sources K, K sets of attribute embeddings $\{\mathbf{x}_{1,v}, \mathbf{x}_{2,v}, \ldots, \mathbf{x}_{K,v}\}$ for entity v can be obtained.

Source-Level Fusion. For each entity v, we follow the similar learning pattern of attribute-level fusion method, but with different neural network att_{src} and query vector $\mathbf{q}_{src} \in \mathbb{R}^{N_d \times 1}$ to compute weights $\omega_{k,v}^{src}$, which are normalized by softmax to obtain $\gamma_{k,v}$, representing each contribution to entity attributes of each source.

Both the attribute-level and the source-level attention distributions are then used as coefficients to integrate attribute embeddings, yielding the ultimate attribute embedding vector $\mathbf{x}_v$ of entity.

$$\mathbf{x}_v = \sum_{k=1}^{K} \gamma_{k,v} \cdot \mathbf{x}_{k,v} \tag{5}$$

where $\mathbf{x}_v$ is one of the inputs for the multi-Channel graph neural network in the subsequent section.

3.3   Multi-channel Graph Neural Network

Multi-Channel Construction. Three representation channels: *single graph*, *sub-graph* and *combined graph*, based on input from multiple graphs. For instance, with a set of knowledge graphs $\mathcal{G} = \{G_1, G_2, \ldots, G_K\}$ and entity set $V = \{V_1 \cup V_2 \cup \cdots \cup V_K\}$, we illustrate this idea with $k = 2$. **(1) The Single-Graph Channel.** It focuses on the internal structure and features of individual graphs ($\mathcal{G}_{sing} = G_1, G_2$) which maintains the integrity and uniqueness of each graph. **(2) The Sub-graph Channel.** It comprises sub-graphs formed by the "intersection" and "difference" of multiple graphs ($\mathcal{G}_{sub} = G_1 \cap G_2, G_1 - G_1 \cap G_2, G_2 - G_1 \cap G_2$) which captures common features and unique characteristics of each graph. **(3) The Combined-Graph Channel.** It represents comprehensive relationships and entity information of combined graphs ($\mathcal{G}_{comb} = G_1 \cup G_2$) which expands the graph's scale, simulating cross-graph neighbor information (Figs. 1 and 2).

Multi-channel Embedding Representation. Each channel has graphs G_k^{ch} representing the kth graph in channel ch, and N is the total number of graphs in this channel. We utilize Unsupervised Knowledge Graph Convolutional Networks (UKGCN) for entity embedding learning in each channel. K-GCN [16] is

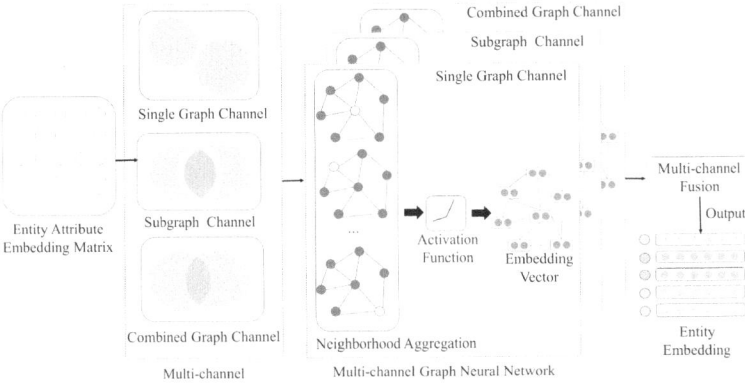

Fig. 2. The framework of Multi-Channel Graph Neural Network (the second part of MCKRL).

the encoder, and a bilinear model is the decoder. The adjacency matrix A_k^{ch} and association matrix M_k^{ch} represent the node connections and node-edge relationships in each graph.

We have obtained the feature matrix X_k^{ch} for graph G_k^{ch} with dimensionality N_d through the embedding representation method from the first part of MCKRL. And the adjacency matrix A_k^{ch} is updated to a weighted matrix S_k^{ch} by using the method in K-GCN.

Next, we input $(S_k^{ch}, M_k^{ch}, X_k^{ch})$ into the UKGCN for encoding, resulting in the feature representation $\mathbf{Z}_k^{ch}$ for G_k^{ch} within this channel.

The feature representations for all graphs in $\mathcal{G}_{ch}$ are $\mathbf{Z}_1^{ch}, \mathbf{Z}_2^{ch}, \dots \mathbf{Z}_N^{ch}$. Then, a bilinear decoder is used to reconstruct the original weighted adjacency matrices:

$$\hat{Z}_k^{ch} = \text{sigmoid}(\mathbf{Z}_k^{ch} \mathbf{W}_k^{ch} \mathbf{Z}_k^{ch\top}) \tag{6}$$

To ensure that the reconstructed $\hat{Z}_k^{ch}$ is close to the original S_k^{ch}, we apply mean square loss error for optimization:

$$\mathcal{L}_{ch} = \sum_{k=1}^{N} \|\hat{Z}_k^{ch} - S_k^{ch}\|^2 \tag{7}$$

By using the described methods, the embedding vectors $\mathbf{Z}_{sing}, \mathbf{Z}_{sub}, \mathbf{Z}_{comb}$, along with their corresponding loss functions $\mathcal{L}_{sing}, \mathcal{L}_{sub}, \mathcal{L}_{comb}$ for the three channels are obtained.

Multi-channel Fusion and Objective Function. We combine embeddings from multi-channel graphs with adjustable weights via graph-level attention.

The resulting attention weights $(\alpha_{sing}, \alpha_{sub}, \alpha_{comb})$ highlight the relevance of each channel from the embedding representations $\mathbf{Z} = \mathbf{Z}_{sing}, \mathbf{Z}_{sub}, \mathbf{Z}_{comb}$.

For node v_i in the combined graph G_{comb}, its embedding $\mathbf{z}_{comb}^i \in \mathbb{R}^{1 \times h}$ (the i-th row of $\mathbf{Z}_{comb}$) undergoes a non-linear transformation, and then the attention score π_{comb}^i is obtained by using a shared query vector $\mathbf{q} \in \mathbb{R}^{h' \times 1}$:

$$\pi_{comb}^i = \mathbf{q}^\top \cdot \tanh(\mathbf{W}_{comb}^{att}(\mathbf{z}_{comb}^i)^\top + \mathbf{b}_{comb}^{att}) \tag{8}$$

where $\mathbf{W}_{comb}^{att} \in \mathbb{R}^{h' \times h}$ and $\mathbf{b}_{comb}^{att} \in \mathbb{R}^{h' \times 1}$ are the weight matrix and bias for $\mathbf{Z}_{comb}$, and π_{comb}^i is the attention score of the i-th embedding in the combined graph channel.

Similarly, We obtain attention scores π_{sing}^i, π_{sub}^i, and π_{comb}^i for the embeddings of node v_i across the channels which are normalized via softmax to get the final weight α_{comb}^i, α_{sing}^i and α_{sub}^i.

For all N_v nodes, we obtain learnable weights $\alpha_{sing} = [\alpha_{sing}^i]$, $\alpha_{sub} = [\alpha_{sub}^i]$, and $\alpha_{comb} = [\alpha_{comb}^i]$, and represent them as $\alpha_{SING} = \mathrm{diag}(\alpha_{sing})$, $\alpha_{SUB} = \mathrm{diag}(\alpha_{sub})$, and $\alpha_{COMB} = \mathrm{diag}(\alpha_{comb})$, then combine the feature vectors in three channels to obtain the embedding $\mathbf{Z}_{att}$:

$$\mathbf{Z}_{att} = \alpha_{SING} \cdot \mathbf{Z}_{sing} + \alpha_{SUB} \cdot \mathbf{Z}_{sub} + \alpha_{COMB} \cdot \mathbf{Z}_{comb} \tag{9}$$

Under graph-level attention, the goal is to accurately reconstruct the combined graph's adjacency matrix, ensuring fidelity to the original structure.

$$\hat{Z}^{att} = \mathrm{sigmoid}(\mathbf{Z}_{att}\mathbf{W}^{att}\mathbf{Z}_{att}^\top) \tag{10}$$

$$\mathcal{L}_{att} = \|\hat{Z}^{att} - S^{comb}\|^2 \tag{11}$$

where S^{comb} denotes the weighted adjacency matrix of combined graph channel.

The objective function is a sum of the loss functions for each channel and the loss function for the graph-level attention mechanism.

$$\mathcal{L} = \mathcal{L}_{sing} + \mathcal{L}_{sub} + \mathcal{L}_{comb} + \mathcal{L}_{att} \tag{12}$$

Then $\mathcal{L}$ employs the Adam optimizer for training the model through backpropagation.

4   Experiments

4.1   Experimental Setup

Dataset. (1) **The DB-UP dataset** integrates DrugBank and UniProtKB, authoritative sources for drug and protein knowledge, respectively. It maps 2,423 drugs from DrugBank to 1,861 UniProtKB proteins, facilitating drug-protein interaction analysis. (2) **The BioSE dataset**, based on Stanford's BioSNAP3, focuses on drug side effects, compiling data from TWOSIDES, STITCH, and the Decagon [30] (Tables 1 and 2).

Table 1. The statistics of datasets. $|E|$ stands for the entity size, $|R|$ denotes the relation size.

Dataset	$|E|$	$|R|$	Entity Categories	Relationship Categories	Feature Categories	Graphs
DB-UP	10,377	1,381,078	2	4	18	2
BioSE	20,379	5,383,743	2	4	1	3

Table 2. The statistics of Entity distribution in the knowledge graph.

Dataset	Knowledge Graph	$|E|$	Associated Knowledge Graph	Shared Entities	Proportion of Shared Entities
DB-UP	DrugBank	4,373	UniProtKB	3,811	87.15
	UniProtKB	9,815	DrugBank	3,811	38.83
BioSE	G1	645	G2	284	44.03
	G2	3,932	G1,G3	3,924	99.80
	G3	19,081	G2	3,640	19.08

Implementation Details. For experimental parameter settings, Embedding dimensions were uniformly set to 64 for attributes, 128 for GNN and final entity embeddings, and 64 for attribute-level, source-level, and graph-level attention hidden layers. The learning rate was fixed at 0.003 and weight decay at 5e-4.

To prevent overfitting, training was subject to Early Stopping, which ceased training if the validation loss showed no improvement of at least 1e-4 over 10 epochs, ensuring the optimal parameters of model and saving the best result before training termination.

All experiments are performed on an Intel(R) Core(TM) CPU i5-9500 with 128 GB of main memory and an Nvidia GeForce RTX 3060.

Performance Metrics. We conduct the evaluation in link prediction, and adopt four widely used metrics, which are **AUROC**, **AUPR**, **Accuracy**, and **F1-Measure**.

4.2   Main Results

From the overall results in Table 3, we summarize our findings as follow:

(1) **Adopting a multi-channel approach offers a more comprehensive and diverse set of graph information.** Our method outperforms G-GCN and Decagon by effectively representing multiple graph structures. It yielded 6.3% and 9.5% higher AUROC and AUPR scores on two datasets, with respective gains of 7.1% and 10.4%.

(2) **Multi-channel graph neural networks improve embedding learning with greater accuracy and flexibility.** On the DB-UP dataset, our

method substantially surpassed RSN in all metrics, with improvements of 4.7–13%. RSN's reliance on manual tuning and shallow feature extraction contrasts with our approach.

(3) **MCKRL's simplified attention parameters help prevent overfitting.** MCKRL outperformed MCGAT on all metrics, with MCGAT's neglect of combined graph information and its extensive attention parameters leading to overfitting.

(4) MCKRL enhances performance over AM-GCN, HetGNN, and MGRL by integrating local and global graph information, addressing issues like data loss and attribute misinterpretation.

Table 3. Results of the link prediction task on the DB-UP and BioSE datasets. Underlined data indicates the best performance among baseline models, while bold data indicates the best performance across all models. Imp (%) denotes the percentage improvement of MCKRL over the best-performing baseline model.

Model	DB-UP				BioSE			
	AUROC	AUPR	ACC	F1	AUROC	AUPR	ACC	F1
R-GCN [13] (2018)	0.804	0.761	0.702	0.746	0.759	0.690	0.677	0.724
Decagon [22] (2018)	0.816	0.788	0.715	0.767	0.771	0.704	0.702	0.755
RSN [6] (2019)	0.758	0.726	0.717	0.742	0.805	0.757	0.728	0.759
HetGNN [20] (2019)	0.829	0.795	0.735	0.759	0.796	0.734	0.697	0.746
AM-GCN [17] (2020)	0.748	0.669	0.624	0.592	0.694	0.652	0.548	0.692
MCGAT [21] (2021)	0.608	0.572	0.502	0.668	0.618	0.574	0.509	0.669
MGRL [2] (2022)	0.832	0.813	0.739	0.768	0.812	0.781	0.714	0.761
MCKRL (Ours)	**0.867**	**0.856**	**0.764**	**0.796**	**0.842**	**0.808**	**0.744**	**0.780**
Imp.(%)	4.207	5.289	3.383	3.646	3.695	3.457	4.202	2.497

4.3   Ablation Studies

The MCKRL model includes a heterogeneous attribute processing module and a multi-channel graph neural network module. Ablation studies were performed on these modules to evaluate the effectiveness of different attribute fusion methods and channel-specific embeddings.

Ablation Study on the Heterogeneous Attribute Processing Module. The models are defined as follows:

– MCKRL: The complete model without any modules removed.
– MCKRL w/o src-level: The source-level attention mechanism is replaced with the summing and averaging method.
– MCKRL w/o atr-level: The attribute-level attention mechanism is replaced with Bi-LSTM.

– MCKRL w/o attributes: The attribute processing module is replaced with randomly initialized vectors.

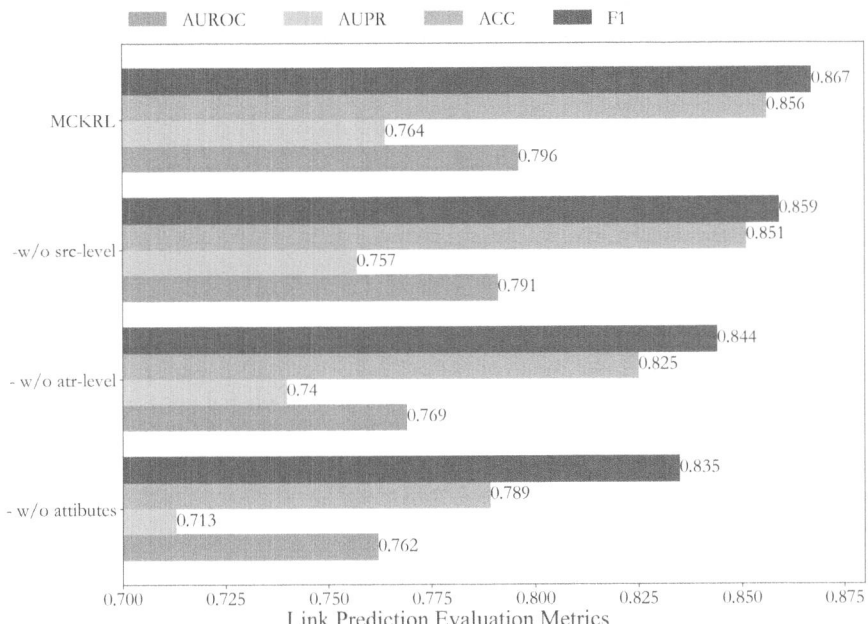

Fig. 3. The ablation study on heterogeneous attribute module of MCKRL.

As shown in Fig. 3, we have the following observations: (1) Compared to the MCKRL w/o attributes model, the MCKRL model exhibits a 4.6% mean improvement in metrics, signifying the criticality of attributes for embedding enhancement. (2) Compared to the MCKRL w/o atr-level model with Bi-LSTM fusion, the MCKRL model's inclusion of an attribute-level attention mechanism leads to a noticeable improvement in all metrics, reflecting its attunement to semantic attribute diversity. (3) Compared to the MCKRL w/o src-level, the advancements in the MCKRL model underscore the necessity of source-level attribute focus for embedding quality improvement.

Ablation Study on the Multi-Channel Graph Neural Network Module. The models are defined as follows:

– MCKRL w/o combined: The combined graph channel is removed.
– MCKRL w/o single: The single graph channel is removed.
– MCKRL w/o subgraph: The subgraph channel is removed.
– MCKRL w/o att: The attention fusion method is replaced with an averaging fusion method.

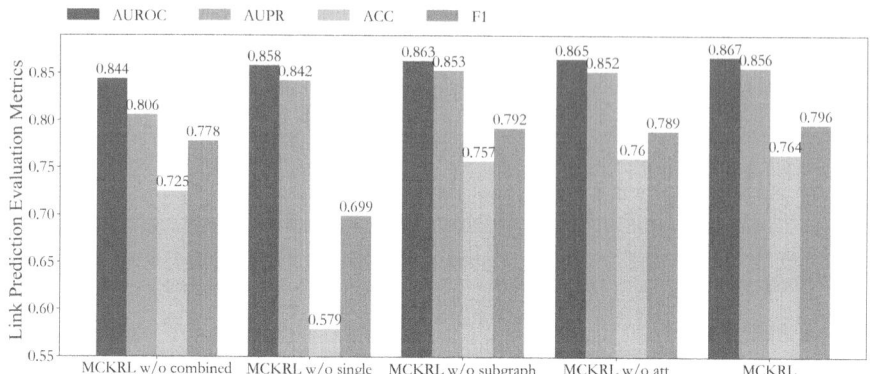

Fig. 4. The ablation study on multi-channel module of MCKRL.

As shown in Fig. 4, the absence of the combined graph channel most affected AUROC and AUPR, underscoring the value of comprehensive node information. The removal of the single graph channel notably impacted ACC and F1, highlighting the necessity of maintaining knowledge distribution within single graphs. The contribution of subgraph channel confirmed the efficacy in capturing graph distinctions and similarities.

4.4   Attention Mechanism Visualization

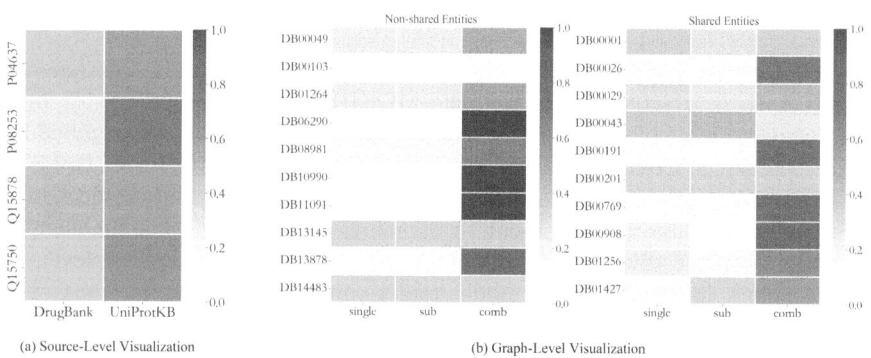

Fig. 5. (a) Visualization of source-level attention mechanism. (b) Visualization of graph-level attention mechanism.

Visualization of Source-level Attention Mechanism: Analyzing four protein entity samples across DrugBank and UniProtKB knowledge graphs in the DB-UP dataset, which indicates that the source-level attention mechanism favors UniProtKB for its comprehensive protein information over DrugBank. This weighting is justified, as MCKRL dynamically integrates relevant details from both knowledge graphs, as shown in Fig. 5.(a).

Visualization of Graph-level Attention Mechanism: For entities in both graphs, the combined graph channel enriches feature representations, while the single graph and subgraph channels provide complementary insights, with the subgraph channel enhancing attention weight precision by capturing graph similarities, demonstrating the multi-channel architecture's effectiveness in integrating diverse graph representations for accurate entity characterization.

5   Conclusion

MCKRL is a model for knowledge representation learning in multi-graph scenarios, consisting of two key components: 1) a hierarchical attention mechanism to encode heterogeneous attributes, and 2) a multi-channel multi-graph framework that captures entity features from distinct viewpoints (single graph, sub-graph, and combined graph channels) and integrates them using graph-level attention. Its efficacy is demonstrated through link prediction tasks, ablation studies.

In the future, we expect to extend this work to scenarios with more complex graphs. Additionally, more scenarios requiring the use of multiple knowledge graphs can be explored, and experiments can be conducted in multiple fields using the proposed method to test its generalizability.

Acknowledgments. This work was supported by the National Key R&D Program of China (2023YFC3806002).

References

1. Catherine, R., Cohen, W.: Personalized recommendations using knowledge graphs: a probabilistic logic programming approach. In: Proceedings of the 10th ACM Conference on Recommender Systems, pp. 325–332 (2016)
2. Chen, K., Wang, G., Fu, S., Hu, J., Liu, L.: MGRL: attributed multiplex heterogeneous network representation learning based on multi-granularity information fusion. Int. J. Mach. Learn. Cybern., 1–16 (2021). https://doi.org/10.1007/s13042-021-01494-3
3. Cui, W., Xiao, Y., Wang, H., Song, Y., Hwang, S.W., Wang, W.: KBQA: learning question answering over QA corpora and knowledge bases. arXiv preprint arXiv:1903.02419 (2019)
4. Dalton, J., Dietz, L., Allan, J.: Entity query feature expansion using knowledge base links. In: Proceedings of the 37th International ACM SIGIR Conference on Research & Development in Information Retrieval, pp. 365–374 (2014)
5. Gilmer, J., Schoenholz, S.S., Riley, P.F., Vinyals, O., Dahl, G.E.: Neural message passing for quantum chemistry. In: International Conference on Machine Learning, pp. 1263–1272. PMLR (2017)

6. Guo, L., Sun, Z., Hu, W.: Learning to exploit long-term relational dependencies in knowledge graphs. In: International Conference on Machine Learning, pp. 2505–2514. PMLR (2019)
7. Hamilton, W., Ying, Z., Leskovec, J.: Inductive representation learning on large graphs. In: Advances in Neural Information Processing Systems, vol. 30 (2017)
8. Kong, C., Gao, M., Xu, C., Fu, Y., Qian, W., Zhou, A.: EnAli: entity alignment across multiple heterogeneous data sources. Front. Comp. Sci. **13**, 157–169 (2019)
9. Le, Q., Mikolov, T.: Distributed representations of sentences and documents. In: International Conference on Machine Learning, pp. 1188–1196. PMLR (2014)
10. Li, Z., Liu, H., Zhang, Z., Liu, T., Xiong, N.N.: Learning knowledge graph embedding with heterogeneous relation attention networks. IEEE Trans. Neural Netw. Learn. Syst. **33**(8), 3961–3973 (2021)
11. Liu, Z., Lin, Y., Sun, M. (eds.): Representation Learning for Natural Language Processing. Springer Nature Singapore, Singapore (2023). https://doi.org/10.1007/978-981-99-1600-9
12. Ran, H., Jia, C., Zhang, P., Li, X.: MGAT-ESM: multi-channel graph attention neural network with event-sharing module for rumor detection. Inf. Sci. **592**, 402–416 (2022). https://doi.org/10.1016/j.ins.2022.01.036
13. Schlichtkrull, M., Kipf, T.N., Bloem, P., Van Den Berg, R., Titov, I., Welling, M.: Modeling relational data with graph convolutional networks. In: The Semantic Web: 15th International Conference, ESWC 2018, Heraklion, Crete, Greece, June 3–7, 2018, Proceedings 15, pp. 593–607. Springer (2018). https://doi.org/10.1007/978-3-319-93417-4_38
14. Valdeolivas, A., et al.: Random walk with restart on multiplex and heterogeneous biological networks. Bioinformatics **35**(3), 497–505 (2019)
15. Velickovic, P., Cucurull, G., Casanova, A., Romero, A., Lio, P., Bengio, Y., et al.: Graph attention networks. Stat. **1050**(20), 10–48550 (2017)
16. Wang, H., Zhao, M., Xie, X., Li, W., Guo, M.: Knowledge graph convolutional networks for recommender systems. In: The World Wide Web Conference, pp. 3307–3313 (2019)
17. Wang, X., Zhu, M., Bo, D., Cui, P., Shi, C., Pei, J.: AM-GCN: adaptive multi-channel graph convolutional networks. In: Proceedings of the 26th ACM SIGKDD International Conference on Knowledge Discovery & Data Mining, pp. 1243–1253 (2020)
18. Wu, Z., Pan, S., Chen, F., Long, G., Zhang, C., Philip, S.Y.: A comprehensive survey on graph neural networks. IEEE Trans. Neural Netw. Learn. Syst. **32**(1), 4–24 (2020)
19. Yang, C., Xiao, Y., Zhang, Y., Sun, Y., Han, J.: Heterogeneous network representation learning: a unified framework with survey and benchmark. IEEE Trans. Knowl. Data Eng. **34**(10), 4854–4873 (2020)
20. Zhang, C., Song, D., Huang, C., Swami, A., Chawla, N.V.: Heterogeneous graph neural network. In: Proceedings of the 25th ACM SIGKDD International Conference on Knowledge Discovery & Data Mining, pp. 793–803 (2019)
21. Zhao, Y., Meng, K., Liu, G.: A multi-channel graph attention network for Chinese NER. In: Mantoro, T., Lee, M., Ayu, M.A., Wong, K.W., Hidayanto, A.N. (eds.) Neural Information Processing: 28th International Conference, ICONIP 2021, Sanur, Bali, Indonesia, December 8–12, 2021, Proceedings, Part I, pp. 203–214. Springer International Publishing, Cham (2021). https://doi.org/10.1007/978-3-030-92185-9_17
22. Zitnik, M., Agrawal, M., Leskovec, J.: Modeling polypharmacy side effects with graph convolutional networks. Bioinformatics **34**(13), i457–i466 (2018)

Author Index

D. F. Wong et al. (Eds.): NLPCC 2024, LNAI 15359, pp. 517–519, 2025.
https://doi.org/10.1007/978-981-97-9431-7

GPSR Compliance

The European Union's (EU) General Product Safety Regulation (GPSR) is a set of rules that requires consumer products to be safe and our obligations to ensure this.

If you have any concerns about our products, you can contact us on ProductSafety@springernature.com

In case Publisher is established outside the EU, the EU authorized representative is:

Springer Nature Customer Service Center GmbH
Europaplatz 3
69115 Heidelberg, Germany

The manufacturer's authorised representative in the EU is Springer
Nature Customer Service Centre GmbH, Europaplatz 3, 69115 Heidelberg,
Germany. If you have any concerns regarding our products, please
contact ProductSafety@springernature.com

Printed and bound by CPI Group (UK) Ltd, Croydon, CR0 4YY
29/04/2026
02099541-0013